THE ORIGINS OF MODERN
RUSSIAN EDUCATION

THE ORIGINS OF MODERN RUSSIAN EDUCATION: AN INTELLECTUAL BIOGRAPHY OF COUNT SERGEI UVAROV, 1786-1855

CYNTHIA H. WHITTAKER

NORTHERN ILLINOIS UNIVERSITY PRESS · 1984

© 1984, 2011 by Northern Illinois University Press

Published by Northern Illinois University Press, DeKalb, Illinois 60115

Manufactured in the United States of America using acid-free,

postconsumer recycled paper

1st printing in paperback, 2010

All Rights Reserved

Design by Joan Westerdale

Library of Congress Cataloging in Publication Data

Whittaker, Cynthia H., 1941–

The origins of modern Russian education.

Bibliography: p.

Includes index.

1. Uvarov, Sergeĭ Semeonovich, graf, 1786–1855. 2. Educators—Soviet Union—
Biography. 3. Education and state—Soviet Union—History. 4. Soviet Union—
Intellectual life—1801–1917. 5. Soviet Union—Social conditions—1801–1917.

I. Title

LA2375.S592U939 1984 370'.92'4 [B] 84-7471

ISBN: 0-87580-100-5 (casebound)

ISBN: 978-0-87580-984-7 (paperback : alk. paper)

The original publication of this book was assisted by a grant from the East/West
Education Fund, Bowling Green University Foundation, Inc.,
Bowling Green, Ohio 43403.

FOR MY HUSBAND,
RICHARD C. WADE

CONTENTS

ACKNOWLEDGMENTS

THIS book requires two separate sets of acknowledgments since it has had an unusual history. Normally, a first monograph expands upon a doctoral dissertation; in this case, however, the monograph refutes the thesis of the dissertation and represents an almost entirely new work of scholarship.

My doctoral dissertation on Sergei Uvarov was completed at Indiana University in 1971. I am grateful that the university's fellowship program enabled me to carry out basic research in the New York Public Library, the Hoover Institution, and the Helsinki Library. Building upon the groundwork laid by Professor Elsie Carrillo of Marymount College (Tarrytown), my professors at Indiana, such as Robert F. Byrnes, William Edgerton, and Peter Scheibert, provided the useful assistance of training me to read critically, to write, and to maintain a healthy skepticism toward sources. However, because of personal circumstances, I was unable to do original research in Soviet archives and my dissertation generally, despite some reservations, reflected the traditional interpretation of Uvarov as a quasi-liberal in his youth who turned reactionary upon reaching full maturity.

A Young Faculty Grant from the International Research and Exchanges Board enabled me to spend six months in 1973 doing research in the USSR. The material explored during that stay transformed my interpretation of Uvarov and led to the inevitable conclusion that the book on him required a fresh start. Truly generous financial support from Baruch College of the City University of New York, including a sabbatical year and scholar assistance funds, enabled me to digest the new material and write this book.

Once the book entered its final stage, Dr. Orest Pelech, the Slavic bibliographer at Princeton University, took the manuscript in hand and meticulously pointed out every scholarly overstatement, grammatical error, or bibliographical omission. Beyond that time-consuming task, he offered me the encouragement and temerity to pursue a revisionist view of a major figure in history.

The scholars and editors involved with the reading of the manuscript at Northern Illinois University also deserve special mention. W. Bruce Lincoln, Allen McConnell, and Patrick Alston offered invaluable advice on honing the book's concepts. Professor Alston, through our long association on the *Slavic and European Education Review*, was, by the way, the first scholar to support the trend of my research. Editors Mary Livingston and Ann C. Bates made valuable emendations with care, consideration, and craftsmanship.

My husband, Richard C. Wade, who acted as my in-house editor, certainly warrants having the book dedicated to him, even, or maybe especially, on nonscholarly grounds. My children, Erica and Andrew Whittaker, deserve grand thanks for their patience and for their love and understanding, as well as for their pride, which often sustained me, in their mother as a scholar.

Cynthia H. Whittaker
New York City
April 16, 1983

INTRODUCTION

*The genesis of Uvarov's ideas remains unsolved and . . . could be an interesting
subject for historical-cultural research.* Gustav Shpet, 1922

SERGEI SEMEONOVICH UVAROV was a Russian statesman of
progressive vision but cautious disposition. His lifetime, 1786 to
1855, spanned a volatile era, one that demonstrated the inevitability
of social, political, and economic changes in European life. Uvarov became
determined to accomplish those changes in Russia gradually and without
revolution. His extraordinary career in public service gave him the opportunity to act upon this view. From 1810 to 1821, he rose to prominence as
the head of one of six educational districts in the empire.[1] From the age of
thirty-two until his death, he served in the prestigious position of president
of the Academy of Sciences. The capstone of his career was to become
Russia's longest tenured and most influential minister of education, a post
he held from 1833 to 1849. Uvarov's accomplishments in office and the
endurance of his policies, *mutatis mutandis*, into modern times mark him as
one of the most important statesmen in nineteenth-century Russia.

In addition, while lacking in formal education, Uvarov earned a reputation as the foremost autodidact of his time. An abbé had tutored him in
the values of the *ancien régime* and left his young charge with the conviction
that the traits of a true nobleman were pursuit of culture and development
of refined taste. True to this ethos, Uvarov published poetry in his teens
and engaged in all the literary quarrels, big and small, of his day. He
developed a facility in seven languages, wrote in four and, during his lifetime, authored over two dozen essays on a variety of literary, historical,
scientific, and scholarly topics that brought him repute throughout Europe.
In retirement, he fulfilled a long-held dream of gaining formal recognition
of his scholarship. He earned a master's degree in classical studies from the

University of Dorpat and then prepared a doctoral dissertation, published only posthumously.[2]

In particular, a keen interest in history provided Uvarov with a foresight, direction, and overview uncommon among bureaucrats. What obsessed him most was the notion that he was living through an age of transition, between two worlds, "one dying and the other yet to be born," in an "epoch at once stationary and progressive."[3] His observation was valid. He was born into a generation nurtured on the rational ideals of the Enlightenment and on the polite society of the old regime, but there then followed more than a half century of searching, a Romantic chaos that alternated between revolution and reaction, both of which Uvarov loathed. He termed revolutions "moral-political ulcers" and reactionaries "cold-blooded fanatics."[4] Instead, Uvarov, even in youth, demonstrated a tendency to seek the middle ground. In 1810 Count Joseph de Maistre, the Sardinian ambassador to Russia, warned Uvarov that in the quest for compromise one "plants oneself up in the middle of two armed enemies, receiving the bullets of one and gibes of the other."[5] De Maistre was surely correct, but, nonetheless, Uvarov spent a lifetime trying to reconcile eighteenth- and nineteenth-century ideals and demands. A modern critic may call this equivocation, but Uvarov considered it principle and purpose.

Drenched in Russian and European turn-of-the-century thought, Uvarov, in the 1810s, devised a theory of universal historical development that provided him with focus and direction for the rest of his life. In his schema, history portrayed the "inexorable march" or "natural progress" of freedom as predestined and guided by Providence. God's greatest bequest to mankind was Christianity with "its great lesson of moral equality" and with the promise of political freedom as its "*last and most beautiful gift*." According to Uvarov, nations achieved this pinnacle only when "mature."

"Young" nations lived under the control of absolute monarchs, but their descendants eventually were to become "enlightened" enough to guide their people patriarchally and peacefully to "maturity." This latter stage would result in a limited monarchy with institutional arrangements designed to prevent the twin historic evils of despotism and anarchy. Its formal constitution would go beyond a *Rechtsstaat* to include three guarantees: some type of representative institution that effected a balance of power among monarchy, nobility, and bourgeoisie; civil rights for the entire populace; and political rights for the educated and propertied elite. In addition, Uvarov believed that maturity brought with it some degree of industrialization and a sure sense of national or cultural identity. He also thought that each country achieved its goals by way of its own organic path, thus lending a certain diversity to historical developments. Uvarov offered, as examples of "mature" societies, the British nation with its unwritten constitution and the French with the Charter of Liberties as upheld by Louis XVIII and

Louis Philippe. The later nineteenth-century goal of universal manhood suffrage remained outside Uvarov's ken.

Uvarov believed that the transition from absolute to limited monarchy was problematic because history is not replete with kings who willingly abdicate power to other groups. Thus, he regarded the devolution of power as supernatural in origin. If kings or peoples tried to veer from Providence's design for gradually achieving a limited monarchy, they would be punished or "devoured" or suffer the "scourge" of revolution.[6] Britain in the seventeenth century, the shortsighted Louis XVI, the Jacobin democracy, the despotic Napoleon, the reactionary Charles X all served as reminders of those who violated historical laws. In Russian terms, Uvarov extolled Peter the Great (1682–1725) and Catherine the Great (1762–1796) for what he considered their enlightened ability to adjust to the inevitable transition from "youth" to "maturity." He was appalled by Paul I (1796-1801), whose recidivism threatened Russia's progress, but he noted that the despot had received the providential sentence of assassination.

Uvarov served under two tsars, Alexander I (1801–1825) and Nicholas I (1825–1855). Alexander, dubbed the "Hamlet on the Throne," dreamed of constitutions and emancipation but, frightened by unrest in Europe, turned to a policy of reaction during the last five years of his reign. The failed Decembrist Revolt of 1825, led by dissatisfied nobility, was again a providential response to repression. Nicholas was basically a military man who tried to fend off unrest by administrative reforms and by a neat and orderly shoring up of the existing institutions of his vast empire. Yet, faced with the widespread European revolutions of 1848–1849, he too chose reaction in his last years. At both times, in 1821 and 1849, Uvarov rejected the new twist in tsarist policy and left office.

Despite the tsars' vacillations, Uvarov remained consistent. Indeed, he once declared that "my principles" were not like "the transient will of the tsar" but offered a "firm and durable system" for Russia's progress.[7] By 1818, Uvarov reached two conclusions: first, that Russia had to devise its own path to "maturity" and, second, that education provided the basic means for progress.

European nations, of course, were far closer to "maturity" than Russia, but Uvarov witnessed during his lifetime the constant stream of violent upheavals that they suffered as a result of their mistaken paths. He believed that his country was still "young"; it would profit from the mistakes of its elders and achieve "maturity" without the pain of revolution: "Providence blessed Russia, having made it last in the assembly of enlightened states."[8]

Uvarov listed several "ailments" among the nations of the West: the "pursuit of incessant change," a "scorn for tradition," an "industrialization . . . that sets one class of people against another," lack of "convictions," "materialism . . . and moral chaos," "self-interest" rather than communal responsibility—all of which was leading to the "rapid downfall of religious and civic institutions in Europe." Nonetheless, Uvarov did not despair. Throughout the 1830s and 1840s, he sanguinely reiterated: "We need not fear for the health of civilization in general, because the law of progress will remain its express condition." In particular, he continued to respect profoundly European achievements in all areas of knowledge, but concluded: "What is needed is a *Russian system* and a *European education.*" He gave the "system" a slogan, "Orthodoxy, Autocracy, Nationality" *(Pravoslavie, Samoderzhavie, Narodnost').* These "sustaining principles" were to guide Russia through what is often called "modernization" or "conservative renovation" and what he called "maturation," while preserving social and political stability and a sense of national pride.[9]

Thus, Uvarov devised a *"Russian system"* for conforming to the providential "law of progress" and at the same time escaping revolution. Its essential characteristic, in keeping with tradition, was autocratic direction: "The autocracy constitutes the *sine qua non* of Russia's political existence." He assumed the patriarchal and disinterested nature of the tsars and believed that only they could bind all classes together during the intersection of tradition and change, by moderating conflicting demands and by insuring a community of belief based upon the Orthodox heritage. Since he considered all lapses on the part of tsars aberrations, he claimed: "Providence has given us a series of tsars who conformed to the demands of the times and fully satisfied the spirit of their century"; they alone "possess all the means to know . . . the real needs of the fatherland" and, as in the past, could best inaugurate needed reform.[10]

Another fundamental premise of the "system" stemmed from Uvarov's perception that the West was lurching ahead too fast, without thought for the "past and future, living only for the present." He was far ahead of his time in recognizing that rapid modernization—accomplished in a generation and involving the imposition of new and often foreign ways upon a people—can result in dislocations that, in turn, can cause revulsion and unrest. Throughout his life, Uvarov waged a constant campaign against "blind imitation of this or that foreign culture" and "stupid envy." To offset this centuries-old propensity, he devised a concept of nationality that enshrined native history, literature, and mores and even attempted to charm the non-Russian subjects of the empire into adopting Great Russian culture. He pointed out that progress should involve a gentle "melding of ancient and new concepts" rather than what he perceived as the West's "passion for reforms" and its universal "dissatisfaction with its present state."

Uvarov insisted that his program did "not necessitate going backward or standing still," but it did demand, above all, "developing slowly." Cautious forward movement dominated his views and policies: Russia should slowly prepare for emancipation so as not to alienate the nobility nor pauperize the peasants; Russia should carefully restrain its industrialization so as not to create a class of proletariat nor neglect agricultural production; Russia should pace the education of its populace, beginning with the elite, so that all eventually would be prepared to handle constitutional rights and responsibilities; Russia should discriminate in its reception of Western trends, so as not to suffocate national consciousness; Great Russian culture should become so alluring that it would stave off nationalist separatism.[11]

In the meantime, Uvarov considered it his duty to educate Russia—and perhaps its tsars—in order to bring it to the "threshold of citizenship." He ranks among the first Russian or even European statesmen to grasp the essential role education played in nineteenth-century development. His name may be easily linked to Guizot in France, Wilhelm von Humboldt in Prussia, and William Tory Harris in the United States. Indeed, Uvarov placed education at the center of a grand national strategy.

> In several . . . abstract questions, the responsibility of the ministry of national enlightenment consisted in going ahead of the other parts of the upper administration, paving the way for others, performing the first experiments . . . and thus facilitating the constant development of other branches of government and the harmonious approach of each to common aims.

In fact, a "mature" or "modern" country, especially one like Russia that aspired to maintain and enhance great-power status, required a literate population, a cadre of economic and administrative specialists, advanced knowledge, and a sense of cohesion, all of which necessitated "the free and fast growth of education in the land." Uvarov, though, understood that only "future generations will reap the fruits of our labor," that he was only laying the foundations for maturity. His aim was clear, if ambitious and complex: "To preserve all the advantages of European enlightenment, to raise the intellectual life of Russia to the level of other nations [but at the same time] to give it national uniqueness, to base it on its own principles, and to make it conform to the needs of the people and the state."[12]

However grand his ultimate vision or moderate his immediate plan, Uvarov bred a hardy band of antagonists: nobles who recoiled at learning; clerics who distrusted secular knowledge; chauvinists who feared Western culture; journalists who resented censorship; defenders of the status quo who quaked at even meek reform; reformers who wanted more rapid change; obscurantists who thought education, as a general matter, bred revolution; radicals who despised the repressive measures that marked even the most progressive of Russian reigns; the public who, once educated, rightfully thought they deserved a voice in government; the tsars, who, when frightened, fled back into the refuge of oppression and tried to curb educational opportunity.

Perhaps the most significant fact in Uvarov's public life was that he fell from power twice, in 1821 and 1849, because he would not support the triumph of reactionary policies. Indeed, the end of the second half of his career presented an eerie replay of the end of the first: undignified attempts to gain wealth and repute, significant contributions to education and culture, the effort to balance conflicting social and political aims, a rousing defense of his policies in letters to the tsars, and defeat at the hands of extremists. Also, in both instances, he had just declared Russia ready for substantial reform. In 1818, he thought a constitution near at hand. In 1847, he believed that at least the educated public was nearing "maturity"; he eased censorship, tried to loosen the university structure, and sensed the "discontent of minds" at the strictness of the regime. In this way, Uvarov's biography exposes the array of options, aspirations, conflicts, and delusions entertained by educated Russians in the struggle to bring their country peacefully into the "modern" world.

Despite opposition and eventual dismissal, Uvarov made solid gains. His tenure as superintendent of the St. Petersburg Educational District, president of the Academy of Sciences, and minister of education bore witness to his talent as an administrator and intellectual: he created two first-rate universities and brought the others to a golden age in terms of faculty, salaries, pension benefits, physical facilities, libraries, laboratories, and student bodies; he revitalized the secondary schools and brought them, too, to a level of excellence; he patronized a new emphasis on technology and science in education; he gave birth to Oriental, Slavic, classical, and philological studies; he organized Russia's historical archives and archeological findings; he turned the Academy of Sciences from a shambles into a renowned center of learning. In the process, Uvarov went far to realize Peter the Great's dream of making education the prerequisite for responsible office and to propagate his own notion that the only good nobleman is an educated nobleman. In fact, an aristocracy of knowledge began to replace an aristocracy of birth in Russia. With pride, but surely some exaggeration, Uvarov declared in 1849 that "respect for a university diploma was equal to that for noble lineage."[13] To use Uvarov's terms, the educational system that had been born only in 1802 was brought from youth to near maturity by mid-century.

It is not hard to see why subsequent scholars overlooked these extraordinary achievements. In catering to the elite and the upper reaches of the educational ladder, Uvarov had too few resources left to pursue reform in the elementary schools equal to that he effected at the higher and secondary levels. Although he sponsored training for lower school teachers and standardized curricula at elementary schools, he relegated the awesome task of educating peasants, roughly 95 percent of the population, to public charity or future ministers. He believed emancipation was distant, and hence there was time to spare.

Also, since Uvarov was still working within the framework of absolutism, he had no qualms about employing some of its traditional and irksome policies in his ministry, including control, censorship, regimentation, inspection, and political indoctrination; in effect, he tried to set himself up as the autocrat of education. In addition, the man had a difficult personality. Contemporaries charged him with opportunism and a sychophantic "groveling before the powers-that-be"; this behavior they connected to his alleged ability to "switch from his own convictions to someone else's."[14] Arrogance, condescension, greed, and flaunting of intellectual credentials rendered Uvarov unpopular throughout his life and prompted a suspicion about the sincerity of his views and of his motives. Furthermore, Uvarov, as chief censor, provoked the hostility of the most articulate and widely published figures in Russian society in his era. Their assessment has prevailed.

Indeed, in the past, Russian, Soviet, and Western historians almost unanimously have agreed that Uvarov, lacking ideas of his own, conveniently mouthed progressive phrases during the "liberal" phases of Alexander I's reign and, in truer form, became an inflexible, crude reactionary during the Nicholaevan era. This dichotomy was reinforced by a similar view of the two reigns on the part of most writers.[15]

However, since about 1970, American scholars of Russian economic, institutional, and educational history have begun to reinterpret the Nicholaevan era and see it much as Uvarov did. They do not consider it a period of utter stagnation, but one of preparation during which some necessary foundations were laid for Russia's future development, even though basic reforms were not forthcoming. Some writers indicate that many of Uvarov's policies, often effected despite the reluctance of the tsars, assisted this transition.[16]

Part of the Uvarovian "system"—promoting monopoly and centralization, assuring political loyalty, muting dissidence, and maintaining educational standards at the highest contemporary levels—endured to the extent that it remains part of the present-day Soviet system. The transitional era became permanent, and the vision was lost: central power has still not been significantly limited, and increases in political and civil rights are still not forthcoming, even in their early nineteenth-century version. In the era of the tsars, Uvarov, in his historic optimism, never envisioned that Russian autocrats would not willingly share their political power even with the educated and propertied members of the populace. In addition, the tsars and their advisers continued to see an inevitable connection between education and revolution—as well they might, since they refused partnership with their schooled and often critically thinking subjects. The fear of a jacquerie persisted and added to the reluctance to educate the entire population. Thus, the process and promise of Uvarov's "Russian system" for reaching "maturity" was never fully realized.

In one sense, then, the Uvarovian "system" endured and, in another sense, it was lost. He "did much," as one contemporary chronicler noted, but "in different circumstances he could have done even more."[17] It seems time to take a fresh look at Uvarov and remember the words of the intellectual historian, Gustav Shpet. In 1922, he suggested that the "genesis of Uvarov's ideas remains unsolved and . . . could be an interesting subject for historical-cultural research."[18]

This new look ought to have three dimensions. First, Uvarov should be viewed as a cultural figure, as one of those many litterateurs in his era who strove to develop a sense of Russian identity and, in his own case, as one who then attempted to impose it on all subjects in the Russian Empire. Second, Uvarov should be viewed as an ideologist whose theories stemmed from his concepts about the direction of universal history in its political, social, and economic facets. Third, Uvarov should be viewed as an educational statesman whose policies demonstrate the implementation of his views and their affect on Russia's contemporary and future development. Perhaps then we can better place Uvarov as a major figure in Russia's public life in the nineteenth century and also assess his legacy to more modern times.

P A R T   O N E

THE REIGN OF ALEXANDER I, 1801–1825

SEARCHING FOR A RUSSIAN
CULTURAL IDENTITY

When very young [I was] by tradition and taste passionately attached to what is called the ancien régime.   Uvarov, 1815

With the reign of the Emperor Alexander, a new era has begun for Russia, even in literature.   Uvarov, 1817

WHEN Uvarov was in his youth, his interests lay almost solely in the realm of culture, where heated debates were being waged about Russia's own literary coming of age. At the beginning of the nineteenth century, the central questions raised were how to relate to the West and how to formulate a modern literary language. The answers provided the foundation for the golden eras of poetry and prose that followed soon after.

Russian men of letters were painfully aware that their nation possessed only a fledgling culture by Western standards, and they feared that it might sink into a lifeless imitation of European literary forms and traditions without ever having made an original contribution.[1] The desire to win an equal place in the European world intensified between 1812 and 1815, a period when Russian victories over Napoleon stimulated national self-consciousness and pride as well as the yearning to add cultural triumphs to those on the battlefield.[2]

Russia's relationship to European culture was complicated by the fact that, during the Napoleonic era, the continent was as much a literary as a military battleground. The French classical and cosmopolitan tradition, whose sacrosanct rules had governed all literary genres during the eighteenth century, gave way to a variety of trends: sentimentalism substituted a cult of feeling for the Enlightenment's cult of reason; neoclassicism sought inspiration in original sources of antiquity rather than in their French imitations; and various romanticisms extolled national or popular traditions, a return to nature, the individual personality, the medieval era, or, especially, free and unregulated creative activity. Fortunately for Russia, most schools of thought at the turn of the century were colored by an incipient nationalism, a belief that each people could and should discover a cultural identity and make a unique contribution to world literature and the arts. Before the 1820s, lines of conflict were not yet sharply drawn, and there arose an exciting era of experimentation.

Russian men of letters urgently tried to digest these trends and to telescope European developments that dated back to the Renaissance. At the same time, they set out to develop a modern literary language, and this attempt produced a virulent conflict between the so-called Old and New Styles that also entailed an acceptance or rejection of Western culture. The origins of this debate lay in the pioneering linguistic work of Michael Lomonosov, a brilliant scholar in a variety of fields, who first analyzed the Russian language in the mid-eighteenth century. Lomonosov equated "low" style with the vernacular and concluded that literature demanded a "high"—soon to be called "old"—style preserving the character of the nonvernacular, medieval Church Slavonic that formed the historic roots of the language. Using a reworked syntax modeled on German and Latin, much of the literature that followed Lomonosov's precepts seemed archaic, cumbersome, and bombastic, because it bore little resemblance to spoken Russian.[3] Nicholas Karamzin, Russia's most important belletrist at the turn of the century, challenged Lomonosov's dicta and advocated a "middle" or "new" literary language that was more simple, lively, and colloquial and incorporated the ease and flow of French syntax. In his own works, which also introduced new genres such as the ballad and short story, Karamzin jettisoned Church Slavonic vocabulary in favor of gallicisms or new Russian words that expressed modern ideas and emotions in more graceful and conversational style.[4]

In 1803, Admiral Alexander Shishkov attacked Karamzin's innovations in his book *An Inquiry into the Old and New Styles of the Russian Language*. A dilettante philologue with a consuming passion for Church Slavonic root words and an equally consuming hatred of the supposed moral depravity and Jacobinism of the West, Shishkov argued that Karamzin's efforts to abandon Church Slavonic and frenchify the language marked a destructive break with tradition and threatened to contaminate national character. Russian men of letters, the xenophobic admiral insisted, must abandon cultural contact with the West.[5]

Both Shishkov's and Karamzin's views found significant support in the Russian literary world. The poets Gabriel Derzhavin, Wilhelm Küchelbecker, and Sergei Shirinskii-Shikhmatov, the fabulist Ivan Krylov, the dramatists Paul Katenin, Alexander Griboedov, Dmitri Khvostov, and Alexander Shakhovskoi rallied to Shishkov's standard, while Karamzin's camp boasted such luminaries as the poets Vasili Zhukovskii, Constantine Batiushkov, Vasili Pushkin, Peter Viazemskii, and eventually Alexander Pushkin, along with the literary dilettantes Dmitri Dashkov, Stephen Zhikharev, Peter Poletika, and the young Uvarov. These men often changed their attitudes, but they all remained steadfast in their search for an answer to the essential questions: How much, what, and from whom, if at all, should Russian literature borrow or seek inspiration in its early development? What were to be the ingredients of its cultural identity? Uvarov's own intellectual odyssey in these years proved typical of his generation.

A CULTURED NOBLEMAN COMES OF AGE

D EBATE over cultural issues remained an aristocratic preserve during the first two decades of the nineteenth century, especially since a number of young Russian lords began to see the pursuit of intellectual and cultural interests as a surer test of their noble spirit than military or civil service. The sentimentalism that Karamzin had imported from the West became popular for its emphasis on spiritual self-fulfillment and on a creative freedom that offered defense against a hostile, artificial world. Salons and literary circles, rather than garrisons or bureaucratic offices, became the central focus of life and provided outlets for the cultural interests of this new type of nobility.[6]

Raised in this atmosphere, Uvarov was taught that there existed a necessary connection between true nobility and cultivated taste or intelligence, and he spent his early years consciously acquiring them. Once he held offices in the educational ministry, he exerted the bulk of his effort driving young noblemen into secondary schools and universities where they might absorb the traits he considered so essential to their station and so important for their calling to nurture the development of Russian culture.

Uvarov himself was not necessarily destined for a life of high culture or high office, but simple luck helped him along. True, as his service record indicates, Sergei Semeonovich was a "descendant of ancient Russian nobility"; he could trace his lineage to a fifteenth-century Tatar, Minchak Kosaev, who joined the service of the Muscovite Grand Princes and one of whose sons adopted the surname Uvarov. The family, though, enjoyed little distinction until the time of Sergei's birth, when Alexander Uvarov, a cousin, aided General Alexander Suvorov in his brilliant military campaigns during the reign of Catherine II. Through this channel, Sergei's father, the inept but ever-humming Semeon—dubbed the "balladeer of the hallways"—was appointed aide-de-camp to the empress in 1783, and she held his infant son, born three years later on August 26, over the baptismal font in the court church. Semeon died in 1788 and left his widow, Daria, with little money to raise Sergei and his brother, Fedor, who eventually became a major general and a noted botanist. Daria, spoiled and unscrupulous, squandered whatever inheritance there was to maintain her place in society, but shrewdly connived that her sons would be educated in the home of her sister.[7] Fortunately for Sergei, his aunt had married into the princely Kurakin family.[8]

While Uvarov grew up a poor cousin in a wealthy family—perhaps the reason why greed later marred his character—he enjoyed the benefit of an excellent tutor. Abbé Mauguin had fled France in horror after the Revolution and inspired his student to become "passionately attached to what is called the *ancien régime.*" Idealizing the educated aristocrat of the eighteenth-century salon, Mauguin tutored Sergei in the discipline of classical languages, the hallmark of European aristocratic education, and also encouraged him to "read a whole library of French poets, writers, and thinkers." Serge d'Ouvaroff, as he now signed his name, soon took himself quite seriously as an intellectual of the salon. Philip Vigel', a well-known raconteur, who is malicious but generally accurate, described his impressions of the vain sixteen-year-old at *soirées.*

> One rather handsome boy appeared to me to be entirely insupportable and annoying; he was presumptuous, arrogant, garrulous and, in a loud voice and without any humility whatsoever, deliberated about French literature and theater.[9]

Sergei was clearly a nobleman of the new school.

Probably in 1802, again due to the generosity of his uncle, Sergei was sent for a *Lehrjahr* in the German-speaking states. Although there is no evidence that he enrolled officially as a student, all accounts of Uvarov's life suggest that he at least attended several classes at Göttingen University and pursued his study of classical languages while at the same time learning German.[10] Upon his return to Russia, Uvarov became a salaried translator in the newly founded ministry of foreign affairs. In 1804, he was also appointed *Kammerjunker*, an honorary court position indicating the tsar's respect for the "family or service of ancestors." Since both posts conveniently involved only perfunctory duties, Uvarov was able to pursue the intellectual life of the salon and literary circles that he and many of his coevals considered of such central importance in their lives.[11]

Uvarov eagerly adopted the then-fashionable sentimentalism. Even as a thirteen-year-old, he worked its themes of nature and emotion into his remarkably proficient pencil drawings, which include sketches of birds, a weeping willow at early morning in front of the Kurakin château, a poet awakening at midnight to jot down an inspiration, and an especially moving portrait of a beggar woman. His first publication, at age eighteen, was in the leading sentimentalist journal of the day; the two poems were heavy with *mal de siècle*. One stanza reads:

> I am a sufferer now—and help I do not see;
> In life I have abandoned hoping.
> Life I hate and the world is cruel in its entirety;
> I drag the chains of my days sobbing and moaning.

Another poem was entitled "Sur l'avantage de mourir jeune"; after reading Goethe, he composed "Sehnsucht," the first line of which was "Dreams of youth, colors of morning, the sounds of the lyre." Uvarov's verses passed from "hand to hand" in society. Zhukovskii, the best poet of the decade, considered him talented but was irked that the young man wrote not in Russian, but in French or German.[12]

At this point, Uvarov was quite typical of Russian noblemen whose education and cultural enthusiasms ignored study of their native tongue and land. And yet, in the next decade and especially during his tenure as minister, he waged a campaign to emphasize an education for the nobility that was rooted in Russian tradition and laid the foundations for Russian and Slavic studies in his homeland.

Four experiences in this first decade of the nineteenth century began to alter Uvarov's attitudes. First, while at Göttingen, Uvarov probably attended the course offered by August-Ludwig Schlözer, because it was the most popular among the many Russian students who attended the university; Uvarov's later writings quote the historian at length. This prominent scholar had lived for a time in St. Petersburg as a member of the Academy of Sciences; while there, he had urged the necessity for publication of Russian historical documents, a project Uvarov later brought to fruition. At Göttingen, Schlözer taught Russian history even before such a course was offered in Russian universities. He considered Russia an integral part of the European family and upheld the Normanist theory of the origin of the first Russian state, namely that the Varangians had brought political organization to this Eastern outpost in the ninth century A.D. In his lectures, Schlözer became a panegyrist for the new reign of Alexander I because he considered the tsar more progressive or "enlightened" than his European counterparts. Student memoirs agree that Schlözer's course did much to engender a new sense of pride in being Russian.[13]

Second, beginning in 1805, Uvarov frequented the home of Maria Naryshkina, the beautiful Pole who was Alexander I's mistress and the mother of his children. There, the tsar "singled him out" and forecast that this gifted young man would one day become his educational minister. Sergei clearly cherished these words, for two years later at a salon he confided that his life's ambition was to fulfill that prophecy. Uvarov, like many noblemen of his generation, desired intellectual self-fulfillment but still felt the moral tug of his class's traditional obligation to serve the state. Uvarov was fortunate early in life to receive the motivation and inspiration—from no less a father figure than the tsar—to fuse these two callings.[14] But Uvarov could hardly aspire to being educational minister while immersed only in French, German, and classical literature and quite ignorant of the direction and needs of Russian culture. Uvarov's intellectual migration home began in another salon.

Uvarov attested, in a memoir written when he was sixty-five years old, that the salon of A. L. Olenin acted as the main influence on his literary views and formation in this decade, because it was Olenin who awakened his interest in Russian culture. He apparently revered the Olenins as surrogate parents and admired the archeologist for his lifelong "love of art and literature" and for the "asylum" he provided for the burgeoning talent of the era. Uvarov remembered the thrill of finding himself in the company of such native talents as Krylov, the classicists Vasili Kapnist and Nicholas Gnedich, the artist Orest Kiprenskii—who later painted the best known portrait of Uvarov—and the most popular dramatist of the time, Valdislav Ozerov.

Olenin russified Uvarov's interest in classicism by convincing him that the mission of men of letters was to develop their own national culture by returning to the ancients for models and adapting classical standards to native art and literature. Olenin likewise encouraged national pride by urging writers to use themes from Russian antiquity. Ozerov's play *Dmitri Donskoi* was written within the salon. It was classical in form, Russian in theme, and modern in language and style, the three literary criteria that guided Uvarov for the rest of his life.[15]

The last factor that drew Uvarov gradually away from being so singularly and "passionately attached to . . . the *ancien régime*," that is, to European, non-Russian culture, was his experiences in Italy and Vienna. In the second half of 1805, he was dispatched as a courier to Naples, a city he found backward and boring. He considered the land poor, the women homely, the climate debilitating, and the people in general noisy, lazy, and poor. Cultured noblemen also seemed lacking; he noted, with some condescension, that even people in "society" did not discourse on intellectual matters but confined their conversation to gossip about "affairs of the heart." Besides learning a "pleasant Italian," he lived up to his own ideals by attending the opera and ballet. Young Uvarov's growing sense of national pride and even superiority led him to regard the Neapolitans as half-savage because at one point he was forced to travel by ox, "a method of transportation not very suitable for a Russian courier." While returning home by way of Dalmatia and Croatia, he chauvinistically attributed his warm reception in these provinces to his country's preeminence among the Slavs: "The very fact that one is Russian awards the right to love and respect among Slavic peoples."[16]

Uvarov's next assignment in the ministry of foreign affairs proved much more exciting and left a deep imprint upon the young man's attitudes. Once Prince Alexander Kurakin was appointed ambassador to Vienna in 1806, Uvarov's mother began beseeching him and a relative, General Fedor Uvarov, who was "beloved by Alexander I," to obtain a position for their relative in the embassy. The entreaties worked: Uvarov became an attaché, he even got a raise, and his mother declared herself "in raptures." He set off early in 1807 for what he would soon call "the best epoch in my life." Uvarov kept a careful diary of his stay in Vienna, "Tablettes d'un voyageur russe," a title probably inspired by Karamzin's *Letters of a Russian Traveler*, the most important example of the genre in Russia.[17]

What Uvarov learned in Vienna was that the *ancien régime* he "loved so much to study," the French standards of culture that Mauguin had taught him to idealize, now merely constituted a "charming world irrevocably lost." He had expected the Austrian capital to be a variant of Louis XIV's Versailles, with a government patronizing the arts, stimulating a golden age in literature, and supported by a cultured nobility. The young man was appalled by what he actually saw.

> The Austrian nation has a taste neither for letters nor for the arts; at least it is excessively rare. . . . In Vienna at this moment there are few artists and not one litterateur or scholar of note. The nobility haughtily drive them off and swathe themselves in ignorance; the government does not protect [the arts]. . . . The nobility's essential vice consists in the bad education that they receive, in their ignorance of all that could elevate and nourish the soul, in their disdain for the arts and learning. [Thus] the people contemn the nobility who, instead of distinguishing themselves by quality and talent, with an unbridled taste for horses and women surrender themselves to the dark vices in which they wallow.

Although the majority of his Austrian acquaintances may have conformed to this bleak pattern, in Vienna as in Italy Uvarov could quickly find solace in the cultural attractions available to him. His diary recounts his joy at strolling along the Prater or Danube, visiting Gothic churches, studying the treasures of the imperial art gallery and library, attending performances of *King Lear* or *Iphigenia*, viewing the porcelains and engravings found in private collections, or listening to the music of Gluck and Mozart. A performance of Haydn's new work, the *Oratorio of the Creation*, was the high point of Uvarov's visit; after hearing it he exclaimed: "Voilà la Sublime dans les Arts."[18]

Another highlight of Uvarov's stay in Vienna was the close friendship he developed with Madame de Staël. She came to the Austrian capital because it remained, in 1807, the only center of anti-Napoleonic politics, and Bonaparte had exiled her as a subversive. Uvarov and de Staël attended balls, *soirées*, and restaurants, enacted French plays in salons, and agreed that Vienna was a cultural bore "with the exception of music." When Uvarov wrote a warm memoir of de Staël in 1851, he admitted he was quite dazzled by her brilliance in conversation and her fame as a novelist and literary critic. At the same time, she challenged another of Uvarov's bases for revering the old regime, French classical literature. Rightfully called the Luther of literature, de Staël supported the new freedom in form and subject matter of the emerging German romanticism as represented by August-Wilhelm and Friedrich Schlegel. Although Uvarov seems to have been more bothered by the competing influence and friendship of the brothers with de Staël, there nonetheless erupted a serious literary quarrel. As Uvarov later put it, they "raised the flag of insurrection against French classicism." On the contrary, at this moment in his life, Uvarov considered it sacrilegious to belittle Racine, whom they singled out for attack, and "barbarism" to jettison the disciplined forms that had their origins among the ancients in the golden age of civilization. The loyal French classicist decried this "new sect that threatens to invade German literature and whose first rule is to disdain all that preceded it." Nonetheless, de Staël forced Uvarov to confront the imminent downfall of another pillar of the *ancien régime*.[19]

Still, the salons of the diplomatic circles in Vienna maintained the flavor of the *ancien régime*, and Uvarov naturally became an habitué. The young man had the advantage of refined good looks; he was of medium build and thin, with dark hair, a high forehead, aquiline nose, piercing eyes, narrow mouth, and, in general, sharp, finely chiseled features that made some contemporaries comment that he looked more French than Russian. He thrived in the salon atmosphere: "Handsome and the general favorite of aristocratic gatherings, he was witty, tactful, gay, a bit vain, but highly educated and truly enlightened." Uvarov also possessed a certain precious quality that sometimes displeased his coevals but attracted older men and women. He easily courted liaisons, apparently platonic, with well-situated women, a habit that began in the Naryshkina salon in St. Petersburg and would continue throughout the next decade.[20] Uvarov also became the darling, the "cher petit," of the two leading salons in Vienna. They were presided over by the former longtime Russian ambassador to Austria, Count Andrew Razumovskii, and Charles-Joseph Prince de Ligne, a prolific author, a master of the *bon mot*, a former general, and the septuagenarian "host of Vienna to all civilized Europe." Both men welcomed Uvarov's tact and refinement.[21]

Uvarov became especially attached to de Ligne because he seemed—as an "intimate of Voltaire, Louis XV, Catherine II, Frederick II, and the Emperor Joseph"—the last relic of the old regime. Upon de Ligne's death, Uvarov wrote a commemorative essay, judged a classic of the genre, in which he rued the passing of an era. Even Uvarov's rendition of heated literary debates in de Ligne's salon assumed a sense of tragedy for the melancholic author: "These conversations seemed to be the last echo of a dying society, the last flight of the French genius." Later in life, he recalled: "In these salons occurred all the revolutions in taste and literary publications." And he rued: "Then a book was an event; a new idea a phenomenon; a philosophical system an epoch; a production of art the symbol of a party." A few years later, he regretted that "one looks in vain for something similar today" since "politics devours everything."[22] Similarly, when Uvarov recalled the Olenin salon, he demonstrated his preference for the aristocratic world of culture over public events.

> Here all the literary news was customarily brought: poetry that just appeared, news about the theatre, about books, paintings, in a word everything that could nourish . . . a love for enlightenment. Ignoring the dreadful events then taking place in Europe, politics did not constitute a central topic of conversation—it always gave way to literature . . . and to peaceful intellectual pursuits . . , even when governments stood on the brink of ruin.[23]

Uvarov's two-year stay in Vienna, then, did not change his belief that culture remained the worthiest vocation for a nobleman and that its pursuit should not be interrupted even if a conqueror's army was sweeping across the European continent. Indeed, Uvarov clearly spent much time in Vienna studying the culture of his host country. In 1810, after first meeting Uvarov, Alexander Turgenev wrote admiringly: "Above all, Uvarov knows German literature so well that he puts me to shame even in history [Turgenev's specialty], and his style is incomparably better" than most.[24]

On the other hand, the stay in Vienna drastically altered Uvarov's cultural views. His nearly total, and typically Russian, reverence for foreign models of behavior and forms gave way first to melancholic disillusion and then to a sure knowledge that the old world, the old regime, "was dying and another had yet to be born."[25] Therefore, only after his stay in Vienna did Uvarov begin seriously to turn his attention to the possibilities of original Russian cultural development and to cease yearning for some reincarnation of Versailles.

Nonetheless, Uvarov, not unnaturally, still wanted to visit France. At the end of 1808 Ambassador Kurakin was transferred to Paris and requested that Uvarov accompany him as secretary. While waiting for his official appointment, which came in October of 1809, Uvarov left Vienna in May of that year and returned to St. Petersburg. During the summer he tried to put his mother's financial affairs in order but discovered that, in order to keep her place in society, she had fallen deeply into debt; in effect, she could not afford to support Uvarov "in a proper manner" if he became an ambassadorial secretary. Purportedly, a carriage was waiting to take him to Paris, but Uvarov reluctantly decided to remain in St. Petersburg; the future foreign minister Nesselrode took his place. In 1810, Uvarov made additional attempts to get to Paris, but they also appear to have failed.[26]

THE POSSIBILITIES OF ORIENTALISM
AND NEOCLASSICISM

ONCE finally settled in St. Petersburg, Uvarov began to act upon his new cultural views. In Vienna, Madame de Staël had correctly chided the young man for "not yet having undertaken anything serious." In the next decade, though, he authored a series of essays, whose central theme was to foster neoclassicism and orientalism as possible bases for building an original Russian culture now that European old regime models seemed spent.

Uvarov's first published essay was entitled *Projet d'une académie asiatique* (1810). While in Vienna, Uvarov had concluded that the major problem in European culture was that it lay "exhausted" and required rejuvenation. His solution was to discover "new strength and freshness" in those "sources, old, forgotten, buried under debris" in the Orient, whence Europe traced its origin.

> And if it is true that we have arrived at one of those epochs, which are not unknown in the history of civilization, epochs where the human spirit, having come to the end of its productive abundance and unable any longer to cope with the fermentation of ideas, returns within itself to gather new forces by analyzing its own riches, then never could the renaissance of Oriental studies encounter more favorable circumstances.

The young author hoped to convince his government to bid for leadership of this endeavor by establishing a scholarly Asian academy in St. Petersburg. Because of its geographic location, the farflung Russian Empire could emerge as a "mediatrix between European civilization and Asian wisdom."[27] Uvarov thus made a dramatic shift: according to him, the needed renovation or renaissance of European culture would be centered in Russia, not the West, since inspiration would come from the East.

In 1810, Uvarov's *Project* could indeed seem a hopeful venture, because the Oriental Renaissance, an intellectual movement that had begun in the last decades of the eighteenth century, appeared as a cultural watershed, at least to its devotees. Just as the rediscovery of Latin and Greek manuscripts had produced the earlier Renaissance, the introduction of Eastern manuscripts might result in a revolutionary expansion of the European *Weltanschauung*. Intellectual perceptions would become truly global once it was recognized that Eastern and Western cultures were equally rich and that, indeed, the latter had its origins in the former.[28] In addition, the colonial interests of European powers provided the impetus for Eastern scholarship as a means of understanding and administering conquered or about-to-be-conquered peoples. In 1784, the British established the Asiatic Society of Calcutta, and its founders began translating monuments of drama, poetry, and legislation from the Sanskrit.[29] In 1795, the French, rivals of the British in the Far East, encouraged Silvestre de Sacy to found a center for Oriental studies in Paris, École des langues orientales, whose graduates produced the scholars and teachers that enabled Eastern studies to flourish in universities throughout Europe.

The fragmented German states had no possibility for Eastern expansion, but their great literary figures, Novalis, Fichte, Schelling, Schiller, Goethe, the Schlegel and Humboldt brothers, all became luminaries in the Oriental Renaissance and hailed it as the beginning of a true *Weltlitteratur.* Indeed, it was Friedrich Schlegel who first studied, appreciated, and formulated the consequences of Orientalism for scholarship in general. In 1808, his famous essay *Über Sprache und Weisheit der Indier* shocked the intellectual world with the startling thesis that Greek, Latin, German, Arabic, and Persian languages and religious ideas were direct descendants of the ancient culture of India. The impact of the book was immediate and widespread. It soon became conventional wisdom that Europe's origins lay in the East, and that the riches of this cultural source had been shamefully ignored. Few poets, linguists, philosophers, or historians remained unaffected.[30]

Of all European countries, Russia in 1810 seemed least affected by the Oriental Renaissance, though paradoxically it had the longest tradition of Eastern involvement. Scythians, Sarmatians, Kumans, and Mongols had mingled with, beset, and often dominated the inhabitants of the central Russian plain until the fifteenth century. In a spectacular reversal, beginning in the sixteenth century, Russia mounted an expansive drive deep into the Far East, Central Asia, and the Caucasus that resulted in the formation of a Eurasian empire. To answer the need for translators, administrators, diplomats, and missionaries trained in the languages of these conquered areas, Peter the Great began to promote Eastern studies, a policy continued by Catherine the Great. The emperor invited leading European orientalists to join his newly established Academy of Sciences, and the empress promulgated the teaching of Arabic, Tatar, Chinese, and Persian in schools in the appropriate border regions, but neither effort produced durable results.[31] In 1733, Academician George Kehr proposed an Eastern institute, as did Lomonosov; and in 1802 the orientalist Jan Potocki repeated the suggestion. All three plans were buried in the archives as "eccentric" or as "not having the smallest hope for success."[32] The first real recognition of the importance of Oriental studies came with the provision made in the 1804 educational statutes for chairs in Eastern languages and literatures in all the newly founded Russian universities as well as in Moscow University, which had been created in 1755 by Lomonosov.

Uvarov was to become the main purveyor of Orientalism in Russia because of his own interest and because he understood the empire's political interest in the East. This young man of Tatar origin asked to accompany the 1805 Golovkin ambassadorial mission to China, a monumental enterprise that became the "only thing people talked about in society." The mission was charged with furthering trade relations, and it included a pleiad of scientists to collect information on botany, astronomy, and mineralogy; but lack of knowledge of protocol prevented the Russians from reaching Beijing. Although Uvarov did not go on the mission, he came into close contact with Golovkin in Vienna; they both frequented the same salons as Count Wenceslas Ryzhevsky, who in 1808 had founded one of the first European journals devoted exclusively to the East, *Fundgruben des Orients*. And, while Uvarov deplored Schlegel's romanticism, he heralded his friend's essay on India, became a convert to his theories, and enthusiastically mailed copies of the first edition of the essay to his acquaintances in St. Petersburg.

In addition, Uvarov's patron, Alexander Kurakin, served as Alexander I's plenipotentiary during the conferences in Tilsit and Erfurt in 1807 and 1808; as the accompanying attaché, Uvarov surely knew that the tsar and Napoleon discussed plans to cripple England by conquering India and to divide up the Ottoman Empire. Convinced of both the intellectual and political importance of the East, Uvarov began seriously to study it. When he returned to the capital, he sought guidance from Ignatius Fessler, a professor of Hebraic literature at the St. Petersburg Ecclesiastical Academy, and from Julius Klaproth, a leading orientalist in the Academy of Sciences; they guided Uvarov's reading and collaborated with him on his *Project*.[33] The resulting essay, although containing no original ideas, displayed the author's talent for synthesis and the fact that he had thoroughly read and assimilated the works of all the prominent English, French, and German orientalists, with Schlegel the chief influence.

This period during which Uvarov became a student and enthusiast of Oriental studies is noteworthy, in the long run, because he supported them tirelessly for the rest of his life. His policies, both as president of the Academy of Sciences and as educational minister, resulted in Russia's emergence as an international center of Oriental scholarship, an esteem the country holds to this day. Indeed, Uvarov brought to Russia the main heritage of the Oriental Renaissance—to recognize and study the East as an essential contributor to world civilization, not as an object of modish exoticism or a practical concern of foreign policy, and to create a self-perpetuating school of scholarly research on the topic.[34]

On a more immediate level, Uvarov's *Project for an Asian Academy* first enunciated his religious and historical views. After 1810, he never doubted that the Orient, in particular India, contained "the cradle of all the civilizations in the universe." He uncritically accepted the notions that Western Christian philosophy echoed Indian metaphysical concepts of creation, conservation, and destruction, and that Sanskrit was a language richer than Latin or Greek. If "grammatical perfection" existed in the "cradle" of civilization, and man had thus arrived on earth fully endowed intellectually, then this line of reasoning offered Uvarov final proof of the biblical account of creation as a special act of God.[35] Study of the Orient would thus "demolish the frail scaffolding of modern materialists," especially Rousseau and his theory of the grunting "savage man" who had to evolve "from an epoch of shadows and stupidity." All of this endowed Uvarov with a religious, though deistic and hence nondogmatic, world view. He neatly charted the flow of moral, philosophical, and religious opinions from India to ancient Greece to Rome and then on to Augustine, Aquinas, Descartes, and Leibnitz. In the next decade, Uvarov developed a progressive philosophy of history based upon this notion that each civilization absorbed the ideas of its predecessors, added to them its own character, and then transmitted them to its heir; soon, Russia would be the successor to Western Europe.

On a scholarly level, Uvarov correctly assumed that, because Oriental studies would illumine the origins of knowledge, they would bring about the rejuvenation of many branches of scholarship, especially comparative philology and the history of philosophy and religion. But, politically and culturally, he was eager to promote study of the East as a salvation from the contemporary "popular abuse of ideas" that caused "a great portion of the human race" to grovel before everything new. He particularly opposed "modern philosophy" for its materialism and rejection of religious values, politics for its love of revolution, and romanticism, at least the understanding of it that he had gleaned in Vienna, for its "disdain" of all past culture. In place of this negativism and love of change, Oriental studies emphasized tradition and channeled "restive intellects" into the peaceful pursuit of "determining the bases of their genealogy." He lectured his generation: "We are called upon not to erect a new edifice, but to reconstruct, to defend the immense remains." This turned out to be the same logic that Uvarov used as minister to encourage Russian youth to investigate their own national origins, which he assumed would support existing values, rather than focus their attention upon revolutionary European ideas.

Indeed, fearing that Europe was either in decay or on the brink of a "total revolution" that would "plunge it into darkness," Uvarov called upon Russia to pick up the mantle of Eastern studies. First, here was a way for a younger Russia to avoid "European contagion" and hence "premature old age." Second, Russia was already "mistress of the entire northern part" of the Asian continent and thus possessed a "clear political interest" in the endeavor. Herein lay the basis for a "new national politics," for the possibility that Russia would become the first modern Eurasian power and would forge a link—as the "*shrewd*" British had done in India—between political domination and cultural leadership: "Never has *raison d'état* been in such perfect accord with the grand designs of moral civilization."

To fulfill this mission, of course, Russia desperately needed teachers, translators, interpreters, and administrators to service Asian portions of the empire as well as to carry on diplomacy with Eastern countries. Uvarov believed that such a cadre could be produced only if training were systematized and centered in a scholarly institution where one would see the "*European critic* alongside the *Asiatic lama*."[36] Despite arguments that emphasized political utility and nationalistic aspirations, Uvarov was among the first to conceive of scholarly research as a major component of Russia's Eastern involvement; indeed, that remains his major contribution in this area. The academy was to offer thirty-one language and twenty-five literature courses in Sanskrit, Chinese, Manchurian, Arabic, Persian, Turkic, Tatar, and Hebrew, and there were future provisions for Georgian, Armenian, Tibetan, and North Asian studies. Uvarov ended the *Project* with a plea for major government funding so that the work of the academy would assume "proportions worthy of the Russian Empire."[37]

Uvarov's *Project* was already well known in the spring of 1810; one hundred copies were printed in November, apparently distributed by the author himself to friends and people of influence, and the young man suddenly acquired fame. He was quickly nominated for membership in the Russian Academy of Sciences. The essay won praise from a diverse audience: Napoleon, the French orientalist Langlès, Grand Duchess Catherine, Friedrich Schlegel, Goethe, and Friedrich Majer, a leading German specialist on India.[38] The reactionary de Maistre congratulated Uvarov for attacking the eighteenth century, "the most infamous epoch of the human spirit," and for boldly professing "good and ancient principles," such as the divine origin of society and speech. However, he attacked Uvarov's efforts to find similarities between Krishna and Christ and between Christian philosophy and Platonism, on the ground that these notions could only lead to a nondogmatic approach to religion and then to secularism.[39]

Others dismissed Uvarov's *Project* as a work of crass opportunism, an attempt to curry favor by appealing to Russian interest in Eastern expansion and immodestly to seek literary fame by sending the essay to luminaries throughout Europe.[40] The charges were in part true, and some of them provide evidence that Uvarov's open quest for "paper immortality" irked even his friends. On the other hand, distribution of one's works was commonplace, and Uvarov's sincere interest in Eastern studies cannot be doubted. At any rate, the *Project* was shelved until the next reign. Zhukovskii effectively squelched Uvarov's idea for fostering Orientalism by correctly pointing out that, while Russian grammar studies were "still in their infancy," talent should not be taken up by an Asian academy.[41]

While its suggestions were not acted upon immediately, Uvarov's essay successfully launched him on a new career, one for which his early experiences and cultural interests admirably suited him. The *Project* was dedicated to Count Alexis Razumovskii, the newly appointed educational minister, the brother of Uvarov's patron in Vienna, and, as of the fall of 1810, Uvarov's father-in-law. Since Uvarov's return from Austria, he had not only tried to put his financial affairs in order and write his essay but had also courted the "not young" (she was five years his senior) but very rich daughter of the count, Catherine.[42] As the Razumovskii family chronicle laconically states: "He married the countess [on September 23, 1810] and soon thereafter [December 31, 1810] was appointed superintendent of the St. Petersburg Educational District."[43] Although his marriage appeared opportunistic, and may have been, he apparently, despite some gossip, proved to be a good husband for the next thirty-nine years and the devoted father of four children; recently one literary critic, offering no proof, avers that Uvarov had a male lover.[44] A charge of nepotism may be warranted, but Uvarov's appointment was also plausible, because, despite his youth, he was clearly gifted. Furthermore, he enjoyed the good will of the tsar, who wanted to offer him some "compensation" for his lost Paris post.

Uvarov's new job, however, as might be expected, did not prevent him from pursuing his cultural interests. While Orientalism held little attraction for Russian men of letters, the other ideas Uvarov expressed in his *Project*—namely that Western Europe was in decay or at least disarray and that Russia might need an original approach to cultural development—were quite in the mainstream of thought. No consensus, though, had yet been reached. A new round in the seminal battle between the Old and New Styles, symbolic of Russia's acceptance or rejection of the West, was just erupting. In 1811, Shishkov, sensing growing antagonism toward the four-year-old Franco-Russian alliance, republished his *Inquiry* and organized a literary society, called the Symposium of the Lovers of the Russian Word (*Beseda liubitelei russkago slova*), to combat foreign influence at court and in culture and to encourage the use of the Old Style in Russian literature.[45]

Karamzin had, in 1803, abandoned belles-lettres for history, but remained the symbol of the New Style he had devised. His followers, most like him against the Napoleonic alliance, nonetheless struggled against the attempt to reject Western cultural contacts that was promoted by advocates of the Old Style. Karamzin's followers demonstrated through parody that the self-educated Shishkov was an ignorant linguist who hopelessly confused Russian, Greek, and Church Slavonic root words. Of greater importance, the poets Zhukovskii and Batiushkov, using Karamzin's models, in the past decade had translated German, English, and Italian poetry into the Russian. The results were so masterful and original in meter and diction that they proved that use of the New Style and assimilation of Western culture produced not sterility or imitation, but the raising of Russian literature to universal standards of excellence.[46] Bemoaning the growing equation of "French armies with French books," Uvarov in early 1812 tried to initiate a literary group in opposition to the Symposium with his acquaintances Zhukovskii and Karamzin, but neither wanted anything to do with this "ink battle."[47]

When the War of 1812 broke out, literary sniping gave way to the military struggle to save the nation. For the moment, Shishkov triumphed as the gallophobe and patriot par excellence. In 1812, Alexander appointed him secretary of state, the highest aide of the tsar, with the order to compose stirring patriotic manifestoes; this he did beautifully. In 1813, he was made president of the Russian Academy and thus was enabled to impose his views on that institutional guardian of the Russian language.[48] His victory was shortlived. The arch literary rival, Zhukovskii, while Napoleon was still in Moscow, wrote a moving poem, "The Poet in the Camp of the Russian Warriors," and thereafter became "the favorite of the nation" with fame extending to the throne.[49] By the end of 1813, when Russia's victory over Napoleon had become a foregone conclusion, gallophobia and consequently the Symposium and Shishkov's influence began to wane.

Nonetheless, the cultural issue remained unsettled. Shishkov had had a point—the Russian tendency blindly to imitate foreign culture and neglect native roots. For all Karamzin's contributions to the Russian literary language, he borrowed extensively from the French, and this practice eventually seemed demeaning. But to accept Shishkov's propositions for basing modern Russian literature on a spent Church Slavonic model in isolation from the West seemed just as inauspicious.[50] Besides looking to the Orient, Uvarov's *Project* suggested another avenue for the development of an original Russian literature, one that he had borrowed from the Olenin salon and from Göttingen professors.

> Russia has an infinite advantage over the rest of Europe. She can take Greek literature as the basis for her national literature and found a completely original school. She should imitate neither German literature, nor the French spirit, nor Latin erudition. The thorough study of Greek will open an inexhaustible source of new ideas, of fecund images for Russia. It will give to history, to philosophy, to poetry, the purest forms and those closest to true models. Further, the Greek language is tied to the religion of the Russians and to Slavonic literature, which appears to be formed from it.[51]

The return to Greek models offered a compromise between the approaches of a Karamzin and a Shishkov. Neoclassicism, as the movement came to be called, could provide the service of bringing Russia into the mainstream of European literary development by allowing the experience of a Renaissance, even if shortlived. The neoclassicists expected original, national works quickly to supersede the reliance on Greek models. Russian men of letters were encouraged in this possibility by the knowledge that a later Renaissance was occurring in Germany, as seen in the towering achievements of Herder, Goethe, and Schiller.

The French classical tradition, it was pointed out in the last quarter of the eighteenth century, asserted rules that were really nonclassical for set styles and genres and stolidly declared their eternal validity. The irony was that the French inherited their suppositions from a Renaissance that emulated Latin sources, which themselves were dusky mirrors of the Greek: hence, an imitation of an imitation. Thus, the task of neoclassicists was to define what Greek culture really meant, which was surely beauty, nobility, and measure in art and life; but the Greek model also represented a freedom from perverse and artificial rules as well as from artistic repression of any sort and a love for the natural and the national. In this way, neoclassicism provided a home for those in many literary camps.[52]

Uvarov became a central figure in Russian neoclassicism by supporting its propositions and encouraging its adherents. As he pointed out to one of his talented literary friends: "I expound the theory . . . and I am an observer—you are the poet."[53] It was Uvarov, in particular, who spelled out the notion that Russian literature was in an organic state of "infancy" *(mladenchestvo)* and, therefore, if it succumbed to "blind imitation" of "this or that contemporary literature," it would "look like an infant carrying all the signs of senility or withered youth." Instead, Russians should turn to the truly original culture of the Greeks, "the most perfect product of the human mind." This was the reason why Uvarov, as superintendent and minister, insisted that the study of classical languages, especially Greek, should form the "basis of all education"; his successful establishment of a classical curriculum in the gymnasia forms a central theme in Russian educational history.

In 1820, along with his fellow litterateurs Batiushkov and Dashkov, Uvarov published a limited edition of the *Greek Anthology*, translated for the edification of the Russian reading public; Batiushkov's renderings are considered masterpieces. As Uvarov pointed out in the introductory article, the translations were done solely with the purpose of acquainting Russians with the "beauty, charm, taste, and voluptuousness" of Greek poetry in order to set literary standards and spark similar creations: "If we take Greek literature as the foundation of our literature, then perhaps we could succeed in substituting for the inadequacy of our own national taste the pure taste of the ancients, the eternal rules of classical literature."[54] The compilation represented an imitation of the Renaissance tradition in that Dashkov, while serving in Constantinople, searched for and sent back new manuscripts to his collaborators in Russia. This spirit of search for new models that would result in original creations renders the *Anthology* the single most representative work of Russian neoclassicism.[55]

Uvarov also encouraged Nicholas Gnedich to translate Homer's *Iliad* into Russian using the original Greek hexameter rather than, in the French manner, using the "boring and dry" Alexandrine verse form. He took the opportunity in a letter to Gnedich to admonish Russian men of letters at last to "stop burdening the infancy of our literature with the heavy chains of French taste" and mindlessly imitating "not only foreign *ideas* but also foreign *forms*." Despite the controversy that ensued, Gnedich complied. When the translation was completed a decade later and hailed a masterpiece, he "blamed" Uvarov for the result; it is still acknowledged as "the most splendid example in Russian poetry of the grand classical style." By 1849, Zhukovskii, also admitting Uvarov's inspiration, completed an equally magnificent rendering of the *Odyssey*.[56] Other talented neoclassicists, such as Alexander Voeikov, celebrated Uvarov's guidance by dedicating their works to him. Batiushkov wanted his works read "only by him" because of the "brilliance of his mind"; he ended a poem in Uvarov's honor with the words: "It seems as though you were in Athens born." Classical scholars in Russia, such as Friedrich Gräfe of the St. Petersburg Ecclesiastical Academy and Christian Matthei of Moscow University, dedicated works to him because he had assisted in their compilation. K. Gerbskii, whose Latin dictionary was hailed by scholars, mentioned that one of the "first-class scholars" with whom he consulted was Uvarov.[57]

Uvarov earned his reputation as a classical scholar through learning and publication. Beginning in 1810, for fifteen years he studied Greek with Gräfe. He acquired and devoured a library on Greek scholarship and published several essays on the topic during this time.[58] Although Uvarov admitted he only wrote for "amateurs of antiquity," he addressed the highly debated issues of the era but without offering a definitive solution. As one reviewer observed: "He rather reads secondary sources and critically points out weaknesses, offering a new synthetic view."[59] However, the erudition evident in the essays and the ability to digest scholarly works in five languages established the author as one of the best-educated Russians of his era. With some condescension Friedrich Schlegel said he could "not get over the fact that a young Russian noble is as learned as he."[60] Uvarov openly continued to work at building his reputation by sending copies of his essays to leading intellectuals in Russia and Europe.

Sensing that his own era was one of transition, Uvarov used the idea of transition as a common theme in his writing. In particular, he displayed a fascination with the fourth and fifth centuries A.D., years when neoplatonism offered an intellectual bridge connecting the two great epochs into which Uvarov believed universal history was divided, the classical and modern (or pagan and Christian). To a lesser extent, he returned to the theme of his *Project* and portrayed the Indic roots of Greek thought. His first work on classicism, *Essai sur les mystères d'Éleusis* (1812), suggested that the ancient pagan rite of the Eleusinian Mysteries—in which "higher truths" about the immortality of the soul and unity of the godhead were revealed to initiates—contained ritual words of Indian origin and were revived in the fourth century as a last stand against Christianity. Twentieth-century scholars still uphold this thesis.[61] In 1817, Uvarov wrote *Nonnos von Panopolis, der Dichter* (1818) about the writer whom he considered the last of the great Greek poets; because Nonnos had converted from paganism to Christianity, Uvarov saw him as personifying the fourth- and fifth-century era of transition. One year later, two more essays by Uvarov appeared: *Über das Vorhomische Zeitalter* (1819) was an appendix to the work just published by the German classicists G. Hermann and F. Creuzer containing correspondence between Homer and Hesiod, the latter a transitional figure between the epic and lyric stages of Greek poetry. A polemic, *Examen critique de la fable d'Hercule* (1817), attacked a French scholar, M. Dupuis, for not recognizing the nature of the apparent affinity between the account of Hercules and the twelve signs of the Zodiac and that of Christ and the apostles: it should be regarded as only another attempt of pagans to reconcile themselves with Christianity in the neoplatonic era of transition. In 1824, Uvarov's *Mémoire sur les tragiques grecs* (1824) correlated the work of Euripides, Sophocles, and Aeschylus and stressed intellectual continuity from the East to Greece and then on to the Christian West.[62]

These essays also endeared Uvarov to Goethe, the unquestioned leader of the European intellectual world. The German poet, who abhorred *Sprachpatriotismus*, applauded Uvarov as a cosmopolitan "scholarly liberal" because he wrote and read in so many languages and announced in his preface to *Nonnos* (dedicated, by the way, to Goethe): "It can be hoped that we have already abandoned that false idea in scholarship of the political excellence of one or another language, . . . when everyone . . . will always choose the language closest to that area of ideas in which he has chosen to write." Uvarov continued a long correspondence with Goethe on various topics, but one aspect was rather amusing. It was well known that Goethe, a poet of unbounded creativity, hated the fetters of grammar: "The rules seemed ridiculous to me." And so, when Uvarov apologized for his grammatical lapses when writing in German, Goethe politely encouraged the author: "Rest in peace from the immense advantage you have in not knowing German grammar; for thirty years, I have tried to forget it."[63] Uvarov treasured this as a compliment to his prose and apparently carried the letter around with him. In the 1830s Alexander Herzen found this curious: "He amazed us by the multitude of languages and the heterogeneous hotch-potch which he knew, a veritable shopman behind the counter of enlightenment. . . . He used to carry in his pocket by way of a testimonial, a letter from Goethe, in which the latter paid him an extremely odd com-

pliment, saying: 'There is no need for you to apologize for your style—
you have succeeded in what I never could succeed in doing—forgetting
German grammar.'" Herzen's profile is keen: Uvarov was surely erudite,
but somewhat vainglorious.[64]

On a more serious level, Uvarov's writing in French and German demonstrated a retreat from the isolationism that reigned in Russia from 1812
until the defeat of Napoleon. Once the threat of the universal monarchy
of the French both in literature and politics had passed, Uvarov, as superintendent, signaled the "new and better order of things" by suggesting in
1815 that Russian writers "must mollify their caustic and coarse tone in
judging other peoples who are now in a completely different relationship
to Europe and to us." He expressed this new and accommodating literary
attitude in a letter to another classicist, Kapnist.

> Without the most basic knowledge and long labors in ancient litera-
> ture, nothing new can exist; without an intimate acquaintance with
> other modern literatures, we will not be in a position to embrace the
> entire field of the human mind—a vast and brilliant field upon which
> all prejudices ought to die and all hatred be extinguished; but without
> forms especially suited to our language, it will be impossible for us
> to have a national literature.[65]

It was because of this balanced, moderate program for Russian cultural
development that neoclassicism, unlike Shishkov's theories, was able to
meld into the growing romanticism in this decade and thus contribute to
the golden age of Russian poetry that immediately followed, an age "far
more *formal*, active, selective—in short *classical*—than any other nineteenth-century school of poetry" in Europe.[66] However, before the arrival
of the golden age, the final episode in the controversy between the protag-
onists of the Old and New Styles and to be played out.

THE DIALECTIC OF THE ARZAMAS
LITERARY CIRCLE

THE entire thrust of Russian cultural development was absorbed,
refined, and transmitted by the members of the Arzamas Literary
Circle during its short life from 1815 to 1818. The society, composed primarily of litterateurs in St. Petersburg, performed the dialectical
function of melding Russian traditions and Western innovations, of holding
them both to universal criteria in taste and form and then producing a
synthesis that resulted in modern Russian culture. The group was founded
by Uvarov and Dmitri Bludov, then an official in the ministry of foreign
affairs and later prominent as minister of justice. The two men reacted to
the popularity of a new play, *Lipetsk Spa*, by Shakhovskoi, that in part
satirized Karamzinists and was, in effect, the swan song of the Old Style

and of objections to any foreign influences in Russian life and art. The most prominent regular members of Arzamas were Zhukovskii and Batiushkov, and, as the group grew to number twenty, it included young (twenty-seven to thirty-seven years of age) government officials from a number of ministries who were also active literary dilettantes. The honorary membership boasted the poets Ivan Dmitriev and Iuri Neledinskii-Meletskii; Ivan Capodistrias, the minister of foreign affairs from 1816 to 1822; and Karamzin, the "older brother" of the regular members who taught them how "to think, work, and write."[67] Karamzin set up a branch of Arzamas in Moscow, where he resided. He often visited the capital and wrote to his wife: "I know no people more intelligent than Arzamas members; with them, one could live and die." The group met at first weekly, and then monthly, at either Uvarov's or Bludov's home; each was spacious and well furnished.[68]

Most scholars fail to discern any underlying unity in the Arzamas Literary Circle, save for a postmortem opposition to Shishkov's literary theories, and some dismiss its gatherings as examples of an empty prank. In part, these observations are correct. By the time Arzamas held its first meeting in October 1815, defenders of the Old Style had so dwindled in number that it had become an act of courage to support its premises; in fact, eight months later, the only ranking Shishkovite, Derzhavin, took the Old Style with him to his grave. Thus, the Arzamas members happily celebrated the uncontested victory of the New Style and in mock eulogies, with a touch of black humor, "interred" any remaining opponents; Zhukovskii and Karamzin, who both loathed polemics, were pleased to belong to the society because they really were no longer necessary. The atmosphere of the meetings seemed indeed prankish. The name was drawn from Bludov's setting for a parody of Shakhovskoi, and the lackluster town was located on Uvarov's familial estates. At meetings, Zhukovskii, the permanent secretary whose ballads provided "Arzamas names" for each member, read the minutes, "hilarious" in their mockery of everything from the Russian Academy to Masonic rites, and ended with the recitation of jovial epigrams. Occasional plans to publish literary almanacs, anthologies, or journals never materialized.[69]

The real point of the Arzamas society was its literary direction, both in the sense of leadership and in its demarcation of the path to follow, but this fact has gone unrecognized. Actually, Arzamas had existed without interruption since 1811 in that a "spiritual brotherhood" had bound young litterateurs in a common worship of Karamzin and Zhukovskii, in a belief in the New Style, and in an antagonism toward the narrow views of the Symposium. Thus, Arzamas simply made concrete an already functioning fraternity.[70] Uvarov had long tried to organize the group and, when Arzamas finally materialized, it seemed he wanted to preside as president; Vigel' noted that he "already saw himself as the leader of a group of elite guards in which were only famous knights and on his brow would sit a crown in which, as the most precious stone, he would place Zhukovskii." It should be pointed out that Vigel', who became a member at the second meeting, was infuriated that Uvarov "forgot" to include him in the original guest list. At any rate, the group voted to have a rotating chairman; although Uvarov was disheartened, he yielded to the "republic."[71]

Probably because he aspired to leadership among the dilettantes of the society, Uvarov's statements provide the best clues as to its purpose. At one meeting, he orated: "Geese, geese, . . . save . . . intelligence, taste, and native literature as your ancestors saved Capitolium." This is a reference to Krylov's most famous fable, "The Geese," written in 1809; furthermore, Arzamas was a town known only for its geese, and a goose dinner preceded each meeting. The fable revolved about a gaggle which argued that they should not be sold at the marketplace because they descended from those whose warning cackles had saved Rome from the barbaric Gauls. An unsympathetic passerby suggested they deserved to be cooked because, in contrast to their ancestors, they had "yet done nothing." Thus, Arzamas was to protect Russian literature at once from the Shishkovite barbarians and from "blind imitation" of the French. At another meeting, Uvarov went on to proclaim the end of the era from Lomonosov to Derzhavin, poets already in "possession of immortality," and the start of a "new era" heralded by Zhukovskii and Batiushkov. But Arzamas members shared a common belief that the "giant steps" made by Russian culture in the past few years could continue only through invigorating and constant contact with other cultures. Most were neoclassicists and saw discernment as their primary function. In 1812, the Arzamas member Dmitri Dashkov cried out: "Our literature is still not at all formed . . . ; our young writers still do not have enough models before them; they do not know what to shun or what they ought to follow."[72]

From this concern flowed the emphasis in the society on the elegance and development of language, on the studied search for and assessment of new forms and fresh sources. Uvarov's memoirs depict these goals exactly.

The direction of this society or, it is better to say, of these amicable meetings, was primarily *critical*. The individuals composing it were concerned with a thorough analysis of literary publications, the adaptation of native language and literature to all sources of ancient and foreign literature, a search for principles to serve as a strong basis for an independent theory of language, etc.[73]

It followed that Arzamas indeed did not advocate any "definite form" or set literary system; it was exploring. In general, the members of Arzamas adhered to Karamzin's original dicta: that artists should be allowed to create and to explore freely on an individual and independent basis and to emphasize literary activity as personal fulfillment. Some members were primarily interested in tone or deeper questions concerning the relation of literature to society. Others, such as Uvarov, Dashkov, and Bludov, stressed precision of language because, as Uvarov put it: "The more a language is perfect, the more a nation who speaks it approaches civilization." This emphasis on form in literature reflected the influence upon Arzamas members of the new science of philology, a seminal nineteenth-century branch of learning that Uvarov was familiar with from his research into the Asiatic Society of Calcutta. Scholars began to enshrine language as the essential vehicle of literature, the reflection of its speakers' entire cultural heritage, and the standard by which a nation's level of enlightenment is judged. Therefore, upon the development of language hinged the development of a national culture.[74]

Arzamas performed an extraordinarily important evolutionary function in the early history of Russian letters. The romanticism long fostered by Zhukovskii blended with the neoclassical modifications of Batiushkov. These styles, along with the stress on the freedom of the artist, were passed on to the poets of the golden age and in particular to Alexander Pushkin, who joined the society in 1817 after his graduation from Tsarskoe Selo Lycée. Critics agree that Russian literature in its golden ages has had such universal appeal because it absorbed the influences of so many foreign literatures in the process of making its own unique contributions—the very point of the Arzamas society.[75] This was also what Uvarov later meant as combining a "Russian *system*" with "European *education*." Thus, while Arzamas possessed no single literary theory, it acted as a signpost for the direction of future literary production—and therein lies its significance.

In 1817, three new members, Michael Orlov, Nicholas Turgenev, and Nikita Murav'ev, fresh from their stay in the West with the army, returned to Russia with a sense of mission to develop not literature, but the government along constitutional lines and to free the serfs. To these ends, they began to establish the secret political societies that led to the Decembrist Revolt of 1825 and tried to inject Arzamas with this new spirit. The majority of members, who held progressive political views, were clearly stung by the accusation that they had "occupied themselves with futilities and literary quarrels" and "exclusively literary programs" while "the state of the country offered a field so vast to the intelligence of all men devoted to the public good." New "Rules" were drawn up and adopted for a New Arzamas, a society not at all lighthearted and complete with strict membership qualifications. There were also to be new duties, especially writing articles for a journal that would not only guard literature but "observe the political and moral situation of Russia and other governments." Nonetheless, the majority, in contrast to the three new members, still favored the original literary bent of Arzamas; the journal, above all, would provide "an opening in the Chinese Wall separating us from Europe" and "define taste."[76]

The new rules became a major cause of the society's dissolution. In 1818, many Arzamas members left St. Petersburg to take up posts abroad, and many who stayed disliked the onerous duties that were now required. Later, Zhukovskii mentioned that he was glad that the "New Arzamas" never materialized, because many members would have been implicated in the Decembrist uprising; he claimed that because of Arzamas' love of literary freedom, it would have been seen as a symbol of a republic while the Symposium would have been regarded as that of the official government.[77] Arzamas met formally once more, in April 1818. The spirit of brotherhood remained throughout that year at occasional informal gatherings, but by 1819 even this camaraderie "had faded into the sky." Uvarov tried to revive the organization with the members remaining in St. Petersburg, but was unsuccessful. Nonetheless, the work of the society seemed to have been accomplished. As Nicholas Turgenev asserted in 1819: "Little by little Russia has finally entered the great European family in all regards; not only the sound of the Russian sword now brings Russia to the attention of Europe," but literature as well. Somewhat earlier, in 1817, Uvarov had announced: "With the reign of the Emperor Alexander, a new era has begun for Russia, even in literature."[78]

Moreover, some elusive quality that came to be called the "Arzamas spirit" remained. It evoked a generosity, a belief in progress and reform, catholic taste, a dedication to the development of all things Russian, a brotherhood not only among members but with other European cultures as well. This spirit was not relegated to the realm of literature alone; it spilled over into the politics of the post-Napoleonic era. While Zhukovskii and Batiushkov and their heir, Pushkin, represented the "Arzamas spirit" in literature, Uvarov embodied it in politics.

On another level, the Arzamas society may be remembered as a blessed event, a moment when literary circles and government ministries could boast the same members and share the same concerns. Uvarov had traveled a typical road from francophilia, sentimentalism, and self-centeredness to a new consuming interest in Russian culture, and then to dedicating his efforts at finding a balance among classical, native, and European sources in order to create a cultural identity for his country. In general, the reign of Alexander I did not yet demand that tortured choice, introduced by men like Orlov, Nicholas Turgenev, and Murav'ev, among serving the self, state, society, or culture—an election made nearly mandatory later in the century. Men like Uvarov could, at the same time, find self-fulfillment, hold government office, participate in intellectual circles, and consider themselves agents of public progress. Uvarov's optimistic theory of history only supported this happy Arzamas mentality.

THE FORMULATION OF A THEORY
OF HISTORY

We, following the example of Europe, are beginning to think about concepts of freedom.   Uvarov, 1818

DURING the first two decades of the nineteenth century, the direction of Russia's political and social development generated as much heated debate as her cultural evolution, and the issues were similar. At their heart lay the problem of Russia's relation to the West. The country's status within the European family of nations reached a zenith in these years. Russia daunted the seemingly invincible Napoleon in 1812, and, soon after, its military leadership appeared proved when Alexander I, acclaimed the Savior of Europe, rode at the head of the coalition that unseated the French emperor. Furthermore, the tsar, although retaining an autocratic form of government at home, became a leading proponent of constitutional government in Europe. In 1818, with pride and amazement, Uvarov wondered: "How has this people, the youngest son in the large family of Europe, in the course of one century surpassed its brothers . . . and now aspires to steal from others both the laurels of military glory and the palm of civic valor?"[1]

This enthusiasm was somewhat premature because momentous questions, "accursed questions," relating to Russia's development remained unresolved. In order to maintain the country's stature in a Europe rife with new political and social aspirations, was it not necessary to alter Russia's own governmental forms and abolish serfdom? If so, how quickly would these changes occur, how would they be effected, and what would be their model? Could the country modernize or westernize without sacrificing its unique national character? Or was Russia's present strength proof of the superiority of her traditional institutions? Indeed, was the West worth imitating? Was it perhaps not bankrupt and spent after the traumas of the revolutionary era?[2]

Uvarov addressed these social and political issues in a series of essays and pamphlets that he published between 1810 and 1818.[3] Although the young man remained outside the inner circle of influence around the tsar, his comments received notice because he occupied the important posts of superintendent of the St. Petersburg Educational District and, as of 1818, president of the Academy of Sciences.

Uvarov's statements provide uncommon insight into the intellectual climate of the era. Although he relished his reputation for erudition, he never pretended to be a professional scholar, historian, or philosopher, but he had the temerity—one rankled contemporary called it the "gall of a charlatan"—to approach these problems from a wide perspective.[4] He had the same end in view as when he discussed cultural topics. In the Arzamas spirit, his purpose was to discover a path by which Russia could come of age within the older European community and borrow the best achievements of this community while retaining a Russian identity. Born, as he himself recognized, "between two worlds," his ideas serve to capture the spirit and concerns of an embattled generation that sought to remove the perceived tension between Enlightenment ideals and absolutism, that wanted neither revolution, reaction, nor stalemate. His lifelong quest for the *juste milieu* and his admitted "love for synthesis" led him to sample and mix the multitude of opinions swirling among the Russian educated public at this time.[5]

The European mentors Uvarov cited in his works constituted a varied grouping: Mauguin had raised him on Voltaire's *thèse royale*, the notion that the "tutelary angel of sweet and wise liberty" was an enlightened, hereditary monarch;[6] at Göttingen, Schlözer and the resident Hannoverian Conservatives taught an abhorrence of revolution, a Burkean respect for tradition—the "standing wisdom of a country"—and reliance on a benevolent ruler and upper classes ready to proffer gradual reforms "as they are required by a new age";[7] Pozzo di Borgo championed the old absolutism while de Staël and Baron vom Stein applauded constitutional monarchies and representative governments that included the bourgeoisie, as did Benjamin Constant and the French Doctrinaires;[8] Bossuet, Bonald, Mallet du Pan, de Maistre, and Chateaubriand upheld the providential design of human affairs;[9] Montesquieu, Herder, Hume, Gibbon, and William Robertson looked to the lessons of history for answers to the *condition humaine*;[10] Johannes Müller and Schiller sought clues among Germanic tribes, while the new school of orientalists looked to Asia;[11] for Uvarov, a host of classical writers remained a constant source of inspiration and the supposedly radical Rousseau the object of derision.[12] Quite remarkably, Uvarov's interpretation of the historical process anticipated many of the propositions that

Hegel presented during the next decade at the University of Berlin, in his lectures on the philosophy of history. Thus, in effect, Uvarov's writings represent something of a catalog or synopsis of the European intellectual trends present in Russia at this time.

Uvarov displayed an equally broad acquaintance with Russian authors and historians. He especially lauded the work of two men whose views are normally considered antithetical, namely Michael Speranskii, the statesman whose name was synonymous with institutional reform along Western lines, and Karamzin, who, as an historian, championed autocratic tradition and shivered at any breeze of change. Because of his family connections and positions, Uvarov was surely at least aware of the ideas of Alexander's young group of advisers, the Unofficial Committee, who in the previous decade had encouraged reform and constitutional projects, although usually to no avail. Also, Uvarov was well acquainted with the diehard opponents of reform, the clique of nobility led for a time by Shishkov. In addition, as superintendent, Uvarov was responsible for the faculty of the Central Pedagogical Institute (later St. Petersburg University), many of whose members discoursed about Adam Smith, the Physiocrats, Rousseau, and Kant. And, it should be noted, Uvarov was raised on the same books as his acquaintances who participated in the Decembrist Revolt of 1825.[13]

From this intellectual pastiche, Uvarov arrived at his own "self-styled"[14] theory of universal historical development that guided him through this decade and for the rest of his life. This theory bore a symbiotic relationship with and complemented Uvarov's attitudes toward cultural development. Both the theory and the attitude portrayed Russia as a young nation still in the process of learning from her older European brothers, but implied her unique and climactic place in the new era Uvarov suspected was dawning.[15] In the course of his life, Uvarov often changed his mind about whether the rest of Europe was in a stage of decaying old age or robust maturity, but he possessed a clear idea of what elements Russia should incorporate in its own historical development. Nevertheless, preferring "the peaceful pursuit of culture," he avoided contemporary political affairs until the French army invaded Russia.

THE TRIAL OF THE REVOLUTIONARY AND
NAPOLEONIC ERAS

IN Vienna, as a matter of course, Uvarov had "like all high society hated Napoleon."[16] After he became superintendent of the St. Petersburg Educational District, he facilitated the publication of anti-French treatises and established patriotic journals such as the *Conservateur impartial*, headed by his tutor Mauguin, and *Son of the Fatherland (Syn otechestva)*.[17] Between 1813 and 1815, he wrote six essays reacting to the Napoleonic threat[18] and in them honed his concepts on European political progress. His conclusions were reflected in all his later writings, including his literary essays, and hence constitute a watershed in his intellectual development.

In these essays, Uvarov tried to make rational sense of his era by melding several eighteenth- and early nineteenth-century concepts: that a study of history explained contemporary events; that progress was the fundamental law of history; that this progress proceeded organically within civilizations and nations; that Providence guided this progress; that the end of progress was a government that reflected the moral, Christian equality of all men before God; and, last, that this government was a constitutional monarchy characterized by representative institutions, universal civil rights, and qualified political rights. Despite the apparent contradictions that would riddle any attempt to reconcile these streams of thought, Uvarov rarely tried openly to resolve them or to define his commonplace but ambiguous terms. Still, he proved able to incorporate all these elements into a neat, if not profound or rigorously logical, synthesis.

Uvarov's turning to history for analysis and explanation of his era reflected a new tendency that had been growing since the mid-eighteenth century. Historical research and writing became tools for causal explanation of the past, for condemning and reforming contemporary abuses, and for discovering criteria and laws for charting future action.[19] The next generation of thinkers even more desperately craved to understand the meaning of history; radicals and conservatives alike interpreted the revolutionary era as a result of "mistakes," of rulers not clearly understanding the thrust of historical development. For instance, Uvarov in 1813 felt distraught because the past and present appeared "chaotic" and the future seemed "hidden from view"; he yearned for the "light of philosophy" to illumine his times. Such common sentiments resulted in a new urgency to discover scientific, Newtonian laws in history that might disclose, in Uvarov's words, the same "constant and tangible order that governs the physical world." He further apotheosized history as the "witness of the times, the light of truth, the life of memory, the tutor of life, the echo of antiquity." He also warned that leaders would be "devoured" by history, "the supreme judge of peoples and tsars," if they "did not follow its directives."[20] On a pragmatic level, Uvarov, both as superintendent and minister, considered the interpretation and teaching of history of such importance and consequence that he insisted they be a strictly "governmental task."

It is understandable that a belief in progress provided the elemental force behind Uvarov's historical theory, because this belief was the central idea of most philosophies of history in the eighteenth century. Its strength held into the nineteenth century, at least after Napoleon was defeated, in its vague sense as an assumption born of modern experience. By the 1820s, Guizot, in his lectures at the Sorbonne on the history of European civilization, confidently told his beaming audience that the idea of progress was "fundamental," based on "common sense," and therefore needed no philosophical underpinning.[21] Similarly, Uvarov assumed that what he called a "law of progress" was operating in nearly all areas of human endeavor, "including mutual relations, public laws, general enlightenment, international trade"; in general, the ever-increasing "accumulation and spread of knowledge" figured as the chief characteristic and cause of the "grand evolution of humanity"—the "progressive march" of what Uvarov liked to call the *"esprit humain."* Although he never espoused the notion of strict, linear development, he adhered, ever ebullient, to a cyclical theory that avoided the despair of degeneration by projecting a spiral wherein no civilization ever really dies; its "spirit," achievements, or "torch" somehow is passed on and "rushes to another part of the globe." He viewed history as an "endless chain," with each generation building upon the accomplishments of all the others.[22]

Uvarov attached to his belief in progress the equally popular notion of organic development. Using the newly resurrected man/society analogy, he suggested that the two civilizations history had thus far produced, the Ancient and the Modern, were each subject to a life cycle. In addition, he accepted the historicist idea that each state within the civilization possessed an individual national spirit as well as functioning as part of the general *esprit humain* and that each developed at its own pace: "States have their epochs of birth, infancy, youth, their actual maturity, and finally old age." In the process, each state retained its unique "physiognomy"—the result of the peculiarities of physical environment, customs, institutions, and communication with other peoples that made it a nation. Furthermore, development or innovation, whether called organic or historicist, is perforce gradual. Uvarov explained that "all great . . . changes are . . . the slow fruit of time" and that "transplanted institutions cannot flourish unless identified by a considerable lapse of time with the soil that received them."[23] In the wake of the French Revolution and Napoleonic era, many contemporaries, of course, saw disaster as the only possible result of a quick break with the past. Slow, organic development, building on national tradition, became the fulcrum around which Uvarov's thought and policy turned for the rest of his life.

Although Uvarov until his death confidently asserted that progress was discernible and organic development its only fruitful course, he never clearly stated how these phenomena occurred; he simply alluded to "natural laws" or "eternal laws of necessity." Neither a philosopher nor a historian, he remained content to solve any mysteries in the universe by turning to Providence: "There is in the course of empires, as in the life of men, one constant law that one could term *Fatality*, if it were not the effect of an eternal and impenetrable Providence. This law is imprinted in the moral world as in the physical world. . . ."[24] Needless to say, Uvarov's reliance on Providence diminished the validity of both a pure theory of progress and one of organic development, both of which necessitate an internal principle inherent in nature. However, in Uvarov's looser narration of historical processes, Providence could handily be harnessed to both theories. Uvarov described progress as working on three levels. First, Providence was the ultimate cause directing human affairs: It "predestined" the final aim of man on earth. Second, Uvarov believed that Providence, to accomplish this aim, usually operated through natural causes, allowing the intrinsic development of the *esprit humain*, which received its potential from "fundamental notions implanted in the human reason by Providence." Normally, Providence was discreet, exerting only a "secret influence on all the actions and efforts" of men: "None knew that he was a blind instrument in the hands of Providence." On a third and direct level, Providence meddled whenever "natural" development veered from the proper path or proved too hesitant. For instance, in Europe, when feudal institutions "began to oppress the growing *esprit* and opposed its predestined progress, then Providence planted the seeds in the womb of feudalism that gave birth to the means for its abolition." In that one statement, Uvarov combined the ideas of progress, organicism, and providential direction. He believed that all peoples or rulers who failed to cooperate with Providence suffered revolution or overthrow.[25]

Uvarov claimed to discern Providence's plan for mankind—the steady development of "true enlightenment," that is, of "the correct understanding . . . of the obligations and rights of a man and a citizen" on the part of rulers and ruled alike. As the dignity and self-respect of individuals grew and the limits of their responsibilities to and expectations of the state became better defined, commensurately higher forms of government evolved in response. Uvarov considered the gradual extension of "civil and political rights"—the working out of an evolving "moral order in the universe"—to be the main theme and rationale of history.[26] The Fall of Man, he claimed, "contains in itself alone the key to all history." Man left Paradise in a marred state but with all his potential "implanted" or innate. Providence called upon man to develop suitable institutions that could accommodate "the immortal soul and the mortal body" and that could reconcile the vice and virtue of fallen nature and the rights and obligations of a creature of God with those of a citizen in a state. This interlocking advance of morality and politics defines, in the abstract, what Uvarov meant by the "marche de l'*esprit humain*" as he traced it through history.[27]

More concretely, in the infancy of ancient civilization, just after the Fall, man had "no sense of his own worth" since he had "lost knowledge of the true God," and government and religion were "cruel," with "throne and altar equally covered with blood." In youth, the *esprit humain* reached a higher level "under the miraculous Grecian sky," but polytheism's "strange combination of morality and depravity" failed to "inform civic life" and resulted in republican government, "a beautiful dream of youth" that fostered only "turbulence," anarchy and "passions." The awesome "durability of Rome's political structure" marked the maturity of ancient civilization but, like the Greek era, was stained by being based on "a most cruel slavery" with no one "defending the rights of mankind" in general. But the "*Emancipator of the world* was born under a straw roof in a forgotten corner of [the Romans'] vast empire" and, slowly but surely, "the curtain lowered" on the ancient world.[28]

Then, according to Uvarov, the *esprit humain* was reborn on a new Christian basis, and modern or European history began. First, Uvarov vaguely asserted, "the half-savage institutions and morals" of German barbarians gave rise to "some kind of superior political formation" that presaged the concept of balance of power. The Middle Ages represented the childhood of Europe, when ancient slavery gave way to the infinitely more humane serfdom, based on "*belonging to the land*" and not on war captivity.[29] Providence next ordained the Crusades as "the last trial of young Europe." Despite "the spilled rivers of blood and tears" in the Crusades, there emerged a new interplay of social and political forces: serfdom as well as "particularly unsubmissive great *vassals and barons*" were gradually weakened, the commercial classes or "third estate" asserted their rights as a corporate body in free cities, and the monarchical power increased its control. These three elements—monarchy, nobility, and bourgeoisie—sought selfishly "to expand their spheres of power," but nonetheless "blindly" acted "to lay the foundation for a balance of all political powers," a trait Uvarov considered basic to an ideal form of government.[30]

Uvarov claimed that from the fifteenth to the eighteenth century all Europe was in transition, struggling to advance from youth to maturity. The stage of youth, by his definition, meant an era of absolute, unlimited monarchy. In this state, Uvarov excused the exercise of autocratic power as "historical necessity" among nations and governments that had developed to only an adolescent level. Thus, a monarch might treat his people as subjects and his realm as private property. But, given the ignorance of the masses and the narrower interests of the other castes, only a king could bind the organic parts of the state and bring unity and cohesion through a leadership that provided for the general welfare. The monarch served as both apex and basis or, in Uvarov's phrase, "the cornerstone of the social edifice and its only rallying point."[31] In addition, he believed that monarchies were best suited to the nature of mankind. Tyrannies and despotisms degraded human nature; democracies and republics gave it too much credit; aristocracies acted for selfish interest and not for that of the whole nation. Uvarov apparently agreed with those who believed that legitimate monarchs only aberrantly degenerated into despots. Chateaubriand had declared about France: "Nine centuries, thirty-three kings, and not one a tyrant." Karamzin saw only two despots in Russian history, Ivan the Terrible in the second half of his reign and Paul I.[32]

Eventually, in Uvarov's view, kings increasingly stopped acting "blindly" in their own interest and became "enlightened." They came to understand that, in order to maintain power, they should not only provide security against an external threat or furnish a corrective authority to punish enemies of the public peace, but should also enact positive measures for the moral and material progress of their nations. Monarchs were called upon to fulfill the economic, social, and legal aspirations of their peoples, who, themselves better enlightened as to their dignity, wanted to be treated as citizens, not subjects, with rights and not simply obligations. In order to accomplish these aims monarchs attempted to govern by sound laws and efficient administration. Thus, the king ruled not just because of his legitimate, inherited authority to do so, but also because of his purposeful activity; he provided for the general welfare of the populace, moderated their interests, and respected their rights. In effect, by establishing norms of legality and social utility, instead of whim, for the exercise of power, the sovereign became de facto limited; and this process could pave the way for a "modern form," to use Uvarov's phrase, of the monarchy. Uvarov exulted that the "tutelage" of kings had brought Europe "four centuries of glory and prosperity"; the "rights of man became known to all and the rights of a citizen were everywhere defined."[33]

The next stage, that of full maturity, would result in "true" monarchy, namely, one limited in power by some type of representative assembly, based on constitutional laws and guaranteeing some measure of civil and political liberty. This model constituted the ideal form of government that Providence intended for all mankind.

This wonderful process of progress, however, had been heinously interrupted by the French Revolution and the Napoleonic era, Europe's last adolescent trial before full maturity. In the eighteenth century, "the rays of a false philosophy," "desolate doctrines," and "philanthropic diseases" had spread among peoples, "shaking the basis of the social world" and causing the "reversal of all moral and political ideas." Uvarov admitted that "the *esprit humain* does not always proceed on a straight, strictly circumscribed path." "The gift of political freedom," he warned, is attended by "sacrifices," "losses," "dangers," "storms," and "delusions": "How many navigators were lost before Columbus! How many unsuccessful attempts before the English constitution!" He considered the revolutionary epoch a "chastisement" allowed by Providence in order to dissipate the false ideas that remained about the direction of human development. However, "the misery and horror," "the shedding of the blood of an entire generation," "the mass of crimes and useless evils" all served to demonstrate the futility of revolution, the disasters of anarchy, and the perversion of interrupting Europe's four-century development.[34]

In particular, Uvarov believed that the Jacobins had once and for all disspelled the myth that the republican form of government was workable in the great states of Europe; it should be added that he never referred to the new United States, except tangentially in his comment that Russia seemed to be "a slumbering bog as distant from advanced Europe as the endless steppes of North America." The other false form of government that reemerged during the revolutionary era, according to Uvarov, was despotism, a form appropriate only in mankind's pagan infancy and immoral in its Christian maturity. He deplored the contemporary embodiment of despotism in the universal monarchy and tyranny of the "satanic" Napoleon Bonaparte, "the destructor of thrones and unpunished violator of all people's rights."[35]

Uvarov could not understand how anyone could fail to recognize Napoleon as embodying a perversion of Providential design. In one essay, stung and angry, he denounced his hero Goethe for having written admiring verses about Napoleon, whom the poet called a "Weltgeist zu Pferde." (Goethe had met him in Jena and was quite charmed.) Uvarov could hardly believe that this "magnificent German genius" could "prostitute his sublime talent" by praising "the evil cause" of one who spread a gloom that "desolated centuries" of enlightenment.[36] Uvarov also chastised Pope Pius VII in an unpublished essay, "Memoir on the Concordat of 1801." He rued the church's capitulation to Napoleon and decried the general's attempt "to conquer religion as he had all Europe." Uvarov then criticized the pope for his act of "fatal condescension" in agreeing to place a crown on the "vulgar" usurper's head.[37]

Another essay, published as a brochure, *Éloge funèbre sur Moreau* (November 1813), summarized Uvarov's interpretation of the bloody events of the era.[38] Quoting Bossuet as the prophet of the moment and, recognizing the confusion and catastrophe in contemporary life, Uvarov found comfort in Providence, "who weighs the destinies of people and kings." Jean-Victor Moreau was a popular French general, the victor at Hohenlinden, and was reputed, unlike Napoleon, to have a deeper concern for his soldiers than for victory. He supported the republic and then the consulate, something Uvarov attributed to the "dizziness of the moment." Moreau became critical of Napoleon's tyranny and was implicated in the royalist conspiracy of 1803–1804. When the emperor banished him, he took his family to settle in Pennsylvania. In all these difficulties, Uvarov found "the finger of God." The émigré hunted, fished, studied, gardened, and was regenerated. As soon as he learned of the 1812 invasion, Moreau returned—"with a favorable wind" engineered by "the visible protection of Providence"—to the continent to save Europe, much, in Uvarov's rendition, like an Old Testament prophet.[39]

Uvarov saw in Moreau's story a microcosm of the events of the era: the hasty enthusiasm for revolution, the moral cleansing from the horrors of the revolutionary era, the final realization of the error of revolution, and the redirection along the correct path of rehabilitation, as pointed out by the hand of Providence. Moreau had realized his mistake and abandoned his "republican dreams and visions." After 1812, he espoused what Uvarov considered the proper political stance.

> Profoundly convinced of the necessity for a monarchical government, he reserved for only a small number of analogous souls that which he called *his imaginary state*. When he examined the situation of Europe, when he examined the needs of this grand exhausted body, he desired for France a legitimate government, in which powerful barriers assured the civil liberty of individuals. He desired for it the return of political moderation and interior stability.

Fighting under Alexander, Moreau was fatally wounded at Dresden. He became a political martyr; his blood, like the blood of Christian martyrs, was to be the seed of the "political liberty of Europe." Rather than condemning France for its costly mistakes, Uvarov considered the revolutionary era a providential event, a purgatory designed to bring in its wake a "regenerated Europe." This belief allowed him to build an optimistic construction around Europe's past, present, and future history.

When Alexander finally defeated Napoleon, Uvarov's optimism knew no bounds. Inspired by Chateaubriand's eulogy, *De Buonaparte et des Bourbons*, he composed a hymn of praise to the tsar entitled *L'Empereur Alexandre et Buonaparte*.[40] The pamphlet rang with patriotism and sang Alexander's praises as the moral and political liberator of all Europe, whose peoples rejoiced "from Cadiz to Kamchatka." After a scathing portrayal of a satanic Napoleon, Uvarov in equally purple prose extolled the tsar as "God's instrument."[41] He blithely excused the defeat at Tilsit by claiming that Alexander, because of his "affection" for his people, "had turned all his attention to the interior of his vast states." In 1812, however, never permitting himself the "quiet submission" of other rulers, he took up arms to lead a "national war" and "to save the liberty and independence of peoples and kings!" A series of defeats displayed Napoleon's "hideous nudity." The Tsar-Liberator marched into Paris and, because of his modesty, simplicity, and generosity, unlike a "vulgar conqueror," he treated the French as "victims, not enemies." Consigning Napoleon to the inner circles of Dante's Hell, Uvarov concluded: "The case of kings has been won by twenty years of revolution. Full of reciprocal esteem and better enlightened as to their own interests, king and nations have made, on the tomb of Bonaparte, the mutual sacrifice of despotism and popular anarchy."[42] Uvarov had buried Napoleon too soon. During the Hundred Days, he once again took up his pen against Napoleon, this time comparing him to Milton's Satan. In anger and disgust, he accused the French of treason and ingratitude for turning their backs once again on the Bourbons: "What a spectacle France presents us!" But he trusted once more that "Providence would not permit the utter triumph of crime"; more pragmatically, he pointed out that "the allies know the road to Paris."[43]

In the end, Uvarov's vision of a renewed Europe "now reconstituted on its bases" was euphoric.

> An insane tyranny will no longer act against the efforts of the *esprit humain*, which will be permitted to flourish on the entire surface of the globe; sciences and letters, banned like virtue and liberty, will be reborn with them. Commerce will unite all nations: foolish barriers opposed to the free exchange of the products of two worlds will fall of themselves. The *esprit humain*, cured of its errors, formed by its disasters, will take a path more analogous to its true grandeur; far from destroying, it will carefully reconstruct the social edifice: religious ideas and monarchical ideas have been purified in the misfortune of peoples and reaffirmed in the fall of kings.[44]

For Uvarov, then, the revolutionary era above all served the providential purpose of presenting the final proof of the proper form of government for a mature Europe and the necessity for monarchical leadership in achieving the desired goals.

After Alexander's defeat of Napoleon and Russia's emergence as a European power, Uvarov's hopes and dreams for his country's development toward maturity seemed to him on the brink of fulfillment. In 1814, he enthused: "A new era is going to be born bearing the name of Alexander!"[45] It was well known that the tsar had toyed with constitutional projects since his ascent to the throne and that, after the defeat of Napoleon, he had forced a very reluctant Louis XVIII to accept the French Charter of Liberties and had sponsored similar documents for other states such as Baden and Würtemberg. Beginning in 1814, journals such as *Son of the Fatherland (Syn otechestva)* and *Northern Mail (Severnaia pochta)*, the organ of the ministry of internal affairs, propagated the ideal of constitutional monarchies on the model of the charter, a document they published in full. The journalist Nicholas Grech, after a stay in France, was also enthusiastic. He commented: "Then again, who among the young people of that day was on the side of reaction? All sang the constitutional song and Emperor Alexander Pavlovich carried the tune."[46]

But, at the same time, xenophobes, obscurantists, and reactionaries appeared to be gaining power at home in the capital. A very powerful clique of nobility had all along feared innovation, progress, and especially constitutions, because these might threaten their power and privilege. There was also a continuing hostility to imported ideas as destructive of national and religious values, though this was surely a lesser concern. As the power of the noble faction grew, Uvarov became so despondent that he became physically ill and had to take a leave of absence from his official duties; this was probably a case of clinical depression, the first of many bouts he suffered in his lifetime.[47] Uvarov described "the despair in [his] soul" to his friend, the progressive German statesman Baron vom Stein.

> Some wish enlightenment without danger, i.e., a fire that does not burn. Others (and these are the greatest number) lump together Napoleon and Montesquieu, the French army and French books. . . . In the end, it is a chaos of cries, of passions, of factions battling one against the other, of exaggerations of parties; it is impossible to sustain the spectacle for any length of time. People throw around the terms *religion in danger*, *moral compromise*, *the falsity of foreign ideas*, *illuminism*, *philosophe*, *Freemason*, *fanatic*, etc. In a word, it is complete irrationality.

Uvarov also complained to Zhukovskii that his strength was drained: "*Even to believe in the possibility of something better* is in our situation an effort, a fantasy, an *ideal;* but to try actually to do something is a herculean task." Early in 1817, Uvarov confided his fears to his Arzamas friends and, later in the year, grumbled about a "century of disappointed hopes" and "how difficult it is to be born on a throne and be worthy of it."[48]

THE PROMISE OF MATURITY

ALEXANDER roused Uvarov out of his melancholy when, on March 15, 1818, after agreeing to rule in Poland as a constitutional monarch, the emperor addressed the first session of the Sejm, or parliament, in Warsaw. Using the same terms and timetable as Uvarov had in his theory of history, Alexander asserted that a constitution lay in Russia's future.

> The tradition existing in your country has permitted me immediately to enact this constitution. I am guided by the principles of constitutionally endowed institutions, which are constantly the object of my thoughts and whose salutory influence I hope, God willing, to extend to all countries entrusted to me by Providence. . . . You have given me the means to show my country what I have been preparing for it for many years and of what it can avail itself when the foundations for such an important event achieve a desired maturity.

He asked the deputies to "prove to your contemporaries that liberal institutions . . . are not at all a dangerous marvel" but, when stripped of "subversive doctrines," that is, revolutionary ideas, "they accord perfectly with order and produce by common agreement the true prosperity of nations."[49]

Bolstered by the tsar's statements, one week later Uvarov delivered a lengthy discourse (immediately published) that still stands as perhaps the single most progressive document ever written by a ranking official of the autocratic government. It is usually claimed that Timothy Granovskii, professor of history at Moscow University from 1839 to 1855 and a thinker deeply influenced by Hegel, "first introduced in Russia the view of world history as a progressive march toward the highest and noblest ideals of humanity"; but, in fact, it was Uvarov who first did so. Uvarov delivered his *Speech of 1818* before a convocation of professors and students of the Central Pedagogical Institute, on the occasion of the establishment of chairs in world history and Oriental culture. The *Speech* conveyed in summary detail his theory of history from the Fall of Man to about 1500 and the formation of the "modern" European world. Its thesis was that Providence intended "freedom" for all mankind, and its climax occurred in the last few pages, in which Uvarov dealt exclusively with Russia.

Uvarov admitted that Russia was "the youngest son in the large family of Europe" and in the past had "participated in none of [its] general changes." However, he did note that Karamzin, alluding to the Normanist theory, contended that Russians had the same historical foundation of reverence for "the holy rights of mankind and citizenship" that other European nations had acquired in the forests of Germany: "Our ancient laws were of Scandinavian origin and had their roots in German laws" and, like the Germanic peoples, those of ancient Rus' "feared slavery more than death." As proof, Uvarov mentioned the eleventh-century Russian Law, still universally regarded as a humanitarian code far ahead of its time. Uvarov attributed Russia's truncated development to the Mongolian domination of the thirteenth to fifteenth centuries: "With us, enlightenment and laws were for a long time victims of enslavement under the barbarians' yoke."[50]

Uvarov implied in the *Speech* and other writings that Russia had emerged from feudalism only in the seventeenth century, when the Romanovs ascended the throne. But since then, Russia had entered the mainstream of European development and had blossomed into the next stage of full autocracy, especially since the time of Peter the Great, whose reign Uvarov equated with that of Louis XIV. Catherine the Great (Uvarov's godmother) had projected an image throughout Europe of being the enlightened monarch par excellence, though her actions may have been self-serving behavior, window dressing, or successful propaganda. Besides her success in foreign policy, Catherine awarded charters to the nobility and towns, at least convoked a legislative assembly, brought greater order into the administration, and corresponded with philosophes. Her son, Paul I, threatened to stop Russia's progress. He ruled by whim and caprice both in foreign and domestic affairs and inaugurated a reign marked by terror and despotism. Paul's assassination—which was expected, welcomed, and carried out with the assistance of Uvarov's uncle, General Fedor Uvarov—indicated that Russians had outgrown this form of government. Alexander himself was appalled by his father's policies and felt compelled to acquiesce in the deed. Educated in Enlightenment ideals by his tutor La Harpe, he announced his intention to rule in the spirit of his grandmother, Catherine.[51] Uvarov concluded that "we, following the example of Europe, are beginning to think about *concepts of freedom*."[52]

Here, Uvarov paused and went to excessive pain to point out, with a facile generalization, that only "the *last* stage" of Europe's development to maturity witnessed the emancipation of the serfs. He underlined the point that, despite their other benefits, "the crusades did not result in *free villagers*." This was an appropriate comment because many progressive Russians believed that victory in the Napoleonic crusade, as it was often called, marked Russia's coming of age and should warrant emancipation. Instead, Uvarov delivered a long lesson in patience to his audience; many professors present taught and wrote that serfdom was the basic flaw in the Russian system and that progress required its abolition. But there was little evidence, Uvarov maintained, that emancipation would occur soon: "And if you ask the reason why, then history will tell you that all great political changes of this kind are the slow fruit of time . . . [and represent] the exchange of mutual gains on the part of all state castes." Thus, Uvarov put off the resolution of this crucial problem indefinitely.[53]

Serfdom notwithstanding, Uvarov assured his audience that Russia would eventually experience "the natural progress of political freedom." At the same time, he delivered another lesson in patience to those who might want the new order to arrive rapidly. In his *Speech*, he quoted the English liberal Lord Erskine as saying: "Political liberty is the *last and most beautiful gift of God*." It was still necessary "first to wear down the unbridled strength of youth" with all its "delusions" and "dreams"—Uvarov's euphemisms for favorable attitudes toward republicanism, democracy, and revolution. Within the Arzamas Literary Circle, Uvarov had just come into contact with the radical ideas of the future Decembrists, and this association may have prompted his cautionary remarks. On the other hand, with an impertinence extraordinary in an autocratic state, Uvarov presumed to warn Alexander that history was the "supreme judge of tsars and peoples" and demanded that the awarding of freedom not be unduly delayed without a harsh sentence, because "the spirit of the time, similar to the terrible Sphinx, devours those who do not understand the meaning of its prophecy!" A tsar could not be "foolhardy" enough to attempt "to enclose a grown youth in the restricted confines of an infant's cradle," that is, to tell citizens ready for political and civil rights that they were to continue as subjects of an absolute monarch.

The theory of government in this instance resembles the theory of child rearing. He is not worthy of praise who succeeds in perpetuating physical or moral youth; but he who is wise is one who mitigates the transition from one age to another, guards over inexperience, early encourages the faculties of the mind, warns of danger and delusion, and, upholding the law of necessity, matures and grows along with a people or with a man.

Uvarov then attempted to alleviate any remaining doubts that Russia would soon enjoy freedom by exclaiming: "Rest at peace! It [freedom] is immortal like the human soul, like eternal justice, like truth and goodness!"[54]

This audacious, open projection of civic and political freedom in Russia staggered the public. One newspaper announced that the speech had become the "object of general attention" and that its "decided success" was demonstrated by the fact that the Academy of Sciences had decided to print it. Two articles were devoted to its content. F. N. Glinka, the future Decembrist, hailed it as "marvelous"; A. P. Kunitsyn, the professor who most influenced the Decembrists, called it "a tribute to the success of enlightenment in Russia." *Conservateur impartial* noted that Uvarov spoke of Russia's rapid development under "hero-tsars" and in general of "the progress of the human spirit, especially in institutions relative to political liberty." Sergei and Nicholas Turgenev considered the address filled with "liberal ideas" that had "never been before spoken in the Russian language." Indeed, its publication was presented as evidence that freedom of speech and press did exist in the country. The reactionary Shishkov carefully and despairingly annotated his private copy. Karamzin worried that it reflected a growing vogue of constitutionalism among Russian youth. Later, Grech wryly noted that if the speech had been given while Uvarov was educational minister, he "would have thrown himself in jail."[55]

Uvarov's *Speech* also hinted at even greater glory for Russia. The problem of backwardness, after all, had its optimistic side, particularly in the context of Uvarov's theory of history. Europe as a whole had developed organically, but each individual state likewise was experiencing a life cycle from birth to old age. Since Western European countries were already supposedly mature or very close to maturity, would they not reach old age sooner than young Russia and would not Russia then become the dominant nation and incarnate the development of the *esprit humain*? Uvarov, both in his literary writings and in his *Speech*, alluded to a parallel between the last and most mature stage of the ancient world, the Roman Empire, and that of the Russian Empire. This rather common cultural myth had developed in the eighteenth century; it envisioned Russia as a future empire of major world influence that would incorporate the ancient Roman principles of political freedom, just laws, and patriotism. Uvarov repeated the myth, but in a way that unhistorically jumbled the eras of the Roman Republic and the Roman Empire to suit his own rhetorical purpose.

He specifically likened the current Russian transition to "civic and political freedom" to the progress of the Romans from "the turbulent years of inexperience to the years of mature and real adulthood." When Uvarov admitted that Russian literature was still a "late flower" compared with the vastness of the realm or the progressive nature of Alexandrine politics, he claimed, with little validity, yet another comparison: "The Romans first of all conquered the world and only subsequently began to think about enlightenment." Furthermore, he attested, both Roman and Russian literatures received their character from the Greeks and neither, because they came late, could be "distinguished by originality" in its early years. But, just as Rome had inherited all the developments of the ancient world and had disseminated them in its last and mature stage, so too might Russia inherit those of the rest of Europe.[56]

Uvarov then proposed, as he had in 1810, that Russia become the center of the Eurasian world and carry European enlightenment back to the now-spent Eastern countries; this function would be similar to that performed for imperial political unity by the "ecumenical throne" of Rome. Uvarov had already proposed that Russians should pursue Eastern studies because Russia "rested on Asia" and indeed occupied one-third of that continent. His plan now, apparently, was to conquer the rest of the continent, but not "by fire and sword," because "this dreadful feat does not belong in our century" and was a "vain, bloody dream." Instead, conquest would now include promoting "respect for mankind, . . . [inaugurating] new and better laws, . . . improving the position of the conquered, . . . propagating the gentle spirit of religion and scholarship and art, education and welfare." These high aims, he declared, were the "single use of conquest" and, perhaps with more honesty, "can in some way *sanctify* the license of intense national glory."[57] In a few short pages, then, Uvarov transformed Russia from a backward country into one soon nearing maturity and anon into an imperialistic global power.

At least in his optimism that Russia would soon reach "maturity," Uvarov was not alone. Similarly, Speranskii, the most important statesman of the era, maintained: "Our state is in the second period of the feudal system, i.e., in the period of absolutism, and the trend is doubtlessly straight in the direction of freedom. Note: In truth, this movement is straighter with us than it has been in other states."[58] Of course, in order to understand what future Uvarov had in mind for Russia or Europe, it is necessary to examine what he meant by the stage of "maturity."

Uvarov described his vision of "maturity" in rather misty terms, but its essential features were clear. First, the monarch would no longer rule "alone," and some degree of "political freedom" would be granted to the educated and propertied classes, those prepared to carry out its responsibilities. A "balance of power" among monarch, nobility, and bourgeoisie would be achieved through some type of representative institution that could prevent the twin evils of despotism and anarchy. After witnessing a session of the Pressbourg Diet in 1809, Uvarov hailed such constituted bodies as "the most beautiful development of human justice" and a "peaceful and periodic revolution" wherein "each has a place."[59] Second, there would be "powerful guarantees to assure the civil liberty of individuals." Uvarov, like the great majority of his contemporaries, accepted the traditional hierarchical organization of society as natural and thus reserved political rights for an elite. However, Uvarov was quite up-to-date in including the bourgeoisie among the elite; he recognized their growing importance, and he and the Arzamas Circle espoused the idea of free trade along with free intellectual communication among peoples. Recognizing the advent of capitalist Europe, in 1840 Uvarov even called for a historical study "of the speculative spirit, both commercial and industrial, up to the time of the entire consummation of the new social system founded in great part on these pivots."

Despite his elite orientation, Uvarov also believed that "modern governments" of the mature Christian era owed "civil rights" (once again, unspecified) to their entire population, because of each person's dignity as a creature of God. And, just as all individuals were equal in the eyes of God, all warranted equality before the law. In particular, all people had a right to demand that the government rule in their best interest because all played a part in national development. Uvarov criticized his friend, Pozzo di Borgo, for his "blindly conservative principles," which insisted that a monarch "rule with a firm hand," and for the Sardinian's "insurmountable aversion to the principles of democracy."[60] But, for Uvarov, popular sovereignty and democracy really meant government for the people in the eighteenth-century framework derived from enlightened absolutism, not necessarily by or of the people in the nineteenth-century sense. He stated flatly that individuals could contribute to society only "in the caste to which they belong and [in the position] where they have been placed by fate." He did allow that the lower classes could work their way into the "third estate."[61] In addition, he considered the Russian Table of Ranks, whereby a person could earn nobility through advancement in the civil or military service, bona fide evidence of "democracy."

Uvarov believed that a constitution should embody and guarantee the various features of a limited monarchy, but it mattered not whether it was written or unwritten. However, he did insist that a valid constitution had to be an organic product of a national past, a compendium of "fundamental laws" that had developed over the centuries. For Uvarov, the eighteenth-century penchant for abstract plans that treated states like machines and attempted to interrupt traditional development by substituting novel political forms "prepared the slow fall of all Europe." In like manner, he condemned Napoleon, who "by chemical manipulation," that is, by combining states as though they were stable physical elements, tried to replace the "German constitution," meaning all that had developed "since the fifteenth century," with the Rhenish Confederation. He also agreed with de Maistre's statement that "a constitution cannot be written," in the sense that it cannot be imposed *ex nihilo* on a state. Uvarov contended that each nation *achieved* a constitution in its own unique way and developed its own version of a limited monarchy, but all would reach that universal goal because this was what Providence intended. Thus, Uvarov tried to combine, again only vaguely, the Burkean view of the word "constitution," which referred to the traditional features of any legitimate body, with the more abstract modern view of a representative ideal that prevented the abuse of power.[62]

Although Uvarov may have been vague as to the exact functioning of his ideal form of government, he had two models in mind. He praised the British constitution of the turn of the century and lauded the French Charter of Liberties and, later, the government of Louis Philippe. Both the British and the French systems subscribed to his model—a balanced, hierarchical, representative, constitutional type of government. It seems doubtful he would ever have accepted as workable or desirable the later nineteenth-century versions of constitutional government that included universal manhood suffrage or the eventual relegation of the monarch to a figurehead.

Uvarov was also quite clear as to what he regarded as "audacious" in government. In Vienna, while he admitted he lacked the courage to debate with Madame de Staël, the daughter of Necker, about political issues—he left the task to wittier men such as di Borgo—he objected to her calling for the abrogation of the French Estates, political equality for all citizens, and an elected assembly coequal to, rather than balancing off, monarchical power.[63] Similarly, while Uvarov had enormous respect for Baron vom Stein—a man who was said to have "the soul of an Arzamas member" and after whom he named a pavilion on his summer estate—he thought vom Stein's reform plan for the German states both too rapid and farfetched, especially its provisions for the immediate abolition of serfdom and for a federation of aristocratic republics presided over by an elected emperor.[64] Last, but surely not least, Uvarov had been brought up to abhor revolutions for their rupture of organic development and the disorder that came in their wake. Schlözer taught that revolution was so dangerous an act that it was better, even with a tyrant, to take a passive stance and wait until "Providence itself wants to free a people from an iron scepter." Uvarov likewise demonstrated a disgust for what he considered were Rousseau's views in support of egalitarianism and revolution (in other words, for the later, more radical version of the Enlightenment) and condemned such thinkers who offered "sophisms" and "who prostituted the beautiful appellation of philosophe."[65]

Two aspects of Uvarov's thinking demand further elucidation: his extraordinary reverence for monarchical power in all the stages he described and projected, whether youth, adolescence, the transitional era, or maturity; and his notion that an enlightened monarch would willingly promote legislation to share his power when his country reached maturity. Although the majority of Uvarov's ideas on historical development were derived from Western European sources, especially as these reflected the theory of enlightened absolutism, his convictions regarding the monarch were rooted more deeply in Russian tradition. Uvarov owed these views to Karamzin and Speranskii, his first two nominations to the Academy of Sciences once Uvarov became its president in 1818.[66]

Strangely enough, Uvarov's assumption that the traditional monarchy would carry Europe to maturity was proved to him in the Russian example by the conservative Karamzin. Uvarov knew and had long admired the literary man and historian and in 1811 sent him a copy of Schlegel's *Lectures on Modern History*, because Schlegel, like Karamzin, stressed the beauty of monarchies and the necessity of preserving tradition in the process of national development.[67] In 1816, Karamzin read passages of his monumental *History of the Russian State*, the first eight volumes of which were published two years later, to his "brothers" in the Arzamas Literary Circle.[68] Uvarov became rapturous and wrote down a short description of the feelings that welled up within him. To Uvarov, the *History* proved once and for all that Russia too played an integral part in the development of the *esprit humain*. It showed Russians what "they have been, how they progressed to the present status quo, and what they can become without resorting to forced change." Then Uvarov formulated the first version of what became known, after it was first pronounced in 1832, as a notoriously reactionary slogan—"Orthodoxy, Autocracy, Nationality." Karamzin's *History*, Uvarov averred, would induce Russians better to love "their fatherland, their faith, their tsar" and would serve "as a cornerstone for Orthodoxy, national development, monarchical government and—God willing—a feasible Russian constitution." Given Uvarov's concept of history, these earlier versions of the tripartite formula were obviously not reactionary statements but exuberant declarations and affirmations that Russia was assured peaceful progress toward a "modern" form of government.

It is also obvious to later scholars that Uvarov had misread Karamzin's intentions. Bludov was closer to the mark when he commented: "What's all this talk about a constitution? Each state has its own constitution, related to it. Our historiographer Karamzin often says this."[69] But Uvarov had taken Karamzin's emphasis on historicism and his description of the autocracy as the institution that had brought Russia to its present greatness and had read into it proof of his own interpretation of Russia's participation in the course of universal history. Uvarov was apparently ignorant, as nearly all Russians were, of Karamzin's *Memoir on Ancient and Modern Russia* (1810). In that document, Karamzin declared the unlimited autocracy perfect as it stood, and asserted that "all novelty in the political order is an evil," and that any "division of authority," "any change in her [Russia's] political constitution has led in the past and must lead in the future to her perdition. . . ." Karamzin objected not only to limited monarchy but to enlightened absolutism, because it entailed government interference in the lives of individuals. Such Enlightenment concepts as political rights, balance of power, or rule by law only weakened the ability of virtuous, self-censoring monarchs to provide the internal and external security of individuals, which should be their only concern.[70] Thus, while Karamzin wrote his *History* to buttress the case for the perfection of unlimited autocracy, Uvarov read into it his own views and found support for the notion that an autocrat would always act in a way beneficial to his nation, that is, would guide it to the maturity of a limited monarchy.

At any rate, the problem with Uvarov's scheme was that he left it to the absolute monarch at the appropriate moment to limit his own authority; he was confident that the ruler would then peacefully agree to effect a balance of power among himself, the nobility, and the bourgeoisie. Uvarov never proposed any criteria by which monarchs could reach this judgment but assumed their ability and willingness to do so. This was a naive notion, because even the most enlightened of absolute monarchs in their heyday in eighteenth-century Europe hoped to broaden the powers of the state, chiefly to bolster their own authority. In the process, they typically further disrupted any balance of power by substituting a private army of bureaucrats for the traditional partnership with the nobility in running the state.

Nonetheless, Uvarov was not working in a vacuum. In the very beginning of his reign, Alexander and his advisers at least contemplated reforms. In keeping with the rationalism and legalism of eighteenth-century thinking, most of their measures were intended to perfect the machinery of state rather than alter fundamental institutions. They believed that new ministries with their inevitable bureaucracies would systematize the administration, establish the rule of law, organize the government according to clear, logical principles, and educate the population. Much like Turgot, they defined a constitution as a regular and orderly structure rather than a system of checks and balances or legal limitations on sovereignty. "Reform" projects were designed to avoid "*arbitrariness* and, consequently, decrease the evil that may result from the difference in talent of those who are at the head of the state." However, none of these measures curbed the power of the autocracy, because the Unofficial Committee believed that reforms could be better expedited by an unfettered central authority. Even emancipation was discussed, although the consensus was to resolve the problem "without shocks." Thus, Uvarov could well believe that enlightened absolutism, in its precise eighteenth-century form, was flourishing in Russia.[71]

Uvarov's view of the way in which an enlightened absolute monarch could foster an era of transition to limited monarchy more than likely came from a plan Speranskii devised in 1809. As secretary to Alexis Kurakin, the future secretary of state tutored young Sergei in Russian grammar, and in 1810 both belonged to the same Masonic lodge. The transitional stages of historical development posited by Uvarov accord perfectly with Speranskii's plan of 1809: both concepts anticipated a first step in the direction of freedom and a true balance in the exercise of power while preserving the autocratic tradition. If enacted, Speranskii's plan would have established a Russian *Rechtsstaat*, a state based on "fundamental laws" and efficiently and honestly administered through a division of legislative, judicial, and executive functions, but united in a single sovereign power. The separate functions would be aided by a series of representative institutions, allowing propertied members of the population, even those of the middle classes, participation (although not power) in government; all Russians were entitled to basic civil rights and the security of person and property. Even serfs were included in the latter provisions, although abolition would come only "gradually." Speranskii aimed "to set up and base on immutable laws the government, which heretofore has been autocratic," and thus to eliminate the dreaded possibility of despotism.

The goal was to limit but not abolish autocratic power. Speranskii's plan preserved for the autocratic institution the initial and final action in nearly all administrative matters. In general, Speranskii cautioned: "Limits of innovation should be restricted by existing traditions and historically developing institutions." Again, as much of the old order as possible should be left intact while social-political development occurred, in order to prevent disruption and dissatisfaction. Both Speranskii and Uvarov agreed that either premature or overdue reform would bring disaster. There seems little question that the two men collaborated and agreed. Speranskii called Uvarov a "first-class mind" and claimed, with some exaggeration, that he and Karamzin were the preeminent learned Russians of all time. Uvarov endorsed Speranskii's governmental projects when he declared in 1819: "May God grant you sufficient strength of mind and body to finish the great task that you began!"[72]

Throughout his life, Uvarov preached what may be called the Arzamas spirit in politics—belief in progress, interest in reform, acceptance of Western standards, and respect for national tradition. The Arzamas members were for good reason dubbed "local Tories" or "government liberals" because, like Uvarov, they above all placed Russia's future in the hands of the autocracy.[73] Also called the "right wing of noble-bourgeois liberalism," they tried to espouse a compromise among the demands of monarchy, nobility, and bourgeoisie. Uvarov was their political spokesman, and, neither a radical, a reactionary, nor a defender of the status quo, he blended the "liberal" and "conservative" principles of the era: he upheld both legal equality and social hierarchy, secular values and Christian culture, constitutional controls and authoritarianism, inevitable progress and gradual development, universal goals and national variation, rationalism and a belief in natural causation alongside trust in Providence's control. His dearest belief—that a reforming autocrat would award guarantees of civil and political rights—also accommodated contrasting political attitudes. In a specifically Russian context, he possessed a warm and welcoming attitude to Western European ideas but warned that they should not be allowed to blemish Russian tradition. He espoused liberal hopes for universal civil rights but believed political rights should be restricted, and he had a conservative, if not callous, attitude toward existing serfdom. And, again in the Russian tradition, he thought that the needs of the state superseded those of the individual.

This mixture of liberalism and conservatism and of rationalism and traditionalism was and is not uncommon. The Hannoverian Conservatives, French Doctrinaires, and German Reform Conservatives were other examples. Originally, with the exception of their attitude toward serfdom, the Decembrists also shared this synthesis and tried to reconcile the political ideas of the eighteenth century with the historicism or nationalism of the nineteenth. They turned to history, according to S. S. Volk, for exactly the reason Uvarov did: "The Decembrists hoped to discover in the history of Russia the basis for the right and capacity of the Russian people for a self-governing political life." By 1821, Alexander had obviously turned his back on "enlightened" reform, and the Decembrists abandoned any faith in gradual amelioration for a new hope in revolutionary change. The Turgenev brothers looked upon Uvarov as possibility for the Decembrist ranks and thought that he might "come over." Uvarov, however, eschewed revolutionary means and continued to hope in the tsars, as did the majority of Arzamas members. Nicholas Turgenev rued this fact: "They want the same aims, but not the means.[74]

Although the Decembrists clearly misread the "spirit of the time" as ripe for revolution, they had foresight in forsaking the Russian autocracy. The Russian educated public had wanted to continue to believe in enlightened absolutism, which Leonard Krieger points out is "a characteristic doctrine of moderate intellectuals," because it represents a peaceful way to resolve the intersection of tradition and innovation in a society. But the doctrine hinges on whether a ruler is willing to adjust his policies to satisfy demonstrably new demands or whether he is inclined to subordinate these demands to the interests of older social groups or absolutism itself. The latter turned out to be the case in Russia. The autocracy tended to coopt its rivals and, contrary to the development so well understood by Uvarov in Western European countries, there were no strong groups or classes— church, nobility, courts, or bourgeoisie—to effect a balance of power or checks on absolutism. Therefore, there existed little possibility of the autocracy moving from its first, fully absolute state to the "mature" second stage, even though it often appeared "enlightened." Even in Europe, the attempts to reconcile benevolent paternalism, legitimate absolutism, and constitutionalism proved awkward. Kant "climaxed the problem . . . by fusing the contradictions and committing himself to an autocratically ruled representative constitution which would itself be both a final end of nature and a means to the moral freedom of man."[75] Uvarov more clearly recognized that the autocracy had to change its "form," but he surely overestimated its willingness to do so.

Overall, Uvarov's enthusiasm for universal norms of progress sets him somewhat beyond Burke's "tendency to preserve with an inclination to improve." However, his concept of progress never extended beyond the early nineteenth-century version of a constitutional monarchy. His timetable for an individual nation, such as Russia, to develop toward that end also places him firmly in the conservative camp. Indeed, this was the rub. Liberal hopes and dreams could be put off indefinitely if a country had not yet achieved a "desired maturity." Thus, Uvarov's politics appeared astoundingly liberal when he thought Alexandrine Russia was on the brink of achieving a modern government, but hopelessly conservative when he understood that Nicholas had a lower opinion of his populace.[76] For this reason, Uvarov has confused both Western and Soviet scholars who try to label him as a liberal in his youth but an inflexible reactionary as educational minister. Instead, he consistently held to the view that Russia was in a transitional era, and he patiently waited for the tsar to signal its end. This was not cynical; it was pragmatic.[77] If revolutions are rejected as scourges of God, if attempts to abandon the path of organic development are seen as self-defeating, if in general tsars appear enlightened, then trust in a reforming autocrat provides the only realistic political position. Furthermore, Uvarov sincerely believed that an educated public constituted the primary basis for a mature government. In this decade and for the rest of his life, he dedicated his own efforts to creating that foundation.

THE SUPERINTENDENT OF THE ST. PETERSBURG EDUCATIONAL DISTRICT

The emancipation of the soul *through enlightenment ought to precede the emancipation of the* body *through legislation.* Uvarov, 1818

UVAROV'S activities as a government official during the Alexandrine era flowed logically from his political, social, and cultural views and represent his attempt to apply his understanding of the historical path of Russian development. From youth, he argued with conviction that education remained the essential prerequisite for progress in every area, and educational level the criterion by which a country should be judged. Especially, inspired by the ancient Athenians, he believed that citizenship should be founded upon education, that "the emancipation of the *soul* through enlightenment ought to precede the emancipation of the *body* through legislation."[1]

These ideas, coupled with Uvarov's own strong intellectual interests, made it natural that he find his service home in the educational ministry. Even Tsar Alexander predicted this future when he met the teenaged Sergei, and the young man worked to make certain that the prophecy was self-fulfilling.[2] In 1810, when only twenty-four, he became superintendent of the St. Petersburg Educational District. This was a prestigious position because there were only six educational divisions in the empire, and their directors possessed powers second only to those of the minister of education. As noted above, Uvarov acquired his post as much through nepotism as demonstrated ability. Once in office, though, he proved the ablest member of his ministry. He apparently disagreed with his father-in-law/minister over policy: all but one of Uvarov's proposed measures—which touched every level of education from primary grades to the university—were set forth only after Razumovskii retired in 1816. But even after 1816, Uvarov still faced opposition; he was forced to defend his concept of education as an instrument of progress against others who feared its danger to throne, altar, and nation, a task he performed with more courage and ire than success. Opponents forced his resignation in 1821.

Uvarov's career in this decade proved noteworthy for two reasons. First, the twists and turns of his tenure in office reflect Alexander's shift from one wing of public opinion to another. Second, the policies of Uvarov the superintendent in the 1810s adumbrated those of Uvarov the minister in the 1830s and 1840s. From the beginning of his rule, the tsar demonstrated great interest in "enlightened" reform projects based on Western norms of progress, and at Tilsit he befriended Napoleonic France; but at the same time he remained attuned to the counsel of the "antireform nexus", as we shall call it, with its undertones of xenophobia or gallophobia and fear of Enlightenment ideals. By about 1820, the members of the antireform nexus had succeeded in bringing Alexander fully into their group. Uvarov's policies during the 1810s attempted to effect a compromise between the two schools of thought, but once one of these had triumphed, such efforts were useless, and he was drummed out of office. The compromise, though, was resurrected after Uvarov returned to duty in the educational ministry in 1826 and became its head in 1833.

Uvarov joined the Ministry of National Enlightenment, to use its official name, only eight years after it was founded, while debates concerning the methods, extent, and nature of education were still in process. Alexander and his advisers in the Unofficial Committee, all products of the Enlightenment, shared that movement's vast vision of the place of education in society. Education promised a panacea for backwardness and provided a sure foundation for future development. Administrative efficiency, military might, a cohesive public spirit, national well-being, economic progress, all demanded the schooling and training of both a professional elite and the working classes. Consequently, eighteenth-century systems of education tended to stress secular, utilitarian subject matter as well as an all-class scope. Peter established the first technical school; Elizabeth, the first university; Catherine, the first elementary and secondary schools; and Paul the first medical college; in doing so these Russian rulers were briskly in step with the "modern" philosophy. Furthermore, given the perceived importance of education and the general trust in enlightened governance, the assumption prevailed throughout Europe, even among revolutionaries, that the state had both the right and duty to direct, define, and fund schooling on all levels. In the words of one historian of French education, everywhere education came to rest on the philosophe postulate that "the state was to assume the responsibility for providing universal schooling from public funds, by teachers it would certify, and for purposes it would decide were conducive to the social good."[3]

In keeping with these theories, Alexander made clear that education held first priority in his reform program and should be considered *the special function of the state.*[4] The Ministry of National Enlightenment was founded on September 8, 1802, and the tsar entrusted the formulation of appropriate educational statutes to a group of his closest friends and advisers, including Speranskii and three of the four members of the Unofficial Committee. The comprehensive school system these men created was not only the first in Russia, but was also, in conception at least, the best in Europe for meeting the needs of a developing nineteenth-century nation.[5]

The reform statutes, as they are often called, were published during 1803 and 1804. They represented an attempt to realize Peter the Great's egalitarian dream of affording opportunities for state service to all classes in society, and an effort to assign position on the basis of mandatory schooling and examined merit rather than noble birth. Permeating the entire system was the basic idea that the unrestrained expansion and promulgation of all learning could bring nothing but benefit to the Russian Empire and its inhabitants. If fully carried into effect, the new educational system would obviously have rattled the existing order of things, and that indeed was the intention. Peter's Table of Ranks, which was instituted in 1722 and lasted until 1917, stipulated that all those who entered military or civil service had to start at the lowest level, Rank Fourteen, and earn their upward progress; the higher the rank, the more difficult were the responsibilities of office and the greater the prestige. All military ranks and Rank Eight in the civil bureaucracy conferred hereditary nobility and carried with it the privileges of exemption from direct taxation, recruitment, and corporal punishment as well as the right to own estates with serfs residing on them. In theory, then, the Table of Ranks could enlarge the nobility by adding people of all classes to its numbers and thus provide a democratic element in the Russian social system.

In practice, however, in the eighteenth century, wealth, class, and connections still provided the easiest and most normal access to higher ranks; a dearth of schools obviated anything but on-the-job training, and the established nobility worked to obstruct newcomers. Nonetheless, there did emerge a recognition that official rank and useful service counted more than noble birth in assessing status in society. L. E. Shepelev, a Soviet historian of the system, summarized: "For contemporaries, rank became a shorthand designation of one's place in the service hierarchy and of one's social standing, and a symbol of one's rights and privileges."[6] Now that a school system was being created, examination was to become necessary before entrance to state service, thus more clearly tying merit to the coveted ranks. The intention was obviously to provide enough well-trained men for the inevitable expansion of bureaucracy in a modern, centralized state.

The new statutes incorporated several progressive foreign models, all of which buttressed the all-class, utilitarian bent of the Petrine ideal. The democrat Condorcet had presented an educational plan to the French Legislative Assembly in 1792; this was intended to make education and its resultant privileges universally available. Similar to Condorcet's, the Russian system was structured like a ladder. Each rung from primary to university level offered an education complete in itself as well as preparation for the next step. Access to all levels depended only on ability; schools were free of charge, and maintenance grants were set aside for the needy.[7]

The reform aimed at providing the state with skilled manpower and a literate, productive populace; in particular, the schools were to train the teachers, doctors, administrators, and technologists the empire so desperately needed. The curricula thus stressed practical "modern" subjects. Purposefully avoiding the monastic bent of the traditional French and Austrian systems, as opposed to the German emphasis on secular training, the reformers snubbed religion and had it taught only at the elementary levels. In 1808, even the ecclesiastical schools were modified to offer practical subjects that would enable graduates to serve in the bureaucracy. Elementary education in the new system was structured to promote better agricultural and industrial or commercial techniques. One-year *prikhodskye*, or parish, schools, located generally in rural areas, had one teacher each to instruct pupils in reading, writing, arithmetic, religion, and the elements of farming. In urban centers the two-year *uezdnye*, or district, schools offered a somewhat more advanced education; in each, two teachers gave instruction in twenty-eight hours per week of geography, history, grammar, technology, and some sciences, depending on the nature of local enterprises. Eight teachers in each of the forty-two *gymnasii*, gymnasia, or secondary schools—located in the capitals of the provinces, the major administrative subdivisions—offered four years of study in an encyclopedic panorama of courses appropriate for either merchants or state servants.[8]

Crowning the network, six universities administered educational activity in their geographical areas, and a superintendent represented their interests in St. Petersburg. Moscow University had functioned since 1755, but the institutions established in Kazan, Kharkov, and eventually the capital were new creations. The Vilna Academy was also transformed into a university, and the ministry revived the German university at Dorpat. According to their charters, formulated on the German model, the universities received privileges highly unusual in an autocracy so that they could function autonomously, with academic freedom. The university councils, made up of faculty members, had the right to elect rectors, deans, and other personnel, to run independent courts of justice, to impose their own censorship, and to choose textbooks. The charter stipulated course offerings in order to direct students into the areas of expertise sought by the state, and each university was expected to disseminate the knowledge needed for the benefit of its surrounding community.[9]

The new educational system could have laid the foundations for a *Rechtsstaat*, eventual emancipation, efficient administration, increased economic productivity, and assimilation of useful foreign ideas. However, although the reform statutes were enacted by fiat, they were only partially put into effect because of lack of resources and because of the opposition they encountered. Matériel and public opinion limit even an autocrat. Actually, the plan warranted considerable criticism on practical grounds alone. Russia was a culturally weak country; the nobility, not to mention the peasantry, were indifferent to the prospect of schooling. Given the lack of qualified teachers, particularly at the university level, the curricula and expansion schemes were overly ambitious, and they forced dependence on foreign talent. Once the nation became embroiled in the Napoleonic wars, financing drained away. Despite these difficulties, the basic organization of the educational system was firmly set in place by the end of Alexander's reign. Nevertheless, the reforming spirit of the original statutes was gradually and spitefully emasculated.

Public opposition to the educational plan came from several quarters and for a variety of reasons. For instance, Karamzin gloried in an educational system as the "cornerstone of a government's greatness" and lauded Alexander's efforts; but he believed its purpose should be not to change society but to preserve the status quo. Many members of the nobility, whose interests Karamzin usually championed, correctly understood that the reform statutes threatened an end to their dominance in state service and in relations with the peasants. They recognized that the primary aim of 1789 had been not so much to limit the monarchy as to end noble privilege and establish equality before the law as well as upward social mobility. There thus arose in Russia an aristocratic resurgence similar to the abortive movement in eighteenth-century France; in Russia the nobility aimed in particular to block the fulfillment of the egalitarian educational reform, upon which further change depended. Early in the reign, the so-called Senatorial Party tried to prevent the tsar from expanding a centralized bureaucracy at the expense of traditional noble control. The attempt was unsuccessful, but the hostility behind it lingered and spilled over into dissatisfaction with the new educational system. According to James Flynn, the historian of universities in this reign, "the self-interest of the nobility represented the most significant factor in blocking the achievement of the goals envisioned by Alexander and his close co-workers."[10]

Self-interest is rendered vastly more powerful when supported—or masked—by ideology. Four strains of opposition to the educational plan emerged during Alexander's reign, and they eventually connected to form the antireform nexus. Those who considered violent social and political revolution the inevitable outcome of Enlightenment thinking rejected the general emphasis of change, reform, and hence education; they vowed a defense of the status quo. Those who contended that national values were being betrayed objected that the educational structure imitated German and French models, as it did, and thus neglected Russian traditions. Xenophobia grew as the tsar accommodated Napoleon at Tilsit in 1807 and then apparently planned to import the Napoleonic civil code and governmental organization. Those who believed that religion should constitute *an*, if not *the*, essential ingredient in education thundered against the secular and materialistic bias of the new system. Last, obscurantists—who insisted that knowledge per se breeds discontent—sought to restrict both the number of those educated and the amount of learning available to them. Put starkly, the fundamental issue was whether education should serve the needs of progress or bolster the status quo; the opposing views coexisted uneasily from the very beginning of the reign.[11]

Alexander never actually abandoned his conviction that Russia needed an educational system from primary to university level, but he wavered as to the purpose of the system. In the course of two decades, he gradually retreated from the reforming spirit of the original statutes; he succumbed to a formidable force of public opinion that upheld, in turn, noble interest, nationalist sentiment, religious fervor, and political reaction. In this regard, the trends during his reign were comparable to those elsewhere in Europe. For instance, in 1819 there was an educational plan under discussion in Prussia that was much like the one proposed in Russia in 1803–1804. A Prussian official recognized, although rather inelegantly, that providing instruction "from the gutter to the university" was necessary in a modern state and was a logical outcome of or a precondition for carrying out the reform program initiated by vom Stein a decade earlier. The plan was defeated because of the threat to noble status and a general hostility to change.[12] When revolutionary disturbances broke out in 1820 in Europe, there arose a consensus that they were the ineluctable result of expanding educational opportunity. In Russia itself, by 1820, Uvarov alone in the educational ministry defended the spirit of the reform statutes, and indeed he became their symbol.[13]

SECONDARY AND ELEMENTARY SCHOOLING

WHEN Uvarov became superintendent on December 31, 1810, he rapidly designed a new plan for secondary education in his district; it was approved one week after its presentation on October 31, 1811, and was extended to the rest of the educational districts by the end of the decade. The reason for its acceptance is clear; it satisfied not only the original spirit of the reform statutes but the objections of their critics as well.

When Uvarov entered office, criticisms of the reform statutes had come to a head on a number of issues. The statutes, as mentioned, stipulated that a link between higher learning and rank was necessary in order to rectify the abysmally low educational level of state servants. In 1809, State Secretary Speranskii, himself the upstart son of a priest, reinforced that link by engineering the Examination Act. It required for promotion to Ranks Eight and Five in the civil bureaucracy, a university certificate or satisfactory performance on university-level tests in fifteen subjects ranging from physics to Russian grammar. The law, Karamzin noted, was "greeted everywhere with sarcastic ridicule," and more likely fear, among the nobility. De Maistre, then in residence in St. Petersburg and an eloquent defender of pre-Enlightenment, pre-Protestant Europe, bitterly pointed out that the French king and nobility had fallen because *la science* had replaced *noblesse* as the status symbol in society.[14] Nonetheless, the law held; this aspect of the reform statutes, after all, was rooted in a century of tradition dating back to Peter.

But, in general, if forced to pursue serious study, the nobility wanted to make secondary and higher education, and hence the upper ranks of state service, their own preserve and not an endeavor in which they were subject to the competition of the masses. Even Speranskii understood this and in 1810 worked to establish Tsarskoe Selo Lycée, a strictly aristocratic institution designed to "educate the children of distinguished nobility for military and civil service."[15] Economic and psychological factors dictated this drive on the part of the nobility to keep out newcomers. The majority of this group needed to engage in state service for its monetary rewards, because in many cases familial serf and land holdings had declined since the eighteenth century and proved too small to provide a life-style appropriate for a privileged class. For instance, in 1833 roughly 60 percent of the nobility had fewer than twenty serfs and another 24 percent less than a hundred; thus, the overwhelming majority of the "privileged" could not afford anything resembling upper-class comfort.[16] Even for the wealthy, self-respect, status, and usefulness in society were judged by position in the Table of Ranks.

In addition, many members of the nobility objected to the "superficial" or "encyclopedic" curriculum in secondary schools as impractical or as promoting the "dangers of half-knowledge," while the absence of religion in the course of study seemed a danger to throne and altar.[17] As de Maistre noted, such knowledge makes a man "argumentative, obstinate," "and renders him a critical observer of government, an innovator in essence"— obviously someone who would foment revolution or at least change. Karamzin, who believed in functional education, wondered why the "superintendent of a lunatic asylum [must know] Roman law." Snobbishness also entered the picture. Noble parents who thought it, first of all, demeaning that their children needed to undergo the arduous process of learning, thought it even worse that they were to do so on the same benches with commoners. In response, in the first decade of the reform, something of a boycott occurred and the nobility patronized domestic, usually foreign, tutors and private boarding schools, also normally run by foreigners, and avoided the state schools. Such a situation troubled Razumovskii and Shishkov, both members of the Old Russian clique of nobility who clung to traditional ways. They cooperated to pass regulations so that at least Russian attitudes and the language would be taught in the private schools. The minister lamented: "In the womb of Russia, they make a foreigner out of a Russian." Furthermore, Razumovskii dealt a major blow to the democratic ladder by requiring serfs to obtain ministerial permission before entering a gymnasium, thus effectively barring them. It should be added that, although Razumovskii and Shishkov shared de Maistre's political and social views, his championship of ultramontane Catholicism and his hope of establishing a Jesuit monopoly over the education of Russian nobility led to a parting of the ways.[18]

Uvarov addressed, and went far to resolve, all these problems in his gymnasium plan; he was more than likely inspired by Wilhelm von Humboldt, vom Stein's colleague, who was in the process of restructuring Prussian education.[19] Uvarov forthrightly accepted the need for higher civil servants to receive a higher education and declared that the essential, if not sole, purpose of secondary schools was to prepare students for the university; he admitted they were failing in this function. In St. Petersburg especially, where a university did not yet exist, the gymnasium and the lycée attempted to compensate by offering subjects appropriate only for "mature and previously prepared" minds but "highly dangerous" for the younger student. Instead of providing fundamental knowledge and the acquisition of intellectual skills, the St. Petersburg gymnasium curriculum put emphasis on the memorization of undifferentiated facts in a variety of useless subjects.

Uvarov's attack on this encyclopedic curriculum was not a mere de Maistrian echo but an opinion shared, he contested, by thinkers in "all states and every century" and for educational, not political, reasons. Schlözer criticized the new fashion, as did the Göttingen philologist Friedrich-August Wolf, whom Uvarov greatly admired and whose educational report of 1811 preceded his. Wolf was adamant that "the daily increasing superficiality and multitude of studies in the schools should be opposed by all possible means," because it led "to the no small injury of youth." Pestalozzi, the humanitarian Swiss educational reformer who was then influential in Europe, likewise argued against the encyclopedic vogue in gymnasium education.[20] Uvarov's plan called for the elimination of such properly university-level subjects as political economy, aesthetics, commercial science, finance, and philosophical grammar. Instead, the curriculum returned to fundamentals by doubling the hours per semester devoted to geography and history and including logic, rhetoric, grammar, mathematics, science, and literature. Furthermore, to provide more basic, less superficial, training, the length of study was extended from four to seven years.

The reform statutes did not include the teaching of religion or Russian in the gymnasia; the omission of these subjects was based on the premise that they were already well covered in the lower schools. Uvarov, however, sympathized with the view, shared by most parents, that continuing religious and moral development properly belonged in the middle schools; he added an average of two hours per week of Orthodox theology to the overall seven-year curriculum. In keeping with his new stress on the urgent need to develop native culture, he included an average of seven hours per week of Russian grammar, history, and literature over the seven years of the curriculum. The study of French and German language and literature continued, but the number of hours was cut by half.

In addition to these modifications in existing subject areas, Uvarov's gymnasium plan also represented a "new era" in Russian secondary education—the introduction of the classical curriculum. A lifelong devotee of Greek and Roman scholarship, he never wavered in the belief that "the teaching of classical languages is the basis of all education." Most European educators held as commonplace that study of the ancients taught one to think, read, write, hone taste, acquire a sense of the beautiful, and learn citizenship. In Russia, however, the study of French culture was preferred. M. N. Murav'ev-Apostol, a neoclassicist, in 1813 compared the typical education of a youth in England and Russia. He presented a devastating, rather humorous, contrast between the Eton/Oxford graduate—a young man of refined taste, classical sensibility, disciplined mind, and civic virtue, educated on classical and native traditions—and the bumpkin Russian, whose great pride was to "chatter" in French "without the slightest foreign accent," fence dashingly, and dance handsomely at balls.[21]

In addition, Uvarov's theory of Russian cultural development dictated that classical education should serve as the only proper basis for national achievement. Because of his philosophy of history, he never thought, as many did, that study of the classics could become a danger to autocracy; he considered republican forms hopelessly inadequate for a large modern state. In fact, Uvarov not only added a third year of Latin study—and made it "central . . . not auxiliary" in the curriculum—but insisted on Greek as well. In this way, he hoped to emphasize the Byzantine roots of Russian culture and develop an understanding of Russia's distinctiveness as compared to the more Latin-based Western cultures. The inclusion of Greek dismayed many, including Wolf, who thought it overly ambitious, and de Maistre and Napoleon, who thought it dangerous because it might lead to the glorification of republics. At the same time, Uvarov hired the noted scholar Friedrich Gräfe to teach classics at the gymnasium in St. Petersburg in order to assure the new curricular emphasis.[22]

Historians of Russian education unanimously agree that Uvarov's plan enabled the gymnasia better to fulfill their original function of preparing students for the universities. It also rectified some glaring deficiencies in the original statutes: the encyclopedic curriculum, the absence of religious training, and especially the lack of attention paid to study of the native language and literature. Thus, de Maistre, Razumovskii, Shishkov, and Speranskii could all approve.

While the 1811 plan represented a genuine improvement in the gymnasium curriculum, there remained a much more fundamental problem— how to attract students. Uvarov's first priority was to encourage the nobility to take advantage of middle and higher education. He had little objection to the possibility that a few talented individuals of the lower classes might rise upward socially through the opportunities afforded by the Table of Ranks. However, along with a score of other progressive Russian and European thinkers, he felt that society was generally, and more or less naturally, divided on a hierarchical basis into the laboring, commercial, and noble classes. Consequently, he supported the attitude that the majority of state servants would be drawn from the privileged ranks, and that these ranks therefore would form the principal clientele in middle and higher schools. But, as Uvarov noted, the nobility "all still regard it [education] distrustfully" and tried to avoid or reduce the period of schooling that preceded state service, or patronized the less taxing, frenchified boarding schools.[23]

Since there was no university in the capital in any case, Uvarov's first step was to convince parents, whatever their class, to encourage their children at least to graduate from secondary schools. In 1816, he noted with exasperation that although about 100 students were enrolled in the lower grades of the First St. Petersburg Gymnasium, only a dozen remained in the upper levels. He proposed offering a sizable enticement. Graduates with a good academic and behavioral record would receive Rank Fourteen immediately, rather than serving first as apprentices; they would also be exempt from the 1809 Examination Act in regard to future promotion. Furthermore, a special eighth year dedicated to jurisprudence offered practical preparation for state service. The ploy worked: the number of students in the district's gymnasia doubled to roughly 600; when the reward was removed after Uvarov fell from office, the number plummeted to its previous level, about 300.[24]

Next, Uvarov clearly understood that the nobility balked at attending schools with commoners, and he proved willing to accommodate them. In 1817, he founded a state-run *pansion*, a university preparatory institution exclusively for the nobility, at the St. Petersburg Pedagogical Institute, which was the highest-ranking educational institution in the capital, given the lack of a university. In this way, the nobility could study among their own kind, receive a first-rate secondary education (institute faculty taught subjects at the higher level), and even pursue upper-class, "refined" courses such as fencing, singing, and dancing. In addition, all graduates, depending on their success in examinations, were entitled to enter state service up to Rank Ten, a privilege normally received only after graduation from a university. This plan also worked, and soon ninety noble scions who had formerly shunned state gymnasia enrolled.

The *pansion*, however, skirted the original intention of the reform statutes in two ways. First, because of the extensive service advantages they possessed, graduates failed to pursue their studies at a university and instead took up positions in the government immediately. Second, the *pansion* severely compromised the earlier premise of equal opportunity through education. The nobility now clearly were getting the edge that they desired and thought they deserved.[25]

While Uvarov catered to the nobility, at the same time he made an attempt to prop up the democratic ladder by improving elementary education for the lower classes. This effort set the superintendent apart from his father-in-law, from Shishkov, and especially from de Maistre, all of whom agreed that learning for commoners resulted in aspirations that led to revolution; once "knowledge is accessible to everyone, the pride of the lower classes of the state will always seize this means to raise itself, and this it is necessary to fear."[26] The new administration that came into power in 1816 under Prince Alexander Golitsyn, on the contrary, supported elementary education, at least at first. Golitsyn encouraged mass literacy so that the entire population could read Scripture and would thus become more virtuous, more accepting of its lot in life, and more loyal to the divinely appointed tsar. Therefore, the new administration rejected the de Maistrian view that education per se was dangerous for the lower orders, but its motives were far removed from the spirit of the 1803-1804 statutes.

Anyone who worried about the subject concurred that the parish schools were in woeful condition. Despite their homage to the "ladder" system, the formulators of the original statutes never provided the first rung. They did, it is true, stipulate that parish schools be established throughout the empire in order to assist the lower classes' moral and physical development and to eradicate prejudices detrimental to people's well-being and economic progress. However, out of an educational budget of 1,319,450 rubles, not one was allocated for this purpose. The erection of parish schools was left to the "well-intentioned" among city, church, or rural organizations and to the serf-owning nobility. Consequently, of the roughly 600 parish schools that were set up, most were located in urban areas, where the value of education seemed more apparent. But in rural Russia, where 95 percent of the population lived, even the schools that started were generally closed down through lack of interest, money, or teachers.[27]

Uvarov's concern for the educational needs of Russia's "ordinary people" was based on his acceptance of the principles underlying the reform statutes. While willing to wait long for emancipation, he fostered education as its first step, the preparation of "souls" for their subsequent new place under a freer political constitution. Although Uvarov's plan to improve elementary schooling was very modest, major Russian educational historians consider that he was at this time the only "liberal" official left in a ministry and in a regime increasingly dominated by the interests of the nobility or by defenders of the status quo. S. V. Rozhdestvenskii attested that Uvarov was "the only fresh air in a flaccid and unprincipled ministry of education" because of his continuing attempts to make the reform statutes fulfill their original promise.[28]

Uvarov recognized, first, that unless parish schools were established throughout Russia, the ladder system existed only on paper and, second, that the shortage of teachers hampered any possible progress. According to the reform statutes, one of the purposes of the gymnasia was to train teachers for the lower schools. But Uvarov had turned the secondary schools into seven-year university-preparatory institutions with a classical curriculum that at best appealed to only the upper and middle classes. Hence, it was unlikely that they would produce students willing to accept the poorly paid, socially inferior position of lower school teacher. Even before his reform, statistics demonstrated that gymnasia graduates preferred any service other than teaching and worked to avoid it. Those who entered the profession left as quickly as possible. Thus, the educational system failed to provide the needed teaching cadre for the lower schools.

Uvarov's first solution, suggested in April 1817, was to try to improve salary and pension benefits in order "to lessen the poverty of school teachers." Realizing that government funds were not available for the purpose, he proposed levying tuition at all school levels, a common European practice. Somewhat condescendingly, Uvarov argued that people, "especially those in the lower classes," value only what they pay for and "laugh off" what comes free; but, he insisted, all revenue should be used "only for teachers' salaries." However, when the measure was passed in 1819, Golitsyn presented the suggestion simply as an additional financial resource for the ministry in general. Thus, Uvarov's intention was subverted, and historians unjustly accuse him of sponsoring the measure for the crass motivation of preventing the lower classes from attending schools.[29]

Uvarov's second recommendation, also presented in April 1817, was to establish a second section in the St. Petersburg Pedagogical Institute to be devoted to the training of elementary school teachers. The program would start slowly. Only thirty students would be accepted, and they would be drawn generally from the children of the poor, who allegedly would least mind the low status of the profession and even find it an avenue for upward mobility. Teachers' children would also be recruited, because "experience" indicated that offspring tended to follow their parents' profession.[30]

Although this was surely a modest proposal that ought to have offended no one, Uvarov's rationale and defense implied that its acceptance would endorse the "ladder" system of education and encourage the "movement," as de Maistre would say, of the common people. Uvarov laid bare the inadequacy of the reform statutes by stating bluntly that "without proper support given to the training of commoners, the entire system of national enlightenment is a building on sand." He went on to declare that, according to the reform statutes, the lower schools were supposed to be "tightly linked to higher educational institutions."

Consequently, good elementary schools promote the flourishing of gymnasia and prepare able students and teachers in always sufficient numbers. The gymnasia themselves serve the universities and from the latter the Academy acquires men with talent and basic knowledge. Thus, the lower schools are the primary seedbeds of enlightenment, and it is essential that they be protected from falling apart. . . . Without good schools for commoners, we shall never have good universities or academies. If a half century before the foundation of academies and universities, we had established modest, humble schools for the training of elementary school teachers, our academies would not now be in ruins and our elementary schools only on paper.

Uvarov rested his argument on what defenders of the status quo feared: upward mobility through education with even the lowest-born able to work their way into the highest reaches of the establishment. Never radical, he went on to say that such training would also "reconcile" the "suffering class by means of religion and knowledge about itself . . . to its fate in society."[31]

Uvarov's proposal for opening an institute for lower school teachers had a very strange fate. The tsar approved it but, when Golitsyn presented it to the Council of Ministers, funds were declared unavailable until January 1819. Uvarov knew he had been betrayed and became irate. He argued that every year was "precious," and that the late opening meant no graduates would be forthcoming until 1823 or 1824. He thundered that "the moral well-being of our largest class of people does not allow us any longer to lay aside this measure, which ought to rank first by virtue of its importance and necessity."[32] His anger was to no avail. As time went on, the ministry and government in general became increasingly skeptical about the benefits of lower school education. The Teachers' Institute of the St. Petersburg Pedagogical Institute (and later of St. Petersburg University), as the second section came to be called, opened only in January 1820 and thereafter came under constant fire until it was closed in 1822, soon after Uvarov was forced to resign.

Another reason for antagonism toward the Teachers' Institute was that it taught the views of both Joseph Lancaster, an English Quaker, and Pestalozzi, the Swiss educational reformer. Tsar Alexander had been impressed with the theories of both men when he met them during the Napoleonic campaigns; however, by 1822, both were accused of fostering revolution. Earlier, though, in 1816, Uvarov sent four students to study their methods.

The Lancastrian system of "mutual instruction" was devised at the turn of the century as a means of resolving the teacher shortage in England. Its essential feature was to have gifted older students instruct younger ones in elementary subjects and also provide them with nondenominational religious training; only one trained teacher was needed for every 1,000 pupils. Cheap, simple, and effective, the method enjoyed popularity first in England, then on the Continent, and then in Russia, where it was regarded in the military and among philanthropic landowners as a cure for illiteracy. By about 1820, though, both critics and proponents in Europe admitted that "mutual instruction" appeared to foster democratic attitudes and religious skepticism; in Russia, the influence of the schools supposedly caused a revolt in the Semenovskii Regiment. Uvarov himself had warned that some undefined aspects of this imported doctrine were both "useless and harmful" in Russia.[33]

At any rate, Uvarov, because of his theory of historical development, and the students he sent abroad, who apparently agreed with his view, preferred the system of Pestalozzi. The Swiss educator, although a believer in the hierarchical arrangement of society, was an ardent proponent of the importance of providing for the full development of the common people's physical, intellectual, and moral faculties, a privilege usually preserved for the elite. This system, once its details were known, came to be seen as appropriate only as a preparation for emancipation in the near future, not for long preservation of the status quo. In this sense, de Maistre was right. If serfdom is to be maintained, education of the lower classes is a dangerous project indeed. As Uvarov himself noted, you cannot expect education to be "a fire that does not burn." In Russia, it needed accompanying political and social reforms.[34]

In summary, in regard to elementary and secondary education, Uvarov tried to keep alive the spirit of the reform statutes while at the same time answering those criticisms of the antireform nexus that he found valid. He offered proposals for maintaining and improving the democratic ladder, the ultimate need of his ideal government; for its proximate need, the creation of an educated elite, he attempted to cajole the nobility into enrolling in state institutions, where they could obtain a rigorous, Russian, Orthodox education as opposed to the instruction offered in the private schools, with their foreign and lax orientation. In keeping with his own particular views, he introduced the classical curriculum into the gymnasia and then sponsored programs for the teaching of Latin in district schools so that even commoners could participate in this general thrust toward a unique national culture. All these ingredients also found their place in his program as minister.

THE DUAL MINISTRY AND THE ESTABLISHMENT OF ST. PETERSBURG UNIVERSITY

ALTHOUGH Uvarov may have been able to effect a compromise between the aims of the reform statutes and the quibbles of the likes of Razumovskii, de Maistre, and Shishkov, the new administration proved harder to deal with. In hindsight, it is clear that the spirit of the 1803–1804 statutes, and hence Uvarov's position, were doomed after 1812, when Napoleon, perceived by many as the embodiment of the Enlightenment, invaded the Fatherland and provoked a moral and intellectual crisis. Still, until about 1820, two voices were heard in the government: one espoused rationalism and progress and the other pietism and the status quo; the tsar, as was his wont, listened to both.

At the turn of the century—a period of rapid change, dislocation, revolution, and war—many Europeans, in a search for solace and anchors, were drawn into a widespread religious revival.[35] Golitsyn perhaps best personified this trend in Russia and, as educational minister from 1816 to 1824, rendered it most significant in terms of policy. A boyhood friend of the tsar, a bonvivant and atheist, he was persuaded in 1803 by Alexander to become over-procurator of the Holy Synod in order to reform administration in the Orthodox Church. Apparently due to his immersion in ecclesiastical affairs, Golitsyn in this decade underwent a string of conversions from deism to regular Orthodoxy and then found peace in a mysticism that sought inspiration in the reading of Scripture and emphasized a universal Christianity superseding particular dogmas. The Moscow fire and the Napoleonic invasion filled the tsar with consternation and, in his own search for solace, he dramatically adopted Golitsyn's religion and declared that God had entered his heart.[36]

The tsar's new religion, best defined as Bible Mysticism, held a multitude of attractions. Tolerant of all Christian sects, it seemed appropriate and enlightened in an eighteenth-century fashion for an empire with a various, multiconfessional population, even though the teachings excluded Moslems and Jews. It ignored doctrinal differences among Christians and stressed their spiritual unity through espousal of the essentially Protestant dogma of universal priesthood, which elevated the layman and promoted equality and brotherhood. While emphasizing the contact of the individual soul directly with God, Bible Mysticism also translated into action. A person could be "born again" by experiencing the direct religious inspiration of the Bible, the sacred book of all Christians. Knowledge of Scripture was considered a first step toward the spiritual regeneration of all society and the establishment of a Kingdom of God on earth, similar to Calvin's experiment in Geneva.

The first practical application of the new faith came almost immediately, when the tsar blessed the establishment of the St. Petersburg Bible Society in December 1812. This was a branch of the British and Foreign Bible Society, which had rapidly spread throughout the Continent since its inception in London in 1804. Its praiseworthy philanthropic aim was to translate the Bible into the vernacular and distribute easily affordable copies to all classes, with the poorest receiving them gratis. Thus the Word of God, and hence regeneration, would spread. The next month, the first meeting of the St. Petersburg branch was held in Golitsyn's home, and he became president. Razumovskii was one of the first six vice presidents and Uvarov one of the first ten directors.[37] Although Uvarov was originally attracted by the society's philanthropic aims, he soon became aware of its mystical tendencies and canceled his membership, an act that proved his undoing.

For the next ten years the Bible Society prospered. It had wide appeal because of its philanthropy and stress on brotherhood and tolerance; also, since the tsar gave warm moral and financial support to the enterprise, nearly every public figure clustered around this new center of power. In time, access to service and court depended on one's standing in the Bible Society. While Bible Society membership ran the gamut from zealots to sycophants, the organization proved enormously successful and soon "fairly dominated the Russian religious scene." By 1822, it had printed 129 editions of the Scriptures in twenty-nine languages and distributed 675,000 copies in the empire.[38]

The second expression of the tsar's new religious inclination came after the fall of Napoleon. It took the form of Alexander's grand vision of the Holy Alliance, whereby he sought to establish a new world order based on Christian brotherhood.[39] While other heads of state signed the document establishing the alliance in 1815 with eyes glancing upward—not from inspiration but amused cynicism—Alexander sought to implement it in Russian internal affairs: "Why support the Holy Alliance if its principles remain isolated and do not penetrate the heart of my people?" Such a penetration could obviously occur only through an educational process. The result was the creation in 1817 of a joint ministry of ecclesiastical affairs and national enlightenment, the Dual Ministry. It combined Golitsyn's two posts, but the aim was not administrative efficiency—indeed the entire education organization remained unchanged. Rather, Golitsyn announced a "new spirit" in educational policy which "recognized that Christian piety would always be the basis for true enlightenment." The clear intention was to establish the supremacy of faith over knowledge and to substitute a simple-hearted reverence for biblical teaching and Revelation in place of the critical thought, rationalism, and secularism that had inspired the reform statutes. Indeed, the other aim of the Dual Ministry was staunchly to defend the political and social status quo. Within a short time, the Dual Ministry and the all-powerful Central School Board, which debated and decided every aspect of educational policy, became staffed almost solely with Bible Society members or opponents of reform. Uvarov was the only important exception, and he rapidly became the *bête noire* of the new administration.[40] Once again, Russian policy was but part of a general European drift. Although a French twin of the Dual Ministry was not established until 1824, it was proposed as early as 1816. In 1819, the Carlsbad Decrees replicated the "new spirit" in the German states.[41]

The members of the Dual Ministry spent most of their time encouraging village Bible schools and, in district and middle schools, policing textbooks and curricula for signs of secularism or attacks on Revelation. But universities, in particular, bedeviled the Dual Ministry, since the purpose of these higher institutions was to encourage knowledge, reason, and a critical intelligence, not faith, Revelation, and piety. During the same week that the Dual Ministry came into existence, the Wartburg Festival in Germany lent credence to the dangers lurking in the pursuit of higher education. Nearly 500 students, members of the *Burschenschaften*, a secret society founded at Jena University in 1815, met to celebrate the tricentennial of Luther's *Theses* and ended with protesting tyranny and despotism. The Dual Ministry thus felt justified in having recently announced its intention to fight Enlightenment politics and "free-thinking," especially at universities.[42]

Included among those newly appointed to the Central School Board was Alexander Sturdza of the foreign ministry. In 1818, he prepared a report ("Mémoire sur l'état actuel de l'Allemagne") for the tsar on the recent political disturbances in Germany. Sturdza's "Mémoire" blamed Germany's problems, which in his view were potentially fatal to the established order, upon the universities. He described them as "aimless," "demoralized," interested only in their academic freedom and corporate exclusiveness. They were supposedly composed of immoral students and demagogic professors who fomented political extremism and disorder. Sturdza advised German leaders to take draconian measures against the universities, to annul their privileges and freedoms, to reduce their number and curricula, and to place their entire operation under police and governmental surveillance. Soon, the Carlsbad Decrees implemented these suggestions. Since Russian universities were in part modeled after the German, Sturdza was suggesting domestic policy as well. As a school board member, he displayed no sympathy for Uvarov's educational attitudes but disliked pietism even more; ill health gave him the opportunity to resign quickly. His points were not forgotten, though, and, like de Maistre's, they became part of the arsenal for battling the reform statutes.[43]

Golitsyn, a sincere man of considerable gifts but little formal learning, felt ill at ease in the area of higher education. His only suggestion—and one for which he surely won few converts—was to require lectures in theology at universities on Saturday so that "students from every faculty could conveniently attend them."[44] Golitsyn always admitted hoping that "a saint from heaven would appear in the department to drive out the unfortunate Minerva bird." In 1818, he thought he had found his "saint" in Michael Magnitskii, actually a Russian Tartuffe. The erstwhile liberal and atheist, noted for his "feverish striving for power, glory, and wealth," in an effort to get to the center of influence donned a "mask of holiness." Upon opening a chapter of the Bible Society on New Year's Day in 1818, with apocalyptic fervor he preached the piety that Golitsyn loved. The powers of darkness, trying to undo those of Christ, had "thought up a new idol—*human reason*. The theology of this idol—*philosophy*. Its priests—*the most famous writers of every century and country*." Napoleon had brought this eighteenth-century idolatry to fruition, and only Russia could successfully battle these evil forces.[45] Golitsyn adopted the orator as his lieutenant and appointed him to the Central School Board along with Magnitskii's "caricature," Dmitri Runich, an "idiot, braggart, and windbag." By mid-1819, of the fourteen members of the Board, four fanatically defended the new religious and political views, seven endorsed the policy, two remained tactically neutral, and only Uvarov was left openly defending the 1803–1804 statutes.[46] Uvarov weakened his own case, moreover, by adopting a strident attitude and a sense of superiority. He lectured his opponents as to the "true" aim of the ministry and displayed his intellectual credentials. As a result, nearly every measure Uvarov proposed received automatically a negative response, a reflex reaction against his support of the reform statutes as well as his abrasive conduct.

What the new board represented was clear. Uvarov called the members "a horde of deformed enemies . . . of humanity and reason." Nicholas Fuss, an academician and a neutral member of the board although an architect of the reform statutes, sorrowed: "My heart bleeds when I compare the present-day position of our schools of higher education with those expectations that we nourished thirteen years ago under the influence of the new currents of life that flowed from the heights of the throne to all spheres of Russian education." Karamzin warned that this Ministry of the Eclipse, as he called it, was reaping a harvest of hypocrites and that "many are worried and forecast grave troubles."[47]

The clash that settled the immediate future of Russian higher education occurred, very naturally, between Magnitskii and Uvarov. In the first week of January 1819, Golitsyn sent Magnitskii to inspect Kazan University, which seemed in poor condition. At exactly the same time, Uvarov won approval from the tsar to set up a university in St. Petersburg, with a charter that would somewhat revise but generally replicate the provisions of the 1803–1804 statutes.

Scholars agree that Kazan, due to tyrannical and incompetent administration, was the least successful Russian university. Results included high faculty attrition and understaffing, a poor physical plant, inadequate laboratories and libraries, unprepared and undisciplined students, and, apparently, embezzlement of funds. Magnitskii reserved his especial horror, however, for what he deemed the poor morality of professors and students and the lack of religious instruction. His solution, not unanticipated by Golitsyn, was to close the university. But rather than dryly explain this as a needed administrative measure, Magnitskii made of Kazan a larger issue, linking university education to immorality and political disorder. The highly publicized murder in Germany the previous month of Augustus von Kotzebue, the German dramatist and Russian agent, prepared receptive ground for Magnitskii's statements. A university student, Magnitskii asserted, had assassinated Kotzebue because of his hostility to German unification, literary romanticism, and political freedom.[48] To make his point, Magnitskii spoke like an evangelist; he told the Central School Board that he had discovered

the abomination of desolation, an all-powerful atheism, and a complete ignorance of Holy Scriptures and of the most essential foundations of the Christian religion. . . . Truly, there is nothing else to do; it is necessary to destroy the university, to abolish this cesspool that infects and poisons an immense country . . . , to raze the buildings, tear down the walls, to strike a terrible blow and give the world a resounding example.[49]

Hostility between Uvarov and Magnitskii had been smoldering both on ideological and personal levels; now the clash broke into the open. Recognizing the differences between the new direction of the ministry and its earlier mission, Uvarov lectured:

The discussion about the future fate of Kazan University exceeds the limits of our normal deliberations. To this point, the Ministry of Enlightenment . . . concerned itself with the foundation and perfection of higher studies and with the propagation of all means of knowledge. Now we are discussing the abolition of one of Russia's universities. . . . I hope that this discussion will be the first and last of its kind.

Uvarov admitted that the academic and administrative abuses at Kazan necessitated corrective measures. But, he asked, is it actually impossible to rectify the situation and is the death sentence warranted, given the evidence? "Because it did not fulfill the hopes of the government, because it seems *unbeneficial*, it does not follow that it should be called *dangerous*, to seek in it a school of deism and immorality. . . . Ought we to judge the spirit of an entire university on *one speech*, in which *one phrase* is underlined?"

Uvarov concluded by saying that he gave his own speech not from personal enmity—which was surely partly the case—but to *"save my own conscience and my own personal judgment."* Although Uvarov alone defied Magnitskii on this issue, his reasoning won the day. Alexander personally intervened, and Kazan remained open, although subject to future reform.[50]

Uvarov, then, still had some assurance that the tsar continued his support for higher education. But, sensing that time was running out, he feverishly set to work to create a new university in the capital. The foundations were already in place: in 1804, the St. Petersburg Pedagogical Institute had been established with the intention that it should serve as the first section of a future university; in 1808, twelve students were sent to study abroad to prepare a core of professors; in 1816, Uvarov expanded the school, renamed it the Central Pedagogical Institute, and made it nearly the equivalent, in course offerings and administration, of a university. In a dramatic effort to underline imperial approval of the original educational statutes, and probably to enhance his own position, Uvarov proposed the establishment of St. Petersburg University at the beginning of 1819; he received permission from the tsar one week later. Uvarov announced the opening on February 14 in a speech that deliberately defined the university as an institution that would be dedicated to the development of the "life of the mind, knowledge, and reason." He then worked "day and night," so that by the end of May he had completed a permanent statute, a document of 345 articles, and presented it to the Central School Board. In a state of exhaustion and exhilaration, Uvarov retired to his country estate for the summer and fall. He had reason to assume approval of the proposal by the time he returned, since the draft was based on the organization of the Central Pedagogical Institute, which the tsar and board had already accepted.[51]

The plan for administration of the proposed university, however, differed from former rules. The new organization (which Uvarov was to adopt when he became minister) attempted to ameliorate the deficiencies of the earlier statutes that had become evident after fifteen years of experience. Uvarov suggested separating academic functions from those concerned with budgets, maintenance, and diurnal supervision of the district's schools, tasks allotted previously to the university professors. He claimed with justice that the former situation had not worked well at all and had proved burdensome to scholars; cleverly citing the example of Kazan University, he agreed that there it had occasioned incompetence, poor academic performance, and an overworked faculty. Karamzin earlier had bewailed: "The best professors, who should devote their time to knowledge, are busy furnishing candles and firewood for the university!"

Instead, Uvarov recommended the creation of the post of director, an innovation borrowed from Halle University. The director would be a permanent government appointee responsible to the superintendent and charged with running the nonacademic features of the university and its district's schools. To clarify lines of responsibility further, a related innovation established a single administrative organ, the directorate *(pravlenie)*, in place of the several committees that characterized the rather chaotic management of the older universities. While only elected university officials sat on earlier directorates, however, the new one would consist of four governmental appointees (the superintendent, who would also be the ex officio chairman; the director; a legal adviser; and the district school superintendent) and only one elected member, the rector. On the other hand, Uvarov insisted that, as earlier, a conference of professors should yearly elect a rector from among their number, decide appointments, and have total control over all academic matters. Even the superintendent would be subject to their judgment in the academic area, and thus the proposal further protected academic prerogatives.

Most scholars analyze Uvarov's novel administrative arrangement as yet another attempt of an autocratic government to circumscribe university autonomy; but the situation was not so simple. Uvarov's strict insistence that all academic matters remain in the hands of the professoriate would legally prevent the firing of teachers and the alteration of curricula by administrative fiat, practices that had become commonplace under the Dual Ministry; the proposal was, then, actually an act of defiance. Defenders of university autonomy could, however, justifiably worry that even Uvarov's plan involved restrictions on faculty power, and some believed that any such infringement meant betrayal. Uvarov himself was anxious and at length underlined the fact that, in the case of St. Petersburg, the proposals meant a curtailment of the powers of the superintendent, who had formerly the "right to act alone, without witnesses, without forms, and without guiding legislation." Instead, the directorate would act openly and collegially; indeed, he maintained, the only power diminished was that of the superintendent—himself, in this instance.[52]

Although the board had not yet approved the new proposal, St. Petersburg University began to function in accordance with a temporary statute in November 1819. Uvarov worked tirelessly to create a first-rate institution and even observed classes. He upgraded admission standards, allowing no one to enroll who was younger than seventeen years old or who did not pass entrance examinations or possess a graduation certificate from a state gymnasium.

The faculty, though small, rivaled even that of Moscow University in quality. Most professors were young, were able to lecture in Russian, rather than the usual Latin or German, and were attuned to the latest ideas in their fields. One group, Carpatho-Ruthenians who had formed the nucleus of the Central Pedagogical Institute, consisted of men about fifty years of age, all of whom were experienced teachers and published scholars: Michael Balug'ianskii, Vasili Kukol'nik, and Peter Lodii taught philosophical and juridical sciences; Karl Hermann wrote the first three Russian textbooks in political statistics and trained Constantine Ars'enev, a younger professor, to write the fourth. Another group included eight men in their thirties who had studied abroad. Among them, Alexander Galich in philosophy and Alexander Kunitsyn in natural law had just published the first books in the Russian language on these topics. Gerasim Pavskii, who held the chair in theology, was a distinguished Hebrew scholar; his courses became noted for their strong intellectual content rather than for their religious preachments. Some foreigners, all celebrated in their fields, were brought to the university by Uvarov and enjoyed his personal protection: Gräfe in classical languages, Vikenti Vishnevskii in astronomy, Demange and Charmoy in Oriental languages, and Karl Raupach in world history. The excellent faculty, along with Uvarov's well-known insistence on high standards, augured well for the new institution. In all, observers noted that Uvarov oversaw the new university like a "benevolent patriarch," and they compared his role to that of Lomonosov at Moscow University.[53]

Uvarov's victory in establishing St. Petersburg University proved to be his last as superintendent. The Central School Board began engineering the downfall of its only dissenting member. Uvarov assisted their plans by making a political mistake. In creating his new statute, Uvarov had promised to consult with experienced university people but instead had acted nearly alone. Thus, he alienated the professoriate, who suspected the apparent infringement on autonomy and misunderstood his motives. In a word, he made the statute synonymous with his own person and views, both of which the majority of the Central School Board were trying to defeat. In this way, Uvarov's desire to make the new university a personal triumph worked toward his fall.

The board understood that defeating the university statute meant Uvarov's own defeat and that of the reforming spirit of 1803–1804. Magnitskii led the attacks by stating that he could "excuse this enormous creation" of a new charter only if the author had the circumspection to end the previous tendency to imitate German universities, a tendency that had led to "danger to social well-being" and to "anarchy," and had produced a generation of Voltaires. Magnitskii's accusations bore special force because, only two weeks before their delivery in September 1819, the Frankfurt Assembly had found it necessary to pass the Carlsbad Decrees.

The Central School Board meeting of December 11, 1819, determined the immediate future of higher education in Russia. Golitsyn officially handed Uvarov a statement of the attacks on his charter, and the statute now began a long and hopeless trek from committee to committee. The professors found administrative arrangements "unclear," salaries too low, the curriculum too heavily defined, and other aspects of the proposal similarly objectionable—all of which could probably have been worked out, but that was not the intention. In late February, a committee composed of Magnitskii, Uvarov, and Balug'ianskii, the rector, was to resolve the issues and prepare a compromise statute. As expected, within the week the group euphemistically admitted it had "difficulty in fulfilling its duties." The board ordered a new committee, composed only of university people, to prepare another statute. The revised document was to conform to the original university statutes, but in their current form as modified by the directions of the Dual Ministry as well as by the new instructions for Kazan University, recently written by Magnitskii. Uvarov objected time and again in "separate opinions," which were sadly futile. Rumors began circulating that he would have to resign.[54]

Underlining his defeat, the board, at the same meeting of December 11 at which it virtually discarded Uvarov's statute, approved Magnitskii's "Instructions for Kazan University" without change. Golitsyn had appointed his sycophant superintendent of the Kazan Education District in mid-summer 1819 and had charged him with reforming the errant institution. In general, the "Instructions" provided a more violent Russian rendition of the Carlsbad Decrees. Magnitskii declaimed:

> *Professors of godless universities spread the poison of skepticism and hatred of lawful powers to an unfortunate youth* and spread it throughout Europe. Happy would be Russia if she could so *separate herself from Europe that even hearing about the atrocities happening there would not reach her ears!*

The board applauded this warning, with only Fuss muttering that "this kind of university does not exist" in Russia. The "Instructions" stressed the importance of maintaining a unity "in the teaching of all knowledge in the university," and specified that the source of this unity was to be "the sole spirit of Holy Scripture." The new curriculum ordered that instruction in philosophy be based on Paul's Letters to Timothy; politics on the examples of Moses, David, and Solomon; history on Bossuet; classical literature on the Church Fathers; literature on the Bible and Lomonosov; science on Genesis. The "Instructions" enforced monastic discipline; officials supervised students' reading Scriptures during meals and performing religious obligations several times a day, and indeed oversaw every action of students "in the course of the entire day." Inspectors checked notebooks, investigated classrooms, approved curricula. In general, students were to learn that "obedience is the first law of education and the citizen." Thus, on December 11, the two views of higher education clashed, and Magnitskii's won.[55]

Besides Uvarov, only the Dorpat professor George Parrot attacked Magnitskii, but he did so in a private letter to the tsar, which received no circulation. Parrot reminded Alexander that the tsar had saved Europe, given Poland a constitution, and planned for his country's progress. In order to fulfill his hopes for Russia, he should continue to respect the reform statutes and enable the educational system to create a cadre of government servants capable of independent activity. The "Instructions" would instead produce slaves, imbeciles, and hypocrites, who would be useless in a modernizing state. Alexander agreed with this advice for a time.[56] In internal matters, the tsar still harkened to moderate voices such as those of Capodistrias, an Arzamas member. In November 1819, Capodistrias called a cabinet meeting in which he declared the Carlsbad Decrees "a mistake made under the simple influence of passion" and disproportionate to the circumstances. He considered that temporary measures in censorship and some surveillance of the universities were all the action that was warranted. Early in 1820, Alexander vetoed a motion made by the Council of Ministers to recall all Russian students enrolled in German universities to save them from contamination. Quite obviously, Alexander still saw no real connection between higher education and threats to throne and altar.[57]

By 1821, however, the tide had turned in both educational and political matters. In 1820, the reactionary Prince Klemens von Metternich, the Austrian prime minister, found his justification for his hatred of reform and for his uncompromising defense of the old order in Europe. Revolutions unexpectedly broke out in Spain, Portugal, the Italian States, and then Greece; finally, a mutiny took place in the Semenovskii Regiment. Assuming his prey was ready, Metternich sent Alexander a "Confession of Faith," dated December 15, 1820. Metternich announced that "evil . . . penetrates into every vein of the social body" due to "presumptions," both in religious and political matters, of the individual to knowledge and to freedom from authority. He claimed that "all reform in France touching the very foundations of the monarchy was soon transformed into revolution." Napoleon had spread the disorder but, even after his defeat, "completely false steps" had been taken in France, steps, of course, that Alexander had initiated. These new attitudes had resulted in the "moral gangrene" of secret societies and the rallying cry of constitution—which, Metternich lectured, "everywhere means change and trouble." Even the Bible Societies, he warned, had replaced an established church with individual reading of Scripture.

Alexander, chastised, now grew cool to his new religion and to projects of reform. Thus, although the Bible Society began a three-year decline, the antireform nexus that it had fostered triumphed. The year 1821, not surprisingly, saw a "parting of the ways" between Alexander and many progressive segments of Russian society; in that year, Marc Raeff points out, the future Decembrists abandoned hopes of gradualism and turned their thoughts to revolution. In terms of education, they came to the conclusion that a true system of enlightenment had to follow freedom, not act as its preparation; otherwise, it only served the status quo.[58]

The stage was also set for Uvarov's dismissal. In June 1820, Uvarov's proposal, strongly supported by St. Petersburg professors, to offer courses to those who were either unwilling or unable to attend a university but who wanted to pursue study in their leisure time was scotched as "harmful." Next, in March 1821, Kunitsyn was forced to resign. His two-volume work *On Natural Law*, completed in 1820, was noted for its "proper caution" in handling "notions that in an unlimited monarchy are impossible to approve," even though he incorporated the ideas of the Physiocrats, Adam Smith, and Rousseau. Runich, hungry for Uvarov's post, used the book as an excuse to attack the supposedly "evil spirit" allowed by the superintendent to reign at St. Petersburg University. He and Magnitskii connected the text of this "enemy of God" with all the horrors of revolutions then occurring in "Lisbon, Naples, Turin, and Madrid."

> Kunitsyn's book is nothing other than a mass of appalling and abominable pseudo-thinking, which, unfortunately, the overly celebrated Rousseau brought into the world and which has agitated and still agitates the hot heads of the defenders of the rights of man and citizen. Marat is nothing other than a sincere practitioner of this doctrine.

It should be added that Kunitsyn and Uvarov generally agreed about the direction that Russia's political, social, and economic development should take.[59] After censure by the Central School Board, Kunitsyn's books were removed from stores and library shelves. Then followed a desperate, and silly, effort to locate all 2,000 copies of *On Natural Law*, and a frenzy when officials found only 1,875. Runich forced Kunitsyn to sign the itemized list and Uvarov, who refused to agree to the censure, to witness the notarization. Uvarov next futilely objected to new censorship proposals that Magnitskii claimed were needed because authors ran about "with philosophical tracts and constitutional charters in their hands."[60]

In March of 1821, Alexander Turgenev, an Arzamas friend and colleague of Uvarov in the ministry, wrote in a letter to his brother that Uvarov "must not only save Kunitsyn but scholarship in general from the inroads of the Magnitskiis and Runiches." Turgenev himself uttered not a word of criticism.[61]

The episode that finally led to Uvarov's departure involved a protest by *pansion* students against the dismissal of a favorite language teacher, Wilhelm Küchelbecker. Since Küchelbecker subsequently became a Decembrist, perhaps authorities had reason to worry about his loyalty, although on the other hand his firing may have provoked his switch from liberalism to radicalism; in any case the Dual Ministry was not interested in making such a distinction. Uvarov considered the protest an isolated incident; even the director, Dmitri Kavelin, called it the work of teenaged "pranksters." But Golitsyn wanted to use the incident to indict and unseat Uvarov. He called it a "crime" and insisted that it "clearly shows weak administration." One contemporary attested that the *pansion* was indeed in a nearly laughable state, "with neither structure, nor order, nor cleanliness, nor even tidiness" and attributed the mess to the director, who was a "nice fellow" but "not cut out to be an administrator." Kavelin proved not even a nice fellow, but he did possess a sense of self-preservation. Although an Arzamas member—Turgenev suggested he be formally expelled for his action—he agreed to become Golitsyn's tool and switched the blame to Uvarov by saying that the liberal arts curriculum promoted by Uvarov filled students' minds with philosophy and hence revolution or at least "a general spirit of willfullness." What was needed was a radical transformation of the institution similar to that proposed, of course, by Magnitskii. Uvarov agreed to tighten up student discipline but would not sanction full-scale reform or, as he put it sarcastically, "teaching political economy on the basis of Revelation." Uvarov finally had had it. He stopped attending board meetings after April 28 and resigned in the summer of 1821.[62]

In July, Uvarov went "far from the capital . . . to recoup moral and physical strength." He once again succumbed to illness in time of crisis and complained that "my infirmities are nearly habitual." In an official letter, he claimed that the only reason he resigned was "to restore my health." Runich, who quickly secured the vacant position, said of Uvarov: "He was simply a mold from those contemporary German universities." Magnitskii was relieved; he would no longer have to suffer through those "terrible arguments" with Uvarov over the "leading figures in German literature and philosophy." Golitsyn wrote gleefully about the "departure" of Uvarov.[63]

Students at the university feared the worst because they recognized that in contrast to Uvarov, who was educated and well-intentioned, Runich was an "unintelligible, canting hypocrite." Indeed, once Uvarov resigned, Runich hastened to enact Magnitskii's "Instructions" for Kazan at St. Petersburg University, and this resulted in "disastrous changes" for the new institution.[64] A reprehensible inquisition and purge of both faculty and students followed. The Golitsyn-Magnitskii clique, with the ardor common to zealots of all ages, sought vindication and attempted to "prove" that they had acted justifiably, that the university was in fact a loathsome place.[65]

Uvarov alone objected to Runich's conclusion—based on illegal, nocturnal interrogations of professors and spurious, unexamined evidence (the notebooks of students)—that the university had become "a corridor of atheism and sedition" as a result of a premeditated plot of the staff. In a letter to the tsar, Uvarov "threw down the gauntlet" in an attempt to unmask these "powerful enemies of public tranquility."

The born enemies of all positive order and consequently the *friends of darkness* give themselves the most holy names in order to seize authority and sap the foundations of the established order; these cold-blooded fanatics are . . . everything but men and citizens and pretend to defend throne and altar against attacks that do not exist and, at the same time, plant suspicion of the real mainstays of throne and altar; these facile comedians take every disguise to trouble every conscience, to alarm every soul, and now create around themselves chimerical dangers in order to prolong their ephemeral existence for a few moments longer.

Uvarov then begged Alexander to examine the evidence himself and proclaimed his trust that once the tsar recognized the truth, this "odious dream" would end and order would be restored in the university.[66] The Council of Ministers, who did review the evidence, chose not to support the findings and, in true bureaucratic fashion, referred the matter to committee; Nicholas I formally closed the case in 1827.

Although Runich's purge of St. Petersburg University never received legal sanction, it achieved the intended result. Very soon after the proceedings, the four professors who had been accused of malfeasance and the six colleagues who had supported their innocence—"the flower of the university," according to historians—resigned or went into early retirement. Their replacements were unknown in their fields and had done no scholarly work. In 1822, Runich demoralized the student body by conducting an equally illegal purge of its members; he expelled roughly half the state stipendiates on the basis of poor moral attitudes. After only one year in office, Runich had crippled, for the moment, what had promised to become one of Russia's most eminent institutions of higher learning.[67]

Nonetheless, Uvarov proved correct when he asserted that the Golitsyn clique would enjoy only an "ephemeral existence." Their next drive, to eliminate the teaching of philosophy altogether, fell on deaf ears; their game had played itself out.[68] In 1824, Alexander dismissed Golitsyn and closed the Bible Society as an "un-Russian phenomenon." He yet again resurrected Shishkov, making him educational minister in order to signal a return to traditional values. In 1826, the sanctimonious Magnitskii was dismissed as superintendent when a government inspector found evidence of embezzlement of funds at Kazan University and declared the institution a shambles. Magnitskii and Runich, ever the opportunists, still tried to save their careers. Runich excused his actions with the eternally weak claim that he was only following orders. As late as 1831, Magnitskii carried on his vendetta and tried to convince Nicholas I that Uvarov was dangerous because he consorted with the likes of Goethe and Pestalozzi. But Uvarov had the last word. Once he resumed activity in the educational ministry in 1826, he declared that the opinions of the Dual Ministry "in changed conditions, now demand no special attention."[69]

The defeat of the Dual Ministry, though, did not entail the defeat of the antireform nexus, which had deeper, more stable roots in Russian society. In terms of both education and politics, the Alexandrine era represented in the end a turning away from a progressive spirit to a defense of the status quo. In an autocracy, education, without accompanying political and social reform, is acceptable only if it is limited in both content and access. It was this attitude that triumphed. For the rest of the century, the more extreme features of the antireform nexus softened into milder variants, although occasionally obscurantism or xenophobia would capture an audience. Golitsyn's pietism and his ecumenism (the one really positive feature of his policies), however, never again became influential. The weakening of the spirit of the 1803–1804 statutes meant a bias toward nobility in educational opportunity, an insistence upon Orthodox morality in student life and the curriculum, a stiffening against European intellectual influences, a retreat into secure Russian political and cultural traditions, and a lingering fear of education in general.

When he became educational minister in 1833, Uvarov was chastened by his experience in the 1810s but not quite converted. He stayed within the general bounds set by the antireform nexus but learned how to circumvent it and thus still manage to press forward gradually and forcefully. He continued to value education for all classes as the essential ingredient in Russia's progress. He expanded greatly the educational system and, with his usual insistence upon high standards, made it one of uncontested quality, equal to those in Western Europe. He devised ways to attract the nobility into the gymnasia and universities and established a new career pattern whereby education preceded state service. In this way, his policies prepared the cadres for technological development as well as for the judicial and administrative reforms of the next half century. Promotion of classical, Oriental, and especially Russian studies remained a hallmark of his administration. At the same time, he fostered ties with the West and brought Russia more fully into the modern intellectual world. Thus, Uvarov as minister generally retained the spirit of the 1803–1804 statutes that he had fought for as superintendent.

P A R T   T W O

THE REIGN OF NICHOLAS I, 1825–1855

THE FRAMEWORK

We are entering one of those epochs of transition . . . , epochs at once stationary and progressive.   Uvarov, 1833

AFTER Uvarov fell from grace in the Alexandrine educational ministry, he kept his social status intact by accepting service in the ministry of finance. He functioned in the unlikely positions of director of manufacturing and internal trade and of state loans and commercial banks, and occupied himself "signing factory reports and drafting foreclosures."[1] Nicholas's ascent to the throne at the end of 1825 brought a quick reprieve. The tsar had long known Uvarov and only months into the reign appointed him a senator and a member of a new ad hoc commission whose task was to reorganize the faltering educational system. In April 1832, Uvarov became deputy minister of education, and in March 1833 acting minister; he was confirmed as minister one year later and held the post until October 1849, thus becoming Russia's longest-tenured minister of national enlightenment. He also proved the most ambitious.

Uvarov's policies represented a pioneering effort at grappling with what is usually called modernization, the vast changes societies undergo when they adapt to the new world created by the myriad scientific, intellectual, social, and political revolutions that began in sixteenth-century Europe.[2] According to Edward Crankshaw's recent study of the prerevolutionary era, Uvarov figured as one of a new breed of officials that emerged in Nicholaevan Russia. They "raised the largest questions" and understood "that they had inherited a problem that was unique in Europe. . . . These men had an immense and backward country to run and to bring forward."[3]

Uvarov himself spoke of transforming Russia from a "young" to a "mature" nation. He contended that education necessarily played the key role in the process, that "the responsibility of the Ministry of National Enlightenment consisted in going ahead of other parts of the upper administration, paving the way for others, performing the first experiments." Indeed, in any modernizing country the educational system must be unified and expanded to create a fully literate elite; to produce a new generation of competent bureaucrats, lawyers, doctors, scientists, teachers, and professors; to provide the knowledge needed for industrialization and improved agricultural production; and to promote a sense of national unity and identity. These elements, Uvarov believed, formed the prerequisites for all other reform. With some temerity, he declared that "my principles" are not like "the transient will of the tsar" but offer "a firm and durable system" for Russia's peaceful progress.[4]

A TIMETABLE FOR DEVELOPMENT

UVAROV had outlined his goals for Russian development by 1818, but subsequent events altered his timetable for their achievement. He originally assumed that an already "mature" West had paved a providentially approved path for this "youngest son of the large family of Europe." He was ebullient and optimistic. He considered that Russia's progress from youth to maturity was already well underway, having begun under Peter the Great, and implied that it might be shorter than Europe's four-century march. Uvarov's hopes for quick development were soon dashed. In the last years of Alexander's reign, reaction and obscurantism triumphed. In December 1825, upon Nicholas I's accession to the throne, scions of leading noble families attempted a revolt that ended in a fiasco. In Uvarov's scheme, as expressed in his writings of the 1810s, such an event meant that even Russia's elite still toyed with the youthful "dreamy vision" of republican governments and/or revolutionary methods rather than understanding the mature process of gradual, organic growth.[5] Uvarov began to lengthen his timetable for Russia's complete entry to modernity and continued to adjust it to conform to the changing character of Nicholas's reign.

At first, the new monarch's policies seemed to hold some promise of progress.[6] Nicholas thoroughly investigated the grievances of the Decembrists and came to the conclusion that their dissatisfaction had a basis in reality and was not simply an ideological importation from the West, as he had at first assumed. Consequently, the first years of the reign witnessed the formation of special committees designed to plan reforms and in a sense to carry on the work begun by Alexander in his own first years in power. There was little anticipation of fundamental change, such as freeing the serfs or granting a constitution, since Nicholas's advisers, like Uvarov, thought these actions premature, even if desirable; the tsar himself believed that social and economic changes were inevitable but drew the line on political reform. Instead, and once again as in the earlier regime, the idea was to make governmental organization more efficient in order to cure Russia's deficiencies. Indeed, the problem of administering a vast empire, of having even simple legislation adopted and executed in provinces distant from the capital, remained acute. The emphasis on increasing administrative efficiency suited Nicholas's character well, since he was, by profession and at heart, a military man and an engineer who appreciated precision and clear lines of command; similarly, he preferred the role of administrator and manager to that of innovative leader.

At the beginning of his reign, Nicholas was clearly of a conservative bent but not necessarily a diehard defender of the status quo. He was surely not a reactionary, and he quickly rid himself of the whole Golitsyn-Magnitskii clique. His first principal adviser was Karamzin, who, until he died in 1826, counseled the young, inexperienced monarch on the beauty of national traditions and on the necessity of autocracy for Russia; still, power had to be used for the general development and happiness of citizens. To supplement this viewpoint, Karamzin recommended his Arzamas "brothers" to Nicholas. Zhukovskii, Bludov, and Dashkov joined the administration, while Uvarov became a member of the new committee set up to reorganize the school system. Speranskii also returned to the center of power, where he carried out the important task of codifying Russia's laws. Speranskii and Karamzin coauthored Nicholas's Coronation Manifesto; its sentiments fit in exactly with Uvarov's views and underscored the basic cohesion of the triumvirate's political attitudes.

> The statutes of the land are perfected, faults are corrected, and abuses are rectified from above and not by daring dreams, which are always destructive. Gradual improvement means that every modest desire for betterment, every idea for strengthening the power of law, for spreading true enlightenment and industry will reach us by a legal path, open to all, and will always be received by us with good will. For we have not, cannot have, any other desire but to see our country on the highest level of happiness and glory predestined by Providence.

In Nicholas's first years in power, contemporaries noted that his "resolute activity produced many changes in internal administration"; as opposed to the "fanatics and adherents of old prejudices," he gave a "positive answer" to the question, "Is enlightenment beneficial to Russia?"[7] Thus, in the first years of the reign, Uvarov concluded that, while the "new era" was not immediately forthcoming, as he had once hoped, it would arrive in about twenty years after Nicholaevan ministers had laid the groundwork:

"If it is not given to us to see the full success of such endeavors, then . . . at least the generation that will soon replace us will gather the fruits of our labors."[8]

The 1830 revolutions, however, which started in France, spread throughout much of Europe, and set all classes in motion, profoundly affected Uvarov's thinking. He had always recoiled from revolutions and regarded them as "moral-political ulcers . . . useful only in the general plan of Providence" for punishing wayward nations or kings that followed an incorrect path. A few years later, he remembered his "despondency . . . at the sight of social upheavals which were at that time shaking Europe and whose echo, weaker or stronger, reached even us, threatening danger."

Nevertheless, several essays, written under the influence of the events of 1830, demonstrated his continuing belief in the essentials of his earlier prognosis. Although deeply troubled by the current "disasters in the political world," he reiterated his faith that "the law of progress cannot cease to be the express condition of our social existence." Recent events indicated to him that "for a large part of Europe the era of aristocratic governments seems to have come to an end"; he saw doom for "the *unconstitutional* monarch"—even if recognized as "legitimate"—who "rules alone" and refuses "to admit the *sovereignty* of his people." For this offense, Charles X, who tried to abrogate the French Charter of Liberties, had been driven from his throne. Furthermore, Uvarov recognized that "the entire consummation of the new social system" would be founded upon a "commercial and industrial spirit." Louis Philippe, the "bourgeois king," also called the King of the French, a title implying that his power originated in the people, replaced Charles, an old regime monarch who considered himself a divine-right King of France.[9]

On the other hand, after 1830 Uvarov's plans for the achievement of "maturity" were tempered by an equally weighty concern—to prevent Russia from undergoing full-scale revolution, "from which both love of the Fatherland and even sensible thinking tell us to flee." Uvarov concluded that the countries of Western Europe had attempted to go too far too fast and thus had caused the unwarranted disruption and suffering that led to unrest. He excoriated those political leaders who tinker with the present order but "do not think about the future" and "imprudently strive forward without glancing backward [or] weighing the past with the future." Instead, Russia would "develop slowly."[10]

Really, there was little choice, because the Revolution of 1830 had pushed Nicholas in the direction of status quo conservatism. Not only did his good friend, Charles X, lose his throne, but his sister's Dutch monarchy lost Belgium and an uprising broke out in Russian Poland. At the end of the year, Alexander Nikitenko, a censor, literature professor, and former serf, moaned in his diary: "The outgoing year has been of little comfort to the forces of enlightenment in Russia. They felt stifled by an atmosphere of repression."[11] The tsar's fear of revolution from below and his post-Decembrist distrust of the nobility led Nicholas to rely on suppression, controls, and personal rule through loyal agents; for this reason, nearly all historians agree that Nicholas's reign is properly considered the "apogee of absolutism."

Reforms continued, though, especially in the 1830s, just so long as they did not breach the fundamental social and political order. Thus, progress occurred in the areas of state peasant administration, justice, finances, and education, but the essential problems of serfdom and autocracy remained untouched. In the phrase of Robert Tucker, Nicholaevan Russia became a "classic case" of arrested but differential modernization wherein progress occurred in some areas but "obstructionist tendencies" slowed the general process of change to "such a creeping pace that the society is, broadly speaking, in a state of stagnation." An earlier educational historian, Thomas Darlington, confirmed that "politically the era was one of arrested progress; educationally it was a time of great advance." Likewise, while agreeing that "movement prevailed over stagnation" in economic, social, and cultural life, Nicholas Riasanovsky rues the recidivism of Nicholaevan politics, which transformed "enlightened despotism into despotism pure and simple."[12]

By 1833, Uvarov had concluded: "It is evident that in all respects we are entering one of those epochs of transition, which are not unknown in the annals of the *esprit humain*, epochs at once stationary and progressive." Paul Annenkov's memoir, *The Extraordinary Decade*, recorded that the men of the 1830s and 1840s "constantly reiterated, even in print, that their generation, as a transitional one, was destined only to prepare the materials for reforms and changes." Mid-twentieth-century historians, with the benefit of hindsight, concur that the Nicholaevan era was indeed a time of preparation during which the groundwork was laid for future reform.[13]

As educational minister, Uvarov set himself a two-pronged and exquisitely delicate task: to facilitate Russia's transition to maturity but to keep the country youthful until it was fully ripe for change, in other words, to go forward while standing still and maintaining the existing social and political structure. Obviously, there were pitfalls in this program. On the one hand, Uvarov correctly discerned that providing increased educational opportunities and a program for development creates a sense of progress, which is, overall, the best antidote to dissatisfaction, disorder, and hostile attitudes toward the existing state. He delighted in quoting Catherine the Great's dictum: "Do you want to prevent revolution? Then spread enlightenment among the people."[14] On the other hand, the social and political aspirations of an increasingly educated public are difficult to contain within the confines of the status quo. The success of using education as a spearhead for general, peaceful development also depends on perceptible responses to the "rising expectations" of society, which in this instance included emancipation of the serfs and some measure of political and civil rights. In his diary, Nikitenko wondered as early as 1827:

> Will the people themselves cast off their bonds or will they receive freedom from the government itself? God save us from the former! But this is inevitable if the government merely educates the people without slackening their bonds as national self-awareness awakens. It is important that educational measures go hand in hand with a new civil code.[15]

Although no "new civil code" was forthcoming, nevertheless the Nicholaevan autocracy enjoyed something of a honeymoon period through the thirties, which were "remarkably calm and quiet." By 1840, however, the Third Section of His Majesty's Own Chancery, the gendarmarie or secret police, reported "a certain general dissatisfaction, which can be expressed in a statement . . . from Moscow: '*I do not know exactly, but something is wrong*,' and this expression we now hear often from the most gentle, the most well-intentioned people."[16] As hopes dimmed for basic reform on the part of the state, an impatient public developed a critical attitude and began fashioning its own programs for Russia's future and challenging the government's desired monopoly.

Uvarov, who had multiplied the ranks of the educated in the belief he could "control the direction of their minds," became ever more frustrated at his inability to leash the new forces for which he was in part responsible and which he still believed necessary, but which the tsar grew to fear more and more.

Faced with the twin challenges of autocratic intransigence and the growing demands of the public, Uvarov took a middle ground and simply called for extensions of the time of transition. In 1835, he recognized that "our liberals" wanted more rapid, fundamental change, but he remained firm. In a famous statement recorded by Nikitenko in 1835, Uvarov expressed his commitment to his program and his anger at not being understood.

> We, that is, the people of the nineteenth century, are in a difficult position: we are living amidst political storms and political unrest. Nations are changing their way of life; they are experiencing rebirth, are in ferment, and advancing. No one [nation] can prescribe its own rules here. But Russia is young and virgin, and she should not taste, at least for the time being, these bitter troubles. We must extend her youth and educate her in the meantime. That is my political approach. I know what our liberals, our journalists and their minions want. . . . But they won't succeed in casting their seeds on to the field that I am sowing and guarding—no, they will not succeed. My task is to keep an eye not only on education, but also on the spirit of this generation. If I can succeed in delaying for fifty years the kind

of future that theories are brewing for Russia, I shall have performed my duty and shall die in peace. That is my theory; I hope I shall realize it. For this I am equipped with both good will and the political means. I know that people are crying out against me, but I do not heed their cries. Let them call me an obscurantist. A statesman must stand above the crowd.[17]

Eight years later, Uvarov repeated his faith in the "correctness of the chosen path" but spoke also of "a distant future, nearly unseen." In one sense, then, Uvarov became a classic example of what George Yaney described as that "persistent tendency among politically conscious Russians to derive their moral identity from future expectations." In Uvarov's case, though, the protracted timetable led to melancholy, frustration, and a loss of enthusiasm. In 1843, he compiled a lengthy review of his accomplishments in ten years in office, entitled *One Decade in the Ministry of National Enlightenment*, and then asked to be relieved of his position. He was persuaded to stay on. The death of his daughter at the time also disturbed him deeply, and he took a trip abroad to cure his depression. On a more opportunistic level, Uvarov was probably reluctant to abandon the corridors of power and seemed willing to trim his sails to suit the mood of the tsar. At any rate, after 1843, the energetic, "indefatigable" minister once filled with endless plans became a coasting and passive man.[18]

By the end of the forties, Uvarov had lost the support of the tsar. Nicholas's response to the Revolution of 1848 in Europe was to become a full-fledged reactionary, to harken back to old regime principles, and to brandish more forcefully the weapons of a police state—all this even though Russia remained quiescent while nearly all Western Europe erupted. Even such a loyal and conservative reformer as Uvarov was declared too "liberal," and he was forced from office. This gruesome period of full-scale repression from 1848 to 1855 was to become a focus of historical literature on Nicholas's reign, to such an extent that the entire reign was generally portrayed in bleak colors, despite the fact that many gifted men had worked conscientiously in the previous two decades for the reform of Russia.

Uvarov's reputation suffered the most. Most scholars have flatly branded him a reactionary, an enemy of all progress. His policies as minister are generally condemned as the "vivid expression" of the worst of Nicholaevan politics in practice, and chapters describing his educational system are often entitled "The Reaction" or "The Long Period of Reaction." But this practice does little to explain the common conclusion that "despite Uvarov's policies," to use a nearly universal phrase, the 1830s and 1840s enjoyed the golden age of universities, the "best period" in the history of the secondary schools, major advances in technical education and scientific knowledge, qualitative development on all levels of schooling, "sky-rocketing" publication figures, the birth of Oriental, Slavic, classical, and philological studies, the organization of historical archives, the explosion of archeological work—indeed, a general cultural renaissance.[19] All these areas were in Uvarov's purview as educational minister. Clearly, the usual portrayal of his tenure in office is simplistic and tendentious.

To some degree, nevertheless, Uvarov deserves his caricature as a reactionary. According to his own confessed theory, his policies were geared, in part and for the time being, to support of the existing social and political order. Consequently, they included censorship, "intellectual dams," class bias in education, political propaganda, ubiquitous inspectors, and curriculum control as well as those hallmarks of Nicholaevan bureaucratization—regimentation, standardization, and hierarchical centralization. Furthermore, Uvarov styled himself the creator and guardian of Russian culture and, with wearisome and nettling repetition, insisted that everyone write, think, and act "in conformity with the views of the government," really of Uvarov. These traits quite naturally grated on the sensibilities of the most articulate in society and earned Uvarov the enmity of Herzen, Bakunin, and Belinskii, who eventually emerged as the heroes of the epoch to those who opposed autocracy. Educational historians, especially those of a libertarian bent, also justly decry the promotion of education as a tool of the state rather than as an humanitarian ideal.

This stress on the repressive features of Uvarov's policies, though, requires modification and the balance of historical perspective. If his actions are analyzed according to the criteria of modernization propounded by recent historians, Uvarov accomplished what was possible and necessary in Russia at that time. He laid the basis for future development by achieving "the goal of a well-educated and wholly literate elite," the essential prerequisite for the full-scale modernization that began under the next tsar, Alexander II, who thus had the trained personnel and bureaucratic and public support to emancipate the serfs, reform the judiciary, and create local organs of self-government.[20] Moreover, Uvarov made these preparations consciously, fully aware that he was living in a "transitional" era. But while Uvarov intended his "system" as a temporary measure, his successors copied it as a final form. He surely never pushed for constitutional reform during the Nicholaevan era—no bureaucrat did—but he assumed its inevitability because of his profound faith in the inexorable, providential march of history and progress. Since this aspect of development never became a permanent feature of Russian life, the vision behind Uvarov's educational policies was lost. What remained was an effective and repressive system that promised simultaneously to advance knowledge and arrest dissidence: to sustain a transitional era made permanent. Furthermore, if Uvarov's policies are compared with those in England, France, or Prussia, it becomes apparent that centralization, state control, class barriers, powerful inspectors, political indoctrination, and the drive to create an homogenized national culture were characteristic of all contemporary school systems.

Those other countries, however, developed into freer societies, with corresponding changes in their educational systems, and so their earlier efforts are regarded with more respect.

Thus, the years following 1848 overshadowed the entire Nicholaevan regime, and Uvarov's policies with it, to the extent that this repressive period became regarded only as the end of an old regime era rather than, in part, as an era of transition to more modern forms. In particular, Uvarov's famous tripartite formula, "Orthodoxy, Autocracy, Nationality," became an eternal and neat symbol of the tsars' unwillingness and inability to change, of the government's hostility to Western ideas, and of the necessity for the February Revolution of 1917. Despite the historical fate and use of the formula, Uvarov's own conception of it was quite different.

THE PRINCIPLES OF DEVELOPMENT

U VAROV was so proud of the success of the motto he had invented in an 1832 report to the tsar that he emblazoned it upon the family shield when he was given the title of count in 1846; by then, it had already become a Russian institution.[21] The phrase, "Orthodoxy, Autocracy, Nationality," was brilliant in its simplicity and accessibility. It raised the flag of old-fashioned patriotism and rang a proud affirmation of native values. It proffered a cogent outline of the dynamism, content, and form of Russian development. On the other hand, the formula lacked precision since its terms allowed a variety of definitions and represented something of a bowdlerization since it remained silent on social and economic issues. For all these reasons, it provided a useful political tool for the faithful as well as a convenient target for the disenchanted.

The inner message of the formula, that Russia was paving its own distinctive pathway to modernity, echoed the contemporary intellectual tone. Since the victories of the Napoleonic era, there had arisen a new sense of national self-worth, a welcome compensation after a century of Western tutelage. The novelist Vladimir Odoevskii in *Russian Nights* could exult: "Europe called the Russian *a savior!*" The 1820s witnessed a penetration of German romanticism and idealism into Russian intellectual life that resulted in the many famous philosophical "circles." At first, there was a stress on those peculiarities of geography, race, or religion that, as Herder had long ago pointed out, divided peoples. By the 1830s many intellectuals were ready for the next step: because of its national characteristics and history, young Russia was superior to the "old enfeebled West" and would enjoy a glorious messianic future. Odoevskii grandly trumpeted this exuberance: "The nineteenth century belongs to Russia!"[22]

Uvarov anticipated these trends in the 1810s, but, as the years progressed, in particular after the revolutions of the 1820s and 1830, he, too, began to place new emphasis on Russia's uniqueness and to question the universal applicability of Western European models of development. While the goals toward which European countries were striving still appeared desirable, the means for achieving them were not. The evidence seemed overwhelming that these countries had steered off course, since the revolutionary movement that began in 1789 still showed no signs of abatement. If the West no longer offered sure guidance for Russia's peaceful development, Uvarov declared, it was necessary to discern and reaffirm the "sustaining principles" that "constitute the unique character of Russia and that belong to her exclusively." Furthermore, she would profit from the mistakes of her elders: "Providence blessed Russia, having made her the last in the assembly of enlightened states." Thus, "Russia, in which everything is new, which bears at this moment the imprint of all the centuries, Russia, which it is impossible to judge either by accepted rules or European theories," would pave its own way to modernity. It would develop a new and original philosophy of history based on "Orthodoxy, Autocracy, Nationality" and avoid the materialism, revolution, and class conflict supposedly rampant in the West.[23]

Orthodoxy

As he had in the 1810s, Uvarov continued to relate the "progress of political bodies and that of the *esprit humain*" and to judge both on their incorporation of Christian principles. "The grand evolution of humanity," he claimed in an article on the philosophy of literature, "will be entirely accomplished when Christianity has penetrated its customs, its conscience, and its spirit." Uvarov went on to express a fear that modern society, rather than remaining true to its Christian heritage, its "center of unity," was instead regressing to the cynicism, skepticism, "materialism," and "moral chaos" of the ancient world: an overweening emphasis on "material progress" reduced "man and things to the same level." Speaking of literature, but implying politics, Uvarov attested that if society "shakes off this providential yoke [of Christian morality], it will destroy itself with its own hands," because Christianity possesses "ideas without which society cannot exist for a moment." The new materialism was thus in part responsible for "the rapid downfall of religious and civic institutions in Europe." In contrast to the growing materialism of the West, Uvarov presented Russia as still "sincerely and profoundly attached to the church . . . , looking upon it as a guarantee of social and familial happiness." He ominously warned: "Without love for the faith of their ancestors, a people as well as an individual must perish."

Uvarov, ever the proponent of the *juste milieu*, enshrined Orthodoxy as a temperate religion. Franz von Baader, one of the few European intellectuals who extolled the Russian creed, complained to the minister in a lengthy correspondence that Roman Catholicism represented a doctrinaire approach to religion that resulted in oppression; in reaction, Protestant individualism led to the skepticism and dissolution that bred revolutionary eras, and it would eventually culminate in atheism.[24] Although Uvarov had no profound views about Orthodoxy, he regarded it as a necessary cultural, ethical, and political source of unity and believed that it increasingly seemed superior to other European religions, especially Protestantism. The Russian church enjoyed a "firm structure."

> In Protestantism it is the opposite; their churches do not contain a Protestant dogma, but the central Protestant principle: *'that each judges by his own conscience the tenets of his own beliefs,'* and this places the churches in a state of eternal ferment. Vainly would one search for an anchor in the midst of this unending agitation; an anchor would be broken on the first day of sailing. It is impossible not to note that the audacity of intellectualization about matters of faith has led, especially since the beginning of the nineteenth century, to skepticism. *Rationalism*, in the sense of the negation of all that is supernatural, has brought and continues to bring forth detestable phenomena. From this phenomenon is born an entire set of sects.

Thus, the Western Christian tradition appeared divided, and the nations and civilizations it should, in its historic role, inspire were seemingly engulfed in conflict and turmoil. In contrast, adherents could still claim that Orthodoxy held the Russian nation together as it had from "time immemorial" and that it "posited the principle of internal unity" in a community of interest that set the standards of behavior and belief for the individual, society, and its tsar. Historically, it had retained its purity despite assaults from the Latin West, pagan East, and Islamic South, and at the same time it counseled peace and cooperation with the existing government, rarely making the Western dichotomy between church and state. Thus, if Christian morality and political structure marched hand in hand, as they did in Uvarov's scheme, the principles of Orthodoxy remained truer to their providential role and provided a better foundation for national development than those of any religion in the West. But to conclude that Orthodoxy, in reality a servant of the state, was capable of inclining the tsar and population to greater civil and political equality, which Uvarov in 1818 attested was an essential mission of Christianity, proved, at best, a naive optimism.[25]

Autocracy and Serfdom

As excessive as Uvarov's confidence in the reforming power of Orthodoxy may have been, in the long run it was even greater wishful thinking on his part to rely so heavily on the tsars to carry Russia to modernity, especially in political terms. This is a judgment made in hindsight, however. In 1830, witnessing class conflicts in the West and the continuing threat of revolution, Uvarov, like the overwhelming majority of the Russian educated public, preferred to look to a "strong, humane, enlightened autocracy" to lead development or proffer reforms. This rather common theme in Russian political theory did not die until Bloody Sunday, 1905, when the tsar was perceived as having broken his bond with the "people." Uvarov rejected the ever-growing "liberal" tendency toward democratic republics or rule by interest groups and called upon Russians "to return to the straight path of the Russian monarchical principle." As always, he claimed: "*Autocracy* constitutes the *sine qua non* of Russia's political existence." The tsar rules for the benefit of all and transcends class interests, thus providing stability, strength, and unity during a time of change. In contrast, "other peoples know no peace and are weakened by discord," while "here the Tsar . . . leads the people like a father who is guided by the Law; and the people do not know how to separate Fatherland and Tsar and see in Him their happiness, strength, and glory."[26] Stephen Shevyrev, a romantic nationalist, agreed entirely.

> To be sure, there is no country in all of Europe which can pride itself on possessing such a harmonious political existence as our own motherland. Almost everywhere in the West, wrangling over principles has been recognized as a law of life, and the entire existence of peoples is consumed by grievous struggle. Only among us do tsar and people comprise one indissoluble entity.

Timothy Granovskii, a Moscow University history professor acknowledged as a "liberal" because he championed Western-style political rights, also commented: "The monarchical principle is at the basis of all great developments in Russian history; it is the root system of our political life and of our political importance in Europe." Other writers regarded the autocracy as an institution "alien to Europe and Asia . . . but our strength"; they spoke of the tsar as a ruler concerned with "the general welfare, who labors only for the good of the entire people" and "goes ahead of all social improvements" based on a principle "patriarchal as well as progressive."[27]

On a practical level, Uvarov believed that an empire "so extended, so varied" required a central power; otherwise, "confusion" and "dilatoriness" would result. How else, he wondered in 1829 when inspecting the province surrounding Nizhnii-Novgorod, could one rule a country at once "so young and so old, so rich and so poor, so weak and so strong, so barbaric and so civilized." He rued the poor and often corrupt performance of provincial officials and the consequent "profound sense of discouragement" that plagued the "public spirit, so neglected and already so powerful." Uvarov's solution was to educate a new type of official who could restore "an absolute trust between the Monarch and His subjects, a trust in the executors of His authority, a trust in His organs of justice, a trust in the rightful power of the country, in its own resources, a trust in the future."[28]

Uvarov never tired, as students noted, of lecturing on "his most favorite theme—that all reforms in our country are going forward and thus any revolution among us has no aim or sense."[29] Whatever the facts, Uvarov and most Russians continued to see a necessary connection between autocracy and enlightenment, the partnership that had provided the historic dynamism in Russian history since the time of Peter the Great. Indeed, attempting to underline the similarities between the reign of the Great Emperor and Nicholas I became, defensively it seems, a near obsession in the era. Peaceful reform led by a "farsighted" patriarchal government was announced as the quintessential, successful Russian path.

In particular, Uvarov avowed the necessity for careful, patriarchal control of the school system. He recognized an innate human drive toward enlightenment but also insisted on the need for supervision in reaching its lofty goals. He reasoned: "If emerging from the rude shadows of ignorance and the constant, further movement toward light is necessary *for man*, then the guiding help of government in this task is necessary *for peoples*. Only the government has all the means to know . . . the existing needs of the Fatherland" and can make sure that "the progress of new ideas conforms to the Faith and institutions . . . of the State" and to the subjects' proximity to the "threshold of citizenship." Thus, the state promotes a development that is "*natural* for its country" in all areas that are "promising, peaceful, appropriate."[30]

Uvarov assumed that the autocracy, since Peter, had outgrown simple despotism and had entered its "enlightened" stage. An article that he commissioned in 1838 repeated: "Our monarchs, true to their calling, kept a vigil over the state, . . . sponsored the sciences, the arts, and industry and led it to a height of glory and prosperity: Peter the Great, Catherine II, Alexander, Nicholas!"[31] But the imperial commitment to progress and eventually even to Uvarov's educational policies was weakened by fear. Count Alexander Benkendorf, the head of the Third Section, offered this shrewd warning to Nicholas.

> Russia is best protected from revolutionary disasters by the fact that in our country, from the time of Peter the Great, the monarchs have always been ahead of the nation. But for this very reason they should not hasten unduly to educate the nation lest the people reach, in the extent of their understanding, a level equal to that of the monarchs and would then attempt to weaken their power.[32]

Benkendorf proved more attuned to the aims of the Russian autocracy than was Uvarov. While progress and reform might occur in many areas, the tsars stubbornly clung to their unlimited power. In this regard, they acted much like their "enlightened" European forebears and did not forge any new political path unless forced to do so.

Uvarov, with typical optimism, believed that autocratic direction would steer Russia around the economic and social problems that had accompanied industrialization in the West. His initial and prescient response to the 1830 Revolution was to assert that it was caused by faulty economic policy. In a lecture delivered at the end of the year and then published, he trenchantly attacked political economists from the eighteenth century to the present and claimed that their theories were all "extreme, equally exclusive, equally extraordinary." The economists of the eighteenth-century Quesnay school had believed that a larger population automatically resulted in greater production as well as a larger corps of consumers. After this eagerly accepted theory was found faulty, there was a rush to the "opposite extreme," according to Uvarov; Malthus found an inherent disproportion between geometric population growth and the arithmetic increase of the products of nature. Odoevskii, writing at the same time as Uvarov, but with a passion more similar to that of Dickens in *Hard Times*, bemoaned the loathsome logic: "Let wars, pestilence, the cold, and mutinies destroy the faulty decrees of nature. Only then can the two progressions fuse and the crime and misery of each member of society will make possible the existence of society itself. . . . Malthus is the last absurdity in mankind."[33]

Uvarov drew a simpler conclusion, namely that European political economists didn't know what they were doing. He anticipated no simple solutions, no "one law, one interpretation" since man, "composed of two opposing principles," had too "complex a nature."

> If we regard him as a mathematical unity, we subject him to rules that are positive, immutable and abstract, and then his other half, feeling and intelligence, throws into confusion the best calculations and flies away from under the knife of *political dissectors*.

Thus, it was best to attend to "the practical needs and existing ailments" of society rather than operate on "mystical notions."

Uvarov went on to deliver a most happy version of the state of the Russian economy, admittedly backward but for that very reason still free of Europe's toubles. While Western economists complained that Russia's productive potential required a larger population, Uvarov insisted that there existed a proper balance with "enough land for hands and enough hands for state needs," whether agricultural or military. He pointed to the rich farm zone of the Southeast, the growth of trade and manufacturing in the central area, and the sky-rocketing land values on the banks of the Volga—the "Nile of Russia" that connected the two parts—as all providing signs of prosperity and balanced development.

Uvarov's central message, though, was that Russia would approach industrialization only slowly. He was understandably appalled at the results of the first stage of the Industrial Revolution in Europe and at the plight of the proletariat, who were constantly threatened with unemployment because of advanced technology or overproduction. Instead, in Russia further industrialization would occur only when "*demand* surpasses *production*." Also, since Russia was entering the industrial age, when machines were already at a late stage of development, she "will not wrest workers from the plow" only to make them slaves to machines that then replace them in the factory and cause unemployment. Thus, "our industrialization will not threaten [to bring about] the dangerous revolution from which the most enlightened states in Europe are suffering." Uvarov, with great foresight, discerned that the "battle of mechanical production with the increasing needs of the lower class contains in itself the germ of the greatest political calamities." Russia would profit from Europe's mistakes and even escape Luddite activity: "It will not be necessary for us to sacrifice one class of people to another class, not less worthy of the attention of the government; thus, our factory people will not destroy machines, for machines will not rob them of their last crust of bread."

True to Russian tradition, Uvarov envisioned the fulfillment of his humane, if impossible, dream through the abandonment of the laissez-faire economics of Adam Smith and one-sided stress on industrial growth, in favor of state intervention and central planning. He maintained that "the government, under the leadership of the Monarch, will protect the simultaneous development of both sources" of national wealth, the agricultural and the industrial, and thus prevent economic dislocation and perhaps show a new way to resolve "one of the most difficult problems of political economy." Although Uvarov did not postulate specific economic policies, he insisted that all further development first demanded the acquisition of the advanced "knowledge" available in Europe, and its adaptation to the Russian principle of state direction.

> Here . . . what is necessary is a *Russian system* and a *European education*; a Russian system—since what is useful and fruitful is only that which conforms with the present order, with the spirit of the people, with its needs, with its political laws; a European education—since more than ever before we are obliged to look intently at what is happening outside the borders of the Fatherland, but to look not in a spirit of blind imitation or stupid envy, but to cure our own prejudices and seek the best discoveries.

Uvarov called upon everyone to assist in the task of economic development, which he singled out as the most important and difficult challenge facing Russia; all officials needed to become acquainted with the laws of commerce and industry. What was required was the support of the "statesmen at the helm of government, the writer in the quiet of his study, the landowner among his villagers, the merchant, the factory owner, the serf."

Both as a private and public man, Uvarov eagerly accepted the challenge of the new technological age. As a "modern" owner of vast estates, he belonged to the Moscow Agricultural Society, one of several such organizations established in the first half of the nineteenth century to promote scientific farming, the use of machinery, and more efficient production methods. He was a student of cattlebreeding and wrote an article on the topic in which he invited other landowners to send their serfs to his own estate of Porech'e in order to learn from his talented overseer. Also in keeping with then-progressive views, he established a fabric factory on his land.

With more far-reaching significance, as minister of education and president of the Academy of Sciences, Uvarov actively promoted the importation and propagation of the European "knowledge" he considered so essential for further economic development; his brief service in the ministry of finance also probably encouraged his interest. In his view, a prime goal of the educational system should be to answer "the technical needs of *handicraft*, *factory*, and *agricultural industries*." Public lectures, new courses and programs at all school levels, and the practice of sending students abroad for study in the sciences became characteristic of Uvarov's ministry. He also enticed some of the best scientific talents in Europe to come to the academy, where they worked to resolve the larger economic problems facing the empire. In addition, a reading of Uvarov's yearly ministerial reports demonstrates that he kept fully abreast of recent scientific discoveries and possessed a sure grasp of which ones were important for Russian development.[34]

Against this ever-so-rational plan of development, there stood the glaring problem of serfdom. Just as autocracy remained intact during the Nicholaevan era, so too did serfdom. Perhaps because over 700 peasant uprisings punctuated the reign—a few on Uvarov's estates and half requiring military action—Nicholas paid more attention to this problem than had any autocrat before him. Between 1826 and 1847, ten ad hoc committees dealt with serfdom, and their work somewhat mitigated and constricted the institution, thus preparing for future emancipation. Through various measures, 1.7 million male serfs were freed during the reign; for example, Uvarov freed his house serfs—but only in his will. These actions fed the rumor mill. In 1841, Nikitenko recorded the news that "this loathsome system of slavery" might be abolished.

It's said that a manifesto on the liberation of the peasants is being prepared for the heir's wedding day. . . . But many educated people consider this measure premature. They say that it will lead to disorders, that one must approach this question gradually, and so on. . . . Though why shouldn't Nicholas do it? He is omnipotent; whom and what is there to fear? What better use could he make of his autocratic power?

The diarist concluded, "I have, however, little hope," and his skepticism was well placed. In 1842, the tsar told the State Council:

> Serfdom in its present situation in our country is an evil, palpable and obvious for all, but to attack it *now* would be something still more harmful. . . . The only answer is thus to prepare the way for a gradual transition to a different order, and, not fearing change as such, to examine cold-bloodedly the advantage and the consequences of change.

The problems were indeed formidable and left Nicholas feeling less omnipotent than Nikitenko thought him.

Nonetheless, public sentiment in favor of emancipation grew steadily during the reign until "by the middle of the nineteenth century, educated or 'enlightened' public opinion was, almost by definition, abolitionist opinion." Not only radical members of the intelligentsia but also the fresh wave of young bureaucrats who began streaming out of the school system anticipated reform soon. However, the Revolution of 1848 arched the back of the tsar, and, as Herzen noted, "All the rumors about the intention of the Tsar to declare the liberation of the peasants, which had become very widespread, . . . instantly ceased."[35]

Uvarov's own attitude toward serfdom has suffered serious distortion from historians. The only source of his views remains four pages of secondhand testimony in Nicholas Barsukov's anthology of biographical material on Michael Pogodin; but scholars have incompletely quoted it so that the minister appears to be a diehard foe of emancipation, with "serfdom the cornerstone" of his policies and "nationality" merely its code word. In fact, Uvarov's views on the subject, as on most matters, were moderate and were based on his concept of historical development. He saw an intrinsic connection between unlimited autocracy and the bondage of serfdom.

> Political religion, like the Christian religion, has its inviolable dogmas; in our case they are autocracy and serfdom. The question about serfdom is closely linked to the question of autocracy and even one-man rule. These are two parallel forces that have developed together, as a single historical principle, and they are equally legitimate. This tree took root long ago; it shades both church and throne. To rip it out by the roots is impossible.

While all these statements have been used to demonstrate Uvarov's eternal hostility to emancipation, the seldom-quoted passage that follows them mitigates the accepted interpretation. He concluded with a prescription that is vintage Uvarov.

> It is necessary to proceed slowly. It is enough now to put this idea [emancipation] into circulation so that generations are prepared gradually to receive it. Only education and enlightenment can prepare [for emancipation] in the best manner.

Uvarov never accepted the more progressive opinion that many Europeans and Russians shared, namely, in Gladstone's words, that "it is liberty alone that fits men for liberty."

Uvarov clung tenaciously to his timetable, believing that a constitutional monarchy and emancipation would arrive simultaneously; but his plan of development was systematic to a fault and demanded more time than was available. A cadre of bureaucrats and teachers had to be trained from among the upper and middle classes, both to devise and carry out reform and to administer and educate the villagers, who then would be prepared for their new freedom. It will become clear that this consideration informed Uvarov's policies as minister and that he was successful in at least producing the administrators. Uvarov, like Nicholas, feared that illiterate peasants, "shocked" by freedom, would foment the "carnage of a jacquerie," and the "building of Peter I would be shaken." At the same time, the "dissatisfaction of the nobility" would cause them to seek "compensations" in some type of Frondist movement, since "there is no place for them to look except in the area of autocracy." Uvarov, like Karamzin, recoiled at "the many-headed hydra of aristocracy" as much as at democracy, which he tended to equate with mob rule; education had to demonstrate that only the monarchical system was feasible in Russia. Furthermore, surveying the emancipation plans of the past twenty years, Uvarov found them all "clumsy" or "one-sided"; "there was even a plan," he added incredulously, "to give all the land to the landowners," leaving peasants only some form of "abstract freedom." But landowners for their part wondered, "How will we live?" At least at the current time, thought Uvarov, peasants felt "somehow tied to their lords" and spoke of estates as "ours," indicating a familial atmosphere. In all, Uvarov concluded, the government had much to lose and nothing to gain by "premature" emancipation.[36]

Nationality

Besides counseling fidelity to Christian values, autocratic direction, judicious economic growth, and distant emancipation, Uvarov championed the principle of *narodnost'*, or nationality, in his program for Russia's evolutionary development. The very use of the term in 1832 displayed astute tactics, since it had just become *au courant* among the educated public. In 1834, Peter Pletnev, a literary critic and professor of Russian literature at St. Petersburg University, noted: "The idea of nationality is the major characteristic that contemporaries demand from literary works"; but, he went on, "one does not know exactly what it means." Indeed, much of Russian intellectual life in the 1830s and 1840s involved groping at this concept in an attempt to discover its inner significance and its implications for Russia's past, present, and future. Annenkov recorded the atmosphere of search and excitement.

> By the 1830s, the educated Russian world had awakened, as it were, for the first time. . . . Everybody with even the slightest inclination to think began about that time to search eagerly, and with the rav- enousness of famished minds, for bases of a fully conscious, rational existence on Russian soil. . . . Only with the help of convictions procured through such an analysis could some idea be formed of the position we occupied among European nations and of the means of self-education and self-definition we needed to choose in order to make that position a worthy one in all respects. Everything sprang into motion.

As Donald Fanger noted in his biography of Gogol, there existed a "sense of awakened expectation," a desire to discover "a collective national *voice*."[37] The intellectual ferment of the two decades naturally bred a variety of responses.

The least inspiring response, but a highly influential one, came from the so-called dynastic nationalists who dominated the court, included the tsar, and found their mouthpiece in the far-flung journalistic enterprises of Fadei Bulgarin, Nicholas Grech, and Osip Senkovskii. Their understanding of *narodnost'* was patriotism, a defensive doctrine used to support the status quo and Russian great-power status. For them, "Russianness," even for Baltic Germans or Poles, basically revolved around a subject's loyalty to the autocrat; in other words, they equated the nation with the state gov- erned by the dynasty, which was seen as both the repository and the bearer of the national culture.[38]

A second group, usually called romantic nationalists, also maintained close ties to official Russia. Professors Michael Pogodin and Stephen Shev- yrev, from their pulpits in Moscow University, led the exponents and propagated their ideas through the journal *The Muscovite (Moskvitianin)*, founded with Uvarov's patronage. The two professors shared the dynastic nationalists' reverence for autocracy as the only possible political system in Russia. They soared well beyond official thinking, however, in their romance with Russia's uniqueness, her poetic richness, the peace-loving virtues of her denizens, and the notion of the Slavs as a chosen people, all of which supposedly bestowed on Russia a glorious mission to save mankind and made her superior to a "decaying" West.[39]

A third group, the Slavophiles, found the clue to Russian nationality in the church rather than the state. Their beautiful, but myth-ridden, dogma was developed in the 1830s and 1840s by Moscow-based landowners who also occupied themselves with philosophy, theology, folklore, and history; this group included Constantine and Ivan Aksakov, Alexis Khomiakov, Ivan and Peter Kireevskii, and George Samarin. For them, the tsar figured simply as a symbol of the unity of the nation, not as an object of blind obedience. In opposition to such Western concepts as individualism, legalism, and majority rule, Khomiakov elaborated the notion of *sobornost'*: a community, much like a church council or *sobor*, should engage in discussion, with the aim of achieving a "chorus" of unanimous decision and thus preserving a spirit of familial love, harmony, and brotherhood. Then, the people would advise the tsar, through some type of *zemskii sobor*, Russia's medieval representative institution or land council. Knowing their "general will," to borrow Rousseau's term, the ruler would act accordingly and in cooperation. This system, the Slavophiles believed, was the "true" Russian way in all things, whether social, political, or religious.[40]

Another group, the Westerners, as their name implies, were far more sympathetic to European values and contributions to civilization than the other nationalists. This was a varied group, including moderates such as Pushkin and Granovskii and the radicals Alexander Herzen, Nicholas Ogarev, Michael Bakunin, Nicholas Nekrasov, and Vissarion Belinskii. The two best "thick" journals (each issue was about 400 pages in length) in the era, *Notes of the Fatherland (Otechestvennye zapiski)* and the *Contemporary (Sovremennik)* reflected their diverse views.

The Slavophiles, romantic nationalists, and Westerners agreed on the necessity for emancipation, legal reform, and freedom of speech and press. The Westerners assumed, however, that while the Russian path of development might differ from the Western prototypes, goals would be achieved in the European context of a constitution and of legal provision for civil and political rights rather than through some form of national mystique.[41]

Granovskii, who had received his education abroad, stressed the notion, derived from the Western humanist tradition, that the individual, not the state or race or church, should be regarded as the bearer of culture and the instrument of progress. In his public lectures at Moscow University, Granovskii was applauded for demonstrating that one could be Russian and European at the same time; Pogodin, his colleague and rival, sneered that Granovskii was only a "German student who's read French newspapers." On the other hand, when Granovskii was confronted with deprecatory attitudes toward Russian customs, he could blurt out "that in our outlook on our Russian nationality and with respect to many other literary and moral questions, I sympathize far more with the Slavophiles than with Belinskii, *Notes of the Fatherland*, and the Westerners." Always moderate and balanced in his views, Granovskii believed that Russia's path to freedom lay in peaceful, gradual measures taken by political authorities and in the slow diffusion of enlightenment from the upper levels of society down to the peasants. While the Romantics extolled the innate virtue of the peasants, Granovskii regarded them, as did most Westerners, as ignorant and superstitious and in dire need of education by their betters.

By the mid-1840s, Granovskii's moderation caused his falling out with the more radical Westerners, who came to support revolution and socialism and stressed atheism and materialism. At the same time, the Slavophile camp broke into factions over the question of partial accommodation with or total rejection of the West.[42] To some extent, this development represented a replay of the battle between the Old and New Styles. The variety of viewpoints lent even more color to an already "extraordinary decade." The term "nationality," which for all these thinkers became a symbolic word incorporating the meaning of Russia's past, present, and future, carried a variety of meanings: a stolid defense of the status quo and crude xenophobia; messianic myths based on "true" Russian religious, social, or political virtues; a native version of European liberalism; or a revolutionary dogma.

Before sides were clearly drawn, the appearance of Peter Chaadaev's famous "Philosophical Letter" in the journal *Telescope (Teleskop)* in 1836 forced a public debate of the issues smoldering beneath the surface. As Herzen noted, the letter had "the effect of a pistol shot in the dead of night," because it jolted the smug, albeit vague, belief that Russia would someday be as great as if not greater than the West. Chaadaev grimly stated that there was no chance of that occurrence. He believed that the progress of the West was bound up with the values of Roman Catholicism and, in language surprisingly similar to Uvarov's, he claimed that Providence had used the Western church to lead the "*esprit humain*" through a series of "moral revolutions" and a "frenzied adolescence" that in "maturity" enshrined "duty, justice, right, and order" and promised unlimited progress. Orthodox Russia, he claimed, remained outside this mainstream. Orphaned by Providence, Russians "live in a narrow present, without a past as without a future, in the midst of a dead calm" with a culture "wholly imported and imitative" and had never "added a single idea . . . to the progress of the human spirit." This outburst offended some Russians' vanity and pride and injected a high emotional pitch into what were formerly gentlemen's debates.[43]

Before the acrimony began in the late thirties, Uvarov raised the banner of nationality in the relatively quiet and searching early thirties. Since his earliest days as a man of letters, Uvarov had railed against the Russian propensity always to pursue "adopted rules or European theories." He applauded the fact that Peter the Great had brought Russia into the European family, while he regretted the accompanying "sacrifice not only of national self-respect but even of a part of our national character." But, he challenged: "This is another era." Russia was still young but had "outlived the period of unconditional imitation." Now on a higher "level of glory and greatness" and recognizing the many ills that have befallen Europe, "she, better than her foreign tutors, knows how to apply the fruits of learning toward her own needs; she clearly can distinguish in the rest of Europe good from evil: we will use the former and not suffer the latter." His message was "to fortify the anchor of our salvation" on native principles that offered "the surest guarantee of the strength and greatness of our Fatherland."[44]

Uvarov's clarion call of nationality was intended to provide a new rallying point—to unite the state, *narod*, and educated elite to join in finding indigenous, and perhaps better, answers to modern problems of development. Rejecting only the views of the radical Westerners, whom he abhorred, and Chaadaev, who had the effrontry to use similar arguments to reach opposite conclusions, Uvarov's own definition of nationality flirted with all conceivable renditions: he was part of the officialdom that clung to dynastic nationalism; he patronized and befriended Pogodin and Shevyrev; he praised Khomiakov and Kireevskii to the tsar for their religious spirit; he "loved" Granovskii and supported his public lectures; and he tolerated *Notes of the Fatherland* and the *Contemporary* because of their intellectual excellence. As usual, Uvarov was somewhere in the middle of what he called the "ultra-European" and "ultra-Russian" schools of thought.[45]

Although scholars usually assert that Uvarov was a dynastic nationalist with a Romantic coloring, Granovskii's views were closest to his. Both expressed an uncommon faith in history and entertained similar historical views: a belief in incremental progress; the perception of freedom as the destiny Providence intended for all mankind; the allowance for differing national paths in reaching that destiny; the use of the man/society analogy; the trust in the Russian monarchy as an agent of reform; the stress on education as the foundation and prerequisite for that reform. They even shared and discussed a special interest in transitional epochs, of which they agreed their age was one. Granovskii often admitted that Uvarov "protected" him from those who disagreed with his progressive, Western-oriented views. The difference between the two men was one of emphasis, but it was of critical importance because it qualified Granovskii as more truly liberal than Uvarov: while the professor's ultimate norm of progress was the free individual, the minister tended to stress the importance of the development of the state within which the individual could thrive.

Uvarov's emphasis upon the state also placed him at odds with the romantic nationalists, whose theory idealizing the *narod* he found fanciful, and with the Slavophiles, whose vision of a polity based on *sobornost'* he

also rejected. In this sense, Uvarov's concept of nationality was much less
"modern" than those of the Romantic groups and closer to the ever more
passé version of the dynasts. Instead of regarding the people as actively
informing the content of nationality and possessing the traits a government
should reflect, Uvarov reversed the flow and believed the state, from its
all-seeing perch, should define, guide, and impose "true" national values
upon a passive and acquiescent population. In a word, his concept of *narodnost'* excluded the creative activity of the *narod*, thus losing the appeal
and vitality the Romantics engendered.

Because of his state-oriented concept of nationality, Uvarov believed it
possible to force Russian culture onto Poles, Balts, Jews, and Asiatic tribesmen and thus turn them into worthy citizens—as it were, to turn non-
Russians into Russians. Blinded by the dream of imperial unity, he even
chastized the Baltic German nobles—who were descended from the Teutonic knights, practiced Lutheranism, and spoke German—for their "illusion" that "their . . . nationality is *German* nationality."[46] His plan was
to use the educational system to capture the minds of the young and thus
to assimilate gradually the disparate populations of the empire. Various
ethnic groups would be merged into a larger entity, to which they would
owe their loyalty and tie their destiny and whose claim to political and
cultural leadership they would recognize. This use of schooling was not
unusual; one scholar of nineteenth-century Europe notes that "everywhere
the inculcation of national ideals became a fundamental goal of public
education."[47]

Among the Great Russians in the empire, the development of a concept
of nationality also served to russify the educated classes, who themselves
were lacking in a sense of national identity. Uvarov, and all the other
nationalists, believed that the search for identity began in a study of "each
page of the history of the Russian Realm." Annenkov noted that the "very
first steps" of the men of the 1830s in their pursuit of "self-definition" led
"to the necessity, above all, of delving into the inner meaning of Russian
history, of arriving at clear conceptions of the old institutions . . . and
arriving at a proper understanding of the new ones." Uvarov agreed that
"all the difficulties" surrounding a definition of nationality "are resolved in
the melding of ancient and new concepts." Consequently, both as educational minister and as Academy of Sciences president, he relentlessly supported the teaching and research of Russian history and culture and even
fostered a Romantic interest in local cultures in the empire.[48]

Besides creating a sense of pride, Uvarov encouraged the promotion of
national studies so that "foreign ideas in the political sense would lose their
enticements." In 1832, he set forth the program he would follow as minister; the program was essentially positive, emphasizing "carrots" rather
than "sticks."

Inspiring young people with a closer inclination to the history of the Fatherland will turn more attention to the knowledge of our nationality in all its various aspects. Not only would an inclination to subjects concerning the Fatherland be useful for its better explanation but it would also divert minds from paths they should not follow; it would pacify the stormy gusts for the alien, the unknown, the cloudy regions of politics and philosophy. I do not doubt that such a direction toward invariable, basic, harmless pursuits would serve as a sort of barrier against the influence of so-called *European ideas*, which threatens us with danger, but whose strength, deceptive to those immature, it is impossible to overcome other than through an inclination toward other concepts, toward other interests and principles. In the light of present-day circumstances and the intellectual state of mind, it is necessary to increase where possible a number of "intellectual dams."

But Uvarov was no xenophobe. He never tired of repeating that Russian culture was "the fruit of [both] the national mind and foreign enlightenment" and that his goal was "to eradicate the incompatibility of so-called European learning with our needs" and to combine "a *Russian system* with a *European education*." He surely intended to use "intellectual dams" to block "so-called" European concepts, meaning disruptive political or "immoral" ideas, but he welcomed the rest of Western culture. Indeed, in 1839, he grew angry with the Slavophile Ivan Kireevskii for his anti-Westernism, his "one-sided and unconditional" concept of nationality. While Uvarov was irritated by the cultural chauvinism that the idea of nationality occasionally generated, he still saw its usefulness:

If this idea is subject to some exaggeration in the minds of those immature and prejudiced, then at least it cures them . . . of an excessive bias to other notions that are more dangerous and contrary to the existing order of the state.[49]

Uvarov, like Granovskii, preferred a Slavophile or a romantic nationalist to a radical Westerner.

Uvarov's hope was to build the national culture that he knew Russia did not yet possess. By 1838, he could sigh: "We are finally beginning to live our own life, to breathe our own principles." He correctly understood that, for Russia "to go not *behind* but at least *on a par* with other European nationalities," she needed to cease being an intellectual colony, to avoid the pitfalls of "blind imitation" and to acquire "intellectual independence." The object was to raise native arts and sciences to Western levels of development. In 1855, after Uvarov's death, Granovskii commented on the "rich successes of every sort" that occurred during Uvarov's tenure, but singled out "one leading idea."

The exclusive and harmful predominance of foreign ideas in educational activity gave place to a system flowing from the deep understanding of the Russian people and its needs. . . . Uncontested facts demonstrate how quickly learning advanced among us in those seventeen years and how independent and self-sustaining it became. . . . The intellectual tie of Russia with European civilization was not weakened, but the relationship changed to our advantage. We continued to learn from our older brothers; we did not repudiate the benefits of enlightenment, but acquired the rights of criticism and independent verdict.[50]

Thus, Uvarov's concept of nationality, despite its conservative aspects, was a "constructive," dynamic idea. As he himself noted, building on "the precious inheritance" of the past did "not necessitate going back or standing still; it does not demand intellectual immobility."[51] On the other hand, Uvarov attempted to pour the new nineteenth-century wine of nationality into the old eighteenth-century bottle of enlightened absolutism. Nationality for him never became an end in itself, a foundation for popular sovereignty, a result of the free and spontaneous creativity of the people, or a distinction based on race. Instead, he wanted to use it to cement the imperial state, so that the state could define the task of nationality and make it synonymous with loyalty to throne and altar. In the first issue of his educational journal, Uvarov reprinted a speech delivered by Pletnev, whose message was: "In the will and action of the Government . . . , here fully will be achieved our History, and with it Nationality itself." Uvarov's cultural program was vast and complex, intended to harmonize new ideas with traditional elements, to learn from the West, perhaps to mediate between Eastern and Western civilizations. While the prosaic Nicholas simply demanded obedience to commands, Uvarov wanted creation on command. He proved wedded, both by tradition and personality, to the notion of state (or Uvarovian) direction in culture, and he feared and resented any movement outside this controlled perspective. Therefore, while he awakened and often led intellectual life in his era, he could not satisfy it because he tried to force it into his own preconceived mold. He attempted to orchestrate individual creativity and never understood the implicit contradiction of such an effort. For this reason, his concept is often pejoratively dubbed "official" nationality.[52]

Censorship

The negative attributes of an "official" nationality were nowhere so pronounced as in censorship activities. Uvarov often spoke of the necessity for "freedom of thought," and Nikitenko believed that the most important feature of his tenure in office was that "not one person by his decree was persecuted for his ideas." Indeed, the universities and "circles" of the "re-markable decade" were aswarm with all manner of theories. However,this "freedom" did not apply to the printed word. As Uvarov flatly declared, "The right to address the public in print is not among the rights possessed by Russian citizens. This is a privilege that the government can give or take away at will" in order to protect itself from the propagation of "de-structive ideas."[53]

Actually, few in Nicholaevan Russia denied the need for some degree of government guardianship over publications. The Slavophile proponents of free press and speech agreed it was needed "to protect the individual" against vilification. Pushkin, whose *bête noire* was censorship, accepted the institution because "what is right for London is early for Moscow." The poet correctly ascertained that censorship and unlimited autocracy went hand in hand. After the newly crowned Alexander II allowed the easing of regulations, he soon complained that "very frequently" opinions about state affairs appeared in print that "are not in agreement with my thoughts, stimulating minds vainly." Even during the most enlightened eras, "the ideal arrangement for officials was one in which the public, through the press, would support and aid bureaucratic initiatives in reform."[54] In fact, the government sought uniformity of thought and will, that spirit of con-sensus which the Slavophiles, for their own reasons, idealized; Uvarov looked forward to the time when "future members of society will form one great family with identical thoughts, with an identical will, with identical feelings." One of the first articles in his educational journal warned of the disasters of a free press.

> There [in Western Europe] the free propagation of all destructive principles is allowed; there, out of varied and dangerous elements, arises the spirit of party that has divided their countries; there, a blinded people thoughtlessly chase after every new theory, after vain dreams, not seeing the abyss to which they are heading.[55]

The essential question in the era was not whether censorship should exist but how strict it should be.

The severity of regulations depended to a great degree on the official in charge. Uvarov, as educational minister, was responsible for censorship activities and, by and large, he took his usual moderate stance. In this "difficult and complicated task," he claimed, "I tried to define a middle ground between the ferreting strictness of censors, of powers used insen-sitively rather than with delicacy, and a gullible lack of vigilance, which if not curtailed could lead to evil." Censors were to be on guard but to act in such a way "that the public has no cause to conclude that the government is hounding culture." In 1835, after receiving a number of complaints, he warned the Moscow Censorship Committee that "a needed strictness should not degenerate into a constraint upon harmless literary activity and place writers in an unfriendly relationship with the censorship."[56] Uvarov himself, though, had trouble treading this middle path, especially when journalists offered critical challenges to his concept of culture and when the quieter thirties gave way to the more vociferous forties.

Uvarov's first foray into censorship in the Nicholaevan era occurred in 1832 when, as deputy minister of education, he inspected Moscow University and delivered his famous report to the tsar in which he called, for the first time, for a culture based on "Orthodoxy, Autocracy, Nationality." He turned his especial attention to the "journalistic filth" coming off the periodical presses, "a branch of literary production," he always rued, "that, unfortunately, more than any other, affects the mass of readers." His complaints and fears were several.

> For a long time, I have shared with many good-thinking people an unpleasant impression produced by the insolent attempts of journalists, especially in Moscow, to exceed the limits of decency, taste, and language and further to extend their encroachments into the most important subjects of state administration and to political concepts, which have already shaken nearly all the states in Europe. When I assumed my duties, I thought that, once restrained from their rash impulses to concern themselves with affairs of state, the journalists could be given complete freedom in discourse about literary matters, despite their vulgar name calling, their careless style, their complete lack of taste and decency; but, after further consideration, I saw that the influence of the journalists upon the public, and especially upon university youth, was not harmless even in its literary aspects; corruption of taste produces corruption of morality.[57]

Uvarov wished the periodical press to be politically loyal and national in bias, to avoid the "polemics that in previous years dominated the journals of both capitals," and in general to subscribe to the aristocratic notion of literary "taste" that he had developed within the Arzamas society.

In effect, Uvarov signaled a retreat from the 1828 statute whereby censors were expected not to judge a work according to its merits but only to check that it contained nothing contrary to church, state, good morals, or the honor of an individual. He returned, in part, to the tenor of Shishkov's "iron statute" of 1826, which asked censors to sniff out "tendencies," to act as arbiters of literary taste, and to check for style, grammar, *doubles entendres*, and unmannerly polemics. These strictures, however, were advised not for literature as a whole but only for the periodical press, since Uvarov's chief goal was "*to raise and ennoble this branch of our culture.*" No wonder that when Uvarov became minister, "the censors went insane" in order to comply with his assumed severity; the traditional punishment for allowing something to slip through the net was confinement from one to several days in the local guardhouse. New regulations included the appointment of two censors, rather than one, for each journal and a prohibition against one person's editing two journals at once and thus having undue influence over the public.[58]

Given these guidelines, it is surprising to find that Uvarov closed only two journals during his ministry. Those incidents, as it happened, had as much to do with personal malice as principle; in each case, Uvarov acted despotically and without "taste and decency." Nicholas Polevoi, editor of the *Moscow Telegraph (Moskovskii telegraf)*, incurred Uvarov's wrath in 1832 by noting in print "the vast number of mistakes" in the Academy of Science's published calendars and by criticizing the academy in general for publishing in German and French rather than Russian. Next, Polevoi, of merchant class origin, edited a collection of essays that satirized aristocratic society. When Uvarov became minister, he warned Polevoi to be "more careful" but the editor refused to "click his heels," an act of independence Uvarov could not abide. In 1833, Uvarov requested the tsar to close the *Telegraph* on the specific grounds that in the July issue a review by Polevoi, "A Glance at the *History of Napoleon*," was unfounded historically and was derogatory to the honor of Russia because of its praise of Napoleon, for whom Uvarov nurtured an undying hatred. Uvarov elaborated to Nicholas that in general the journal contained articles that "not only [are] alien to taste and decorum but that bring false and evil opinions to bear on political subjects." The tsar found the review of *A History of Napoleon*, a book authored by his favorite novelist, Sir Walter Scott, "more foolish than disloyal" and dismissed the charges.

Uvarov, unwilling to accept defeat, ordered a member of his staff to prepare a dossier so that he would be ready to strike again at the proper moment. An opportunity arose in 1834, when Polevoi criticized as banal a new play by N. Kukol'nik entitled *The Hand of the Most High Has Saved the Fatherland*. This was an eminently patriotic play, presented with great pomp, and Nicholas loved it. Upon learning of his mistake, Polevoi tried to stop publication of the issue in which his review appeared, but it was too late. He was summoned to St. Petersburg, where Uvarov conducted an inquisition and accused the drama critic of using "the play as a pretext for deriding the most elevated feelings." During the inquiry, Uvarov constantly referred to the thick notebook he had compiled, and he presented this to the tsar. It contained examples of Polevoi's "perfidy": his "revolutionary direction of thought"; his praise for revolution in the Netherlands, of equality in France, of Stenka Razin and Pugachev; and his complaints of Siberian exile.

Some agreed with Uvarov's assessment; Pushkin called Polevoi's views "Jacobinism under the very nose of the government." The journal was closed and Polevoi's name forbidden to appear in print, although he continued to write and edit journals. Not satisfied, Uvarov, a terrible grudge bearer, hounded Polevoi to the point that Benkendorf had to come to Polevoi's rescue to allow publication of his translation of *Hamlet*, which then, to Uvarov's chagrin, received a signet ring as an award from the tsar.

Uvarov attempted to defend his actions against the *Telegraph* to Nikitenko, but his words ring with a certain hysteria, especially since even the Third Section considered Polevoi "a good and clean citizen."

> It is a vehicle for revolution. He has been systematically disseminating destructive principles for several years now. He doesn't like Russia. . . . It is well known that there is a group in our country which hungers for revolution. The Decembrists were not destroyed and Polevoi wanted to be their organ. . . . This man is a fanatic. He is ready to suffer anything for an idea. With him, one must take firm measures.

Clearly Uvarov could not tolerate Polevoi's type of independence of mind. In a later entry, Nikitenko observed that "the authorities acknowledge the existence of a policy of oppression, but consider it a policy of firmness. And they are wrong. No matter how you look at it, oppression is still oppression, particularly when it is born of anger."[59]

Uvarov's next outburst occurred in 1836, when the *Telescope*, another journal he found incorrect in "spirit," published the first of Chaadaev's "Philosophical Letters," whose conclusions ran in the face of every aspect of Uvarov's cultural views. He ranted that they "breathe an absurd hatred for the Fatherland and false and outrageous opinions about history as well as about the present and future existence of the state." The journal was banned, Chaadaev was officially declared insane, the censor was relieved of all his posts, and the editor was exiled to Ust-Syslotsk to live on forty kopecks a day. Uvarov "behaved very harshly," reacting with particular severity because the censor and editor were Moscow University professors—whom he called with great exaggeration "university anarchists"—whose high position in his own ministry cast a shadow over his administrative judgment.[60]

Pushkin also irked Uvarov because he challenged the minister's ability and right to control the direction of literature and the periodical press. The poet held a privileged position in that he had the tsar as his own personal censor. But Uvarov intrigued to have only Pushkin's manuscripts scanned by the tsar, while his published works were to be treated under general regulations, and the minister freely used his blue pencil. Pushkin further irritated Uvarov by trying to seize the leadership in effecting liaisons between literary men and the government. His plan was to establish and edit a private journal, the *Contemporary*, around which he "would group writers of talent and in this way would bring closer to the government men who still shy away in the mistaken belief that it is hostile to enlightenment."

Only with Benkendorf's help did Pushkin receive permission to establish the journal in 1836. Uvarov concluded that Pushkin had a "harmful way of thinking." Matters of principle, however, did not breed as much enmity between the two men as did Pushkin's epigrams that publicly ridiculed Uvarov's posturing. So, the minister hounded the poet until Pushkin's premature death in 1837. Uvarov then forbade students and professors from attending the funeral and banned the publication of any more of the laudatory obituaries that had immediately sprung up in the press. A vengeful Uvarov asked one editor: "Why a black border around the news of the death of a man not ranked, not occupying any position in the government service? Was Pushkin a general, a military leader, a minister, a statesman?" Nikitenko laconically noted, "Uvarov cannot forgive even a dead Pushkin" for his epigrams.[61]

Both for reasons of literary taste and because of a desire for control, Uvarov had equally poor relations with the notorious publishing triumvirate of Grech, Senkovskii, and Bulgarin. He considered them venal hacks, which they were, and detested their "mercenary" attitude toward literature, which they possessed. In fact, in this era, as Riasanovsky has noted, "journalism was the only industry . . . that operated along sophisticated capitalist lines and responded promptly and effectively to market conditions." Uvarov could only sneer at Senkovskii's definition of literature as "light and pleasant reading . . . intended for the transitory delectation of the educated man." In contrast, Uvarov admired only "high" culture, the sort that thrived in elite salons and concerned itself with "serious" topics. He found it disgusting that the *Reader's Library (Biblioteka dlia chteniia)*, the intellectual equivalent of the American *Reader's Digest*, pandered to "common" tastes. Early in his ministry, he waged a campaign against its editor, Senkovskii, for his "gutter jokes" and his cynical attitude toward journalism. Uvarov despotically forced him to resign, although Senkovskii continued to manage the journal's affairs. The aesthete Uvarov especially disliked the name calling, discrediting of rivals, and self-promotion in which Senkovskii and the others indulged. He often reminisced about the "old days" in Arzamas when literature was "respectable." On another level, Bulgarin and Grech infuriated Uvarov by hiring Polevoi, once the minister had discredited him, as an unofficial editor of their publications *Northern Bee (Severnaia pchela)* and *Son of the Fatherland (Syn otechestva)*. It was also rumored that the triumvirate acted as spies for the Third Section, informed on any devious trends in literature, and often accused the educational ministry of dereliction of duty. The animosity between Uvarov and the triumvirate grew to the point that they plotted his downfall in 1848–1849.

In general, the three hacks understood the Russian reading public better than Uvarov did. They recognized the existence of a new readership who preferred "relevant" topics, literary fireworks, and light novels to "serious" subjects. Indeed, the class monopoly and aristocratic tenor of culture—to which Uvarov was attached and which, as minister, he himself did much to break—was gone forever. While Viazemskii might complain that the triumvirate was "corrupting the reading public, both morally and intellectually," their publications enjoyed the largest circulations and profits of any in the era. Thus, Uvarov was unable to oppose them effectively because of the immense popularity of their periodicals, their protection in high places, and especially Nicholas's approval of their smarmy brand of patriotism, which is often erroneously equated with Uvarov's concept of nationality; in that regard they surely got the last laugh, at least for a century and a half.[62]

Uvarov presented two "models for Russian journalists." He founded the *Journal of the Ministry of National Enlightenment (Zhurnal Ministerstva narodnago prosveshcheniia)* in 1834. It was intended to serve educators throughout the empire, but also stood as one of the era's most ambitious "thick" journals in its attempt to educate the public through scholarly, well-written, and intellectually significant articles on the sciences as well as on the history, literature, and philosophy of Russia, the East, the ancient world, and Europe, all "serious" subjects with which Uvarov thought the general public should occupy itself. He also encouraged Pogodin and Shevyrev to publish the *Muscovite* in an effort to offset the "dark power" of the triumvirate's publications as well as to replace the *Telegraph* and *Telescope*. The project was approved in 1837 but, due to Pogodin's lack of enthusiasm, the journal did not appear until 1840. It, too, was nonpolemical and was occupied chiefly with national history and literature, reflecting the viewpoints of both romantic nationalists and Slavophiles, who briefly took over the editorial board in 1845. Because of the mercurial Pogodin, however, the *Muscovite* never became the significant intellectual force Uvarov had envisioned. Bulgarin and Grech's newspaper, *Northern Bee*, enjoyed 4,000 subscribers and the *Reader's Library* an unheard-of 7,000 at a time when Western European publications considered a circulation of 1,000 respectable. The *Muscovite's* high was 500 in its first decade, and the educational journal averaged, outside the required subscribers within the ministry, a rather dismal 135, even though it was one of the most popular of the eighteen government journals during the era.[63]

The two private journals that did compete effectively with the triumvirate's publications were the progressive Westerner organs the *Contemporary* and *Notes of the Fatherland*, whose subscribers numbered from 3,000 to 4,000. The editors of these publications transformed Russian journals into forums for the most advanced segment of the educated public. For instance, they featured such writers as Belinskii and published the first series of articles on socialist economics. Uvarov approved the publication of the *Contemporary*, edited by Pletnev, year after year, since it was "beneficial to literature," and he admitted that the two serials represented "the best examples of Russian journalism." The minister also probably considered them a safety valve for public opinion, especially in the forties when criticism of the government's unwillingness or inability to reform began to mount. Indeed, if care were taken, writers could publish a good deal of criticism, albeit muted, by developing the cryptic art of Aesopian language; they used implications, code words, and allusions to get their points across to a public who knew well how to decipher the messages. This did not mean that censors and officials were fools; many, like Nikitenko or Uvarov, simply cooperated to find a middle ground between a muzzled and a free press, to discover a balance that the tsar could accept.[64]

Uvarov himself did not enjoy a free hand in censorship. Since 1832, any new journal required Nicholas's personal approval, and he was stingy in granting it. When Uvarov endorsed a scholarly journal for Kharkov University or a literary anthology to be published by Andrew Kraevskii and Odoevskii or another journal by Granovskii, Nicholas typically replied, "there are plenty without this one." He allowed publication of the *Muscovite* only because "the strongest possible surveillance" was guaranteed. On the other hand, light publications such as *Illustratsiia*, *Album des petites soirées*, and *Reader's Library* were approved in record time as "useful publications." The military governor of Moscow, V. Androssov, was also permitted to publish the *Moscow Observer* (*Moskovskii nabliudatel'*) because he was considered a man "of excellent moral quality," of "highly titled nobility" and "with no interest in politics"—a perfect indication of the preferred criteria.[65]

The tsar and Uvarov, however, were in full agreement on one issue. They opposed the production of inexpensive books or periodicals such as "penny magazines" because the lower classes could afford them; Uvarov considered this possibility a poor idea, both politically and intellectually. His tight, logical system demanded that first only the upper and then slowly the middle and only finally, "in the distant future," the lower classes should be the beneficiaries of enlightenment. If the lower classes had access to literature before emancipation was declared, dissatisfaction with the existing order might ensue; if they received their information from "cheap" journals, they would absorb only the "superficial knowledge" that supposedly fomented revolutions and they would not study "serious" topics. Furthermore, in Gogol's judgment, these "skinny, little things . . . who are multiplying so quickly and so abundantly in Russia" possess a character of "utter childishness." Noting the unwelcome trend, in 1834 Uvarov argued:

Cheap periodical publications are now more incompatible [with the existing social structure] because the predilection for reading and, in general, literary activity, which formerly was confined to the upper classes, at the present time has filtered into the middle classes and its bounds are spreading *even* further. Moreover, independent of this political incompatibility of cheap literature for the people, it not only does not bring any actual use for true intellectual development and enlightenment but, on the contrary, will sooner serve as an obstacle to it; good-thinking people have recognized that this literature is harmful in those countries where it arose and was established; for the easy acquisition of incomplete information about many subjects takes away from basic studies and spreads superficial knowledge, which, consequently, is harmful to it.

In 1834, Prince L'vov attempted to print inexpensive books for the lower classes, for the elevated reason of teaching them about religion and the Russian government; Uvarov refused permission, reasoning "that to put the lower classes in any way in motion and to encourage them to make any efforts is not only useless but harmful." He perhaps recalled the nightmares of the Bible Society era. The only books he allowed to be distributed among the serfs were those related to methods for improving agricultural production, since these conformed to the peasants' position in society.[66]

Uvarov's dreams of full control of the press and culture were hampered not only by the tsar but by other ministries that meddled in censorship affairs. The right of preventive censorship by separate ministries was first established in the 1826 and 1828 censorship statutes; articles in which individual ministries were discussed could not be printed without the approval of the ministries concerned. A test case occurred in 1831 when A. N. Golitsyn, the postmaster general, objected to an article entitled "Reports on the Post Office" by Keppen of the Academy of Sciences, because it criticized postal delivery, that eternal problem, and postulated reform. Golitsyn stated that "this is an example of the liberal spirit of Western Europe," where the press was allowed to challenge the authorities. Keppen was reprimanded, and similar articles were ordered sent to the post office for approval. During Uvarov's ministry, the same privilege was acquired by the Holy Synod; by the ministries of war, finance, foreign affairs, and justice; by the Second and Third Sections of His Majesty's Own Chancery; and by the departments of roads and public construction, of orphans, and of horse breeding, to mention only a few. By 1848, despite Uvarov's objections, the right of preliminary censorship was officially granted to all ministries and departments. Rozhdestvenskii summarized: "In a word, pure poetry and belles-lettres alone came under the authority of the [regular] censorship committees; all other [types of material] were given to some department or other for their examination." Stroganov correctly complained that this multiplicity of censors in every area of intellectual pursuit or contemporary interest "holds back our writers in the publication of their works."[67] In fine, censorship in the Nicholaevan era was something of a muddle.

Despite all this, according to Riasanovsky's statistics, the periodical press "spurted ahead": a yearly average of forty-six periodicals was published between 1831 and 1837, and by 1850 the number had reached eighty-three. Much of this growth was due to the proliferation of government publications in response to the technical needs of the various ministries, while at the same time private specialized journals responded to growing public interest in the arts and sciences, such as music, numismatics, agricultural economy, and manufacturing.[68]

Book publishing also prospered. Uvarov took great pride in the fact that the number of original publications in the Russian language per year rose from roughly 700 to 900 during his ministry, thus indicating the development of a national culture. As further proof of the growth of an educated reading public that Uvarov applauded for its interest in "the languages and culture of foreign countries," the number of imported books increased from 280,000 in 1833 to roughly 830,000 in 1847; only .2 percent were "denied entry." These statistics are astounding for a government usually described as xenophobic. As one historian commented about a future radical, "Under Nicholas I, the young Chernyshevsky could sit in St. Petersburg tea houses and read the *Journal des Débats* and other Western publications." Furthermore, Uvarov instituted the practice of establishing public libraries in district and provincial towns, generally with the assistance of private financial support. These libraries were, of course, under strict government supervision so that books contrary to "religion, government, or morality" would not find a place on the shelves; catalogs were inspected annually for "doubtful" literature. Nonetheless, forty-six libraries were opened during his ministry, and one, in Tambov, by 1843 contained 13,000 volumes.[69]

The number of translated books, however, decreased during the reign from an average of 120 in the thirties to half that in the forties. Uvarov closely scrutinized this area of publication because he feared the propagation of the French novels of Balzac, Hugo, or Paul de Kock among those Russians who were less educated and hence capable of reading them only in translation. He objected that these novels describe "the weak side of human nature, moral outrage, uncontrollable passions, and strong vices and crimes." Although copies in the original French proliferated and although Uvarov had warm praise, for instance, for *Notre Dame de Paris*, he thought that it was "too early" for the dissemination of such books to the general public. Furthermore, he disliked the public's "passion" for this genre in contrast to elevated reading and works by Russian authors. In fact, he cited the decrease in the number of translations as evidence of the growth of native literature and the public's diminishing interest in foreign fiction; the former development, of course, was real, while the latter was not.[70]

At any rate, despite Uvarov's efforts, by the 1840s his whole censorship "system" had gotten out of control. In 1843, as he got angrier and angrier with both Kraevskii and Bulgarin for their abusive name calling and began ordering firmer steps to stop it, Bulgarin retaliated. He attacked *Notes of the Fatherland*, Kraevskii's journal, and Uvarov in one blow by accusing the minister of allowing the journal to print articles that led to "the overthrow of the existing order of things," claiming that he was either a "simpleton or a champion of liberalism." Grech chimed in by saying that "everyone" knew that the journal spread "disrespect for altar and throne" and "only Uvarov sees and hears nothing." Uvarov, fearing for his position, warned censors "to be on their guard" and asked the tsar for increased powers to stem abuses. Nicholas responded icily: "Censors have sufficient authority—they have pencils: these are their swords." Rebuffed, Uvarov tried to increase his vigilance and unsuccessfully tried to obtain a new code, but he had neither the power nor the will to institute an epoch of terror such as the one that was to follow his fall from power in 1849. Instead, he harassed writers and censors on an erratic basis, but generally let matters slide. He is said to have confided in utter frustration: "I hope that finally Russian literature will cease . . . [and] then I will sleep peacefully."[71] In fact, on this question he had no peace. So obsessed was Uvarov with creating and directing his own brand of culture, he scarcely realized that a golden age in literature had blossomed during his tenure. His policies failed to satisfy the public, the journalists, and the court, and he was attacked by all.

Uvarov found himself in a trap of his own making. Through the expansion of the school system at all levels and among all classes, he worked to create the educated public that the nation needed to emerge from backwardness. But that public understandably became more mature, independent-minded, and resentful of the government's telling them what and how to think and obstructing a free flow of information on issues of concern to all. The lack of freedom of the press coupled with the lack of political parties isolated many of the most progressive and talented intellectuals and pushed them into the egocentric role of dreamers whose only outlet was the circles' "feast of friendship." Private societies became something resembling a government-in-internal-exile in opposition to the "official nationality."

On the other hand, what Belinskii dubbed "our Tatar censorship" allowed many dissenters, including Belinskii, to flourish, at least until 1848.[72] According to a biographer of Nicholas I, "Most educated Russians . . . found it possible to work successfully and creatively within the framework of Official Nationality,"[73] and this was so mostly because of Uvarov's "allowances." Professor Igor Vinogradoff lamented the usual judging of Nicholas's reign on the basis of the "panic period of 1848–1855"; he offered, as partial vindication, the thought that "one should not forget that his Minister of Public Instruction was Uvarov . . . , who did an immense amount to spread education through the Empire at all levels, and that he made Pushkin possible (even if he pinpricked him) and that he was delighted with [Gogol's play] 'Revisor.' A great literature blossomed in his reign." Indeed, the new respect for Russia's past, present, and future inspired "a whole phalanx of unquestionably gifted people" in poetry, painting, journalism, and theatre.[74] Thus, a golden age in Russian culture emerged from the "remarkable decade," as well as a good deal of dissent and dissatisfaction. Uvarov shared some responsibility for both the grandeur and the disillusion.

THE PERSONALITY

ECAUSE of his "temperate views,"[75] his fence straddling, his apparent belief that politics is indeed the art of compromise, Uvarov's principles escape neat ideological categories. His character was equally slippery; it apparently careened between heroic and craven. In objective terms, Uvarov was surely one of the better high officials of the era. Of all Nicholas's ministerial choices, he was one of the youngest, certainly the most learned, and he possessed the highest scholarly credentials. Unlike the typical bureaucrat who moved from ministry to ministry or from military to civil service, Uvarov had long experience in his field: he had been president of the Academy of Sciences since 1818, superintendent of the St. Petersburg Educational District from 1810 to 1821, and member of the ad hoc educational commission of 1826. Like Kiselev in the ministry of state domains, Kankrin in finance, and Bludov in justice, the ministers with whom he is best compared, Uvarov worked hard and responsibly for Russia's development and was dedicated to its interests. Like these men, he was moderate in his political and social beliefs, accepting the leadership of the autocracy and the existence of a stratified class structure along with the notion that the era in which he lived was one of transition. In background, Uvarov shared with over three-quarters of high officials the advantages and privileges of noble birth; he began life in the "court elite" pattern described by Walter Pintner, which ensured a propitious start to a career, and ended life as one of only forty-three Russians in the era to reach Rank Two in the Table of Ranks.

Unlike the great majority of Nicholas's appointees, Uvarov lacked a military background, which the tsar favored in part because of his own training and perhaps also because of his belief that soldiers were more given than others to duty, loyalty, and obedience. Since the tsar's inclination in this regard is well known, historians tend to view Nicholas's officials as having been subservient executors of his wishes, but this position exaggerates the truth. Nicholas surely preferred working with individuals whom he knew and with ad hoc committees composed of men whom he trusted, but he reached decisions in conference with these ministers, not alone. Uvarov surely had control of educational policy; although previous school systems had been given the names of the reigning emperors and empresses, in Nicholas's era the system was called Uvarovian.[76]

Nicholas apparently felt ill at ease in educational matters, perhaps because he had disliked his own schooling, and he generally followed Uvarov's advice. He was clear on two matters, however: that education should safeguard the autocracy and that it should maintain the class system. Apparently one could manipulate within this framework; Benkendorf complained that "although the emperor's name is constantly on his [Uvarov's] lips, he has in his orders weakened the force of many laws signed by the tsar." In fact, one early apologist for the reign offered "proof" that Nicholas did not act like an obscurantist since "an obscurantist would not have appointed Uvarov as minister of national enlightenment and tolerated him in this office for more than fifteen years." But all ministers knew they needed the full and enthusiastic support of the tsar on every issue or else they and their plans were doomed. In 1849, when Uvarov tried to prevent the repressive measures planned against the universities and appealed to public opinion in an article, Nicholas's response was typical of a martinet: "One must *obey* and keep his arguments *to himself*"; on this sour note, Uvarov left office.[77]

Scholars have often noted that Nicholas's appointees seemed to lack moral fortitude. Uvarov, in particular, seems to have possessed a flawed character. His negative traits were so pronounced that they set him up for ridicule when he might have been praised, eventually made him an unpopular public official, and meant that even his accomplishments were only grudgingly recognized. From the time he was a young man performing in frenchified salons, contemporaries noted his vanity, pride, boastfulness, greed, anxious currying of favor, and servility toward his betters. They also commented on his inclinations to worm his way into high social circles by cultivating the friendships of well-placed women, and to flaunt himself constantly as a man of letters.

These unattractive traits became more prominent after he left office in 1821, a departure that, it should be noted, resulted from an act of courage, because he alone had attacked the reactionaries who triumphed in his ministry. The actions that followed, however, were anything but heroic. Uvarov did not need a new position for financial reasons, but, possessing the mentality common among the nobility, he still considered it a social necessity and duty to hold office. By cultivating the friendship of the Dowager Empress Marie and the Empress Elizabeth, he became acquainted with Count D. A. Gur'ev, the notoriously inept but well-connected minister of finance. Uvarov presented him with a snuffbox and a portrait of the Empress Marie; an appointment as director of manufacturing and internal trade followed in July 1822. When Gur'ev retired the next year, he asked that Uvarov, along with fifty others, receive an award for their service; only Uvarov and one other were refused, lending force to the gossip of the time that he had "managed to bankrupt several factories" and even "hurt his own private interests." It probably also indicated that he had lost imperial favor.

When Egor Kankrin took Gur'ev's place, Uvarov engaged in a version of back-door politics by cultivating the wife of his new superior. His friend Alexander Turgenev commented: "He knows all the wet nurses at the Kankrins' and even feeds the children oatmeal." Another colleague noted that "he visits the minister's wife and carries her children around, in a word, in a base way is paving his road to honors." Similarly, Pushkin was revolted that "his baseness goes down to running errands for the Kankrins." Another appointment as director of state loan and commercial banks followed. No wonder gossips had relished his earlier fall from power.[78]

One wag noted of the self-styled professor and litterateur: "He's fallen from the lap of the learned into those of the factory owners." Another snide commentator in the capital "lamented": "Except for Uvarov's regulations, there's no literary news here." Somehow even a contemporary eulogistic biographical sketch of Uvarov made the new appointment as director of banks a cause for sneering rather than feeling a man's talents were being ill-used: "Of course, the learned academician found himself ill at ease in a milieu of figures and tables. Arithmetic hardly blends with poetry, and the pen busy in the service of the muses does not voluntarily wish to sign factory reports and draft foreclosures."[79]

Uvarov did not quite drop out of the realm of the muses, but his literary activity took a curious turn. Whether because of sincere emotion, an attempt to curry favor, or his extraordinary talent in the genre, between 1824 and 1828 Uvarov published five eulogies upon the deaths of Alexander, Empress Elizabeth, Dowager Empress Marie, Uvarov's uncle Fedor, and Princess Lieven. Each, of course, described the deceased in heroic terms and was replete with the usual doleful, purple language. The adulation of the princess could seem suspicious since, at the time of her death in 1828, her husband had just become head of the educational ministry, a post he held until Uvarov took it over in 1833.[80]

Uvarov's connections with the nobility, however, did not depend wholly on such literary efforts. He and his wife were, in fact, active in aristocratic circles and in socially appropriate charitable projects, such as caring for orphans and combatting the cholera epidemics of 1824 and 1830–1831. Uvarov returned to imperial favor once Nicholas ascended the throne; because of Uvarov's connection with the young monarch's mother and grandmother, he had been in his company frequently for over a decade. Only four months into the new reign, Uvarov received the Order of St. Anne, First Class, and in the summer of 1826, the tsar appointed him a senator, which must have pleased, if not satisfied, Uvarov.[81]

Uvarov was greedy, not only for honors, rank, and recognition, but for money as well. A good deal of gossip circulated in 1810 to the effect that he married for all these reasons, since his wife was slated to inherit enormous wealth. The rumors were probably in part true. A short time before, Uvarov, whose fondest dream was to go to Paris, had obtained through connections an official appointment as secretary in that city. He either went to Paris for only two months or never went at all, and Nesselrode took his place (the only official, by the way, that reached Rank One in Nicholaevan Russia, perhaps to Uvarov's chagrin). In either case, the problem was money, and Uvarov's disappointment may have left its psychological mark. He was also especially sensitive to the importance of money because, after his father died, he had been brought up as a poor cousin among rich relatives.

Eventually, in 1822, Razumovskii did die and Uvarov inherited 10,945 "souls," or taxable male serfs, and six estates. And yet, in an undignified way, he bickered with the other heirs and complained, even to the Dowager Empress, that his father-in-law had neglected to pay his bills "in the last epoch of his life" and had left Uvarov responsible.[82] In all, through inheritance and purchase, Uvarov possessed landholdings that included 14,186 "souls" centered in Porech'e near Moscow, a wooden house in St. Petersburg, a lavish summer home, and a factory; he was thus one of the richest men in Russia. This wealth must surely, at least unconsciously, have affected his attitude toward serfdom. Despite his riches, Uvarov never rose above the rampant corruption that characterized the era. Once he became minister, he enjoyed an immense office whose walls were covered with embroidered red silk and rare paintings; it was dominated by a French chimney that he liked to stoke, and it was filled with plush sofas and chairs.[83] Rumor had it that Uvarov, not satisfied, in the best tradition of the craven official filched firewood from the state and had government metal craftsmen work on his own property. For these reasons, apparently, even his Arzamas friends broke with him; Dashkov, upon seeing Zhukovskii and Uvarov strolling along the Nevskii Prospect, asked the poet: "Aren't you ashamed to be seen in public with such a man?"

Another Arzamas brother, Pushkin, also broke with him. They had remained close until Uvarov, as minister, became jealous of the poet's independent position in literary life. At the beginning of 1835, Pushkin was furious that Uvarov made snide comments about his most recent publication, which had received the approval of the tsar: "In public, they're inveighing against my Pugachev, but what is worse, they're not buying it—and Uvarov's the villain." "Yes," he went on, "the Doge likes it, but the dog doesn't."[84] Later that year, Pushkin got revenge. A wealthy relative of Uvarov was on his deathbed, and Uvarov's wife figured as the heir; the minister was reputedly already calculating his huge new fortune when the man, D. N. Sheremetev, miraculously recovered. Pushkin published a poem, "The Recovery of Lucullus: A Translation from the Latin," whose point, including a snipe at Uvarov's classical scholarship, was clear to everyone. In one stanza, the heir "thinks to himself":

No more at the home of a grandee
Must I the kiddies nurse;
I myself a grandee will be,
'Cause there's plenty in his purse.
Now being honest will be a cinch!
My wife I'll no longer plunder
And I'll even forget how to pinch
Those cords of good state lumber![85]

Benkendorf, in his annual summations of observations made by the secret police, regularly reported on Uvarov's progress in office. At first, he admitted, the public greeted the appointment with enthusiasm; great things were expected of Uvarov, and soon there was general agreement that he had given his ministry "a new life." By the 1839 report, though, Benkendorf repeated Pushkin's sentiments.

Although there is no doubt of Uvarov's intelligence, capability, and encyclopedic knowledge, his character limits him from producing the results that might be expected from his mental abilities. He is vain, proud, boastful, in an eighteenth-century French way, and this hurts him in the public eye. His former friends, Bludov and Dashkov, do not respect him; they say he is willing to sacrifice anybody and anything to his own aggrandizement. Society, subordinates, and the public do not trust him, and this tends to paralyze the progress of affairs.

The chief of police then quoted the French ambassador as saying: "From far away, he's something—close up, he's nothing."[86]

Uvarov's vanity was probably his most irksome and demeaning trait. While he did in fact possess the most logical and comprehensive plan for Russia's development at that time, he pompously refused to brook any answers to problems other than his own and hounded anyone, like Pushkin, who claimed to be independent of his power. Partly because of his arrogance, Uvarov suffered such a loss of public respect and support that he became one of the least-liked government officials. Fortunately for himself, as president of the Academy of Sciences and minister he enjoyed total jurisdiction and was indeed an "education czar," as he might have been called in American politics. A survey of his administrative and appointive measures will indicate that he generally used his powers well and possessed a keen eye for quality and promise.

But, once again, this talent was offset by a negative trait, this time his tendency to surround himself with sycophants. The worst of the type was probably Professor Ivan Davydov of Moscow University, who accepted "gifts" when he inspected schools. Davydov also christened his new-born son Sergei and wrote to each of four powers-that-be (Uvarov, Stroganov, Golitsyn, Gagarin) that he was the one for whom the child was named. The permanent secretary of the Academy of Sciences, Paul Fuss, and its vice-president, Michael Dondukov-Korsakov, as well as Musin-Pushkin, superintendent in Kazan and then St. Petersburg, were devoid of qualifications for their jobs, except that they did Uvarov's bidding; they were called "stooges" and "lackeys," and the last two sounded and acted like characters out of Gogol. Pushkin, of course, could not let this situation pass unnoticed. When Prince Dondukov-Korsakov was appointed to the elite academy, the poet penned an epigram, playing on the prince's name and *dunduk*, the Russian word for blockhead, and through anal allusion invoking the rumor that Uvarov and the prince were lovers.

> When the Academy meets,
> Prince Dunduk finds there a seat.
> People say it isn't fitting
> That Dunduk this honor has.
> Why then do we find him sitting?
> Just because he's got an ass.

Pogodin cited another example of Uvarov's inclination to dominate those around him. When Uvarov approached him to head the chancery of the ministry, the professor noted, Uvarov tried to act as his "adviser and even nanny" and wanted "only a loyal, unquestioning and able executor of his decrees and a mouthpiece for his ideas." Apparently, scholars and subordinates were left alone if they performed the necessary servilities and did not challenge Uvarov's authority, but someone like the noted zoologist Christian Pander left the academy because he refused to kowtow.[87]

The eminent historian Sergei Solov'ev, whom Uvarov hired at Moscow University, sketched the most devastating profile of the minister.

> Uvarov was indisputably a man of brilliant gifts, and because of these gifts, because of his education, because of the liberal mode of thinking which he derived from the society of the Steins, the Kochubeis, and of the other luminaries of the epoch of Alexander, he was capable of occupying the position of the minister of education, of the president of the Academy of Sciences, etc. But in this man the qualities of the heart did not at all correspond to the qualities of the mind. Acting the part of a noble landlord, Uvarov had nothing truly aristocratic in him. On the contrary, here was a servant who had acquired pretty good manners in the house of a pretty good master (Alexander I), but who remained a servant at heart. He spared no means, no flattery to please his master (Emperor Nicholas). He instilled in him the thought that he, Nicholas, was the creator of some new enlightenment based on new principles, and he devised these principles, that is the words: Orthodoxy, autocracy and nationality; Orthodoxy—while he was an atheist not believing in Christ even in the Protestant manner, autoc-

racy—while he was a liberal, nationality—although he had not read a single Russian book in his life and wrote constantly in French or in German. Decent people close to him, indebted to him and loving him, admitted with sorrow, that there was nothing so low that he was incapable of doing, that he was soiled on all sides by dirty acts. When talking to this person, often in the course of an intellectually brilliant conversation, one was struck by his extreme egotism and vanity. On such occasions one would be expecting that the next moment he would say that at the creation of the world God consulted him concerning the plan.

The portrait is astute; the last sentence, for instance, recalls the fact that Uvarov did seem to think that he had divined Providence's plan for Russia and all mankind. Solov'ev exaggerated in two respects: Uvarov was no atheist, although he emphasized religion more as a cultural than a spiritual value; and his library was not only filled with Russian books, but he even wrote in an elegant style in his native tongue. But what rings true is that Uvarov was "liberal" in his vision of Russia's emancipated, constitutional future but that he closeted his views in a nervous—and pragmatic—effort to remain in power. Since his generally progressive policies belied his stance, his ruse backfired; his enemies successfully discredited him in the reaction after 1848. Nikitenko considered Uvarov "intelligent and truthful" but lacking in "moral strength":

Seeking influence and favors at the court, he tied himself hands and feet and at the same time lost the respect of both the court and the public. He sought to sacrifice the latter to the former and made a severe error. . . . Uvarov constantly got bogged down in the subtleties of his mind. He tries to catch a fly in his web and diligently spins the threads, not noticing that they only serve to show his enemies the path to his nest.[88]

Despite all this, Uvarov showed the courage of his convictions twice. Both in 1821 and 1849, he left office rather than oversee the destruction of the "system" and the institutions he had publicly, and rightfully, proclaimed as his monuments.

Overall, the difficulties of assessing Uvarov's performance in office are enormous. Clearly, he was an intriguing, complicated person, a man of "brilliant gifts," lofty vision, and low character, a man of abilities and debilities, of achievements and misdemeanors. His vanity, his greed, his fawning, his policy of creeping development, his hostility to independent views all earned him a bad press among contemporaries and a bad name among historians. What remains to be seen is how his talents and his traits affected Russian educational development.

C H A P T E R 6

THE LOWER AND MIDDLE SCHOOLS

Public education in institutions opened by the government and operating under its constant surveillance and direction is, of course, the chief instrument for the enlightenment and moral life of the people. Uvarov, 1843

NICHOLAS I and his advisers recognized that the causes leading to the 1825 revolt were many and complex, but they singled out faulty education. The men of December were young and schooled. One general concluded, ironically writing his report in French, that this was a generation "toute gangrenée" by the infection of foreign ideas transmitted by French tutors, German professors, and allied soldiers. The poet Pushkin, claiming an ideological distance from his many Decembrist friends, in a memorandum to Nicholas agreed that the revolt was caused by an "alien ideology," a lack of respect for Russian culture, and an "absence" of proper upbringing. The tsar announced his conviction that "foreign influences" and "a fatal indulgence in pseudo-knowledge" had led to the insurrection.[1]

Not surprisingly, then, only five months into his reign, Nicholas established an ad hoc School Committee to address the problem of education. As a start, the ten members of the committee, one of whom was Uvarov, were to rework and make uniform the laws governing the system from the elementary to the university level. The mandate was not fulfilled until 1835, although the statute of 1828 regularized lower and middle schools. Nicholas soon lost patience with the septuagenarian and now torpid Shishkov, the minister of education from 1824 to 1828 and hence the chairman of the committee, and he was forced to retire. Prince Karl Lieven, a former superintendent of the Dorpat Educational District and a pious, decent person, succeeded him, but he left no special mark on the ministry and retired for reasons of health in 1833.[2]

Uvarov, who had been deputy minister of education since April 1832, became acting minister in March 1833 and was confirmed as minister one year later. His unusually extensive scholarly credentials and his experience in the ministry made him an excellent choice for the office. In addition, all the important measures drafted by the School Committee, which Uvarov would have to carry out, were in fact his inventions. This is not to say he dominated the committee's proceedings; in fact he attended only roughly one-third of the meetings.[3] Rather, the committee's actions between 1826 and 1835, which essentially constituted the refinements and reversals of the 1803–1804 statutes, had been foreshadowed by Uvarov's decisions as superintendent of the St. Petersburg Educational District. These decisions included: the introduction of tuition at middle and higher educational institutions; increases in teachers' salaries; promotion of teacher-training colleges; development of the classical gymnasium curriculum; a new emphasis on Russian studies at all levels; an enhanced role of superintendents in supervision of schools and universities; and efforts to entice young people from the upper classes into state schools so that they might be better prepared for civil service.

Of more interest and importance to Nicholas, though, was Uvarov's presentation of a dynamic program for an educational system that would be instilled with a new national "spirit" and that promised to preserve the "existing order." Four months before his appointment as acting minister, Uvarov reported on conditions at Moscow University. Although representative of his long-held views, his observations shrewdly played upon Nicholas's fear of another revolt and his search for an educational ideology that offered positive measures to prevent a recurrence.

> I maintain that in a general sense the spirit and disposition of the minds of the young await only a well-considered direction in order to mold the great majority of them into useful and sincere instruments of the government, that this spirit is ready to bear the imprint of a loyal love for the existing order. . . . I firmly believe that we have the means . . . gradually to rule the minds of the young as much through decree and gentle exhortation as through strong and astute surveillance, to lead them nearly imperceptibly to that point where we ought to accomplish one of the most difficult tasks of the era: [to provide] an education that is proper, basic, and necessary in our century with a profound respect and warm faith in the truly Russian sustaining principles of Orthodoxy, Autocracy, and Nationality, which constitute the last anchor of our salvation and the surest guarantee of the strength and greatness of our Fatherland.[4]

Neither Nicholas nor Uvarov invented the use of schools as tools of the state; the practice was common throughout Europe in the nineteenth century. Two fundamental principles were at work in educational systems:

governmental control for the purposes of ensuring political stability and of channeling resources to match the needs of the state; and class barriers to maintain the existing structure of society. In his study of German education, Friedrich Paulsen has pointed out that throughout Europe the right of state control was deemed an "obvious truth" because the future of a nation depends on its "rising generation"; by the end of the century, all systems were state-funded and state-directed. In a comparative essay, another scholar has commented that control next led to indoctrination: "No longer content with merely supervising the schools, states also began actively to use them to mold the political ideas of all children." In 1833, a bill introduced to the Reformed Parliament in England called for a system of national education in order to "promote political tranquility."[5] The same principles informed educational policy in Russia under Uvarov. Their operation is most clearly demonstrated in the measures relating to middle and lower education in the Great Russian provinces of the Russian Empire; measures relating to the subject nationalities require separate discussion.

THE PRINCIPLE OF STATE CONTROL

THE Russian government was the first in the nineteenth century flatly to declare education "a special function of the state." Other European countries soon followed, but came somewhat more slowly to this conclusion because they faced jealous opposition from religious bodies which regarded instruction as their own fiefdom—in contrast to the acquiescent and coopted Orthodox clergy. But when education became recognized as a proper and necessary preparation for work and life for all classes in a modernizing society, the task was clearly too mammoth and too important for anything less than national supervision. The Russian system, although in place, had developed somewhat erratically in its quarter-century existence. When Nicholas established the School Committee, he singled out lack of "necessary uniformity" as a basic problem and repeated the complaint to Uvarov when he took office.[6]

The Drive for Uniformity

Uvarov accepted the challenge and, according to his own testimony, spent his first six years in office reorganizing, expanding, and unifying the school system so that a new structure was set up "so to speak, in the rough." In 1843, he reported:

In the reign of Your Majesty the major task of the ministry of national enlightenment consisted in gathering and uniting in the hands of the government: all intellectual resources, which up to that time had been fragmented; all public and private means of education, which remained without respect and in part without surveillance; all elements that had taken an unwanted or even false direction; [then] to adapt the development of minds to the needs of the state and to link, as much as it is given to human understanding, the future with the present.

His next self-imposed task was simply to "perfect" the existing schools and to "administer" a period of "constant but quiet development." Uvarov stated clearly that he chose the criterion of quality rather than quantity because he believed his vocation as minister was to create firm foundations. Given the continuing lack of teachers, textbooks, money, and often public interest, his policy was eminently sensible, if conservative. Also, this attitude coincided with his historic view that the aim of the Nicholaevan era consisted in laying the groundwork for future development. The historian Hugh Seton-Watson grants him success and concludes that he provided "the material foundations of a modern system of education in Russia."[7]

Uvarov's first years in office witnessed the laying of those "foundations." A fundamental characteristic was hierarchical, centralized organization. As superintendent, Uvarov had presented a plan for replacing the former administration of middle and lower schools by university professors with their supervision by district superintendents. The School Committee suggested a similar revision, and Uvarov put it into effect in 1835. The change represented a clear improvement. As Uvarov noted, "thirty years experience" demonstrated "evident incongruities and inconveniences." Most professors either lacked the talent for or disliked the burdens of administering schools. Furthermore, the necessity of doing so "distracted them from their real and major occupation in scholarship and teaching."

The 1835 statute placed all schools under the care of the superintendent, now a resident of the district he administered rather than of the capital, a stipulation that permitted more "direct action" and control. But, Uvarov stressed, "The consultative aspect was retained." An advisory council assisted the superintendent; its members included the deputy superintendent, university rector, school inspector, director of schools, one or two gymnasium directors, and an honorary superintendent drawn from the ranks of the local nobility. The superintendent was also expected to continue to seek the advice of university councils on purely academic matters. Nonetheless, power and initiative resided with the superintendent, who took his orders from the minister.[8]

Centralization allowed standardization, another hallmark of Uvarov's system. As Granovskii noted, and with approbation, "The duties of the Russian teacher, from the university professor to the village instructor, were defined with all possible precision." Strict regulations governed the curricula and choice of textbooks at all school levels. Entrance examinations for district schools and the gymnasia attempted to ensure the proper level

of preparation for incoming students. "Detailed manuals" spelled out testing procedures for teachers in order to "protect educational institutions
from those unfit." By law, the ministry controlled what was taught only
through its system of surveillance and stipulation of course titles, but syl-
labi were not provided. The *Journal of the Ministry of National Enlightenment*
further served to standardize schools throughout the empire by systematically publishing new legislation and offering guidelines even for the
content of courses.[9]

Uvarov's journal presented not only academic but also, in his words,
"moral" or "political" guidelines. His first circular as minister demanded
that subjects be taught "in conformity with the views of the government"
by teachers who were "worthy instruments in the hands of the government" and who would "act in the spirit of the government and for aims
indicated to them" by the central ministry. Any school system, of course,
is expected to reflect, not undermine, its society, and educational ministers
in France or Prussia preferred similar exhortations and insisted upon intense centralization and control even after democratic institutions developed in those countries.[10] However, Uvarov's hectoring qualities, his self-
righteous pretension that he alone knew the needs of Russian culture, and
his tiresome incantation of the tripartite formula often irritated others and
caused him to be cast more in the role of ideologue than educator.

The insistence on academic and political conformity necessitated an inspectorate. Uvarov took special care to attract "capable and trustworthy"
people to this new arm of the ministry by awarding high civil service rank
and setting well-defined criteria for appointments. At all school levels,
inspectors became powerful officials, responsible for carrying out the curricula, the "spirit of teaching," and especially the discipline and morality
of students. The stress on inspection resulted in part from the connection
officials tended to see between education and revolution. In France, Guizot,
as minister of education from 1832 to 1837, created an inspectorate that
had similar responsibilities and that rapidly grew to a battalion of 153 men.
In 1834, the Committee on Education in England concluded: "Next in
importance to the system of training would be a system of inspection.
There should be . . . a vigilant eye everywhere. Schools cannot be too
much inspected and examined."[11]

Uvarov used centralization, standardization, and inspection as much to
improve the school system as to maintain control. When he first entered
office, he ordered a survey of all institutions under his jurisdiction. He
concluded, as he had as superintendent, that the problem of teachers was
fundamental: they were too few in number to allow desired expansion, too
ill-trained to improve quality, too impoverished to be held in any esteem.
A reading of Uvarov's yearly reports to the Emperor, which were published
in the *Journal*, indicates that his major concern was instilling a "new spirit"
among youth. Next to this objective, however, the solution of the teacher

problem captured his greatest enthusiasm, and his efforts in this area led to an extraordinary amount of legislative activity. Uvarov's first answer, once again a repetition of his work as superintendent, was "to free them [teachers] of concern for a comfortable living" by raising salaries, establishing pension funds and death benefits for teachers and their families, exempting them from the onerous poll tax, and improving their progress through the ranks. Special provisions made for those serving in the hardship posts of Siberia and the Caucasus included educational subsidies for their children.[12]

In order to create a "self-sustaining teaching profession," Uvarov energetically promoted the Central Pedagogical Institute, which the School Committee had reestablished in 1828 especially to prepare gymnasium teachers. He oversaw the draft of the statutes for the institute, which were identical with those he had sponsored in 1816 except that they made additional provision for a hundred state stipendiates. During his ministry, he paid great personal attention to the institute by attending exams and lectures and even reporting yearly to the tsar on student grades. He also sent students abroad to study in such fields as Slavic studies, law, and technical chemistry. Also, in his administration the first separate chairs in pedagogy were instituted in all Russian universities as well as pedagogical institutes, with twenty state stipendiates each for teacher training. Uvarov's interest in quality led to one other measure. "For the stimulation of scholarly activity among gymnasium teachers," he exorted each (probably to the utter distress of most) to present examples of their work—translations, articles on pedagogy, or scholarly treatises; university panels would judge them and publish the best, with promotion an additional reward.[13]

Neither was the training of lower school teachers neglected. In 1838, Uvarov trumpeted as his "biggest joy" and one of the greatest accomplishments of his ministry the reestablishment of a Second Section at the St. Petersburg Institute, which he had sponsored as superintendent. He rued the closing of the earlier institution: "The time lost cannot be retrieved; but it therefore becomes even more necessary to compensate for it." Otherwise, he declared, "parish schools cannot grow." But events repeated themselves. Like the 1820s, the 1840s witnessed a growth of hostility toward teacher-training institutes, because candidates tended to come from the lower classes and thus seemed to challenge the social order; they received Rank Fourteen upon graduation. In 1844, Uvarov was forced to bar admission of members of "obliged" classes to the institute, supposedly because there were enough candidates from the "free"; the enrollment dropped by half. In 1847, the Second Section was abolished once again and in 1858 the entire institute. Teachers were now to receive training at the universities, whose student body was more largely drawn from the upper classes.[14]

Uvarov's policies as well as his difficulties in regard to teacher training were common in Europe. France, Prussia, and England increased salaries, accredited teachers, and together erected over 130 "normal" schools in an effort to raise the level of instruction. Guizot, both as educational minister and as prime minister in France, like Uvarov encountered great difficulties in establishing normal schools, because many French officials also regarded them as threats to the social order; in Germany, the Revolution of 1848 was in part blamed on the "irreligious" and "pseudo-educated" lower-class graduates of teacher-training schools. Whatever the similarities, Uvarov's results were paltry compared with those, for instance, of Guizot; in 1838, 2,500 teacher trainees were enrolled in France and only 200 in Russia. Although the number of teachers and other personnel on the middle and lower levels rose by one-third during Uvarov's ministry, the teacher shortage remained acute.[15]

With somewhat more success, Uvarov attempted to improve physical conditions in the educational system. Particularly in his first ten years in office, he devoted constant attention to purchasing, constructing, and refurbishing buildings, both because of growing enrollment and because many buildings were decrepit—often, according to reports, in a state of "complete physical ruin." Indeed, in that era, one-half the budget was used for such purposes, and Uvarov enticed donations from the upper classes that equaled two-thirds of the state's outlay, a welcome sign of the public's new interest in education. Local architectural committees advised on design, but Uvarov always preferred, as can be expected, a simple classical motif; this became known as the "Uvarov style." He devoted a good deal of attention to the acquisition of textbooks and teaching materials and often commissioned university professors to create or translate works needed for instruction on the lower and middle level, especially for courses in language training or new technical courses. Medical facilities were improved at all school levels by granting doctors civil service rank that carried with it financial gain and social status.

At first, Uvarov's efforts to improve schools were supported by handsome government funding; figures demonstrate a dramatic rise from roughly 5,089,000 to 9,149,000 assignat rubles between 1833 and 1839 and an increase of .5 percent (from 1 to 1.5 percent) of the total budget as compared with a 2 percent drop for the military. However, in the second period the percentage was gradually reduced to less than 1 percent by 1848 and showed no improvement until the next reign.[16]

Uvarov's attempts at centralization and standardization, of course, applied only to the schools under the control of his ministry. In 1837, schools maintained by Tatar, German, or Jewish communities, as well as those under the auspices of other governmental ministries such as those of the Holy Synod, war, roads, justice, and finance, enrolled 374,872 students as compared with only 85,707 in the educational ministry. Once the ministry of state domains under Kiselev turned its attention to the education of state peasants in the 1840s, its schools counted roughly 100,000 pupils, twice the number in parish schools (49,101) run by the educational ministry.[17]

Private Education

While Uvarov simultaneously sought to raise the quality of instruction and to create a "new spirit" or "morality" among youth, Nicholas was primarily concerned with a "morality even higher" than "learning or erudition." For the tsar, "morality" served as a code word for loyalty to the autocracy, belief in Orthodoxy, and a pride in being Russian, all of which was to help prevent revolution and create domestic stability. But such "morality" could not be "under constant surveillance and direction" except in "institutions of public education"—domestic and private education threatened the desired monopoly and control.[18]

The employment of domestic tutors was common among the upper classes throughout Europe, but in Russia tutors tended to be foreigners and hence, as Uvarov put it, were typically "alien to our beliefs, laws, and customs." Humorously, in Pushkin's novella *The Captain's Daughter*, the valet of a young nobleman laments his turning to drink.

> Who is to blame for all this? That accursed "Monsoo." He was perpetually running round . . . with *"Madame, zhe voo pree, vodkyoo."* Well there's *zhe voo pree* for you! It can't be denied, that son of a bitch taught you some pretty habits! And that infidel tuor had to be engaged for you—as if the master hadn't enough of his own people![19]

To Nicholas, though, the phenomenon was no laughing matter. Fearing the potential hazards of foreign ideas, soon after the Revolution of 1830, he forbade students to study abroad until they reached eighteen; if younger, more impressionable people acquired their learning outside Russia, they might, "perhaps with reason," read the edict on foreign study and return with a critical attitude toward their own state. In 1831, regulations demanded that embassies strictly investigate the background of anyone who wished to enter Russia as a tutor. In 1834, with Nicholas's prodding, Uvarov took up the campaign in earnest and declared "it time to strengthen in private homes a truly national education."[20]

Uvarov, however, never had any intention of forbidding domestic education, only of cleansing it. He believed that the state should not and could not interfere in the sphere of "sacred blood ties and parental power" and should use only "indirect means." His legislation in 1834 set up sixty-nine criteria "to help parents" in selecting tutors. In order to attract Russians to this "obscure and modest occupation," and to cater to the universal quest for ranks, Uvarov elevated tutors to civil service in his ministry and also set up a pension fund so that "weak old age and the helplessness of their orphans would not frighten them." For reasons of both maintaining quality and eliminating foreigners, tutors required government certification attesting to their moral, intellectual, religious, and social qualifications; failure to comply meant prosecution for a Russian and expulsion for a foreigner. Uvarov also seems surreptitiously to have set up a quota system: from 1835 on, always 10 percent of those certified—anywhere from 300 to 500 each year—were aliens. In 1845, the tsar requested more stringent measures, and the next year only 11 of the nearly 400 certified were foreigners. In 1848, after the revolution in Europe, foreigners who wished to become tutors were no longer admitted into Russia.[21]

Private schools, which had grown in popularity and number since the time of Catherine the Great, posed an even more serious challenge to a state-controlled system of education. When Shishkov was minister, he simply advised closing all private schools. Although the School Committee unanimously opposed private education, the majority believed that it had to be tolerated as a "necessary evil" until the state had enough schools to fill the gap. Thus, the 1828 statute provided only that private institutions should be more closely scrutinized and that their courses of study should be made to conform to that prescribed for state schools; in 1831, teachers in private schools required government certification.[22] Nicholas, still not satisfied, informed Uvarov that control of private education should constitute a first priority.

Uvarov took swift action and presented comprehensive legislation subjecting private institutions to vigilant supervision. In 1833, regulations stipulated that new private schools could be opened in the capital only "in cases of extreme necessity" and in other cities only if "special need," such as the absence of state institutions, was demonstrated; Uvarov served as the judge in both instances. The ministry next appointed special inspectors, drawn from the ranks of professors or academicians, to check morality, religious atmosphere, student accomplishment, textbooks, and curricula in these institutions. Furthermore, teachers were to lecture in Russian, rather than the more usual French, and stress "national subjects" such as Russian history, geography, and literature.[23]

French newspapers deplored what they considered discrimination against their nationals. But an article commissioned by Uvarov in his educational journal stated flatly: "The formation of the entire system of education, both public and private, must be *in the spirit of our own institutions and in agreement with our own national feelings.*" In France, the article declared with much exaggeration, officials allowed the teaching of "all destructive principles" and created "a spirit of party" while a "dazzled population flippantly rushes after every new theory, after vain dreams." Thus, measures that "take away the preponderance of foreigners in the area of national education" were warranted in order to prevent the foreign disturbances from which "Providence has preserved us to this point."[24]

If private schools were supervised and regulated and if the teaching staff were increasingly native, Uvarov believed, there would be little harm in private education. In 1843, he triumphantly announced that in the previous year seventy-one more schools had been opened, even though forty-one of them were private. During his ministry, the rate of growth in the private and the public sector was identical, each registering a 50 percent increase; private schools maintained a steady proportion of 27 percent of the total, and by 1848 they numbered 601 of 2,190 institutions. To the tsar, Uvarov attempted to downplay this fact, and referred to private schools as a "small fraction" of the total.[25]

In Great Russia, private institutions were concentrated in the two capitals and especially in St. Petersburg, where they increased during Uvarov's ministry from 97 to 195. Statistics indicate that these schools were primarily providing an education for the middle classes, who were not encouraged to attend the predominantly upper-class state gymnasia, and for females, who were barred from them. For instance, in 1842, in Moscow and St. Petersburg, roughly 65 percent of the 4,812 pupils attending private schools were female and 54 percent were non-noble. Although the type of education offered women was meager and was geared toward preparing them as wives and mothers, the increased number of women students surely was one cause of the eagerness and readiness of women to attend universities in the next reign. For young men of non-noble origin, since the curriculum in a private gymnasium was supposed to be identical with the state's and since an entrance examination was all that was required for university entrance, private schools became a route to higher education and hence high positions in civil service. Uvarov welcomed both developments. He applauded the new interest on the part of the public in educating women because it was "important for family life and through it for the state as well," and he declared even the most mediocre private institutions "useful" because they afforded educational opportunity for the middle classes.[26]

In general, then, Uvarov looked upon private education benevolently and thought that it would continue to serve a need until more state schools were in operation. Nicholas apparently did not share this view, but by the mid-1840s his objections to private schooling were based on its "democratic" rather than foreign character. To allay the tsar's fears, in 1845, Uvarov announced to him, using suspect statistics, that the number of private institutions was dropping because of the "growth in popularity" of state schools. Two years later, he was forced to note the "extraordinary increase" of private schools and issued a regulation that a new one could not open unless another closed. Nonetheless, in 1848, sixty more appeared and only forty-six ceased operation.[27] Uvarov was playing a dangerous game; the autocrat came to believe that the educational ministry was allowing too much private initiative and thus contributing to class movement.

THE CLASS QUESTION

B ECAUSE Nicholas was highly concerned with stability and understood that revolutions erupt from social as well as political causes, he was insistent that the Russian educational system in no way challenge the existing class structure. Accordingly, he objected to the "democratic ladder" concept and the "open admissions" policy written into the 1803–1804 statutes. As the School Committee debated this issue, the tsar delivered a rescript despairingly noting that serfs had made their way even into higher educational institutions. The contradiction between their advanced learning and low status would create "intolerable burdens" that would result in "fatal dreams or low passions," the euphemism for revolutionary thinking. Thus, while Nicholas saw the necessity for an education for all classes, each person should receive only "the knowledge most necessary to improve his lot, not falling below his social position but not striving above that class in which in the general run of events he is fated to serve."[28]

Throughout Europe, educational systems were constructed so that they would reflect, confirm, and reproduce existing social divisions; there existed little, if any, allegiance to the principle of upward mobility through education. In 1831, Victor Cousin reported to the French educational ministry on the dangers of allowing lower and even middle classes into gymnasia:

> There these young men acquire connections and tastes which make it difficult or even impossible for them to enter into the humble careers of their fathers; whence comes a race of disturbed men, discontented with their own and other's position, enemies of the social order ready to hurl themselves, their knowledge, their more or less real talent, and their vaunting ambition into the paths of servility or revolt.

Frederick William III of Prussia, presiding over the most expansive educational system in Europe, agreed: "We do not confer upon the individual or upon society any benefit when we educate him beyond the bounds of his social class and vocation, give him a cultivation which he cannot make use of, and awaken in him pretensions and needs which his lot in life does not allow him to satisfy." Andrew Bell, one of the founders of the Lancastrian movement, warned that it was a mistake to educate children too much and thereby "render them discontent and unhappy in their lot." Schools were in fact designed to stifle the ambitions of the lower classes and thus, in the words of one historian, became "central instruments of social control." This policy was carried out, as another scholar maintains, "without a bad conscience" because the governing elite accepted a hierarchical social order as natural.[29]

Nicholas was, then, not unusual in envisioning a clearly defined social structure wherein, as in the military, each person knew his place, performed his duties, and received a training appropriate for his rank. Despite their vaunted all-class character, the 1803–1804 statutes also decreed that schools were established "for the moral education of citizens in keeping with the duties and uses of each estate," and the revised statute of 1828 repeated this formula nearly verbatim.[30] Under Alexander, the all-class principle was modified so that anyone from the "non-free" classes who wished to enter middle or higher educational institutions had to obtain an official release from his former obligations. Under Nicholas, the legal situation remained the same, although the rules were periodically restated. This relative permissiveness is surprising, because the tsar clearly would have preferred a more strict social segregation with middle and higher schools reserved for children of the upper classes, with others absolutely confined to the district and parish school level.

The problem remained that the social structure in Russia, as it had developed since the time of Peter the Great, was not given to easy regimentation.[31] Peter had dictated that everyone in society owed service to the state and that schooling and merit alone warranted entry into the Table of Ranks. Since rank could be acquired through service, the nobility was not a closed caste. It included newcomers like former Secretary of State Speranskii and ranged from impoverished rural gentry to wealthy court aristocracy. In 1762, Peter III excused the nobility from their service obligations, thereby making them the only really "free" class in Russian society. However, for economic reasons and because Peter I had successfully managed to instill the notion that one's position in society depended solely on one's rank, most noblemen continued to serve. Ranked officials and the few wealthy merchants of the first guild were also considered "free," but they retained the obligation to work; they, plus the nobility, were counted in the upper classes during Nicholas's reign.

Other groups, while still serving in some occupational capacity, were deemed "free" if they were released from corporal punishment, the poll tax, recruitment, and the residency requirements of an artisan's society, merchants' guild, peasant commune, or landowner's estate. Such a release was difficult to obtain since those remaining had to shoulder the tax and military obligations of the departing member, but one could buy one's way out. Consequently, movement or crossovers occurred, and the number of classes multiplied into the dozens as various occupational groups sought to improve their legal position, and the government tried to define more clearly the obligations of the varying strata in society. The attempt at precision led only to confusion, and, as Lieven pointed out to the School Committee, the possibility of organizing schools on the basis of heredity was no longer viable, because the class structure was too fluid. He pointed out that, in Russia,

where a well-off peasant may at any time become a merchant, and often is both at the same time, where the nobility extends from the foot of the throne at one end and nearly merges into the peasantry at the other, where every year many from the citizen and from the peasant class enter the ranks of the nobility by achieving the necessary rank in the military or civil service—in Russia it is very difficult to organize the school in that way [that is, on the basis of hereditary class].[32]

Because of Lieven's arguments, the School Committee decided to compromise and to organize the school system in such a way that each level was arranged "chiefly," but not "exclusively" as Nicholas would have preferred, according to class needs, thus allowing for some social mobility but not making it "the object of general endeavor" or expectation.

In Russia, as elsewhere, upward mobility through education was "comparatively rare," accessible only to those individuals of the lower orders who possessed "manifest talent." In Western Europe, the vaunted "career open to talent" remained as much window dressing as was the promise of elevation through the Table of Ranks in Russia. Uvarov nevertheless strongly believed in the latter; in 1847, when an ad hoc committee investigating the civil service raised the possibility of abolishing ranks, Uvarov presented a memorandum to the tsar. The table, he asserted, provided *"equality before the law"*; upon entering service, the son of a poor man competed on equal terms with the sons of magnates, and only through "constant zeal" could one "work his way" to the prestigious upper levels. Furthermore, the system gave even the autocracy a "moral value" in that the nation was united in the ideal of service and functioned with common purpose under the leadership of the tsar.[33] In general, from the beginning to the end of his tenure, Uvarov voiced the necessity to spread "education among all classes and in all places" and "to attend to the needs of all levels of society."[34] But he set priorities in favor of the upper and urban classes, since resources were limited and those segments of the population would gain most from an education and would most benefit the state. Whatever the rationale, this situation rendered disservice to the other classes.

Parish Schools

Since its foundation in 1802, the educational ministry had paid notoriously little attention to Russians living in rural areas, although they formed the bulk of the population. As in 1803–1804, the one- or two-year curriculum of parish schools was limited to reading, writing, arithmetic, and religion, the four Rs of Russian education, and after 1828 the ministry supervised the selection of textbooks, teaching methods, and course content. The statute of 1828 reiterated that the state would take no financial responsibility for parish schools, intended primarily for serfs and sometimes factory workers, and left their education to the goodwill of local landowners, clergy, and town councils. Amazingly enough, according to official statistics, the number of such schools nearly doubled during Uvarov's ministry, and increased from 583 to 1,030, with an enrollment of roughly 100,000.[35] While this growth still barely touched the needs of a general population of sixty million, nonetheless, it did indicate a new recognition of the importance of education on the part of private citizens, a development already noted in their willingness to sponsor private schools or to contribute to building funds.

While Uvarov applauded this new "zeal" because he considered parish schools "necessary" for raising the general level of citizenship, the tsar grew fearful.[36] Even in Western Europe, as one scholar noted, it was widely believed that there was "nothing more frightening" than giving a general education to the lower classes, because it disturbed their social docility and humble resignation. One English pedagogue wanted to limit lower schooling to reading, on the theory that if a student learned to write he might pen criticism of religion or government. The institution of serfdom, of course, and the hundreds of peasant uprisings that occurred during the reign compounded the situation in Russia and made it all the more ominous. Oblomov, a character in the eponymous novel by Goncharov, recoiled when a progressive landowner suggested that he set up a school on his estate: "Isn't it too soon for that? Education is bad for the peasant: if he starts learning, he will probably stop plowing."[37]

The rare possibility, and the difficulties, of upward mobility for a serf were demonstrated in the case of Ivan Petrov, from the village of Ragozin. The young lad was a "mathematical genius" (in seventeen minutes, he solved twelve problems such as $875 \times 35 \times 5 = 153,125$). His mistress, a widow with eight children and only seventy serfs—a number too small to support the large family—was reluctant to free him so he could enter a gymnasium; finally the tsar gave her 2,000 rubles as recompense, and she emancipated him. But then, she queried, since the tsar was good enough to raise her serf "from a nobody," could he not perhaps provide a proper education and stipends for her own children? At any rate, Ragozinskii, as he chose to call himself, enrolled at a gymnasium in Moscow, completed the course, and went on to Moscow University, with Uvarov dutifully itemizing his every course and "gentle and modest" behavior to the tsar. Another serf, Frolov, was allowed into the same gymnasium as a reward for an act of bravery during a fire. These were the only two cases noted by Uvarov in his annual reports to the tsar during his ministry.[38]

District Schools

The difficulties of arranging the tiers of the school system according to class lines is seen most clearly in the district schools that were established in the main towns of the provinces. The School Committee, the 1828 statute, and various rescripts in the 1830s and 1840s all declared that these schools were intended "primarily" for the children of the "obligated" or "non-free" urban classes such as artisans or merchants of the lower guilds. In fact, however, they became all-class schools and accepted serfs whose landowners wanted them trained at state expense. Also, the poorer nobility, bureaucrats, and merchants of the upper guilds hoped that the district schools would prepare their children for the gymnasia.[39]

In contrast to the parish schools, which were left nearly unchanged, the 1828 statute made significant improvements in district schools. The state took over responsibility for their financing and made them subject to uniform regulations. Attendance was gratis, although contributions were encouraged from town councils or citizens. The number of teachers rose from two to five in each school; their salaries were raised and pension funds made available. The number of district schools during Uvarov's administration rose only from 406 to 450, but this meant that nearly every district town possessed its own school.[40]

The 1828 statute changed the duration of the curriculum from two to three years and included the "Four Rs" along with geometry, geography, history, and drawing; courses in physics, natural history, and technology were dropped from the earlier syllabus. This change meant that the district school curriculum was identical, although narrower in range, to the first three years of the seven-year gymnasium course, except that it did not include training in Latin, French, or German. Since many children from "free" classes attended, however, parents who wanted to keep their children in the district town for three years before sending them away to the provincial gymnasia, which required tuition and board, requested the addition of classical and modern languages. Uvarov's yearly reports indicate that by the end of his ministry, about one-fifth of the district schools had courses that prepared students for the gymnasia. He accepted, however, only individual petitions; he refused to allow language study as a "general rule," since that would have fully reestablished the democratic ladder that had been rejected by Nicholas and the School Committee. Nonetheless, some students from non-free classes, including serfs, were clearly getting an education on the lower level that equipped them to handle gymnasium work; this was one reason why the flow of these classes into the gymnasia could only be discouraged, not stopped.

With financial backing from the ministry of finance, Uvarov encouraged a policy of responding to "local needs" by setting up additional district-school courses in bookkeeping, trade, commerce, mineralogy, mechanics, architecture, shipbuilding, and agriculture, all to increase the trained man-power needed in those areas. He also promoted Sunday school classes, generally for adult artisans, in such courses as mechanical drawing because of "the great need for technical knowledge." Even members of the nobility were encouraged to attend, because "all classes" had need of such training.

In the course of Uvarov's ministry, district schools were set up in six cities in the manufacturing areas of the empire specifically to stress scientific training in an effort to "increase and strengthen factories," and Uvarov supervised the provision of texts, models, and supplies for these courses.[41]

The increased attention to "practical" instruction in the district schools served two functions. It promoted the education of the lower classes for their station in life and hence could have a beneficial effect on trade, industry, and agriculture. Stressing scientific training at this level, however, made the majority of district schools terminal institutions; their graduates were unprepared for the gymnasia. Beginning in 1833, Guizot established "higher primary schools," nearly identical with the Russian district schools but lacking supplementary instruction in technology, for the avowed purpose of satisfying the growing desire for education but keeping the lower orders out of the middle schools.[42]

Gymnasia

Uvarov was the sole architect of middle education in Nicholaevan Russia. He dominated the discussions of the School Committee on this topic, and the 1828 statute generally repeated the curricular plan he had devised in 1811. As then, Uvarov's first aim was to attract the upper classes into state gymnasia. Given the generally hierarchical nature of Russian society, it was natural to assume that the existing upper classes, and in particular the nobility, would continue to occupy leading positions in the civil service. Uvarov referred to "noble youth" as "the best flower of the maturing generation, destined by their very origin and opportunities in life to tasks of the greatest responsibility in the state." Thus, if Russia were to modernize and to be well administered, it needed a well-trained nobility. "Noble youth," however, tended to resist serious educational pursuits and to prefer the indulgence of private schools or domestic tutors followed by promotion through the ranks on the basis of longevity. The traditional call to arms remained strong, and hence staffing the country's armed forces was not a problem; in 1837, 179,981 students were enrolled in military schools at all levels. But in civilian life, trained men were needed to replace the ignorant, incompetent, corrupt officials that had become both legion and legendary in the central and especially provincial bureaucracy.[43]

In the first years of his ministry, Uvarov proved the strong suspicion of nearly all the leading members of the educational ministry since its inception that the principal obstacle to inducing the nobility to enter the state gymnasia was the "democratic" character of these schools. In the 1820s, roughly 60 percent of the enrollment came from the "other" classes. On a visit to Moscow University in 1832, Uvarov heard the "complaints of parents" concerning this issue and their desire for a "special education" for their children—for which they were even willing to pay. Uvarov sided with the parents, and, only two months after his appointment as minister, he issued a circular that declared:

> The experience of many years has fully shown that . . . by opening these [gymnasia] to people of all estates, we have been forced to combine in them children of nobility with children of *raznochintsy* and other middle and lower classes. From this diversity . . . followed the consequence that our gymnasia all too rarely held the respect of the noble estate . . . , and the nobility prepared their children for higher education by means of domestic education or private *pansions*.[44]

Uvarov proposed two solutions. The first of these, for which the School Committee had provided legislation in 1826 but which was of little interest to either Shishkov or Lieven, was the building of noble boarding schools, or *pansions*, alongside the gymnasia. According to this plan, students would attend regular lessons with the "other classes" but would spend their leisure time among their own kind and receive instruction in subjects "more pertinent for the education of the upper classes" such as fencing, dancing, riding, music, and conversational French. State subsidies would be available, but basically the nobility was expected to finance the new endeavor. They responded with extraordinary enthusiasm. Forty *pansions* were established during Uvarov's ministry, to add to the existing seven; by 1843, the nobility had spent 13 million rubles on the erection and maintenance of these schools; local assessments usually were made on the basis of taxable serfs. Uvarov was right to declare this development a "miracle." His other solution was less successful, probably since it was too costly. He proposed establishing, again at the nobility's expense, institutes for the upper aristocracy similar to Tsarskoe Selo Lycée. At these elite institutions, noble students would live and learn in an exclusive atmosphere; but only six such schools were established.[45] The nobility may have wanted a "special" education for their children, but not one where they would have to pay the entire bill.[46]

Because of their noble bias, the School Committee and Uvarov paid particular attention to the needs of their poor brethren, members of the noble caste with too little land or too few serfs to maintain a standard of living commensurate with their social standing. State stipends, with help from local nobles, were provided for 10 percent of *pansion* students, or roughly 800 per year. The aim clearly was to attract as many promising young people from the nobility as possible into the civil service, especially the notoriously inept provincial bureaucracy; generally the poor nobleman anxious to improve his lot opted for the military, where stipends were readily available. Uvarov also instituted stipends for students in the border provinces because of the "need for educated civil servants in distant places." In Siberia, he created twenty-two new state scholarships for preparing students to become teachers by studying in their local gymnasia and then transferring to Kazan University; he looked forward to a "new epoch" when this plan should bear fruit. Again in "distant places," special *pansions* were created for sons of officials and even unranked chancellery workers so that their children would receive a good education and, it was hoped, be better trained than their fathers. If students received stipends from the state or nobility, they were expected to serve six to eight years in the province in which the gymnasium they attended was located.[47]

In general, Uvarov catered to the social sensibilities of the upper classes. The inclusion in the *pansions* of subjects that provided polish gave the institutions a finishing-school aspect, and the minister clearly intended these features as sops or bribes to attract the proper clientele. Uvarov's primary object, though, was to create a corps of educated, trained civil servants, and he therefore wished to push the sons of the privileged into the universities which they had been loath to attend. Uvarov flatly declared that *pansions* were solely "preparatory schools for attending lectures in the universities."[48]

The 1828 statute drawn up by the School Committee advocated a gymnasium curriculum that was nearly identical to that set up by Uvarov in 1811, although the committee's decision was not reached without some controversy. Of great importance for improving the bureaucracy was the measure extending the curriculum from four to seven years; the normal age of a graduate entering service, then, would be eighteen rather than fifteen, and his preparation deeper and broader. The seven-year curriculum served the dual function of offering a course of study that would prepare a young man to enter the university or to go into service directly upon graduation. However, the School Committee, and especially Uvarov, preferred that as many students as possible pursue higher education.

The first hallmark of the gymnasium curriculum was its emphasis upon classical studies, a development that represented a singular victory for Uvarov. Only one other member of the School Committee endorsed his long-held view that "classical learning [represents] the most perfect and effective means for intellectual development" and is properly the "foundation of all education." Pushkin, probably speaking for the majority of the nobility, considered study of Latin and Greek a "luxury," and parents had long objected that it demanded too strenuous study and was "superfluous" for future civil servants or students preparing for most other vocations. But Uvarov held his ground and produced his former tutor and one of Russia's foremost scholars, Gräfe of the Academy of Sciences, to support his view. The arguments were successful to such a degree that the committee agreed to require, for the sake of uniformity, both Latin and Greek for all gymnasia students.[49]

Uvarov, however, to the surprise of his colleagues, argued against the inclusion of Greek in all schools until a sufficient number of teachers were well prepared; in the meantime, he suggested the teaching of Greek only in university towns and "perhaps Riga and Mitau." Once again demonstrating that his chief concern was quality, Uvarov asked: "What advantage can we expect from weak, immature, superficial instruction in the Greek language in our distant provinces? Where shall we find capable teachers of the subject?" Nicholas intervened and decided in Uvarov's favor but for the wrong reason, namely that he simply considered Greek a useless "luxury."

Nonetheless, by the end of Uvarov's ministry, Greek was taught at forty-five of the seventy-nine gymnasia, but at only nine about five years after he left office. Incentive, "an undoubted encouragement," was given to study Greek by awarding those who pursued it Rank Fourteen immediately upon graduation, rather than after the normal one-year wait. However, the usual picture of Uvarov as a fanatic defender of the classical curriculum at the expense of other subjects scarcely holds. In gymnasia where Greek was taught, 29 percent of the curriculum was devoted to the classics, and where it was not taught, only 16 percent; by comparison, the Prussian curriculum, which served the School Committee as a general model, demanded 46 percent.[50]

Toward the end of Uvarov's ministry, the classical curriculum came under attack, as it did throughout Europe at mid-century, either because it was seen as failing to meet the needs of an industrializing economy or because, allegedly, the study of ancient republics fomented revolution. Eventually, egalitarians came to see the classical curriculum as a reactionary ruse designed to discourage the lower classes from gymnasium attendance. However, in the 1830s, study of the classics remained a universal tradition in secondary education in Europe. Classical study was prized because it was thought to improve the whole person, both intellectually and morally; to offer the best mental exercise, knowledge of a major pinnacle in civilization, and preparation for university study; as well as to provide examples of honor, duty, and public service, the virtues of a ruling class. In truth, classical learning served to provide a unifying common tradition among the elites of all European countries; it was a sign of distinction without which the Russian upper classes could not hope to achieve equality with their peers abroad in either intellectual or social terms. Furthermore, within countries, it served as an agent of acculturation for new entrants into the elite; for instance, the French middle classes rushed to classical learning despite its rigors or even impracticality because they recognized it as a *sine qua non* for blending in with the established social strata.[51]

In 1855, Granovskii, reacting to the assault on the Uvarov gymnasium after 1848, posited that contemporary literature and circumstances, not the study of the classics, created revolutions, and that socialism had nothing whatsoever to do with the Latin-Greek world. Furthermore, he noted, in France and Austria more revolutionaries had graduated from technical schools than from the classical gymnasia. When Dmitri Tolstoi, as minister of education from 1866 to 1880, later revived the classical curriculum, he argued that its abandonment had resulted in "materialism, nihilism, and a most ruinous egotism" among youth.[52]

Two other features of the Uvarov gymnasium reflected the minister's view that Russians should be educated in their own culture but should not lose contact with the study of Western European civilization. In the new curriculum, 36 percent of the course hours were devoted to the study of the Orthodox religion, to Russian language and literature based on readings from Lomonosov to Pushkin, to history based on Karamzin's interpretation, and to geography and statistics; this change marked the end of the cosmopolitan tendency of the 1803–1804 course of study and supported the new sense of national pride and independence. At the same time, Uvarov tried to augment the instruction of French and German but encountered considerable opposition in the committee, especially from the old gallophobe Shishkov. Nicholas intervened and declared French "a necessity." Thus, 11 percent of the curriculum in gymnasia that taught Greek was devoted to the two modern languages, and 19 percent in gymnasia without Greek, whereas only 4 percent of the Prussian curriculum was allotted to nonclassical languages. Another 12 percent of the Russian curriculum, or 16 percent in gymnasia without Greek, centered on mathematics and physics and the remainder on drawing, calligraphy, and logic. Thus, the Uvarov gymnasium provided a general, liberal arts, humanistic education especially suited for university preparation. In addition, Uvarov stressed the need to develop the student's mental facilities and discouraged the use of rote learning.[53]

Despite the range of subjects taught, Uvarov guaranteed that the curriculum was "safe." Subjects such as political economy and philosophy were dropped from the earlier curriculum because of the effect they might have on "immature" minds and their propensity for "erroneous application." In 1846, as reaction was setting in, even logic was eliminated. Apparently Uvarov thought this move an overreaction, because he immediately ordered that logic must then be taught to every university student. To train independent intellects and keep them supporting the existing order can often breed conflict and hypocrisy. As one scholar maintains, teachers had to rely on "omission, selectivity, and distortion of facts to conform" to upholding the status quo.[54]

But overall, scholars agree that Uvarov performed the herculean feat of putting the Russian gymnasia on a par with the best in Europe. In particular, he was at the forefront in his recognition that middle schools should not only train the governing elite, but also satisfy "the ubiquitous and more general endeavors in *industry*." He opened a German-type *real* section at St. Petersburg University in order to train teachers for subjects such as technology, architecture, applied mathematics, drawing, and chemistry. Although this was a modest program, it represented an important pioneering effort. In general, Uvarov tended to respond to local demands, as he had in district schools. Practical mechanics, chemistry, and technology were introduced in the gymnasia of Tula, Vilna, and Kursk in order to improve factories; forestry was taught in Mitau; in Archangel, a trading center, courses in bookkeeping, commercial mathematics, trade, Russian commercial law, and English found a place in the curriculum; in Odessa, commercial law and Italian were instituted to meet the needs of merchants. Completion of such courses brought the right of the obligated classes to buy exemptions from recruitment or corporal punishment.

Encouraged by the ministry of finance, in 1838 the educational ministry opened the Third Moscow Gymnasium with the particular purpose of improving technical knowledge. The curriculum of the new school offered two parallel courses of study, beginning in a student's fourth year—one that remained classical and another that taught natural history, chemistry, technology, mechanics, accounting, and commercial law and was intended especially for the children of merchants and artisans. Uvarov called the establishment of this school a "first assault" on spreading technical education throughout the middle and lower educational system. By 1842, he boasted that each year either a new *real* course or a new *pansion* was being opened, thus indicating his commitment to answer the various vocational needs of the different classes of a modernizing state. In addition, teacher-training programs were organized in technology and the sciences.[55]

Although Uvarov believed that the gymnasia should primarily provide preparation for university study, many graduates of these schools went directly into service. Such students were allowed to substitute courses in French and German for Greek, but no specific courses trained future civil servants except in Siberia and the Caucasus, where all gymnasia taught jurisprudence and legal procedure. Local nobility began to request and pay for lectures in jurisprudence in Pskov, Tula, Novgorod, and Kishniev, in order to educate better bureaucrats. In 1848, in cooperation with the ministry of justice, Uvarov agreed to the introduction of juridical studies in the last three years of the curriculum. This program was intended especially for the provinces, where as few as 10 percent of gymnasium graduates entered the university, and at first was limited to five cities.

Similarly, in order to prepare bureaucrats and also because of his special interest in Oriental studies, Uvarov from the first year of his ministry established training in Arabic, Persian, Tatar, Turkish, Mongolian, and Chinese in the First Kazan Gymnasium; fourteen of eighty state stipendiates followed this course of study. Among them, Uvarov enthused, were Asiatic tribesmen; hence enlightenment was spreading "among these nomadic and half-savage people." In appropriate areas, Persian, Georgian, and Armenian were also taught, and Uvarov proudly announced that graduates were as a result serving in responsible posts in various ministries and embassies.[56]

Although Uvarov agreed that "primarily" sons of noblemen, government officials, and merchants of the first guild should study at gymnasia, his policies made little dent in the class composition of the student group, and James Flynn has demonstrated that he had little intention of making one. The rescript of 1827 and the statute of 1828 had really only one effect, namely to forbid the entry of serfs to the middle schools. Otherwise, all classes were admitted, including emancipated serfs, but in the case of the "obligated," only upon presentation of a release certificate.

In 1833 the upper classes provided roughly 78 percent of the total enrollment, with 2 percent drawn from the clergy and the rest from the lower and middle classes; while the number of gymnasia students tripled during Uvarov's ministry, the percentages remained nearly identical. The numbers of students enrolled in 1833, when compared with those for 1826, indicate a 9 percent increase for the upper classes but a 6 percent increase for those middle and lower. Uvarov's primary concern was to attract the upper classes into state gymnasia, and he used positive measures to achieve that goal, but he applauded all interest in education. Both in 1836 and 1844, Uvarov welcomed the new love for learning and "the striving of higher and middle classes" for a gymnasium education, as well as the "rush to education" that inspired the higher and even lower members of the middle class to enroll their children in secondary schools, as they did in increasing numbers each year. Furthermore, he set up special courses to meet the needs of the middle and lower classes, another indication of their acceptance.[57]

Nicholas, however, was reluctant to accept the presence of these classes in the gymnasia and even closed one in Pskov when he discovered not a single noble in attendance; he also criticized the First St. Petersburg Gymnasium for being "too democratic." At Nicholas's request, Uvarov raised tuition in 1845 in order "to keep the striving of youth for education in some proportion with the civic existence of the various classes," although the poor still received exemptions. In that same year, for the first time in his annual reports, Uvarov singled out the need to provide education "especially for the nobility" rather than repeating his usual phrase, "for all classes in society."

Uvarov had always favored the European tradition of charging tuition for secondary education, a practice based on the concept that education at this level was a privilege, not necessary for everyone. But he scrupulously allotted the funds obtained in this manner among teaching awards, pensions for lower-school teachers, and general maintenance. By the 1840s, tuition had acquired a political and social purpose, especially after Nicholas asked: "Are there no other means of making entry into the gymnasia more difficult for *raznochintsy*?" Uvarov replied that he had already presented the Committee of Ministers with a resolution requiring "liberation certificates" from non-free classes before entrance so that the gymnasia "will become primarily a place of education for the children of nobility and government officials [and merchants of the first guild]: the middle class will turn to the district schools." This was, of course, the same rule that had

been in operation since the 1810s and apparently was still being circum-
vented, as indicated by Uvarov's use of the future tense. As one Russian
historian suggested, the ideal of obtaining an education was such a powerful
stimulus to many Russians that regulations were "of almost no avail to
those who had seriously determined to obtain it."[58]

Nicholas was really in a quandary, and it is sobering and uplifting to
note the limitations on even autocratic power when confronted with the
quiet but strong demands of public opinion, with the needs of the state,
and with the necessity of keeping pace with developments in other countries. Nicholas accepted the idea that it was necessary for a strong state in
nineteenth-century Europe to maintain a school system, but he would have
preferred to organize it absolutely along class lines, with no lower- or
middle-class students in the gymnasia, and to eliminate private education.
He could fulfill neither wish without antagonizing the very classes that
might help develop Russia's resources or without making Russia appear
hopelessly antediluvian in the eyes of Europe. Even the tsar's advisers
planned to encourage the development of a middle class as one antidote to
economic backwardness; in 1827 Kochubei suggested to Nicholas that his
views in regard to the class question be issued as a rescript of the educational
ministry rather than as an imperial decree in order to avoid the criticisms
of Europeans who held aloft the principle of the "career open to talent."
Furthermore, Russian statistics in regard to middle education made the
system look sufficiently backward without compounding this impression
through statements of restrictive policy: France and Germany enrolled 1.65
students in secondary schools per 1,000 population and Russia only .33,
despite the fact that under Uvarov the number of state schools had grown
from 65 to 79 and since 1826 the number of students from 6,533 to 20,474.
Unfortunately, there are no statistics to indicate how many of the 601
private schools were at the secondary level. Nonetheless, by comparison,
France had 481 public and 1,089 private secondary schools with an enrollment of roughly 85,000.[59]

To Uvarov's credit, given the lack of coherent imperial policy, he mas-
terfully crafted a program that went far toward satisfying the biases of the
tsar and upper classes in education while at the same time not discouraging
the other sectors of the population. *Pansions*, noble institutes, stipends, the
insistence on a firm connection between at least secondary education and
rank, a prestige bred of high scholastic standards, all made the gymnasia
more attractive, especially to the nobility, than was previously the case. If
education were needed for promotion in the ranks, it behooved the nobility
to acquire it in order to maintain their monopoly on public office and
prestige in society. By 1850, according to Walter Pintner, over three-quarters of high officials in central agencies were of that class and the same
percentage had received at least a secondary education; career success came
to the nobility, whether rich or poor, because they were most encouraged

and, at long last, most inclined to take advantage of educational opportunities. Poor noblemen, especially, saw education as a way to advance and differentiate themselves from other equally poor but non-noble Russians. The upper classes throughout Europe and even in America were similarly drawn to education in an effort to justify their status and the existing social structure: "In a masterful act of social and ideological manipulation, the higher schools had united the elitist notion of breeding with the democratic belief in 'career open to talent' to create what was known throughout Europe as an 'aristocracy of intelligence.'" And everywhere, school systems showed more concern for training an elite for leadership than the masses for citizenship.[60]

What is more surprising is how quickly the value of obtaining at least a middle education filtered down into the "other classes" and became a general social endeavor. The financial contributions of landowning nobility were largely responsible for doubling the number of parish schools during Nicholas's reign and for supporting forty-seven *pansions* and six noble institutes. At the same time, non-nobles also contributed to the gymnasia and, along with various strata of the "obligated" middle classes, supported private institutions, which came to represent 27 percent of all the schools under the educational ministry. Indeed, by the end of Uvarov's ministry, there were 601 private schools but only 529 state district schools and gymnasia, most of them aided by subsidies of private citizens; and the 1,030 parish schools were not state-financed. These facts show clearly the extensive popular support of education and diminish the concept of Nicholaevan Russia as a purely statist society.

To this new popular support of education, Uvarov contributed his encouragement; he allayed the fears of the tsar by assuring him that widespread education was "safe" for the autocracy, and he ensured the quality of schools by insisting on standards of excellence both in private and public institutions. The minister correctly divined and welcomed a "rush to education" and "a new recognition of its importance," believing these developments to be evidence of a "new, visible trend" among the upper and urban classes. Uvarov's partnership in this trend does much to explain the intellectually "remarkable decade" of the 1840s. What was accomplished during the ministry was the creation of a literate elite, the first essential step in a nation's modernization. As the historian Darlington has noted:

> It was not a mere historical coincidence that, of the scholars and men of letters or of action who distinguished themselves in the next reign, especially during the "period of great reforms," a very large proportion had passed through the Uvarovskian gymnasia.[61]

THE RENAISSANCE OF THE UNIVERSITIES AND THE ACADEMY OF SCIENCES

The ministry is guided by one leading concept: to preserve all the advantages of European enlightenment, to raise the intellectual life of Russia to the level of other nations [but at the same time] to give it national uniqueness.   Uvarov, 1843

D URING Uvarov's tenure as minister of education, Russia's institutions of higher learning underwent a renaissance. In 1833, the universities were ailing economically and academically; they still suffered from the results of the fervid campaign waged against them in the early 1820s. A slow recovery had begun, but official reports and memoirs continued to complain of inadequate financing and physical facilities, poor teaching, lax standards, vacant chairs due to the dearth of Russian scholars, and a lack of public esteem. Similarly, when Uvarov became president of the Academy of Sciences in 1818, the post had been vacant for eight years and its occupant for the previous eight years, Nicholas Novosiltsev, was apparently too busy with other official duties to pay much heed to those pertaining to the academy. Consequently, the academy was literally in a state of disintegration: two floors of its building on the Neva River had decayed to the point that they were uninhabitable. In startling contrast, the historian Alexander Vucinich, who is generally hostile to Uvarov, concludes that by 1848

the universities were well established as scientific institutions and as organic components of their respective communities, [and] the Academy of Sciences enjoyed a reputation as a great intellectual center recognized by Western scholarship as well as the growing ranks of native intellectuals.[1]

This astonishing transformation was but one aspect of a dramatic explosion of intellectual energy that occurred in the late 1830s and 1840s, the long-awaited blossoming of a national culture. In a variety of fields, for the first time Russians began to make significant and original contributions to world civilization: Pushkin, Lermontov, Gogol, Nekrasov, Dostoevskii, Ivan Turgenev, and Griboedov in literature and drama; Briullov in art; Shchepkin in acting; Glinka in music; Lobachevskii in mathematics; Struve in astronomy; Belinskii in literary criticism; Herzen and Bakunin in revolutionary thought—and these giants were backed by a host of lesser talents. The ranks and interests of the educated public, while still limited, expanded to support a growing number of learned societies, theatres, public lectures, publishing ventures, and schools at all levels. In the private world of the now-famous "circles," the more intense intellectuals heatedly debated German idealist philosophy, French socialism, and Russia's past, present, and future. It was, indeed, "a remarkable decade."

Uvarov thus had the good fortune to preside over the educational ministry when a pride of new and original talent appeared to fill chairs and lecture halls. Furthermore, as Goncharov noted, even the least enlightened members of the upper and middle classes had to accept the fact "that people could not make their way in life—that is, acquire rank, orders of merit and money—except through education."[2]

Encouraging this mood, Uvarov went one step further and made the universities and Academy of Sciences respectable and prestigious, both intellectually and socially, as such institutions had become in Western Europe.[3] His policies served to attract even wealthy aristocrats into the universities. At the same time, a new crop of public-spirited professors forged closer ties with their surrounding communities through "circles," consulting work, and the public lectures that Uvarov mandated as regular features of university life. According to Annenkov, Granovskii's public lectures on history at Moscow University in 1843 attracted "the whole *educated* class of the city, from old men straight from the card tables to young misses still breathless with their success on the dance floor, and from governor's aides to private noblemen."[4] Similarly, as the Academy developed into an eminent center of research, government officials began to turn to its members for advice, and, for the first time in the institution's one-hundred-year history, academicians became numbered among the social elite.

In part, the universities, and to some extent the academy, gained public respect because they were perceived as "cultural oases" or "sanctuaries" for "persecuted ideas." One Soviet scholar concedes that, "despite" a reactionary government, "universities continued to act as centers of scholarship, culture, progress, and enlightenment" but only because "the progressive part of the university professoriate and . . . progressive youth . . . did not allow tsarism to turn the universities into organs of obscurantism." This attribution of power to professors and students hardly seems a likely explanation for conditions under a government widely regarded as a police state, but the "despite thesis" is nearly universal.[5]

Censorship of teaching and research was generally negative. As Isaiah Berlin described it, "The tsarist censorship imposed silence but it did not directly tell professors what to teach." Everyone knew that criticism of throne, altar, or fatherland was not allowed, but the rules were "consistently applied" and there existed no reign of terror or sense of suffocating rigidity until 1848. For instance, the celebrated battle among romantic nationalists, Slavophiles, and Westerners was carried on openly in public lectures, and German idealist philosophy, supposedly anathema to officials, was all the rage in the universities. Enterprising and "daring" games were played with the censorship structure. Annenkov described Granovskii's lectures as a "political event" despite the esoteric topic (the late Merovingian and early Carolingian dynasties) because "of his adroit arrangement designed to skirt areas still not open to free investigation. . . . He said everything that could and should have been said in the name of science and *sketched in* everything that could not yet be said in the simple form of an idea."

Uvarov was as shrewd as anyone and apparently chose deliberately to be lenient in this case; he was known to be a close friend of Granovskii and invited the historian often to his summer home for lengthy vacations. In 1845, right-wing officials denounced Granovskii three times as a man dangerous to the state and religion, but Uvarov protected him.[6] He probably considered these lectures, and others like them, a safety valve for public opinion and a preparation for the "distant" awarding of greater freedom in tsarist Russia.

In general, Uvarov's objective was not to enforce rigidly some ideological orthodoxy, but to stimulate learning. In this regard, the shrewdness in Uvarov's character served the universities well. He believed that they should become institutions dedicated to the teaching and research of all the arts and sciences and that at least some academic freedom was necessary to fulfill this mission, but he also understood the limits of learning in an unlimited autocracy.

University enrollment more than doubled between 1833 and 1848; in order to achieve this growth, Uvarov was obliged continually to assure Nicholas that higher education had been made safe for the autocracy. Since about 1815, European governments, while forced to accept higher education to fill manpower needs, had feared, in Metternich's words, that at universities "a whole generation of revolutionaries could be formed."[7] Indeed, so embedded was the notion of a close relationship between education and revolution that Nicholas's response to the Polish Revolt in 1830 was to close the universities in Vilna and Warsaw; after the outbreak of revolution in Europe in 1848, he threatened to shut down all the universities in the empire. In the time between these two episodes, Uvarov walked a tightrope, balancing the benefits and dangers of higher education.

There is no doubt that inspectors supervised student life in minute detail, and Uvarov made abundantly clear the need for lecturers to treat respectfully Russia's "peculiar institutions." Furthermore, the curriculum was rearranged so as to give it a more practical, less abstract, hence less dangerous orientation. In this way, Uvarov could argue that although all liberal arts, including supposedly dangerous courses in philosophy and classics, were being taught, these subjects represented no threat and indeed would produce the well-informed, decisive intellect the government would like to see among its bureaucrats. Both Nicholas's fears and Uvarov's trust were well founded. As Martin Malia has noted, the best definition of the revolutionary intelligentsia is "student youth trained in the various establishments of the Ministry of National Enlightenment"; Daniel Brower's sample of radicals at mid-century indicates that 62 percent who were active between 1840 and 1855 had received a university education.[8] In far greater numbers, though, the universities produced the loyal statesmen and reformers that were to revitalize the empire in the next reign, at least for a time.

Uvarov gained support for a policy of expansion because it caught the mood of a public—and a tsar—even more hungry for establishing Russia's place in the world. For instance, in areas of strategic importance, such as the sciences, technology, Eastern studies, and jurisprudence, Uvarov intended to create intellectual foundations for teaching and research so that instruction in these fields would reach modern standards and provide the personnel so desperately needed. Four different scholars attest the accomplishment of various parts of this goal: "The 1840s laid the groundwork for the scientific triumphs of the 1860s, the years of Russia's scientific emancipation from the West"; "an intellectual foundation for technology was built" in the first half of the nineteenth century; "from the 1820s to the 1840s a solid scholarly basis for the further development of Russian Eastern studies was created"; "the institutional and educational reforms of the first half of the nineteenth century prepared the way for a fundamental change in the character and attitudes of legal personnel."[9]

Uvarov approached the task of revitalizing Russia's institutions of higher learning with the zeal of a missionary. He sincerely believed that anyone who aspired to sit behind an official desk should first sit on a university bench and that Russia's progress absolutely depended on an aristocracy of knowledge. He also presumed that intellectual quality and the possibilities for expanding educational opportunities would trickle down from the upper to the lower levels of the system. Thus, not only did higher education demand priority in its own right, but its improvement would assure the development of secondary and elementary schools. Finally, since he had spent nearly a lifetime in the ministry, Uvarov knew precisely what he wanted to accomplish in the area of higher education. Within twenty-four hours of becoming minister, he wrote to the local superintendents:

> I trust you will join me in raising the [universities] to the highest possible level and that professors will act in the unifying spirit of Orthodoxy, Autocracy, and Nationality and that each will endeavor to raise the teaching of his subject to the desired perfection, showing constant work and indefatigable diligence toward the education of youth. For my part, turning constant attention to the condition and progress of the [universities], with special pleasure I will take part not only in general administrative measures but also in the individual efforts of each of their members.[10]

Thus, immediately, Uvarov raised the flags of quality, loyalty, and direct control.

UNIVERSITY ADMINISTRATION

UVAROV'S intention to supervise higher education personally manifested itself within one month of his taking office. The School Committee had plodded along since mid-1828 in preparing a university statute to accompany the new regulations it had already effected for primary and secondary education; the final redaction was ready by the summer of 1832. But once Uvarov became minister, he reworked the draft. Indeed, with Nicholas's approval, he shifted the locus of power in the educational ministry from the School Committee, which rapidly became unimportant, to himself and his staff, who now alone formulated policy and projects, although in consultation with superintendents and academic officials. Thus, the final statute for the Great Russian universities of Moscow, Kazan, Kharkov, and St. Petersburg, put into law on July 26, 1835, contained both the fruit of the School Committee's work and Uvarov's own slant.[11] The two other universities, Dorpat and St. Vladimir's in Kiev, warrant separate discussion because of their German and Polish composition.

The fundamental issue facing the School Committee in its deliberations about the universities concerned administration. Few argued for maintaining the 1804 statute's provision for the full retention of autonomy, but, on this question, the university regulations of 1835 went further in the direction of bureaucratic centralization than the 1832 draft.[12] The most important innovation of the 1835 statute—and one that reflected Uvarov's long-held belief in "clear lines of responsibility" and centralized control—was the expanded power of the superintendent of each district. No longer an absentee official residing in the capital, he became the "chief head" of the district schools, formerly under university control, and the district university itself was "entrusted to his special jurisdiction." He held primary responsibility for "bringing the university to a flourishing condition, for strictly observing that all personnel without fail fulfill all the responsibilities of their positions," and for attending to their "ability, morality, and loyalty," Uvarov's favorite trinity of attributes. To implement this general task, the superintendent had the power to reprove or fire "untrustworthy" teachers. He could also chair the university council—composed of the elected rector and the chair-holding full professors—if he so chose and receive its monthly minutes and yearly reports. Other surveillance included the presence of the university lawyer, or syndic, at all council meetings; this official was formerly chosen by the rector from among professors of jurisprudence but was now appointed by the superintendent from the ranks of civil servants.

The principal function of the superintendent within the university was administrative. He chaired a board that the School Committee agreed should handle the budget, maintenance, staff, and paperwork; he thus possessed the ever-awesome power of the purse. But whereas the 1832 draft had suggested that the board be composed only of civil servants, Uvarov added the rector and deans as members. The board also took over the policing functions in the university. The former judicial powers of the university were abrogated as "not in keeping with the general arrangement of the state structure," and professors or students who ran afoul of the law were subject to the authority of the local legal system. In addition, the superintendent, rather than the rector, now chose the student inspector from among bureaucrats rather than professors.

Article 80 of the 1835 statute represented a glaring infringement on academic autonomy, since it allowed the minister, if he found properly qualified candidates, to share the university council's previously exclusive right to appoint professors.[13] Uvarov's action was motivated by the fact that he wanted the power to mold the universities according to his own qualitative plan; in truth, in those institutions where the professors were inferior, they could hardly be expected to select highly qualified colleagues. Uvarov had already used emergency appointive powers to fill all the chairs at St. Vladimir University, which he created in 1833 to replace the one closed at Vilna, and to distribute newly trained scholars throughout the system. He most likely agreed with the Kharkov superintendent who attributed the large number of empty chairs to "the spirit of party and intrigue that so often cripples the activity of learned estates." At Kazan, for instance, in 1834 only eighteen of twenty-eight chairs were filled.[14] Somehow, despite what should have been a chastening experience in St. Petersburg in the 1820s, Uvarov never understood that government power could more quickly "cripple" an institution than professorial pettiness. Nonetheless, when Uvarov asked university councils and the six superintendents for opinions, both groups responded favorably and both showed more concern for improved teaching standards than the question of autonomy.

Despite restrictions intended to bring universities under more direct governmental control, they still enjoyed a decent measure of academic autonomy and respect as learned institutions. As before, faculty meetings determined course distribution and reviewed textbooks, awards, and instructional methods. The council retained strict supervision of the academic sector of the university.[15] Professors retained their privileges of importing materials free of duty or censorship regulations and self-censorship over dissertations, faculty writings, and the publications of the state-supported university press; however, materials used by students in courses were still subject to ministerial approval. Also, although course titles were stipulated, content was not. The university council elected the rector and deans of faculties from among their ranks to four-year terms, subject to confirmation, respectively, by the emperor and minister. The status of the rector was enhanced to include the new power of reprimanding and disciplining professors and even bureaucratic officials if he thought them derelict. Furthermore, of great moment for the future of universities in Russia, professors were relieved of administrative duties—which they had performed poorly anyway—just so they could better carry on research for their scholarship and teaching.[16]

As Rozhdestvenskii has pointed out, on the question of autonomy the 1835 statute fell in a middle ground between the 1804 rules and the blatant, numbing interference that was instituted by the Golitsyn-Magnitskii clique and that only proved academic freedom was largely mythical. Even the liberal historian, V. S. Ikonnikov, conceded that the statute was "more liberal than that of German universities," where all professors were government appointees and lacked freedom from censorship; their vaunted *Lehrfreiheit* and *Lernfreiheit* were dead letters, applying at best to technological research, and in reality Russian professors and students fared better. In France universities, in the sense of learned corporations engaged in teaching and research, did not exist, and officials regarded higher educational institutions merely as "agents of the state that granted certificates and degrees" to prospective civil servants.[17]

In general, until disaster struck in 1848, Russian universities fared well under their new statute. Count Sergei Stroganov, the superintendent of the Moscow district, ruled like a "despot," but a benevolent one, and the university enjoyed its golden age. Incidentally, Uvarov and Stroganov hated each other; neither strong personality could abide taking advice from the other, and each took credit for Moscow's successes. At Kazan, the superintendent until 1845, Musin-Pushkin, was described as an uncouth "fool" whose only interest, as a former colonel in the Hussars, lay in discipline; but he allowed the rector, Lobachevskii, who served from 1827 to 1846, a free hand to turn the university into a first-rate institution. At St.

Petersburg another dunce, although a nice fellow, Dondukov-Korsakov, was called the "beloved superintendent," again because he rarely interfered in university matters, and the institution entered a period of "startling growth" and "general prosperity." In Kharkov the university, which in 1834 showed "all the signs of moral decay," was slowly but not completely restored under the leadership of a well-educated martinet, I. A. Golovkin. "In the second quarter of the nineteenth century," the French scholar Alain Besançon asserted, the Russian universities "were not far at all" from being among the best in Europe.[18]

With or without a benevolent administration, the four Great Russian universities would have remained intellectual backwaters if forced to remain at their 1834 budget level of 645,900 rubles. The School Committee unanimously agreed that the government should increase expenditures by 200 to 300 percent but met resistance from the grim financial minister, Kankrin, a notorious fiscal conservative. Nonetheless, Uvarov persevered and won an allotment of 1,466,450 rubles; this figure included a tripling of funds for the two weakest institutions, Kharkov and Kazan. The first priority was raising faculty salaries and pensions in order to attract qualified people. Because of the higher cost of living in the capitals, professors' salaries went from 3,000 to 5,000 rubles in Moscow and St. Petersburg but only to 4,000 in the other cities; and Uvarov then forbade, except with special permission, the common practice of holding several posts simultaneously. Physical facilities, laboratories, libraries, and university presses were all marked for expansion. For example, the number of volumes in the four university libraries, with a tenfold increase in funds, nearly doubled between 1834 and 1848; at St. Petersburg University the numismatic collection rose from 205 to 2,772 pieces while the chemistry collection expanded by 2,443 items; 9,170 minerals were added to the laboratory in Moscow; at Kazan, the physics and chemistry laboratory, an observatory, an anatomical theatre, a clinic, and a botanical garden were either refurbished or built, all in Uvarov's favorite Corinthian style.[19]

While enrollment in the four Great Russian universities rose from 1,295 to 2,746 during Uvarov's ministry and, if St. Vladimir and Dorpat Universities are included, from 1,834 to 4,006, the increase represented only a modest gain given the manpower needs of the state. By comparison, for instance, German universities, in 1845, enrolled 11,800 students or .34 per 1,000 population, while the Russian ratio was .075. Clear financial and political reasons accounted for this slow growth. Uvarov could squeeze very little more from the state budget, and soon it failed to cover even maintenance costs and Uvarov felt compelled to introduce tuition. Also, Nicholas would hardly condone large increases in expenditures to support growth in university enrollments, given his ambivalent position on the uses and abuses of higher education. Furthermore, beginning in the 1830s, after two decades of university expansion, officials in England, France, and

Germany perceived an "excess of educated men" and cut back enrollment for fear of creating an "intellectual proletariat" among dissatisfied junior civil servants and other graduates. In 1847, Uvarov expressed the fear that unless educated young people were quickly absorbed into the Table of Ranks, they would become part of "a caste already numerous among us, of people without a past or future, who have their own peculiar orientation and distinctly resemble the proletariat. . . ."[20] Consequently, even if resources had been available, Uvarov probably would still have chosen his usual policy of "constant but slow development."

UNIVERSITY FACULTIES

THE single most important action taken to prepare the renaissance of Russia's universities was the establishment of the Professors' Institute at Dorpat University. Universal agreement existed among School Committee members that both the quality of instruction and the number of native teachers had to be raised. At first, the universities had relied upon invited foreigners, but language barriers and national pride precluded the continuation of this system. With success, the government, until the Golitsyn era, had sent some students abroad to train as professors, but the problem remained that Russian universities were not preparing their own future teachers. The combined result of these circumstances was either aging and often incompetent staffs or severe understaffing.

In 1827, the School Committee, with Nicholas's blessing, authorized the Professors' Institute. The starting enrollment of twenty would include the most promising students from each of the universities. Those selected were to earn their doctoral degrees by studying for two years at Dorpat University, which, because of its location in the German-speaking Baltic provinces, had achieved high standards by drawing upon the services of the neighboring German scholarly community. The students were next to study in Paris or Berlin for two years to perfect their specialities, and then to return to Russia to serve as professors for a minimum of twelve years. Typically, Nicholas sent the first class off to Dorpat with the command, "Return Russians!" The experiment proved an unqualified success. The two sets of institute graduates, those enrolled in 1828 and 1832, produced twenty-two first-rate professors in a variety of specialities, and each university dated its revitalization from the time these young men entered the lecture halls. One student at Kharkov noted:

The year 1835 was remarkable in the history of Kharkov University: some kind of rejuvenation was experienced. The various faculties received fresh, young forces, new people returning from abroad, where they were sent by the minister to finish their education.[21]

In this way, Uvarov obtained the native scholars with which to build higher education in Russia.

The institute closed its doors in 1838, because by that time Uvarov had concluded, with some patriotism and self-congratulation, that Russian universities, now "renewed and reformed," were capable of "preparing their own future teachers" and possessed "an independent scholarly class" whose "intellectual activities were free from the influence of foreign systems and examples." Nonetheless, Uvarov continued to encourage professors and doctoral students to study abroad.

> These scholarly journeys of young people serve as a continuous and living link between learning in the Fatherland and the development of the arts and sciences in Europe and constantly raise the Russian scholarly class and Russian universities to the high level of knowledge of people who formerly outstripped us on the path of education.

On the average, each university had two of its members studying abroad at government expense each year of Uvarov's ministry; roughly half the projects were in the humanities and half in the sciences. Indeed, there emerged a pattern by the late 1830s of students' receiving at least an undergraduate degree in Russia and then spending two or three years in Europe for doctoral or postdoctoral work. In 1844 passport fees, which had just been raised, were waived for university personnel, and in 1846 study abroad began to count as time in civil service so that it would not hold back promotion and retirement.[22]

To improve the quality of teaching and also to assure the greatest proportion of "native Russians" among faculty members, Uvarov forced the retirement of older teachers. In 1833, he clarified regulations that a professor had to retire, although with full salary, after twenty-five years of service, unless the university council or minister granted an exemption. The 1835 statute demanded that full professors possess doctoral degrees and allowed one year for those who were already employed but did not hold doctorates to defend publicly a dissertation, although they were not obliged to undergo preliminary examinations. Nikitenko noted that thirteen professors at St. Petersburg University quickly found themselves out of a job because of the "purification system" designed to rid the universities of incompetents. In a reversal that made this intention clear, in 1839, since vacancies continued to plague the system, a special rank of *dotsent* was created for young native Russians who had not yet completed the doctoral degree but were still able to perform the teaching duties of an adjunct professor. Student memoirs recorded relief at being freed from doddering, old-fashioned teachers who read lectures in a monotone directly from books and, in paternalistic fashion, addressed students in a familiar, often disrespectful, fashion. By the 1840s, at Kazan, only five of thirty-eight full professors were holdovers; three-quarters of the faculty members were new at St. Petersburg; foreign professors dropped from 39 to 13 percent of the faculty at Kharkov; and sixty-six new, young professors had taken up duties at Moscow University.[23]

Uvarov's main achievement in regard to the universities was enhancing their function as true institutions of higher learning while still accommodating "the needs of the state" and the "views of the government." Although the 1835 statute abandoned the encyclopedic curriculum of the past, students in each of the three faculties were still required to take "core courses," especially in national subjects such as Russian history and literature, in order to produce well-rounded and patriotic citizens. The statute also provided for a new, separate chair in theology, church history, and law, courses made mandatory for all the Orthodox as yet another guarantee of turning out loyal subjects. Non-Orthodox were exempt from these courses, and there were no religious qualifications for admission. At any rate, the direction of the statute was not unusual. For instance, at "Oxbridge," students were expected to leave the university with "a respect for and a love of English traditions, and an abiding sense of moral responsibility, particularly to the state and the Church, involving active participation in the service of each."[24]

The Philosophical Faculty: Division of History and Philology

Uvarov worked hard to develop every facet of the university curriculum, but the innovations that Pogodin thought would make him "immortal" were in the area of Russian and Slavic studies.[25] The 1835 statute provided for new departments in Russian history, Russian language and literature, and the comparative history and literature of Slavic peoples; none of these fields, astonishingly, had before been deemed worthy of an independent chair.

The history and literature professors of the 1830s and 1840s were profoundly affected by the new interest throughout Europe in "scientific" history based on the study of original documents. Systematic research was made possible because the Academy of Sciences, again under Uvarov's zealous patronage, began unearthing and publishing the country's rich archival lodes. Although all scholars agreed on the need for organizing research materials, the varying interpretations of documents led to the lively quarreling so typical of the "remarkable decade." Michael Kachenovskii of Moscow University founded the "skeptical school" of Russian historians and questioned the authenticity of such early (pre-1200) works as "Russian Justice" and "The Lay of Prince Igor" (still a subject of controversy). Offended, Pogodin, the first holder of the chair in Russian history at Moscow, mercilessly attacked his colleague and upheld the theory of the Varangian origins of the state found in those early documents. He even criticized the nearly sacred works of Karamzin on the ground that he had slighted Peter, who was the founder of modern Russia and who was idolized by Pogodin, and many other dynastic and romantic nationalists, as the engineer of "the most radical, wide, and prolonged revolution in history." Pogodin, although a serious scholar and not a sycophant, also won official plaudits for his intense nationalism, his support of throne and altar, and his belief that history should serve as the "preserver and guardian of social tranquility"; in 1835, he authored an official text on Russian history for the gymnasia.[26]

Nicholas Ustrialov, the most prominent historian at St. Petersburg University and one of Uvarov's "discoveries," also supported Pogodin's views. In 1836, he published his dissertation, *A Pragmatic System of Russian History*, which proposed to demonstrate the influence of one event upon another with a discussion of the reasons for and consequences of these events in contemporary terms, and to explain how and why Russia had developed into her present structure. The themes Ustrialov postulated were consistent with official ideology: as compared with the West, Russia had developed "under completely different principles and under the influence of different circumstances"; Orthodoxy and Autocracy were responsible for her greatness.[27]

Ustrialov was asked by Uvarov to write the official history text for the universities, and he became the historian laureate of the empire. Uvarov commented that, whereas previously Russian history had been treated in a "one-sided and old-fashioned manner," Ustrialov's text served the dual need of "bringing historical science to the attention of youth" and "leading them harmoniously and safely to the central results of the history of the Fatherland." While Russian history professors were expected to teach "according to Ustrialov's plan," they embellished it with their own perspectives. A. I. Stavrovskii of St. Vladimir's, for instance, supplemented it with readings from Polevoi's *History of the Russian People*, even though Uvarov naturally found the latter work suspect; P. P. Gulak-Artemovskii of Kharkov, the university catering to the Ukrainian provinces, added lectures on local culture.[28]

Although Uvarov lent support and protection to strongly nationalistic professors, he equally applauded the work of Granovskii, with whom they incessantly argued because of his view that Russia was more a part of Western civilization and "liberal" progress than they cared to believe. What especially irked Pogodin and Shevyrev was that Granovskii's public lectures made him an idol in society and were far more popular than theirs—even though, they complained, he said "little about Orthodoxy" and "exalt[ed] the West." Solov'ev and K. D. Kavelin joined the Moscow faculty in the mid-1840s, and their more "scientific" investigation of Russia's past eventually became the principal models for historians, although they offered little in the way of new interpretations.[29]

The professors who held chairs in Russian literature generally upheld the patriotic view that their field also should support the existing state and thus should "include all that directly leads man to this civic purpose"; nonetheless, this inclination did not prevent them from teaching or doing research as serious scholars. Neither Pletnev at St. Petersburg, Shevyrev at Moscow, nor G. S. Suvortsov at Kazan could be called literary hacks of the Bulgarin-Grech school. Indeed Shevyrev, working together with academician Alexander Vostokov, laid the scholarly foundations for the historical and comparative study of Russian literature.[30]

In the infant field of comparative Slavic studies, it was clear that "a new generation [of scholars] had to be prepared." Uvarov sent Pogodin, F. I. Buslaev, and O. M. Bodianskii of Moscow, P. I. Preis and P. A. Kulish of St. Petersburg, I. I. Sreznevskii of Kharkov, and V. I. Grigorovich of Kazan to visit, for as long as five years in some cases, all the Slavic countries as well as to study under foremost Slavicists throughout the capitals of Europe, including P. J. Šafařik, F. L. Čelakovsky, and V. V. Hanka; Uvarov's interest in the field led him to carry on a lengthy correspondence with Hanka. The minister sent off Sreznevskii with the admonition: "Work, young man! Know that every step of yours not only can, but should have an impact on the next generation." These pioneers more than repaid Uvarov's confidence through their publications, teaching, and inspiration of students. For instance, Sreznevskii earned the first Russian doctorate in Slavic-Russian philology and wrote 300 works in his lifetime, while Buslaev taught the first Russian courses in the comparative grammar of Indo-European languages. Uvarov justified his promotion of Slavic studies as an additional means for "fathoming *Russian narodnost'*," in order to "give more vigor to the Russian spirit." At the same time, however, it had the unintended result of awakening Pan-Slav or Ukrainian separatist feelings detrimental to the imperial ideal. Nonetheless, Uvarov had successfully nurtured a school of self-sustaining scholarship in the field.[31]

In general, Uvarov had to guarantee publicly and to the tsar the "safety" of subjects taught, especially in the sensitive historical-philological section of the philosophical faculty. Chairs in philosophy, Roman and Greek culture, and political economy and statistics were all considered "dangerous"—as evidenced by their curtailment after 1848—but without them a university would not be worthy of its name. By law, the ministry controlled what was taught only through its system of surveillance and its stipulation of course titles. In addition, Uvarov used the educational journal as a device both to influence the content of courses and to cut off potential criticism of them as dangerous.

In particular, many prominent Russians, heirs of the antireform nexus, regarded the teaching of philosophy with deep suspicion, since it conjured up the ghosts of Rousseau, the philosophes, and the French Revolution. In 1827, Magnitskii subjected the School Committee to a strongly worded memorandum, once again warning of an intellectual apocalypse if rationalist philosophy should gain entrance into the university curriculum. Lieven and Uvarov dismissed the declamation out of hand, although Novosiltsev thought the curriculum should perhaps exclude Kant, Fichte, and Schelling—because they were boring. The 1835 statute placed no official limits on teaching philosophy, for which it established a chair and after which it named the faculty of liberal arts and sciences. But, at least in Uvarov's eyes, a public relations campaign was required in support of the discipline, and he waged this campaign in the educational journal for a year before the statute was issued. Professor A. A. Fisher of St. Petersburg University echoed Uvarov's contention that it was "false patriotism" to think that a truly national, Orthodox education necessitated the negation of European ideas and, because of their often revolutionary results, to consider philosophy "empty and fruitless," a "destructive force of pseudo-education" or an "empty dream." Instead, philosophy could serve to support throne and altar.

To alleviate any remaining fears of philosophy, Abbé Bautain's *De l'enseignement de la philosophie au dix-neuvième siècle* was endorsed by Uvarov as a university textbook. Bautain attacked all contemporary philosophical schools as godless because they neglected their true basis in Christian religion and Revelation. The rector of Kharkov University, I. Kroneberg, continued this theme by claiming that the history of philosophy was dangerous and "banal" because it became involved in political questions, whereas pure philosophy "aspired to religion." Taught in its latter mode, philosophy confirmed in students "a holy respect for religion, a firm belief in the monarch, and an unconditional obedience to existing laws." From one point of view, attitudes like Magnitskii's triumphed: university teaching of philosophy generally became the province of clergymen who concentrated upon the theological ramifications of their subject. On the other hand, they lost their audience.[32]

Beginning in the 1820s, Russian intellectuals, especially in Moscow, became absorbed in German idealist philosophy and avidly discussed the ideas of Kant, Fichte, Schelling, and then Hegel. Lecture halls were not immune. Professors, recognizing the old-fashioned bent of the teaching of philosophy, brought the subject into their own classes and continued its discussion in "evenings" held with students. Thus, M. G. Pavlov expounded Schelling's *Naturphilosophie* from his chair in agronomy while "la mode hégélienne" nearly "dominated" the university in the 1840s and structured the lectures, for instance, of Granovskii, Peter Redkin, Nikita Krylov, and Kavelin in history and law. In literature, Davydov introduced students to "all the philosophers." In the early 1840s, he wrote an article eulogizing

German idealist philosophy. He focused especially on Hegel, by then the student favorite, but warned that Russians should not regard Hegel's system as "the final word." Taking the historicist view, Davydov maintained that each people created its own laws, science, art, and philosophy as a "consequence" of its national life; and soon Russia would have its own Schelling and its own Hegel. The article constituted a neat defense of both the principle of nationality and the study of philosophy.[33]

Although the classics had always formed part of the university curriculum, Uvarov, as could be expected, wished to provide further encouragement for classical scholarship. At his insistence, two chairs in each university were devoted to Latin and Greek culture. To offset the lingering association of classics with republics, revolution, or lack of utility, three articles in the educational journal defended their inclusion. Kroneberg wondered how an educated man could ignore the accomplishments of the ancients as well as their "role as an instrument for the education of mind and taste." Snegirev of Moscow University stressed that study of classical culture "contains in itself all science, all art, political history, mythology, and literature." M. Rozberg got more to the point when he advised a religious spirit in approaching classical knowledge so that republican ideas would not capture the imagination of the young.

In a more positive vein, Uvarov sought to increase the competence of both secondary school and university teachers in the classics by publishing lengthy articles on the topic in nearly every issue of the educational journal. University teaching of the classics at Moscow and Kharkov was enhanced by two alumni of the Professors' Institute. Kriukov, who was "under the influence of Hegel," acquainted students at Moscow with ancient history and "all new ideas," while A. O. Valitskii, heralded as one of the best teachers at Kharkov, held "evenings" for students.[34]

The Juridical Faculty

One of the major functions of the universities was to provide the cadre of trained officials so sorely needed in the central and especially provincial bureaucracies. Indeed, in 1836, amid much grumbling, university graduates had to serve three years in a provincial post before being allowed to take a position in the more attractive capitals. Both Alexander I and Nicholas I dreamed of instituting a *Rechsstaat*, but, as Speranskii often pointed out, an efficient administration based on rule of law required educated men who understood and were prepared to apply the laws. To provide this first step became the function of the new juridical faculty. Formerly, the study of law had been subsumed in the moral-political division of the university. In that division, as the name implied, instruction stressed the historical and philosophical foundations of law and its general guiding principles, with little attention to Russian law. In contrast, the new program had a more functional slant, centering around the statutory details of Russian civic, financial, criminal, police, and administrative laws. Some scholars have rued the apparent shift from educating students of law to turning out technocrats. However, charges of such a major change are only in part true, because the faculty also included chairs in Roman, international, and encyclopedic law, and students took a whole range of core courses in the first year. Nonetheless, the curriculum was indeed designed to meet the practical needs of the state. In addition to the university faculties, Uvarov reorganized three provincial lycées (the Richelieu in Odessa, the Prince Bezborodko in Nezhin, the Demidov in Iaroslavl) so that they had a clear concentration in Russian law. The School of Jurisprudence in the capital, founded by Prince Peter Oldenburg in 1835 under the auspices of the ministry of justice, proved another successful source of well-trained administrators.[35]

From a political standpoint, government officials considered the more practical university curriculum more "safe." Nicholas especially feared abstract concepts of justice because, with their dissemination, "not rarely are born new theories about the structure and direction of the state." Pursuing this theme, the statistician V. P. Androssov in 1834 supported the notion that juridical courses should deal with practical application of law rather than toy with "metaphysical fanaticism." Three years later, Professor A. V. Ivanovskii of St. Petersburg University reiterated: "The beginning of reform belongs exclusively to the government; it is for private individuals only to use every strength and all possible zeal to assist in its noble vision." Without the unifying force of the autocracy, reform would scatter in a "thousand different directions." These statements, of course, reflected Uvarov's viewpoint as well.[36]

Despite the prevalence of such opinions and the practical drift of statutory regulations, dissonant voices were heard in the lecture halls. Like other faculties, that of jurisprudence received its lifeblood from teachers educated abroad. In 1828 and 1829, Speranskii, recognizing the lack of professors trained in Russian law, took twelve students under his charge, made them interns in the Second Section of His Majesty's Own Chancery, which was working on the codification of laws, and had them take courses at St. Petersburg University. He then sent them to study in Berlin under Friederich Savigny, the famous exponent of the historicist school of jurisprudence, where the majority became Hegelians as well. Upon their return in 1832 and 1834, just as the new juridical faculties were being set up, these men received the doctorate and were assigned to various universities, forming the first corps of Russian law professors. Because of their excellence, this group provided a solid basis for the future development of the legal profession and legal studies in Russia.

As Richard Wortman's study has pointed out, the new professors "regarded the law in exalted terms." They instilled in their students "the notion of the high calling of the legal official" and, therefore, a desire to change the existing legal system, which was so clearly incompatible with their ideals. Redkin of Moscow University, a charismatic lecturer whose courses were filled with "liberalism," told students their vocation was to defend justice in Russia and to elevate legislation "to universal principles of law." Krylov, also of Moscow, became the first scholar to develop "a philosophical approach to early Russian legal institutions." Krylov criticized serfdom, as did Tikhon Stepanov, the eminent professor of political economy at Kharkov University, as well as a syndic and dean, who took a generally unfavorable attitude toward the status quo. P. I. Meier, in courses on Russian civic law at Kazan University, stated flatly: "It is clear that freedom must be given the serfs." At St. Petersburg, Professor V. S. Poroshin's lectures contained a good deal of sympathy for socialist economics. The upshot of all this, again according to Wortman, was that a new type of official trained in the law and critical of the existing order emerged from the juridical faculties of universities and later engineered the Great Reforms.[37]

The Philosophical Faculty: Division of Physics and Mathematics

The second section of the philosophical faculty, the physical-mathematical, profited from the fact that Uvarov possessed a deliberate policy in regard to the sciences and technology. He believed that the educational system had the responsibility for making the "first assault" and providing the "intellectual capital" for answering the "needs of *handicraft, factory*, and *agricultural industries*." To this end, the 1835 statute expanded the curriculum at each university to include the study of agronomy, forestry, technology, and architecture. The new budget allotted the substantial amount of money required to erect or furnish modern laboratories and libraries, to import the equipment needed for teaching and research, and to finance travel abroad for professors and students so that they could become aware of the latest theories and techniques.[38]

A modest basis for scientific study had been developing since the eighteenth century, but in the 1830s and 1840s there emerged an unprecedented and powerful confluence of public interest, government support, and native talent. Kazan University, overcoming its distant location and past history of poor administration, developed in a spectacular fashion. Lobachevskii, who never studied beyond its walls, became the greatest mathematician Russia ever produced and the world's leading pioneer in non-Euclidian geometry.

Under his leadership and with the new chemistry laboratory mandated by the 1835 statute, Kazan, which had not even had a chemistry professor before 1832, developed a superb "school" that won an "honored place" for Russian chemistry in Europe; in addition, its physics laboratory became one of the best on the continent. Karl Klaus, for two decades beginning in 1832, attracted students to his courses in inorganic chemistry and achieved renown for his discovery of the element ruthenium. In the 1840s, N. N. Zinin's "model" lectures, filled with observations on the philosophical ramifications of chemistry, also inspired a large following. His most important scientific achievement was to reduce aniline from nitrobenzene, thus making possible the industrial production of drugs and dyes; his work on explosives attracted the attention of Alfred Nobel, whom he subsequently tutored. Although Zinin was stolen away by St. Petersburg University and the Medical-Surgical Academy in 1847, the Kazan School of Chemistry continued to prosper. Kazan also published an excellent scientific journal, established with Uvarov's patronage in the 1830s.[39]

Moscow, at once the oldest, largest, and most intellectually exciting of the universities, had the surest foundation in science and technology by the 1830s. Because of its location near the industrial centers of the empire, since the turn of the century it had encouraged a practical orientation in its science curriculum, and its professors contributed to industrial and agricultural development as well as writing for popular or student consumption. R. G. Heimann, for instance, emphasized technological and industrial applications in his chemistry courses, advised the government, created a laboratory in the late 1830s used by factory owners, supervised a private plant that produced stearine candles, delivered widely attended public lectures on technical chemistry, and also wrote a textbook on applied chemistry. His colleague A. A. Ivovskii published a basic treatise on analytical chemistry that established a native vocabulary for the field. M. F. Spasskii, who experimented with heat, light, and electricity, made significant contributions to the fields of geophysics and climatology. D. M. Perevoshchikov, who worked principally in applied mathematics, authored a mathematical encyclopedia as well as two textbooks in astronomy. His more famous colleague N. D. Brashman pioneered in the field of practical mechanics and developed a course—one of only four in Europe—on the subject. Brashman's student A. S. Ershov adapted the subject even more closely to the needs of Russian factories and advised the government on machine production.

In contrast to its practical bent, Moscow University also became known as the leading exponent of Schelling's *Naturphilosophie*, which emphasized the search for metaphysical truths, rather than experimentation, as a means of attempting to answer the riddle of the universe and provide its theoretical unity. Pavlov, the pioneering agronomist, injected philosophy into his lectures to such a degree that Herzen attended regularly even though he was thoroughly bored by agricultural science. Pavlov's best student, Ia. A. Linovskii, like his mentor, wrote textbooks, specialized in the development of experimental farms and soil reclamation, and in 1846 created an agricultural laboratory at the university that became a model of its kind; neither agronomist saw any intrinsic contradiction between experimentation and Schelling's philosophy.

The fashionable condescension toward experimentation reached its peak in 1836 with D. M. Vellanskii's heralded textbook on physiology, the first in Russia. He taught at the Moscow Medical-Surgical Academy, soon joined to the university, and expounded strict Schellingianism. Nicholas Pirogov, an 1828 graduate, recalled: "I received a physician's diploma and had mastery over life and death without ever having seen a single typhus patient and without ever having had a lancet in my hands!" Pirogov went on to attend the Professors' Institute; he became a renowned anatomist and surgeon and a pioneer in Russian medical practice.

In the same year as Vellanskii's triumph, a younger professor at the university, A. M. Filomafitskii, who had also studied at the Professors' Institute, published a textbook that championed experimental physiology and led to the demise of *Naturphilosophie* at the same time the trend was being reversed in the rest of Europe. Like their counterparts in the West, Russian researchers returned to the experimental method, but with a Schellingian heritage of healthy respect for theory; this combination laid the foundations for modern developments in the sciences. This movement, by the way, paralleled developments in the social sciences that led away from Hegelianism to a stress on archival work.[40]

Despite its youth, St. Petersburg University in the late 1830s managed to surpass Moscow in the fields of mathematics, physics, and chemistry, because of both its location and Uvarov's nurturing of the institution to which he gave birth. In 1835, he recruited the brilliant Heinrich Lenz of Dorpat University to become a member of the Academy of Sciences and a professor at St. Petersburg University, where he founded a school of physics. As a dean and then rector, Lenz created a laboratory, developed public lectures, encouraged scientific organizations, inspired students to study the sciences, and wrote two textbooks. As a scholar, he was peerless in the fields of electricity and physical geography.

The mathematics department at St. Petersburg counted three men of international reputation: Victor Buniakovskii built computing instruments and developed the theory of probability and applied it to demographic trends and insurance and banking statistics; Pafnuti Chebyshev performed important work in prime numbers, worked on devices to transform motion, and applied the theory of probability to recruitment and insurance rates; O. I. Somov studied elliptic functions and wrote the first Russian study of this branch of calculus. In other areas, A. A. Voskresenskii was dubbed the "grandfather of Russian chemistry" because of his large student following; he pioneered in the analysis of Russian coal deposits and the application of chemistry to agriculture. S. M. Usov—the one scholar of those mentioned besides Lobachevskii who received his education only in Russia—

taught scientific agriculture and technology, constructed model farms, edited industrial and agricultural journals, managed a factory, and advised government agencies.[41]

In the study and teaching of science and technology, St. Petersburg University had the advantage of being able to draw upon the resources of a host of institutes in the capital, such as the Academy of Sciences, the Medical-Surgical Academy, the Mining Institute, the Institute of Transport Engineers, and the higher-level military schools. In addition, during the reign, various ministries sponsored the creation of the Michael Artillery School (1830), the first schools in civil engineering and architecture (1830 and 1832), the first agricultural college, named the Gorygoretsk Institute (1836), and the first technological institute (1828), one of the world's earliest. The mere attempt to coordinate higher education with the technological needs of the state and with the demands of modern science placed Russia in the forefront of this movement in Europe, second only to Prussia. Indeed, England, despite its industrial preeminence, made no effort until the 1870s to bring education into line with scientific and technological developments; and France, by 1840, had ceded her leading position in science to Prussia because of the failure of her educational system to modernize in this direction.[42]

In addition, Uvarov sought to attract general interest in the sciences by sponsoring public lectures at the universities as well as in major cities where no institute of higher education existed. For monetary assistance, he enlisted the support of the ministries of finance and of state domains; he also devised strict regulations so that study of the sciences would bring no "moral harm." Each year in his official report, Uvarov proudly boasted of his ministry's efforts to spread knowledge "in keeping with the needs of the time" in such diverse areas as paleontology, agronomy, practical mechanics, applied chemistry, geometry, astronomy, and bookkeeping. Lecture series at Dorpat, Uvarov reported, attracted about 350 auditors yearly, mostly artisans. In Moscow, Heimann delivered an annual set of lectures on technical chemistry for eighteen years. He was a gifted popularizer and his audience grew to 500, including nobility, factory managers, merchants, and "even peasants." According to Herzen, K. F. Rouillier's lectures on animal psychology helped transform attitudes toward education; Rouillier also earned a place among the precursors of Darwin by questioning the immutability of the species. In St. Petersburg, Lenz taught physics and electromagnetics, accompanying his lectures with experiments. His colleague S. S. Kutorga, another product of the Professors' Institute, became a great popularizer in each of the varied fields that he embraced; in particular, the geological trips he conducted through the St. Petersburg area attracted large numbers of participants.[43]

Public lectures enabled the universities to become centers for the dissemination of knowledge in their communities and to gain increased recognition for their value to society. Even in regard to the sciences, however, suspicion lingered as to their "safety." Investigation of natural causality, for instance, in the newer fields of geology and physiology, might leave scant room for a Creator. In 1835, in the educational journal, Kutorga felt the need to defend science against charges of materialism. He did so by contending that the scientist came particularly close to God because his study of nature gave him a sense of wonder and led him to approach his Creator with "humility and love." In 1840, in a lead article in the journal, V. F. Fedorov of St. Vladimir University stated that it was the Christian scientist's duty "to expose the false opinion of those who oppose the truths of the Christian religion to the truths of science."[44]

Besides attending lectures, the general public demonstrated its new and growing interest in science and technology by joining learned societies in which amateurs and scholars cooperated to make contacts with similar groups abroad, to expand the number of Russians engaged in scientific pursuits, to explore Russia's resources, and to disseminate knowledge through their publications. The number of societies was far below those in Germany, where Berlin alone counted twenty-five scientific societies as opposed to seventeen in Russia as a whole; Bavaria had a membership of 18,000 in agricultural societies while Russia had only 1,175. Nonetheless, according to Vucinich, the learned societies in Russia represented a "grass-roots movement clamoring for—and supporting—the idea of Russia's national independence in the world of science," and they helped "science achieve an honored place in Russian culture." In general, they present yet another witness to the intellectual explosion of the 1830s and 1840s and the growth of a technical and scientific intelligentsia. In addition, the most popular journals of the era, the *Reader's Library* (1834–1865) and *Notes of the Fatherland* (1839–1884) carried regular and long sections on science, agriculture, and industry, as did the educational journal, which also proselytized concerning Russia's need to develop manufacturing and trade.[45]

During the 1830s and 1840s about 16 percent of those undergraduates who enrolled or graduated were in the physics-mathematics divisions of their universities; this proportion may seem small, but it is the same as that for American universities in the 1970s. In general, students preferred the juridical or medical faculty, indeed the areas also of the government's greatest manpower shortage. In the next reign more interest in the sciences would develop, and the government meanwhile had already laid the groundwork to cultivate and satisy it. Vucinich and Blackwell noted that because of the "comprehensive and up-to-date training" provided by the universities, these institutions "laid the indispensable foundations for the training of Russian scholars and for a triumphant emancipation of Russian sciences during the 1860s."[46]

The Medical Faculty

The 1835 statute provided for medical faculties at each university except St. Petersburg; the capital already was the site of the Medical-Surgical Academy. Like instruction in so many other fields, medical education in Russia in the 1830s and 1840s underwent a slow transformation during which it freed itself from foreign tutelage, began to produce its own professional leaders, and thus "prepared" itself for making "substantial contributions to science." The School Committee considered the expansion of medical education a primary goal of the university statute, but Uvarov, as minister, personally argued the case for increasing the number of chairs in the medical faculty to ten and for awarding 180 scholarships for advanced study in newly created medical institutes. His personal concern may have stemmed from his relief work during the cholera epidemics of the previous decade, when dreadful mortality rates caused fear and peasant riots and demonstrated that there was a "tragic" shortage of medical personnel.[47] Nicholas supported Uvarov's plan because he saw it as helping to provide for the medical needs of his beloved military.

Uvarov's efforts in regard to medical education were characteristic. Both in 1838 and 1845, stiff new regulations were promulgated for the certification of doctors, pharmacists, veterinarians, dentists, and midwives, thus causing a drastic, although short-lived, drop in the number of degrees awarded; for instance, after 1845, 50 percent fewer diplomas were granted to general practitioners. In 1840, Uvarov established a Temporary Medical Commission to assist him in future planning. Subsequently, proposals were adopted to increase the number of chairs and scholarship students and improve the civil service privileges of medical personnel. In that same year, for administrative efficiency, the medical-surgical academies in Vilna and Moscow, formerly under the jurisdiction of the ministry of internal affairs, were incorporated into the medical faculties at St. Vladimir and Moscow Universities, respectively. The commission worked to establish a "model" clinic at Moscow in the old academy building and erect the most modern medical facilities possible at St. Vladimir's; both schools were to rival "the contemporary status of medical sciences in Europe." By 1846, Uvarov announced that medical education in Russia was on a level of "real excellence." In addition, a new pharmacy institute was established at Dorpat in 1842 and programs were developed for veterinary institutes at both Dorpat and Kharkov.

Despite these general improvements, the major center of teaching and research in these fields, and a notorious pirate of university talent, remained the capital's Medical-Surgical Academy, founded by Emperor Paul in 1798 and still administered by the ministry of internal affairs. In general, Russia long remained behind Western European countries in medical services. For instance, in 1882: Italy numbered one doctor per 2,280 people and Russia one per 18,000; England had one military surgeon per 3,118 population and Russia one per 12,400; Prussia counted one hospital for every 22,000 people and Russia one for every 176,000.[48] But, as in so many other areas, a start had been made.

THE UNIVERSITIES AND STUDENTS

BECAUSE of the ever-lingering identification of students with revolutionaries, universities were always obliged, above all else, to guarantee political reliability. In his annual report for 1836, Uvarov noted the expansion of the student body but quickly added that discipline and surveillance saved this group from the "contagion" infecting the younger generation in other states. Furthermore, he attested, the 1830 Revolution in Europe served as a "strong lesson" for inculcating into students the primary principle of "unlimited devotion to the government and laws of the land."[49] Besides being influenced by political considerations, universities (in Russia as elsewhere, generally until the 1960s) considered themselves *in loco parentis* and disciplined students accordingly. For both these reasons, a new university bureaucracy was established in Nicholaevan Russia that closely kept watch over student behavior and even appearance.

Nicholas in fact paid inordinate attention to student appearance. Having the soul of a drill sergeant, he somehow believed that if students were "pulled up and buttoned up," they would march in step. Consequently, although the wearing of uniforms had been required but not really enforced since 1804, the first piece of educational legislation under Nicholas insisted upon dress codes, at lectures and in public, including regulations for the length of hair; even parade uniforms were issued, along with nine pages of regulations that set up protocol for marching. Indeed, when the tsar visited universities, he seemed to notice little else except dress and social behavior. In 1840 at St. Vladimir's, he was displeased with the "external appearance" of students who, in further proof of their lack of morality, could not dance or fence well; additional funds were quickly allotted for these optional subjects, as well as gymnastics. *Soirées* were arranged in dormitories to accustom students to "society." At Moscow, the best of the universities, Nicholas was disgusted with the ragged look of students, and the rector had to explain apologetically that many were aspiring doctors from the lower orders. But at Kharkov, the weakest of the institutions, he was delighted because the young men there looked like "born cuirassiers." Despite Nicholas's rationale, many students liked the uniform because it provided a sense of *esprit de corps* and of the new dignity of their calling, and also lessened the differences between the rich and the poor. Furthermore, the navy-blue outfits were quite handsome, complete with gold buttons, sewn gold buttonholes, and three-cornered hats.[50]

By the terms of the 1804 statute, students were answerable for their conduct only to professor-inspectors and the autonomous university court. Nicholas distrusted this apparently lenient system and set a precedent in 1827, after a clash between the Moscow city police and rowdy students, by subjecting the students to local authorities. The 1835 statute sanctioned and regularized the new rules of conduct and inspection that had developed since the beginning of the reign. The chief inspector at each university was to be a highly ranked, highly salaried official drawn from either civil or military service, with anywhere from four to fourteen deputies as well as assistants, really spies, who could go to taverns and "other houses" where it was not seemly for bureaucrats to be seen. According to Musin-Pushkin, the inspector earned his pay.

> From nine in the morning to midday, the inspector is always found in the lecture halls; then he visits the rooms of either sick students or those absent from class or those with poor behavior; in the evening he attends dances, the theatre, balls, and gatherings so that he rarely returns home before midnight; earlier in the morning the inspector listens to the explanations, complaints, and requests of the students.[51]

Inspectors were to make sure that students were pious, hardworking, and clean-living. The young men with state scholarships lived in a dormitory with a resident deputy inspector who was supposed to supervise their coming and going, pass judgment on their friends, and assure their attendance at morning and evening prayers and their keeping of church rituals, such as the Lenten fast. Non-stipendiary students were scattered around town in apartments that were regularly inspected for lapses in cleanliness and for evidence of cards, liquor, questionable literature, or unsavory associates, whether male or female.

Infraction of rules carried penalties ranging from oral reprimands and written complaints to incarceration for one day or an entire vacation, with regular meals or with only bread and water. Repeated or very serious misconduct meant expulsion for self-supporting students and dreaded military service for state stipendiates. Inspectors also sat in on examinations. Without their approval students could not pass from one class to another, receive awards, or continue to receive financial assistance.

The enforcement of rules depended on the university. Kazan and Kharkov stressed discipline because of the local superintendents, and there "a poor mark in behavior" could undo "a whole student career," while universities in the capitals were more lenient. Inspector Fittstum at St. Petersburg made reprimands tactfully, and when an occasional "flare up" occurred with the police, he "always rescued the students." In the extensive memoir literature that Moscow students produced, the "beloved" inspector, Platon Nakhimov, emerges as a saint and hero. An old navy officer, an "officer-father" with a "heart of gold," he apparently lent money to the needy, escorted home those who were drunk so that they could avoid the police, and, while carrying on a continuous war with long hair, would turn his back on the yet-unbarbered so as not to have to issue a written complaint; the detention cell was never used during his long stay.[52] It is said that Maksim Maksimich in Lermontov's *A Hero of Our Time* was modeled after the Moscow inspector: Maksim/Platon, of impeccable conduct himself, because of his kindness could never condemn anyone, even the amoral, cynical, ungrateful Pechorin.

While comportment was generally good, the Shakeev affair at St. Petersburg University demonstrated that students did not necessarily become the disciplined cadets envisioned in the regulations. M. S. Kutorga, brother of the scientist, taught world history to underclassmen, who idolized him because of his liberalism. The history professor I. P. Shulgin tried to replace him with his protégé Shakeev. At Shakeev's first lecture, a "huge throng" of students from all the faculties appeared and stamped their feet and whistled, both forbidden acts. The rector and superintendent tried to quell the disorder, and Uvarov threatened military service if it continued. Instead, passive resistance was employed; only two or three students showed up at Shakeev's lectures, and he finally quit. When Kutorga returned, he was applauded (though applause was also forbidden) and carried from the hall in triumph.

As another example of less than strict discipline, when the popular Granovskii attempted a public defense of his dissertation and was subjected to an inquisition by his ideological rivals, the romantic nationalists, students whistled and heckled; Nakhimov simply asked them to hiss more quietly. Word flew to Uvarov, who suggested dismissing all those in attendance; Stroganov, the superintendent, replied, "I myself was there" and thus the matter ended.

Students seemed able to circumvent or ignore the regulations condemning corporations, large gatherings, or the frequenting of taverns. Beginning in the late 1830s, St. Petersburg students began imitating their German counterparts by forming fraternities that picnicked, sang, and ate together. About one-fifth of the student body belonged to some fraternity, including Uvarov's son and the son of the local superintendent. Inn-keepers typically asked students to throw bottles out the back window rather than the front in order to avoid trouble with police or inspectors—it all reads like a scene out of Sigmund Romberg's *The Student Prince*. At Moscow, student study circles proliferated and were organized according to ideology, nationality, or social division.[53]

Whether a student were intellectually serious or not, Uvarov expected him to work, and he instituted strict regulations to this effect. In contrast to the general leniency of earlier years, inspectors checked class attendance, quiet hours for study, and conduct during lectures (no eating, drinking, or noise). At the end of each year, students had to pass examinations in each subject in order to proceed to the next level. One could remain at one level for only two years, a provision eliminating incompetent and "eternal" students and also, in Uvarov's words, "compelling them to use educational time with zeal and industry."[54]

In order to make sure that the baccalaureate degree would be "accessible only through long and constant work," in 1837 Uvarov set stiffer requirements for graduating from the philosophical and juridical faculties and later from the medical; these changes involved course work, oral and written examinations, and theses. At the same time, he elevated standards for receiving master's and doctoral degrees by requiring examination in both related and major fields of study, and he instituted a requirement that all recipients must write dissertations, which were to be defended publicly and published. As an example of examination requirements, a master's degree in philosophy demanded testing as well in world history and literature and Greek and Roman history and literature.[55]

Uvarov not only made it tougher to graduate, he also made it more difficult to get in. First, students had to be sixteen years of age; higher education would be a "useless waste of time" for a younger person and, for the university, "an unprofitable burden." Second, entrance examinations, required of all students who had not graduated from a state gymnasium with good grades, were made more stringent. The immediate effect was that approximately only half the applicants were admitted, causing a temporary drop in enrollment. In 1833, Uvarov discovered Kharkov not in compliance with the regulations in admitting 124 students, most of those who applied; in the next year, only 55 of 115 applicants were allowed to matriculate at that university.[56]

By the early 1840s, Uvarov so believed in the "trustworthiness" and "maturity" of the universities and student body that he allowed *Lehrfreiheit* and *Lernfreiheit* to be included in the 1842 statute for St. Vladimir University, and five years later he tried to incorporate them at all the universities; other officials defeated his proposal as "disruptive of university life." The new system would have introduced a two-semester system and a single examination at the end of four years, rather than annual testing. For the first year, students would follow an established curriculum that included theology; they would then take a minimum of seven courses of their own choosing, although their choices would require the approval of the faculty dean. Professors could develop new courses but still could not teach outside their chairs.[57] These proposed changes would have represented a true liberalization of university rules, increasing the freedom of students and professors alike.

Under Uvarov, enrollment in the four Great Russian universities more than doubled, while the social composition remained constant. Sons of nobility, junior officials, and priests—the elite group—accounted for about

70 percent; separately, the nobility provided roughly 45 percent of the total. The remaining student body was drawn from the families of freed peasants, foreigners, and merchants, but especially from *déclassé* elements, the *raznochintsy*, which supplied roughly 25 percent of the enrollment. By comparison, the University of Halle, a typical German institution, on an average enrolled 66 percent of its students from the elite group, and Cambridge 90 percent. The fact that Russian universities did not become more elitist is startling given Nicholas's fear of educating *déclassé* elements, his regular flow of proposals (1828, 1837, 1840, 1844) to discourage their attendance, and his desire that only nobility acquire the benefits of rank and prestige that accompanied higher learning. Despite the tsar, as Herzen noted, but with nostalgic extravagance, "Until 1848, the organization of our universities was purely democratic" with students drawn "from all classes of society" and with enrollment open to anyone who could pass the admission test.[58]

Herzen's statement is exaggerated; in fact, the system barred serfs and encouraged enrollments from the elite group at both secondary and higher levels. Uvarov admitted that, although universities were in a broad sense institutions "in which the youth of various classes receive a final education," his intention was as far as possible "to attract the children of the upper class of the empire" in order "to put an end to their false education at home at the hands of foreigners."

Once adopted, the 1835 statute instituted a "new order" in the universities. Uvarov waged a successful public relations campaign to attract the aristocracy; and, beginning in 1835–1836, contemporaries noted the influx of student names such as Shcherbatov, Golitsyn, Dolgorukov, and Kochubei. Although the aristocrats wore the student uniform, they stood out and were resented even by the other nobility, because they arrived in carriages, spoke French, attended dress balls, had money, imperiously sat in the front of lecture halls, and generally broke what was considered the "democracy" and "solidarity" of student life. Nonetheless, Uvarov proudly announced that "children from the best families, sons of the highest dignitaries sit on student benches"; he welcomed them especially because, by virtue of birth and wealth, they were destined for and now would be prepared for high positions.[59]

Overall, though, in Russia as in Germany, only a small proportion of university enrollment came from the aristocracy of birth and wealth. Instead, there developed a newer aristocracy of learning whose ranks were drawn from the lesser nobility—distinguished by birth but not wealth—and who were joined by members of the professional classes, officialdom, and *déclassé* elements. The "democratic" aspect of the universities may be gleaned from a few statistics. Approximately one-third of the student body were granted state stipends, that is, received full room, board, and tuition. The majority were aspiring doctors, teachers, or Oriental special-ists—that is, students in the areas that had the greatest manpower needs and that were, Uvarov always maintained, generally attractive only to ambitious young people of little means. Indeed, Uvarov instructed medical faculties to disregard social background when accepting students; gradu-ating physicians and surgeons received Rank Eight, as did those with doc-toral degrees, and this status conferred personal nobility. Furthermore, since medical students were generally from the "needy" classes, Uvarov awarded each graduate a gift of the "best medical publications" to get him started. When moderate tuition fees were introduced in 1839 for all but those who could demonstrate inability to pay, anywhere from 70 to 90 percent received at least partial exemptions; for instance, at Moscow in 1848, only 85 of 1,165 students paid full tuition. Contemporaries noted that the families of the majority could not support them, and students relied on state or privately funded assistance and worked as tutors.[60]

While Uvarov was no democrat and believed in a class system, in which children generally follow in their parents' vocations, as the natural order of society, he just as firmly believed that status should follow from merit and service and that the well-born should earn their place. He agreed that talented non-nobles, which he assumed few in number, should have some opportunity. He boasted about his "system" both at home and abroad and about his stimulation of the desire for education among all classes. How-ever, the social ramifications of his policy began coming to the attention of the tsar, the gendarmarie, and the ministry of internal affairs. In 1837, for example, the tsar felt the need to issue a rescript reiterating that edu-cational and social levels should be commensurate. In 1840, Nicholas vis-ited St. Vladimir's, the most elite of the universities with a 75 percent noble enrollment, but the nobility in that area tended to be impoverished. Since he was displeased with the poor students' "external" appearance, ironically he told Uvarov to admit only "young people with a noble back-ground." In 1842, when scanning a list of students from St. Petersburg University, the tsar rued: "How few well-known names!"

Uvarov, in 1840, issued a circular to superintendents, but warned them to keep it secret so as not to arouse public feeling. He advised them "to turn some attention to the background" of prospective students and, be-cause graduates were destined to high calling in state service, to use "plau-sible excuses" to keep out those "unable to compensate for their lack of external polish by excellent academic ability." Uvarov admitted that "it is difficult to establish a firm rule," but, he nevertheless insisted, "The time has come to make sure that, given the rising aspiration for education every-where, these excessive aspirations to higher subjects of learning do not upset in any way the order of civic estates and raise in young minds a rush to the acquisition of luxurious knowledge." These are nearly direct quotes, by the way, from Nicholas's Coronation Manifesto and his other rescripts concerning the class question. At any rate, Uvarov did nothing more about the issue for the next four years.[61]

As enrollments grew, the tsar grew more fearful and in 1844 ordered Uvarov to present a program to "moderate the flow of youth to higher educational institutions." None of the minister's suggestions would have much altered class composition. First, he forbade tax-paying citizens to enter the teaching profession "except in cases of extreme necessity," which in fact existed everywhere, since a teacher shortage was endemic; he then suggested keeping out unprepared gymnasia students, as he had already done. His third suggestion was to raise tuition for self-supporting students. He had already introduced tuition in 1839, but strictly for the purpose of getting funds desperately needed both for routine maintenance and scholarships. Stipendiates, poor students, and faculty children received exemptions; the rules were even more generously redrawn in 1841.

In 1845, Uvarov advised raising tuition from 28.59 assignat rubles to 40 in the capitals and from 14.29 to 20 in the other cities. One of his arguments implied that an increase might curtail "the rising influx of young people, in part of those from the lower strata of society, for whom higher education is useless, only a luxury that removes them from their original class, without advantage to them or the state." On the other hand, the money was to be used only for poor students, regardless of class origin, a provision nullifying any but the slightest change in the universities' social composition. But the tsar escalated his demands and suggested a near doubling of the tuition in the capitals to 50 rubles and a near tripling to 40 rubles in the other cities; he also insisted on sterner measures to keep the *déclassé* element out of the gymnasia and hence the universities. Uvarov simply had the Committee of Ministers reiterate the old restrictions and won a postponement of Nicholas's tuition increases as "dangerous" to the progress of general education.[62]

Uvarov was surely uneasy with these measures. He asked superintendents to implement them "quietly and secretly" so that the general social order would be preserved but there would be no appearance of "violating the central principles" upon which the state had acted for a century. He feared that if the public perceived any threat to these principles, that is, to the practice of allowing all who qualified into the universities, "the most enormous difficulties" could arise. But if carried out secretly, "Then the views of His Majesty will be achieved without agitations, which are always useless, often dangerous, and without holding back the true progress of general education." Uvarov played both sides since he agreed in part with each, with the tsar's general desire to maintain the existing social order but also with the public's demand for higher education.

By the late 1840s, however, Uvarov's moderate policies came under increasing attack from high government officials, and Nicholas was growing impatient. In 1846, the Senate demanded stricter legal proof of social origin for university admission. In June 1847, it passed a measure eliminating the status of auditor, originally intended for those in civil service who could not enroll as regular students because of full-time positions. Private auditors were virtually outside the control of normal university surveillance; they could enter without passing qualifying examinations, did not have to take examinations to pass from one course to another, and were not under the inspector's supervision, but could take the final tests to get a degree. If one could not obtain a proper certificate of social origin, the status of auditor provided a loophole. At St. Petersburg, one-third of the *raznochintsy* were auditors and at Kazan one-half. Henceforward, this status was abolished, although members of the free classes, after passing the qualifying entrance examination, could attend lectures in isolated subjects if these were "necessary for their work." At the same time, the number of state stipendiates at St. Petersburg was reduced, and recipients had to be Christian, native, and noble. None of these measures, however, could erase the results of past policies.[63]

During the 1830s and 1840s, the universities had produced a new type of graduate who altered the face of the bureaucracy. University professors—"new models for noble manhood," according to Wortman—apparently managed to instill in their students and in "progressive officials" who attended their *soirées* a sense of the necessity of reform, of a new ethos in service, and of a new social conscience. Graduates who continued to uphold the status quo were better trained and they experienced school contacts outside their narrow elite circles, while their reform-minded opposites formed the "first generation of Russian intelligentsia." The educational ministry had especially stimulated higher education for the lesser and middle nobility who had few if any serfs and hence were not financially or emotionally tied to the old social order. Of the total group of mid-century officials sampled by Walter Pintner, 50 percent were nobles, and 50 percent of this group of nobles were serfless, so that 75 percent of the officials in Pintner's sample possessed no serfs at all. Lacking serfs, these men had no personal opposition to emancipation; thus, the regime of Alexander II came "to have at its disposal a cadre of officials both capable and willing to undertake the sweeping changes in Russian institutions that were involved in these 'Great Reforms.'"[64]

As another example of change, Zaionchkovskii's sample of the 1853 membership of the State Council, Senate, and Committee of Ministers, bodies in which the majority of members were over sixty years of age, indicates that an average of only 21 percent had received a university education, while 59 percent had received the lax domestic education that offered little preparation for state service. In contrast, among the younger deputies, aged thirty to sixty, 71.8 percent had received a higher or middle education and only 28.2 percent the domestic; of seventeen bureau chiefs in 1849 in the Ministry of Justice, the average age was twenty-seven, and fourteen had a higher education, fifteen were noblemen, and most were serfless. Between 1847 and 1856, the bureaucracy grew by 30 percent; and the same percentage started somewhere in the Table of Ranks, a status indicating possession of a gymnasium or university diploma. By the early 1850s, more than 60 percent of middle-level officials in central agencies had a university or lycée education, as did 83 percent of the top officials. Of those at the bottom, only 19.6 percent had a higher education. Thus, while the nobility continued to dominate the civil service despite its minute proportion of the total population, it warranted its status because of the educational advantages it had received.[65] There had finally developed that connection between rank and education of which Peter had dreamed and which Uvarov had worked to make a reality.

In 1862, Professor Ivan Andreevskii of St. Petersburg University summarized the monumental achievements that had been accomplished in the previous era.

> One must give the universities credit for preparing a whole generation to reject serfdom in their hearts, thus enabling the government to realize the greatest political act of Russian history—emancipation. They also bred a generation that recognized the necessity for reform of the judicial system and the legal procedure and one that is ready and able to help the government transform the idea into action. And finally, they equipped an entire generation with the rational tools for broad, critical investigation of the historical, ethnographical, geographic, cultural, and economic foundations of our national life—in a word, they introduced all the branches of science for which both state and society have so desperate a need.[66]

THE ACADEMY OF SCIENCES

WHEN Uvarov became president of the Russian Imperial Academy of Sciences in 1818, a post he held until his death in 1855, he was understandably appalled. He complained to Minister Golitsyn, to whom he was responsible, of a host of deficiencies: not enough money; "no trace" of intelligent administration; buildings in poor repair; the library and collections "in terrible condition"; "a spirit of anarchy" in the academic sector; among the academicians, "a lack of respect for public opinion" and personal animosities on an enormous scale. Nicholas Fuss, the permanent secretary of the academy until his death in 1826, agreed in every detail and noted that Uvarov's arrival ushered in "l'époque de la regénération." Subsequent scholars agree that Uvarov, the first president with a scholarly background, through his "devoted work" saved the academy from disintegration and raised it to one of the premier institutions in the world.[67]

Despite his eventual achievements, Uvarov's original efforts were hampered because, at just about the time he became president, he fell out of favor with the Golitsyn ministry. Nonetheless, he did manage to create the Asiatic Museum in 1818 and began to transform the academy into a respected Oriental studies center. He also started trying to transform the image of the academy by appointing as honorary members Speranskii, Karamzin, Capodistrias, Gräfe, Zhukovskii, Alexander Humboldt, de Sacy, and Langlès, all of whom were deserving but were also Uvarov's friends or correspondents. In his first year in office, he also suggested publishing the findings of eighteenth-century expeditions, complete with plates, maps, and text, as a start for "renewing the glory of the academy." However, after this initial burst of energy, Uvarov did little until the next reign.[68]

Nicholas's first year in power was also the centenary of the Academy of Sciences, and Uvarov used the occasion wisely and shrewdly. He obtained money to refurbish two buildings, finish a third, and acquire a fourth. He personally planned every facet of the jubilee celebration, a glittering affair held on December 29, 1826, with the emperor and his family in attendance. Uvarov opened the ceremony with a speech eulogizing the founder of the academy, Peter the Great, as the "wise reformer of Russia" who understood the impact that arts and sciences had on the power and fate of a nation. Then followed an historical survey of each tsar's contributions and the presentation of a medal—designed by the famous craftsman F. P. Tolstoi and representing a Greek goddess laying a laurel wreath on Peter—to the Emperor, making clear that he next had to earn the crown. Fifty-two new honorary and corresponding members were added to the academy and, as an indication of Uvarov's direction, these included some of the foremost scholars in the world: Champollion, Malthus, Sir Humphrey Davy, Goethe, Heeren, Barthold Georg Niebuhr, August Schlegel, and Sir Roderick Murchison.[69]

In 1828, Uvarov performed his greatest feat. He recruited four stars into the academy, all of whom would have been, in contemporary terms, Nobel Prize winners: Lenz in physics, Karl von Baer in zoology, Herman Hess in chemistry, and Michael Ostrogradskii in applied mathematics. Friedrich von Struve soon joined the constellation. As von Baer's biographer noted, these additions were the result not of "luck" but of a "conscious" policy of attracting people "full of energy, creative ideas, and seriousness of purpose," and they contributed much to the "quick renewal" and "flowering" of the academy.[70]

Even before joining the Academy of Sciences, von Baer, while on the faculty at Königsberg University, had won acclaim as the discoverer of the mammalian ovum and as a founding father of the field of comparative embryology. A universal genius, von Baer is credited as the leading force in the modernization of Russian scientific investigation in a variety of fields, because of his rigorous empiricism and his championing of the need to unify the facts, once gathered, into an understanding of organic life in the process of change. Von Baer's achievements were monumental: he pioneered in the scientific study of Russia's natural resources and to that end participated in numerous expeditions and founded a journal; he became Russia's first physical anthropologist; he stimulated the growth of physiological studies through his lectures at the Medical-Surgical Academy; he wrote a historical study of Peter I's contributions to geography and formulated a number of laws in physical geography; and he authored ichthyological studies that suggested means of improving fishing methods in the Caspian, Baltic, and Azov Seas. Furthermore, he did much to awaken public interest in science by helping to found two learned societies, in the fields of geography and entomology.[71]

Hess won international fame as the founder of thermochemistry, as a pioneer in the development of the atomic theory, and as the discoverer of four minerals, one of which he named "uvarovite" in the president's honor. He was a superb teacher who lectured at various institutes in the capital. He also wrote the first modern chemistry textbook in Russian, a work that came to be widely adopted throughout the school system.

Under Lenz, the Russian Academy soon rose to international leadership in the new field of electromagnetics. He formulated the law on the direction of induced current and pioneered in the application of mathematics to experimental data. Like his colleagues, he also contributed to Russian scientific progress by developing curricula and by employing his ability as a lecturer to inspire students and the general public. Other academicians joined the effort to adapt scientific findings to the practical needs of the state in industry and communication networks. Moritz Jacobi, for instance, invented galvanoplastics, made Russia the world leader in its study, and applied it to the handicraft industry; he also developed an electrically powered boat. P. L. Schelling, another member of the academy, invented the electric telegraph ten years before Samuel Morse.[72]

The academy was particularly rich in the field of mathematics, even though the chair had been vacant since 1813 and even though Lobachevskii, who was far ahead of his time and therefore largely went unrecognized, was never elected to its ranks. Buniakovskii, Chebyshev, and Somov became academicians after they had proven themselves as scientists and inspirational teachers at St. Petersburg University and had gained recognition in the West. Ostrogradskii also lectured at various institutes in the capital but carried out his research within the academy. As a young man, he had studied in Paris and had been quickly recognized for his brilliance; he had won election to several academies including the American Academy of Arts and Sciences. With fame in hand, then, he came to the academy at the age of twenty-seven; it was said he was kept under police surveillance because of his stay in the revolutionary capital. His principal contribution was in the study of the mathematical foundations of physics and in research on the theory of heat; he also participated in practical projects for the government, such as introducing the Gregorian calendar and piping pure water into the capital.[73]

Uvarov credited the academy's long tradition of "expeditions for all that we know about the geography, statistics, and natural condition of Russia," and during his presidency he sponsored over seventy such expeditions, half of those that took place during the nineteenth century. The government was especially interested because of its constant expansion both south and east. In 1829, for instance, Uvarov had Nicholas invite Alexander von Humboldt to conduct an expedition to the Altai, Urals, and Caspian Sea areas, and this provided many additions to the academy's collections; a grateful Humboldt praised Uvarov as one who "patronizes and aids in everything that leads to the expansion of our spheres of knowledge," and he kept up a correspondence with Uvarov about his work. Humboldt's findings were published in 1843 under the title *Asie centrale*. This work broke new ground in the empirical, detailed, multifaceted study of geographical data and provided a vast store of information on and analysis of Russia's soil, climate, mountain formations, sea levels, organic life, and minerals. Using Humboldt's modern techniques, Alexander Middendorff, a professor of zoology at St. Vladimir University and then an academician, conducted an expedition to explore the vast, uncharted resources of Siberia. It proved to be the most ambitious and most fruitful project sponsored by the academy in the nineteenth century. After three decades of analysis, the material collected resulted in a four-volume "scientific encyclopedia" of the region, the first of its kind and a classic of the genre. Other expeditions provided information on such diverse subjects as ancient Crimean architecture, statistics on Central Russia, maps of Lapland, and the flora of Irtysh.[74]

Uvarov sponsored yet another enterprise of monumental importance. Academician Paul Stroev approached the president after his 1827 annual presidential speech praising the work of expeditions, which were usually scientific in nature. Stroev suggested the need for gathering archival materials in order to document the nation's history. Within days of this request, Uvarov won approval from the tsar and the Committee of Ministers—and 10,000 rubles—to proceed with the project. From 1820 to 1834, Stroev searched through 200 uncatalogued libraries and archives in fourteen provinces of North and Central Russia and unearthed 3,000 documents of crucial significance covering the fourteenth to the seventeenth centuries. Four volumes of manuscripts were ready by 1832. Uvarov presented them to the tsar, who, he related, read them "from cover to cover"; at Uvarov's behest, Stroev soon received a medal and a pension. Given this imperial enthusiasm, Uvarov set up an Archeographical Commission in 1834 to continue editing and compiling the enormous collection as well as to carry out further expeditions. His objective was to produce a "systematic and complete collection of the sources of national history" that would form the basis for "a truly national enlightenment." By 1834, the tireless commission had managed to publish twenty volumes of manuscripts, and these became the foundation upon which the study of Russian history, literature, jurisprudence, and numismatics was laid.[75]

Uvarov also demonstrated a special interest, as he had in the universities, in developing the libraries and other physical facilities of the Academy of Sciences; in fact, he set aside a majority of the budget for this purpose. Under his personal direction, the academy's library quadrupled its holdings through either purchase or regular exchange of materials (without censorship until 1850) with English, French, German, and American academies. The library was reorganized, its archives were readied for use, its books properly catalogued, and its resources publicized; the polymath von Baer served as a bibliographer from 1835 to 1862 and produced a systematic catalog that ran to twenty-four volumes. Once in order, the library was daily (from 11 A.M. to 3 P.M., except Sundays and holidays) open to the public, as it had not been previously, and in this way it served its social and intellectual milieu. A network of specialized libraries and museums was also founded in the fields of botany, minerology, ethnography, Asian studies, and zoology, with the collections in the latter two areas becoming among "the richest in the world." These museums were also open to the public.[76]

The crown of the new endeavors was the Pulkovo Observatory. In 1830, von Struve, already an eminent professor of astronomy at Dorpat University and after 1832 an academician, approached the tsar with a request to build a modern observatory. Nicholas approved and turned the project over to Uvarov with instructions to make it "the best in the world." The government spent 2 million rubles to establish it. Struve was sent abroad to buy instruments from "the best-known craftsmen and first masters in Europe," and these efforts "created an epoch in the annals of mechanical and optical arts." With an annual allotment of 60,000 rubles, the observatory was also able to create, in five years, a first-rate astronomical library of 5,699 volumes. Under the direction of Struve and his superb staff, Pulkovo became, in the words of an American scientist, "the astronomical capital of the world." It attracted foreign scholars because of its unsurpassed ability to provide data and star statistics; for instance, after only three years of operation, it identified 461 new double stars, whereas only 654 had been known before. In addition, the observatory served as a center for training young Russian astronomers and provided the experts needed for scientific expeditions as well as the information required for transportation, military, and colonization efforts in the empire.[77]

In 1836, after four years of work by a commission, Uvarov promulgated a new statute for the academy, which was defined as "the most important scholarly body in the Russian Empire." Its tasks were to expand the horizons of learning, to propagate new knowledge, and to advance "practical application." To this end, its budget was doubled, from 120,000 to 239,400 rubles. To allow academicians ample time for research, they were largely relieved of their century-old teaching function, although they were allowed to hold part-time positions in universities or institutes so that students could benefit directly from the academy's talent. The number of full academicians rose from eighteen to twenty-one, fifteen of whom were in the sciences and six (one each) in Latin, Greek, Russian, and Oriental languages and literature; political economy; and statistics. Full members were expected to produce two dissertations for presentation and publication each year, while adjuncts, young assistants who were "preferably Russian," presented one. Despite the fact that the vice president and permanent secretary served as Uvarov's watchdogs, the statute left the academy a self-governing, autonomous institution under the direction of a conference of its members. Academicians also enjoyed freedom from censorship regulations, although all publications needed the imprimatur of the permanent secretary.[78]

The only other change until 1927 in the academy's organization occurred in 1841. On April 10 of that year, finally, Shishkov, who had seemed eternally resurrected by appointments to public office, died. He had been the long-time president of the Russian Academy, an offical literary institution that had served as the established guardian of the "purity" of the Russian language and that had become notorious as a foe of contemporary literary trends. On April 11, Nicholas ordered Uvarov to incorporate the Russian Academy—sixteen of whose seventeen members were Great Russians but not of great caliber—into the Academy of Sciences, where German names predominated. Uvarov was apparently appalled at this dilution of his academy's talent and prestige. After a good deal of procrastination, he finally presented Nicholas with a plan: a single academy divided into three sections—exact sciences, Russian and Slavic civilization, and history and antiquities. But Uvarov asked "for this time only" to appoint all twenty members of the Second Section, as the division of Russian and Slavic languages and literatures came to be called, and his appointees were generally of high quality. They included the eminent literary men Krylov, Zhukovskii, and Viazemskii; university professors such as Pogodin, Davydov, Pletnev, Shevyrev, and Kachenovskii; the truly great philologue and historian Vostokov; and the historian and archivist Stroev. The three corresponding members were the highly respected linguists Vladimir Dal',

Šafařik, and Vuk Karadzič. Uvarov encouraged the Second Section to work on much-needed grammars and dictionaries, and by 1847 it had readied a seminal dictionary of Church Slavonic. Nonetheless, Uvarov always treated the Second Section as something of a bastard child. Members were not encouraged to participate in general Academy of Sciences affairs, nor did they receive salaries or pension rights; they were not even called academicians but merely "members" of the Second Section of the academy, unless, like Berednikov or Stroev, they were elected to the "regular" academy because of their scholarly achievements. In this way Uvarov stubbornly preserved the original scientific character of the academy.[79]

Indeed, it is to Uvarov's credit that he considered a policy of nativism ludicrous in regard to the academy. Discounting the Second Section, of the forty-six men appointed during Uvarov's tenure, thirty-two were non–Great Russians with ten drawn from the Baltic provinces;[80] the academy thus retained the "German flavor" that it had possessed since its foundation and that the tsar apparently disliked. But native talent had not yet developed to the extent that it could make contributions of international significance; relying upon natives would have condemned the academy to a second-rate existence, except in mathematics. Instead, the array of great scientists that Uvarov recruited raised the standards of the academy to a phenomenal degree. Furthermore, most of these men became Russianized and encouraged public interest and native scholarship in their fields while at the same time fulfilling their duty to adapt their research to the practical needs of the empire. The Academy of Sciences, like the universities, took up the task of ushering Russia out of its backwardness and contributed in no small part to the "remarkable decade."

Uvarov's own achievements in regard to the universities and the Academy of Sciences were as remarkable as the decade itself. Because of his logic of development and his elite concept of culture, he showered his attention upon Russia's institutions of higher learning. He assumed their gains would filter down to the rest of the schools. Along with a brittle insistence on control, he imparted a certain vitality bred of a respect for the significance of intellectual pursuits. Fundamentally, his policy was one of attraction; he endlessly wooed talent, public support, students, and official backing and, once these were won, used them well to improve the system. In the end, his insistence on high standards, coupled with his considerable administrative skills, accomplished one of the greater feats of the imperial era—to turn inconsequential and mediocre institutions into serious and first-rate centers of higher learning whose benefits redounded to the society at large.

C H A P T E R 8

THE SUBJECT NATIONALITIES: A POLICY OF
CULTURAL IMPERIALISM

My aim is to unite the various elements and have sit together on school benches Russians and Poles and Italians and Germans and French and Moldavians and Jews and Turks and Tatars and Armenians and Greeks and Bulgarians. This demands, without a doubt, not a little work and good sense so as, through education, not only to make them good and useful citizens, but also to make them understand and love our Fatherland. Uvarov, 1837

Instead of oppressive, unconditional commands, . . . I tried to satisfy the just demands of the locale, to inspire minds with a respect for Russian education, with a faith in the views of the government, and with an accurate, although not transparent, awareness of the good intentions of the ministry. Uvarov, 1843

UVAROV was the first minister of education to construct a coherent policy for dealing with the empire's subject nationalities. Poles, Baltic Germans, Jews, Moslems, and Asiatic tribesmen were generally located in the border provinces, outside the central core dominated by those whose native language was Russian and who professed Orthodoxy, that is, the Great Russians. If one adds the Ukrainians and White Russians, the group constituted 55 percent of the imperial population. Considerations based on politics and administrative efficiency necessitated the integration of these peoples into the mainstream of Russian life. Internal and external security demanded the cementing of ties between the central government and the border minorities and the inculcation of allegiance solely to the autocracy; any sense of unity with "brothers" in other states posed a threat to stability. Also, the polyglot empire needed a common language for purposes of trade, communication, and administration. In addition, the military and economic strength of Russia depended on the government's ability to develop and draw upon manpower resources from all its people.

Alexander I, in eighteenth-century fashion, was content to let the various peoples of his empire simply cohabit; he demanded only dynastic loyalty. Nicholas I, in contrast, had absorbed the Romantic notion of reverence for his own Great Russian culture. However, he possessed no Romantic sympathy for the value of other people's cultures, especially if these were contained within the borders of the Russian Empire. He openly expressed his contempt for Poles, Jews, and Tatars and feared the territorial separatism and aspirations for autonomy that so often accompanied feelings of nationalism. His inclination was to use the stick and to force outright russification in order to achieve a homogeneous empire.

Uvarov possessed a more subtle plan which, interestingly enough, resembles Soviet doctrine.[1] He managed to convince the tsar that the educational ministry could "go at the head of other parts of the administration" and achieve peaceful integration in about a generation; as in so many other areas, his intention was to lay the groundwork, not necessarily reach the goal. Uvarov advised Nicholas that "in my opinion, the measures thus far taken little conformed to their aims, since they too abruptly and too prematurely displayed the views of the government." The essential point was to move ahead slowly and "cautiously" so as not to arouse "local passions and prejudices."[2]

Indeed, another aspect of policy entailed a respect for, not an attack on, local culture, once again so as not to provoke antipathy. For instance, Uvarov put extraordinary effort into patronizing fledgling Slavic scholarship and research and spent a lifetime promoting Oriental studies. Also, to borrow Lenin's memorable image, Uvarov happily used "old bricks" to construct new, imperially directed schools among Jews, Poles, and Balts.

The goal remained, though, assimilation—the creation of a Great Russian identity among the varied subjects of the tsar. Uvarov's was a policy of cultural imperialism: what the sword had conquered and what had been won at the green tables of diplomacy, the schools would incorporate indelibly into the imperial fold. For him, a russified citizen was one who spoke the language fluently, worked in the military or civil service, and swore fealty to the autocracy; although he assumed Orthodoxy's innate superiority and considered adherence to it another aspect of "belonging" to the Great Russian fold, he did not view open religious proselytization as his function. He did insist that all imperial subjects under his domain as educational minister recognize the superiority of Great Russian culture.[3]

His policy entailed, first, the state's gradually taking over the education of all subject peoples, for the usual reasons of control and administrative unity. Second, since Uvarov firmly believed in the power of ideas, the government would use the school system to conduct a "battle for minds" and try to coopt youth by acquainting them with "the basic study of Russian language and literature and an understanding of Russian institutions and establishments."[4] Uvarov intended to appeal to both pride and ambition; the state schools would be made superior to private and religious institutions, and graduation would carry the promise of quick promotion through the ranks of imperial service and thus of a comfortable life.

Uvarov applied his policy differently to each major minority group, and hence each requires separate discussion. In the western provinces, he created a first-rate university, St. Vladimir's in Kiev, to serve as the center for the dissemination of Russian culture; he then waged a war on private education and made mandatory the use of the Russian language in all schools in order to enhance a sense of Great Russian identity. In the Baltic provinces, Uvarov also attempted to enforce use of the Russian language as the weapon of russification, but successful opposition convinced him to reduce his efforts nearly to a standstill. For the Jews, Uvarov spent his ministry trying to establish an entirely new set of state schools that aimed openly at cultural assimilation and secretly at conversion. At the same time, Uvarov made beginning efforts to attract the youth in the south and east of the empire into regular state schools, where they could learn to become Great Russians, but most of his emphasis lay in building a scholarly school of Orientalism in the Academy of Sciences and the universities.

In general, Uvarov's rather quixotic policies were geared to earning the respect of national minorities for Great Russian culture and thereby achieving voluntary assimilation; he wanted all imperial subjects to "love" the "Fatherland." Uvarov was not blind to the spirit of separatism and nationalism that enflamed so many peoples in the nineteenth century, but he underestimated the strength of these impulses.

THE POLES

IMMEDIATELY upon appointing Uvarov minister, Nicholas presented him with the problem of the Poles. "You commanded me," Uvarov remembered in 1843, "quickly to study all measures that would lead . . . to a rapprochement between these two hostile elements," namely the Russians and Poles, and to end "the long mutual hatred of one language toward the other, of the Roman church to the Orthodox, of Western civilization to the Eastern," a hatred "reflected in every page of our past and present history"; indeed, the hostilities had gone on for roughly 600 years. The contemporary problem was most acute in the western "provinces returned from Poland," to use the official euphemism. In fact, during the past century the independent country of Poland had been partitioned among Austria, Russia, and Prussia. This dismemberment was indeed, to the Poles, a tragedy not easily forgotten; a nation of cultural richness and vast resources had been destroyed. Only the Russians, although full partners in the crime, could claim with historical justification a "liberating" role, in that the lands they acquired had once been part of the ancient Kievan state and were populated principally by Orthodox Ukrainians and White Russians. Although the Vienna Congress of 1815 following the Napoleonic wars allowed for a Kingdom of Poland (or Congress Poland) with its own rather "liberal" constitution, that part remained under Russian "protection." Meanwhile, the dreams of Poles for a truly independent, republican, and restored nation that would reincorporate the lost lands flourished.

Russia's western provinces were inhabited by White Russians, Lithuanians, and Ukrainians as well as by Jews; the so-called Eastern Slavs, according to 1850 population statistics, included 7,586,607 males, a sizable 25 percent of the total in the empire.[5] Commoners had retained their Eastern Slav identity over the ages, but the local nobilities had assimilated the culture of their former Polish masters. The Polish identity of this group was no small problem because, while the percentage of nobility to the general population hovered in the rest of the empire at less than 1 percent, the nobility in the western provinces reached proportions as high as 7 percent. Furthermore, in the Kiev province, of 43,597 nobles and 955 civil servants, only 189 were Great Russian in the 1820s.[6] Uvarov noted that, despite sixty years of Russian rule, "the Russian language was hardly heard in this vast area."[7] Instead, the schools were dominated by a spirit of Catholicism, dreams of freedom, and Polish nationalism, terms hardly compatible with Orthodoxy, Autocracy, and Nationality.

Previous administrations had carelessly allowed this situation to develop. Since the inception in 1803 of the Vilna Educational District, which was centered in Vilna University and included the western provinces, the district had been left under the care of the zealous Polish patriot Prince Adam Czartoryski. An inspection in 1823 revealed that "in a word, the entire system of learning had only this as an object, to inculcate in youth republican principles and to nourish in them the hope for the restoration of former Poland." Although Czartoryski was then dismissed, the revolutionary agitation of 1830–1831—which took the army under General I. F. Paskevich one year to quell—demonstrated the policy's results; the schools and university were closed.[8]

The closing of Vilna University, in the words of a recent historian, constituted no simple administrative action, but "one of the worst examples of cultural genocide in history." The university had become the thriving center of Lithuanian, White Russian, and Ukrainian culture and the symbol and source of Polish civilization in the annexed territories. Since 1808, Vilna had enjoyed the largest enrollment of any university in the empire; in 1830, it could boast 1,322 students while Moscow, the second largest, had only 814. Clearly, the destruction of Vilna University represented a staggering blow to cultural development in the western provinces and one intended to kill Polish influence in the area.[9]

The typical response of Nicholas and his trusted viceroy, Paskevich, was to use "the strength of the bayonet and police" to render Poles obedient imperial subjects. The clear intention was to absorb administratively even the Kingdom of Poland into the empire through forcible means—to destroy its institutions, such as its state council, supreme court, and criminal code; to secularize the lands of the Catholic church and put priests on fixed state incomes; to dictate the use of the Russian language; and to pressure conversion to Orthodoxy.

Uvarov approached the problem in cultural rather than political terms and preferred an "intellectual fortress" to a military one. He advised that "a political rapprochement cannot have any beginning other than an intellectual and moral rapprochement." He believed neither in militantly suppressing the Poles nor in allowing local nationalism to win converts, but thought it best "to go, so to speak, *on a middle path* between the two extremes of opinion, both equally one-sided and dangerous."[10]

The fulcrum of Uvarov's strategy and the clearest expression of his policy was the establishment in Kiev of St. Vladimir University, fully Uvarov's own creation. While he accepted the abolition of Vilna University as a "natural consequence" of the 1830 revolt, he promoted the new institution as a center for the moral and cultural renovation of the western provinces, now divided into the Kiev, Odessa, and White Russia Educational Districts and subject to general imperial regulations. The reorganization served the aim of bureaucratic uniformity and, at the same time, that of russification:

> The new university ought, as much as possible, to smooth over those sharp characteristic traits that differentiate Polish from Russian youth and in particular to suppress the idea of particularist nationalism, to bring them closer to Russian concepts and morals, to transfer to them the general spirit of the Russian people.

Kiev—the first seat of the state of Rus' and the centuries-long meeting ground of Polish and Russian culture—was chosen as the site because it could provide an historical bridge as a city "equally precious to all Russia, the cradle of the Holy Faith of our ancestors, the place of the first witness of its civic self-government." The name St. Vladimir itself was chosen in honor of the tenth-century Grand Prince of Kiev who brought Christianity to Rus'. Therefore, Kiev was enshrined as the seat of Orthodoxy, as St. Petersburg was that of Autocracy and Moscow of Nationality, thus neatly underlining the essential historical unity and development of the empire. On a less poetic note, Benkendorf noted that Kiev, while "the ancient cradle of Orthodoxy," was also "the headquarters of the First Army, which offered all the necessary facilities for the surveillance of a large gathering of young people."[11]

When the university was established in 1833, Uvarov appealed to local sentiments by allowing Polish professors, students, and Catholicism to dominate; in practical terms, Russians were not available to fill positions. The Volyn' Lycée in Kremenets was transferred to Kiev and became the university's nucleus; since the lycée's establishment in 1805, it had flourished as a center of Polish culture and was equal in quality to a higher educational institution. Because of a lack of qualified Russians, one-half of the university chairs were filled by Polish professors from the lycée. There was also little attempt to regulate the nationality or religion of the student body. Of the 267 students in attendance in 1838, 164 were Catholic and only 93 Orthodox; the Catholic and Orthodox chairs of theology were coequal in the university structure.[12]

However, Uvarov designated "Russians," most really Ukrainians, to university chairs in fields that touched upon sensitive issues. The most significant appointment was that of M. A. Maksimovich, another of Uvarov's "discoveries," as professor of Russian language and literature and first rector of the university. Maksimovich was a former professor of botany at Moscow University and a Ukrainian who dabbled in his region's folklore but also participated in Moscow literary circles; he thus typified in his person the aim of the new institution.[13] His course in Russian philology stressed the common origins of the Slavic peoples and reinforced the theme of Polish-Russian unity by calling "Muscovite and Kievan Rus'—two aspects of one Russian world." O. M. Novitskii, a Russian, taught Slavic literature and supported this view.

Uvarov also appointed "Russians" to the chairs of Slavic and world history. V. F. Tsykh taught world history with an emphasis on the cosmopolitan development of the moral nature of man, in an attempt to avoid national issues. Upon Tsykh's premature death due to overwork, Gogol, still a young man in his twenties, attempted, through the "pull" of Zhukovskii and Pushkin, to gain an appointment as full professor ("and 6,000 rubles outright for the payment of his debts"), despite his total lack of experience. To Uvarov's credit, he rejected the demand even though Gogol's roots in the area would have made him an excellent political choice; once again, quality took precedence. It should be added that Uvarov did succumb to pressure when a vacant post arose at St. Petersburg; Gogol was appointed assistant professor of history, but he quickly became "the laughing stock of the students" because of his ignorance and was fired.

A. I. Stavrovskii took over the chair in world history at Kiev and introduced a course on Russian history. His appointment came the same year as the publication of Ustrialov's *Pragmatic History*; Stavrovskii taught with the latter's format, supplemented by the works of Karamzin and Polevoi. In 1837, when Uvarov visited the district, he was so impressed by V. F.

Dombrovskii, a gymnasium teacher, that he took him to St. Petersburg to study under Ustrialov and then appointed him adjunct to the chair in world history in Kiev. One of the major purposes of Ustrialov's history was to "decide in the most positive way the great contemporary question about Poland and its sometime subjection of western Russia." In particular, Ustrialov gave a new view to the history of the Lithuanian Principality, underscoring its differences from Poland and the prominent role of Rus' in its formation. The consequence was to claim western Russia as Rus' and not Poland and thus provide a scholarly basis for the attempt to impose Russian national principles in the area. Despite this authority, Stavrovskii and Dombrovskii found it difficult, if not impossible, to lecture openly on the subject because of the intense feelings surrounding it.[14]

The juridical school was opened in 1835 and, because of the system-wide emphasis on practical Russian law, its faculty was overwhelmingly Russian in composition. It contained only one professor from the Volyn' Lycée, but he was one of the outstanding jurists in Europe, A. N. Mickiewicz, brother of the poet. Although Mickiewicz was soon transferred to Kharkov, the remaining faculty at Kiev was strengthened by the inclusion of four graduates of Speranskii's juridical school, the most promising of whom was Nevolin. In five years, it became one of the best faculties in Russia and thus attested to the success of Speranskii's endeavors. Uvarov exulted that these professors "give evidence that Russian enlightenment is going forward with rapid strides and thus in them is supported a respect for the high level of Russian learning."

Culturally, the juridical faculty was inbred; the Poles largely avoided it, and therefore Russian students dominated in a proportion of three to one. It thus created a "silent army" of Russian bureaucrats in the provinces. The Poles concentrated themselves in the Second Section of the philosophical faculty, the physical-mathematical, which was composed almost entirely of professors from the lycée; in it, Polish students outnumbered Russians by a proportion of six to one.[15] The university at first clearly did not accomplish its aim of moral-political rapprochement.

Nonetheless, the university at Kiev made great strides in its first years. Uvarov appointed Egor von Bradke as superintendent, and he proved to be an excellent choice. His main qualification was that he was German and hence above the Polish-Russian cultural struggle. Contemporaries agreed that for von Bradke "Russians, Germans and Poles didn't exist: only competent and incompetent people." While he considered himself an executor of the imperial will, he managed to be remembered by Poles and Russians alike as an enlightened administrator, humane in his dealings with faculty and paternal in his relationship with students. Von Bradke interfered little with the academic sector of the university, allowing it to be run by the usual committees. From 1834 to 1838, the university council and board held a numbing total of 1,160 meetings in order to organize the curricula, hire professors, erect seven new buildings, and establish public lectures in technology, bookkeeping, and practical mechanics.[16]

In the White Russian, Odessan, and Kievan Educational Districts, Uvarov brought private education under ministerial supervision in order to make it conform with general statutes. Of greater concern, private schools had long been regarded as notorious breeding grounds of Polish national feeling. To bring youth under the control of the state, Uvarov sponsored dozens of noble *pansions*, state dormitories, and "model" schools for girls in an attempt to wrest education from the hands of nuns and priests who were "filled with national prejudices."[17] Uvarov's most dramatic measure in the area was the abolition of Polish as the language of instruction in the middle and lower schools, except in the teaching of the Catholic religion. Separate teachers had been maintained for instruction in Polish, but in 1836 a law excluded them from all school staffs, including that of the university, and each gymnasium was required instead to employ two teachers of Russian language and literature. Russian history was then taught from the third year on, rather than only in the last year, to make sure that "dropouts" did not escape its preachments. Furthermore, to receive the fourteenth rank, "a perfect knowledge of the Russian language and excellent success in Russian literature" was necessary. Uvarov considered the policy successful by the 1840s and claimed, with exaggeration, that where before the Russian language was "hated and alien," it "is now learned with love, enthusiasm, and unusual success. . . . That great agent of Russian nationality has received uncontested superiority in this area."[18] Uvarov attested, after a personal inspection of the district in 1837, that in his war of ideas, "The field of battle, especially for the consciousness of the enemy, stands in the hands of the government."[19]

In 1838, however, a considerable amount of revolutionary propaganda was found circulating among St. Vladimir students at the same time that Simon Konarski, a former hero in the Polish revolt of 1830–1831, was apprehended and then executed for his underground activities throughout Russia in support of a new revolt. Von Bradke had received warnings but thought them exaggerated. The tsar did not. He dismissed von Bradke as a person of "weak character" and replaced the moderate Gur'ev with the militant D. G. Bibikov as governor-general of the district.

In January 1839, local authorities even shut the university down, but Uvarov interceded so that it could reopen within the year. However, he was forced to replace all the Polish professors, one-half of the university's faculty, with Russians. The whole student body of 275 was released; about 150 transferred to other schools, 30 entered civil service, and 36 were expelled, of whom two-thirds received twenty-five-year terms in the army. Nonetheless, Nevolin, the rector, kept the university faculty on hand for the fall semester. In admitting the first class for the reopening, an attempt was made to insure its "trustworthiness." Of 126 students, for the first time those who were Orthodox outnumbered Catholics; 41 stipendiates were retained from the class of 1839 and, of these, 37 were Orthodox. However, by 1848, Catholics outnumbered Orthodox by a three-to-one majority.[20]

Despite constant warnings from the tsar that he should be more vigilant, Uvarov refused to believe that the institution he had created was anything less than loyal and reliable; he claimed that any disorder was the work "of a handful of desperate enemies of order," and he was right—most "affairs" turned out to be innocent. In 1842, he prepared a new statute for St. Vladimir University in which the only punitive measure was that the university council lost its right to elect the rector; instead, the council presented two nominees to the minister, and the tsar, on the advice of the minister, appointed one of them. Uvarov even awarded the university *Lehrfreiheit* and *Lernfreiheit*—although the system of inspection remained intact—and nearly doubled its budget and the number of volumes in the library; he provided for the student body to increase by more than one-half.

The 1842 statute also greatly expanded the faculty. The number of chairs increased from twenty to thirty-seven; chairs in Russian history, the history and literature of Slavic peoples, and political economy were established. The Vilna Medical-Surgical Academy, the last refuge of "pseudo-patriotism" in the area, according to Uvarov, was transferred to St. Vladimir's. This medical component, together with the juridical faculty, contained half the total university chairs, thus setting a tone of practical education. In order to fill some of the new chairs established by the statute, Uvarov sent five Polish St. Vladimir students abroad for training under a plan devised by the university council. His action was surprising in view of the recent revolutionary disturbances, but it underlined Uvarov's undaunted belief that foreign influences would not harm students with a firm and loyal political background. Uvarov had asked other universities for candidates to fill the vacancies, but none of the nominees seemed promising. Rather than accept poorly qualified Russians, then, he sent the five Polish students to Western Europe for further education. They returned in 1846 and, like their forebears in the Professors' Institute, began to inject new life into St. Vladimir's. Their influence was short-lived, however, because the events of 1848 made their European education suspect.[21]

The tsar had even greater suspicions about the loyalty of the Kingdom of Poland. Because of the 1830 Revolt, Poland's 1815 constitution was replaced by the Organic Statute of 1832, which reduced the country from semiautonomy to the status of an imperial province. The provisions in the statute for civil liberties and local self-government were never put into effect because of the hostile dictatorship of Nicholas's trusted Paskevich. At any rate, Uvarov noted the "slipshod system of national education" in the Warsaw province and blamed it on Jesuit influence, free-thinking, and revolutionary nationalism. In 1840, the Warsaw Educational District was organized, and all its institutions, with their 70,000 students, were made to conform with general imperial regulations. The district was placed under the surveillance of a resident superintendent and a Council of National Education, which Paskevich eyed closely. So did Uvarov. He visited the district in 1839, 1840, 1842, and 1843.[22] Nonetheless, in 1841 and 1846 new secret societies appeared, and students from other parts of the empire were forbidden to study in the Warsaw district for fear of contamination. Then, the three upper grades of the Warsaw gymnasia were closed except for the *Realschule*-type courses, which were retained because their practical emphasis appeared to make them relatively unsusceptible to revolutionary propaganda.

To offset the lack of educational facilities in the district, and especially because of the abolition of both Warsaw and Vilna Universities, Uvarov, in the face of much opposition, allowed a limited number of Polish students to study in imperial universities for preparation as gymnasia teachers or as administrators for the Kingdom of Poland or the western provinces. His assumption was that they would imbibe a spirit of loyalty to the autocracy and propagate it among their fellow Poles; in fact, before serving in their native territory, they were expected to serve a five-year apprenticeship in the Great Russian provinces, thereby even further proving their imperial allegiance. St. Petersburg and Moscow Universities became centers for the training of Polish jurists, and both added appropriate chairs in these disciplines. By 1845, regular stipends amounting to 32,000 rubles were allocated for these students, much to the chagrin of some, like Stroganov, who resented expenditures on Poles when Russian students were in need.[23]

Although there was constant threat of revolutionary activity in the Warsaw district, Uvarov resolutely opposed more repressive policies. He required the study of Russian at all school levels but attacked the idea of an all-out battle for cultural assimilation: "In the political sense, language can be compared to a weapon that inflicts a wound on the hand inexperienced in wielding it." Uvarov felt that it was possible in the western provinces to say to Russian subjects, "Learn Russian!"; but in the Kingdom of Poland, which possessed a national history and tradition independent of Russia's, more caution and a special path were necessary.

> This path lies between two extremes: between an *ultra-Russian* feeling, understandable but useless and fruitless, of clear disdain for a people, and an *ultra-European* inclination, which has been made, in the eyes of this people, the subject of their blind enthusiasm. Here, as in nearly all state affairs, the middle path alone appeared firm and promised success.

Thus, Uvarov set forth his general plan, to go "with firmness but without threat and without persecution."

Uvarov's middle-of-the-road policy was attacked by both militant Russians and nationally minded Poles. He complained of his lack of support from Russian "society," and especially from Bibikov and Paskevich.

> They do not want to understand that education is not a political policy that can be deemed successful merely if [students] appear to behave properly; they also do not want to understand that, during a time of intellectual upheaval, harsh actions only prevent the government from fulfilling its central aims . . . and might awaken opposition among the local people. [Then] they would keep their children out of state schools, and hence it would be impossible to give the next generation a correct education.

The Poles, better than the Russians, recognized the significance of Uvarov's educational policy and "saw in it a greater assault than the exploits of Paskevich." Czartoryski, from his exile in Paris, agreed that eradication of the native language was more dangerous than the threat that had existed "when the Russians fought with sword in hand."[24] For the Russians, the problem of the Poles seemed, and seems, to defy solution.

THE BALTIC GERMANS

THE Poles remained troublesome, but it was the Baltic Germans who had the most ammunition with which to resist attempts at russification; although small in number—in 1850, 790,242 out of a population of 60,000,000—this group withstood effectively what Uvarov himself called a "siege." Their nobility, numbering only 5,389, were descendants of the Teutonic knights, and they met the siege with tactics of passive resistance. Their century-long record of unblemished support for the dynasty, both as caretakers of their own provinces and as high officials in the army and central bureaucracy, gave them every presumption that they need not further prove their loyalty by adopting Russian culture. Besides, they believed their own culture superior. The stage was set for an inevitable clash between the Baltic German nobility and the equally arrogant Uvarov.[25]

At first, Uvarov took the offensive and, with sure optimism, presented Nicholas in 1836 with a secret plan aimed at achieving "a decisive rapprochement" of the Dorpat Educational District with the Great Russian districts. His plan, not surprisingly, centered on "the introduction of teaching and execution of affairs in the Russian language and, consequently, replacing the majority of professors, teachers, and clerks with Russians." He admitted that full execution of this design, so necessary for imperial "unity" and "uniformity," was "premature," because so few in the provinces knew Russian well. He suggested eight lines of assault to rectify the situation. The object was to have the "Russian language learned with love and diligence."[26]

The first item simply applied the change, made in the regular university statute of 1835, for placing the supervision of district schools under a superintendent rather than the local university council. Uvarov appointed G. B. Krafstrem to the post. Since Krafstrem was a martinet dedicated to fulfilling the letter of the law, the minister had full confidence that he and his staff, consisting solely of Great Russians, would obediently enact the remaining measures. They tried, but failed.

Five items in the plan demanded that, within three years, all the district's middle and elementary schools would conduct classes in Russian, that administrative vacancies would be filled only by those proficient in the language, and that all the work of the educational ministry would be conducted in Russian. Although a dozen students were dispatched from the Central Pedagogical Institute to the Dorpat District, they could barely dent the phalanx of 250 stubbornly German-speaking teachers and clerks busily meeting the needs of four gymnasia, twenty-four district schools, and eighty-five elementary schools. Although the teaching of Russian was strengthened and expanded, the lack of trained personnel for even the Great Russian districts prevented the release of people to Dorpat who could alter the cultural composition of the school staffs. Amusingly, when Krafstrem sternly ordered the university council to deal with him only in Russian, they simply hired a translator to make bilingual copies of all transactions.[27]

The seventh item in Uvarov's agenda stipulated that no one could receive a degree from or be admitted to Dorpat University, the jewel of the district, without a knowledge of Russian. Despite this imperial order, the university did nothing whatsoever to prepare students in Russian, and Uvarov was forced to entreat the tsar for a five-year extension of the deadline; the legislation was put into effect only in 1845. The eighth measure allowed the minister to fill university vacancies with qualified scholars who could lecture in Russian. However, this objective also proved impossible to attain, because of a lack of professors. The only three Russians at Dorpat, N. I. Pirogov, I. Varvinskii, and A. S. Zhitaev, taught in German because the students could not understand Russian. Soon, M. P. Rozberg was appointed to the chair in Russian language and literature—which the university council had left vacant for six years—and lectured in Russian. In 1842, Russian law was taught in the commensurate language but Russian history continued to be offered in German. Such was the fate of Uvarov's eight-point plan. In 1848, when he visited the district for an inspection, he had to admit that knowledge of Russian remained generally deplorable.[28]

Uvarov's attempts in the 1830s to bring Dorpat University more into line with the 1835 general administrative regulations brought equally meager results. Efforts to wrest juridical rights and student supervision from the university council met with resistance, and the council, despite orders, continued to hear 200 cases a year and to keep the student inspector responsible to it rather than to the superintendent. The council's legal position was that its separate 1820 statute and its 200-year-old traditions superseded the diurnal regulations of the ministry. Uvarov would surely have taken sterner measures except for his satisfaction that the roughly 600 university students were thoroughly loyal and "not at all interested in contemporary politics"; "they have pranksters but not political dreamers," he concluded. Uvarov did, however, pass special rules to offset the German "propensity for dueling and loud merrymaking out-of-doors." Strict regulations forbade, among other things, graffiti, crimes against women, surreptitious smoking in the botanical gardens, gambling, and hard drinking, the last proscription leading to a marked decrease in the number of taverns in the Dorpat vicinity. The traditional German student corporations were allowed to exist even though there occurred one *Burschenshaft* scare. Benkendorf maintained that there was no cause for fear, but the tsar, as preventive medicine, ordered the incarceration of forty-two students during winter vacation, on a diet of bread and water.[29]

The main reason that Dorpat escaped the usual censure befalling a maverick institution was its high educational quality, the trait Uvarov most cherished. He would declare: "I am the greatest friend of the Germans and the only support of Dorpat University." The university dated back to 1632, had been open intermittently until 1710, and was resurrected under Alexander I in 1802. Because of its ability to draw upon established scholars from Germany, it rapidly became one of the best institutions in the empire and Europe, especially in the sciences. The Professors' Institute attested to that reputation and made the university the seedbed for Russian scholars. Uvarov's policies facilitated Dorpat's growth and led to its "golden age." The minister oversaw the opening of veterinary, forestry, and pharmacy institutes, and he provided for an unusually high budgetary allocation and 50 percent increase in library holdings; public lectures attracted the support of the community and led to the establishment of two learned societies and four journals. The university thrived until the next minister, in 1852, forbade hiring foreigners to fill vacant chairs, a measure that diminished its stature as an institution of higher learning.[30]

The fact that the university thrived could hardly console Uvarov for his failure to sow the seeds of Russian nationality among the Baltic Germans. The minister was clearly aware that the task demanded the utmost "circumspection" and that full revelation of the final, albeit distant, plan for complete russification would provoke anger. Consequently, his reports were delivered in secrecy to the tsar and even kept from other members of the ministry. Alas, they leaked to the press; for instance, a full reprint of the 1836 plan and a similar one of 1838 made their way to both the *Allegmeine Zeitung* and the *Neue Hamburgische Zeitung*.[31] In 1839, in response, Parrot wrote a stinging letter to the tsar. He asserted that as much attention was given in Dorpat University to teaching the Russian language as was possible in a place dedicated to scholarship; he added that Balts were learning Russian as fast as Russians were learning "science." Parrot commented that the Balts had no desire to become "closer in character and customs to native Russians," a direct quote from Uvarov's "secret" plan, because it would be a step down for them: "The level of development of the Baltic provinces is higher than in the rest of Russia." He avowed that all educated Russians knew this and that it would be "false patriotism" to contradict such a self-evident truth.[32]

In his ten-year report, Uvarov angrily refuted Parrot's argument with notions borrowed in part from the romantic nationalists' arsenal of anti-German sentiment. Uvarov snidely allowed that "this handful of people of another origin . . . much helped our development," and that therefore in the past the government had "indulged their prejudices" and false sense of superiority. However, times had changed: *"They do not understand the Russia of Nicholas I,"* and they "do not perceive that *Russia has grown up*"—once again, Uvarov's favorite theme of "maturity." Their welfare as imperial subjects, he noted, demanded knowledge of the Russian language; but, because of their "arrogance," they found such study "distressing" and wallowed in the "illusion" that "their alleged nationality is *German* nationality." No statement better defines Uvarov's attitude toward the subject nationalities.

He concluded his statements on a sour note, namely that his plans "long ago" would have delivered "youth to the hands of the government," since the young "obviously are drawing near to our way of thinking"; however, the lack of cooperation of local officials prevented progress: "As with the builders of ancient Jerusalem, it is necessary to create with one hand while repulsing the blows of enemies with the other." Despite his militaristic language, Uvarov to the end suggested patience and enticement; he insisted that "compulsory measures would bring more harm than good." He acclaimed his results, though admittedly modest, as still notable, given the fact that Russian was "not native, not a mother tongue, not used in society."[33] Uvarov's successor, P. N. Shirinskii-Shikhmatov, abandoned the policy of gradualism and executed more stringent russification measures, again to no avail. The whole campaign was realistically abandoned in the next reign, although it was resumed in the 1880s.[34]

THE JEWS

UVAROV'S interest in the Jewish question was long-standing. On the very day the tsar appointed him acting minister, he was commissioned to sit on a panel charged with drawing up a new statute for this minority group. Among his first acts as minister, he prevented the suggested closing of nearly all Jewish presses, opposed censorship of ancient sacred texts, and even commended "the astounding increase in the number of Jewish books." It became known that Uvarov "undoubtedly possessed a sympathy for the Jews," a proclivity very unusual among high Russian officials. Even more than Poles or Balts, the Jews lived in isolation from the rest of the Russian population.[35] Their dress, language, confinement to the Pale of Settlement in the western region, poverty, religious differences, autonomous administration through local *kahals*, and occupation restrictions all contributed to denigrate them as "non-citizens" of the empire. Nicholas called them "regular leeches" but decided to try to bring them into the Russian community with an 1827 decree that abrogated their former exemption from military service; good soldiers, apparently, made good citizens. The law was applied with such abuse and cruelty that it only served further to alienate Russian Jews; in 1837, one odd ukase allowed a Jew to obtain freedom from the twenty-five-year tour of duty by either engaging in classical studies or becoming a farmer—quite a choice. The 1835 Jewish Statute merely codified restrictions, including prohibitions against Jewish employment of gentiles. The members of a new commission in 1840 suggested deporting the Jews to Siberia, and only Uvarov and Kiselev urged some "Christian charity."[36]

Uvarov had his own moderate plan for effecting "the rapprochement of the Jews with the rest of the population," based, of course, upon his ministry's school system. The 1804 educational statute permitted Jews to attend all state schools without discrimination. At Uvarov's behest, the 1835 Jewish Statute repeated this allowance with the added concession that university graduation would bring freedom from restrictions and would lead to the same status in the Table of Ranks as for non-Jewish graduates. The Jews, however, failed to accept the government's invitation; they preferred to educate their children in community schools, called *heders*, supervised by teachers or *melameds*. These presented no threat to the traditional Jewish way of life, since only religious and no secular subjects were taught, and they were successful in promoting literacy, which became nearly universal among male Jews. In 1840, out of 80,017 students in lower and middle schools, only 48 were Jewish, and in 1835, of 1,906 university students only 11 professed the Jewish faith.[37]

The 1840 Jewish Commission agreed to let Uvarov draw up a program for special school systems for Jews, similar to those already established by Austria in 1781 and by Prussia in 1824. While Uvarov in the early thirties was cool to this idea of special education, the initiative of Jewish intellectuals made him reconsider his position. In 1836, progressive Jews from Riga, Odessa, and Kishniev successfully petitioned for approval to open *kahal*-sponsored secular schools in which Jews would be taught "modern" subjects such as Russian and other foreign languages. The Riga *kahal* was fortunate in obtaining as its first principal an energetic and zealous young German rabbi, Max Lilienthal, who had just recently completed his doc-

toral studies at the University of Munich. Under him, the school prospered, and, when Uvarov visited it one year later, he was greatly impressed,
calling it "a fresh seeding ground of enlightenment" and expressing confidence in its "happy, bright future." Uvarov's patronage succeeded in getting the school imperial approval in 1839. With his eye for talented tools,
the minister also befriended Lilienthal.

In early 1841, Uvarov summoned Lilienthal to St. Petersburg to assist
him in formulating a general program for the state education of Jews. The
minister explained to the awed twenty-four-year-old what was at stake in
"this immense task of reforming this highly gifted people." He claimed
that the tsar's patience was wearing thin with Jewish "lethargy" and the
stubborn refusal of Jews to join the Russian mainstream. Uvarov warned
that if Jews did not accept a new proposal to attend state schools, "I fear
bad, very bad, times will be in store for them, while the brightest future
is awaiting them if they seize this opportunity of amalgamating themselves
with European civilization." The plan was to establish a whole system of
special state schools for Jews so that they could simultaneously study their
religion and learn the Russian language and other national subjects; in this
way, it was thought, they might lose their hostility to gentile culture and
become contributing members of Russian society. Uvarov feared that Jews
might oppose this plan, considering it to be meddling by the state in the
education of youth, and he asked Lilienthal's advice for avoiding such
antagonism. The rabbi quickly replied: "Every obstacle will be overcome
readily if His Majesty will grant the Jews at once full and complete emancipation." Uvarov, of course, demurred; as with the serfs, education must
precede freedom. At any rate, Lilienthal was won over and in raptures
wrote to Dr. Samuel Luzzatto of the Jewish Institute in Padua.

> [Uvarov] is at present occupied in an attempt to avoid the collapse of
> the elementary and secondary schools of our coreligionists in Russia
> and Poland by preparing them, through cultural training, for a better
> future. He also desires to institute a similar school for rabbis who are
> later to become leaders of the people. . . . Once they have attained
> culture, they are offered emancipation; in the wake of knowledge—
> the rights of man.

Lilienthal's description of the government's plans were received so enthusiastically by his correspondents that Uvarov's next yearly report could
speak of "the ecstasy of foreign Jewish intellectuals with my plans" and
with the impression of enlightenment that Russia was imparting to Europe.
The ministry received 200 applications from European Jews to work in the
proposed schools.[38]

In March 1841, Uvarov presented his first report to the Jewish Commission. The introduction reiterated his usual preference for cultural rather
than military assault. He rued that the Jewish "majority still stagnates in

inherited prejudices and centuries of humiliation" and that only state schooling could help this "unlucky people," whose "modern history began at the foot of Golgotha." In the state schools, a *"purification of their religious concepts"* would occur that could, in the short run, bring them into the Russian mainstream and could ultimately extend to conversion to Christianity.

> Little by little, the *fanaticism for separatism* must be abolished among the Jews and *bring them into the general source of citizenship.* In this matter, they cannot go wrong, for is not the religion of the Cross the purest symbol of international citizenship?[39]

Lilienthal, who of course had no knowledge of Uvarov's secret statements, went to Vilna and Minsk to seek cooperation for the new school system. At Vilna, the young rabbi told a gathering of 100 Jews of the government's education plans, calling Uvarov their "friend." The progressive, younger Jews approved, but their elders suspected a first step to conversion. They warned the foreigner, Lilienthal, of the religious policy of the Russian government.

> The course pursued against all denominations but the Greek proves clearly that the government intends to have but one church in the whole empire; that it has in view only its future strength and greatness and not our own future prosperity.

In Vilna, 4,000 Jews protested during Passover against the new government policy and were quieted only by a fire brigade. At Minsk, Lilienthal was not even allowed a hearing and was told:

> So long as the government does not accord equal rights to the Jew, general [Russian] culture will only be his misfortune. . . . The Jew who is educated and enlightened, and yet has no means of occupying an honorable position in the country, will be moved by a feeling of discontent to renounce his religion.[40]

As Lilienthal noted, Uvarov "preferred to see [his plan] favored by the Jews themselves." Therefore, he organized a commission dominated by Jewish members to set up the new state schools, a clever move that indeed appeased many in the community, especially since the commission was an imperial one and hence implied the tsar's support. By 1844, the official plan was ready. The schools were of three types, with their curriculum identical to that of the three types of regular state schools except that study of the Jewish language and religion was included; teachers were drawn from both the Christian and Jewish populations. Thus, parish and district schools were put into operation as well as rabbinical schools, which were similar to the regular gymnasia and were intended to prepare lower-school teachers and rabbis. Jewish private schools and domestic tutors were also incorporated under the general regulations in force in the empire, and thus were subject to strict surveillance and certification; the stipulation that *melameds* needed training in general education, as well as religion, soon reduced their number by half, from 1,009 to 504. In order to insure the "proper direction" of the schools, Christians were hired as administrators. A tax on Sabbath candles and the profits from Jewish printing shops substantially helped to finance the endeavor. The hope was that Jews would flock to the state schools, which seemingly offered the best of the religious and secular worlds and would provide an avenue out of the ghetto; the tsar hoped their success would bring an end to Jewish private education altogether. When the state schools for Jews opened in 1847, the *heders* enjoyed an enrollment of 50,000; by 1855, the state operated only its original 106 schools with 3,488 pupils,[41] an enrollment that hardly competed with the traditional Jewish schools and indicated a boycott of the secular schools.

The government was never able to win the trust of the Jewish population, who correctly suspected a threat to their religion and way of life in the state schools. Even Lilienthal felt duped and grew to understand that the government had no intention of emancipating the Jews. He had warned Uvarov that if the education plans were nothing other than a "farce, a pretext for wholesale proselytization," he would resign. It is not actually clear why he left the Russian service, but the most common theory is that, once he learned of the secret circulars that spoke of conversion, he left for America and rued that "the Jews must bow before the Greek cross—then the tsar will be satisfied." In fact, probably personal considerations, namely a new wife and the fear that his ambitions could not be satisfied in Russia, prompted his resignation. In truth, Lilienthal had failed to construct a bridge between himself and either the traditional or the reform wing of the Russian-Jewish population, and so, in effect, his mission was doomed.[42]

Uvarov also failed in his own personal mission; he had hoped to integrate Jews into the Russian community through the school system, a tactic that had worked in West European countries and that also promised a better life for the Jews. He may have hoped for ultimate conversion, but he was intent on proceeding gradually "without repressive measures of any kind"; this notion, of course, reflected his general political stance as well as his historical theory that Christianity and citizenship were inexorably correlated. Because Uvarov thought of religion as a cultural factor rather than a belief system, he never acted in the spirit of blatant anti-Semitism that inspired most Russian tsars and their ministers. As with the Poles and the Balts, Uvarov acted in the spirit of a good administrator bent on imperial unity and uniformity. He believed assimilation of the Jews through the school system would draw them out of a ghetto of ignorance, poverty, and discrimination and thus benefit both themselves and the state. In this way, he anticipated their "moral and civic rebirth."[43] Uvarov's policy may have been more "enlightened" and well-intentioned than other imperial programs, but it was based on a misguided concept of national and religious feelings and aspirations as well as an innate sense of Great Russian and Orthodox superiority.

TRANSCAUCASIANS AND SIBERIANS

UVAROV'S policies in regard to the peoples of Transcaucasia and Siberia enjoyed more success than was the case with other subject nationalities, but mostly because his measures took a much more scholarly direction, were limited in scope, and met little resistance. As with the Poles, Germans, and Jews, he hoped to attract the loyalty of Transcaucasians and Siberians by acquainting them with Russian laws, language, and institutions while still allowing for the study of their local culture. In 1835, he pointed out with pride:

> On the one hand, inhabitants of the Polish provinces are finding their way into Russian schools opened up for them, and at the other end of the empire, the sons of half-savage inhabitants of the Asian steppes have finally decided to attend our educational establishments in order to acquire there both a knowledge of the Russian language as well as a correct study of their own dialects.[44]

Furthermore, in an attempt to emulate British rule in India, Uvarov singlehandedly encouraged scholarship in this area and laid the foundations for Russia's development as an international leader in the study of the East. In these regions he encountered little opposition because generally these peoples were the most backward and remotely located in the empire and had not yet developed the sense of separatism and local pride that usually accompanied nineteenth-century versions of nationalism; 4 to 5 percent of the empire's population resided in the expanses of Siberia and only 11 percent of the population was Turkic-speaking. Consequently, a Romantic interest in local culture and the practical need for imperial unity marched easily hand in hand, and the collisions so noticeable between other, more numerous and developed minorities and the Great Russian government were avoided.

Uvarov's own interest in the East was lifelong. From the time he published his *Project for an Asian Academy* in 1810, he became one of the leading representatives in Russia of the Oriental Renaissance that was sweeping through European intellectual life. He proposed establishing an Asian Academy in St. Petersburg that would centralize research and student instruction and be staffed by leading specialists in each language and literature. Its scholarly purpose would be to investigate topics relating to

Asian studies, to translate the monuments of Eastern literature, and to compile grammars and dictionaries. Its practical purpose would be to train the personnel needed by various ministries in their dealings with Eastern peoples. Uvarov never succeeded in establishing his academy, but through his educational posts, he attempted to fulfill its purposes.[45]

Immediately upon becoming president of the Academy of Sciences in 1818, Uvarov began the transformation of the institution into a major European Oriental center by sponsoring the creation of the Asiatic Museum. Because of Peter the Great's interest in the East, from its foundation the academy had collected manuscripts and ethnographical and archeological objects, especially coins of the Chinese, Manchurian, Japanese, Mongolian, and various Muslim peoples; these treasures, however, were uncatalogued and therefore useless to scholars. Nonetheless, they attracted the attention of Christian Frähn, an Eastern numismatist and Arabic scholar who, after ten disappointing years as a professor at Kazan University, decided to accept a position in his native Germany. En route, he stopped to examine the Academy's Eastern collection and was astounded by its richness. Uvarov had also just arranged the purchase of 700 Arabic, Persian, and Turkish manuscripts from a French diplomat, George Rousseau; this collection proved to be one of the best acquisitions made in Europe in the nineteenth century. The new president convinced Frähn to stay in Russia, to put the collection in order, and to pursue his research using its resources; he granted him the position of academician as well as director of the Asiatic Museum.

Frähn remained in Russia for the rest of his life, and his accomplishments were several: he made the Asiatic Museum, although the first devoted to Eastern studies in Russia, one of the best research institutions of its kind in the world; he created a school of Eastern numismatics in Russia; and his research and teaching resulted in an enduring school of historiography that articulated Arabic and Russian historical developments. After Frähn retired in 1841, his work was carried on by Boris Dorn, whom Uvarov had appointed to the academy for this purpose in 1839 and who directed the museum until his death in 1881. The collection continued to expand and acquire international recognition, a development that, as Dorn pointed out in his histories of the institution, was due largely to Uvarov's patronage.[46]

In addition, roughly half the academy's expeditions during Uvarov's tenure were concerned with the East; the largest and most fruitful of these was that of Middendorff to Siberia. Academicians accompanying the expeditions produced classics in their fields, for example, Leopold Shrenck's ethnographical study of tribes in the Amur Basin and Otto Böhtlingk's study of the Iakut language. Also, beginning in 1818, Uvarov commissioned the publication of catalogs describing the Oriental holdings of the academy's libraries, and in 1839 he instituted a program for publishing collections of articles relating to Russia and the East.[47]

In general, the academy's research projects began to stress Oriental topics. In 1830 a new statute provided that two of the twenty-one chairs in thirteen areas be allotted to Eastern history and literature (only mathematics, with three, fared better). Of greater importance, in 1841 a new division of Eastern literature was created within the academy, representing the first substantial organization of Eastern scholars in Russia. Having come of age, the academy could retain such scholars as Jacob Schmidt and Nikita Bichurin (Tibetan, Chinese, and Mongolian), François Charmoy (Persian and Arabian), Marie Brosset (Georgian and Armenian), Andrew Sjögren (Caucasian), Böhtlingk, Robert Lenz, and Friedrich Adelung (Sanskrit), Dorn (Near Eastern), and Anton Schiefner (Tibetan). Uvarov personally commissioned Schmidt to write the first Mongolian grammar and dictionary.[48]

As educational minister, Uvarov continued to give systematic and serious attention to Eastern studies. Although the 1804 university statutes provided for teaching Arabic and Persian at Moscow and Kharkov, lasting results were not forthcoming. However, at Kazan, the easternmost Russian university, Arabic, Persian, and Tatar were taught; and, as superintendent, Uvarov invited two gifted students of de Sacy, Charmoy and Demange, to teach Eastern languages at St. Petersburg University. Nonetheless, the fact that Foreign Minister Nesselrode felt compelled to open a school for Eastern language instruction in his own department in 1823, under the leadership of the eminent orientalist Adelung, demonstrated that regular state schools were not producing the trained manpower needed in this area.[49]

At Uvarov's behest, the 1835 university statute provided for the teaching of Turkish, Arabic, and Persian at Moscow, Kharkov, and St. Petersburg. In keeping with his viewpoint, it was stressed that "the political and literary life of the peoples be taught as well as the mechanics of the languages." Nonetheless, the universities at Moscow and Kharkov suffered from a lack of teachers even after Uvarov waived degree requirements. The flamboyant Senkovskii, however, who taught at St. Petersburg, attracted a considerable following and is considered the founder of the school of orientalism there. In 1829 and 1832, along with Frähn and Charmoy, Senkovskii proposed plans for a full, special section of Eastern languages in the university, but the suggestion was rejected both for lack of money and because of Uvarov's hostility to Senkovskii's other life in journalism. Nevertheless, in the next decade, the university added Mongolian, Tatar, Georgian, and Armenian to the curriculum, and offered public lectures in Sanskrit.[50]

Uvarov hoped to center the teaching of Eastern studies at Kazan University where, because of its location, they were a "living" science, not confined to the classroom. Fortunately, both the superintendent, Musin-Pushkin, and the rector, Lobachevskii, were completely committed to Eastern studies. In 1833, Kazan became the first university in Europe to teach Mongolian; in preparation, Uvarov had sent P. Popov and Osip Kovalevskii to Irkutsk and Beijing to study, and upon their return he encouraged them to prepare Mongolian grammars and anthologies. In the next decade, the university offered Chinese as well, for the first time in Russia. Two students from the Beijing Spiritual Mission, Daniel Sivillov and Osip Voitsekhovskii, assisted. The curriculum also included Armenian, which was taught by Stepannos Nazariants, a native of Tiflis, after he had been trained by Frähn at Uvarov's direction. The minister, still filled with his fantasies about India, personally supervised the training of A. V. Popov so that he could fill a chair in Sanskrit in 1842. The curriculum of Kazan University thus offered the widest range of courses available in Europe for the study of Eastern languages.[51]

Lobachevskii and Musin-Pushkin had a more grandiose scheme for establishing an Eastern institute at Kazan, an idea that Uvarov could not help supporting, but for reasons still unclear the proposal was never adopted. Indeed, in 1854, the entire Eastern faculty of Kazan, including professors, students, the library, and a numismatic collection, was transferred to St. Petersburg University, where the division prospered. Most likely, several factors prompted the move. First, the new location was more convenient and comfortable for students and faculty alike. It was difficult to attract professors, especially those of European origin, to vacant chairs in Kazan, and the number of students enrolled had dropped from 42 in 1848 to 16 in 1852, whereas the St. Petersburg division opened with 44; indeed, 79 of the 197 graduates of the historical-philological faculty at St. Petersburg from 1839 to 1852 were in Eastern studies. Second, the St. Petersburg faculty could draw upon the resources of academicians and the Asiatic Museum. Third, because of its location in the administrative center of the empire, the faculty enjoyed closer contact with the ministries it was expected to serve; students trained at Kazan had difficulty obtaining government appointments, because the ministries preferred hiring those who had been trained and proven in the capital in their own institutes of Eastern languages. Finally, and perhaps of greatest importance for the quick change, when both Musin-Pushkin and Lobachevskii left Kazan in 1847 and Uvarov retired under fire in 1849, Kazan was left without patronage. In 1855, a separate Faculty of Eastern Languages of St. Petersburg University was opened. While it did not precisely fulfill Uvarov's dream of 1810, it did centralize Oriental studies in one city, although not in one institution.[52]

Uvarov was also the first minister of education systematically to carry on the tradition begun by Catherine the Great of encouraging the study of Eastern languages in gymnasia and district schools. As in higher education, his efforts were centered upon the Kazan Educational District. In 1836, the First Kazan Gymnasium introduced courses of study in Arabic, Persian, Turko-Tatar, Chinese, and Mongolian, with the expressed aim of training teachers for the educational ministry; translators and interpreters for the ministry of foreign affairs; and administrators, tax collectors, and border guards for the ministries of finance and internal affairs. Fourteen of the eighty state students enrolled in this Eastern curriculum, including one Buriat, Dorzhi Banzarov; Uvarov condescendingly cited him as an example that education could "be a possession even of the half-savage sons of the Mongolian steppes" and looked forward to a "new epoch" when the East would become educated. As a means of promoting this program, teachers in Transcaucasia and Siberia received salary bonuses. By 1843, Uvarov could boast that graduates had positions in the capital, Kazan, Tobolsk, Omsk, Orenburg, Astrakhan, Odessa, Tiflis, and Irkutsk, and in embassies and missions in Asia. Depending on local needs, gymnasia and district schools serving the eastern and southern portions of the empire introduced Persian, Armenian, Tatar, or Georgian. With pride, Uvarov pointed out that "in distant Siberia, in a school in Nerchinsk, the Mongol language has been introduced because of the desire of the merchant class of that city."

Further, Uvarov, along with internal affairs minister Alexis Orlov, fought for the upgrading of the Lazarev Institute in Moscow, a private school founded in 1800 by the merchant Ivan Lazarev for the study of his native Armenia. Uvarov and Orlov sought, with success, to have this school accredited as an institute of Eastern languages and then as a lycée with an eight-year course intended for translators, missionaries, and teachers as well as commercial consultants. Intense interest in conquering the Caucasus aided this effort. In addition, in 1847, Uvarov called for the establishment of state-sponsored Muslim schools in Tiflis so that children could learn their own religion as well as Russian language, customs, and laws, a policy similar to that undertaken among Jews. In 1848–1849, Uvarov, understanding he was about to fall from power, worried that he had not yet fully organized the Eastern aspect of his school "system"; in those years, he enacted over a dozen pieces of legislation increasing the number of schools serving Eastern Causasian peoples.[53]

Uvarov rightfully enjoyed a sense of pride in his contributions to Eastern studies in Russia. In 1843, he boasted:

> Foreign scholars who not very long ago accused Russia, both in public and private, of a lack of fundamental research on the East, to which it was contiguous and by which it was influenced, now unanimously and with amazement glorify the Russian government's institutions and the services their scholars have rendered in this area in such a short time and with such indubitable success.[54]

While his aim, as with other subject nationalities, was assimilation of Eastern peoples into a unified and uniform empire, his policy surely seemed humane compared with militant russification. Indeed, later ministers would complain that "the students of the faculty of Oriental languages of

St. Petersburg University and of Lazarev Institute are unsuited for our Asiatic areas, since they study the literature, history, and ethnography of the Asiatic peoples objectively and carry to them their own sympathies." This "sympathetic" attitude resulted in part from Uvarov's policies, based as they were on a profound respect for Eastern cultures fostered by the impact of the Oriental Renaissance. But, of course, he also expected Eastern subjects to reciprocate, with loyalty to the "enlightened" empire.[55]

In retrospect, it seems evident that Uvarov's policies among the border peoples scored mostly scholarly successes. He unquestionably deserves credit for his creation of St. Vladimir University, for his support of Dorpat, and for his contributions to Oriental and Slavic scholarship in Russia. However, his policy of cultural imperialism, of assimilating the various minorities into a Great Russian imperial family, achieved only meager results and was abandoned shortly after his fall. Then again, militant russification, the attack on local cultures and the forcible imposition of Great Russian culture on subject nationalities, was hardly a more successful policy—as the rest of the century proved. The problem was probably unsolvable; it still festers, and even more virulently, in the Soviet Union today. Nikitenko, always so observant, clearly saw the limitations of a policy of nationality and understood that *Realpolitik* on both sides could forge the only lasting links.

> Can the Germans, Poles, Moslems, and others be united with Russia in a mechanical way? They can be kept side by side, but it isn't possible to blend them into one indivisible, spiritual whole. They should feel content in their cohabitation with Russia, for they do have one thing in common under these conditions: their unity of interests.[56]

Even Uvarov's moderate approach antagonized ethnically conscious Poles, Balts, and Jews, since he still insisted upon Great Russian cultural and religious superiority. The simple request to adopt a common language, a rational necessity in any nation, met resistance, although some movement in this direction occurred. On the other hand, true respect for the culture of a subject nationality can foment revolutionary separatism; it was this implicit threat in Uvarov's policy that led in great part to his downfall in 1848–1849.

THE FALL FROM POWER

---

*The character of our century is the ubiquitous fermentation of minds, a dissatisfaction
with the present, and a striving for incessant changes.*   Uvarov, 1848

THROUGHOUT the 1830s and 1840s, Uvarov worked simultaneously to cultivate educational development and to maintain loyalty to the autocracy. Of the many ironies in Russian history, one is that his "system" generally succeeded, while his reputation and career suffered ill fortune. Although revolutions erupted throughout Western Europe in 1848 and 1849, peace continued to reign in the empire, in its schools and among the educated public. However, the occurrence of these "events," as officials euphemistically called the outbreaks, panicked the imperial government and seemed to demand new and rigorous measures for crushing any hint of domestic unrest. As a result, Nicholas began to cast aside Uvarov's moderate policies in regard to nationality, censorship, the universities, and the gymnasia. Only the Academy of Sciences, scrupulously maintained as a purely scholarly, apolitical institution, was left intact. Uvarov, of course, contributed to his own fall. He made enemies, both for good and bad reasons: he insisted on his own panaceas for Russia's development and problems and clung tenaciously to power; on the other hand, as Granovskii noted, he fought off the "wild beasts" of reaction and would not succumb to the new hysteria.[1] He remained moderate to the end.

Uvarov grasped the expanding demands of the educated public. Indeed, in 1847, he seemed to think that Russia was finally nearing the goal of "maturity," when civil and political rights would be forthcoming. In that year, talk of emancipation was rife, and the country appeared prosperous and secure. Uvarov himself proposed a new university statute that would have greatly enhanced the freedom of both professors and students and loosened their structured existence. He apparently discerned some "discontent" over the tight and perhaps now superfluous regulations that aimed at assuring the "trustworthiness" of the community. In addition, as Isaiah Berlin noticed, 1847 "marks the highest point of relative toleration on the part of the censorship."[2] However, the government and Uvarov's position in it were somewhat shaken by the disclosure, early in the year, of revolutionary, separatist sentiments in the Ukraine, a result, apparently, of renewed interest in local culture.

THE SOCIETY OF STS. CYRIL AND METHODIUS

UVAROV bore some responsibility for this unwelcome development, since he was the first minister of education systematically to encourage Slavic studies. From a Romantic and historical standpoint, such studies served to discover, create, and glorify interest in the roots and past of the premier Slavic power, Russia. In addition, they could act as a healthy antidote to the usual portrayal of the West as the only notable agent of civilization in the contemporary world. Russian pride warranted moving the center of this scholarship to the empire from Prague, the seat of most great Slavists of the day.

Especially in the provinces bordering on or once belonging to Poland, Slavic studies also seemed a political asset. Officials fondly believed and Ustrialov confidently preached that Ukrainians, White Russians, and Lithuanians would learn that their origin and fate, while of a certain uniqueness and charm, were most naturally and legally tied to those of their Great Russian brothers and protectors. At the same time, the legitimist Russian government frowned upon pan-Slavism, but shrugged if off as the dimmest possible revolutionary dream in the empire. Other states, however, interested in maintaining the existing balance of power, worried that promotion of Slavic studies in Russia foreshadowed an imperialistic thrust. To allay these fears, from the early 1840s Nicholas ordered censors to pay "especially strict attention" to publications in this area, including the works of the Moscow Slavophiles. Nothing "harmful" surfaced, and early in 1847, as luck would have it, Uvarov officially welcomed the arrival of a Bulgarian in Kiev to study at a gymnasium, and called the event "a sign of brotherhood among Orthodox Slavs."[3]

The discovery of the Society of Sts. Cyril and Methodius in Kiev later that year demonstrated where such "brotherhood" could lead. Uvarov seemed compromised. At first glance, the society, named after the ninth-century apostles who brought both Christianity and an alphabet to the Slavs, appeared revolutionary indeed, although it was committed to nonviolence in the pursuit of its aims. Its statute and a proclamation addressed to "Brother Ukrainians" cited "unity" as the "true destiny" of all Slavs. In the future, each Slavic group would enjoy political and cultural independence, a republican form of government, and a classless society. However, a *sobor*, or general assembly, would bind the various "tribes" together; the society's members admitted that they had modeled their dream of a Slavic federation upon ancient Greek republics and the United States of America. A set of eleven rules enjoined members to disseminate their views through the peaceful means of educating youth, publishing tracts, and attracting confederates.

Another document, *Scripture (Zakon Bozhii)*, attempted, in ten pages, to present a universal philosophy of history. It argued, like Uvarov, that equality was the central message of Christianity, but it went on to condemn all nonegalitarian forms of government, whether Eastern despotisms or contemporary autocracies, as perversions of God's law. Not surprisingly, since the society was composed of Ukrainian romantic nationalists, it enshrined the Cossacks, with their supposedly classless and freedom-loving sense of brotherhood, as the only remaining body of the faithful; and it made of the Ukraine God's only comfort: "Not one country in the world prayed so sincerely to God, nowhere did husband so love his wife, and children respect their parents." The Ukraine, of course, was to lead her brethren—despite the fact that many of them had "crucified and divided her"—to a glorious future of "Slavic union, universal equality, brotherhood, peace, and love of our Lord Jesus Christ."[4] Thus, the program of the Cyril-Methodius society blended Cossack romanticism, Christian democracy, and republican pan-Slavism, while simultaneously attacking tsarism, serfdom, Great Russian nationalism, and international political order.

Despite the rhetoric found in their unpublished documents, upon investigation the group appeared pretty harmless, even to the members of the secret police—at least once the latter concluded to their satisfaction that the society had no connection with Polish nationalist revolutionaries nestled in Paris. Like so many "circles" in this era, the society met informally during one year, 1846, held heated discussions into the night, in this instance about the glories of the Ukraine, proposed a practical program, and then disbanded because career opportunities caused the dispersal of members; much the same had happened with Arzamas. In fact, the brotherhood had more or less collapsed just before an impoverished St. Vladimir University student informed on it in the hope of receiving some monetary reward. Count A. F. Orlov, head of the Third Section since Benkendorf's death in 1843, reported: "The evil did not mature, [but] partially destroyed itself, and the rest was intercepted by government measures." In the end, the evidence warranted penalizing ten young men.

All the men had—either through professsors of Slavic studies, the works of Gogol, or the general influence of the Romantic era—developed an enthusiasm for Ukrainian and other Slavic cultures and a desire to give them respectability. They also shared, indeed with the government, an aversion to Polish influence in the Ukraine. Of the ten, Taras Shevchenko, Nicholas Kostomarov, and Panteleimon Kulish, all about thirty years old at the time of their arrest, made the most substantial contributions to Ukrainian culture. Shevchenko, already a noted artist and poet in the capital, was not part of the brotherhood but was implicated through correspondence as an influence. He was sent into the military, which destroyed his health, because of the discovery of a notebook filled with a harsh cycle of poems, "Three Years," that accused Russians of being "murderers" and "cannibals" and lamented the russification of the Ukraine. Kulish, in 1847 a novelist, poet, Russian teacher, and budding Slavist, was also not an active member of the society, since he resided in St. Petersburg. But, because of his similar sympathies, he was jailed for four months and exiled to Tula; by 1853, he was back in the capital, where he worked to develop Ukrainian prose and literary criticism. Kostomarov was an historian who stressed the creative role of the people as opposed to their leaders and wrote a master's thesis on folk poetry, emphasizing Ukrainian songs. He actively participated in the brotherhood and was jailed for one year and then exiled. Despite his continuing stress on Ukrainian themes, in 1859 he managed to replace Ustrialov at St. Petersburg University. Of the other seven, two spent some time in jail or exile, the rest were exonerated, and all soon resumed active and productive lives.[5]

The episode, however, put Uvarov on the defensive and marked the beginning of the end of his career. While Orlov dismissed the sociey as "no more than learned delirium" on the part of young people, he implied a stinging criticism of Uvarov's vigilance. He pointed out that, since nearly all the accused had been in some way or other involved in the educational ministry, "they had the opportunity to sow corruption among the growing generation and prepare future disturbances." "Luckily," Orlov added, the Third Section intervened; in truth, though, it discovered the "conspiracy" only through an unsolicited informer. Of the ten who were charged, four were students or recent graduates of St. Vladimir University, Uvarov's "own creation," and one was a Dorpat University product, but also a functionary in Bibikov's office. Furthermore, in 1843 the ministry had blessed Kulish's historical poem on the Ukraine by ordering copies for all libraries in the district; at the moment of arrest, he and another member, V. Belozerskii, were en route to a two-and-one-half year tour of Slavic lands funded by the Academy of Sciences. Shevchenko's published works had passed all censors, and, as luck would have it again, just days before his arrest, Uvarov had appointed him professor of drawing at St. Vladimir University.

In addition, after Dombrovskii's recent death in 1845, Kostomarov had taken over the sensitive and influential chair of Russian history at St. Vladimir's. Uvarov approved the appointment despite the fact that as a student the young scholar had shown a decided lack of political judgment. In 1840, he wrote a dissertation on the still-sensitive topic of the Uniate Church in the Western provinces. (In 1839, in yet another attempt further to eradicate Polish cultural ties, the government had suppressed the Uniates in a messy process that included some violence and arrests.) Uvarov allowed Kostomarov to write another thesis, but Kostomarov never repented; in 1862, he was removed from his next post at St. Petersburg University because he continued, unlike Ustrialov, to stress the differences rather than the similarities between Ukrainians and Great Russians. At any rate, the men of the brotherhood were obvious products of Uvarov's "system" and front-line warriors in his battle against Polish influence in the border provinces. The minister encouraged local patriotism as a defensive weapon, but it obviously could be turned offensively against the empire itself.[6]

Clearly, Uvarov had to justify his policy of nationality. In a lengthy report to the tsar, dated May 8, 1847, the minister repeated an assertion he had made in the early 1840s, namely that there existed two "Slavisms." One was destructive of state order and the other the inspiration for and object of legitimate historical investigation. He agreed that among Slavs living under foreign domination, the two often went hand in hand. Fifty years ago, he suggested, scholars in Bohemia had originated the idea that someday there should be a "purely Slavic state." While generating interest "everywhere in the languages, history, antiquities, in a word, for all evidence of Slavic originality," this striving "could not long remain within the peaceful borders of scholarship and pure brotherhood." Uvarov added that when he visited Prague and corresponded with Czech scholars, he applauded them for their work, but warned them that their perhaps natural turning to Russia for help in "breaking their oppression" would find "neither echo nor sympathy." Unfortunately, Uvarov rued, the pan-Slav "dream," usually pinning its hopes on Russia to go to war with Prussians, Austrians, and Turks to free her brethren, continued to find adherents to its "errors" and denigrated Slavism to a "pretext" or "cover" for revolutionary ideas.

In his report, Uvarov treated the ideas found in the *Scripture* of the Cyril-Methodius society with total condescension and dismissed them as a perversion of all Slavisms. He saw the document as the jejune product of a *"provincial spirit,"* not a "Slavic spirit," and a mere "echo of Ukrainian prejudices" in its claim of the superiority of one Slavic branch over another. Uvarov attributed this provinciality to the tendency of the society's members to "grieve over past independence, their Hetmanate, their rakish Cossacks, the enserfment of their free inhabitants, the loss of local privileges, perhaps, over the loss of the free sale of alcohol." Unlike other Slavs, the "Ukrainophiles" called not for Slavic unity under one government, but for the fragmented existence of each tribe and, more alarmingly, for the *"dismemberment of Russia."* Uvarov concluded that the "rhapsodical, good-natured Moscow Slavophiles," with whom he enjoyed friendly relations, would never agree with the society's program, nor would other Ukrainians. He was, in fact, correct; both groups looked upon the brotherhood as a "small number of mindless children."

Nonetheless, these errant "children" were all part of the ministerial family. Despite his many character flaws, Uvarov always took full responsibility for his actions and admitted that the "affair" had "the closest ties with the ministry." But, he added, and cited Bibikov's concurrence, the ideas of the society had been gleaned not from university teaching but from "hidden conversations in secret societies," that is, their development should have been checked by the Third Section. Even if Uvarov squirmed out of the charge of lack of vigilance, his educational policies remained open to criticism. The European press began to call him a "démasqué" propagandist for pan-Slavism since his school system sponsored Slavic studies. Such attacks placed the legitimist Nicholas, the "gendarme of Europe," in an awkward foreign policy position.

Scholarly Slavism and interest in local color did, often, seem only one step removed from revolutionary pan-Slavism and nationalist separatism. Uvarov, a true believer in an imperial *narodnost'*, attempted to avoid the "complex" dilemma. For Russian subjects, Slavism could only mean "the Russian spirit, the source of our state principle, that cornerstone on which rests throne and altar." He boasted of having created among youth—"without recourse to coercive measures"—a devotion to a truly Russian nationality.

> What weapon has rendered us more service than the awakening of the spirit of the Fatherland under the triple formula: Orthodoxy, Autocracy, Nationality? If our sons know the native language better than we, if they are more familiar with our history, with our traditions, with the way of life of the people, does this not prove that their education has, in every way, received a Russian orientation? If, to the banks of the Niemen and beyond, everyone has begun to speak Russian, if everyone studies according to Russian models, if even in the Baltic provinces the supremacy of national education grows stronger every day, is it not the Russian language, the Russian spirit that has produced and that continues to produce this happy result?

Uvarov then vindicated Slavic studies as a logical consequence of his measures.

> In order to give more vigor to this spirit, the ministry necessarily turned toward that which is its very source: the basic study of the ecclesiastical Slavic language and related Slavic dialects. This is why, with the authorization of Your Majesty, Russian universities have created chairs of Slavic languages, and the study of these languages has been made obligatory even in secondary schools. The principal

monuments of our ancient Slavic-Russian literature have been lifted from oblivion, a great number of documents that serve the study of history have been published at the expense of the government. At the same time, the ministry has unceasingly been on guard to keep this movement within the limits of legality and good order.[7]

About three weeks after his personal report to the tsar, Uvarov, "by imperial command," sent a circular to all superintendents that they were to read to their university councils. It outlined the tenets of "true" Slavism and contained instructions for "*preventive* measures" so that revolutionary ideas would not blossom in the schools. Uvarov's arguments followed the line of the earlier commentary and defended Slavic studies as an apolitical investigation of the "general hereditary" background of the Russian people. But he also inserted a new stress on Russia's "own personality" as a "special idea of Providence" and on the fact that Russia alone among Slavic states had "preserved its independence." Apparently at the behest of the emperor, Uvarov, for the first time in his career, made a strongly patriotic distinction between a "Slavic-Russian" and "pure Russian" nationality; only the latter was permissible.

> Therefore, independent of general Slavism. . . we ought to follow our own fortunes . . . in our own native principle, our own national personality, our own faith, devotion to the throne, in language, literature, in history, in our own laws, morals, and mores; we are obliged to uphold the vital principle of the Russian mind, Russian valor, Russian feeling.[8]

Uvarov reiterated his set pronouncement that Peter advised his subjects to "remain Russian in spirit and heart, but to equal Europeans in education." He then preached that the rest of Slavdom was of no concern to Russia.

> Holy Russia lived through distress and suffered alone; alone she shed her blood for the Throne and for the Faith; alone she advanced with a firm and rapid step on the course of her civic development; alone she rose to fight the twenty nations that invaded her borders with fire and sword in their hands. Everything that we have in Russia belongs to us alone, without the participation of other Slavic peoples who now stretch their hands toward us and beg for protection, not so much from an inspiration of brotherly love as from the calculations of a petty and not always disinterested egoism.[9]

Such crude intellectual chauvinism was not Uvarov's style, but through Orlov the tsar told him to do as he said, "not asking the reasons." Confusion followed in the censorship department; articles about Slavism, for which three days previously authors had been thanked, were now banned. For the rest of the era, the secret police even felt obligated to hound the harmless Moscow Slavophiles.

Sergei Stroganov, of the Moscow Educational District, balked at the order to read the circular even though Uvarov, anticipating trouble from a man with whom he did not get along, accompanied it with a palliative note written in French (Stroganov had trouble with the Russian language). The superintendent insisted that he needed, before addressing his university council, full information about the Cyril-Methodius society, and he maliciously cited Uvarov's 1842 directive that "the question of Slavic propaganda far exceeded the limits" of his department. Nicholas abhorred insubordination and, despite his personal liking of Stroganov, found the obstinate response "disgraceful and incongruous." Stroganov then resigned his post on the grounds that "my concepts of service to Your Majesty cannot be reconciled with the concepts held by the minister of national enlightenment."[10] This proved a pyrrhic victory for Uvarov, since Stroganov then joined the forces working to unseat him.

1848 AND THE CENSORSHIP

DESPITE the embarrassment of the whole Cyril-Methodius affair, Uvarov's position might still have proved tenable if revolution had not broken out in France in February 1848. The French monarchy fell; a republic was declared. Unrest rapidly spread eastward and reached Russia's borders with clarion calls for political and civil freedom, independence for national minorities, and better conditions for the working classes. In reality, the Russian government had little to fear; open dissidence seemed remarkably absent, although there did exist a smoldering disquiet among the educated classes because of the lethargic movement of change or reform. People were getting anxious. In November 1847, when cannon shots warned the capital's population of rising water levels—the flooding of the Neva River was a constant problem in this city built on a swamp— the Third Section reported that many believed a revolution had begun, that the people were rising instead of the water. But Belinskii had a keener eye: "The people need potatoes, but not a constitution in the least; that is wanted by the educated urban classes, who are incapable of doing anything."[11]

Nonetheless, Nicholas began to panic and especially to fear a jacquerie. In March 1848, he reached back into the arsenal of old-regime weapons and held out "the hand of friendship" to the landed nobility, long neglected as a partner in government in favor of the more modern bureaucratic elite. He called upon the gentry to become his "police" in the countryside; to guard "the thoughts and morality of young people" they knew; to prevent their house servants from hearing news of European upheavals; to treat their serfs well and report on "cruel" masters so that causes for unrest might be avoided. The serf owners gladly cooperated because, as one contemporary noted, they were "more scared" than any other group in the population. Although the government in general tried to mute talk of the revolution, Baron Modest Korf reported that people in the capital became "preoccupied," "afraid"; "whenever two people met," they argued about "freedom of the press, national representation, or nationalist uprisings." Even without the "events" in Europe, the year 1848 was star-crossed for Russia: a universally bad harvest produced the worst famine of the era; a dreadful cholera epidemic struck, on the average, one of every twenty-eight Russians, and "terror reigned everywhere," emptying the cities; a dry summer increased fires by 25 percent, causing more death, alarm, and economic turmoil.

Nicholas responded to these crises by becoming more and more frightened and more and more reactionary. His first concern, and logically so, was over the possibility that the revolutionary infection would spread to the Kingdom of Poland and the border provinces. Hundreds of thousands of soldiers were moved to form "a solid cordon from the shores of the Baltic to the Black Sea." The tsar urged Uvarov to take swift measures to assure the loyalty of students, who so recently had been suspect, but the minister calmly and correctly asserted that all was in order; he merely issued circulars of warning to superintendents to watch for "echoes" of the "events" in Europe.

Bibikov and Paskevich, not satisfied, began policing the school system and enacting stricter measures; for example, at St. Vladimir's, one student wrote: "For a joke, one is expelled, and this never happened before; we're being squeezed to nothing." Uvarov, angry at this infringement on his domain and still opposed to militant russification, complained: "They want to let blood and think that I will stand and hold the basin." The minister's comment reached the tsar, who sided with his governor-general and viceroy, and, it was reported, "from that day onward did not like Uvarov." At the same time, the Baltic Germans at court complained that Uvarov's policies had intensified the enmity between them and the Slavic population and that his "Slavophilism" could cause separatist sentiment in their home provinces.[12]

The fact that the revolutions had started in France also compromised Uvarov's position. Since 1830, Nicholas had shown an open dislike for the France of Louis-Philippe, the "bourgeois king" whom he considered illegitimate, as well as foolish for agreeing to rule as a constitutional monarch. The drift of Russian foreign policy had been to isolate France, break the *entente cordiale* that loosely aligned it and Britain, and win over the English as an ally of the Eastern powers. By 1846, these goals seemed well on their way to accomplishment since, in that year, the incident of the so-called Spanish Marriages alienated Britain and France from each other. Lord Palmerston returned to the British foreign office; he was amenable to the

Russian policy, although suspicious, as he always had been, that it masked expansionism.

Uvarov, on the contrary, maintained a certain "progressive" sympathy for the government of Louis-Philippe and his prime minister, Guizot, with whom he corresponded; some foreigners and Russians perceived Uvarov as the leader, albeit discreet, of a pro-French faction at court. Since his youth, he had always revered France as the center of European intellectual life, and he relished being applauded in its press for his peerless erudition and his ability to write in French "better than any non-native outside the country." As further proof of his intellectual prowess, in 1845 Uvarov published a volume of his collected essays, *Études de philologie et de critique*, in Paris.[13]

Uvarov's next "literary" foray involved sending a dozen anonymous copies to the French capital of an essay he had published in a limited edition in St. Petersburg, *Stein et Pozzo di Borgo* (which, curiously, bore no censorship imprimatur). Uvarov was either naive or devious, but surely imprudent. The essay reminisced about the two leaders of anti-Napoleonic politics when Uvarov knew them in 1809. Stein dreamed about a "liberal" unified Germany; Pozzo looked toward a new and "legitimate" European order based on Russian hegemony, although in partnership with a restored France.

The brochure, published in 1846 at that delicate moment in Russian-French-British relations, caused a furor in France and frowns in all the foreign offices. The author, of course, was immediately exposed. Editorials in the French press reached diverse conclusions about the "meaning" of the essay, but in general discovered "a political secret on each page." Some considered Uvarov a spokesman for the emperor and the essay, in its clear hostility to Napoleon, an affront to "amour propre." Others feared further evidence of the attempt to elevate an expansionist Russia once again as Europe's "savior" and to deprive France of her "intellectual supremacy and material domination" on the continent. One typically condescending editorial considered it "folly" to suggest that "a barbaric, enslaved Russia, without commerce, without agriculture, without poetry, without theatre, without literature, without art, and without sun" should exert leadership in Europe. Others interpreted the brochure as a clue that Russia wanted an alliance with France, not England, and was stretching out a hand for partnership, especially since the two countries had just negotiated a commercial treaty.

Because of the controversy, Uvarov felt compelled to have the essay translated into English and published in London. The translator included prefatory remarks that attacked the Parisians for "gratuitously ascribing to the publication objects altogether foreign to it, . . . as having especial reference to certain grave political questions which now occupy the attention of European cabinets."[14] Instead, he advised, the reader should regard the essay as a simple, and very well-written, memoir. At about the same time, after a meeting with Metternich, Uvarov advised the tsar not to "quarrel" with the pope since he still enjoyed enormous support from Catholic nations. Nicholas tersely remarked at a *soirée*, "Uvarov is meddling in things that are none of his business."[15]

Unfortunately for Uvarov, even things that were his business began coming under attack. As Nikitenko later recalled the events of 1848: "At that time it became customary to blame everything on the ministry of education." Russian officials, including the minister, possessed an awesome belief in the power of ideas and hence of the printed word. Thus the revolutions of 1848 immediately threw the domestic spotlight on censorship matters. Uvarov's policy of compromise and of making "allowances" could hardly quell the growing paranoia that began to grip the government. In addition, again as luck would have it, another of Uvarov's collections of essays, with the compromising title *Esquisses politiques et littéraires*, appeared in Paris just after the revolution began; a rhapsodic introduction praised this "friend and admirer" of all things French.[16]

Also ominous, in the two months preceding the news of revolution, Bulgarin began stepping up his decade-long battle against the "liberalism" reflected in *Notes of the Fatherland* and the *Contemporary*, especially because these publications had just denigrated his quarter-century career in publishing as one long act of "self-promotion." At the end of 1847, a young lieutenant from the Mining Institute admitted to the Third Section that he had imbibed his progressive ideas and then disrespect for all things Russian from *Notes of the Fatherland*. Bulgarin and his "spies," in Nikitenko's phrase, used the opportunity to spread "the blackest slander" about both journals.

In mid-February of 1848, the secret police received three anonymous memoranda. The first condemned Belinskii, who had written for first one and then the other journal. The detractor claimed that the author's criticism of old Russian writers and his praise for "only Gogol" could lead to a negation "both of power and of the existing order and even of the tsar," as it had in the case of the young officer. Furthermore, although the fact was not specifically noted in the memorandum, the *Contemporary* had just published a long series of articles by a young economist, Vladimir Miliutin, on socialism, which he described as an infant science and still a dreamy ideal. In denouncing the *Contemporary*, the memorandum did not portray the journal as intentionally communistic, but it warned: *"There exists in its articles something similar to communism and the young generation can, from them, become completely communistic."* The second report condemned the *Notes* in similar fashion.[17]

The third memorandum focused a direct, personal attack on Uvarov. The January 1848 issue of the *Northern Review* (*Severnoe obozrenie*) contained a translation of the minister's article "Vues générales de la philosophie de la littérature." It presented his usual thesis that there were two historical literary epochs, the pagan and the Christian. In the former, art was "democratic" and "chaotic" since it reflected a materialistic society, while in the latter era in was "aristocratic" and impregnated with the unity of religious values. But Uvarov also took pains to praise such foes of the authoritarian state as Cato, Brutus, and Socrates, just at the time when censors were ordered to expurgate their names from textbooks. Again with an unfortunate sense of timing, Uvarov reiterated his belief in "the grand evolution of humanity" and his confidence that the "genius of Christian civilization," meaning equality, would soon penetrate the "new social system" now emerging. These passages were quoted in the memorandum to demonstrate that Uvarov bore "an indubitable resemblance to our fashionable young journalists," especially of the *Contemporary* and *Notes;* indeed, Uvarov had also recently published in the former a translation of his essay on the Eleusinian Mysteries. The memorandum listed the minister's sins: he composed in a modish literary "style," wrote "obtusely," used "words of foreign origin," and babbled on forever without saying "anything of importance." The closing lamentation stung: "It is a shame that our young writers, in composing their senseless works, have an example and even support in the minister of national enlightenment."[18]

On February 23, the morning after the tsar had received news that a republic had been declared in France, Orlov presented him with a summary of the reports. The head of the Third Section tried to excuse his own department by maintaining that no overt threat to the established order was to be found in the journals' articles; he assigned the blame for any revolutionary potential to the laxity of Uvarov's censors. In the future, they should ferret out "allusions" and "doubtful expressions" and "stop the filthy works of the Natural School in literature." The latter's emphasis on social and moral evil threatened to harm "public morality, the taste of educated people, and the Russian language." Everyone in the government seemed to fancy himself a literary critic.

The next day, Korf, an educated man who apparently wanted Uvarov's post for himself, used his connections as a tutor in the royal family to present the tsar with a previously prepared critique of the censorship establishment. "In the light of the dreadful events in Europe," he warned, it was necessary to "preserve our lower classes from the incursion of dangerous concepts." The periodical press was "in everyone's hands" and was read in "taverns," but "why should a lackey or a shopkeeper know that a throne has been toppled in Paris?" He suggested a thorough investigation of both newspapers and the "thick journals." The latter, in particular, often exceeded their officially approved "programs" and size; they spoke about and praised forbidden foreign books (the works of Lamartine, Michelet, and Blanc were used as examples). Korf complained that, contrary to regulations, the journals even published political news.

Stroganov, himself publicly perceived as a "progressive aristocrat" with close ties to Granovskii and other Westerners, sought revenge for his dismissal at Uvarov's hands. He entered the fray with a comment to Nicholas "on the liberalism, communism, and socialism reigning in the censorship and in the entire ministry of national enlightenment." Bulgarin, not letting the opportunity slip, followed with a note on "communism in Russia": "Among us there is more material for a revolution than many think." He placed the blame squarely on Uvarov for allowing the *Notes* and the *Contemporary* to continue publication and for his execrable choice of censors: Professor Krylov was an "idiot," science professor Kutorga only "knows about cows," Nikitenko was a "former serf and liberal," while Sreznevskii was a "Little Russian." But what could one expect, Bulgarin concluded, since for Uvarov "Orthodoxy, Autocracy, Nationality" were "only words," and he "himself writes little brochures and little articles." The tsar, dumbfounded and panicked, within the week created a special committee to investigate the periodical press.[19]

On February 27, Nicholas resolved that his new committee should "discern whether or not the censorship is functioning properly" and should bring him directly any information of "dereliction of the censorship and its office, i.e., the ministry of national enlightenment." There lingered few doubts that this represented a direct attack on Uvarov. Prince A. S. Menshikov, after whom the committee was named, took over its chairmanship. A bibliophile, admiral, and one of the tsar's few close personal friends, he hesitated to accept this duty because, he admitted, the committee smacked too much of an "inquest over Uvarov"; later he tried to convince Uvarov that he himself was "not an inquisitor." At any rate, Menshikov called the investigation "an altogether unpleasant job." Indeed, other members of the committee were Uvarov's outright enemies: Korf, Count D. P. Buturlin, head of the Imperial Public Library and a man of right-wing views, and Alexander Stroganov, brother of the erstwhile superintendent. The other two appointments to the committee included the more neutral General Dubelt of the Third Section and the jurist Paul Degai, but they were added only as afterthoughts.

The Menshikov Committee operated for a month, until March 29. It forced Uvarov to open the entire censorship archive and to carry out the committee's measures; but because he was not consulted on these, and poorly understood them, the result was confusion. The committee asked for his comments only on March 24. In the meantime, it bypassed the minister. It summoned the editors of various journals and, as a preventive measure, frightened them with the news that they were to be held responsible for any "bad direction" in articles, even if this was accomplished by "indirect allusions" and even if the material had already been cleared by regular censors. It should be noted that as early as 1843 Uvarov had suggested to Nicholas involving editors in the censorial process.

The committee members investigated several journals and, as expected, singled out the *Contemporary* and *Notes of the Fatherland* for articles that were "imprudent" and "blameworthy" but that stopped short of criminal intent. Nonetheless, the Menshikov Committee discerned suspicious tendencies of the journals to concentrate on the mitigation of social evils, to criticize contemporary Russian life, and, through "allusions," perhaps to squeeze in a "secret aim" of attacking the autocracy. The government, of course, considered such public discussion of problems and solutions an encroachment on its desired monopoly. In the end, the committee advised not closing the journals, for fear of public outcry, but drawing up a new, and presumably more severe, code. In the meantime, censors should maintain strict vigilance and prohibit outright any articles dealing with actual or proposed government measures. A last suggestion called for doubling the salary of censors, a move Uvarov thought overdue; he had long complained that censors were overworked, underpaid, and hence not held in a sufficient degree of esteem to attract much talent into their ranks.[20]

Despite the weight of personal attacks on his administration, Uvarov, in his presentation before the Menshikov Committee, managed a strong and intelligent defense of his censors. Everyone, he claimed, underrated the "difficulties" of their position. "Eighteenth-century sophists," he explained, were easy to handle because they flaunted their revolutionary ideas, but "contemporary writers," at least those in the West, "slowly pour their teachings sweetened with sugar into the educated public," which is therefore unsuspecting. And yet, he insisted, Russian writers needed an acquaintanceship with Western European literature in order to improve their own quality and remain abreast of developments abroad—thus, the ministry made "allowances." "The character of our century," he went on, "is the ubiquitous fermentation of minds, a dissatisfaction with the present, and a striving for incessant changes." The only Russian journals that had adopted this "character" were the *Telegraph* and *Telescope*, and he had long ago closed them. He implied that the new vitality of the contemporary intellectual scene made it impossible to weed out every potentially dangerous idea without destroying national literature itself.[21]

The Menshikov group proved to Nicholas's satisfaction that the periodical press had indeed gone astray. On April 2 the tsar ordered the creation of a permanent watchdog committee composed of Buturlin, Korf, and Degai. Nicholas considered the committee "the supreme purveyor of the spirit and direction of our publishing in regard to its moral and political aspects." In establishing it, he introduced dual censorship into Russia. Preliminary censorship was left to regular ministerial channels, while the Buturlin Committee would examine what appeared in print, acting as "the eyes" of the tsar and reporting directly to him. Uvarov knew nothing about this new institution until April 16. For the previous two weeks, he worked under the assumption that he was only to author a new censorship code and slap the hands of the editors of the two "untrustworthy" journals,

Kraevskii and Nikitenko (who promptly and quakingly recanted their past "sins" to the Third Section), and that there the matter ended.

Once Uvarov learned of the creation of the Buturlin Committee, he was shaken. Pletnev had dinner with him in April and described him as a "pitiful man" who "trembles like a timid *chinovnik*." In truth, the committee had the single responsibility of making sure Uvarov did his duty as a censor; thereafter, it hounded him for records, reprimanded him for infractions, and ordered him to explain every detail of his censorship activity. In general, the Buturlin Committee, operating in secret, banned so many types of articles and used such harsh tactics that its tutelage, lasting to the end of the reign, became known as "the epoch of censorship terror."

Uvarov, knowing he had nothing to lose, defiantly inaugurated "the most liberal period of his reign in censorship matters"—and these are the words of a generally harsh critic. He passed articles and books that his colleagues thought "contrary to law" or "impermissible," such as an illustrated almanac with caricatures of public figures, an article on Peter the Great that contained "historical inaccuracies" (but these were corrected in footnotes by Ustrialov), and a translation of Chateaubriand that dealt with revolution.[22] But in one instance, Uvarov used his remaining power and the new atmosphere to be ruthlessly severe, and did so only out of a desire for revenge.

Testifying before the Menshikov Committee, Uvarov dismissed as "ridiculous" the opinion that articles on pre-Petrine Russia and discussions of Peter's reforms were really mirrors for advocating changes at the present moment or for disparaging the contemporary autocracy. He adopted a different position, however, six months later, when Giles Fletcher's highly critical essay of 1588 on Russian despotism and barbarism appeared in the October 1848 issue of Moscow University's *Readings of the Society of Russian History and Antiquities (Chteniia obshchestva istorii i drevnostei Rossiiskikh)*. Uvarov then orchestrated an "affair." He informed the tsar that the manuscript contained "deprecatory remarks" about the Russian government and clergy and would have a "pernicious effect" on the public. Uvarov's point was that Stroganov, while superintendent and hence censor, had performed his job poorly in approving Fletcher's essay. Stroganov, on the other hand, complained that the whole furor was a result of "Uvarov's personal enmity toward me" and that "not one line could be related to contemporary Russia." The tsar, probably correctly, agreed with Uvarov that there was a relationship and gave Stroganov a severe reprimand, much to Uvarov's satisfaction.[23]

Whatever the cruel, comic relief of "tit for tat," the post–1848 era did, to use Nikitenko's words, become one of "terror": "People were gripped by a panicky fear. . . . Terror gripped everyone who thought or wrote. Secret denunciations and spying complicated the situation even more." While there are no statistics available for the number of those persecuted, the oppressive atmosphere was pervasive. Another famed memoirist, Gleb Uspenskii, despaired:

> One could not move, one could not even dream; it was dangerous to give any sign of thought—of the fact that you were not afraid; on the contrary, you were required to show that you were scared, trembling, even when there was no real ground for it—that is what those years have created in the Russian masses. Perpetual fear . . . was then in the air, and crushed the public consciousness and robbed it of all desire or capacity for thought. . . . There was not a single point of light on the horizon—"You are lost," cried heaven and earth, air and water, man and beast—and everything shuddered and fled from disaster into the first available rabbit hole.

Annenkov, who returned from Paris to St. Petersburg in October 1848, was stunned by the new atmosphere. He wrote that

> the situation in Petersburg seems extraordinary: the government's fear of revolution, the terror within brought on by the fear itself, persecution of the press, the buildup of the police, the suspiciousness, the repressive measures without need and without limit, the setting aside of the peasant question only just then due for consideration, the struggle between obscurantism and enlightenment, and the expectation of war. . . . Buturlin comes on the scene with his hatred for expression, thought, and freedom, preaching limitless obedience, silence, discipline. Extraordinary theories of education are laying the first stones for a grievous corruption of minds, characters, and natures.

Indeed, in that very month, rumors began circulating that the tsar intended to shut down the universities and gymnasia.[24]

THE ATTACK ON EDUCATION

THE gymnasia and universities remained open, but they underwent radical alteration beginning in 1849. The changes proved tantamount to a rejection of Uvarov's entire "system." Attacks were leveled in a variety of directions. Only three days after news of the French revolution reached Russia, Orlov ordered his police to check "the style of thought" of private school inspectors, who were usually academics drawn from the local university professoriate. This move implied distrust of Uvarov's method of surveillance and ushered in the Third Section's meddling with educational matters, something the minister had long fought. In addition, the tsar still looked askance at the fact that the private sector under Uvarov had continued to operate one-quarter of the schools in Russia. Furthermore, Stroganov, in his letter on censorship, accused Uvarov of "everywhere sowing the seeds of democracy" by leveling classes through education, especially at the middle level. Although the charge was a vengeful exaggeration, it was indeed true that Uvarov had not transformed secondary schools into fully elite bastions, as Nicholas had desired and as European administrators had generally succeeded in doing.[25]

In March 1849, Nicholas forced Uvarov to underwrite legislation that nearly demolished his lifelong work in the gymnasia. The new order abandoned the classical curriculum as the core of secondary education. The study of Latin was now required only for those intending to enter a university, and the number of hours stipulated was cut by half. Greek remained compulsory only for prospective students of philology. In 1848, forty-five of the seventy-nine gymnasia offered Greek, but, by 1852, it had disappeared except in university towns and in places like Taganrog and Nezhin that had a Greek population. A new, practical orientation was substituted for Uvarov's notion that the gymnasia serve primarily to funnel students into the universities. The changes were hastily enacted and were really negative in design; as a result, the "gymnasia proved incapable of providing either a broad cultural background or specialized instruction."

Several reasons accounted for this dramatic reversal in educational policy. In general, many youngsters, their parents, and even the tsar regarded the strenuous study of "dead" languages as useless and preferred more "modern" or practical subjects such as natural sciences or jurisprudence. The establishment in Germany of *Realschule* testified to a similar trend in the rest of Europe. However, the post-1848 panic lent ideological support to opponents of classical studies, who long regarded them as a potential source of subversion, republican ideas, and even atheism.

Yet another motivation led to the attack on the classical curriculum and its encouragement of students to pursue university studies. The tsar, according to his sister, the Grand Duchess Elena Pavlovna, was seriously concerned about the number of vacant positions for military officers and the growing preference among the nobility for a civil service career, a trend Uvarov did much to encourage. By the late 1840s, Nicholas had determined, especially because of the mobilization he thought necessary to fight revolution in the West, to deflect noblemen into military institutes after their gymnasium education. He echoed old-regime attitudes in announcing:

Children of the nobility, as descendants of the knights of old, should look primarily to the military service in preference to civil service. For this end, they have the choice of either entering military-educational institutes or going directly into the ranks of the army, and for this *a university education is not necessary.*

As it stood then, Uvarov had little hope of preserving his concept of the gymnasia, and Nicholas even refused him a hearing on the subject.[26]

Nicholas designed his new policy toward the gymnasia partly in order to discourage attendance at universities, which he still clearly regarded as the most probable source for revolutionary propaganda and recruitment; he even remarked to his advisers that universities might be "premature" for Russia. As seeming proof, heavy student involvement and often leadership characterized the revolutionary "events" in 1848–1849 in Western Europe. The minister himself was nervous, although still confident that the universities would remain calm. While he immediately banned foreign travel for scholarly purposes, he waited one month after hearing news of the European uprisings to issue a secret circular to superintendents reacting to the "latest events in Western Europe" that had "gradually spilled over into Germany." "In order that the pernicious philosophizings of criminal innovators not penetrate our numerous educational institutions," he advised close guard over "the spirit of teaching, . . . the conduct and style of thought of students . . . . the loyalty of officials . . . , and private institutions run by foreigners." His instructions were of a general nature.

> Of course, the most important means for preserving youth from the contagion of freethinking is: first, in the explicit teaching of the Scripture with direct emphasis on the unswerving duties of loyal citizens; second, in not allowing in the teaching of other subjects anything that might weaken the Faith in as yet immature minds or lessen conviction of the necessity and usefulness of the basic institutions of our government; and third, in vigilant and intense surveillance over the morality of students.

A few days later, Uvarov advised abridging sensitive courses, such as state law, political economy, history, and Slavic studies. He suggested "eliminating all that is unwarranted, superfluous, and out of place with present conditions, all that could, although in an indirect or inadvertent manner, contribute to the delusion of inexperienced minds," but, he added, these changes should be made "without disturbing the aims of teaching and without detriment to scholarship." Uvarov obviously clung to the hope that he could still effect that accommodation between autocratic politics and learning that had been the hallmark of his "system."

All the superintendents reported on the "good spirit" of their districts but admitted that the "events" in Europe were the topic of the day, and "each chatters about them from his own point of view."[27] In order to confirm this "good spirit," Uvarov visited Dorpat in the spring and Moscow in the fall of 1848. As was his habit during these inspections, Uvarov listened to lectures, had conferences with each professor, attended students' examinations, toured the gymnasia, clinics, and *pansions*, and awarded medals. The only problem he noted was that students exhibited a "corporate identity" and felt a right to be "subject to their own laws," a penchant he ordered eradicated lest they begin—needless to say, as students had done in all the countries undergoing revolution—to take "events" into their own hands. He did not confide this fear to the tsar, but only presented a luminous portrait of "the spirit of university youth" as "entirely trustworthy." Indeed, he accurately reported, despite the "impropitious events" in Europe, not only was "order not disturbed" but "everywhere conduct improved." It was true, for example, that St. Petersburg University, from 1845 to 1847, expelled nineteen students for smoking, playing cards during lectures, or not wearing proper uniforms; but in 1848, no one risked expulsion—probably because it meant a quick transfer to the army. Uvarov admitted that some "discontent of minds" had existed before the European revolution but claimed that it had now "abated."

> This volte-face in concepts is displayed more or less in all classes of society. It seems that minds, frightened by external horror, gather more closely around national principles and institutions. Everywhere is heard the echo of a general consciousness that, in the midst of upheavals disturbing neighboring states, Russia, guided by its firm and stable principles, presents a majestic calm, commensurate with its dignity and strength. Aversion to the sad events in Western Europe can be called general.

Uvarov concluded that his policies had "cured [students] of unthinking foreign imitation," and indeed the blessed calm precluded the necessity for any unusual measures. In his general report for 1848, the minister called the year "one of trial and testing" that his administration had passed with glowing colors.

> Providence, always kind to Russia, blessed our diligence and precautionary measures with success, not only preserving the public institutions of the ministry but further giving youth a new burst of respect for our basic state institutions and to the holy Person of Your Majesty.

His Majesty was quoted as replying, "I don't believe it."[28]

Despite Uvarov's assurances, Buturlin had the upper hand, and he called for "the full liquidation of the universities." Nikitenko recorded that the "university community is frightened and depressed."

> What a fantastic place is our Russian land! For 150 years we feigned a yearning for education. It seems this was all sham and pretense, for we are bolting backwards faster than we have ever gone forward. . . . [Buturlin] operates in such a way that it is becoming utterly impossible to write or publish anything at all. . . . Barbarism is celebrating its savage victory over the human mind, which was just beginning to think, and over education, which was just be-

ginning to come into its own. . . . What is fashionable now is the patriotism that rejects everything European, including science and art. . . . Patriots of this type have no understanding of history and think that the presence of physics, chemistry, astronomy, poetry, painting, etc., in the world is responsible for France's having proclaimed herself a republic and for Germany's revolt. . . . And now simple-hearted folk are sighing: "Well, you can see that science is really a German affair and none of our business." . . . Secret, underground swamp reptiles have crawled out again.[29]

Indeed, the whole stream of events had a strange aura of *déjà vu*, a repetition of the end of Alexander's reign and the undoing of Uvarov's whole compromise, then and now, between autocracy and enlightenment.

Still unable to accept the fact that his whole life's work was crumbling, Uvarov jousted as "the primary defender of the rights of the universities." He asked his friend Davydov, whom Bulgarin had recently described as "Hegelian" and therefore "anti-Christian," to write an article in defense of the universities and publish it posthaste in the *Contemporary*, one of only two journals with an effect on progressive public opinion. Davydov admitted to Pogodin, "You may have guessed *how* this article was written," namely upon dictation from Uvarov. In fact, the short essay rang as an angry defense of the minister's whole tenure in office and a call to the public to render its verdict or at least calm down. Uvarov was concerned that anonymous memoranda on closing the universities, apparently the handiwork of Grech and Buturlin, "profoundly upset minds in an epoch when calm ought to be a necessity." The article is vintage Uvarov in its message, but lacks his literary style.[30]

Uvarov/Davydov put their enemies on the defensive; recent calls for the "reform" of the universities represented nothing other than Western infection among "light-thinking superficial dreamers": "In the West, the passion for reforms, the dissatisfaction with their present state, the scorn for traditions are the general ailment of people without a past and a future, living only for the present." The authors pointedly added that such individuals were "drugged by love of power and self-interest." True Russians, on the contrary, respected tradition. Since the founding of Moscow University in 1755, they had nurtured such a strong heritage of higher education that soon "respect for a university diploma was equal to that for noble lineage." During his ministry, of course, Uvarov had worked for precisely that outcome. Nicholas, the article claimed, inherited this love for education and allowed for "the striving of all classes to enlightenment," even among Jews, Poles, Balts, and women. Statistics proved the success: 784 new educational establishments, 35,000 more students, 2,000 more teachers, 40 scientific expeditions, over 7,000,000 Russian books printed. The essay also cited the monumental work of the Archeographical Commission.

Thus, according to the article, for 100 years universities had been considered "necessary" for Russia's development. But now, "frivolous people" deem them "premature" and declare that specialized institutes in military, mining, or pedagogy can answer the country's needs. "But," the authors asked, "who will breathe life into and feed all these institutes? University professors and officials. And it cannot be otherwise: knowledge in its fullness is taught only in universities." The essay then heatedly defended "universal knowledge" and liberal arts as the only true sources of specialized knowledge and professors as proven responsible agents for their propagation among the entire population.

Next, Uvarov/Davydov warned against those who attacked the teaching of Greek and Latin: "A new battle of darkness with light!" They treated with utter contempt those who made "latinists" equivalent to propounders of "atheism, anarchy, revolution, and debauchery." On the contrary, "events" in Europe clearly indicated that among the "bloodthirsty" the specialists predominated—doctors, astronomers, jurists, and chemists, not classical scholars. Those who studied classics, the authors lectured, included such cultural giants as St. Augustine, Dante, Shakespeare, Lomonosov, Speranskii, and Zhukovskii. Certain contemporary writers, such as Strauss and Feuerbach, corrupted minds, but all art and knowledge flowed from the ancients. The Russian educational system was striving to educate the "whole man," to develop fully his moral and intellectual capabilities, to make "knowledge powerful as Bacon said," and thus to enter the "one great family of civilization." This objective could be accomplished only through thorough study of both ancient and modern subjects and only in the universities.

This courageous, indeed suicidal, defense of knowledge became more subdued in the last two pages. Uvarov, who had two years earlier proposed introducing *Lehrfreiheit* and *Lernfreiheit* into Russian universities, now claimed that their absence made native institutions superior. The intricate system of surveillance, lecture and curriculum guidelines, uniforms, and propaganda about Faith, Tsar, and Fatherland in the Russian universities belied any comparison between these institutions and their German counterparts. Furthermore, the "desperate proletariat" did not occupy Russian student benches. Mostly, children of nobility, civil servants, and clergy attended universities; "even half the professors are noble." The latter was a startling admission; it meant that half the professors came from the "other classes."

In January 1849, the Third Section forced Uvarov to divulge the exact social origin of all university students. By including the clergy, he was able to produce a rather happy 67 percent elite enrollment, although the figure would have dropped to 63 percent if he had excluded the poor sons of priests. Uvarov was trying simultaneously to save the universities and his own career. He really didn't do either. In the short run, however, he managed to assuage fears that universities would be closed and, as Nikitenko observed, "Everyone calmed down"—except for Buturlin. Uvarov planned to have the article, which had been so well received by the public, reprinted in the *Muscovite;* he quickly changed his mind.[31]

The article aroused the wrath of the special censorship committee. Buturlin admitted that, on the surface, the article was loyal, even patriotic, and often spoke of love for Russia, subjection to the autocracy, gratitude toward the government, etc.

> But if one grasps *its internal meaning*, then it is clear that here is a meddling, out of place for a private person [*sic*], in the affairs of government. Such submission of a governmental question to public judgment, such an appeal to public opinion constitutes a development as novel as it is intolerable in our social order. If similar articles are allowed, then any plans of the government, if somehow made known to the public, could be refuted . . . and the journals would set themselves up as judges in matters of state.

The tsar, taken aback by Buturlin's report, asked; "How could such a thing be allowed?" Uvarov received an imperial reproof and used this as a pretext to defend his honor and vent his long-seething hostility against the activities of the Buturlin Committee. Uvarov's letter to the tsar, dated March 22, 1849, began with a defense of his reasons for permitting the article. He said that rumors of closing the universities "could lead to no good" and, since he knew only of the tsar's good wishes for the universities, he had decided to quell the gossip. Furthermore, the article "was written with loyalty, sincere devotion to the government, knowledge of the subject, and finally with a love for true and beneficial enlightenment." Uvarov rebutted the various points in Buturlin's attack and concluded with a plea to end the dual system of censorship that had occasioned this clash.

> Sire! The article in the *Contemporary* was presented to me and approved by me. If someone must be held responsible for it, then that responsibility, in conscience and by law, ought to fall exclusively on me. In such a state of affairs—when on the one hand the ministry, conducting business with its own statutes and instructions and openly carrying legal responsibility, functions in a defined sphere while, on the other, a committee created outside the ministry . . . makes conclusions that, upon imperial approval, carry the strength of law—bewilderment and clashes have been and will be inevitable. In the course of the entire year, I made every effort to forestall such clashes and meekly awaited the end of this state of affairs, not troubling Your Imperial Majesty with premature solicitations. Now, with the full conviction and frankness with which in the course of sixteen years I have always conducted myself before Your Majesty, I dare to ask if

it would not be more satisfactory to give the conduct of censorship a steady course and put an end to the clashes inevitable under the present conditions?

Nicholas responded with displeasure to Uvarov's complaints and, taking them as a personal accusation, pronounced the article *"improper."* The tsar informed his minister: "One must *obey* and keep his arguments *to himself.*" He then forced Uvarov to underwrite an order forbidding any further discussion in the press of the universities, whether positive or negative.[32]

The end was clearly near; the arrest of the group known as the Petrashevtsy, on April 22, 1849, meant that Uvarov's luck had finally run out. The group's leader, Michael Butashevich-Petrashevskii, was a young official in the ministry of foreign affairs who had been educated at St. Petersburg University. The Petrashevtsy represented essentially a "conspiracy of ideas," with one small branch hoping for the overthrow of the regime and the rest interested in reform of the censorship, serfdom, and the court system. Its leader had become enamored with the socialist ideas of Charles Fourier and evangelically spoke of the promise of dividing the planet into phalansteries, or self-sufficient communes. Petrashevskii tried to inject formality into the group's meetings, held on Fridays at his home; they were usually dominated by a merry, public-spirited atmosphere. Then, like other groups of its kind, the Petrashevtsy began to split into factions over the knotty question of means and ends, but the secret police had already infiltrated the membership. Unfortunately for the educational system, of the fifty-one members exiled and the twenty-two sentenced to death (a sentence the tsar later commuted), many were university or lycée students or lecturers. Hence, the connection between education and revolution appeared reconfirmed. In addition, the arrests seemed to invalidate Uvarov's optimistic conclusions about his schools' "trustworthiness," which he had published only the previous week in his ministerial report for 1848.[33]

Eight days after the arrest of the Petrashevtsy, the tsar presented Uvarov with an imperial command to limit the number of students in each university to 300 and to make sure that all those retained possessed "outstanding morality." The real intent was to eliminate the "lower orders." Officials mistakenly believed that students from this group were likely to cause the most unrest; they had yet to understand the revolutionary potential of the conscience-stricken nobleman or the conservatism of the upwardly mobile student from the lower classes who strove only to "belong." In effect, the tsar's order meant dropping the number of students from 4,467 to 1,800; admissions were to be halted until the desired number was reached. In 1848, only Kazan even approached the limit, with 325 enrolled, while Moscow had 1,165 students, St. Petersburg 731, St. Vladimir 656, Dorpat 604, and Kharkov 525. In one sense, Uvarov had anticipated an order of this sort; in 1848 he had demanded "especial strictness in entrance examinations" for the next year's class and rejected the notion that "the well-being" of the universities was demonstrated by a simple increase in numbers; however, he never expected such drastic reductions.

Uvarov began maneuvering. Within the week, he approached Nicholas with a request to exclude the 674 state stipendiates from the quota. He reminded the tsar that their conduct was beyond reproach and that they tended to be prospective teachers, so desperately needed in the empire, or natives of Polish, Caucasian, and Siberian provinces who could profit from the russification provided in universities. Uvarov also asked that medical faculties receive total exemption because of the dire shortage of doctors. He shrewdly played on Nicholas's central concern of the day, his army, and warned that "if even for only one year" medical students were excluded, this action "could significantly lessen the number of doctors now awaited by the office of the military." Nicholas eventually acceded to these requests and agreed that restrictions would apply only to self-supporting students in the philosophical and juridical faculties. The tsar again reasoned that more young men should enter the military rather than civil service in the current state of emergency.

For the first time in his ministry, Uvarov began a secret circular with the phrase "the Emperor considers it necessary" and then stated the enrollment quotas for the universities. By 1850, the total number of students had dropped to roughly 3,000, with each university chopping its enrollment by about 25 percent. St. Petersburg, faring the worst, was left with only 387 students because it lacked a medical faculty; in other schools, young men craftily enrolled as prospective doctors, no matter what their career interests, and then tried to transfer to other faculties, a ruse stopped in 1850.

According to Korf, this policy of contracting the universities was "one of the most unpopular in the reign of the Emperor Nicholas." The normally Cassandra-like Bulgarin suddenly reversed his attitude and announced the quotas unnecessary since "never had there been a democratic spirit" in the universities. He also feared that the measure would give Russia a bad press in Europe, not exactly Nicholas's concern at the moment, nor Bulgarin's ever before. Apparently, the right wing of opinion began to sense that policy had gone amok; even Korf began to find the actions of the Buturlin Committee "sickening."

The nobility, who not long before had resented the idea that their children had a need for serious education, began begging Uvarov not to reverse his long-held policy, but to continue to allow their offspring to enter the universities as the best preparation for their careers—and as a means of advancing in the ranks or, perhaps, of avoiding the military. The minister could only sigh that the nobility needed to approach the tsar directly. Indeed, Uvarov had no influence left. As Rozhdestvenskii commented, the minister had become the "passive executor of measures that destroyed the system he had created." Another scholar, Vladimirskii-Budanov, sympathetically remarked that Uvarov was like "a captain trying to save his ship by jettisoning his valuable cargo overboard."[34]

Next, personal misfortune struck. Uvarov's wife died on July 14, 1849, "after a long and cruel illness." The widower mourned that he could "only take up the pen with effort" to announce her "ceasing to live"; "her death was Christian like her life," he reflected. Apparently, without her support Uvarov himself "lost his spirit," and he succumbed to a stroke on September 6 that paralyzed his right arm and leg and impaired his ability to speak. He recovered within ten days but resigned as minister on October 20. Grand Duchess Elena Pavlovna had advised him to do so, because her brother "was angry with him in general." Indeed, Uvarov received a decidedly cold letter from the tsar accepting his resignation, although Nicholas had constantly inquired about his health. With even less grace, Davydov wrote to Pogodin, in apprehension lest Uvarov should die, "What will become of us?" Like the tsar, Davydov and Pogodin constantly inquired about the minister's health.[35]

With Uvarov gone from office, the character of the ministry changed. Rather than espousing a positive program for the encouragement, improvement, and steady expansion of education, it adopted a negative policy of merely purging and policing the schools under its jurisdiction. Except for establishing a veterinary institute at Kharkov and expanding the number of pedagogical courses at universities, projects both planned by Uvarov, little constructive legislation occurred until the next reign. Even before Uvarov's resignation, the tsar had created the Bludov Committee to reassess the whole educational system, and he strongly pressured it to place the universities in an "obscurantist straitjacket." Fortunately, it took no action, and its suggestions were impractical; Alexander II disbanded it in 1856. As Nikitenko noted in 1853: "The idea of reforming the ministry of education grew out of the panicky fear aroused by events in Europe in 1848. . . . The emperor received several proposals for its reform which were completely amateurish. Some of them were even remarkable for their amazing illiteracy."[36]

Prince Platon Shirinskii-Shikhmatov, who had served as deputy minister of education since 1842, became acting minister upon Uvarov's retirement. On January 26, 1850, he presented the tsar with a memorandum that struck a note ominously harkening back to the 1820s: "Theology is the single strong foundation on which all useful education is based." The tsar gleefully exclaimed: "Why look for a minister of education? Behold, he has been found!" On January 27, Nicholas appointed him. A decent enough nonentity, the former naval officer was a good second-in-command since his forte was taking orders and not making innovations; his only memorable quote was: "You should know that I have neither a mind nor a will of my own—I am merely a blind tool of the Emperor's will." One pundit remarked that he was reminiscent of Luka Lukich Khlopov, the obsequious inspector of schools in Gogol's *Inspector General*.[37]

Shirinskii-Shikmatov resembled Buturlin in his se 'se of grave responsibility to conduct a "Christian crusade against knowledge" and to maintain the status quo. This inclination inspired his list of negative, repressive legislation, which was similar to the postrevolutionary Falloux Law of 1850 in France.[38] University philosophy courses, except for logic and psychology (now taught by Orthodox priests), were cancelled because "the usefulness of philosophy has not been proven, but the possibility of its being harmful is a fact." European state law and ancient history were dropped from the curriculum as "too sensitive." The new administration discouraged Slavic studies, and russification became a military and administrative policy rather than a cultural one. University councils lost their elective powers, with the minister now empowered to appoint rectors and deans. The Buturlin Committee had earlier suggested and the ministry now announced the need for professors to file lithographed copies of their lectures; these were forbidden to contain discussions of paganism, the *veche*, or the Reformation. Foreigners could no longer fill chairs, although 32 of 137 were vacant. The rights of university self-censorship and free importation of books went by the wayside. Public lectures and public defenses of dissertations were nearly discontinued. Legislation reiterated the aim of keeping the "lower classes" out of secondary and higher educational institutions and once again raised tuition. To prevent graduates from crossing over the "slippery threshold into journalism," they were obliged to enter civil service immediately upon leaving the university. In general, university attendance was discouraged.[39] The new direction was clearly evident.

To the credit of Uvarov and the educated public, the system of schools was too strong to be destroyed, but intellectual life and educational development in this era entered a state of attenuation. A popular pun in the capital ran: "Shikhmatov is *shakhmat* (checkmate) to all education." More gloomily, Pogodin smelled "the quiet of a graveyard, rotting and stinking, both physically and morally." The censorship terror achieved its mark. In 1850, Nikitenko visited the regular censorship committee to inquire about new literary works: "There were no books."

The cries of discontent rose, although not in the press, and were only exacerbated by Russia's humiliating defeat in the Crimean War. Kavelin wrote to Granovskii:

> Indeed, only here does one fully feel the disgrace, the humiliation, and the shameful slavery in which this egotistic, degenerate, Prussian-militaristic foreign dynasty . . . holds us. . . . This type of absolutism that we now have only dulls the embryo of independent national life.[40]

Thus, by 1855, the scene was set for reform, an objective that now had an educated public, the trained personnel, and a tsar at least temporarily dedicated to carrying it out. Uvarov, though, died only six months into the new reign and never knew that, in part at least, he assisted the plans of the "reforming tsar," Alexander II.

RETIREMENT

UVAROV spent the remaining six years of his life after his resignation quite happily and industriously. He kept his tongue about the post-1848 administration, but one poem he copied from Byron perhaps reflected his resentment and his belief in the correctness of his path.

> What shall I say to Ye;
> Since my defense must be your condemnation?
> You are at once offenders and accusers,
> Judges and executioners!—Proceed
> Upon your power![41]

These sentiments indeed applied to his treatment at the hands of extremists both in the early 1820s and late 1840s. But he well knew that progressive sorts attacked him as well.

Granovskii, who stayed with Uvarov at his summer estate during 1848 while the historian's wife recovered from an illness, gave heart to the aging and beleaguered minister. He lectured him on "transitional eras," a topic they both loved and a phenomenon they believed they were experiencing. Granovskii commented that there were two types of figures in these eras of "tragic beauty." One "goes daringly ahead" and earns "the right of victory, the right of historical success." The other receives "more personal sympathy" from the historian, the one "in whom is personified all the beauty and all the dignity of the outgoing era." From these two strains, both necessary, "Providence fashions an unexpected and unseen outcome." Uvarov could hope, as one who embodied a little of both types, to be treated better by history than by contemporary opinion.[42]

During his retirement, Uvarov published several essays. They returned to the favorite themes of his intellectual life, and most were defiantly published in the *Contemporary*. Two essays in 1851 poignantly reminisced about the old days in the Arzamas society, of whose members only he and Bludov survived. He remembered that time as one of burgeoning creative activity, the moment of birth of modern Russian literature, and fondly recalled Karamzin, Zhukovskii, Pushkin, and Olenin as well as their Shishkovite opponents. Nostalgically, he wrote Bludov: "We ought to feel gratitude toward Providence, who has given us in the sunset of life the ability to enjoy together both the fruits of a half century of experiences and a game of adolescent fantasy."

In another commemorative essay in 1852, Uvarov rued the passing of the great classical philologists, such as Heyne and F. A. Wolf, and now the death of Russia's greatest Hellenist, Gräfe. Uvarov had known the latter scholar for forty years and had studied Greek and Latin with him; he recalled, in the midst of war, reading Thucydides (in the original) with him and vom Stein. Uvarov took the opportunity to chastize the younger generation for not sufficiently respecting classical culture, "the source of European civilization." Two years earlier, he remembered, Gräfe, while staying at Porech'e, had suddenly cried out "avec transport": "My God, what a pity you became minister! . . . Because I believe you would have made an excellent Hellenist . . . if only you had better learned your grammar, which you never esteemed enough." The statement also harkened back to Goethe's criticism of Uvarov's German in the 1810s, a teasing slap on the hand that the polyglot minister apparently enjoyed.[43]

Another essay in 1850 rushed to defend ancient history from the charge that, since it was written before the invention of the printing press, it could only be classified as "conjectural." On the contrary, Uvarov celebrated the "truth" of ancient history, while he objected to the "new historical school" that had originated in Germany. He believed that German historiography had gotten so caught up in the "anarchical" wealth of material that it failed to bring "order out of the chaos" of its facts and concentrated upon too-narrow topics. He claimed that the "human mind is inclined to synthesis." Thus, the historian is obligated to use "moral principles or values" when presenting his material and to have a broad sweep that describes the entire society, not one small facet of it. He lamented that contemporary historians, in their quest for impartiality and objectivity, "fear to announce a moral principle" and become skeptics; this inclination leads "to a negation of good and evil, the exiling of Providence from history, and the substitution for the great laws of social order of some sort of artificial mechanism that is born of chance and lessens the dignity of man by depriving him of his best hopes." He found it especially painful that this new "school" had yet produced nothing "worthwhile" on the French Revolution, "the last and greatest event of mankind." Instead, it tended to deify Napoleon as "an apostle of democracy and a propagator of liberal ideals"—a portrait, Uvarov said, he knew from personal observation was totally absurd. The problems of selectivity and objectivity, of course, remain for historians, who continue to reinterpret the revolutionary era and Napoleon. What is interesting, in viewing Uvarov's position, is that he still clung to his philosophy of history: all mankind in all its aspects was moving ahead toward God-given goals based on Christian teachings, and Providence continued to direct the grand unfolding of events. Contemporary setbacks would not succeed in "depriving him of his best hopes."[44]

Uvarov also never abandoned serious research. In 1853, he publicly defended a master's thesis on the origin of the Bulgarians, complete with citations from Šafařik, Schlözer, Solov'ev, Karamzin, Tatishchev, and Boltin as well as from Latin, Greek, and Armenian sources. In addition, he cooperated from 1851 until his death in editing collections of articles on classical scholarship with Granovskii, Kudriavtsev, and Kutorga. Another book on ancient history, apparently prepared as a doctoral dissertation, and an article on the affinity between Marlowe and Shakespeare appeared posthumously.[45]

More than likely, Uvarov's son Alexis, who became a distinguished archeologist, arranged for the last publications. He also established, in 1858, five annual Uvarov Prizes in honor of his father's "special love for the history of the fatherland and philological research." Their aim was to encourage native writers in the field of Russian and Slavic history and drama; the entries had to be written in the Russian language and to relate to some past or present theme in national life. It seemed a fitting tribute.[46]

A particular comfort to Uvarov in his retirement was his beloved summer estate of Porech'e, located about ninety miles northwest of Moscow.[47] Even during his ministry, he retreated there as to an "oasis in my stormy life" where he could imbibe "different thoughts born from different feelings and impressions"; thoughts of "truth, goodness, and beauty" seemed to him "refurbished" in the countryside. Indeed, friends noted that "Uvarov was totally different in Porech'e" than in Moscow or St. Petersburg: he was happy, a good host who allowed his guests total freedom, spoke "openly" like a boon companion, and argued about a wealth of topics, but also listened attentively to others' opinions. The guest list was revealing; it included only academics, authors, and artists, never court officials. For this reason, participants called Porech'e the "Russian Athens" and likened it to "Plato's Academy." Porech'e, of course, also recaptured the "Arzamas spirit."

Uvarov lived in "tsar-like luxury" on the estate, which he fashioned into a monument attesting to his intellectual interests. Besides the Stein Pavilion and the bronze memorial to Zhukovskii, unveiled with fanfare in 1853, the winged mansion was surrounded by a forest and a formal garden of rare flowers and tropical trees, the work of Uvarov's brother, a noted botanist. The house itself was done in "exquisite taste" and tellingly lacked a ballroom, the usual center of aristocratic homes. Instead, the main hall was a "sanctuary of art" designed by an Italian architect in collaboration with Karl Briullov, the best artist of the day. In it, paintings and sculpture were "harmoniously displayed" to take advantage of a breathtaking belvedere. Uvarov had collected most of his *objets d'art* on a trip to Italy in 1843. His most precious possession, which he had discovered in an abandoned Jesuit church, was a sarcophagus, attested by the classical scholar Winkelmann to belong to the "high" period of Greek art and decorated with the figures of Dionysius, Ariadne, Pan, and Hercules; scholars also conjectured that it had some relation to the Eleusinian Mysteries, one of Uvarov's favorite scholarly topics. In 1854, he described his treasure in an article, which he also published as a pamphlet.

Two arches from the central hall led to Uvarov's library, his "sanctuary of knowledge." It was modestly decorated but contained busts of Raphael, Michelangelo, Dante, Tasso, Ariosto, and Machiavelli. The 12,000 catalogued volumes constituted one of the best classical libraries in Europe. The authors on the shelves were a testimony to Uvarov's wide interests: Herodotus, Livy, Niebuhr, Guizot, Shakespeare, Schiller, Goethe, Scott, the Eastern and Western church fathers, Hume, Gibbon, Fox, Pitt, Burke, Robertson, Voltaire, Racine, Molière, Montesquieu, and even Rousseau; there were also rare editions of Pindar, Virgil, and the Bible. It was in this setting that Uvarov liked to reproduce with his guests the intellectually stimulating atmosphere of the salon that he treasured from his youth.[48]

Despite friends, intellectual activity, and exposure to country air, Uvarov's health remained unsteady. He continued to suffer from rheumatism, hemorrhoids, and the aftereffects of his stroke, all of which led to weakness; he was also bothered by eye trouble. His French and English physicians prescribed iron pills, a salt-free diet, port, and moderate horseback riding, but he slowly grew worse. In 1853, he could not even attend the celebration of his fiftieth anniversary in state service. In mid-1854, he asked to be relieved of his remaining post as president of the Academy of Sciences, since he thought the institution needed "new life and vigor" that "I can no longer give it." Stroganov was offered the post but fortunately declined, and Uvarov suffered one less humiliation. Bludov was appointed after Uvarov's death, but in his acceptance speech, incomprehensibly, said not one word about the Academy's president of thirty-seven years.[49]

In the late summer of 1855, Uvarov came to Moscow from St. Petersburg to celebrate his sixty-ninth birthday on August 25 with his two surviving children, Alexis and Princess Alexandra Urusova.[50] He had been unable to go to Porech'e that summer for fear of dying on the road. He grew increasingly ill in Moscow and soon called for a priest; but even on his deathbed he asked news of literature, politics, and science. On September 2, he suffered another stroke and never regained consciousness; he died "quietly" two days later. Six students stood watch over the body day and night, and Uvarov had what was described as a "rather splendid" funeral on September 10. After his body was carried by students through the old Arbat merchant district, a service was fittingly held in the Moscow University chapel. Memorials celebrated his Greek and Latin scholarship, his days in Arzamas, his work as minister of education, and, in general, his "love for knowledge and art." Professors, students, and the Grand Duchess Elena Pavlovna attended. He was buried in the village of Kholm near Porech'e; only his son, daughter, and the faithful Pogodin accompanied the body. As Stroev remarked: "The former pilgrims to Porech'e chose to stay at home—*sic transit gloria mundi.*"[51]

ABBREVIATIONS USED IN NOTES
AND BIBLIOGRAPHY

GIM   Gosudarstvennyi istoricheskii muzei (State Historical Museum, Moscow)

PD   Pushi:.skii dom (Pushkin House, Leningrad)

ROBIL   Rukopisnyi otdel Biblioteki imeni Lenina (Manuscript Division of the Lenin State Library, Moscow)

TsGAOR   Tsentral'nyi gosudarstvennyi arkhiv oktiabr'skoi revoliutsii (Central State Archive of the October Revolution, Moscow)

TsGIAL   Tsentral'nyi gosudarstvennyi istoricheskii arkhiv v Leningrade (Central State Historical Archive in Leningrad)

SPMNP   Sbornik postanovlenyi po Ministerstvu narodnago prosveshcheniia (Collection of Decrees of the Ministry of National Enlightenment)

ZMNP   Zhurnal Ministerstva narodnago prosveshcheniia (Journal of the Ministry of National Enlightenment)

RA   Russkii arkhiv (Russian Archive)

RS   Russkaia starina (Russian Antiquity)

NOTES

CHAPTER 1

1. When the ministry of national enlightenment was created in 1802, the empire was divided into six districts, each headed by a superintendent residing in St. Petersburg. They included Moscow, St. Petersburg, Kharkov, Kazan, Dorpat, and Vilno.

2. For a listing of Uvarov's works, consult Part 1 of the bibliography; he mastered Russian, French, German, Italian, Latin, Greek, and English.

3. S. S. Uvarov, "Le Prince de Ligne" (1815), in *Esquisses politiques et littéraires* (Paris, 1848), p. 41; and *Notice sur Goethe* (St. Petersburg, 1842), p. 5.

4. S. S. Uvarov, "Predislovie," *ZMNP* 1, No. 1 (1834): iv–v; M. I. Sukhomlinov, *Materialy dlia istorii obrazovaniia v Rossii v tsarstvovanie imp. Aleksandra I* (St. Petersburg, 1866), p. 198.

5. J. de Maistre, "Lettre critique sur le Projet" (December 8, 1810), in S. S. Uvarov, *Études de philologie et de critique* (St. Petersburg, 1843), p. 63.

6. S. S. Uvarov, *Rech' prezidenta Im. A. N. popechitelia Peterburgskago uchebnago okruga v torzhestvennom sobranii Glavnago pedagogicheskago instituta 22 marta 1818* (St. Petersburg, 1818); *Goethe*; and "Vues générales sur la philosophie de la littérature" (1840), in *Études*, pp. 339–51. The italics in quotations throughout this book are those found in the original sources.

7. A. V. Nikitenko, *Dnevnik* (entry of March 21, 1843), I (Leningrad, 1955), p. 264.

8. S. S. Uvarov, "O narodonaselenii v Rossii," *Chteniia Imp. Akademii nauk*, I (St. Petersburg, 1831): 126: and *Appel à l'Europe* (St. Petersburg, 1815).

9. S. S. Uvarov, "O tsenzure" (March 24, 1848), TsGIAL, fond 1611, opis' 1, no. 208b, p. 173; "O narodonaselenii"; and *Desiatiletie Ministerstva narodnago prosveshcheniia, 1833–1843* (St. Petersburg, 1864), p. 2; I. I. Davydov/S. S. Uvarov, "O naznachenii russkikh universitetov i uchastii ikh v obshchestvennom obrazovanii," *Sovremennik* 14, No. 3 (March 1849): 37. The tripartite formula was first expressed in Uvarov's "S predstavleniem otcheta tainago sovetnika Uvarova po obozreniiu Imp. Moskovskago universiteta i gimnazii," *SPMNP*, II, 1: 511–12 (December 4, 1832). (References to *SPMNP* carry the date of the document. Entries consist mainly of decrees, laws, and reports.) On conservative renovation, see the

excellent study of D. T. Orlovsky, *The Limits of Reform: The Ministry of Internal Affairs in Imperial Russia, 1802–1881* (Cambridge, Mass., 1981), pp. 202–4.

The quotation on the "law of progress" is in *Goethe*, pp. 22–23. The *Notice sur Goethe* was first read at a meeting of the Academy of Sciences on March 22, 1833, and published in its *Chteniia*; it was then printed as a separate pamphlet in St. Petersburg in 1842; in 1843 and 1848, it was included in Uvarov's two volumes of collected essays, the *Esquisses* and the *Études*.

10. Uvarov, *Desiatiletie*, p. 3; *Rech'*, p. 61; and "Predislovie," p. iv.

11. Davydov/Uvarov, "O naznachenii," p. 37; Uvarov, "O narodonaselenii"; *Desiatiletie*, p. 3 and passim; N. P. Barsukov, ed., *Zhizn' i trudy M. P. Pogodina*, IX (St. Petersburg, 1888–1906), pp. 305–8.

12. S. S. Uvarov, "Predislovie," p. iv; *Desiatiletie*, pp. 46, 75–76; "O narodonaselenii," p. 127; and *Otchet za 1843* (St. Petersburg, 1844), pp. 93–94. A. Kornilov, *Nineteenth-Century Russia* (New York, 1917), p. 207.

13. Davydov/Uvarov, "O naznachenii," p. 43.

14. F. F. Vigel', *Zapiski*, II (Moscow, 1892), p. 76. A. I. Turgenev is quoted in M. Stepanov and F. Vermale, "Zhosef de Mestr v Rossii," *Literaturnoe nasledstvo* 29–30 (1937):677.

15. For examples of this as accepted Soviet dogma, see K. V. Ostrovitianov, ed., *Istoriia Akademii nauk SSSR*, II (Moscow, 1964), p. 20; S. N. Durylin, "Drug Gete," *Literaturnoe nasledstvo*, 4–6 (1932): 186–217; O. V. Orlik, *Rossiia i frantsuzskaia revoliutsiia 1830 goda* (Moscow, 1968), p. 164; "S. S. Uvarov," *Bolshaia sovetskaia entsiklopediia*, XXVI (Moscow, 1977), p. 438. A. M. Skabichevskii gave one of many similar interpretations in the nineteenth century in *Ocherki istorii russkoi tsenzury, 1700–1863* (St. Petersburg, 1892), p. 231. American scholars also share this view; see N. V. Riasanovsky, *Nicholas I and Official Nationality in Russia, 1825–1855* (Berkeley, Calif., 1967), pp. 70–72; and P. Alston, *Education and the State in Tsarist Russia* (Stanford, Calif., 1969), pp. 33–34.

The last biographical essay devoted to Uvarov, M. P. Pogodin's "Dlia biografii grafa S. S. Uvarova" (*RA* 9 [1871]: 2103–7), was published in 1871. The best of four earlier essays is P. A. Pletnev, "Pamiati grafa S. S. Uvarova, prezidenta Imperatorskoi Akademii nauk," *Uchenye zapiski Imp. Akademii nauk po I i III otdeleniiam* 2 (1856): liii–cxxv. Soviet scholars tend to ignore Uvarov, but many earlier works on Russian education describe his policies and influence; the best of these is still S. V. Rozhdestvenskii, *Istoricheskii obzor deiatel'nosti Ministerstva narodnago prosveshcheniia, 1802–1902* (St. Petersburg, 1902).

16. C. Black, *The Dynamics of Modernization: A Study in Comparative History* (New York, 1966), pp. 64, 121; W. Blackwell, *The Beginnings of Russian Industrialization, 1800–1860* (Princeton, N.J., 1968); R. Wortman, *The Development of a Russian Legal Consciousness* (Chicago, 1976); J. Flynn, "Tuition and Social Class in the Russian Universities: S. S. Uvarov and 'Reaction' in the Russia of Nicholas I," *Slavic Review* 35, No. 2 (June 1976): 232–48; W. B. Lincoln, "The Genesis of an 'Enlightened' Bureaucracy in Russia, 1826–1856," *Jahrbücher für Geschichte Osteuropas* 20, No. 3 (September 1972): 321–30; and Lincoln, *Nicholas I* (Bloomington, Ind., 1978); W. Pintner, "The Social Characteristics of the Early Nineteenth-Century Bureaucracy," *Slavic Review* 29 (September 1970): 429–43; and Pintner, "The Russian Civil Service on the Eve of the Great Reforms," *Social History*, Spring 1975, pp. 55–68.

Two books prepared the ground for this new school of thought by turning attention to nonradical aspects of Russian culture and development: M. Raeff, *Michael Speransky: Statesman of Imperial Russia* (The Hague, 1957); and Riasanovsky, *Official Nationality*.

17. Barsukov, *Zhizn' Pogodina*, X, p. 543.

18. G. Shpet, *Ocherk razvitiia russkoi filosofii* (Petrograd, 1922), p. 240.

CHAPTER 2

1. C. Corbet, "Iz istorii russko-frantsuzskikh literaturnykh sviazei v pervoi treti XIX v.," in *Mezhdunarodnye sviazi russkoi literatury*, ed. M. P. Alekseev (Moscow, 1963), pp. 193–94; and S. A. Zenkovsky, Editor's Foreword to D. I. Chizhevskii, *History of Nineteenth-Century Russian Literature*, I (Nashville, 1974), p. viii; also consult O. V. Orlov and V. I. Fedorov, *Russkaia literatura XVIII veka* (Moscow, 1973); and V. I. Krasnobaev, *Ocherki istorii russkoi kul'tury XVIII veka* (Moscow, 1972).

2. For the interpretation of the War of 1812 as a dividing line in Russian culture, consult V. Belinskii, *Polnoe sobranie sochinenii*, VI (Moscow, 1955), p. 163; V. Kozhinov, *Kontekst—1972* (Moscow, 1973), pp. 291–93; P. K. Christoff, *The Third Heart: Some Intellectual-Ideological Currents and Cross-Currents in Russia, 1800–1830* (The Hague, 1970), pp. 39–43; and V. V. Poznanskii, *Ocherki istorii russkoi kul'tury pervoi poloviny XIX veka* (Moscow, 1970), pp. 44–54, 78–88.

3. Some of the many works covering this topic include Chizhevskii, *History*, pp. 1–96; D. S. Mirsky, *A History of Russian Literature* (New York, 1958), pp. 41–126; D. D. Blagoi, *Istoriia russkoi literatury XVIII veka* (Moscow, 1951), pp. 261–81; and Krasnobaev, *Ocherki*, pp. 133–275.

4. On Karamzin's early life and education, see R. Pipes, "Karamzin as Bellettrist and Poet (Until 1801)," in *Karamzin's Memoir on Ancient and Modern Russia: A Translation and Analysis* (Cambridge, Mass., 1959), pp. 21–43; and J. L. Black, *Nicholas Karamzin and Russian Society in the Nineteenth Century: A Study in Russian Political and Historical Thought* (Toronto, 1975), pp. 3–33.

On his influence, consult A. I. Iatsimirskii, "N. M. Karamzin," in *Istoriia russkoi literatury XIX v.*, ed. O. N. Ovsianiko-Kulikovskii (Moscow, 1910), pp. 124–31; A. Kirpichnikov, "Karamzin kak literator," *Entsiklopedicheskii slovar'*, XXVII (St. Petersburg: Brokgauz-Efron, 1890–1906), pp. 443–45; A. S. Sturdza, "Vospominaniia o N. M. Karamzine," *Moskvitianin* 9 (1846): 145–54; V. Belinskii, *Pol'noe sobranie sochineniia*, III (Moscow, 1884), p. 132; and R. V. Iezuitova, "Ballada v epokhu romantizma," in *Russkii romantizm*, ed. K. N. Grigor'ian (Leningrad, 1978), 138–63.

5. The single best study of Shishkov's theories is in N. N. Bulich, *Ocherki po istorii russkoi literatury i prosveshcheniia s nachala XIX veka*, I (St. Petersburg, 1902), pp. 119–221. Also see N. K. Piksanov, *A. S. Griboedov* (St. Petersburg, 1911); A. Borozdin, "Shishkov," *Entsiklopedicheskii slovar'*, LXXVIII, pp. 611–15; S. T. Aksakov, "Vospominaniia ob A. S. Shishkove," *Sobranie sochinenii*, III, pp. 333–95; Iu. N. Tynianov, *Arkhaisty i novatory* (Leningrad, 1929), pp. 87–118; and L. G. Leighton, *Russian Romanticism: Two Essays* (The Hague, 1975), pp. 55–60.

6. R. Wortman, *Russian Legal Consciousness*, pp. 91–94; and M. Raeff, *Origins of the Russian Intelligentsia: The Eighteenth-Century Nobility* (New York, 1966), pp. 122–47.

The prototype of these circles is described in Raeff, "Russian Youth on the Eve of Romanticism: Andrei I. Turgenev and His Circle," in *Revolution and Politics in Russia: Essays in Memory of B. I. Nicholaevsky*, ed. A. and J. Rabinowitch (Bloomington, Ind., 1972); and in V. Istrin, "Druzheskoe literaturnoe obshchestvo 1801 g.," *ZMNP* 8 (1910): 271–307. See also Iu. Veselovskii, "Sentimentalizm v zapadnoevropeiskoi i russkoi literature," *Entsiklopedicheskii slovar'*, LVIII, pp. 536–39; P. N. Sakulin, "Literaturnye techeniia v Aleksandrovskuiu epokhu," *Istoriia russkoi literatury*, pp. 80–82; and N. D. Kochetkova, "Russkii sentimentalizm (N. M. Karamzin i ego okruzhenie)," in *Russkii romantizm*, pp. 18–37.

7. Biographical information on Uvarov can found in the following sources: "Gramota S. S. Uvarova" (entry dated January 30, 1798), GIM, fond 17, uncatalogued; "Gerb roda Uvarovykh," GIM, fond 17, no. 336; *Sankt-Peterburgskiia vedomosti* 48 (July 16, 1783); V. P., "Uvarovy," *Entsiklopedicheskii slovar'*, LXVII, p. 420; P. V. Dolgorukov, *Rossiiskaia rodoslovnaia kniga*, II (St. Petersburg, 1854–1857), p. 179; "Pis'ma V. F. Bogoliubova k kniaziu Aleksandromu B. Kurakinu" (June 4, 1806), *RA* 10 (1893): 244; Vigel', *Zapiski*, IV, pp. 169–70; L. Leduc, "Un Essai biographique et critique," in Uvarov, *Esquisses*, p. 7; "Graf S. S. Uvarov," *Vsemirnaia illiustratsiia* 59 (1870): 123; I. I. Davydov, "Vzgliad na zhizn' Uvarova, kak muzha gosudarstvennago, kak pisatelia i kak cheloveka," *Izvestiia Imperatorskii Akademii nauk* (1856): 14.

8. At this time, Alexander Borisovich was vice-chancellor of the college of foreign affairs; and Alexis Borisovich, who was married to Daria's sister, was procurator-general of the senate.

9. Uvarov, "Le Prince de Ligne," in *Esquisses*, p. 120; S. d'Ouvaroff, "Albom"; "Mélanges, 1798"; "Extraits, Notes, Remarques, Observations, etc., etc."; "Traductions de Ciceron," GIM, fond 17, no. 1–5; Vigel', *Zapiski*, IV, p. 164.

10. On life at the university, see M. L. Wischnitzer, "Gettingenskie gody N. I. Turgeneva," *Minuvshie gody*, 1 (1908), No. 4:184–218; No. 5–6: 216–41; and *Die Universität Göttingen und die Entwicklung der liberalen Ideen in Russland im ersten Viertel des 19 Jahrhunderts* (Berlin, 1907).
There is some confusion as to the date and length of Uvarov's *Lehrjahr*, but a study of his service record indicates that it could only have occurred between the latter half of 1801 and March 1803. Susini's comments on Uvarov claim a three-year stay (1803–1806), but this is impossible (E. Susini, ed., *Lettres inédites de F. von Baader*, III [Paris, 1942], pp. 405–6).

11. "Formuliarnyi spisok o sluzhbe" (entry of June 27, 1799), and "Gramota" (entries for 1798–1804), GIM, fond 17, uncatalogued; Leduc, "Essai," p. 11; "Pridvornye chiny," *Entsiklopedicheskii slovar'*, XLIX, p. 156; L. E. Shepelev, *Otmenennye istoriei chiny, zvaniia i tituly v rossiiskoi imperii* (Leningrad, 1977), p. 49. Some sources indicate that Uvarov attended the Moscow Boarding School for the Nobility, but its roster does not contain his name (H. Seton-Watson, *The Russian Empire, 1801–1917* [Oxford, 1967], p. 171).

12. Uvarov, "Stikhi: 'Byvalo vse—i vse proshlo' i 'Moi zhrebii'," *Severnyi vestnik* 8 (November 1805): 188–192. "Sur l'Avantage de mourir jeune" was published in the 1813 *Almanach des Muses* ("Iz staroi zapisnoi knizhki, nachatoi v 1813 gode," *RA* 10 [1876]: 161). Alexander Turgenev, a sometime literary critic, considered him more talented than the most fashionable French poet of the era, Jacques de Lille: A. I. Turgenev, "Pis'ma k N. I. Turgenevu v Gettingen" (June 23, 1810), *Arkhiv brat'ev Turgenevykh*, II (St. Petersburg, 1911), pp. 421–22; P. A. Viazemskii, *Staraia zapisnaia knizhka*, *Polnoe sobranie sochinenii*, VIII (St. Petersburg, 1883), p. 490; "Pis'ma V. A. Zhukovskago k A. I. Turgenevu" (September 12, 1810), *RA* 33 (1895): 62–63. On the literary era, consult N. I. Mordovchenko, *Russkaia kritika pervoi chetverti XIX veka* (Moscow, 1959), pp. 95–99.

13. Istrin, "Russkie studenty," pp. 80–144; Wischnitzer, "Gettingenskie gody," pp. 199–200; A. Vucinich, *Science in Russian Culture: A History to 1860* (Stanford, Calif., 1963), pp. 167, 194.

14. Leduc, "Essai," p. 9; "Iz zapisok damy," *RA* 1 (1882): 206: "Otryvok iz zapisok starago diplomata," *Bibliograficheskie zapiski* 10 (1858): 297; Raeff, *Origins*, pp. 139–40.

15. Uvarov, "Literaturnye vospominaniia," *Sovremennik* 27, No. 6 (1851): 39–42; Sakulin, "Techeniia," pp. 83–90; Aksakov, *Sobranie*, III, pp. 209–10, 262;

N. N. Bulich, *Ocherki*, I, pp. 254–58; L. Maikov, *Batiushkov, ego zhizn' i sochineniia* (St. Petersburg, 1896), p. 224; A. V. Arkhitova, "Istoricheskaia tragediia epokhi romantizma," in *Russkii romantizm*, pp. 163–87. Later, Uvarov worked with Olenin on a committee to refurbish the Imperial Academy of Art and also corresponded with him on the study of antiquity ("Pis'mo A. N. Golitsyna k A. N. Oleninu" [August 24, 1816], ROBIL, fond 3626; "Pis'mo A. N. Olenina k Uvarovu" [March 4, 1836], ROBIL, fond 3622; A. N. Olenin, *O knemadakh u drevnykh grekov, ili ponozhkakh: Pis'mo A. N. Olenina k S. S. Uvarovu* [May 25, 1815], [St. Petersburg, 1875], 30 pp.). Kiprenskii's portrait of Uvarov now hangs in the Tret'iakovskii Museum in Moscow.

16. A. B. [Uvarov], "Puteshestviia: Otryvok iz zapisok 1805 goda," *Syn otechestva* 8, (1829), No. 47:43–52; No. 48:109–16. Whenever Uvarov published an article anonymously, he used this rather unimaginative pseudonym.

17. Uvarov, "Tablettes," GIM, fond 17, uncatalogued, p. 90; "Pis'ma Bogoliubova" (May 17, 1806), p. 244. Although the entries in the "Tablettes" are well written, they are fragmentary, and it cannot be considered a polished work; probably for this reason Uvarov never published the diary.

General F. P. Uvarov helped the tsar seize the throne in 1801 and then participated with distinction in the Napoleonic wars; his portrait now hangs next to the epoch's military hero, M. I. Kutuzov, in the Gallery of 1812 in the Winter Palace.

18. Uvarov, "Tablettes," pp. 14–15, 19, 26, 31–32, 37–39, 43, 58–59, 62, 81, 120.

19. Ibid., pp. 46, 48, 78; Uvarov, "De Stal'," as quoted in S. N. Durylin, "G-zha de Stal' i ee russkie otnosheniia," *Literaturnoe nasledstvo* 33–34 (1939): 224, 238–39. Uvarov's essay was written in 1851 but not published; it is located in GIM, but I was not allowed to see it. On de Staël, also consult P. R. Zaborov, "Zhermana de Stal' i russkaia literatura pervoi treti XIX veka," in *Rannie romanticheskie veianiia: Iz istorii mezhdunarodnykh sviazei russkoi literatury*, ed. M. P. Alekseev (Leningrad, 1972), pp. 168–221.

20. "Vospominaniia grafini A. D. Bludovoi," *RA* 26, No. 1 (1889): 61; "Iz zapisok kniazia N. V. Dolgorukova," *RA* 11 (1892): 265; Durylin, "De Stal'," pp. 233–34. Vigel' stated that Uvarov's mannerisms made him a laughingstock at male assemblies in St. Petersburg (*Zapiski*, IV, p. 170). S. Karlinsky, a noted literary critic, asserts (though offering no proof) that Uvarov and Vigel' were well-known homosexuals (*The Sexual Labyrinth of Nikolai Gogol* [Cambridge, Mass., 1976], pp. 56–57).

21. A. A. Vasil'chikov, *Semeistvo Razumovskikh*, III (St. Petersburg, 1882), p. 465; Durylin, "De Stal'," p. 225; Uvarov, "Le Prince de Ligne," p. 126.

22. Uvarov, "Le Prince de Ligne," pp. 119–120, 123, 126–127, 132. De Ligne asked Uvarov to edit some of his essays, no small task (de Ligne, *Mélanges militaires, littéraires, sentimentaires*, 37 vols. in 12 [Paris, 1827]). Also see V. du Bled, *Le Prince de Ligne et ses contemporains* (Paris, 1890). Uvarov made the comment on politics to Speranskii ("Pis'mo k Speranskomu" [December 1, 1819], *RA* 9, No. 2 [1871]: 158).

23. Uvarov, "Literaturnye vospominaniia," pp. 39–42.

24. "Pis'ma A. I. Turgeneva k N. I. Turgenevu" (February 16, 1810), *Arkhiv*, II, p. 412.

25. Uvarov, "Le Prince de Ligne," p. 41.

26. "Pis'ma Bogoliubova" (October 5, 1809), p. 313; and Leduc, "Essai," p. 9; Vigel', *Zapiski*, IV, p. 170. Uvarov made a second try to go to Paris in the spring of 1810; but since he was in Russia in February, May, June, and Septem-

ber, it seems impossible that he succeeded. See "Pis'ma A. I. Turgeneva," *Arkhiv* 1 (February 16, 1810), 394; and "Pis'ma A. I. Turgeneva," *Arkhiv* 2 (May 4, 1810), 416; and, in the same volume, the letters of June 23, 1810, p. 421; and October 15, 1810, p. 427. Some sources—Susini, *Lettres*, III, p. 408; and Pletnev, "Pamiati grafa S. S. Uvarova," p. lvii—nonetheless indicate that he did get to Paris. It would seem unusual that Uvarov would not have written anything about his stay in Paris, given his love of things French. No details are found in written documents about the extent of Daria Uvarov's debts or her son's financial status at this time.

27. S. S. Uvarov, *Projet d'une académie asiatique* (St. Petersburg, 1810); Durylin, "De Stal'," pp. 237, 251.

28. R. Schwab's book, *La Renaissance orientale* (Paris, 1950), most extensively covers the topic and contains a thorough bibliography. V. V. Barthol'd's *Istoriia izucheniia vostoka v Evrope i Rossii* (Leningrad, 1925) is also useful; it appeared in a French translation, *La Découverte de l'Asie* (Paris, 1947). Also consult the recent monograph by Edward Said, *Orientalism* (New York, 1979).

29. For instance, Warren Hastings, the governor-general of India, asked the Society to translate the *Code of Manu*, the greatest of Hindu lawbooks, so that he could draw up a law code for the Indians (H. G. Rawlinson, "India in European Thought and Literature," in *The Legacy of India*, ed. G. T. Garratt [Oxford, 1937], p. 31.)

30. On Schlegel's influence, see Schwab, *Renaissance*, pp. 74–86; A. L. Willson, *A Mythical Image: The Ideal of India in German Romanticism* (Durham, N.C., 1964), pp. 199–220; H. Glasenapp, "Indien in der Dichtung und Forschung des Deutschen Ostens," *Schriften der Königlichen deutschen gesellschaft zu Königsburg Presse* 5 (1930): 5–47; S. Sommerfeld, *Indienschau und Indiendeutung romantischer Philosophen* (Zurich, 1943); A. F. J. Remy, *The Influence of India and Persia on the Poetry of Germany* (New York, 1966).

31. N. A. Smirnov, *Ocherki istorii izucheniia Islama v SSSR* (Moscow, 1954), pp. 22–26; A. P. Baziiants, *Lazarevskii institut vostochnykh iazykov* (Moscow, 1959), p. 5; R. N. Frye, "Oriental Studies in Russia," in *Russia and Asia: Essays on the Influence of Russia on Asian Peoples*, ed. W. Vucinich (Stanford, Calif., 1972), pp. 33–34; P. E. Skachkov, *Ocherki istorii russkogo kitaevedeniia* (Moscow, 1977), pp. 15–18; *Russkokitaiskie otnosheniia 1689–1916: Ofitsial'nye dokumenty* (Moscow, 1958), pp. 9–11.

For other eighteenth-century developments, consult I. Iu. Krachkovskii, *Ocherki po istorii russloi arabistiki* (Moscow, 1950), pp. 42–47; N. I. Veselovskii, "Svedeniia ob ofitsial'nom prepodavanii vostochnykh iazykov v Rossii," in *Trudy tret'iago mezhdunarodnogo s'ezda orientalistov v S.-Peterburge, 1876*, ed. V. V. Girgor'ev, I (St. Petersburg, 1879–1880), pp. 99–103, 105–106; B. M. Dantsig, "Iz istorii izucheniia blizhnego vostoka v Rossii (vtoraia polovina XVIII v.)," *Ocherki po istorii russkogo vostokovedeniia* 6 (1963): 139–40.

32. Uvarov had no knowledge of any one of the plans in 1810. On Kehr's project, see P. Savel'ev, "Predpolozheniia ob uchrezhdenii vostochnoi akademii v S. Peterburge, 1733 i 1810," *ZMNP* 2 (February 1856): 27–36. The first publication of Potocki's "Zapiska ob obrazovanii Aziatskoi akademii" was in P. V. Tairova's "Proekt I. O. Pototskogo otnositel'no sozdaniia Aziatskoi akademii v Rossii," *Narody Azii i Afriki* 2 (1973): 202–7.

33. Uvarov may have studied with H. L. Heeren while at Göttingen University, for he praised his views; this noted orientalist, in 1804, republished his two-volume *Ideen über die Politik, den Verkehr, und den Handel der vornehmsten Volker der alten Welt*. Uvarov's contacts are drawn from the following sources: Skach-

kov, *Ocherki*, p. 89; V. S. Vorob'ev-Desiatovskii, "Russkii indianist G. S. Lebedev (1749–1817)," *Ocherki po istorii russkago vostokovedeniia* 2 (1956): 57–62; Gal'perin, "Russkaia nauka," p. 25; Bartol'd, *Istoriia*, p. 236; Durylin, "Drug Gete," 192; "Vyderzhki iz staroi zapisnoi knizhki," *RA* 11 (1873): 1979–80; "Otryvok iz zapisok starago diplomata," p. 294; V. V. Grigor'ev, *Imperatorskii S.-Peterburgskii universitet* (St. Petersburg, 1870), p. 8; "Pis'ma S. S. Uvarova k V. A. Zhukovskomu" (April 21, 1811), *RA* 9 (1871): 158; "Pis'ma N. M. Karamzina k S. S. Uvarovu" (July 1, 1811), *XVIII vek* 8 (1969): 351; "Pis'ma Bogoliubova" 313; (October 5, 1809), *RA*, p. 313; Vigel', *Zapiski*, II, 103–4; and Vigel', *Zapiski*, IV, p. 170.

34. For a synopsis of Uvarov's lifelong interest in the Orient, consult C. H. Whittaker's "The Impact of the Oriental Renaissance in Russia: The Case of Sergei Uvarov," *Jahrbücher für Geschichte Osteuropas* 26, No. 4 (1978): 503–24.

35. Uvarov, *Projet*, pp. 2–6, 10–14. Scholars consider this linguistic discovery still to be the most important contribution of the nineteenth century to the study of the ancient world; see, for example, Rawlinson, "India," p. 35.

36. Uvarov, *Projet*, pp. 8, 21–23.

37. Ibid., pp. 6, 8, 14–19, 21–24, 30. For N. V. Riasanovsky's assessment of Uvarov's enthusiasm for the East, see his two articles: "Asia through Russian Eyes," in *Russia and Asia*, ed. Vucinich, pp. 11–13; and "Russia and Asia: Two Nineteenth-Century Views," *California Slavic Studies* 1 (1960): 170–82.

38. Leduc, "Essai," p. 12; "Pis'ma N. I. Turgeneva k A. I. Turgenevu" (March 12, 1810), *Arkhiv* 1 394; Vasilchikov, *Semeistvo*, II, p. 228; J. Körner, *Briefe von und an Friedrich und Dorothea Schlegel* (March 13, 1811) (Berlin, 1926), p. 132; G. Schmid, "Goethe und Uwarow, und ihr Briefwechsel" (August 17, 1811), *Russische Revue* 28, No. 17 (1888): 138–43; Susini, *Lettres*, p. 410. The *Projet* was translated into German and Russian: S. S. Uwarow, *Ideen zu einer asiatischen Akademie*, trans. A. von Hauenschild (Berlin, 1811); and Zhukovskii, *Vestnik Evropy* 1 (1811): 27–52; the Zhukovskii translation was concluded in *Vestnik Evropy* 2 (1811): 96–120.

39. De Maistre, "Lettre critique sur le Projet" (December 8, 1810), in Uvarov, *Esquisses*, pp. 49–65. The rest of the correspondence is reprinted in M. Stepanov and F. Vermale, "Pis'ma Zhozefa de Mestra k S. S. Uvarovu" (December 8, 1810–July 1, 1814), *Literaturnoe nasledstvo* 29–30 (1937): 677–712.

40. This is, in particular, the thesis of Durylin, who sees the essay as a political ploy or masquerade for Russian foreign policy interests and denies any scholarly motivation whatsoever; this extreme view is even criticized by Soviet scholars: see Durylin, "Drug Gete," pp. 190–97; Stepanov and Vermale, "De Mestr'," p. 677.

41. This was the characterization of Alexander to his brother, Sergei Turgenev; it is quoted in Stepanov and Vermale, "De Mestr'," p. 677; "Pis'ma Zhukovskago k A. I. Turgenevu" (December 4, 1810), pp. 80–83.

42. The gossipy Vigel' declared her to be twelve years Uvarov's senior; Vigel' probably confused Catherine with her sister, Barbara (1778–1864), who married Nicholas Repnin-Volkonskii and patronized female education with her wealth (Vigel', *Zapiski*, IV, p. 170; also see M. L. E. Lehmann, *Freiherr vom Stein*, V [Leipzig, 1905], p. 587).

43. Vasilchikov, *Semeistvo*, III, p. 465.

44. Catherine died in 1849, and soon after Uvarov suffered a stroke. The four children were Aleksei (1824–1884), who became a famed archeologist; Alexandra (1813–1865), who married Prince P. A. Urusov; Natalia (1820–1843), who married I. V. Baladin and whose early death caused Uvarov to suffer what might

now be called a nervous breakdown; and Elizabeth (n.d.), who remained unmarried. Uvarov left documents that related only to his public life and kept his private life just that. On his alleged homosexuality, consult Karlinsky, *Gogol*, pp. 56–57.

45. E. Kovalevskii, *Graf Bludov i ego vremia* (St. Petersburg, 1866), pp. 103–5; Sturdza, "Beseda liubitelei russkago slova i Arzamas," *Moskvitianin* 6, No. 21 (1851): 3–22; A. N. Pypin, *Obshchestvennoe dvizhenie v Rossii pri Aleksandre I* (St. Petersburg, 1900), pp. 38–40; and A. N. Shebunin, "Brat'ia Turgenevy i dvorianskoe obshchestvo aleksandrovskoi epokhi," in *Dekabrist N. I. Turgenev: Pis'ma k bratu S. I. Turgenevu* (Moscow, 1936), pp. 27–31; B. Hollingsworth, "Arzamas: Portrait of a Literary Society," *Slavonic and East European Review* 44, No. 103 (1966): 310–12.

46. S. S. Uvarov, "Coup d'oeil sur l'état de la littérature russe," *Le Conservateur impartial* 77 (September 25, 1817): 380; Iu. D. Levin, "O russkom poeticheskom perevode v epokhu romantizma," *Rannie veianiia*, 222–46; V. I. Kuleshov, *Literaturnye sviazi Rossii i zapadnoi Evropy v XIX veke (pervaia polovina)* (Moscow, 1965), pp. 20–31; Leighton, *Romanticism*, pp. 1–9.

47. L. Maikov, *Batiushkov, ego zhizn' i sochineniia* (St. Petersburg, 1896), pp. 101–4; M. Aronson and S. Reisner, *Literaturnye kruzhki i salony* (Leningrad, 1929), pp. 52–53; E. Sidorov, "Liternaturnoe obshchestvo 'Arzamas,'" *ZMNP* 335, No. 6 (June 1901): 361–74; Shebunin, "Brat'ia," pp. 29–31; Vigel', *Zapiski*, III, p. 153; and *Zapiski*, IV, pp. 170–73; Poznanskii, *Ocherki*, pp. 71–72.

48. N. A. Politsyn, "Manifesty, napisannye Shishkovym v otechestvennuiu voinu, i patrioticheskoe ikh znachenie," *RS* 150 (June 1912): 477–91. On the Russian Academy, consult M. I. Sukhomlinov, *Istoriia Rossiiskoi akademii*, I–VIII (St. Petersburg, 1874–1888); and Vucinich, *Science*, pp. 164–66.

49. S. S. Uvarov, "Littérature russe: Essai en vers et en prose par M. de Batushchoff," *Le Conservateur impartial* 83 (October 16, 1817): 414. Zhukovskii eventually became tutor to the future Alexander II and the court poet as well; he was introduced at court by Uvarov, who was close to the empress and who believed that the great poet's talent was being stifled by his poor living conditions. "Pis'ma S. S. Uvarova k V. A. Zhukovskomu" (July 29, 1815), *RA* 9 (1872): 0165; "Pis'ma Zhukovskago k A. I. Turgenevu" (August 4, 1815), *RA* 33 (1895): 143–151; "Neizdannye pis'ma V. A. Zhukovskago" (May 4, 1811), *RA* 3 (1900): 11.

50. "Pis'ma Zhukovskago k A. I. Turgenevu" (December 4, 1810), pp. 80–83.

51. Uvarov, *Projet*, pp. 26–27.

52. Shishkov and his adherents are often called classicists, but in the sense that they upheld the eighteenth-century views of Lomonosov. On classicism at the turn of the century, see G. Highet, *The Classical Tradition: Greek and Roman Influences on Western Literature* (Oxford, 1949), pp. 355–61; and de Staël, *Ten Years of Exile*, trans. D. Beik (New York: 1972), p. 189.

53. S. S. Uvarov, "Otvet V. V. Kapnistu na pis'mo ego ob ekzametre," *Chteniia v Besede liubitelei russkago slova* 17 (1815): 62.

54. The English also transferred their study of the ancients from Latin to Greek: M. L. Clarke, *Classical Education in Britain, 1500–1900* (Cambridge, Eng., 1959), p. 76; R. Jenkyns, *The Victorians and Ancient Greece* (Cambridge, Mass., 1980); S. S. Uvarov, "Pis'mo k N. I. Gnedichu o Grecheskom ekzametre," *Chteniia v Besede liubitelei russkago slova* 13 (1813): 57, 61, and 66; Uvarov, *Rech'*, pp. 24–25; I. M. Murav'ev-Apostol, "Pis'ma iz Moskvy v Nizhnii Novgorod," *Syn otechestva* 10, No. 48 (1813): 97–101. For a discussion of Uvarov's classicism in educational policy, see chaps. 4 and 6.

55. Only seventy copies of *O grecheskoi antologii* (St. Petersburg, 1820) were printed. *Sochineniia Batiushkova* 1 (1885–1887): 421–34; V. K. Kiukhel'beker, "Novye knigi: O grecheskoi antologii," *Syn otechestva* 50, No. 12 (March 20, 1820): 269–75; *Syn otechestva* 62, No. 23 (June 5, 1820): 145–51; "Knizhnyia redkosti," *RA* 2 (1892): 252.

56. Uvarov, "Pis'mo k Gendichu"; "Otvet Gnedicha," *Chteniia v Besede liubitelei russkago slova* 13 (1813): 69–72; Gnedich, "Rozhdenie Omera: Poema," *Syn otechestva* 35, No. 1 (January 6, 1817): 24–27; "Pis'mo V. V. Kapnista k S. S. Uvarovu," in *Sochineniia Kapnista* (Moscow, 1849), pp. 600–618; Uvarov, "Otvet Kapnistu," pp. 45–67; "Zapiska Gnedicha k Uvarovu" (November 3, 1826), *Bibliograficheskie zapiski* II (1859): 623; "Pis'mo Uvarova k V. A. Zhukovskomu" (November 10, 1847), PD, fond 265, opis' 1, no. 44, p. 281; A. N. Egunov, *Gomer v russkikh perevodakh XVIII–XIX vekov* (Moscow: 1964), pp. 174–77; and V. E. Vatsuro, "Russkaia idillia v epokhu romantizma," in *Russkii romantizm*, pp. 118–38.

57. A. Voeikov, "Poslanie k S. S. Uvarovu," *Vestnik Evropy* 104, No. 5 (March 1819): 15–24; C. Matthei, *Varia Graeca* (Moscow, 1811); "Annonce littéraire: Bucolicos Graecos par M. Gräfe," *Le Conservateur impartial* 3 (June 11, 1816): 16; "Materialy dlia biografii Uvarova," ROBIL, fond 233, no. 50, ed. 9, pp. 9, 15, 19; "K S. S. Uvarovu," *Sochineniia Batiushkova* 438 (May 1817). Although Batiushkov had become insane in 1821, his poem was republished in the fifth issue in 1841 of *Moskvitianin*.

58. S. S. Uvarov, *Lettre à M. le Sécrétaire perpétuel de l'Académie imperiale des Sciences. Lué à l'Académie le 6/18 février 1852* (St. Petersburg, 1852), pp. 1–13; and "Biblioteka," GIM, fond 17, no. 29.

59. J. Christie, "Observations Occasioned by Mr. Ouvaroff's Essay on the Eleusinian Mysteries," in Ouvaroff, *Essay on the Mysteries of Eleusis*, trans. J. D. Price (London, 1817), p. iv.

60. Durylin, "De Stal'" (September 10, 1815), p. 298.

61. S. S. Uvarov, *Essai sur les Mystères d'Éleusis* (St. Petersburg, 1812). For a similar treatment of the topic, see G. Mylonas, *Eleusis and the Eleusinian Mysteries* (Princeton, N.J., 1961). Uvarov's *Essai* was translated into Russian by I. I. Vvedenskii, "Issledovanie ob elevsinskikh tainstvakh," *Sovremennik* 2 (February 1846): 77:108. It was favorably reviewed in the British *Classical Journal* ("Notice of: Essai sur les Mystères d'Éleusis," 13, No. 26 [1816]: 399–406; and No. 27 [1816]: 165–71; and No. 28 [1817]: 117–23). All the prefaces to the various editions are reprinted in Uvarov, *Études*, pp. 67–191.

62. Uvarov, in *Études*, "Nonnos von Panapolis, der Dichter," pp. 163–250; "Über das Vorhomerische Zeitalter," pp. 252–71; "Examen critique de la fable d'Hercule," pp. 275–98; and "Memoire sur les tragiques grecs," pp. 299–317. The "Memoire" was first read to the Academy of Sciences on November 24, 1820, and later reviewed and translated by F. Somov in *Syn otechestva* 10 and 11 (1825): 134–47 and 282–93, respectively; also see G. D'Ippolito, *Studi Nonniani* (Palermo, 1964).

63. Uvarov, "Nonnos," pp. 165–66; and *Lettre*, p. 11. Goethe, *Kunst und Alterthum* 1, No. 3 (1817): 63; R. Friedenthal, *Goethe: His Life and Times* (London, 1963), p. 25; Schmid, "Goethe und Uwarov" (March 28, 1817–August 10, 1819), pp. 154–60.

64. A. Herzen, *My Past and Thoughts* (New York, 1974), pp. 99–100; and Durylin, "Drug Gete," 204–8.

65. "Dva predlozheniia S. S. Uvarov Spb. tsenzurnomu komitetu, 12 dekabria 1814 g. i 13 maia godu," in *Bumagi otnosiaschiesia do otechestvennoi voiny 1812*

goda, X, ed. P. I. Shchukin (Moscow, 1908), p. 374; Uvarov, "Pis'mo Kapnistu, p. 63.

66. Mirsky, *Russian Literature*, pp. 73–74.

67. Vigel', *Zapiski*, IV, p. 171. Vigel' also attended the opening of the play on September 23, 1815, along with Dashkov, A. Turgenev, and Zhukovskii. B. Malnich, "A. A. Shakhovskoi," *Slavonic and East European Review* 32, No. 78 (December 1953): 29–51; Sidorov, "Arzamas," pp. 46–60; Shebunin, "Brat'ia," pp. 31–32; D. Blagoi, "Sotsial'no-politicheskoe litso Arzamasa," in *Arzamas i arzamasskie protokoly* (Leningrad, 1933), pp. 5–20.

68. Karamzin, *Neizdannye sochineniia i perepiska*, I (March 2, 1816) (St. Petersburg, 1862), p. 165; "Pis'ma N. M. Karamzina k A. I. Turgenevu" (March 30, 1816), *RS* 2 (1889): 471.

69. Hollingsworth, "Arzamas," p. 314; N. Kushelev, "Unichtozhenie masonskikh lozh v Rossii," *RS* 18 (April 1877): 645; S. V. Veselovskii, ed., *Arzamasskie pomestnye acty (1578–1618 gg.)* (Moscow, 1915), p. 608; Kovalevskii, *Bludov*, pp. 107–10. The various aborted plans for publication are recorded in Aronson, *Kruzhki*, p. 259; Mordovchenko, *Russkaia kritika*, p. 283; Sidorov, "Arzamas," pp. 73–74; P. A. Viazemskii, "Pis'mo k A. I. Turgenevu" (September 27, 1816), in *Ostaf'evskii arkhiv kniazei Viazemskikh*, I, ed. S. D. Sheremetev (St. Petersburg, 1899), p. 53; Maikov, *Batiushkov*, pp. 187–88.

70. "Perepiska Kristina s kniazhnoi Turkestanovoi, 1813–1815," *RA* 2 (1882): 161; A. Kirpichnikov, "Novye materialy dlia istorii 'Arzamasa' (po dokumentam Porechenskago arkhiva)," *RS* 30, No. 5 (1899): 338; M. I. Gillel'son, *P. A. Viazemskii: Zhizn' i tvorchestvo* (Moscow, 1969), p. 28; and *Molodoi Pushkin i arzamasskoe bratstvo* (Leningrad, 1974), pp. 141–42

71. Vigel', *Zapiski*, IV, pp. 170–74; S. S. Uvarov, "Rech' S. S. Uvarova pri prieme v Arzamas D. A. Kavelina," *Arzamasskie protokoly*, p. 179; and "Os'moe ianvaria 1851 goda," *Sovremennik* 26, No. 3 (1851): 3.

72. Kirpichnikov, "Novye materialy," pp. 340; *Arzamasskie protokoly*, p. 122; Uvarov, "Coup d'oeil," p. 380; "Littérature russe," p. 414; and "Literaturnye vospominaniia," pp. 37–38. "Pushkin o Batiushkove," *RA* 1 (1894): 528.

73. Uvarov, "Literaturnye vospominaniia," pp. 37–38.

74. Good descriptions of the different attitudes toward literature are found in Hollingsworth, "Arzamas," pp. 318–20; Uvarov, *Projet*, p. 14; Leighton, *Romanticism*, p. 73; M. I. Sukhomlinov, "Osobennosti poeticheskago tvorchestva A. N. Maikova," *RS* 92 (March 1899): 483; and Wortman, *Russian Legal Consciousness*, p. 94.

75. Sidorov, "Arzamas," p. 87; Bulich, *Ocherki*, pp. 108–23; P. V. Annenkov, *Materialy dlia biografii A. S. Pushkina*, I (St. Petersburg, 1855), pp. 50–52; P. F. Iusupov, *Russkii romantizm nachala XIX veka i natsional'nye kul'tury* (Moscow, 1970).

76. The actual order of events in Arzamas, beginning with the twentieth meeting, is somewhat in dispute because the minutes are only partial after the nineteenth meeting on April 22, 1817, thus further indicating that the society was in a state of crisis. See N. I. Turgenev, *La Russie et les Russes*, I (Paris, 1847), pp. 172–73; *Arzamasskie protokoly*, p. 224; V. Pushkin, *Sobranie sochinenii* (St. Petersburg, 1893), p. 86; *Arkhiv brat'ev Turgenevykh*, III, No. 93 (September 8, 1817); Kirpichnikov, "Novye materialy," pp. 341–50 contains the "Rules."

77. A. Turgenev, "Pis'ma k Viazemskuiu" (September 25, 1818), *Ostaf'evskii arkhiv*, p. 124; "Zapiska V. A. Zhukovskago o N. I. Turgeneve," *RA* 3 (1895): 24.

78. Sidorov, "Arzamas," p. 83; *Ostaf'evskii arkhiv*, I, pp. 99, 353; Uvarov, "Coup d'oeil," p. 380.

CHAPTER 3

1. S. S. Uvarov, *Rech'*, pp. 50–51.

2. For a current restatement of these issues, see E. Drauze, "An Interview with Isaiah Berlin," *Partisan Review* 50, No. 1 (1983): 10–16.

3. For an overview, see C. H. Whittaker, "The Ideology of Sergei Uvarov: An Interpretive Essay," *Russian Review* 37, No. 2 (April 1978): 158–76. Uvarov's writings include *Rech'*; "Smes': O stikhotvorenii Gete," *Syn otechstva* 4, No. 9 (February 27, 1813): 134–36; *Éloge funèbre de Moreau* (St. Petersburg, 1813); *L'Empereur Alexandre et Buonoparte* (St. Petersburg, 1814); *Appel à l'Europe* (St. Petersburg, 1815); and *Le Prince de Ligne* (St. Petersburg, 1815).

4. "Pis'ma mitropolita Evgeniia Bolkhovitinova k V. G. Anastasevichu. 1820" (September 3, 1820), *RA* II (1889): 368.

5. S. S. Uvarov, *O prepodavanii istorii otnositel'no k narodnomu vospitaniiu* (St. Petersburg, 1813), p. 13; and "Le Prince de Ligne (1815)," in *Esquisses*, p. 141.

6. Serge d'Ouvaroff, "Elle te peindra la Patrie," in "Mélanges: 1798," GIM, fond 17, no. 2; P. R. Zaborov, "Vol'ter v Rossii kontsa XVIII–nachala XIX veka," in *Ot klassitsizma k romantizmu*, ed. M. P. Alekseev (Leningrad, 1970), pp. 63–194; P. Gay, *Voltaire's Politics: The Poet as Realist* (New York, 1965).

7. The best descriptions of the Hannoverian Conservatives are found in K. Epstein, *The Genesis of German Conservatism* (Princeton, 1966), pp. 546–90; and R. Aris, *History of Political Thought in Germany from 1789 to 1815* (London, 1936), pp. 55–60. On Burke, consult A. Cobban, *Edmund Burke and the Revolt against the Eighteenth Century* (New York, 1960) and J. C. Weston, "Edmund Burke's View of History," *Review of Politics* 33, No. 2 (April 1961): 203–29.

8. S. S. Uvarov, *Stein et Pozzo di Borgo* (St. Petersburg, 1846); Uvarov's praise of Constant is found in the *Appel*; de Staël had a liaison with Constant for many years and spread his brand of "bourgeois liberalism." On Constant's influence in general, consult S. S. Landa, *Dukh revoliutsionnykh preobrazovanii . . . Iz istorii formirovaniia ideologii i politicheskoi organizatsii dekabristov 1816–1825* (Moscow, 1975), pp. 23–25, 135–36; V. I. Kuleshov, *Literaturnye sviazi*, pp. 155–67; G. Vernadsky, *La Charte constitutionnelle de l'Empire russe de l'an 1820*, trans. S. Oldenbourg (Paris, 1933), pp. 141–44; "Golos blagarodnago frantsuza," *Syn otechstva* 21 (1815).

On the French Doctrinaires, consult D. Johnson, *Guizot: Aspects of French History, 1787–1874* (Toronto, 1963), pp. 24–87; C. Muret, *French Royalist Doctrines since the Revolution* (New York, 1933); C. Pouthas, *Guizot pendant la restauration* (Paris, 1923); R. de Nesmes-Desmarets, *Les Doctrines politiques de Royer-Collard* (Paris, 1908); L. Krieger, *The German Idea of Freedom* (Chicago, 1975), p. 78.

9. Uvarov quoted all these men throughout his *Rech'*, *Projet*, and *Eloge*.

10. These writers began having influence in Russia in the latter half of the eighteenth century. Hume, for example, served as the model for the historian Michael Shcherbatov (A. Lentin, ed., *Prince M. M. Shcherbatov: On the Corruption of Morals in Russia* [Cambridge, Eng., 1969], p. 57). The Decembrists saw in Montesquieu a major influence (S. S. Volk, *Istoricheskie vzgliady Dekabristov* [Moscow, 1958], pp. 34–38). Also see R. Ergang, *Herder and the Foundations of German Nationalism* (New York, 1931); L. Schapiro's excellent *Rationalism and Nationalism in Russian Nineteenth-Century Thought* (New Haven, Conn., 1967), pp. 1–28; Vucinich, *Science*, pp. 30–31, 62–65, 166–71.

11. Uvarov, *Projet*; *Rech'*, pp. 38–39. Hegel ridiculed the forest theory, but Guizot applied it to French history (S. Avineri, *Hegel's Theory of the Modern State* [Cambridge, Eng., 1972], pp. 228–29; and F. Guizot, *Historical Essays and Lectures* [Chicago, 1972], pp. 286–303).

12. Uvarov attacked both the materialism and philosophies of the eighteenth century and Rousseau's *Discourse on Inequality* in *Projet*, pp. 10–13, and in *Rech'*, pp. 26, 40.

13. For an overview of Russian intellectual trends, see A. Walicki, *A History of Russian Thought from the Enlightenment to Marxism*, trans. H. Andrews-Rusiecka (Stanford, Calif., 1979), pp. 1–70. Studies useful for demonstrating the similarities between the Decembrists' concerns and Uvarov's include Volk, *Vzgliady;* M. Raeff, Introduction to *The Decembrist Movement* (Englewood Cliffs, N.J., 1966), pp. 1–29; and Christoff, *The Third Heart*. Besides Arzamas acquaintances, one Decembrist, Lunin, was a relation of Uvarov on his wife's side and often visited their home ("Zapiski N. V. Basargina," in P. I. Bartenev, *Deviatnadtsatyi vek, Istoricheskii sbornik*, I [Moscow, 1872], p. 145).

14. The phrase is from V. V. Pugachev, who, in *Evoliutsiia obshchestvenno-politicheskikh vzgliadov Pushkina* (Gorky, 1967), has written the most balanced Soviet analysis of Uvarov's political views; especially see pp. 39–49; also see his "Predistoriia soiuza Blagodenstviia i pushkinskaia oda 'Vol'nost'," *Issledovaniia i materialy*, IV (Moscow, 1962), pp. 94–139; and "K voprosu o politicheskie vzgliadakh S. S. Uvarova v 1810-e gody," *Uchenye zapiski seriia istoriko-filologicheskaia Gor'kovskii g. universitet, im. N. I. Lobachevskogo* 72 (1964): 125–32.

15. Uvarov, "Goethe," in *Esquisses*, p. 206.

16. Uvarov, *Stein et Pozzo*, p. 6.

17. Lehmann, *vom Stein*, III, pp. 699–700; J. R. Seeley, *Life and Times of Stein*, II (Boston, 1879), p. 112; A. N. Shebunin, *Dekabrist*, p. 403; N. I. Grech, *Zapiski o moei zhizni* (St. Petersburg, 1886), pp. 231–32; N. P. Sidorov, "Syn otechestva," in *Otechestvennaia voina i russkoe obshchestvo, 1812–1912*, V, ed. A. K. Dzhivelegov (Moscow, 1912), pp. 140–42; "Dva otnosheniia S. S. Uvarova," p. 373; Uvarov, "Pis'mo k baronu Shteinu," *RA* 9, No. 2 (1871): 132; "Pis'mo S. S. Uvarova—grafu A. K. Razumovskomu: Pervonachal'naia pros'ba Pezaroviusa o razreshenii emu izdavat' ezhenedel'nyi zhurnal," *RS* 32 (January 1902): 175–76. Pesarovius also belonged to the same Masonic lodge as Uvarov and Speranskii, the Polar Star.

18. Besides those mentioned in n. 3 of this chapter, Uvarov in 1846 wrote yet another essay, "Des Vues de Napoléon sur l'Italie," which concluded that Bonaparte had a Romantic passion for the country but no set policy and hence "retarded rather than prepared the hour for Italy's political regeneration" (*Esquisses*, p. 92).

19. Any number of books analyze this general trend. See Volk, *Vzgliady;* G. P. Gooch, *History and Historians in the Nineteenth Century* (Boston, 1959); H. White, *Metahistory: The Historical Imagination in Nineteenth-Century Europe* (Baltimore, 1975); C. Becker, *The Heavenly City of the Eighteenth-Century Philosophers* (New Haven, Conn., 1961), pp. 71–118; H. Trevor-Roper, "The Historical Philosophy of the Enlightenment," in *Studies on Voltaire and the Eighteenth Century*, XXVII, ed. T. Besterman (Geneva, 1963), 1667–88; and a good survey is found in F. Baumer, *Modern European Thought: Continuity and Change in Ideas, 1600–1950* (New York, 1977), pp. 237–55, 288–301.

20. Uvarov, "Mémoire sur les tragiques grecs," in *Esquisses*, p. 179; *O prepodavanii*, pp. 13, 24; and *Rech'*, pp. 15, 41, 53.

21. The classic study of this concept remains J. B. Bury, *The Idea of Progress: An Inquiry into Its Origin and Growth* (New York, 1932); Guizot is quoted on pp. 273–75. Also valuable are J. Schapiro, *Condorcet and the Rise of Liberalism* (New York, 1934), pp. 234–70; J. Barzun, *Darwin, Marx, Wagner* (New York, 1958), pp. 38–55; and Volk on the Decembrists, *Vzgliady*, p. 85. H. Vyverberg's *Historical Pessimism in the French Enlightenment* (Cambridge, Mass., 1958) demonstrates the remains of less optimistic thinking.

22. Uvarov, "Goethe," p. 225; *Projet*, p. 19; *Éloge*, p. 1; *O prepodavanii*, p. 17; and *Rech'*, pp. 29, 50, 52–53.

23. Uvarov, *Essay on the Mysteries of Eleusis*, trans. J. D. Price (London, 1817), p. 20; *Rech'*, pp. 20, 41–43, 48, 50–53. The analogy of a state to a living organism originated with Plato and became a predominant mode of thought by the turn of the century, but in Uvarov's casual way. See F. Coker, *Organismic Theories of the State: Nineteenth-Century Interpretations of the State as an Organism or as Person, Studies in History, Economics and Public Law*, XXXVIII (New York, 1910); Herder, *Auch eine Philosophie der Geschichte zur Bildung der Menschheit* (n.p., 1774), p. 190. Other contemporaries who used this imagery included Karamzin, in R. Pipes, *Karamzin's Memoir on Ancient and Modern Russia: A Translation and Analysis* (Cambridge, Mass., 1959), p. 204; M. Speranskii, "O vosrastakh obshchestv i o soobrazhenii s nimi mer zakonodal'nykh," *V Pamiat' grafa M. M. Speranskago, 1772–1872* (St. Petersburg, 1872), p. 800; N. M. Murav'ev-Apostol, "Pis'ma iz Moskvy v Nizhnii Novgorod," *Syn otechestva* 48 (1813): 97; Alexander I, as quoted in A. McConnell, *Tsar Alexander I* (New York, 1970), p. 138; K. Welcker, *Die Letzten Grunde von Recht, Staat, und Strafe* (Giessen, 1813), pp. 1–20.

24. Throughout his *Rech'*, *Projet*, *Éloge*, and *Alexandre*, Uvarov saw Providence as the unifying principle of history. Some Decembrists and French liberal historians also spoke of Providence but equated it with fatalism, a concept Uvarov definitely rejected; see Volk, *Vzgliady*, pp. 92, 253; E. Kovalevskii, *Graf Bludov i ego vremia* (St. Petersburg, 1866), p. 253; Z. A. Kamenskii, *Filosofskie idei russkogo prosveshcheniia* (Moscow, 1971), pp. 126–27; K. Raupach, "La Science de l'histoire," *Le Conservateur impartial* 25 (March 26, 1818), p. 109.

25. For Burke's similar reconciliation of providential and human causation, see Weston, "Burke," pp. 208–17; and Uvarov, *O prepodavanii*, pp. 14, 24; *Projet*, p. 19; and *Rech'*, pp. 43–47.

26. Uvarov, *Rech'*, p. 25; "Vues générales," in *Esquisses*, p. 243; "Mémoire sur les tragiques grecs," in *Esquisses*, pp. 179–80. Becker considers the unity of politics and morality the essential feature of eighteenth-century historical writing (*Heavenly City*, p. 104). P. D. Cherevin, a Decembrist, expressed the same point of view in "O prepodavanii istorii detiam," *Vestnik Evropy* 1 (January–February 1825): 117–29.

27. Uvarov, *Eleusis*, p. 32; and *Projet*, pp. 7, 10–14.

28. Uvarov, *Rech'*, pp. 3, 11–12, 26–27, 29–30, 35–38; here, Uvarov most resembles Montesquieu in his *Spirit of the Laws* (New York, 1949), p. 14. Hegel shared Uvarov's attitude toward Rome; see Avineri, *Hegel*, p. 227.

29. Uvarov, *Rech'*, pp. 34–42; and *O prepodavanii*, pp. 17–19. Robertson, Turgot, and the Decembrists shared this interpretation of the Middle Ages (Baumer, *Modern Thought*, pp. 250–55; and Volk, *Vzgliady*, p. 237).

30. Robertson also admired the balance of power as "the great secret of modern politics" (*The Progress of Society in Europe*, ed. F. Gilbert [Chicago, 1972], p. xvi).

31. Uvarov, *Rech'*, pp. 40–50; Uvarov is quoted in M. I. Sukhomlinov, *Issledovaniia i stati po russkoi literature i prosveshcheniiu*, I (St. Petersburg, 1889), p. 198. For similar views of the monarchy, see K. Baker, *Condorcet: From Natural Philosophy to Social Mathematics* (Chicago, 1975), pp. 202–14.

32. Chateaubriand, "De Buonaparte et des Bourbons (30 mars 1814)," in *Oeuvres complètes de Chateaubriand*, III (Paris, 1828), p. 16; Uvarov, "Mnenie Uvarova ob 'Istorii gosudarstva Rossiiskogo' Karamzina" (document dated March 1816), PD, fond 265, opis' 2, no. 2907.

33. On this concept, see J. Gagliardo, *Enlightened Despotism* (New York, 1967); R. Birn, *Crisis, Absolutism, Revolution: Europe, 1648–1789/91* (Hillsdale, 1977); L.

Krieger, *An Essay on the Theory of Enlightened Despotism* (Chicago, 1975); Uvarov, *Rech'*, pp. 40–50.

34. Uvarov, *Rech'*, pp. 41–42; "De Ligne," p. 119; *Moreau; Alexandre;* and *Appel*. Coleridge also regarded the revolution as a "chastisement" meted out to France because of the "arrogance" of philosophes who treated states like "machines" (*The Statesman's Manual*, ed. W. G. Shedd, in *Complete Works*, I [New York, 1884], p. 440).

35. Uvarov, *O prepodavanii*, p. 20; "Des Vues," in *Esquisses*, p. 78; *Appel*, p. 2; *Alexandre;* and Preface to the Second Edition of *Eleusis*, p. ix.

36. Uvarov, "Smes'," pp. 134–36. The article was originally published anonymously in German, in *Der Patriot;* in 1851 Uvarov admitted to Grech that he had written it (Gennadi, "Materialy dlia biografii," ROBIL, fond 5, opis' 233, no. 50, vol. 3 [compiled in 1856]).

37. The memoir was apparently not published, and I was not permitted to see it in the archives; but it is discussed in the Stein-Uvarov correspondence of June 7, 1813, and October 6, 1813, in Lehmann, *Stein*, IV, pp. 177–78, 273–74; it was also mentioned in Uvarov's *Alexandre*, pp. 14–16. Stein defended the pope as a victim of Napoleon's perfidy. Nonetheless, he congratulated Uvarov on his "knowledge and style" and facility in matters of canon law.

38. When Moreau died of battle wounds in 1813, Prince Repnin, Uvarov's brother-in-law, erected a monument to him, and Uvarov himself arranged for his burial in St. Catherine's Church in St. Petersburg; the funeral lasted eight hours and was attended by the tsar (Susini, *Lettres de Baader*, III, p. 412; R. de Journel, *Un Collège de Jésuites a Saint-Pétersbourg, 1800–1816* [Paris, 1822], p. 203). Uvarov sent the German translation of the *Éloge* to Goethe (G. Schmid, "Goethe und Uwarow," p. 150).

39. Bossuet's *Universal History* is still considered the classic statement of the providential view of history. The *Éloge* was also translated into English and published in New York and Boston in 1814; it was translated into Russian for *Russkii invalid* and *Vestnik Evropy* in the same year and, after Napoleon's downfall, it appeared in *Moniteur universel* in Paris.

40. Uvarov published the pamphlet simultaneously in Russian and French. Chateaubriand claimed that he himself had won the crown for Louis XVIII by demonstrating his legitimacy; Louis agreed that it was better than 100,000 soldiers (*The Memoirs of Chateaubriand*, trans. R. Balick [New York, 1961], p. 260). Also see O. V. Orlik, *Peredovaia Rossiia i revoliutsionnaia Frantsiia* (Moscow, 1973), pp. 38–39.

41 Alexander also considered himself the instrument of Providence and announced this in the New Year's Day manifesto of 1816 (N. K. Shil'der, *Imperator Aleksandr pervyi: Ego zhizn' i tsarstvovanie* [St. Petersburg, 1898], pp. 1–2).

42. *Alexandre*, p. 38.

43. *Appel*, p. 3.

44. *Alexandre*, p. 39.

45. Ibid.

46. "Konstitutsiia frantsuzskago korolevstva," *Syn otechestva* 17 (1814) and 25 (1814): 193–97, 259–70. N. K. Piksanov lists the many articles on constitutionalism in the Russian press ("Publitsistika Aleksandrovskoi epokhi," *Istoriia russkoe literatury XIX v.*, ed. D. N. Ovsianiko-Kuliokovskii [Moscow, 1910], p. 47). On the vogue in general, consult Vernadsky, *Charte*, and Grech, *Zapiski*, p. 446.

47. "Sluzhba S. S. Uvarova," PD, fond 234, opis' 1, no. 42.

48. The letter is reproduced in "Pis'mo S. S. Uvarova k Baronu Shteinu" (November 18, 1813), *RA* 9 (1871): 0129–34; "Pis'ma k Zhukovskomu" (August 17, 1813), *RA* 9 (1871): 161; A. Kirpichnikov, "Novye materialy," pp. 339–40; N. I. Turgenev, *Dnevniki i pis'ma* (n.d., 1817), III (Petrograd, 1921), p. 83.

49. Alexander's speech is republished in *Ostaf'evskii arkhiv*, I, pp. 472–75.
50. Uvarov, *O prepodavanii*, p. 17; and *Rech'*, pp. 24, 48, 39, 60–61.
51. For a Soviet interpretation of enlightened absolutism as a "transitional stage," see I. A. Fedosov, "Prosveshchennyi absoliutizm v Rossii," *Voprosy istorii* 9 (1970):34–55; also consult N. M. Druzhinin, '24oosveshchennyi absoliutizm v Rossii," in *Absoliutizm v Rossii (XVII–XVIII vv.)*, ed. N. Druzhinin (Moscow, 1964).
52. Vucinich, *Science*, p. 274; Uvarov, *Rech'*, pp. 60–61.
53. Uvarov, *O prepodavanii*, p. 17; and *Rech'*, pp. 24, 48. Along with Radishchev, St. Petersburg University professors were considered the major Russian influence on the Decembrists (Volk, *Vzgliady*, pp. 38–40).
54. Uvarov, *Rech'*, pp. 27, 41–43, 51–53. On Erskine, see L. P. Styker, *For the Defense: Thomas Erskine, The Most Enlightened Liberal of His Times, 1750–1823* (New York, 1947); also see A. Kunitsyn, "O konstitutsii," *Syn otechestva* 45 (1818): 206.
55. "Littérature russe," *Le Conservateur impartial* 37 (May 7, 1818): 172; F. N. Glinka, "Podrobnyi otchet drugu o priiatnom vechere v obshchestve prosveshchennykh liudei," *Syn otechestva* 19 (March 29, 1818): 23; Kunitsyn, "Razsmotrenie rechi," *Syn otechestva* 46 (1819): 191; N. I. Turgenev, "Pis'ma k S. I. Turgenevu" (March 23, 1818), *Dekabrist*, p. 254; S. I. Turgenev, "Pis'mo k N. I. Turgenevu" (June 12, 1818), as quoted in Pugachev, *Evoliutsiia*, p. 45; Kovalevskii, *Bludov*, p. 102; *Le Conservateur impartial* 25 (March 26, 1818): 109; N. Barsukov, "S. S. Uvarov i admiral Shishkov," *RA* 6 (1882): 226–28; *Pis'ma N. M. Karamzina k I. I. Dmitrievu* (April 29, 1818), (St. Petersburg, 1866), pp. 236–37; Grech, *Zapiski*, p. 365.
56. Uvarov, *Rech'*, pp. 1, 36, 21–25, 48, 53. On the myth, see S. L. Baehr, "From History to National Myth: *Translatio imperii* in Eighteenth-Century Russia," *Russian Review* 72, No. 1 (January 1978): 1–14. Karamzin also intoned "Rome in its greatness . . . never equaled this state" (Karamzin, "Foreword," p. 118).
57. Uvarov, *O prepodavanii*, p. 17; and *Rech'*, pp. 24, 38, 39, 60–61.
58. "Introduction to the Codification of State Laws by M. M. Speransky (1809)," as quoted in M. Raeff, *Plans for Political Reform in Imperial Russia, 1730–1905* (Englewood Cliffs, N.J., 1966), pp. 93–94.
59. Uvarov, "Tablettes d'un voyageur russe," GIM, fond 17, no. 6, pp. 31, 64–66.
60. Uvarov, *Stein et Pozzo*, pp. 3, 6, 12. Pozzo later admitted he tried to argue Alexander out of awarding a constitution to Poland (*Iz besedy Potstso di Borgo s baronom Meiendorfom v Vene v 1832 godu* [St. Petersburg, 1910], pp. 1–4). Also see "Zametka gr. Potstso di Borgo o nem samom," *Sbornik Imperatorskago russkago istoricheskago obshchestva* 2 (1868): 158–63.
61. Uvarov, *Rech'*, p. 53.
62. Uvarov, *O prepodavanii*, pp. 22–23; *Mysteries*, p. 20; *Alexandre*, pp. 7–8; and *Rech'*, p. 50. Stepanov and Vermale, "DeMestr," p. 705; de Maistre, "The Generative Principle of Political Constitutions," in *The Works of Joseph de Maistre*, ed. J. Lively (New York, 1965), p. 161.
63. A. Durylin, "G-zha de Stal' i ee russkie otnosheniia," *Literaturnoe nasledstvo* 33–34 (1939): 240.
64. N. Turgenev's quotation, saying Stein had "the soul of an Arzamas member," is in *Ostaf'evskii arkhiv kniazei Viazemskikh*, I, ed. S. D. Sheremetev (St. Petersburg, 1899), p. 398; Uvarov, *Stein et Pozzo*, pp. 17–36.
65. Uvarov, *Projet*, pp. 6, 10–14; Schlözer is quoted in V. Istrin, "Russkie studenty v Gettingene v 1802–1804 gg. (po materialam arkhiva brat'ev Turgenevykh," *ZMNP* 7 (1910): 133.
66. "Pis'ma Speranskago k A. A. Stolypinu" (March 5, 1818), *RA* 7 (1869): 1693; "Pis'mo N. M. Karamzina k S. S. Uvarovu," *Syn otechestva* 44, No. 8 (1818): 79–80.

67. M. I. Gillel'son, "Pis'ma N. M. Karamzina k S. S. Uvarovu," *XVIII vek*, p. 8; and *Derzhavin i Karamzin v literaturnom dvizhenii XVIII–nachala XIX veka* (Leningrad, 1969), pp. 351–54. Karamzin found Schlegel somewhat "obscure" and "mystical," but Uvarov was right about the similarity of their views. *A Course of Lectures of Modern History* was published in Vienna in 1811 and *The Philosophy of History* in 1828.

68. The parts that were read included the general introduction and the fall of Novgorod (Karamzin, *Istoriia gosudarstva rossiiskago*, I–VIII [St. Petersburg, 1818–1819]; "Mnenie Uvarova," p. 2).

69. E. Kovalevskii, *Graf Bludov i ego vremia* (St. Petersburg, 1866), pp. 102, 248–55, 266–67. Bludov, though, agreed with Alexander's reforms and representative government on the English model.

70. The following monographs are especially useful in defining Karamzin's thought: R. Pipes, "Karamzin's Conception of the Monarchy," *Harvard Slavic Studies* 4 (1957): 35–58; J. Black, *Nicholas Karamzin and Russian Society in the Nineteenth Century: A Study in Russian Political and Historical Thought* (Toronto, 1975); L. G. Kisliagina, *Formirovanie obshchestvenno-politicheskikh vzgliadov N. M. Karamzina, 1785–1803 gg.* (Moscow, 1976); A. N. Pypin, *Obshchestvennoe dvizhenie v Rossii pri Aleksandre I* (St. Petersburg, 1900), pp. 407–412.

71. For the best treatments of Alexander's political attitudes, consult Raeff, *Speransky*, pp. 29–48; and G. Vernadsky, "Reforms under Czar Alexander I: French and American Influences," *Review of Politics* 9, No. 1 (January 1947): 47–64. Also consult Baker's *Condorcet*, p. 203. This school of thought could agree with B. G. Niebuhr's statement of 1815: "Freedom depends much more on administration than on constitution" (Krieger, *Idea*, p. 217). The term *Rechsstaat* was first used by Adam Müller in his 1808 Berlin lectures and by Welcker, *Die Letzten*, pp. 1–20. On the Plan of 1809, see Raeff, *Speransky*, pp. 138–40; and *Plans for Reform*, pp. 119–69; see also D. Christian, "The Political Ideals of Michael Speransky," *Slavonic and East European Review* 54, No. 2 (April 1976): 192–213.

72. *V pamiat'* (January 12, 1819), p. 233; M. A. Korf, *Zhizn' grafa Speranskago*, I (St. Petersburg, 1861), p. 39. They belonged to Professor Ignatius Fessler's lodge, the Polar Star (T. Bakounine, *Le Répertoire biographique des Francs-maçons russes* [Brussels, 1940], pp. 524, 578, 631; V. F. Ivanov, *Ot Petra Pervago do nashikh dnei: Russkaia intelligentsia i masonstvo* [Kharbin, 1923], p. 276).

73. Shebunin called them "conservatives of the English wrinkle, i.e., independent, self-standing people not inimical to gradual progress"; he sees Uvarov's pamphlets as the characteristic expression of this attitude (*Brat'ev*, pp. 31–41). Also see Piksanov, "Publitsistika," pp. 45–52; and Pugachev, *Evoliutsiia*, p. 46.

74. Raeff, *Decembrists*, p. 16; Volk, *Vzgliady*, pp. 66–68; *Dnevnik N. I. Turgeneva* (entry of November 12, 1816), III (St. Petersburg, 1913), p. 7.

75. Krieger, *Essay*, pp. 48, 77, 90.

76 For a similar case of adjusted timetables, see Christian, "Speransky," p. 213.

77. Peter Gay makes the same point about the *thèse royale* (*Politics*, p. 333); Raeff depicts this as a "traditional form of Russian political psychology" (*Speransky*, p. 221).

CHAPTER 4

1. S. S. Uvarov, *Rech'*, p. 48.
2. P. A. Pletnev, *Perepiska Ia. K. Grota s P. A. Pletnevym*, II (St. Petersburg,

1896), p. 15; "Otryvok iz zapisok starago diplomata, 1855," *Bibliograficheskiia zapiski* 1, No. 19 (1858): 297.

3 The quotation is in J. N. Moody, *French Education since Napoleon* (Syracuse, N.Y., 1978), p. 5; J. G. Gagliardo, *Enlightened Despotism*, pp. 77–79. For a summary of the direction of Russian educational policy in the eighteenth century, consult N. Hans, *History of Russian Educational Policy, 1701–1917* (New York, 1964), pp. 8–32; Alston, *Education*, pp. 3–20; J. L. Black, *Citizens for the Fatherland: Education, Educators and Pedagogical Ideals in Eighteenth-Century Russia* (Boulder, Colo., 1979); M. F. Shabaev, ed., *Ocherki istorii shkoly i pedagogicheskoi mysli narodov SSSR: XVIII v.—pervaia polovina XIX v.* (Moscow, 1973), pp. 19–192.

4. *Polnoe sobranie zakonov rossisskoi imperii . . . 1649–1913* (Petrograd, 1830–1916), 1803, n. 20597 (italics in the original).

5. For overviews of educational policy during the reign, consult Rozhdestvenskii, *Obzor*, pp. 30–161; Vucinich, *Science*, pp. 184–244; Alston, *Education*, pp. 20–30; Hans, *Policy*, pp. 33–60.

6. On the complicated question of ranks, consult Shepelev, *Otmenennye istorii chiny* (the quotation is on p. 58); P. A. Zaionchkovskii, *Pravitel'stvennyi apparat samoderzhavnoi Rossii v XIX v.* (Moscow, 1978), pp. 24–205.

7. For Condorcet's historical views, which were remarkably similar to Uvarov's, see his *Esquisse d'un tableau historique des progrès de l'esprit humain* (Paris, 1966); J. S. Shapiro, *Condorcet and the Rise of Liberalism* (New York, 1934), pp. 196–204; C. Steinger, "Condorcet's Report on Public Education," *Social Studies* (January 1970), pp. 20–25. A venerable error, namely that Condorcet presented his "Report" to the National Assembly, apparently originated with Hans and is repeated by all subsequent historians.

8. On the planning of the new system, the best survey is Rozhdestvenskii, *Obzor*, pp. 30–74; also see Hans, *Policy*, pp. 43–49; and Shabaev, *Ocherki*, pp. 195–210.

9. M. I. Sukhomlinov, "Materialy dlia istorii obrazovaniia v Rossii v tsarstvovanie imperatora Aleksandra I," *ZMNP* 127, No. 10 (1865): 132; Vucinich, *Science*, pp. 193–94.

During the reign, expansion brought two more universities into the empire, those in Turku (transferred to Helsinki in 1827) and Warsaw (closed after the Polish Revolt of 1830). Since Congress Poland and the Grand Duchy of Finland operated under a special administrative status, their universities were not subject to the educational ministry and will be treated only briefly in this monograph.

10. J. T. Flynn has done extensive research on gentry attitudes toward education; for a concise statement, see "The Universities, the Gentry and the Russian Imperial Services, 1815–1825," *Canadian Slavic Studies* 2, No. 4 (Winter 1968): 486–503; the quotation is on p. 492. Also relevant is A. Sinel, *The Classroom and the Chancellery: State Educational Reform in Russia under Count Dmitry Tolstoi* (Cambridge, Mass., 1973), pp. 4–9. On Karamzin's attitudes toward education, see Black, *Nicholas Karamzin*, pp. 5–10, 49–51; and Pipes, *Karamzin's Memoir*, pp. 48–49, 66–67.

11. Rozhdestvenskii, *Obzor*, p. 36; Alston, *Education*, pp. 221–22; Grand Duke Nicholas, *P. A. Stroganov*, II (St. Petersburg, 1903), p. 226; Sukhomlinov, *Materialy dlia istorii obrazovaniia v Rossii v tsarstvovanie imp. Aleksandra I* (St. Petersburg, 1866), pp. 5–6.

A dispute even erupted over the naming of the new ministry in 1802 because no single Russian word describes the general learning process. Some preferred *vospitanie*, which implies character development, disciplining or moral training, the adaptation of the student to his environment. Others insisted upon *obrazo-*

vanie since it stresses instruction, intellectual development, and the widening of horizons. Victor Kochubei, a member of the Unofficial Committee, worried about the latter term "in view of the widespread feeling that it is dangerous to shed too much light." The more neutral term, *enlightenment (prosveshcheniie)*, provoked less commentary despite its reminder of the eighteenth-century movement. In the end, a clumsy compromise was reached: the title of the new offices included all three terms and was called the Ministry of National Enlightenment, the Training of Youth, and the Propagation of Knowledge. As this was too lengthy for use, the last two phrases were dropped, but the controversy did not cease.

12. The quotation and discussion are found in E. H. Reisner, *Nationalism and Education since 1789: A Social and Political History of Modern Education* (New York, 1923), pp. 141–44.

13. For a well-balanced introductory essay on these years, see Flynn, "S. S. Uvarov's 'Liberal' Years," *Jahrbücher für Geschichte Osteuropas* 20, No. 4 (1972):481–91.

14. C. Galskoy, "The Ministry of Education under Nicholas I, 1826–1836" (Ph.D. diss., Stanford University, 1977), p. 16; M. A. Korf, *Zhizn' grafa Speranskago*, I (St. Petersburg, 1861), p. 179; Shepelev, *Chiny*, pp. 58–59; Zaionchkovskii, *Apparat*, pp. 29–34; Pipes, *Karamzin's Memoir*, pp. 160–62. De Maistre's many works on Russian education include "Cinq lettres sur l'éducation publique en Russie," in *Lettres et opuscules inédits* (Paris, 1851), pp. 299–360; *Quatre chapitre inédites sur la Russie* (Paris, 1859), pp. 45–55; and "Observations sur le Prospectus Disciplinarum ou plan d'étude proposé pour le Seminaire de Newsky par le Professeur Fessler" and "Mémoire sur la liberté de l'enseignement publique," in *Oeuvres complètes*, VIII (Lyons, 1886), pp. 233–275.

15. See especially E. K. Shmid, *Istoriia srednikh uchebnykh zavedenii v Rossii* (St. Petersburg, 1877–1878), pp. 81–82; M. Raeff, *Speransky*, pp. 60–62; D. F. Kobeko, *Imperatorskii Tsarskosel'skii litsei* (St. Petersburg, 1911), pp. 6–7; E. Kolbasin, "I. I. Martynov—perevodchik grecheskikh klassikov," *Sovremennik* 56 (March 1856): 41. Martynov drew up the Lycée statutes.

16. V. V. Poznanskii, *Ocherk formirovaniia russkoi natsional'noi kul'tury: Pervaia polovina XIX veka* (Moscow, 1975), pp. 14–25.

17. Noble attitudes are documented in N. P. Malinovskii, "Ocherk po istorii reformy srednei shkoly," *Russkaia shkola* 11 (November 1910): 43; Rozhdestvenskii, *Obzor*, pp. 76–78; Shmid, *Istoriia*, pp. 92–93; A. Borozdin, "Shishkov," *Entsiklopedicheskii slovar'*, LXXVII (1903), p. 613.

18. De Maistre, "Lettres," p. 310. For Razumovskii's sponsorship of de Maistre, see Vasil'chikov, *Semeistvo Razumovskikh*, II, pp. 69–74. The most thorough study of de Maistre's stay in Russia is Stepanov and Vermale, "De Mestr," pp. 577–726; also see A. N. Popov, "Graf Mestr' i Iezuity v Rossii," *RA* 6 (1892): 160–96; De Journel, *Un Collège de Jésuites*, pp. 191–204. Flynn, in "The Role of the Jesuits in the Politics of Russian Education, 1801–1820" (*Catholic Historical Review* 56, No. 2 [July 1970]: 249–65), offers a very good interpretation of the interconnections among the Jesuits, de Maistre, and gentry interests. D. W. Edwards's article, "Count Joseph Marie de Maistre and Russian Educational Policy, 1803–1826," is excellent on de Maistre's thinking, but the evidence for his influence in Russia is circumstantial and flimsy (*Slavic Review* 31, No. 1 [March 1977]: 54–75).

19. The German influence is documented in K. von Raumer, *Contributions to the History and Improvement of the German Universities* (New York, 1859), pp. 59–64; Seeley, *Stein*, II, pp. 73–74; P. R. Sweet, *Wilhelm von Humboldt*, II (Columbus, Ohio, 1980), pp. 3–106. Russian policies are outlined in I. Aleshintsev,

Istoriia gimnazicheskago obrazovaniia v Rossii (St. Petersburg, 1912), pp. 57, 61; Rozhdestvenskii, *Obzor*, pp. 69–70; Hans, *Policy*, p. 50; and Rudakov, "Gimnaziia," pp. 688–99.

20. Wolf is quoted in Henry Barnard, ed., *Memoirs of Eminent Teachers and Educators with Contributions to the History of Education in Germany* (Hartford, 1878), pp. 492, 569–570; and Pestalozzi's views are expressed on pp. 491–92.

21. Schmid, "Goethe und Uwarow" (March 28, 1817), p. 156. M. L. Clarke, *Classical Education in Britain, 1500–1900* (Cambridge, Eng., 1959), p. 76; H. T. Parker, *The Cult of Antiquity and the French Revolutionaries* (New York, 1965), p. 86; I. M. Murav'ev-Apostol, "Russkoe vospitanie i obuchenie v nachale nashego veka (1813)," in M. N. Katkov, *Nasha uchebnaia reforma*, ed. M. N. Katkov (Moscow, 1890), pp. 137–49.

22. De Staël recorded that, under Napoleon, Greek was "positively forbidden" (*Ten Years of Exile*, trans. D. Beik [New York, 1972], p. 47). "Ob utverzhdenii plana ucheniia dlia S.-Peterburgskoi gimnazii i ob uchrezhdenii v onoi trekh klassov dlia prepodavaniia Latinskago iazyka" (October 31, 1811), TsGIAL, fond 733, opis' 20, ed. kh. 110, pp. 2–17; Rozhdestvenskii, *Obzor*, p. 89; Barnard, *Memoirs*, p. 563; de Maistre, "Lettres," p. 316; "Ob opredelenii v Pedagogicheskii institut osobago professora Latinskago iazyka i slovesnosti," *SPMNP*, I, 1: 1802–25 (St. Petersburg, 1864), n. 176. (References to *SPMNP* carry the date of the document. Entries consist mainly of decrees, laws, and reports.) See also "Pis'mo Uvarova k V. A. Zhukovskomu" (November 10, 1847), PD, fond 265, opis' 1, no. 44, p. 281. On Gräfe, see J. E. Sandys, *A History of Classical Scholarship*, III (New York, 1964), pp. 384–89.

23. Uvarov is quoted in Rozhdestvenskii, ed., *S.-Peterburgskii universitet v pervoe stoletie ego deiatel'nosti, 1819–1919: Materialy po istorii S.-Peterburgskago universiteta: 1819–1835* (vol. I) (Petrograd, 1919), p. xi; V. V. Pugachev, *Evoliutsiia obshchestvenno-politicheskikh vzgliadov Pushkina* (Gorky, 1967), pp. 39–49. For instance, Ivan Pnin and Ivan Martynov argued for a class-based system of education; Martynov, editor of the progressive *Severnyi vestnik*, supported a constitution along with a traditional class structure; European "liberals," such as Guizot and Destutt de Tracy, supported education structured along class lines (N. N. Bulich, *Ocherki*, I, pp. 84–100; I. I. Pnin, "Opyt o prosveshchenii otnositel'no k Rossii," in *Sochineniia* [Moscow, 1934], pp. 121–61; S. C. Ramer, "The Traditional and the Modern in the Writings of Ivan Pnin," *Slavic Review* 34, No. 3 [September 975]: 539–59; Poznanskii, *Ocherk*, pp. 71–74; Malinovskii, "Ocherki," pp. 92–93; D. Johnson, *Guizot: Aspects of French History, 1787–1874* [Toronto, 1963], pp. 111–15; Tracy, "Observations sur le système actuel d'instruction publique [1801]," in *Histoire de l'enseignement en France, 1800–1967*, ed. A. Prost [Paris, 1968], p. 10.)

24. "O iskhodataistvovanii primushchestvo dlia S.-Peterburgskoi gubernskoi gimnazii" (October 21, 1816), TsGIAL, fond 732, opis' 1, no. 15, pp. 205–6; A. Voronov, *Istoriko-statisticheskoe obozrenie zavedenii S.-Peterburgskago uchebnago okruga c 1715 po 1828 g.* (St. Petersburg, 1849), pp. 159–63.

25. C. Steinger, "Government Policy and the University of St. Petersburg, 1819–1849" (Ph.D. diss., The Ohio State University, 1971), pp. 58–60.

26. De Maistre, "Lettres," p. 303.

27. The best treatment of this problem is S. V. Rozhdestvenskii, "Vopros o narodnom obrazovanii i sotsial'naia problema v epokhu Aleksandra I," *Russkoe proshloe* 5 (1923): 35–49; see also Sukhomlinov, *Izsledovaniia*, pp. 169–70.

28. Rozhdestvenskii, "Vopros," p. 39. Others share this view; see Shmid, *Istoriia*, pp. 116–21; Malinovskii, "Ocherki," pp. 84–96.

29. "Ob ustanovlenii platy za uchenie," in TsGIAL, *Zhurnal Glavnago prav-*

leniie uchilishch (hereafter cited as *Zhurnal*), meeting of April 13, 1817, fond 732, opis' 1, no. 16, pp. 72–73; these minutes of the Central School Board are among the best sources for these years. "Ob opredelenii platy za uchenie v Sanktpeter-burgskoi gimnazii, prikhodnykh i uezdnykh uchilishchakh," *SPMNP*, I, 957–62 (June 14, 1817); five rubles were charged in parish schools, ten in district, and fifteen in the gymnasia of the district. Also see Hans, *Policy*, pp. 53–55; and Rozhdestvenskii, *Obzor*, pp. 133–37.

30. "Ob uchrezhdenie pri Glavnom pedagogicheskom institut vtorago razria-da, dlia obrazovaniia uchitelei prikhodskikh i uezdnykh uchilishch," *SPMNP*, I, 1:1011–22 (October 25, 1817); discussions are recorded in the *Zhurnal* (April 17, 1817), fond 732, opis' 1, no. 16, pp. 75–84; Rozhdestvenskii, "Vopros," pp. 38–43; Malinovskii, "Ocherki," pp. 94–97.

31. Uvarov is quoted in Rozhdestvenskii, "Vopros," p. 38; and in *Zhurnal*, April 17, 1817.

32. As quoted in Rozhdestvenskii, "Vopros," p. 41; N. Vessel', "NaKh. Ves-sel', "Nachalnoe obrazovanie i narodnaia uchilishcha v zapadnoi Evrope i Ros-sii," *Russkaia shkola* 6 (December 1891): 27–28.

33. On the system, consult J. C. Zacek, "The Lancastrian School Movement in Russia," *Slavonic and East European Review* 45, No. 105 (July 1967): 343–67; B. Hollingsworth, "Lancastrian Schools in Russia," *Durham Research Review* 5 (1966): 59–74; A. N. Pypin, *Obshchestvennoe dvizhenie v Rossii pri Aleksandre I* (St. Petersburg, 1900), pp. 335–40; "O metode Belia i Lankastera," *Syn otechestva*, 96, No. 21 (1817): 26–35.

"Proekt ustava otshchestva uchrezdeniia uchilishch po metode vzaimnago obucheniia Belia i Lankastera (1818)," *RS* 1 (1881): 180–82; F. P. Tolstoi, "Zap-iski," *RS* 21 (1878): 205–36. The Central School Board, in 1817, wanted to start promoting Lancaster schools, but the tsar suggested waiting for the return of Uvarov's students: "O Lankasterovoi metode ucheniia," *Zhurnal* (June 13, 1817), fond 732, opis' 1, no. 16, p. 136. Uvarov is quoted in Rozhdestvenskii, *Obzor*, p. 145; "Pis'ma I. I. Davydova k A. A. Prokopovichu-Antonskomu" (January 27, 1819), *RS* 19, No. 3 (1889): 553; Johnson, *Guizot*, pp. 114–16. M. F. Orlov began a school when disillusioned with Arzamas and Toryism (A. N. Shebunin, "Brat'ia Turgenevy i dvorianskoe obshchestvo aleksandrovskoi epokhi," in *De-kabrist N. I. Turgenev* [Moscow, 1936], p. 66).

34. On Pestalozzi, see K. Silber, *Pestalozzi: The Man and His Work* (New York, 1960); R. R. Rusk, *Doctrines of the Great Educators* (London, 1918); Rozhdestven-skii, "Vopros," pp. 44–49. Kant, for instance, in "What is Enlightenment?" insisted that freedom had to precede widespread education (in *The Enlightenment: A Comprehensive Anthology*, ed. P. Gay [New York, 1973], p. 385); on this ques-tion, also see Rozhdestvenskii, "Vopros," pp. 35–37; Sukhomlinov, *Izsledovaniia*, pp. 208–11; and Zacek, "Lancastrian School," pp. 364–67.

35. For accounts of the general religious revival, see Zacek's excellent "The Russian Bible Society, 1812–1826" (Ph.D. diss., Columbia University, 1964), pp. 1–32; G. V. Florovskii, *Puti russkago bogosloviia* (Paris, 1937), pp. 128–47; Walicki, *A History of Russian Thought*, pp. 71–74.

36. Several works analyze Golitsyn as man and minister: Rozhdestvenskii, *Obzor*, pp. 105–15; S. P. Mel'gunov, *Dela i liudi aleksandrovskogo vremeni* (Berlin, 1923), pp. 235–300; P. von Goetze, *Fürst Alexander Nikolajewitsch Galitzin und seine Zeit* (Leipzig, 1882); W. W. Sawatsky, "Prince Alexander N. Golitsyn (1773–1844): Tsarist Minister of Piety" (Ph.D. diss., University of Minnesota, 1976).

37. On the Russian Bible Society, consult Zacek, "Bible Society"; S. R. Tompkins, "The Russian Bible Society—A Case of Religious Xenophobia,"

American Slavonic and East European Review 7 (October 1948): 251–68 (the article misses the cosmopolitan aspect of the movement); "Rossiiskoe bibleiskoe obshchestvo, 1812–1826 gg.," *Vestnik Evropy* 4, No. 8 (1868): 639–712; 5, No. 9 (1868), 231–37; 6 (1868): 222–85; and 6 (1868): 708–68; A. N. Pypin, *Religioznye dvizheniia pri Aleksandre I* (Petrograd, 1916), pp. 1–144; Sukhomlinov, *Izsledovaniia*, 167–72; and Florovskii, *Puti*, pp. 147–76.

38. The quotation is in Zacek, "Bible Society," p. 81; C. S. Dudley estimated that a million copies were distributed in the empire in twenty-six languages through 196 branches (*An Analysis of the System of the Bible Society throughout Its Different Parts* [London, 1821], p. 47).

39. Alexander continued this tone in his New Year's Day manifesto in 1816 (Shil'der, *Aleksandr Pervyi*, p. 1; M. Bourguin, *Histoire de la Sainte Alliance* (Geneva, 1954), provides an overview.

40. "Uchrezhdenie Ministerstva dukhovnykh del' i narodnago prosveshcheniia," *SPMNP*, I, 1:1058–97 (October 24, 1817). The new educational trend is described in V. Ikonnikov, "Russkie universitety v sviazi s khodom obshchestvennago obrazovaniia," *Vestnik Evropy* 11 (1876): 73–77; Zacek, "Bible Society," pp. 172–248; Rozhdestvenskii, *Obzor*, pp. 105–16; and N. Kutuzov, "O prichinakh blagodenstviia i velichiia narodov," *Syn otechestva* 59, No. 1 (1820): 3–20.

41. Johnson, *Guizot*, p. 110; Prost, *Histoire*, p. 26. A. Koyré insists these men sought to create a new religious philosophy that would conform to their political dogma (*La Philosophie et le problème national en Russie au début du XIXe siècle* [Paris, 1929], pp. 49–84), as does Sukhomlinov, *Izsledovaniia*, pp. 159–61, 188, 193–94.

42. Zacek, "Bible Society," pp. 197–222; Flynn, "The Universities in the Russia of Alexander I: Patterns of Reform and Reaction" (Ph. D. diss., Clark University, 1964); "The Universities, the Gentry"; "V. N. Karazin, The Gentry, and Kharkov University," *Slavic Review* 28, No. 2 (1969): 209–20; H. Kuhn, *Das Wartburgfest* (Weimar, 1913); W. Oncken, *Wartburg* (Berlin, 1907).

43. Sawatsky, "Golitsyn," pp. 258–62; Sukhomlinov, *Izsledovaniia*, pp. 181–84.

44. "O vvedenii po vsem uchilishcham chteniia Novago Zaveta," *Zhurnal* (April 24, 1819), fond 732, opis' 1, no. 18, p. 175; "O vvedenii v universitetakh prepodavaniia Bogopoznaniia i Khristianskago ucheniia," *Zhurnal* (January 30, 1819), fond 732, opis' 1, p. 83.

45. Magnitskii's speech was featured in *Russkii invalid* (March 28 and 30, 1818), pp. 293–95 and 302–5, respectively; *Moskovskiia vedomosti* (March 29, 1818); and *Dukh zhurnalov* (April 3, 1818). On Magnitskii, see Pypin, *Religiozyne dvizheniia*, pp. 144–51; Korf, *Zhizn' Speranskago*, I, p. 283; "Vospominaniia N. I. Sheniga: O Magnitskom," in *Russkie universitety v ikh ustavakh i vospominaniiakh sovremennikov*, I (St. Petersburg, n.d.), pp. 121–22. In *Magnitskii*, the first volume of *Materialy dlia istorii prosveshcheniia v Rossii*, E. Feoktistov gives the most thorough account of Magnitskii's adventures ([St. Petersburg, 1865], pp. 1–6). On the man as a complete opportunist, not an ideologue, see Flynn's overly generous "Magnitskii's Purge of Kazan University: A Case Study in the Uses of Reaction in Nineteenth-Century Russia," *Journal of Modern History* 43, No. 4 (1971): 598–614. Sawatsky quotes Golitsyn's hopes for "a saint" on p. 416.

46. N. I. Grech, "Vospominaniia starika," in *Peterburgskii universitet, 1819–1895*, vol. 1 of *Leningradskii universitet v vospominaniiakh sovremennikov* (Leningrad, 1963), pp. 17–18; Sawatsky, "Golitsyn," pp. 219–20, 257–58; Sukhomlinov, *Izsledovaniia*, pp. 239–55; Pypin, *Religioznye dvizheniia*, pp. 97, 143–45.

47. Uvarov is quoted in Kirpichnikov, "Novye materialy," pp. 339–40; Fuss and Karamzin are quoted in Vucinich, *Science*, p. 232.

48. Sukhomlinov, *Materialy*, p. 19.
49. Feoktistov, *Magnitskii*, pp. 34–54, 186; Sukhomlinov, *Izsledovaniia*, pp. 216–35; A. P. Shchapov, "Sotsialno-pedagogicheskiia usloviia umstvennago razvitiia russkago naroda," in *Sochineniia*, III (St. Petersburg, 1908), pp. 172–76.
50. Feoktistov (*Magnitskii*, pp. 55–63) reprints Uvarov's speech.
51. Uvarov, "Rech' S. S. Uvarova, proiznesennaia v chrezvychainom sobranii konferentsii Glavnago pedagogicheskago instituta 14 fevralia 1819 g.," TsGIAL, fond 733, opis' 20, ed. khr. 219, pp. 39–41; Rozhdestvenskii, *Materialy*, pp. 13–14; Uvarov's speech was also praised and reprinted in the liberal gazette *Severnaia pochta* 16 (February 22, 1819) and 17 (February 26, 1819). "O sluzhbe popechitelia Peterburgskago uch. okruga S. S. Uvarova," TsGIAL, fond 733, opis' 20, ed. khr. 80, pp. 18–19; according to the *Zhurnal* of May 24, 1819, Uvarov was allowed a several months' leave, and Magnitskii was entrusted to take his place on standing committees (fond 732, opis' 1, no. 18). For a detailed analysis of these events, see C. H. Whittaker's "From Promise to Purge: The First Years of St. Petersburg University," *Paedagogica Historica* 18, No. 1 (1978): 148–67.
52. Sukhomlinov, *Materialy*, pp. 72–75; Rozhdestvenskii, *Materialy*, pp. 3–13; "Pervonachal'noe obrazovanie Sankpeterburgskago universiteta," TsGIAL, fond 744, opis' 1, ed. khr. 10, pp. 10–18; "Obrazovanie Sankpeterburgskago universiteta," TsGIAL, fond 733, opis' 20, ed. khr. 219, pp. 1–8; Pipes, *Karamzin*, p. 159.
53. Shmid, *Istoriia*, p. 118; Pypin, *Obshchestvennoe dvizhenie*, pp. 422–23; Grigor'ev, *Peterburgskii universitet*, pp. 10–21; Rozhdestvenskii, *Materialy*, pp. ix–x, xiv–xvii, xxi–xxiii; Sukhomlinov, *Materialy*, pp. 72–89; "Graf S. S. Uvarov," *Vsemirnaia illiustratsiia* 59 (1870): 123. On Uvarov's personal attempt to attract a faculty, see "Ob uchrezhdenii pri Glavnom pedagogicheskom institute kafedry vostochnykh iazykov," TsGIAL, fond 733, opis' 20, n. 184, pp. 1–18; "Ob uchrezhdenii pri Glavnom pedagogicheskom institute kafedry astronomii," *SPMNP*, I, 1:1111–12 (January 8, 1819); Grech, "Vospominaniia," pp. 17–18; Florovskii, *Puti*, pp. 193–201. Two biographies of the professors are noteworthy: A. Nikitenko, *Aleksandr I. Galich, byvshii professor S.-Peterburgskago universiteta* (St. Petersburg, 1869); and E. M. Kosachevskaia, *M. A. Balug'ianskii i Peterburgskii universitet pervoi chetverti XIX veka* (Leningrad, 1971).
54. All the criticisms and some commentary are in Rozhdestvenskii, *Materialy*, pp. xxix–xxxvii, 63–108. "Predstavlenie S. S. Uvarova Ministru ot 10 dekabria 1819 goda s otvetom na zamechaniia chlenov Glavnago pravleniia uchilishch po povodu proekta ustava S.-Peterburgskago universiteta," ibid., pp. 108–10. At meetings in the next three months, Uvarov himself recognized the death of his statute (*Zhurnal*, January 15, February 26, and March 3, 1820, fond 732, opis' 1, no. 19). The rumors concerning his resignation were noted in "Pskovskiia pis'ma mitropolita Evgeniia Bolkhovitianova k Peterburgskomu bibliografu i arkheologu V. G. Anastasevichu 1820 g." (September 3, 1820) *RA* 7 (1889): 368. For similar attitudes toward higher education throughout Europe, consult P. Gerbod, *La condition universitaire en France au XIXᵉ siècle* (Paris, 1965); and Reisner's *Nationalism*.
55. "Dva mneniia popechitelia Kazanskago uchebnago okruga, M. L. Magnitskago," *RA* 11 (1864): 321–25; Magnitskii, "Instruktsiia k D. M. Makshevu," *RA* 5 (1867): 1643–46; "Instruktsiia" (decree of January 18, 1820), *SPMNP* I, pp. 1317–37; *Zhurnal*, fond 732, opis' 1, no. 18, 1819, p. 506; Ikonnikov, "Universitety," pp. 74–78.
56. Feoktistov, *Magnitskii*, pp. 143–47; Zacek, "Russian Bible Society," p. 206; Pypin, *Religioznye dvizheniia*, pp. 161–62.

57. Rozhdestvenskii, *Obzor*, p. 117; M. Shugurov, "Cherty russkoi politiki v 1819 godu," *RA* 4 (1867): 862–878.

58. "Metternich's Political Confession of Faith," in *Memoirs of Prince Metternich, 1815–1829*, III (New York, 1970), pp. 453–76; Raeff, *The Decembrist Movement*, p. 10; Volk, *Vzgliady*, pp. 95–96.

59. Sukhomlinov, *Izsledovaniia*, pp. 205–8; Schapiro, *Rationalism*, pp. 48–50. Kunitsyn's lecture notes are reprinted in A. M. Gorchakov, "Litseiskie tektsii: Entsiklopediia prav," *Krasnyi arkhiv* 1, No. 80 (1937): 90–129; and a summary of *Natural Law* can be found in B. Hollingsworth, "A. P. Kunitsyn and the Social Movement in Russia under Alexander I," *Slavonic and East European Review* 43, No. 100 (1964): 126–29. The comments of Runich and Magnitskii are in Feoktistov, *Magnitskii*, pp. 8–18.

60. The stupidity of the affair can be gleaned only from reading the archival sources: "O knige Professora Kunitsyna *Estestvennoe pravo* i voobshche o sei nauke," TsGIAL, fond 734, opis' 1, no. 139, pp. 1–67.

61. "Pis'ma" (March 1, 1821, A. I. Turgenev), in *Dekabrist*, p. 65.

62. Rozhdestvenskii, *Materialy*, pp. xxxix–xliii, 131–41; Sawatsky, "Golitsyn," pp. 274–75; Flynn, "Liberal Years," p. 488; Zacek, "Bible Society," pp. 213–14; "Pis'ma Davydova," p. 550; Uvarov's resignation is in TsGIAL, fond 733, opis' 87, no. 114, p. 14.

63. "Zapiska Runicha," *Sbornik otdeleniia russkago iazyka i slovesnosti Imp. AN* 9 (1872): 62; "Pamiatnye zametki Vologzhanina," *RA* 5 (1867): 1695; "O sluzhbe Uvarova" (May 3–July 5, 1821), TsGIAL, fond 733, opis' 12, no. 175, pp. 22–30; "Pis'mo Uvarova k neizvestnomu" (July 1, 1821), PD, fond 1179, no. 1; "Perepiska A. N. Golitsyna c Z. Ia. Karneevym" (November 9, 1821), *RA* 2, No. 5 (1893): 131–39.

64. M. G. Ustrialov, "Vospominanie o moei zhizni: Peterburgskii universitet v 20-kh godov," in *Russkie universitety*, pp. 102–3.

65. The documents concerning the proceedings of the "trial" have been fully published (Rozhdestvenskii, *Materialy*, pp. xlvi–lxii; Grigor'ev, *Peterburgskii universitet*, pp. 35–67; Kosachevskaia, *Balug'ianskii*, pp. 135–50).

66. The letter is printed in Sukhomlinov, *Materialy*, pp. 195–200.

67. Rozhdestvenskii, *Materialy*, pp. lxii–lxv; Grigor'ev, *Universitet*, pp. 42–67.

68. Z. A. Kamenskii, "Osveshchenie istorii zarubezhnoi filosofii v russkoi prosvetitel'skoi literature pervoi chetverti 19 veka," *Vestnik istorii mirovoi kul'tury* 6 (November–December 1961): 136–50; Feoktistov, *Magnitskii*, pp. 153, 201.

69. N. Popov, "Obshchestvo liubitelei otechestvennoi slovesnosti i periodicheskoi literatury v Kazani s 1805 po 1834 god," *Russkii vestnik* 23 (1859): 89–92; "Zapiski Runicha," pp. 61–69; P. Artemev, "Biblioteka Kazanskago universiteta," *Russkii vestnik* 15 (1851): 102; N. M. Shil'der, "Dva donosa v 1831 godu: Vsepoddaneishiia pis'ma M. Magnitskago imperatoru Nikolaiu ob illiuminatakh," *RS* 97 (March 1899): 610–11. On the plots against Golitsyn, see Sawatsky, "Golitsyn," pp. 404–41; and Zacek, "Bible Society," pp. 249–327; and Zacek, "The Russian Bible Society and the Russian Orthodox Church," *Church History* 35, No. 105 (July 1967): 343–67.

CHAPTER 5

1 L. Leduc, "Essai," in Uvarov, *Esquisses*, pp. 57–58.

2. For an introduction to the concept of modernization, see Black, *The Dynamics of Modernization*; also consult the more recent explanation of conservative renovation in Orlovsky, *The Limits of Reform*, pp. 202–4.

3. E. Crankshaw, *The Shadow of the Winter Palace: The Drift to Revolution, 1825–1917* (New York, 1976), p. 73.

4. Uvarov, *Desiatiletie*, p. 46; and "O narodonaselenii," p. 126; Nikitenko, *Denvnik* (entry of March 21, 1843), I, p. 264.

For Uvarov's conception of the enormous tasks of the educational ministry, see S. Shevyrev, *Istoriia Imperatorskago Moskovskago universiteta, 1755–1855* (Moscow, 1855), pp. 468–69.

5. See chap. 3 and Uvarov, *Rech'*.

6. For general treatments of the reign, consult Lincoln, *Nicholas I*; Riasanovsky, *Official Nationality*; A. E. Presniakov, *Emperor Nicholas I of Russia: The Apogee of Autocracy, 1825–1855*, ed. and trans. J. C. Zacek (Gulf Breeze, Fla., 1974); and M. A. Polievktov, *Nikolai I: Biografiia i obzor tsarstvovaniia* (Moscow, 1918).

7. The manifesto was published in full in *Severnaia pchela* 85 (July 17, 1826); Nikitenko, *Diary* (entry for January 1, 1829), p. 27. Nikitenko's *Dnevnik* has been translated and abridged; *Diary of a Russian Censor*, ed. and trans. H. S. Jacobson (Amherst, 1975) is used wherever possible.

8. Uvarov, "O narodonaselenii," p. 127.

9. Uvarov, "Goethe," in *Esquisses*, pp. 205–6, 226; "Vues générales," in *Esquisses*, p. 245; "Predislovie," *ZMNP* 1, No. 1 (1934): iv–v; and *Desiatiletie*, p. 2.

10. Uvarov, *Desiatiletie*, p. 2; "Predislovie," p. iv; and "O narodonaselenii," p. 119; also see the article on movement and stability by A. Ivanovskii, "O nachalakh postepennago usovershenstvovaniia nashego gosudarstva," *ZMNP* 13, No. 1, (January 1837): 1–15.

11. Nikitenko, *Diary* (entry for December 30, 1830), p. 30.

12. R. Tucker, *The Marxian Revolutionary Idea* (New York, 1969), pp. 112–13; T. Darlington, *Education in Russia: Special Reports on Educational Subjects*, XXIII (London, 1909), p. 76; Riasanovsky, *A History of Russia* (New York, 1969), p. 377; Riasanovsky, "Nicholas I and the Course of Russian History," in Presniakov, *Nicholas I*, p. xxxvi; Marquis de Custine, *Journey for Our Time*, ed. and trans. P. P. Kohler (Chicago, 1951), p. 135.

13. Uvarov, "Goethe," in *Esquisses*, p. 206; N. A. Ratynskii, "Dvor i pravitel'stvo v Rossii sto let nazad," *RA* 2 (1886): 164; and P. V. Annenkov, *The Extraordinary Decade: Literary Memoirs*, ed. A. P. Mendel, trans. I. R. Titunik (Ann Arbor, 1968), p. 85. Although I use this convenient translation of Annenkov, I prefer Isaiah Berlin's rendition of the title, "A Remarkable Decade," in *Russian Thinkers*, ed. H. Hardy and A. Kelly (New York, 1978), pp. 114–209.

The newer interpretation of the Nicholaevan reign may be found in Black et al., *The Modernization of Japan and Russia: A Comparative Study* (New York, 1975); Blackwell, *Russian Industrialization*; Wortman, *Russian Legal Consciousness*; Lincoln, "Genesis," pp. 321–30; Lincoln, *Nicholas I*; Pintner, "Social Characteristics," pp. 429–43. This view also coincides with V. Kozhinov's new system of Soviet periodization that interprets the reign as the last stage of absolutism as well as the beginnings of the Russian version of the Enlightenment (A. S. Mesniakov, ed., *Kontekst—1972* [Moscow, 1973], pp. 276–302).

14. Uvarov, "Predislovie," p. iv.

15. Nikitenko, *Diary* (entry for April 5, 1827), p. 15.

16. As quoted in Riasanovsky, *A Parting of Ways: Government and the Educated Public in Russia, 1801–1855* (Oxford, 1976), pp. 249–50.

17. Nikitenko, *Diary* (entry for August 8, 1835), p. 62.

18. Uvarov, *Desiatiletie*, p. 1; G. Yaney, *The Systematization of Russian Government: Social Evolution in the Domestic Administration of Imperial Russia, 1711–1905* (Chicago, 1973), p. 392; G. V. Grudev, "Pis'mo k Pogodinu" (February 21, 1842), ROBIL, fond 231, ed. 58; A. Benkendorf, "Obozrenie raspolozheniia umov i razlichnykh

chastei gosudarstvennago upravleniia v 1838 godu," TsGAOR, fond 109, op. 85, ed. khr. 3, p. 165.

19. Polievtkov, *Nikolai I*, p. 203; Hans, "The Reaction," in *History*, pp. 61–91; W. Johnson, "The Long Period of Reaction," in *Russia's Educational Heritage* (Pittsburgh, 1950), pp. 87–108; Shmid believed Uvarov "saved" the middle schools (*Istoriia*)); see also Riasanovsky, *Parting*, p. 276.

For examples of the reactionary thesis as accepted Soviet dogma, see Ostrovitianov, ed., *Istoriia*, II, p. 20; Durylin, "Drug Gete," pp. 186–217; Orlik, *Rossiia i frantsuzskaia revoliutsiia*, p. 164; "S. S. Uvarov," *Bolshaia Sovetskaia entsiklopediia*, XXVI (Moscow, 1977), p. 438; Skabichevskii, *Ocherki*, p. 23. American scholars also hold this opinion; see Riasanovsky, *Nicholas I*, pp. 70–72; and Alston, *Education*, pp. 33–34.

20. On this question, see Black, *Modernization*, p. 102; A. Sinel, "Problems in the Periodization of Russian Education: A Tentative Solution," *Slavic and European Education Review* 2 (1977): 54–61; and P. Meyers, *The Modernization of Education in Nineteenth-Century Europe* (St. Louis, 1977).

21. The tripartite formula was first expressed in "S predstavleniem otcheta Tainago Sovetnika Uvarova po obozreniiu im Moskovskago Universiteta i gimnazii," *SPMNP*, II, 1 (St. Petersburg, 1876), pp. 511–12 (December 4, 1832). (References to *SPMNP* carry the date of the document. Entries consist mainly of decrees, laws, and reports.) Also see Poznanskii, *Ocherk*, pp. 141–54.

22. V. F. Odoevskii, *Russian Nights*, trans. O. Koshansky-Olienikov and R. Matlaw (New York, 1965), pp. 210–12.

On the general issues, see P. N. Sakulin, *Iz istorii russkago idealizma, Kniaz' V. Odoevskii* (Moscow, 1913). On the early circles, consult V. Sechkarev, *Schellings Einfluss in der russischen Literatur der 20er und 30er Jahre des XIX Jahrhunderts* (Berlin, 1939); E. J. Brown, *Stankevich and His Moscow Circle, 1830–1840* (Stanford, Calif., 1961); M. Malia, *Alexander Herzen and the Birth of Russian Socialism* (New York, 1961), pp. 69–98; A. Walicki, *The Slavophile Controversy: History of a Conservative Utopia in Nineteenth-Century Russian Thought*, trans. H. Andrews-Rusiecka (Oxford, 1975), pp. 64–82; Florovskii, *Puti*, pp. 234–85; D. I. Chizhevskii, *Gegel' v Rossii* (Paris, 1939), pp. 36–49, 231–37; J. Frank, *Dostoevsky: The Seeds of Revolt, 1821–1849* (Princeton, 1976), pp. 101–2; Riasanovsky, *Parting*, pp. 152–59; V. P. Gorodetskii, *Istoriia russkoi kritiki* (Moscow, 1958), pp. 352–56.

23. Uvarov, "O narodonaselenii," p. 126; and "S predstavleniem," p. 511. Uvarov also debated calling the principles "saving" or "national" ("Otchet v obozrenii Moskovskago universiteta," TsGIAL, fond 735, opis' 10, no. 2739, p. 203 [handwritten copy of original report]).

24. Uvarov, "Vues générales"; *Desiatiletie*, p. 2; and "Venise," in *Esquisses*, pp. 258–59. Riasanovsky, *Official Nationality*, pp. 78–96; A. N. Popov, *Snoshenie Rossii s Rimom s 1845 po 1850 god* (St. Petersburg, 1871), p. 4; I. I. Panaev, *Literaturnye vospominaniia*, I (Moscow, 1950), p. 56; M. Maksimovich, "Ob uchasti i znachenii Kieva v obshchei zhizni Rossii," *ZMNP* 16 (Oct 1837): 1–29; Susini, *Lettres de Baader*, I, pp. 451–61; and, ibid., III, pp. 320–39; D. Chizhevskii, "Baader i Rossiia," *Novyi zhurnal* XXXV (1953): 301–10.

25. Uvarov, *Desiatiletie*, pp. 53–54; and "Pravoslavie," TsGIAL (September 26, 1839), fond 735, opis' 10, ed. 293, p. 587; see chap. 3.

26. Uvarov, *Desiatiletie*, pp. 3, 107; "O narodonaselenii," p. 126; and *Obshchii-otchet predstavlennyi ego Imperatorskomu Velichestvu po Ministerstvu narodnago prosveshcheniia za 1838 god* (St. Petersburg, 1839), p. 14. (These annual reports will hereafter be labeled *Otchet za. . . .* if published the following year or "Otchet za. . . ." if only reprinted in April of the following year in the *ZMNP*).

27. S. P. Shevyrev, "Vzgliad russkago na sovremennoe obrazovanie Evropy,"

Moskvitianin 1 (1841): 292–93 (Lincoln translates this in *Nicholas I*, p. 243); M. Stasiulevich, "O 'Zapiske' i 'Programma uchebnika vseobshchei istorii,' sostavlennykh v 1850 g. T. N. Granovskim," *Vestnik Evropy* 3 (September 1866), p. 12; Ivanovskii, "O nachalakh," pp. 11–15; Riasanovsky, *Official Nationality*, pp. 96–123.

28. Uvarov, "De l'Administration de la plupart des gouvernements de la Russie centrale," *Materialy sobrannye dlia vysochaishei uchrezhdennoi Komissii o preobrazovanii guvernskikh: Uezdnykh uchrezhdenii*, I (St. Petersburg, 1870), pp. 68–72; also see S. F. Starr, *Decentralization and Self-Government in Russia*, 1830–1870 (Princeton, N.J., 1972), pp. 3–50.

29. A. A. Chumikov, "Peterburgskii universitet polveka nazad," *RA* 2 (1888): 136.

30. Uvarov, "Predislovie," pp. iv–v.

31. Ivanovskii, "O nachalakh," p. 15.

32. Benkendorf is quoted in Schil'der, *Nikolai*, II, p. 287 (translation from Riasanovsky, *Official Nationality*, p. 142).

33. Odoevskii, *Nights*, p. 51; Uvarov, "O narodonaselenii," pp. 114–28; the speech was first read to the Academy of Sciences on December 29, 1830.

34. Uvarov, "O skotovodstve voobshche i o sostoianii onago v Porech'e, podmoskovorom imenii G. pochetnago chlena S. S. Uvarova," *Zemledel'cheskii zhurnal* 23 (1828): 198–227; "Pochetnye chleny Imp. Mosk. Obshch. sel'skago khoziaistva," *Zemledel'cheskii zhurnal* 22 (1828): 52; *Desiatiletie*, p. 21; and "De l'Administration," p. 69; A. Pogozhev, "Votchinnye fabriki i ikh fabrichnye," *Vestnik Evropy* 4 (July 1889): 19; M. Tugan-Baranovskii, *Russkaia fabrika v proshlom i nastoiashchem*, I (St. Petersburg, 1898), pp. 108–9; see chap. 7.

35. Uvarov freed all serfs in his personal service in his will and asked his son to give them a "monetary award" ("Zaveshchanie," October 30, 1849, GIM, fond 17, no. 9).

"Pis'ma Speranskogo k A. A. Stolypinu" (1818), *RA* 9 (1871): 437; "Iz drevnykh-zapisok V. A. Mukhanova," *RA* 35, No. 1 (1897): 47; S. Hoch and W. Augustine, "The Tax Censuses and the Decline of the Serf Population in Imperial Russia, 1833–1858," *Slavic Review* 38, No. 3 (September 1979): 403–25; V. I. Semevskii, *Krest'ianskii vopros v tsarstvovanie Imperatora Nikolaia*, III (St. Petersburg, 1888). P. I. Bartenev, *Deviatnadtsatyi vek. Istoricheskii sbornik*, II (Moscow, 1872), p. 183; Nikitenko, *Diary* (entry of April 9, 1841), p. 81. The tsar is quoted in Seton-Watson, *The Russian Empire*, pp. 227–28. Also see T. Emmons, *The Russian Landed Gentry and the Peasant Emancipation of 1861* (Cambridge, Mass., 1968), p. 33. Herzen is quoted in Frank, *Dostoevsky*, p. 249; also consult Ia. I. Linkov, *Ocherki istorii Krest'ianskogo dvizheniia v Rossii v 1825–1861 gg.* (Moscow, 1952), pp. 7–92.

36. Barsukov, *Zhizn' Pogodina*, IV, pp. 38, 82–85, and especially pp. 305–8 of volume IX. The following historians have incompletely quoted Uvarov: Vucinich, *Science*, p. 268; Presniakov, *Apogee*, p. 23; T. Masaryk, *The Spirit of Russia*, I (New York, 1968), p. 136; Riasanovsky, *Official Nationality*, pp. 140–42; and *Parting*, pp. 262–63; S. P. Mel'gunov, "Epokha 'ofitsial'noi narodnosti' i krepostnoe pravo," *Velikaia reforma: Russkoe obshchestvo i krestianskii vopros v proshlom i nastoiashchem*, III, ed. A. K. Dzhivelegov (Moscow, 1911), pp. 1–21; and T. Schiemann, *Geschichte Russlands unter Kaiser Nikolaus I*, IV (Berlin, 1919), p. 9.

37. Pletnev, "O narodnosti," *ZMNP* 1, No. 1 (1834): 2; Annenkov, *Decade*, p. 85; D. Fanger, *The Creation of Nikolai Gogol* (Cambridge, Mass., 1979), pp. 26–27. For overviews, consult Koyré, *Philosophie*, pp. 197–208; A. I. Pypin, *Kharakteristiki literaturnykh mnenii, 1820–1850* (St. Petersburg, 1906), pp. 93–135; V. Ivanov-Razumnik, "Obshchestvennye i umstvennye techeniia 30-kh godov," in *Istoriia russkoi literatury XIX v.*, I, ed. D. N. Ovsianniko-Kulikovskii (Moscow, 1909), pp.

247–75; A. N. Pypin, *Istoriia russkoi etnografii*, I (St. Petersburg, 1890–1891), pp. 17–202.

38. S. Allister, "The Reform of Higher Education in Russia during the Reign of Nicholas I, 1825–1855" (Ph.D. diss., Princeton University, 1974); Masaryk, *Spirit*, pp. 109, 192 ; Schapiro, *Rationalism and Nationalism*, p. 62.

39. On the romantic nationalists, consult A. G. Dementev, *Ocherki po istorii russkoi zhurnalistiki 1840–1850 gg.* (Moscow, 1951); Riasanovsky, *Official Nationality*, and his "Pogodin and Shevyrev in Russian Intellectual History," *Harvard Slavic Studies* 4 (1957): 149–67; Thaden, "The Beginnings," pp. 500–21, and his *Conservative Nationalism in Nineteenth-Century Russia* (Seattle, 1964), pp. 1–32; P. N. Sakulin, "Russkaia literatura vo vtoroi chetverti veka," *Istoriia Rossii v XIX veke*, II (St. Petersburg, 1910), pp. 448–61; S. E. Shatalov, ed., *Istoriia romantizma v russkoi literature, 1825–1840* (Moscow, 1979).

40. Annenkov, *Decade*, pp. 122–26; Malia, *Herzen*, pp. 278–312; M. Raeff, *Russian Intellectual History: An Anthology* (New York, 1966), pp. 174–251 (contains excerpts of writings of Ivan Kireevskii, Khomiakov, and Constantine Aksakov). In general, consult Riasanovsky, *Russia and the West in the Teaching of the Slavophiles: A Study of Romantic Ideology* (Cambridge, Mass., 1952); Walicki, *Controversy*, especially pp. 121–283; and *Literaturnye vzgliady i tvorchestvo slavianofilov (1830–1850 gody)* (Moscow, 1978).

41. On the intellectual development of the Westerners, consult Malia, *Herzen*, pp. 57–133; and Pypin, *Belinskii, ego zhizn i perepiska* (St. Petersburg, 1876); S. L. Frank, *Pushkin kak politicheskii myslitel'* (Belgrade, 1937); A. G. Netting, "Russian Liberalism: The Years of Promise: 1842–1855" (Ph.D. diss., Columbia University, 1967), pp. 303–46, 421–60; Chizhevskii, *Gegel'*, pp. 50–143.

42. Ch. Vetrinskii, *T. N. Granovskii i ego vremia: Istoricheskii ocherk* (St. Petersburg, 1905), pp. 76–106; Annenkov, *Decade*, pp. 132–35, 141–43, 157–63; Schapiro, *Rationalism*, pp. 59–84; Walicki, *Controversy*, pp. 394–455; Netting, "Liberalism," pp. 198–247; Chizhevskii, *Gegel'*, pp. 144–52.

43. M. O. Gershenzon, ed., *Sochineniia i pis'ma P. Ia. Chaadaeva*, I (Moscow, 1914), pp. 74–93; the first letter is also contained in Raeff's *Anthology*, pp. 160–73. Riasanovsky, "On Lammenais, Chaadaev, and the Romantic Revolt in France and Russia," *American Historical Review* 82, No. 5 (December 1977): 1165–86; Schapiro, *Rationalism*, pp. 29–58; Walicki, *Controversy*, pp. 83–117; Florovskii, *Puti*, pp. 246–48.

44. Uvarov, "Predislovie," p. v; "O narodonaselenii," pp. 126–27; *Desiatiletie*, pp. 4, 106–7; and "S predstavleniem," p. 511. For the only previous study of Uvarov's ideas, consult Shpet, *Ocherk*, pp. 236–78. Also see V. Zavitnevich, "Znachenie pervykh slavianofilov v dele uiasneniia idei narodnosti i samobytnosti," in *Trudy Kievskoi dukh. Akademii za 1891* (Kiev, 1891), pp. 16–17.

45. N. Barsukov, "Zametka ob A. S. Khomiakove," *RA* 3 (1885): 158–60; Vetrinskii, *Granovskii*, p. 302; Uvarov, *Desiatiletie*, p. 68.

46. Uvarov, *Desiatiletie*, pp. 47–52.

47. On this question, consult R. F. Iusufov, *Russkii romantizm nachala XIX veka i natsional'nye kul'tury* (Moscow, 1970); quoted from J. Mulhern, *A History of Education: A Social Interpretation* (New York, 1959), p. 427.

48. Uvarov, *Desiatiletie*, p. 3; Annenkov, *Decade*, p. 84; Ivanovskii, "O nachalakh," p. 19; Kireevskii, "On the Nature of European Culture and Its Relation to the Culture of Russia," in *Anthology*, ed. Raeff, pp. 179–80; *Otchet o pervom prisuzhdenii nagrad grafa Uvarova: 25 sent. 1857 g.* (St. Petersburg, 1859), p. 8.

49. Uvarov, *Desiatiletie*, pp. 96–97, 106; "S predstavleniem," p. 511; "O narodonaselenii," pp. 119, 126; and "I. V. Kireevskii," *RA* 2 (1894): 340.

50. Uvarov, *Otchet za 1838*, pp. 111–12; and *Desiatiletie*, p. 107; Granovskii,

"Oslablenie klassicheskago prepodavaniia v gimnaziakh i neizbezhdeniia posledstviia etoi sistemy (1855)," in *Nasha uchebnaia reforma*, ed. M. N. Katkov (Moscow, 1890), p. 152. For a similar statement, see *Universitet i politika*, p. 39; Riasanovsky, *Parting*, p. 296.

51. R. Hare, *Pioneers of Russian Social Thought* (New York, 1964), p. 335; "Dlia biografii P. I. Sakharova," *RA* 6 (1873): 15; Uvarov, *Desiatiletie*, pp. 1, 3.

52. Pletnev, "O narodnosti," p. 29. On this issue, consult M. Raeff, "The Well-Ordered Police State and the Development of Modernity in Seventeenth- and Eighteenth-Century Europe: An Attempt at a Comparative Approach," *American Historical Review* 80, No. 5 (December 1975): 1221–43; Pypin, *Etnografii*, pp. 233, 314.

53. Nikitenko, *Diary* (entry of April 9, 1834), p. 48; and *Dnevnik* (entry of March 21, 1843), I (Leningrad, 1955), pp. 264–65. For an overview of censorship in theera, see C. A. Ruud, *Fighting Words: Imperial Censorship and the Russian Press, 1804–1906* (Toronto, 1982), pp. 52–96.

54. K. Aksakov, "On the Internal State of Russia," in *Anthology*, ed. Raeff, p. 250. Pushkin is quoted in Lincoln, *Nicholas I*, p. 238; D. Balmuth, *Censorship in Russia, 1865–1905* (Washington, D.C., 1979), pp. 2, 139–44.

55. Uvarov, "O slavianstve," in "Ob ukraino-slavianskom obshchestve: Iz bumagi D. P. Golokhvostova," *RA* 23, No. 7 (1892): 348; and "Zamechaniia frantsuzkikh gazet' kasatel'no rasporiazheniia Russkago pravitel'stva o chastnykh pansionakh," *ZMNP* 2, No. 4 (1834): 142.

56. Uvarov, *Desiatiletie*, p. 96; Nikitenko, *Diary* (entry of April 16, 1833), p. 12; "Pis'mo Uvarova k D. P. Golokhvastovu" (March 1, 1835), GIM, fond 404, ed. 15.

57. Uvarov, *Desiatiletie*, p. 96; and "S predstavleniem," pp. 511–14.

58. On this issue, consult Rozhdestvenskii, *Obzor*, p. 335; *Istoricheskiia svedeniia o tsenzure v Rossii* (St. Petersburg, 1862), p. 46; "Iz pisem brat'ev Polevykh k V. K. Karlgofu" (December 30, 1833), *RA* 3 (1912): 421; Skabichevskii, *Ocherki*, p. 308; Sakulin, "Literatura," p. 445; M. Lemke, *Nikolaevskie zhandarmy i literatura, 1826–1855 gg.* (St. Petersburg, 1907), pp. 83–85. On the "iron statute," see S. Monas, "Shishkov, Bulgarin and the Russian Censorship," *Harvard Slavic Studies* 4 (1957): 127–47; V. Rozenburg and V. Iakushkina, *Russkaia pechat' i tsenzura v proshlom i nastoiashchem* (Moscow, 1905), pp. 47–53; L. Stilman, "Freedom and Repression in Prerevolutionary Russian Literature," in *Continuity and Change in Russian and Soviet Thought*, ed. E. J. Simmons (Cambridge, Mass., 1955), pp. 416–20. On the reading public, see the excellent chapter by Fanger in *Gogol*, pp. 24–44.

59. The sources recording this episode are many: Lemke, *Zhandarmy*, 87–97; Skabichevskii, *Ocherki*, 232–43; "Tsenzura v tsarstvovanie Imperatora Nikolaia I," *RS* 34, No. 3 (1903): 577–80; N. K. Kozmin, "Nikolai Polevoi i ego otnosheniia ktsenzure," *RS* 30, No. 2 (1900): 415–32; V. N. Orlov, *Nikolai Polevoi: Materialy po istorii russkoi literatury i zhurnalistiki tridtsatykh godov* (Leningrad, 1934), pp. 322–23; K. A. Polevoi, *Zapiski* (St. Petersburg, 1888), pp. 319–29, 337–47, 361, 389–401; N. V. Zdobnov, *Istoriia russkoi bibliografii ot drevnogo perioda do nachala XX veka*, I (Moscow, 1944–1948), pp. 181–82; *Letters of Pushkin* (May 13, 1834), III, p. 684; Nikitenko, *Diary* (entry of April 9, 1834), pp. 47–48.

60. N. K. Kozmin, "Nikolai Ivanovich Nadezhdin," *ZMNP* 361 (September 1905): 1–41; "Pis'mo Uvarova k A. Kh. Benkendorfu" (November 5, 1836), *PD*, fond 93, opis' 3, nos. 1367–69; Uvarov, "S predstavleniem," p. 513; Nikitenko, *Diary* (entries of October 25–December 11, 1836), pp. 65–66. "Tsenzura," pp. 583–84; "Istoriia 'Teleskopa,'" *RA* 21, No. 2 (1884): 453–61; Uvarov, "Vsepoddaneishaia dokladnaia zapiska o stat'e 'Filosoficheskiia pis'ma' v zhurnale 'Teleskop' ot 20 okt. 1836 g.," *RA* 3–4 (1884): 459–61.

61. *Dnevnik Pushkina, 1833–1835*, ed. B. L. Modzalevskii (Moscow, 1923), p. 26; *Letters of Pushkin*, III (letters from c. April 1835 and February 1836 appear on pp.

711–12 and 749, respectively); "A. S. Pushkin," *RA* 2 (1884): 375–440; A. P. Piatkovskii, *Iz istorii nashego literaturnago i obshchestvennago razvitiia* (St. Petersburg, 1889), pp. 266–67; Stilman, "Freedom," pp. 420–21; "Iz avtobiografii N. I. Ivanitskago," *RA* 10 (1909): 135; Nikitenko, *Diary* (entry of January 31, 1837), p. 69.

62. Nikitenko, *Diary* (entries of January 16, 1834, and August 8, 1835, pp. 45and 62, respectively); Crankshaw, *Shadow,* p. 100; Riasanovsky, *Parting,* pp. 276–77; and *Official Nationality;* Fanger, *Gogol,* pp. 39–44; Panaev, *Vospominaniia,* pp. 85–86; "Iz pisem kniazia Viazemskogo k Zhukovskomu" (April 14, 1833), *RA* 3(1900): 373; N. I. Grech, "F. V. Bulgarin," *RS* 4 (1871): 483–523.

63. The tenor and statistics of the journalistic enterprises were gleaned from the following sources: Uvarov, "Pis'ma k M. P. Pogodinu" (January 19, 1841), ROBIL, p. 34, n. 4; P. Karatygin, "Severnaia pchela, 1825–1859," *RA* 2 (1882): 241–303; "Pis'ma I. V. Kireevskago k A. S. Khomiakovu" (April 10, 1844), *RA* 5 (1909): 109–114; Zdobnov, *Istoriia,* p. 216; Barsukov, *Pogodin,* VI, p. 22; Dementev, *Ocherki,* pp. 185–99; "K istorii tsarstvovaniia imperatora Nikolaia I," *RS* 26, No. 6 (1896): 556–57; "Knizhnye redkosti," *RA* 30, No. 2 (1892): 251; "Pis'ma M. A.Obolenskago k V. A. Polenovu," *RA* 19, No. 1 (1882): 275; Netting, "Liberalism," pp. 33–88.

64. V. E. Maksimov, *'Sovremennik' v 40–50 gg.* (Leningrad, 1934); V. I. Kuleshov, *'Otechestvennye zapiski' i literatura 40 kh godov XIX veka* (Moscow, 1958); Frank, *Dostoevsky,* p. 253. For a short biography of Pletnev, see O. Pelech, "Toward a Historical Sociology of the Ukrainian Ideologues in the Russian Empire of the 1830's and 1840's" (Ph.D. diss., Princeton University, 1976), pp. 82–88. Netting's "Liberalism" contains an excellent discussion of the development of Russian journalismin the 1840s and early 1850s.

65. "Tsenzura," pp. 585–91. Androssov also wrote an article in the *ZMNP* in which he rhapsodized about the divine origin of monarchical power (4, No. 12 [1834]: 367–85); A. P. Mogilianskii, "A. S. Pushkin i V. F. Odoevskii kak sozdateli," *Izvestiia AN SSSR* 6, No. 3 (1949): 209–26.

66. Lemke, *Zhandarmy,* p. 85; *Istoricheskiia svedeniia,* p. 52; W. B. Lincoln, *In the Vanguard of Reform: Russia's Enlightened Bureaucrats 1825–1861* (De Kalb, Ill., 1982), p. 50; Fanger, *Gogol,*pp. 33–34.

67. *Istoricheskie svedeniia,* pp. 47–51; Rozberg and Iakushkina, *Pechat',* pp. 53–54; N. A. Engel'gardt, "Ocherki Nikolaevskoi tsenzury," *Istoricheskii vestnik* 86, No.10 (1901): 169; Rozhdestvenskii, *Obzor,* p. 336. Nikitenko, *Diary* (entry for December 12, 1842), pp. 88–89, offers another specific example of interference.

68. Riasanovsky's statistics are in *Parting,* pp. 267–83; remaining statistics are compiled from the yearly reports in the *ZMNP;* complete statistics for 1848 are included in "Delo o razsmotrenie v osobom Komitete deistvii tsenzury periodicheskikh izdanii," TsGIAL, fond 1611, opis' 1, no. 208b, p. 21. (There were sixty-four journals in all, twenty-seven privately owned in Moscow and St. Petersburg, eighteen government periodicals, and the rest provincial publications.)

69. Uvarov, *Desiatiletie,* p. 96; F. C. Barghoorn, "Some Russian Images of the West," in *Continuity and Change,* p. 575; Rozhdestvenskii, *Obzor,* p. 333; S. V. Luppov, ed., *Istoriia biblioteki Akademii nauk SSSR* (Moscow, 1964), pp. 163–64; Blackwell, *Russian Industrialization,* pp. 349–50; Vucinich, *Science,* p. 262. On censors' attitudes toward foreign authors, see I. Aizenshtok, "Frantsuzskie pisateli v otsenkakh tsarskoi tsenzury," *Literaturnoe nasledstvo* 33–34 (1939): 769–858; L. Grossman, "Bal'zak v Rossii," *Literaturnoe nasledstvo* 31–32 (1937): 150–73; S. N. Kulikov, "Bal'zak: Neopublikovannye pis'ma," *Zven'ia* 3–4 (1934): 289–98. On the origins, consult G. J. Marker, "Publishing and the Formation of a Reading Public in Eighteenth-Century Russia" (Ph.D. diss., University of California, 1977), and Netting, "Liberalism," pp. 61–65.

70. Uvarov's attitudes are discussed in the following sources: "Tsenzura,"

(March 1903), pp. 571–72; Nikitenko, *Diary* (entry of April 9, 1834), p. 47; "Tri bumagi S. S. Uvarova," *RA* (1866), pp. 1066–69; "Pis'mo Uvarova k Gogoliu" (March 27–May 2, 1845), PD, fond 652, opis' 2, no. 33; N. V. Gogol, "Pis'ma k Uvarovu," *Pol'noe sobranie sochinenii*, X, (Moscow, 1940), especially pp. 459–70; "Pis'ma kniazia V. Odoevskago k Uvarovu," in *Otchet imp. Publichnoi biblioteki za 1892 god* (St. Petersburg, 1895), pp. 53–57; "Zapiska Uvarova k I. A. Krylovu," PD, fond 142, opis' 2, nos. 27–28.

71. Nikitenko, *Diary* (entries of December 7–21, 1843), pp. 96–98; ibid. (entry of October 18, 1845), p. 105; ibid. (entry of January 2, 1846), p. 107; "Zapiski N. I. Grecha," *RA* 11 (1873): 685; S. V. Maksimov, "Literaturnye ekspeditsii," *Russkaia mysl'* (February 1890), p. 18; Skabichevskii, *Ocherki*, p. 333.

72. Frank, *Dostoevsky*, pp. 220–22; Belinskii, "Letter to N. V. Gogol," in *Anthology*, ed. Raeff, p. 258; Malia, *Herzen*, pp. 64–65.

73. Lincoln, *Nicholas I*, p. 239.

74. G. F. Kennan (*The Marquis de Custine and His Russia in 1839* [Princeton, 1971], p. 119) quotes Vinogradoff. Vetrinskii, *Granovskii*, p. 60. Also see Balmuth, "TheOrigins of the Tsarist Epoch of Censorship Terror," *American Slavic and East European Review* 19 (December 1960): 497–99.

75. Pypin, *Kharakteristiki*, p. 107.

76. Pintner, "The Russian Higher Civil Service," pp. 56, 62. On the bureaucracy in general, consult Pintner, "Social Characteristics"; M. Raeff, "The Russian Autocracy and Its Officials," *Harvard Slavic Studies* 4 (1957): 77–91; H. J. Torke, "Continuity and Change in the Relations between Bureaucracy and Society in Russia, 1613–1861," *Canadian Slavic Studies* 5, No. 4 (Winter 1971): 457–76; Torke, *Das russische Beamtentum in der ersten Hälfte des 19 Jahrhunderts* (Berlin, 1967); P. A. Zaionchkovskii, "Vysshaia biurokratiia nakanune Krymskoi voiny," *Istoriia SSSR* 4 (July–August 1974): 154–64; S. Monas, "Bureaucracy in Russia under Nicholas I," in *Russia: Essays in History and Literature*, ed. L. Legters (Leiden, 1972), pp. 100–16; Lincoln, "Genesis"; and "The Ministers of Nicholas I: A Brief Inquiry into Their Backgrounds and Service Career," *Russian Review* 34, No. 3 (July 1975): 308–23.

77. V. Shiman, "Imperator Nikolai Pavlovich," *RA* 3 (1902): 469; Benkendorf, "Obozrenie" (1839) d. 4, p. 117; M. Iuzefovich, "Neskol'ko slov ob imperatore Nikolae," *RA* 8 (1870): 1002; A. Nifontov, *1848 god v Rossii* (Moscow, 1931), pp. 199–200.

78. This gossip is found in "Pis'ma Speranskago" (May 8, 1822) in *V pamiat'*, p. 641; Lehmann, *Freiherr vom Stein*, IV, p. 308; Grech, *Zapiski*, p. 289; *Dnevnik Pushkina* (Moscow, 1923), p. 245; "Zapiski senatora K. I. Fishera," *Istoricheskii vestnik* 3, No. 1 (1908): 459; *Ostaf'evskii arkhiv*, III, p. 33; V. R. Zotov, "Peterburg v sorokovykh godakh," *Istoricheskii vestnik* 39 (1890): 35.

79. *Ostaf'evskii arkhiv*, II, 188–94 (April 26, 1821); "Iz pisem A. Ia. Bulgakova k bratu. 1821" (August 8, 1822), *RA* 3 (1901): 445; Leduc, "Essai," in *Esquisses*, pp. 57–58; "Pis'mo A. A. Bestuzheva-Marlinskogo k P. A. Viazemskomu" (March 23, 1823), *PD*, fond 68, ed. 54.

80. Uvarov's service record is located in TsGIAL, fond 733, opis' 12, no. 775, pp. 36, 38, 39, 42. Uvarov, *À la mémoire de l'Empereur Alexandre* (St. Petersburg, 1826), and republished the same year in *Journal de St. Pétersbourg*, *Severnaia pchela*, *Syn otchestva*, and *Révue encyclopédique*; "À la mémoire de l'Imperatrice Elisabeth,"*Journal de St. Pétersbourg* 83 (July 8, 1826), and reprinted and sold to benefit the poor; *À la mémoire de la Princesse Lieven* (St. Petersburg, 1828); *À la mémoire de l'Imperatrice Marie* (St. Petersburg, 1829). Uvarov, "Posledniia minuty zhizni generala-ot-kavalerii F. P. Uvarova, uchastnika Otechestvennoi voiny 1812 g.," *RS* 44, No. 8 (August 1913): 353–54.

81. A. Gavriila, *Istoriia russkoi filosofii* (Kazan, 1840), pp. 114–16; V. Ostroglazov,

"Kholera v Moskve v 1830 godu," *RA* 9 (1893): 93–106; V. V. Timoshchuk, "Imperatritsa Elisaveta Alekseevna," *RS* 4 (April 1910): 163. Uvarov and his wife occasionally spent summers at Pavlovsk with Maria Feodorovna and Nikolai Pavlovich (Shil'der, *Aleksandr pervyi*, p. 94).

On Uvarov's court contacts, also consult "Pis'ma Elizavety k Uvarovu," PD, fond 274, opis' 3, no. 44; "Raskaz V. A. Zhukovskago o pervom ego predstavlenii imperatritse Marii Feodorovni," *RA* 3 (1865): 803–6; "N. M. Karamzin," *RA* 2, No. 8 (1911): 591.

82. "Pis'mo Uvarova" (April 26, 1822), PD, fond 123, opis' 1, no. 825, p. 3.

83. Uvarov's office is described in Lilienthal's *My Travels in Russia* (New York, 1937), pp. 190–92. On Uvarov's wealth, see C. Galskoy, "The Ministry of Education under Nicholas I, 1826–1836" (Ph.D. diss., Stanford University, 1977), pp. 120, 160–61.

84. *Dnevnik Pushkina*, pp. 69, 361; Pushkin, *Polnoe sobranie sochinenii*, I, ed. V. Briusov (Moscow, 1920), p. 370.

85. "Na vyzdorovlenie Lukulla: Podrazhanie latinskomu," in Pushkin, *Epigrammy* (Moscow, 1974), pp. 139–41. (My translation.)

86. Benkendorf, "Obozrenie" (1833) d. 1, pp. 211–12; (1834) d. 2, p. 14; (1835) d. 2, p. 78; (1839) d. 4, p. 117.

87. A. N. Afanasev, "Moskovskii universitet 1843–1849 gg.," *RS* 8 (August 1886): 390; "Iz zapisok S. M. Solov'eva," *Russkie universitety*, p. 464; A. S. Pushkin, *Polnoe sobranie sochinenii*, III (Moscow, 1958), p. 353. Pogodin is quoted in N. Barsukov, *Zhizn' i trudy P. M. Stroeva* (St. Petersburg, 1878), p. 372; B. E. Raikov, *Russkie biologi-evoliustionisty do Darvina*, II (Moscow, 1951), p. 217; Zotov, "Peterburg," p. 35; *Letters of Pushkin* (April 26, 1835), III, p. 707; Nikitenko, *Diary* (entry of March 31, 1837), p. 72; F. M. Delariu, "D. M. Delariu i A. S. Pushkin," *RS* 9 (September 1880): 219; Pushkin, *Epigrammy*, p. 143; *Pushkin bez tsenzury* (London, 1972), p. 353; Karlinsky, *Gogol*, pp. 57, 218.

88. Solov'ev is quoted in Riasanovsky, *Official Nationality*, pp. 70–71; Nikitenko, *Dnevnik* (entry of May 20, 1843), I, 267–68.

CHAPTER 6

1. N. K. Shil'der, *Imperator Nikolai pervyi: ego zhizn' i tsarstvovanie*, I (St. Petersburg, 1903), pp. 427–28; Nicholas is quoted from his Coronation Manifesto, published in *Severnaia pchela* 85 (July 17, 1826); Darlington, *Education in Russia*, p. 64; A. S. Pushkin, "Zapiska o narodnom vospitanii," *Deviatnadtsatyi vek* 2 (1872): 209–18; A. Tseitlin, "Zapiska Pushkina o narodnom vospitanii," *Literaturnyi sovremennik* 1 (January 1937): 266–91; I. L. Feinberg, *Nezavershennye raboty Pushkina* (Moscow, 1958): 278–91; N. Vasil'kov, "A. S. Pushkin o vospitanii," *Russkaia shkola* 5–6 (May–June 1899): 75–92.

2. On the ministries of Shishkov and Lieven, consult Rozhdestvenskii, *Obzor*, pp. 162–219; *SPMNP*, II, 1: 200–257 (December 8, 1828). (References to *SPMNP* carry the date of the document. Entries consist mainly of decrees, laws, and reports.)

3. Galskoy, "The Ministry of Education," p. 169.

4. S. S. Uvarov, "S predstavleniem," pp. 502–32.

5. F. Paulsen, *German Education Past and Present* (London, 1908), p. 273; Meyers, *The Modernization of Education*, pp. 3–4; M. Sturt, *The Education of the People* (London, 1967), p. 67.

6. *SPMNP*, II, 1: 25–28 (May 14 and May 21, 1826).

7. S. S. Uvarov, *Obshchii otchet predstavlennyi ego Imperatorskomu Velichestvu po Ministerstvu narodnago prosveshcheniia za 1818 god* (St. Petersburg, 1839), p. 111.

Hereafter, unless otherwise noted, Uvarov's yearly reports, always published the following year either separately or in the April issue of the *ZMNP*, will be cited as *Otchet za 18—* or "Otchet za *18—*," *ZMNP*. *Otchet za 1839*, p. 104; *Otchet za 1843*, pp. 93–94; *Otchet za 1844*, p. 95; *Otchet za 1848*, p. 139; Seton-Watson, *The Russian Empire*, p. 220.

8. *SPMNP*, II, 1: 955–62 (June 16, 1835); and 1084 (February 28, 1836); Uvarov, *Otchet za 1835*, pp. v–vi; Shmid, *Istoriia*, p. 295; S. A. Kniazkov and N. I. Serbov, *Ocherk istorii narodnago obrazovaniia v Rossii do epokhi reformy Aleksandra II* (Moscow,1911), pp. 200–7.

Steven Allister's cogent analysis of the workings and debates of the School Committee based on his reading of the committee's journal, located in TsGIAL, is the best study in any language ("The Reform of Higher Education in Russia during the Reign of Nicholas I, 1825–1855" [Ph.D. diss., Princeton University, 1974], pp. 19–74). Galskoy also used these same sources in his dissertation, "Ministry of Education," but Allister's work is definitely superior.

9. Uvarov, *Desiatiletie*, pp. 7, 28; and "Otchet za 1835," *ZMNP*, p. cxxviii; T. Granovskii, "Oslablenie klassicheskago prepodavaniia v gimnaziakh i neizbezhniia posledstviia etoi sistemy (1855)," in *Nasha uchebnaia reforma*, p. 152; Allister, "Reform," pp. 205–6.

10. Uvarov, "S predstavleniem," p. 505; "Tsirkuliarnoe predlozhenie G. upravliaiushchego Ministerstvom narodnago prosveshcheniia nachalstvam uchebnykh okrugov, 'O vstuplenii v upravlenie Ministerstvom,'" *ZMNP* 1 (January 1834): xlix; Uvarov, "Otchet za 1836," *ZMNP* (April 1837): cxxviii; and "Obozrenie istekshago piatiletiia," *ZMNP* (April 1838): 8; F. K. Ringer, *Education and Society in Modern Europe* (Bloomington, Ind., 1979), p. 114; Mulhern, *A History of Education*, p. 541.

11. *SPMNP*, II, 1: 1324 (February 15, 1838): 561–62 (March 9, 1833); 894 (March 5, 1835); 1078 (January 20, 1836); 1324 (February 15, 1838). Aleshintsev, *Vopros*, pp. 158–62; Sturt, *Education*, p. 71; Prost, *Histoire*, p. 92.

12. Uvarov, *Desiatiletie*, pp. 27–28; and the following from *SPMNP*, II, 1: 708–11 (February 20, 1834); 762 (April 18, 1834); 782–880 (February 4, 1835); 887–88 (February 26, 1835); 897 (March 21, 1835); 946 (May 31, 1835); 998 (September 17, 1830); 1162–73 (September 6, 1836); 1256 (April 27, 1837); 1300 (October 19, 1837); 1306–9 (November 23, 1837); 1386 (July 26, 1838); 1464 (January 17, 1839); 1533 (September 5, 1839); 1561–65 (November 18, 1839); and *SPMNP* II, 2: 56 (June 18, 1840); 273–74 (August 26, 1841); and 581–602 (January 9, 1845).

13. Uvarov, *Desiatiletie*, pp. 29–30; Uvarov, "Otchet za 1835," *ZMNP*, pp. c–ci; "Otchet za 1836," *ZMNP*, p. xci; *Otchet za 1837*, p. 104; *Otchet za 1838*, p. 87; *Otchet za 1840*, pp. 7, 76; and *Otchet za 1841*, p. 62; Allister, "Reform," pp. 62–64; Johnson, *Heritage*, pp. 109–33; *SPMNP*, II, 1: 157–90 (September 30, 1828); and 993–94 (July 26, 1835); *SPMNP*, II, 2: 6 (January 28, 1840); M. F. Shabaev, ed., *Ocherki istorii shkoly i pedagogicheskoi mysli narodov SSSR: XVIII v.–pervaia polovina XIX v.* (Moscow, 1973), pp. 270–89.

14. Uvarov, *Desiatiletie*, pp. 30–31; *Otchet za 1838*, pp. 88, 114; *Otchet za 1839*; *SPMNP*, II, 2; 872–74 (July 26, 1847).

15. Sturt, *Education*, p. 71; Prost, *Histoire*, pp. 137–40; Paulsen, *German Education*, pp. 199, 237–39; Reisner, *Nationalism and Education*, pp. 50, 60, 137. The figures here and throughout this chapter are drawn from my own compilation of statistics located at the end of each annual report.

16. Uvarov, *Desiatiletie*, pp. 7–8, 99–101; Uvarov, "Otchet za 1835," p. xv; *SPMNP*, II, 1: 777 (June 5, 1834); 920 (May 14, 1835); 1132 (May 12, 1836); 1204 (December 1, 1836); 1213 (January 21, 1837); 1302 (October 28, 1837). J. G. Bloch, *Finansy Rossii XIX stoletiia: Istoriia-Statistika*, IV (St. Petersburg, 1882), pp. 236–39; *Ministerstvo finansov, 1802–1902*, I (St. Petersburg, 1902), pp. 620, 628–29.

17. A. Krusenstern, *Précis du système, des progrès et de l'état de l'instruction publique en Russie* (Warsaw, 1837), pp. 308–426; Blackwell, *Russian Industrialization*, p. 435, provides a convenient summary of Krusenstern's statistics; Schmid, *Istoriia*, p. 381; Hans, *History*, p. 84; Uvarov, *Otchet za 1837*, pp. 22–23.

18. Uvarov, *Desiatiletie*, p. 14; Nicholas is quoted in P. F. Kapterev, *Istoriia russkoi pedagogii* (St. Petersburg, 1897), p. 156.

19. Nicholas is quoted from his Coronation Manifesto in *Severnaia pchela*; Shil'-der, *Nikolai*, I, p. 428; Pushkin, "Zapiska," p. 211; Allister, "Reform," pp. 56–68; *The Complete Prose Tales of Alexandr Sergeyevitch Pushkin*, trans. G. R. Aitken (New York, 1966), p. 344. On the question of domestic education, consult I. V. Chu-bashev, *Ocherki po istorii doshkol'nogo vospitaniia v Rossii* (Moscow, 1955), pp. 46–83.

20. Shil'der, *Nikolai*, II, p. 407; Uvarov, *Desiatiletie*, pp. 16–17; and *Otchet za 1834*, pp. 19–20; *SPMNP*, II, 1: 438–441 (June 12, 1831); 755–56 (March 25, 1834); 784–99 (July 1, 1834); 845 (November 27, 1834); 849 (December 11, 1834); 850 (December 11, 1834); 1147–50 (June 23, 1836).

21. Uvarov, "Otchet za 1835," *ZMNP*, p. cii; *Otchet za 1839*, pp. 6–7; *Otchet za 1848*, p. 110; the figures are constructed from the *otchety* for the years 1838–1847. Uvarov's attitude toward domestic education was fully elucidated in the article by S. Shevyrev, "Ob otnoshenii semeinago vospitaniia k gosudarstvennomy," *Mosk-vitianin* 4, No. 7 (1842): 36–124; also see Darlington, *Education*, p. 71.

22. Allister, "Reform," pp. 56–59; Rozhdestvenskii, *Obzor*, pp. 204–6; Kapterev, *Istoriia*, pp. 149–52.

23. Uvarov, *Desiatiletie*, pp. 14–15; Uvarov, "Otchet za 1835," *ZMNP*, p. xxxi; *SPMNP*, II, 1: 641–47 (November 4, 1833); 685–87 (December 26, 1833); 753–54 (August 27, 1834); 868–69 (January 30, 1835).

24. "Zamechaniia frantsuzskikh gazet' kasatel'no rasporiazheniia Russkago prav-itel'stva o chastnykh pansionakh," *ZMNP* 2 (April 1834), pp. 138–45.

25. Uvarov, *Desiatiletie*, p. 34; and *Otchet za 1843*, p. 92; statistics drawn from tables attached to *otchety* for 1834, 1838, 1842, and 1847.

26. Uvarov, *Otchet za 1842*, p. 110; *Otchet za 1845*, p. 105; *Otchet za 1846*, p. 125. On women's education, consult C. H. Whittaker, "The Women's Movement during the Reign of Alexander II," *Journal of Modern History* 48, No. 2 (June 1976): 35–69; Shabaev, *Ocherki*, pp. 255–69.

27. Uvarov, *Otchet za 1834*, p. 17; *Otchet za 1839*, p. 6; *Otchet za 1845*, p. 102; *Otchet za 1848*, p. 10.

28. Allister, "Reform," pp. 42–44; *SPMNP*, II, 1: 71–73 (August 19, 1827).

29. Reisner, *Nationalism*, p. 143; Prost, *Histoire*, p. 10; Meyer, *Modernization*, p. 8; Sturt, *Education*, pp. 5, 18, 28; J. Moody, *French Education*, pp. 33–34; R. Rath, "Training for Citizenship in the Austrian Elementary Schools during the Reign of Francis I," *Journal of Central European Affairs* 4, No. 2 (1944): 147–64.

30. V. I. Charnoluskii, "Narodnoe obrazovanie v pervoi polovine XIX veke," in *Istoriia Rossii v XIX veke*, IV (St. Petersburg, 1910), pp. 71, 97.

31. *SPMNP*, I, 1: 759 (November 10, 1811); and 855–56 (September 9, 1815). For an excellent discussion of the topic and reference to further reading on this topic, consult J. Flynn, "Tuition and Social Class in the Russian Universities: S. S. Uvarov and 'Reaction' in the Russia of Nicholas I," *Slavic Review* 35, No. 2 (June 1976): 232–48; on the question of ranks, see Shepelev, *Chiny*, pp. 47–101.

32. As quoted in Flynn, "Tuition," p. 236; P. Keppen, *Deviataia reviziia: Issle-dovanie o chisle zhitelei v Rossii v 1851 godu* (St. Petersburg, 1857), pp. 182–86.

33. M. Vaughan and M. Archer, *Social Conflict and Educational Change in England and France, 1789–1848* (Cambridge, Eng., 1971), p. 210; P. W. Musgrave, *Society and Education in England since 1800* (London, 1968), p. 25; Ringer, *Education*, p. 78; R. Anderson, "Secondary Education in Mid-Nineteenth-Century France," *Past and*

Present 53 (November 1971): 123–26. Uvarov's memorandum is reprinted in V. Ia. Stoiunin, "Konservatory sorokovykh godov," *Istoricheskii vestnik* 7, pp. 1–28.

34. Uvarov, "Otchet za 1835," *ZMNP*, p. cxxxv; and *Otchet za 1844*, p. 95.

35. Uvarov, *Otchet za 1834*, p. 149; Kniazkov and Serbov, pp. 212–14; *SPMNP*, II, 1: 1037–39.

36. I. Aleshintsev, *Soslovnyi vopros i politika v istorii nashikh gimnazii* (St. Petersburg, 1908), pp. 33–36, 142; *SPMNP*, II, 1: 1258–60 (May 9, 1837); 1283 (June 5, 1837); 1348–73 (May 31, 1838); 1401 (September 27, 1838); *SPMNP*, II, 2: 306–7 (February 10, 1842).

37. Ringer, *Education*, p. 22; Musgrave, *Society*, p. 10; I. Goncharov, *Oblomov*, trans. A. Dunnigan (New York, 1963), p. 195.

38. Uvarov, "Otchet za 1835," *ZMNP*, p. xlvii; "Otchet za 1836," *ZMNP*, p. xxxvii; *Otchet za 1838*, p. 28; *Otchet za 1839*, p. 19; *Otchet za 1841*, p. 21; and "Perepiska Uvarova i A. G. Priklonskago s E. A. Voltatis' po povodu eekrest'ianskago mal'chika Ivana Petrova iz dereveni Ragozina," PD, fond 265, opis' 2, no. 2908, pp. 1–10.

39. Rozhdestvenskii, *Obzor*, pp. 282–83.

40. Uvarov, *Desiatiletie*, p. 10; Charnoluski, "Narodnoe obrazovanie," pp. 97–100; Kniazkov and Serbov, *Ocherk*, p. 205; *SPMNP*, II, 1: 200–57 (December 8, 1828).

41. Uvarov, *Desiatiletie*, pp. 21–22; "Otchet za 1836," *ZMNP*, p. viii; *Otchet za 1839*, pp. 6, 20, 22, 41; and *Otchet za 1844*, p. 5; Rozhdestvenskii, *Obzor*, pp. 282–83. Cosgrove is quoted in Ringer, *Education*, p. 22. Shabaev, *Ocherki*, pp. 232–36.

42. On Guizot, see Reisner, *Nationalism*, pp. 52–55. Uvarov, "Otchet za 1835," *ZMNP*, pp. xcii–xcviii; *Otchet za 1837*, p. 91; and *Otchet za 1838*, p. 83.

43. Uvarov, *Desiatiletie*, p. 8; Blackwell, *Russian Industrialization*, p. 435; Allister, "Reform," pp. 35–56; *Avtobiografiia N. I. Kostomarova*, ed. V. Kotel'nikov (Moscow, 1922), as quoted in Pelech, "Ukrainian Ideologues," pp. 123–24.

44. Uvarov, "S predstavleniem," p. 520; Shmid, *Istoriia*, pp. 302–3; Rozhdestvenskii, *Obzor*, pp. 197–98; Kniazkov and Serbov, *Ocherk*, pp. 209–10; *SPMNP*, II, 1: 538–39 (February 22, 1823).

45. Uvarov, *Desiatiletie*, pp. 8, 35; Rozhdestvenskii, *Obzor*, p. 280; *SPMNP*, II, 1: 44 (December 19, 1826); 538–40 (February 22, 1833); 563 (May 9, 1833); 1117–26 (May 6, 1836); 1415 (October 7, 1838).

46. Uvarov, *Otchet za 1841*, p. 101; Rozhdestvenskii, *Obzor*, p. 272; Aleshintsev, *Vopros*, pp. 29–31.

47. Uvarov, *Desiatiletie*, pp. 8–10; "Otchet za 1835," *ZMNP*, p. xvi; and "Otchet za 1836," *ZMNP*, p. xxiii; Hans, *History*, p. 74; *SPMNP*, II, 1: 996 (August 27, 1835); and 1301 (October 28, 1837).

48. Uvarov is quoted in Aleshintsev, *Vopros*, p. 30.

49. Allister, "Reform," pp. 50–53; Uvarov, *Desiatiletie*, p. 20.

50. Uvarov, *Desiatiletie*, p. 20; "Otchet za 1835," *ZMNP*, p. xii; and "K istorii klassitsizma v Rossii: Mnenie S. S. Uvarova (1826)," *RA* 35 (December 1899): 465–68; Darlington, *Education*, p. 65; Shmid, *Istorii*, pp. 261–62; A. I. Georgievskii, *Predpolozhennaia reforma nashei srednei shkoly* (St. Petersburg, 1901), pp. 22–24; Ringer, *Education*, p. 34.

51. Allister, "Reform," pp. 51–53; Rozhdestvenskii, *Obzor*, p. 277; Prost, *Histoire*, p. 54; Anderson, "Education"; Moody, *Education*, p. 33; Ringer, *Education*, pp. 7, 19; Musgrave, *Society*, p. 10; Meyers, *Modernization*, p. 8; from J. Armstrong, *The European Administrative Elite*, the chapter entitled "The Classics Barrier" (Princeton, N.J., 1973), pp. 127–48.

52. Granovskii, "Oslablenie," pp. 154–60. See the excellent chapters on classicalstudies in Sinel, *Count Dmitry Tolstoi*, pp. 130–213; the quotation is on p. 144.

53. Uvarov, *Otchet za 1834*, p. 42; Allister, "Reform," pp. 51–52; Darlington, *Education*, p. 70.

54 . Rozhdestvenskii, *Obzor*, pp. 199–200; Kniazkov and Serbov, *Ocherk*, pp. 205–6, P. Miliukov, *Ocherki po istorii russkoi kul'tury*, II, pt. 2 (Paris, 1932), p. 782; Uvarov, *Otchet za 1846*, p. 8; Vucinich, , p. 254; *SPMNP*, II, 2: 833–34 (December 19, 1846).

55. Uvarov, *Desiatiletie*, p. 21; "Otchet za 1836," *ZMNP*, p. viii; *Otchet za 1838*, p. 8; *Otchet za 1839*, pp. 6, 19, 21, 28, 104; *Otchet za 1841*, p. 16; and *Otchet za 1842*, p. 105; Darlington, *Education*, p. 77; M. Lalaev, *Imperator Nikolai I, zizhditel' russkoi shkoly* (St. Petersburg, 1896), p. 112; N. Vessel', "Nachal'noe obrazovanie i narodnyia uchilishcha v zapadnoi Evrope i Rossii," *Russkaia shkola* 2, No. 5 (1891): 12–44; Allister, "Reform," pp. 162–63; Blackwell, *Russian Industrialization*, pp. 366–67; Shabaev, *Ocherki*, pp. 228–32. On the German *realschule*, consult F. Schnabel, *Erfahrungswissenschaften und Technik*, pp. 292–330, vol. III of *Deutsche Geschichte im neunzehnten Jahrhundert* (Berlin, 1929–1937).

56. Shmid, *Istoriia*, p. 352; Uvarov, *Desiatiletie*, pp. 13, 23–24; "Otchet za 1835," *ZMNP*, p. lxv; *Otchet za 1838*, p. 22; and *Otchet za 1847*, p. 6; *SPMNP*, II, 1: 948–52 (June 5, 1835); 1039–42 (January 2, 1836); 1340 (May 10, 1838); 1403–10 (October 4, 1836); and 1486–93 (March 29, 1838); *SPMNP*, II, 2: 875–76 (September 2, 1847).

57. Hans, *History*, pp. 73–74; Aleshintsev, *Vopros*, p. 39; Uvarov, "Otchet za 1836," *ZMNP*, p. cxxvi; and *Otchet za 1845*, p. 105. The quotation is located in A. Besançon, *Éducation et société en Russie* (Paris, 1974), p. 25.

58. Uvarov, *Otchet za 1838*, p. 11; and *Otchet za 1845*, p. 125; Rozhdestvenskii, *Obzor*, pp. 272–73; Charnoluskii, "Narodnoe obrazovanie," p. 101; Aleshintsev, *Vopros*, p. 144; Shmid, *Istoriia*, p. 346; Lalaev, *Nikolai*, p. 66; *SPMNP*, II, 2: 629–32 (June 11, 1845).

59. Shil'der, *Nikolai*, II, p. 32; Prost, *Histoire*, pp. 32–34; Reisner, *Nationalism*, p. 61–62; Ringer, *Education*, pp. 34, 132.

60. Anderson, "Education," p. 124; Meyers, *Modernization*, p. 8; Mulhearn, *History*, p. 507; Pintner, "Social Characteristics," pp. 429–43.

61. Uvarov, *Otchet za 1841*, p. 104; Darlington, *Education*, p. 77.

CHAPTER 7

1. M. P. Fuss, "Coup d'oeil historique sur le dernier quart-de-siècle de l'existence de l'Académie impériale des Sciences de Saint-Pétersbourg," *Recueil des actes des séances publiques de l'Académie impériale des Sciences* (St. Petersburg, 1843), pp. 185–88; Vucinich, *Science*, p. 371.
As a sample of criticism of the universities, consult F. Buslaev, "Vospominaniia," *Vestnik Evropy* 6, No. 11 (1891): 1–56; S. Ashevskii, "Iz istorii Moskovskago universiteta," *Mir Bozhii* 14, No. 3 (1905): 109–16; Vetrinskii, *Granovskii*, p. 148; V. O. Kliuchevskii et al., *Vospominaniia o studencheskoi zhizni* (Moscow, 1899), p. 46; M. K. Korbut, *Kazanskii gosudarstvennyi universitet imeni V. I. Ul'ianova-Lenina za 125 let: 1804/05–1929/30* (Kazan, 1930), p. 36. Archival reports from the early 1830s speak of "complete physical ruin" (quoted in Galskoy, "The Ministry of Education," p. 63).

2. *Oblomov*, as quoted in D. Brower, *Training the Nihilists: Education and Radicalism in Tsarist Russia* (Cornell, N.Y., 1975), p. 56. On the general growth of culture, consult Poznanskii, *Ocherk*, pp. 154–210.

3. Ringer, *Education*, pp. 32–33; Paulsen, *German Education*, pp. 184–91.

4. Annenkov, *The Extraordinary Decade*, p. 81.

5. Iu. N. Egorov, "Russkie universitety i studencheskoe dvizhenie vo vtoroi polovine 1830 do 1850 gg. XIX veka" (unpublished candidate's diss. [Leningrad State University, 1958], p. 5). A similar view is expressed by I. N. Borozdin, "Universitety v Rossii v pervoi polovine XIX veke," in *Istoriia Rossii v XIX veke*, II (St. Petersburg, 1910), pp. 368–74. For the "sanctuary" idea, see Kliuchevskii, *Vospominaniia*, p. 46; I. A. Goncharov, "Iz studencheskikh vospominanii," in *Russkie universitety v ikh ustavakh i vospominaniiakh sovremennikov*, ed. I. M. Solov'ev (St. Petersburg, 1914), p. 123; and G. A. Kniazev and A. V. Kol'tsov, *Kratkii ocherk istorii Akademii nauk SSSR* (Moscow, 1964), p. 33.

One interesting exception to the "despite thesis" is *Universitet i politika* (St. Petersburg, 1906), a book written in 1905 by liberal professors lamenting the fact that their institutions were being turned into "political circuses." They singled out Uvarov "as a sincere champion of enlightenment" since under him "it seemed we were standing at a point from which we would steadily grow and develop progressive activity in the universities." However, in 1848, repression "replaced . . . the spirit of Uvarov's system," that is, a respect for "the scholarly meaning of the university"; but, they rued, this aim "remains as before not understood."

6. Berlin, "A Remarkable Decade," p. 147; Darlington, *Education in Russia*, p. 78; Annenkov, *Decade*, pp. 81–82; A. Stankevich, *Granovskii: Biograficheskii ocherk* (Moscow, 1914), p. 140; Uvarov, "Pis'mo k Granovskomu" (January 2, 1850), GIM, fond 345, ed. 5.

7. Metternich, *Memoirs*, III, pp. 286–87.

8. M. Malia, "What Is the Intelligentsia?" in *The Russian Intelligentsia*, ed. R. Pipes (New York, 1961), p. 14; Brower, *Nihilists*, p. 37. On the importance of the "university question" to the autocracy, consult K. Meyer, "Die Entstehung der 'Universitätfrage' in Russland. Zum Verhältnis von Universität, Staat und Gesellschaft zu Beginn des neunzehnten Jahrhunderts," *Forschüngen für Osteuropaischen Geschichte* 25 (1978): 229–38.

9. Vucinich, *Science*, p. 364; Blackwell, *Russian Industrialization*, p. 407; Gal'perin, "Russkaia istoricheskaia nauka," p. 3; Wortman, *Russian Legal Consciousness*, p. 50.

10. "O vstuplenii tovarishcha ministra tainogo sovetnika Uvarova v prava i obiazannosti ministra narodnago proveshchenniia," TsGIAL, fond 735, opis' 1, no. 449, p. 13.

11. Uvarov's copy of the statute is preserved in "Proekt obshchego ustava rossiiskikh universitetov, s sobstvennymi ispravleniiami S. S. Uvarova," TsGIAL, fond 737, opis' 1, no. 4.

12. For a comparison of the 1804 and 1835 statutes, see D. I. Bagalei, *Opyt istorii Khar'kovskago universiteta*, I (Khar'kov, 1894), pp. 1–28; *Sravnitel'naia tablitsa ustavov universitetov 1884, 1863, 1835 i 1804 gg.* (St. Petersburg, 1901); *SPMNP*, II, 1: 476–78 (May 1, 1832); 533–36 (December 14, 1832); 647–57 (November 8 and December 13, 1833); and 667–84 (December 25, 1833).

13. Rozhdestvenskii, *Obzor*, pp. 243–44; Allister, "Reform," pp. 117–23; Uvarov, "Otchet za 1835," p. vii; *SPMNP*, II, 1: 981 (July 26, 1835).

14. Rozhdestvenskii, *Obzor*, pp. 185–86; Bagalei, *Opyt'*, p. 117; Korbut, *Kazanskii universitet*, p. 31.

15. *SPMNP*, II, 1: 972–88 (July 26, 1835); Rozhdestvenskii, *Obzor*, p. 246.

16. Bagalei, although he complains of the reduction of autonomy, admits professors would have more time for scholarly work (*Kratkii ocherk istorii Khar'kovskago universiteta za pervye sto let ego sushchestvovaniia* [Khar'kov, 1906], pp. 117, 125).

17. Rozhdestvenskii, *Obzor*, p. 185; V. S. Ikonnikov, "Russkie universitety v sviazi s khodom obshchestvennago obrazovaniia," *Vestnik Evropy* 62 (November 1876): 90–92; Reisner, *Nationalism*, pp. 32–33, 121–22, 130–31, 203; Mulhern,

History of Education, p. 536; Paulsen, *German Education*, pp. 185–91; Moody, *French Education*, p. 24.

18. Vetrinskii, *Granovskii*, p. 146; V. Iakushkin, "Iz istorii russkikh universitetov," *Vestnik vospitaniia* 7 (October 1901): 42; Buslaev, "Vospominaniia," pp. 513–48; Bagalei, *Kratkii ocherk*, pp. 121–26; Korbut, *Kazanskii universitet*, p. 25; A. A. Chumikov, "Studencheskiia korporatsii v Peterburgskom universitete v 1830–1840 gg.," in *Russkie universitety*, p. 157; Steinger, "Government Policy," pp. 200, 206; Besançon, *Éducation*, p. 52; B. G. Kuznetsov, *Lomonosov, Lobachevskii, Mendeleev* (Moscow, 1945), pp. 138–55.

19. Uvarov, *Desiatiletie*, p. 27; and *Otchet za 1838*, p. 10; "Otchet za 1835," *ZMNP*, pp. xxxviii, xli; "Shtaty i prilozheniia," *SPMNP*, II, 1: 18–19, 34–38; Allister, "Reform," p. 78; Blackwell, *Russian Industrialization*, p. 374; Egorov, "Russkie universitety," p. 205; Korbut, *Kazanskii universitet*, p. 67; S. P. Shevyrev, *Istoriia Imperatorskago Moskovskago universiteta, 1755–1855* (Moscow, 1855), p. 489; Steinger's "Government Policy" contains a compilation of statistics on library and laboratory acquisitions (pp. 208–12).

20. Lenore O'Boyle, "The Problem of an Excess of Educated Men in Western Europe, 1800–1850," *Journal of Modern History* 42 (1970): 471–95; Uvarov, "Zapiska," quoted in V. Ia. Stoiunin, "Konservatory sorokovykh godov," in *Istoricheskii vestnik*, VII, pp. 22–23; Ringer, *Education*, pp. 46, 50, 291.

21. Galskoy contains a good analysis based on archival sources ("The Ministry of Education," pp. 228–32). Rozhdestvenskii, *Obzor*, pp. 186–87, 251–53; Ikonnikov, "Universitety," *Vestnik Evropy* 10 (1876): 529; *SPMNP*, II, 1: 95–101 (October 14, 1827); 107–11 (November 29, 1827); 131–34 (February 20, 1828); *SPMNP*, II, 1: 662–67; *Avtobiografiia Kostomarova*, p. 141, as quoted in Pelech, "Ukrainian Ideologues," p. 147.

22. Uvarov, *Desiatiletie*, pp. 31–32, 82–86; and "Otchet za 1836," *ZMNP*, p. cxxiv. *SPMNP*, II, 2: 751–58 (January 3, 1846); *SPMNP*, II, 2: 647, 994; Shevyrev, *Istoriia*, pp. 493, 509; Bagalei, *Kratkii ocherk*, p. 146; "O litsakh, komandirovannykh ministerstvom narodnago prosveshcheniia za granitsu dlia prigotovleniia k zvaniiu professorov i prepodavatelei s 1808 po 1860 god," *ZMNP* 121 (1864): 335–60, a list supplemented by the yearly *otchety*.

23. Uvarov, "Otchet za 1835," *ZMNP*, pp. ix, xxxiii, xxiv; Uvarov, *Otchet za 1838*, p. 6; *Otchet za 1846*, p. 9. *SPMNP*, II, 1: 988–93 (July 26, 1835); *SPMNP*, II, 2: 405–8 (June 28, 1843); N. K. Kozmin, "N. I. Nadezhdin—professor Moskovskago universiteta," *ZMNP* 5 (1907): 124–25; Korbut, *Kazanskii universitet*, p. 52; Bagalei, *Opyt*, pp. 26–27; Johnson, *Heritage*, p. 105; A. A. Kizevetter, "Moskovskii universitet (Istoricheskii ocherk)," in V. B. El'iashevich et al., *Moskovskii universitet, 1755–1930* (Paris, 1930), p. 101; Nikitenko, *Diary* (entry of May 12, 1832), p. 38.

24. *SPMNP*, II, 1: 972 (July 26, 1835); R. G. McPherson, *Theory of Higher Education in Nineteenth-Century England* (Athens, Ga., 1959), p. 17.

25. Pogodin, *God v chuzhikh kraiakh* (Moscow, 1844), p. 7.

26. L. A. Ushakova, *T. N. Granovskii i ego rol' v ideinoi bor'be Rossii 30kh–40kh godov XIX veka* (Tomsk, 1956), pp. 89–103; "A. I. Turgenev v ego pis'makh—1844," *RS* 34 (May 1882): 457; Ostrovitianov, *Istoriia*, II (Moscow, 1964), pp. 190–93; *Letters of Pushkin* (c. September 30, 1832), II, p. 560; Pogodin, *Kratkoe nachertanie russkoi istorii* (Moscow, 1838).

27. N. Ustrialov, *O sisteme pragmaticheskoi russkoi istorii* (St. Petersburg, 1836), 84 pp.; "Vospominaniia o moei zhizni," *Drevnaia i novaia Rossiia* (January 1877): 26–42; and ibid., (August 1880): 603–86.

28. Ustrialov was also encouraged to write a history of the reign of Nicholas I which was published in 1847 and translated into Polish, Swedish, English, and

German and censored by Nicholas himself; Ustrialov compared the tsar, as usual, with Peter the Great. He also got unprecedented permission from Uvarov to have access to all archival documents for a history of Peter the Great (Uvarov, *Desiatiletie*, p. 87; "Iz novonaidennykh zapisnykh knizhek V. A. Mukhanova," *RA* 38, No. 2 [1900]: 316; V. V. Grigor'ev, *Imperatorskii S.-Peterburgskii universitet* [St. Petersburg, 1870], pp. 222–24; "Ocherki i vospominaniia N. M. Kolmakova," *RS* 70, No. 5 [1891]: 468; Ustrialov, *Russkaia istoriia* [St. Petersburg, 1839]; and *Istoricheskoe obozrenie tsarstvovania gosudaria imperatora Nikolaia I* [St. Petersburg, 1847]; *Khar'kovskii gosudarstvennyi universitet im. A. M. Gor'kogo za 150 let* [Khar'kov, 1955], p. 32; Pelech, "Ukrainian Ideologues," pp. 59–62; "Tsenzura," pp. 427–31).

29. Ushakova, *Granovskii*, pp. 115–18; Schapiro, *Rationalism*, pp. 73–80; Vucinich, *Science*, pp. 277–79; N. M. Tikhomirov, ed., *Istoriia Moskovskogo universiteta*, I (Moscow, 1955), pp. 167–71, 322–24; Iu. Sokolov, "Granovskii i Shevyrev," *Golos minuvshago* 3 (March 1913): 212–16. On Granovskii, Kavelin, and Solov'ev as historians, consult Netting, "Liberalism," pp. 198–302; Pypin, *Istoriia russkoi etnografii*, II, pp. 1–47.

30. Ostrovitianov, *Istoriia*, pp. 182–98; Pletnev, "O narodnosti," pp. 1–30.

31. G. Luciani, *Le Livre de la genèse du peuple ukrainien* (Paris, 1956), p. 79; K. Grot, "K istorii slavianskago samosoznaniia i slavianskikh sochuvstvii v russkom obshchestve (Iz 40 kh godov XIX stoletiia)," *Pravitel'stvennyi vestnik*, nos. 195–98; Pogodin, *Istoriko-politicheskie pis'ma i zapiski vprodolzhenii voiny*, 1853–1856 (letters to Uvarov from 1839 to 1842 on his visits to Slavic countries) (Moscow, 1874), pp. 15–39; Ostrovitianov, *Istoriia*, pp. 198–208; A. A. Kochubinskii, *Nachal'nye gody russkago slavianovedeniia* (Odessa, 1888); V. Frantsev, *I. I. Sreznevskii i slavianstvo* (Petrograd, 1914), p. 74, as quoted in Pelech, "Ukrainian Ideologues," p. 80; Pypin, *Etnografii*, II, pp. 75–109; and *Etnografii*, III, pp. 88–113.

32. A. S. Fisher, "O khode obrazovaniia v Rossii i ob uchastii, kakoe dolzhna prinimat' v nem filosofiia," *ZMNP* 6, No. 1 (1835): 28–68; A. Kraevskii, "Sovremennoe sostoianie filosofii v Frantsii i novaia sistema sei nauki, osnovyvaemaia Botenom," *ZMNP* 1, No. 3 (1834): 317–77; I. Kroneberg, "O izuchenii slovesnosti," *ZMNP* 8, No. 11 (1835): 256; Allister, "Reform," p. 54; I. I. Panaev, *Vospominaniia* (Moscow, 1950), p. 56.

33. Vetrinskii, *Granovskii*, p. 152; Besançon, *Éducation*, p. 54; F. I. Buslaev, "Vospominaniia," *Russkie universitety*, p. 142; Davydov, "Vozmozhna li u nas germanskaia filosofiia?" *Moskvitianin* 2, No. 3 (1842): 385–401; "Pis'mo I. I. Davydova k M. P. Pogodinu" (March 12, 1841), PD, fond 231, ed. 5; Z. A. Kamenskii, *Russkaia filosofiia nachala XIX veka: Shelling* (Moscow, 1980), pp. 3–15; Chizhevskii, *Gegel'*, pp. 222–26.

34. Kroneberg, "O izuchenii slovesnosti," p. 269; I. Snegirev, "O predmete i tseli drevnostei rimskikh," *ZMNP* 8, No. 11 (1835): 301–13; M. Rozberg, "Glavnyia svoistva grecheskoi i rimskoi slovesnosti," *ZMNP* 3, No. 7 (1834): 1–26; Uvarov, *Desiatiletie*, p. 20; "Moskovskii universitet" and "Iz zapisok S. M. Solov'eva," in *Russkie universitety*, pp. 175 and 165, respectively.

35. Wortman, *Russian Legal Consciousness*, pp. 45–46, 49–50; Grigor'ev, *Universitet*, pp. 109–12. On the lycées, see Allister, "Reform," pp. 139–45, 281; Nikitenko, *Diary* (entry of December 30, 1836), p. 66; A. A. Sinel, "The Socialization of the Russian Bureaucratic Elite: Life at the Tsarskoe Selo Lyceum and the School of Jurisprudence," *Russian History* 3 (1976): 1–31; Uvarov, *Desiatiletie*, p. 17; *SPMNP* II, 1: 490–95 (October 7, 1832); 627–31 (August 2, 1833); and 1264–82 (May 29, 1837); *SPMNP*, II, 2: 30–37 (April 24, 1840); and 668–80 (November 22, 1845).

36. Grigor'ev, *Peterburgskii universitet*, p. 112; Rozhdestvenskii, *Obzor*, pp. 246–47; Bagalei, *Khar'kovskii universitet*, pp. 15–17; "Ob ustroistve juridicheskikh fakul'tetov v inostrannykh universitetakh," *ZMNP* 1, No. 1 (1834): 331; K. Nevolin,

"O soedinenii teorii s praktikoiu v izuchenii zakonov i v deloproizvodstve," *ZMNP* 8, No. 12 (1835): 455; V. Androssov, "O predelakh, v koikh dolzhny byt' izuchaemy i prepodavaemy prava politicheskoe i narodnoe," *ZMNP* 4, No. 12 (1834): 367–85; A. V. Ivanovskii, "O nacahalkh postepennago usovershenstvovaniia nashego gosudarstva," *ZMNP* 13, No. 1 (1837): 1–15.

37. Wortman, *Russian Legal Consciousness*, pp. 95, 224–27; *SPMNP*, II, 1: 131–32 (February 20, 1828); Shevyrev, *Istoriia*, pp. 174–77; "Moskovskii universitet i disput Granovskago po vospominaniiam A. N. Afanaseva," in *Russkie universitety*, pp. 168, 179; J. Frank, *Dostoevsky*, p. 241.

38. Uvarov, *Desiatiletie*, pp. 21–22; and *Otchet za 1834*, p. 76; Grigor'ev, *Peterburgskii universitet*, p. 109; Vucinich, *Science*, 332–33; Egorov, "Reaktsionnaia politika tsarizma v voprosakh universitetskogo obrazovaniia v 30–50kh gg XII v.," *Istoricheskie nauki* (1960): 75; *SPMNP*, II, 1: 971 (July 26, 1835); and "Shtaty i prilozheniia," pp. 34–38.

39. Vucinich, *Science*, pp. 322–26, 329, 331–33; Blackwell, *Russian Industrialization*, p. 370; Ostrovitianov, *Istoriia*, pp. 132–33, 349–55.

40. Shevyrev, *Istoriia*, pp. 131–60; Tikhomirov, *Istoriia*, pp. 133–34, 141–45, 152–61; Blackwell, *Russian Industrialization*, pp. 356–61; S. S. Dmitrev, "Le Voyage agronomique du professeur Iu. A. Linovskii en France en 1842–1844," in *La Russie et l'Europe: XVIᵉ–XXᵉ Siècle* (Paris, 1970), pp. 103–23; Kamenskii, *Shelling*, pp. 28–267. Pirogov is quoted in Vucinich, *Science*, p. 342; also see pp. 280–86, 335–37. Mudrov is quoted in R. E. McGrew, *Russia and the Cholera, 1823–1832* (Madison, Wis., 1965), p. 33. Also see Paulsen, *German Education*, p. 192.

41. Grigor'ev, *Peterburgskii universitet*, pp. 86, 92, 180–85, 190–96, 208–13; Blackwell, *Russian Industrialization*, pp. 357, 366–71, 384; Vucinich, *Science*, pp. 301–5, 308–9, 326–31, 345; Ostrovitianov, *Istoriia*, pp. 47–51, 66–77, 281–306, 345–53; Uvarov, "Otchet za 1836," *ZMNP*, pp. vii–viii; and *Otchet za 1838*, p. 9; Steinger, "Government Policy," pp. 191–95.

42. Polievktov, *Nikolai I*, pp. 241–42; F. B. Artz, *The Development of Technical Education in France, 1500–1850* (Cambridge, Mass., 1966); Meyers, *Modernization*, p. 10; Musgrave, *Society and Education*, pp. 17–18, 53; Moody, *French Education*, p. 41; Paulsen, *German Education*, pp. 196–97; Shabaev, ed., *Ocherki*, pp. 236–54.

43. Uvarov, "Otchet za 1836," *ZMNP*, pp. vii–viii; *Otchet za 1837*, pp. 12, 62; *Otchet za 1838*, pp. 7, 27, 44, 54; and *Otchet za 1839*, p. 5; *SPMNP*, II, 2: 567 (November 14, 1844); *SPMNP*, II, 2: 137, 231, 310, 329, 339, 763; Shevyrev, *Istoriia*, p. 569; Vucinich, *Science*, p. 331; B. E. Raikov, "Evoliutsionnaia ideia v trudakh russkikh akademikov XVIII i pervoi poloviny XIX veka," *Vestnik Akademii nauk SSSR* 3 (1946): 37–46.

44. Uvarov, *Otchet za 1840*, pp. 7, 24; *SPMNP*, II, 1: 978 (July 26, 1835); S. Kutorga, "Vzgliad na izuchenie estestvennoi istorii," *ZMNP* 8, No. 11 (1835): 290–300; V. F. Fedorov, "Rech'," *ZMNP* 25, No. 1 (1840): 112; Kizevetter, "Moskovskii universitet," p. 99.

45. On learned societies, consult Vucinich, *Science*, pp. 348–60; E. V. Soboleva, *Borba za reorganizatsiiu peterburgskoi Akademii nauk v seredine XIX veka* (Leningrad, 1971), p. 15.

46. Ringer, *Education*, p. 51; Blackwell, *Russian Industrialization*, p. 32; Vucinich, *Science*, p. 360; Paulsen, *German Education*, p. 193; Allister ("Reform," pp. 288–89) has compiled a table of graduates.

47. *SPMNP*, II, 1: 971–72 (July 26, 1835): McGrew, *Cholera*, pp. 27–28, 130; Allister, "Reform," pp. 183–90; Shevyrev, *Istoriia*, pp. 161–63; A. Val'ter, "Shkoly i stremleniia v russkoi meditsine," *Russkii vestnik* 23 (1859): 247–52.

48. Uvarov, *Desiatiletie*, pp. 71–73; *Otchet za 1838*, p. 7; *Otchet za 1839*, p. 26; *Otchet za 1840*, p. 34; *Otchet za 1841*, p. 11; and *Otchet za 1846*, p. 123. Uvarov took

a personal interest in the architecture of the buildings: "Pis'ma Shchedrinu" (December 17, 1842; February [n.d.] 1843; and March 4, 1843), GIM, fond 404, ed. 15; *SPMNP*, II, 1: 687 (January 2, 1834); and 1437–58 (December 28, 1838); *SPMNP*, II, 2: 47 (April 27 and 29, 1840); 85–86 (July 22, 1840); 91–98 (August 20, 1840): 173–74 (December 4, 1840); 189–90 (January 2, 1841); 190–91 (January 3, 1841); 226–27 (March 13, 1841); 296–302 (December 30, 1841); 360–66 (October 14, 1842); 687–711 (December 7, 1845); and 720–48 (December 18, 1845). Also consult N. M. Frieden's seminal study, *Russian Physicians in an Era of Reform and Revolution, 1856–1905* (Princeton, N.J., 1981), pp. 29–36.

49. Uvarov, *Desiatiletie*, pp. 19–20; and "Otchet za 1836," p. cxxviii.

50. *SPMNP*, II, 1: 1–3 (December 29, 1825); Buslaev, "Vospominaniia," p. 51 E. A. Matisen, "Vospominaniia iz dal'nikh let," *RS* 5 (1881): 154–57; N. OzhedeRankur, "V dvukh universitetakh," *RS* 26, No. 6 (1896): 571–73; P. D. Boborykin, "Moi vospominaniia," *Russkaia mysl'* 5 (1906): 75; Egorov, "Politika," pp. 68–69; Bagalei, *Kratkii ocherk*, p. 102; TsGIAL, fond 733, opis' 69, ed. 514, pp. 1–2.

51. Uvarov, *Desiatiletie*, pp. 19–20; *SPMNP*, II, 1: 73–74 (September 1, 1827); 742–46 (February 27, 1834); 826–42 (October 18, 1834); 977–78 (July 26, 1835); and 1245–47 (April 8, 1837); Rozhdestvenskii, *Obzor*, pp. 188–89, 258; Tikhomirov, *Istoriia*, p. 111; Musin-Pushkin is quoted in Egorov, "Politika," p. 68.

52. Afanasev, "Moskovskii universitet," pp. 358–61; Ashevskii, "Iz istorii," in *Russkie universitety*, pp. 108–09, 112; N. A. Popov, "Iz vospominaniia starago studenta. Pamiati P. S. Nakhimova," in *Russkie universitety*, pp. 136–37; Kizevetter, "Moskovskii universitet," pp. 116–17; N. Dmitriev, "Studencheskie vospominaniia o Moskovskom universitete," *Otechestvennye zapiski* 119, Nos. 8, 9, and 10 (1858–1859), pp. 81–95, 1–15, and 1–14, respectively; V. V. Mavrodin, ed., *Peterburgskii universitet, 1819–1895*, vol. I of *Leningradskii universitet v vospominaniiakh sovremennikov* (Leningrad, 1963), pp. 42–44. On the strict rules at Kharkov, see Galskoy, "Ministry," pp. 266–68.

53. Afanasev, "Moskovskii universitet," p. 393; Mavrodin, *Leningradskii universitet*, pp. 43–44; A. A. Chumikov, "Studencheskiia korporatsii v Peterburgskom universitete v 1830–1840 gg.," *RS* 2 (1881): 367–80; Ozhe-de-Rankur, "V dvukh universitetakh," p. 573; "Iz avtobiografii N. I. Kostomarova," in *Russkie universitety*, p. 154; Afanasev, "Disput," pp. 169–70.

54. Kozmin, "Nadezhdin," pp. 125–28; Vetrinskii, *Granovskii*, p. 146.

55. Uvarov, *Desiatiletie*, pp. 17–19; and *Otchet za 1841*, p. 104; *SPMNP*, II, 1: 1252–56 (April 26 and 28, 1837). N. N. Kalugin, "Studenty moskovskago universiteta v byloe vremia," *RA* 11 (1907): 427; Johnson, *Heritage*, pp. 103–4; Shevyrev, *Istoriia*, p. 509; *SPMNP*, II, 2: 476–85 (April 6, 1844).

56. Uvarov, "Otchet za 1834," *ZMNP*, p. cl; B. Frommett, *Ocherki po istorii studentchestva v Rossii* (St. Petersburg, 1912), pp. 18–21; Rozhdestvenskii, *Obzor*, pp. 188, 253.

57. M. F. Vladimirskii-Budanov, *Istoriia Imperatorskago universiteta Sv. Vladimira* (Kiev, 1884), pp. 317–18; "Ob ukraino-slavianskom obshchestve: Iz bumagi D. P. Golokhvostova," *RA* 23, No. 7 (1892): 334; *SPMNP*, II, 2: 331–48 (June 9, 1842); Buslaev, "Vospominaniia," p. 139.

58. For charts on 1836, 1843, and 1848, consult Egorov, "Politika," pp. 61–63; and Allister, "Reform," pp. 240–41, 284–87; P. N. Miliukov, *Ocherki po istorii russkoi kultury*, II (St. Petersburg, 1899), pp. 329, 348. For Halle, see Ringer, *Education*, pp. 81–82, 232–36. On the "democracy" of the universities, see Ashevskii, "Iz istorii," pp. 123–25; Kizevetter, "Moskovskii universitet," p. 115; and Herzen, *My Past and Thoughts*, p. 82.

59. "Uvarov, "Otchet za 1835," *ZMNP*, p. cxxxv; Aksakov, *Vospominaniia*, pp.

37–39; Ozhe-de-Rankur, "V dvukh universitetakh," p. 571; Korbut, *Kazanskii universitet*, p. 70; A. A. Chumikov, "Peterburgskii universitet polveka nazad," *RA* 3 (1888): 125–26; W. B. Lincoln, "The Ministers of Nicholas I," p. 314; Shepelev, *Chiny*, pp. 67–68.

60. Uvarov, *Otchet za 1839*, pp. 2–5; *Otchet za 1841*, p. 6; and "O denezhnom sbore s svoekoshtnykh studentov i vol'noslushatelei universitetov," TsGIAL, fond 733, opis' 23, ed. 70, pp. 19–56 ; Tikhomirov, *Istoriia*, pp. 112–13; Mavrodin, *Leningradskii universitet*, p. 266; Bagalei, *Kratkii ocherk*, p. 157; N. V. Shelgunov, *Vospominániia* (Moscow, 1923), p. 266; Egorov, "Russkie universitety," p. 137. Roughly 20 percent of the nobility were in the medical faculty, compared to a figure as high as 60 percent of the *raznochintsy*.

61. Rozhdestvenskii, *Obzor*, pp. 253–58; Egorov, "Politika," pp. 62–64; Uvarov, "Tsirkularnoe predlozhenie," TsGIAL, fond 733, opis' 69, ed. 514, p. 16. On the whole tuition question, refer to the excellent article by James Flynn, "Tuition and Social Class in the Russian Universities: S. S. Uvarov and 'Reaction' in the Russia of Nicholas I," *Slavic Review* 35, No. 2 (June 1976): 232–47; Nikitenko, *Diary*, (entry of December 22, 1842), p. 91.

62. *SPMNP*, II, 2: 629–32 (June 11, 1845); and 632–34 (June 14, 1845).

63. Uvarov, *Otchet za 1847*, pp. 4–6; *SPMNP*, II, 2: 762–81 (March 1, 1846); and 862–866 (June 16, 1847); Egorov, "Politika," p. 64; Allister, "Reform," p. 246.

64. Wortman, *Russian Legal Consciousness*, p. 223; Pintner, "Russian Civil Service," p. 55; also see Pintner's "Social Characteristics," pp. 429–33. For similar conclusions see Starr, *Decentralization*, pp. 122–38; Lincoln, "Genesis," pp. 321–30.

65. Zaionchkovskii, "Vysshaia biurokratiia," pp. 154–64; and Zaionchkovskii, *Pravitel'stvennyi apparat samoderzhavnoi Rossii v XIX v.* (Moscow, 1978), pp. 106–78; Wortman, *Russian Legal Consciousness*, p. 70; Brower, *Nihilists*, pp. 55–56.

66. *Zhurnaly zasedaniia uchenago komiteta Glavnago upravleniia uchilishch po proektu obshchago ustava rossiiskikh universitetov* (St. Petersburg, 1862), pp. 3–16, as quoted in Alston, *Education*, p. 52.

67. Uvarov, "Kratkaia zapiska ob Imperatorskoi akademii nauk v Peterburge," *Chteniia v Imperatorskom obshchestve istorii i drevnostei rossiiskikh pri Moskovskom universitete* 3 (1865): 336–39; Vucinich, *Science*, p. 239. For laudatory summaries of Uvarov's activity as president, see "Pamiati Grafa Sergeia Semenovicha Uvarova, 1855," *Sochineniia i perepiska P. A. Pletneva*, III, ed. Ia. Grot (St. Petersburg, 1885), pp. 149–226; and "Iubilei prezidenta AN, S. S. Uvarova," *Moskvitianin* 2, No. 3 (1843): 265–86.

68. Pletnev, "Pamiati," pp. 166–69; Ostrovitianov, *Istoriia*, p. 254; P. Savel'ev, *O zhizni i trudakh de Sasi* (St. Petersburg, 1839).

69. *Sobranie aktov torzhestvennago zasedaniia Imp. Spb. AN byvshago po sluchaiu prazdnovaniia stoletniago eia sushchestvovaniia 29 dekabria 1826 goda* (St. Petersburg, 1827); Pletnev, "Pamiati," p. 167; Ostrovitianov, *Istoriia*, pp. 21–22; Rozhdestvenskii, *Obzor*, pp. 96–97; Fuss, "Coup d'oeil," p. 191; Kniazev, *Kratkii ocherk*, p. 29; "Séance solennelle de l'Académie tenue en l'honneur de son président M. S. d'Ouvaroff le 12 Janvier 1843," *Recueil des actes des séances publiques de l'Académie imperiale des sciences* (St. Petersburg, 1843), p. 176.

70. V. I. Vernadskii, "Pamiati akademika K. M. fon Bera," *Trudy Komissii po istorii znanii* (Leningrad, 1927), pp. 5–6.

71. B. E. Raikov, *Karl Ber, ego zhizn' i trudy* (Moscow, 1961); Ostrovitianov, *Istoriia*, pp. 103–4, 113–14, 150–54; Vucinich, *Science*, pp. 296–99.

72. Uvarov, *Desiatiletie*, p. 87; Ostrovitianov, *Istoriia*, pp. 66–77, 129–39; Vucinich, *Science*, pp. 299–304; Blackwell, *Russian Industrialization*, pp. 398–401.

73. Ostrovitianov, *Istoriia*, pp. 34–52; Vucinich, *Science*, pp. 308–14.

74. Uvarov, *Desiatiletie*, pp. 78–86; Barsukov, *Stroev*, pp. 158–59; V. F. Gnuchev, *Materialy dlia istorii ekspeditsii Akademii nauk v XVIII i XIX vekakh* (Moscow, 1940), p. 163; *Perepiska Aleksandra Gumbol'dta s uchenymi i gosudarstvennymi deiateliami Rossii* (November 23, 1829, and to 1842) (Moscow, 1962), p. 95; Ostrovitianov, *Istoriia*, pp. 109–17; Vucinich, *Science*, pp. 304–5.

75. Uvarov, *Desiatiletie*, pp. 89–94; "Otchet za 1836," p. cxviii; A. A. Kotliarevskii, *Sochineniia*, IV (St. Petersburg, 1895), pp. 247–48; *Arkheograficheskaia ekspeditsiia Akademii nauk, 1828–1834. Sbornik materialov*, I (Leningrad, 1930); Gnuchev, *Materialy*; Vucinich, *Science*, p. 353. For cumulative listings of the work of the commission, see its reports in *ZMNP* 24, No. 4 (1842): 79–126; and *ZMNP* 60, No. 1 (1849): 11–20; Barsukov, *Zhizn' Stroeva*, pp. 158–59, 217–44, 257–93; P. Pekarskii, *Istoriia AN v Peterburge* (St. Petersburg, 1870), p. 401.

76. "Biblioteka Akademi nauk v pervoi polovine XIX v.," in *Istoriia biblioteki Akademii nauk SSSR*, ed. S. P. Luppov et al. (Moscow, 1964), pp. 162–224; Uvarov, *Desiatiletie*, pp. 76–77; Pletnev, "Pamiati," p. 210; *Ocherk istorii muzeev Imperatorskoi Akademii nauk* (St. Petersburg, 1865); Ostrovitianov, *Istoriia*, pp. 30, 237–43.

77. Uvarov, *Desiatiletie*, pp. 87–89; *SPMNP*, II, 1: 761–62 (April 12, 1834); 1276–1382 (June 19, 1838); the file is located in TsGIAL, fond 733, opis' 2, no. 40; E. I. Vintergal'ter, *Sto let Pulkovskoi observatorii* (Moscow, 1945); Ostrovitianov, *Istoriia*, pp. 84–101.

78. Uvarov, *Desiatiletie*, pp. 75–76; *SPMNP*, II, 1: 1046–74 (January 8, 1836); Kniazev, *Kratkii ocherk*, pp. 30–35; Ostrovitianov, *Istoriia*, pp. 15–17, 21–23, 254; Vucinich, *Science*, pp. 295–96 Soboleva, *Borba*, pp. 37–38; Polievktov, *Nikolai I*, p. 229.

79. Uvarov, *Desiatiletie*, pp. 77–78; *SPMNP*, II, 2: 256–66 (June 12 and October 19, 1841); Soboleva, *Borba*, p. 96–98; Ostrovitianov, *Istoriia*, pp. 24–26; Ia. K. Grot, *Piatidesiatiletie otdeleniia russkago iazyka i slovesnosti Imp. Akademii nauk, 1841–1891* (St. Petersburg, 1892), pp. 2–5; Barsukov, *Stroev*, VI, pp. 243–44.

80. Drawn from "Spisok deistvitel'nykh chlenov Akademii nauk s 1803 po 1917 g.," in Ostrovitianov, *Istoriia*, pp. 712–18.

CHAPTER 8

1. On this question, consult H. Carrère d'Encausse, *Decline of an Empire: The Soviet Socialist Republics in Revolt* (New York, 1980).

2. Uvarov, *Desiatiletie*, pp. 36, 46, 68–69.

3. See chap. 5 and 7, as well as this chapter.

4. Uvarov, *Otchet za 1837*, p. 95.

5. Lithuania and White Russia included the provinces of Vilna, Grodnonsk, Kovensk, Minsk, Mogilev, and Vitebsk; the Left Bank Ukraine consisted of those of Kharkov, Chernigov, and Poltava, with the Right Bank provinces being Kiev, Volyn', and Posolia. The statistics are drawn from V..M. Kabuzan, *Narodonaselenie Rossii v XVIII–pervoi polovine XIX v.* (Moscow, 1963), pp. 160–62.

6. Kabuzan and S. M. Troitsskii, "Izmeneniia v chislennosti, udel'nom vese i razmeshchenii dvorianstva v Rossii v 1783–1858 gg.," *Isto riia SSSR* 4 (1971): 153–69; D. Beauvois, *Lumières et société en Europe de l'est: L'Université de Vilna et les écoles polonaises de l'empire russe, 1803–1832* (Paris, 1977), p.619.

7. Uvarov, *Desiatiletie*, pp. 35–36.

8. I.N. Borozdin, "Universitety y Rossii v pervoi polovine XIX veke," in *Istoriia Rossii v XIX veke*, II (St. Petersburg, 1910), p. 36 7; Kniazkov and Serboy, *Ocherk*, pp. 222–29; Charnoluskii, "Narodnoe obrazovanie," in *Istoriia Rossii*, IV, pp. 88–91, 113–14; "Protasov k Uvarovu" (June 13, 1834), TsGIAL, fond 735, opis' 10,

ed. khr. 293a, 1. 242; *SPMNP* II, 1: 476–79 (May 1, 1832). (References to *SPMNP* carry the date of the document. Entries consist mainly of decrees, laws, and reports.) On this question in general, consult V. Ia. Shul'gin, "Istoricheskoe obozrenie uchebnykh zavedenii v iugozapadnoi Rjossii s kontsa XVIII veka do otkrytiia universiteta v Kieve: Istoriia Universiteta Sv. Vladimira," *Russkoe slovo* 10 (October 1859): 1–62.

9. Beauvois, *Lumières*, pp. 214, 399, 888, 911.

10. Uvarov, *Desiatiletie*, p. 45; and "Dva pis'ma k shefu zhandarmov grafu A. Kh. Benkendorfu" (October 14, 1832, and March 29, 1833), *RA* 1 (1885): 366–69; Vladimirskii-Budanov, *Istoriia*, p. 163.

11. See chap. 7; Uvarov, *Desiatiletie*, pp. 37–40; M. Maksimo vich, "Ob uchastii i znachenii Kieva v obshchei zhizni Rossii," *ZMNP* 16 (October 1837): 1–29; S. I. Ponomarev, " M. A. Maksimovich," *ZMNP* 158 (October 1872): 217; Vladimirskii-Budanov, *Istoriia*, p. 83; Borozdin, "Universitety," p. 371; I. I. Davydov, "Izvestiia zhizni i deiatel'nosti byvshego prezidenta akademii nauk Grafa Uvarova," in *Otchety Imp. AN po oteleniiu russkago iazy ka i slovesnosti za* 1852–1865 (St. Petersburg, 1866), pp. 166–67; Shil'der, *Nikolai Pervyi*, II, p. 60; *SPMNP*, II, 1: 533–36 (December 14, 1832); 540–42 (February 28, 1833); 554–55 (May 1, 1833); 562 (May 5, 1833); 564 (May 14, 1833); 578 (June 6, 1833); 634 (September 5, 1833); 636 (September 26, 1833); 647–58 (November 8, 4, and 13, 1833); 660 (November 14, 1833); 668–84 (December 25, 1833); 688–90 (January 3, 1834); 711 (February 20, 1834); 799–803 (July 5, 1835); 1154–56 (July 6, 1836); 1183 (October 14, 1836); 1457 (January 1, 1839).

12. *SPMNP*, II, 1: 574–78 (May 23, 1833); 1084–85 (March 3, 1836); and 1093–94 (March 20, 1836); Vladimirskii-Budanov, *Istoriia*, pp. 65–74.

13. On Maksimovich, see Pelech, "Ukrainian Ideologues," pp. 92–96, 109–13; Pypin, *Etnografii*, III, pp. 15–37.

14. Nikitenso, *Diary* (entry of January 21, 1835), pp. 59–60; Gogol, "Plan pre-podavaniia vseobshchei istorii," *ZMNP* 1, No. 2 (February 1834): 189–209; *Letters of Pushkin* (May 13, 1834), II; Vladimirskii-Budanov, *Istoriia*, pp. 83–86, 103–17; V. I. Shul'gin, *Istoriia universiteta sv. Vladimira* (St. Petersburg, 1860), pp. 25–29, 66; Ustrialov, *O russkoi istorii*, p. 3; "M. A. Maksimovich," *RA* 9, No. 12 (December 1874): 1975–76; Kostomarov, *Avtobiografiia*, pp. 190–92.

15. Uvarov, *Desiatiletie*, pp. 46–47; Rozhdestvenskii, *Obzor*, pp. 304–5; Vladi-mirskii-Budanov, *Istoriia*, pp. 91–95; Shulgin, *Istoriia*, pp. 38–51.

16. "Avtobiograficheskiia zapiski E. F. von Bradke," *RA* 3 (1875): 257–94; Shul'gin, *Istoriia*, pp. 66–68.

17. Uvarov, *Desiatiletie*, pp. 43–44; "Otchet za 1835," *ZMNP*, P. lxxxvii; *Otchet za* 1840, p. 8; *Otchet za* 1841, p. 9; *Otchet za* 1843, pp. 8, 103 ; and *Otchet za* 1845, p. 105; Rozhdestvenskii, *Obzor*, pp. 306–8; Shabaev, *Ocherki*, pp. 389–447. *SPMNP*, II, 1: 953–54 (July 16, 1835); and 1423–30 (December 7, 1838); *SPMNP*, II, 2: 12 (March 5, 1840); 158–59 (November 6, 1840); 291–92 (November 18, 1841); 327–30 (May 26, 1842); 403–5 (June 15, 1843); 39 (April 23, 1840); 82 (June 26, 1840); 83–84 (July 17, 1840); 281 (October 22, 1841); and 186–90 (December 16, 1840).

18. The number of students in the Odessa district tripled during Uvarov's ministry (from 3,245 to 9,059) and rose substantially in Kiev 6,203 to 10, 759) and in White Russia (from 10,700 to 13,645). See Uvarov, *Desiatiletie*, p. 37; "Otchet za 1835," *ZMNP*, p. lxxxvi; *SPMNP*, II, 1: 481–82 (July 7, 1832); 560 (May 9, 1833); 661 (November 14, 1833); 1012 (November 2, 1835); 1014 (November 1, 1835); 1080 (January 29, 1836).

19. Uvarov, *Desiatiletie*, pp. 46; Rozhdestvenskii, *Obzor*, pp. 299, 304–5; "Mak-simovich," *RA*, p. 1075; *SPMNP*, II, 1: 899–902 (March 25, 1835).

20. Uvarov, *Desiatiletie*, pp. 40–41; Pelech, "Ukrainian Ideologues," pp. 113–14; "Bibikov k von Bradke" (May 25, 1838), TsGIAL, fond 735, opis' 10, ed. khr. 293,

p. 480; Vladimirskii-Budanov, *Istoriia*, pp. 127–31, 138–55; Shul'gin, *Istoriia*, pp. 129–33; *SPMNP*, II, 1: 1496–1503 (April 25, 1839); and 1383 (June 28, 1838); A. F. Smirnov, *Revoliutsionnye sviazi* (Moscow, 1962).

21. Uvarov, *Desiatiletie*, pp. 40–44; "Pis'ma studentov Kievskago universiteta k studentam universiteta Gel'zingforskago" (March 2, 1841–August 7, 1843), TsGIAL, fond 733, opis' 69, ed. 617, pp. 1–51; Egorov, "Russkie universitety," pp. 249–50; see Vladimirskii-Budanov, *Istoriia*, pp. 174–297, for the whole renewal period; *SPMNP*, II, 2: 331–48 (June 9, 1842).

22. "Iz pis'em Imperatora Nikolaia Pavlovicha k kniaziu I. F. Paskevichu, 1839" (October 17, 1839), *RA* 3 (1910): 346; "De l'Instruction publique en Pologne et en Russie," *Le Courrier françgis*, November 14, 1838, p. 318; Kniazkov and Serbov, *Ocherk*, pp. 229–37; Rozhdestvenskii, *Obzor*, pp. 310–17; Polievktov, *Nikolai I*, pp. 119–45; M. T. Florinsky, *Russia: A History and an Interpretation*, II (New York, 1947), pp. 757–65; A. E. Presniakov, *Emperor Nicholas I of Russia*, ed and trans. J. Zacek (Gulf Breeze, Fla., 1974), pp. 48–51; Uvarov, *Desiatiletie*, pp. 61–67; *Otchet za 1839*, pp. 61–65; *Otchet za 1843*, pp. 95–97; *SPMNP*, II, 1: 1561–65 (November 20 and December 2, 1839); and 1570–71 (December 19, 1839); *SPMNP* II, 2: 19 (March 31, 1840); 57–65 (June 19, 1840): 99–152 (August 31, 1840); 161–64 (November 22, 1840); 166–72 (November 28, 1840); 182–84 (December 10, 1840); 196–215 (January 18, 1841); 314–23 (April 2, 1842); 387–95 (March 10, 1843); 453–58 (February 22, 1844).

23. J. T. Flynn, "Tuition," p. 244; Steinger, "Government Policy," p. 175; Grigor'ev, *S Peterburgskii universitet*, pp. 116–18; *SPMNP*, II, 1: 588–90 (June 13, 1833); *SPMNP*, II, 2: 22–27 (April 10, 1840); 645–50 (August 11, 1845); 803–4 (June 17, 1846); 809–11 (July 21, 1846).

24. Uvarov, *Desiatiletie*, pp. 41, 46, 67–69; Vladimirskii-Budanov, *Istoriia*, pp. 76, 168.

25. Uvarov, *Desiatiletie*, p. 52; K. Lander, "Pribaltiiskii krai v pervoi polovine XIX veka," in *Istoriia Rossii*, II, p. 327–49; O. deBre, "Vospomonaniia—Imperator Nikolai i ego spodvizhniki," *RS* 109 (January 1902): 115–39; Kabuzan, *Narodona-selenie*, pp. 160–62.

26. *SPMNP*, II, 1: 1213–15 (January 20, 1837); Shavaev, *Ocherki*, pp. 465–90; the provinces included Liveland, Estland, and Kurland.

27. Uvarov, *Desiatiletie*, pp. 57–60; and *Otchet za 1837*, pp. 65–66; Rozhdestven-skii, *Obzor*, pp. 323–28; *SPMNP*, II, 1: 712–15 (February 20, 1834); 1215 (January 22, 1837); 1264 (May 18, 1837); and 1566–67 (December 15, 1839); *SPMNP*, II, 2: 3 (January 14, 1840); 356–58 (August 18, 1842).

28. The number of students in the district rose under Uvarov from roughly 59,000 to 81,000 (Uvarov, "Otchet za 1836," *ZMNP*, pp. lviii–lxiii; and *Otchet za 1848*, pp. 91–92); E. V. Petukhov, 1802–1865, vol. I of *Imperatorskii Iur'evskii, byvskii Derptskii, universitet za sto let ego sushchestvovaniia (1802–1902)* (Iur'ev, 1902), pp. 424–30, 445–49; P. Maikov, "Vvedenie russkago iazyka v Otstzeiskikh guberniakh," *RS* 38, No. 4 (April 1907): 60; *SPMNP*, II, 1: 590–602 (June 24, 1833); 1209 (December 19, 1836); 1282 (June 1, 1837); 1527 (July 8, 1839).

29. Uvarov, *Desiatiletie*, pp. 56–57; "Otchet za 1834," *ZMNP*, p. xxii–xliv; and "Otchet za 1838," pp. xxi–xxxix; A. A. Chumikov, "Letopis' zabav i shalostei derpt-skikh studentov," *RS* 55 (February 1890): 341–70; "Iz vospominanii E. I. Elagionoi, *RA* 3 (1902): 476–80; *Staticheskiia materialy dlia opredeleniia obshchestvennago polozheniia lits, poluchivshikh obrazovanie v Imperatorskom universitete s 1802–1852 goda* (St Petersburg, 1862), pp. 3–7; Shabaev, *Ochewrki*, pp. 483–489. *SPMNP*, II, 1: 639–41 (October 31, 1833); 718–45 (February 21, 1834); 1038 (December 20, 1835); 1209 (December 16, 1836); 1374 (June 4, 1838); and 144 (October 4, 1838); *SPMNP*, II, 2: 401–2 (June 3, 1843).

30. Uvarov, *Otchet za 1837*, pp. 62–63; Petukhov, *Universitet*, pp. 378, 399, 417–30, 445–49; Chumikov, "Letopis'," p. 367; Vucinich, *Science*, p. 190; *SPMNP*, II, 1: 715–17 (February 20, 1834); 808–10 (July 29, 1834); and 1527–30 (July 8, 1839); *SPMNP*, II, 2: 880–94 (January 14, 1848).

31. The reports were leaked by the director of the office of the superintendent and a teacher in the Mitau gymnasium; the former was exiled to Viatka and the latter to Ufa (Petukhov, *Universitet*, pp. 426–33).

32. M. Mordar'ev, "Pis'ma i zapiska G. I. Parrota k imperatoram Aleksandru I i Nikolaiu I," *RS* 25, No. 4 (April 1895): 214–17.

33. Uvarov, *Desiatiletie*, pp. 47–52, 59; and *Otchet za 1848*, pp. 91–92; Riasanovsky, *Official Nationality*, pp. 144–46; Petukhov, *Universitet*, pp. 378, 417–19; Chumikov, "General-Guvernatorstvo kniazia A. A. Suvorova v pribaltiiskom krae," *RA* 28, No. 3 (March 1890): 83.

34. Uvarov, *Desiatiletie*, pp. 52–56; *SPMNP*, II, 1: 898 (March 24, 1835); Seton-Watson, *The Russian Empire*, p. 270; A. Plakans, "Peasants, Intellectuals, and Nationalism in the Russian Baltic Provinces, 1820–1890," *Journal of Modern History* 46, No. 3 (1974): 445–75.

35. In 1810, Uvarov attributed their large population, as only a patriot could, to the "marvelous tolerance . . . practiced by the Russian people," those "natural Good Samaritans" ("Tablettes d'un voyageur russe," GIM, fond 17, no. 6, p. 6). The most recent historian of the question of the Jews' status in Nicholaevan Russia, Michael Stanislawski, interprets Uvarov's policies as the most enlightened of any statesman in the era (*Tsar Nicholas I and the Jews: The Transformation of Jewish Society in Russia, 1825–1855* [Philadelphia, 1983], pp. 10, 45–47, 59–69).

36. When I did research in the Soviet Union in 1973, the Soviet authorities issued a central directive that no American scholar could see any information on the Jewish question, in my case, TsGIAL, fond 744, on the education of Jews from 1833 to 1839.

Nicholas is quoted in Seton-Watson, *Empire*, p. 273; "O vstuplenii tovarishcha ministra Uvarova k pravami obiazannosti ministra narodnago prosveshcheniia" (March 18, 1833), TsGIAL, fond 735, opis' 1, no. 449, p. 10; Uvarov, "Otchet za 1836," *ZMNP*, p. cxv; V. Stasov, "Tsenzura v tsarstvovanie imperatora Nikolaia I," *RS* 34, No. 6 (1903): 659–66.

37. *SPMNP*, I, 1: 13–21 (January 24, 1803); "Sravnitel'noe sostoianie," *ZMNP* 12, No. 11 (November 1836): 330; *ZMNP* 32, No. 12 (December 1841): 32–45; A. Dikii, *Evrei v Rossii i v SSSR* (New York, 1967), pp. 69–73; S. M. Ginzburg, "Russkoe pravitel'stvo i vopros ob obrazovanii evreev v pervoi polovine XIX veka," in *Kazennye evreiskie uchilishcha*, I (Petrograd, 1920), pp. xxv–xliii; S. M. Dubnow, *History of the Jews in Russia and Poland*, II (Philadelphia, 1918), pp. 47–50; S. G. Lozinskii, *Opisanie del vyshego arkhiva Ministerstva narodnago prosveshcheniia: Kazennye evreiskie uchilishcha* (Petrograd, 1920), p. 6.

On the general questions, also consult S. Posner, *Evrei v obshchei shkole* (St. Petersburg, 1914); Z. Halevy, *Jewish Schools under Czarism and Communism: A Struggle for Cultural Identity* (New York, 1976); A. V. Beletskii, "Vopros ob obrazovanii russkikh evreev v tsarstvovanie imperatora Nikolaia I-go," *Russkaia shkola*, No. 1 (January 1893), pp. 12–28; No. 2 (February 1893), pp. 9–20; No. 3 (March 1893), pp. 10–31; No. 4 (April 1893), pp. 13–33; No. 5 (May 1893), pp. 13–29; No. 7 (July 1893), pp. 12–27; and No. 11 (November 1893), pp. 10–28.

38. Max Lilienthal, *My Travels*, pp. 182–83, 190–97, 246–47; I. Levitats, *The Jewish Community in Russia, 1772–1884* (New York, 1843), pp. 20–45, 69–86, 188–97; D. Philipson, *Max Lilienthal, American Rabbi: Life and Writings*, (New York, 1915); *SPMNP*, II, 1: 1506–12 (May 10, 1839).

39. Lozinskii, "Ob obrazovanii evreiskoi natsii," in *Kazennye evreiskie uchilishcha*,

I, pp. 27–29; Ginzburg, "Russkoe pravitel'stvo," pp. xxxviii–xxlix; Ginzburg, "Max Lilienthal's Activities in Russia: New Documents," *Publications of the American Jewish Historical Society* 35 (1939): 40; M. G. Morgulis, "K istorii obrazovaniia russkikh evreev," *Evreiskaia biblioteka* I (1870): 136–37, 147–48; S. W. Baron, *The Russian Jew under Tsars and Soviets* (New York, 1964), p. 42; D. Philipson, "Max Lilienthal in Russia," in *Hebrew Union College Annual, XII–XIII* (1937–1938), p. 828; N. Hans, *History of Russian Educational Policy*, 1710–1917 (London, 1931), p. 86; J. Hessen, "Die russische Regierung und die westeuropaischen Juden," *Monatsschrift für Geschichte und Wissenschaft des Judentums* 57 (1913): 265–71; Uvarov, *Otchet za* 1841, pp. 102–3; and *Otchet za* 1842, pp. 9–10; Rozhdestvenskii, *Obzor*, pp. 294–96; Lozinskii, "Nachala i sredstva preobrazovaniia evreiskago naroda v Rossii," *Kazennye evreiskie uchilishcha*, I, pp. 39–40; *SPMNP*, II, 2: 7 (February 1, 1840); and 227–43 (March 17, 1841).

40. Ginzburg, "Max Lilienthal," p. 41; Lozinskii, "Nachala," pp. 62–63; Dubnow, *Jews in Russia*, pp. 53–54; Morgulis, "K istorii," pp. 149–50; Levitats, *The Jewish Community*, pp. 72–74; Max Lilienthal, "Aufenthalt in Russland," *Allgemeine Zeitung des Judentums* 41 (1842): 605; Lilienthal, *My Travels*, pp. 322–30.

41. Uvarov, *Desiatiletie*, pp. 73–74; *Otchet za* 1845, pp. 10–12; and *Otchet za* 1847, pp. 96–102; Rozhdestvenskii, *Obzor*, p. 295; Levitats, *Jewish Community*, pp. 75–76; Dubnow, *Jews in Russia*, p. 54; Lilienthal, *My Travels*, p. 323; Beletskii, "Vopros," *Russkaia shkola*, No. 5 (May 1893), p. 24; *SPMNP*, II, 2: 349–52 (June 22, 1842); and 485–93 (April 17, 1844); 518–66 (November 13, 1844); 651–60 (September 1, 1845); 680–86 (November 27, 1845).

42. See Stanislawsky, *Nicholas and the Jews*, pp. 69–96.

43. Uvarov, *Desiatiletie*, p. 73; Lilienthal, *My Travels*, p. 246; Hans, *History*, pp. 86–87; Ginzburg, "Russkoe pravitel'stvo," p. lxxxi; *Otchet za* 1845, pp. 6–11.

44. "Ob usilenii prepodavaniia vostochnykh iazykov v uchilishchakh Kazanskago okruga," *SPMNP*, II, 1: 727 (June 5, 1835).

45. See chap. 1 and C. H. Whittaker, "The Impact of the Oriental Renaissance in Russia: The Case of Sergei Uvarov," *Jahrbücher für Geschichte Osteuropas* 26 (1978): 503–24.

46. J. Klaproth, *Archiv für Asiatische Literatur, Geschichte und Sprachkunde* (St. Petersburg, 1810); Ostrovitianov, *Istoriia*, II, p. 219; Tairova, "Proekt I. O. Pototskogo," p. 203; Frye, "Oriental Studies in Russia," in *Russia and Asia*, pp. 35, 40, 46; Ostrovitianov, *Istoriia*, pp. 221–23; *Istoriia biblioteki Akademii nauk SSSR*, 1714–1964 (Moscow, 1964), pp. 172–73; *SPMNP*, II, 1: 1172 (May 5, 1839). On the Asiatic Museum's development, see T. V. Staniukovich, *Kunstkamera Peterburgskoi Akademii nauk* (Leningrad, 1953); *Aziatskii muzei Rossiiskoi Akademii nauk*, 1818–1918 (Petrograd, 1920); B. Dorn, *Das Asiatische Museum der kaiserlichen Akademie der Wissenschaften zu St. Petersburg* (St. Petersburg, 1846); Dorn, "Aziatskii muzei," in *Ocherk istorii muzeev Imperatorskoi Akademii nauk* (St. Petersburg, 1865), pp. 76–86; P. S. Savel'ev, *O zhizni i uchenykh trudakh Frena* (St. Petersburg, 1855).

47. V. F. Gnucheva, *Materialy dlia istorii ekspeditsii Akademii nauk v XVIII i XIX vekakh* (Moscow, 1940): 307–8; Vucinich, *Science*, pp. 305–6; *Istoriia biblioteki*, pp. 166, 202–3; "Katalog kitaiskim i iaponskim knigam, v Biblioteke imp. Akademii nauk khraniashchimsia, po porucheniiu gospodina prezidenta onoi Akademii Sergeia Semenovicha Uvarova vnov' sdelannyi Gosudarstvennoi kollegii inostrannykh del perevodchikami, kollezhskimi asessorami: Pavlom Kamenskim i Stepanom Lipovtsovym," unpublished ms., *Katalog izdanii Imp. Akademii nauk*, pt. I (St. Petersburg, 1912).

48. N. I. Veselovskii, "Svedeniia ob ofitsial'nom prepodavanii vostochnykh iazykov v Rossii," *Trudy tret'iago mezhdunarodnago s'ezda orientalistov v S.-Peterburge*, 1876, ed. V. V. Grigor'ev, I (St. Petersburg, 1879–1880), pp. 107–9; A. L.

Gal'perin, "Russkaia istoricheskaia nauka o zarubezhnom dal'nem vostoke v XVII v.–seredine XIX v.," *Ocherki po istorii russkogo vostokovedeniia* 2: 26; Schwab, *La Renaissance orientale*, pp. 92–95; Staniukovich, *Kunstkamera*, pp. 216–17; Uvarov, "Otchet za 1835," p. lx; Krusenstern, *Précis du Système*, pp. 81, 124–31.

49. Veselovskii, "Svedeniia," pp. 109–11, 114–15; I. Iu. Krachkovskii, *Ocherki po istorii russkoi arabistiki* (Moscow, 1950), p. 73; N. P. Barsukov, "Dragoman: Posviashchaetsia pamiati grafa S. S. Uvarova," *RA* 24 (1886): 219; Whittaker, "Uvarov," pp. 108–30.

50. A. V. Boldyrev studied with de Sacy and in 1811 took up a position as professor of Arabic and Persian at Moscow University; he published and edited texts but left no school; when he retired in 1837, no one replaced him. Krachkovskii, *Ocherki*, pp. 73, 100; Frye, "Oriental Studies," p. 46; Bartol'd, "Vostok," p. 5; "Ob uchrezhdenii pri vostochnom otdelenii S. Peterburgskago universiteta prepodavaniia gruzinskago, armianskago i tatarskago iazykov," *SPMNP*, II, 2: 378 (July 24, 1844); "Po soobshcheniiu II otdeleniia D. N. P. otnositel'no uchrezhdeniia novykh kafedr vostochnykh iazykov v S. P. B. Universitete" (November 30, 1838), TsGIAL, fond 733, opis' 87, no. 382. Uvarov is quoted in Korbut, *Kazanskii*, p. 116; Bartol'd, *Istoriia izucheniia vostoka*, p. 5; P. E. Skachkov, *Ocherki istorii russkogo kitaevedeniia* (Moscow, 1977), pp. 191–92; A. M. Kulikova, "Proekty vostokovednogo obrazovaniia v Rossii (XVIII-1-ia. pol. XIX v.)," *Narody Azii i Afriki* 4 (1970): 137–39; Steinger, "Government Policy," p. 189.

51. Krusenstern, *Précis*, p. 81; Korbut, *Kazanskii universitet*, pp. 25–30, 113–31; "Obozrenie khoda," pp. 57–73; Gal'perin, "Russkaia nauka," pp. 27–28; G. F. Shamov, "Deiatel'nost Kovalevskago," in *Ocherki*, pp. 118–77; "O prepodavanii mongol'skago iazyka v Kazanskom universitete," *SPMNP*, II, 1: 457–58 (July 25, 1833); "Ob uchrezhdenii pri Kazanskom universitete kafedry kitaiskago iazyka," *SPMNP*, II, 1: 980 (April 11, 1837); "Ob uchrezhdenii kafedry armianskago iazyka pri Kazanskom universitete," *SPMNP*, II, 1: 1159 (March 22, 1839); "Ob uchrezhdenii pri Kazanskom universitete kafedry sanskritskago iazyka," *SPMNP*, II, 2: 249 (August 27, 1842); Uvarov, *Desiatiletie*, pp. 23–24; A. N. Kononov, *Istoriia izucheniia tiurkskikh iazykov v Rossii dooktiab'skii period* (Leningrad, 1972), pp. 127–38.

52. Veselovskii, "Svedeniia," pp. 112–13, 117; Korbut, *Kazanskii universitet*, pp. 51, 119–31; Grigor'ev, *S. Peterburgskii universitet*, pp. 123–25; Ostrovitianov, *Istoriia*, I, p. 5; *Materialy dlia istorii fakul'teta vostochnykh iazykov*, I, (St. Petersburg, 1905), pp. 3–8; Uvarov, *Projet*, p. 9; and *Desiatiletie*, p. 24. Nesselrode strongly backed locating oriental training in the capital ("Pis'mo Nessel'rode k Uvarovu" [November 10, 1838], TsGIAL, fond 733, opis' 87, no. 382).

53. Krusenstern, *Précis*, pp. 79–80; *Materialy*, pp. 2–3, 8–10; Veselovskii, "Svedeniia," pp. 120–32; Uvarov, *Desiatiletie*, p. 25; "Polozhenie o prepodavanii v pervoi Kazanskoi gimnazii Vostochnykh iazykov," *SPMNP*, II, 1: 801–3 (January 2, 1836); "Ob otpuske dobavochnoi summy na soderzhanie pri Simferopol'skoi gimnazii uchilishchnago otdeleniia dlia obrazovaniia Tatarskikh uchitelei," *SPMNP*, II, 1: 1040 (decree of May 3, 1838); "O predostavlenii Moskovskomu armianskomu lazarevskomu institutu vostochnykh iazykov dopolnitel'nykh prav i preimushchestv, naravne s uchebnymi zavedeniiami 2 razriada," *SPMNP*, II, 1: 1037 (April 26, 1838); Baziiants, *Lazarevskii institut vostochnykh iazykov* (Moscow, 1959); Uvarov, "Otchet za 1835," *ZMNP*, p. xcvii; Shabaev, *Ocherki*, pp. 493–562; *SPMNP*, II, 2: 217–21 (January 31, 1841); 348 (June 9, 1842); 445–97 (November 30, 1843); 510–11 (August 28, 1844); 760–61 (January 31, 1846); 848–58 (April 13, 1847); 915–41 (May 10, 1848); 898–904 (April 2, 1848); 904–6 (April 14, 1848); 907–8 (April 29, 1848); 942 (May 11, 1848); 942 (May 18, 1848); 975–1008 (December 18, 1848); 1029–34 (February 1, 1849); 1077–98 (June 11, 1849); and 1098 (July 4, 1849).

54. Uvarov, *Desiatiletie*, pp. 23, 26.

55. Krusenstern, *Précis*, pp. 99–102; "Ob usilenii prepodavaniia vostochnykh iazykov v uchilishchakh Kazanskago okruga," *SPMNP*, II, 1: 723–27 (June 5, 1835); "Ob otkrytii shkol' dlia detei Tatar' i idolopoklonnikov," *SPMNP*, II, 2: 379 (August 28, 1844); "Ustav Tiflisskago musul'manskago uchilishcha alieva ucheniia," *SPMNP*, II, 2: 683–93 (April 18, 1847). The statement is quoted from a letter written in the name of Konstantin Pobedonostsev, Procurator of the Holy Synod, in September 1884 (B. V. Lunin, *Sredniaia Aziia v dorevoliutsionnom i sovetskom vostokovedenii* [Tashkent, 1965], p. 56).

56. Nikitenko, *Diary* (entry of April 16, 1849), p. 124.

CHAPTER 9

1. Granovskii is quoted in D. P. Golokhvastov, "Ob ukraino-slavianskom obshchestve: Iz bumagi D. P. Golokhvastova," *RA* 30, No. 7 (1892): 359.

2. On Russia in the 1847–1848 period, consult Lincoln, *Nicholas I*, pp. 269–90; I. Berlin, "Russia and 1848," in *Russian Thinkers*, p. 9; also see chaps. 7 and 8.

3. Uvarov, *Otchet za 1847*, p. 53; "Instruktsiia," ROBIL, fond 231, no. 41; E. Solov'ev, *Ocherki iz istorii russkoi literatury XIX veka*, II (St. Petersburg, 1896), p. 13. In general, see A. A. Kochubinskii, *Nachal'nye gody russkago slavianovedeniia* (Odessa, 1888). On the origins of Slavic studies, consult I. V. Iagich's classic, *Istoriia slavianskoi filologii* (St. Petersburg, 1910), pp. 1–185, 237–345.

4. A. I. Bortnikov, "Kirillo-mefodievskoe obschestvo: Glavnye idei i tseli," *Trudy istoricheskogo fakul'teta Kievskogo universiteta* 1 (1940): 221–71; "Iz istorii 'Obshchestva sv. Kirilla i Mefodiia' (1847): Ustav i pravila, proklamatsii," *Byloe* 1 (February 1906): 66–68. On the society in general, consult G. Luciani, *Le Livre de la genèse du peuple ukrainien* (Paris, 1956); Kostomarov, *Avtobiografiia*, pp. 170–97; P. A. Zaionchkovskii, *Kirillo-mefodievskoe obshchestvo* (Moscow, 1959); P. Goncharuk, *Istoricheskie vzgliady Kirillo-mefodievtsev*, 1846–1847 (Kiev, 1970), pp. 197–245; Pelech, "Ukrainian Ideologues," pp. 197–245.

5. V. I. Semevskii, "Kirillo-mefodievskoe obshchestvo, 1846–1847," *Golos minuvshago* 5, Nos. 10–12 (October–December 1918), pp. 150–51; V. V. Aristov, "Dissertatsii kirillo-mefodievtsa I. A. Posiady," *Opisanie rukopisei nauchnoi biblioteki im. N. I. Lobachevskogo* 11 (1962): 21–39; Iagich, *Istoriia*, pp. 485–534, 658–91; Nikitenko, *Diary* (entry of June 1, 1847), p. 112. The most accessible and critical treatment is Pelech, "Ukrainian Ideologues," pp. 119–96, 226.

6. Luciani, *Le Livre*, pp. 74–85; Skabichevskii, *Ocherki*, pp. 327–28; Pypin, *Etnografii*, III (St. Petersburg, 1892), pp. 20–21, 156–57; D. I. Bagalei et al., *Kratkii ocherk istorii Khar'kovskago universiteta za pervye sto let ego susbchestvovaniia* (Khar'kov, 1906), p. 127. On Kostomarov, see M. I. Sukhomlinov, "Unichtozhenie dissertatsii N. I. Kostomarova," *Sbornik statei iz 'Drevnei i novoi Rossii'*, 3, No. 9 (1875): 42–55; J. Flynn, "The Affair of Kostomarov's Dissertation: A Case Study of Official Nationalism in Practice," *Slavonic and East European Review* 52, No. 127 (April 1974): 188–96; Starr, *Decentralization*, pp. 100–104.

7. "Doklad grafa Uvarova Imp. Mikol I-mu," *Nashe minule* 2 (1918): 171–77; *Le Constitutionnel* (July 28, 1847); *Le Siècle*, November 5, 1847.

8. "Predpisanie Uvarova k popechiteliu Kievskago uchebnago okruga" (May 27, 1847), ROBIL, fond 265, opis' 2, no. 93, pp. 147–52; Golokhvastov, "Bumagi," pp. 347–49; Barsukov, *Zhizn' Pogodina*, IX, pp. 236–37.

9. Uvarov, "O slaviantsve," in Golokhvostov's "Bumagi" (pp. 349–50), as translated in Riasanovsky, *Official Nationality*, pp. 163–64.

10. Golokhvastov, "Bumagi," p. 351–57; Semevskii, "Obshchestvo," p. 150; Nikitenko, *Diary* (entry of June 1, 1847), p. 113; "Pis'ma Uvarova k Golokhvastovu" (December 16, 1847 and February 1, 1848), GIM, fond 404, ed. 15, p. 54; S. A. Belokurov, *'Delo Fletchera,' 1848–1864 gg.* (Moscow, 1910).

11. Belinskii is quoted in Lincoln, *Nicholas I*, p. 272. The Third Section report is in TsGAOR, fond 109, opis' 85, ed. khr. 12 (1847), p. 149. M. A. Korf, "Iz zapisok barona M. A. Korfa," *RS* 31, No. 2 (1900): 561–62; Nikitenko, *Diary* (entry of August 22, 1848), p. 117; V. P. Zavadovskii, "Imperator Nikolai Pavlovich v ego rechi k deputatam S.-Peterburgskago dvorianstva," *RS* 39 (1883): 593–96.

12. A. S. Nifontov, *1848 god v Rossii* (Moscow, 1931), p. 98; "O merakh k okhraneniiu uchebnykh zavedenii ot vrednago vlianiia po nastoiashcem polozheniiu del' v zapadnoi Evropy," TsGIAL, fond 733, opis' 70, ed. khr. 181, pp. 1–44, and ed. khr. 236; "Iz razskazov G. V. Grudeva," *RA* 11 (1898): 427, 433; A. A. Mikhailov, "Revoliutsiia 1848 goda i slavianofil'stvo," *Uchenye zapiski Leningradskogo gosudarstvennogo universiteta* 73 (1940): 48–74; T. Schiemann, *Geschichte Russlands unter Kaiser Nikolaus I*, IV (Berlin, 1919), p. 150; Korf, "Zapiski," p. 562; Iu. N. Egorov, "Russkie universitety," pp. 253–54, 276–77; *SPMNP*, II, 2: 1188–89 (May 2, 1850). (References to *SPMNP* carry the date of the document. Entries consist mainly of decrees, laws, and reports.)

13. Uvarov, *Études de philologie et de critique* (Paris, 1845), first published in St. Petersburg in 1843; R. Bullen, *Palmerston, Guizot and the Collapse of the Entente Cordiale* (London, 1974).

14. Uvarov, *Stein et Pozzo di Borgo* (St. Petersburg, 1846); *Stein et Pozzo di Borgo* (Paris, 1847), 36pp.; *Stein and Pozzo di Borgo, As Portrayed by Count Ouvaroff*, trans. D. F. Campbell (London, 1847); *Shtein i Potstso-di-Borgo*, trans. M. Rozberg (Dorpat, 1847); *Le Corsaire*, October 29, 1846; *La Presse*, October 31, 1846; *Le Courrier français*, November 18, 1846; *Revue indépendante*, April 10, 1847.

15. Uvarov, "Metternich," GIM, fond 17, no. 10; F. A. Golubinskii, *Biograficheskie ocherki* (Moscow, 1855), pp. 5–8; "Iz zapisok damy," *RA* 1 (1882): 206.

16. Nikitenko, *Diary* (entry of June 2, 1853), p. 136; Uvarov's *Esquisses politiques et littéraires* (Paris, 1848) includes an introduction by L. Leduc, "Essai biographique et critique," pp. 1–73.

17. A. Dementev, *Ocherki po istorii russkoi zhurnalistiki, 1840–1850* (Moscow, 1951), p. 167; Nikitenko, *Diary* (entries of January 17 and 22, 1848), p. 114; "Dnevnik I. M. Snegireva" (entry of February 12, 1848), *RA* 3, No. 9 (1903): 90; V. Semevskii, "Materialy po istorii tsenzury v Rossii: Zashchita Bulgarina tsenzuroiu," *Golos minuvshego* 3 (March 1913): 218–19.

18. Uvarov, *Obshchii vzgliad na filosofiiu slovesnosti* (St. Petersburg, 1848), also included in *Esquisses*, pp. 229–46; "Issledovanie ob elevsinskikh tainstvakh," *Sovremennik* 2 (February 1846): 77–108; Nifontov, 1848, pp. 181–82; Maksimov, *Sovremennik*, pp. 213, 235–36; M. Lemke, *Nikolaevskie zhandarmy i literatura 1826–1855 gg.* (St. Petersburg, 1907), p. 177; Semevskii, "Materialy po istorii tsenzury v Rossii," *Golos minuvshego* 4 (April 1913): 227–28.

19. Skabichevskii, *Ocherki*, p. 331; Balmuth, "The Origins," pp. 497–99; Maksimov, *Sovremennik*, pp. 236–37; Nikitenko, *Diary* (entry of April 25, 1848), p. 116; Korf, "Iz zapisok," pp. 571–73; "Grudeva," p. 434; Barsukov, *Pogodin*, IX, pp. 241–42, 280; Shil'der, *Nikolai*, II, pp. 632–33; P. V. Annenkov, "Dve zimy v provintsii i v derevne (1840–1851)," *Byloe* 18 (1923): 18; "Delo o razsmotrenii v osobom komitete deistvii periodicheskikh izdanii," TsGIAL, fond 1611,

opis' 1, no. 208, pp. 11–18. Semevskii prints the Korf and Bulgarin memoranda ("Materialy," pp. 219–28).

20. Shiemann, *Nikolaus*, IV, p. 150; Shil'der, *Nikolai*, pp. 634–36; Balmuth, "Terror," pp. 508, 511–19; Nifontov, *1848*, pp. 183–84; "Pis'mo Menshikova k Uvarovu" (March 8, 1848), TsGIAL, fond 1179, no. 11; "Delo," pp. 9–223.

21. Uvarov, "O tsenzure," TsGIAL, fond 1611, opis' 1, no. 208b, pp. 168–80 (March 24, 1848); "Zhurnal Komiteta, vysochaishe uchrezhdennago dlia razsmotreniia deistvii tsenzury periodicheskikh izdanii, 29 marta 1848 g.," *Golos minuvshego* 4 (April 1913): 212–19.

22. "Delo," pp. 233–37; "Pis'mo k Uvarovu" (April 10, 1848), TsGIAL, fond 1189, no. 12; "Ob ustave i shtat'e tsenzury," TsGIAL, fond 1149, opis' 3 (1849), nos. 43 and 84, pp. 1–134; "O novom tsenzurnom ustave," fond 1611, opis' 1, no. 61 (July 6–October 17, 1849); *Proekt tsenzurnago ustava vnesennyi v gosudarstvennyi sovet grafom Uvarovym, v 1849 godu, i neodobrennyi sovetom* (St. Petersburg, 1864); L. Lekhtblau, "Revoliutsiia 1848 goda i tsarskaia tsenzura," *Istorik-marksist* 7 (1940): 4–5; Rozhdestvenskii, *Obzor*, pp. 337–38; Lemke, *Zhandarmy*, p. 177; Nifontov, *1848*, pp. 181–202; Stilman, "Freedom," pp. 423–25; *Perepiska Ia. K. Grota s P. A. Pletnevym*, III (St. Petersburg, 1896), p. 203; V. Stasov, "Tsenzura v tsarstvovanie imperatora Nikolaia I," *RS* 8 (1903): 411–15; M. Chistiakov, "Chateaubriand," *ZMNP* 61 (February 1849): 1–52.

23. Uvarov, "O tsenzure," p. 175; "Pis'ma Uvarova" (October 2–6, 1848), GIM, fond 404, ed. 15; "O nedozvolenii Moskovskomu obshchestvu istorii i drevnostei pechat svoi chteniia," TsGIAL, fond 735, opis' 10, ed. 293b, pp. 663–68; fond 772, opis' 1, no. 2158, pp. 7–8; "Knizhnye redkosti," *RA* 30, No. 2 (1892): 233–58; "K istorii Moskovskago universiteta: D. P. Golokhvastov," *RA* 24, No. 2 (1887): 247; "Pis'ma kniazia M. A. Obolenskago k V. A. Polenovu," *RA* 19, No. 1 (1882): 275; *O razsylke nekotorym mestam sochineniia Fletchera, "O gosudarstve Russkom"* (n.p., 1864); G. Fletcher, *Of the Russe Commonwealth*, 1591 (Cambridge, Mass., 1966).

24. Nikitenko, *Diary* (entries of April 25 and December 1, 1848), pp. 116–17; Berlin quotes Gleb Uspenskii in "1848," p. 14; Annenkov, *Extraordinary Decade*, p. 239; P. A. Valuev, "Dnevnik, 1847–1860" (entry of April 1891), *RS* 70: 172; "Ocherki po istorii Moskovskago universiteta," *Uchenye zapiskie. Moskovskii gosudarstvennyi universitet* 50 (1940): 53–54.

25. Stroganov is quoted in "Delo," p. 11; Gobkhvastov, "Bumagi," pp. 355–57.

26. Koyré, *La Philosophie*, p. 202; Shmid, *Istoriia*, pp. 367–93; Georgievskii, *Reforma*, pp. 22–24; Nifontov, *1848*, p. 182; Luciani, *Le Livre*, pp. 99–103; Rozhdestvenskii, *Obzor*, pp. 263–64, 278; Egorov, "Reaktsionnaia politika," pp. 71–75. Nicholas is quoted in Darlington, *Education*, pp. 84–85.

27. "Ob usilenie nadzora po vospitaniiu v uchebnykh zavedeniiakh," TsGIAL, fond 733, opis' 90, ed. 114, pp. 1–3 (March 19, 1848); TsGIAL, fond 733, opis' 88, ed. 28, pp. 3–5 (March 29, 1848); "Instruktsiia," TsGIAL, fond 733, opis' 90, ed. 124, p. 6 (October 4, 1848) and ed. 115, p. 1 (May 11, 1848); "Prepodavanii v universitetakh nekotorykh chastei politicheskikh i iuridicheskikh nauk," TsGIAL, fond 733, opis' 88, ed. 27, pp. 1–22 (October 27, 1848–January 14, 1849); TsGIAL, fond 735, opis' 10, ed. khr. 293, pp. 670–76 (April 2, 1849); A. Pelikan, "Vo vtoroi polovine XIX veka," *Golos minuvshago* 3 (March 1914): 191–92.

28. Uvarov's quotations are taken from "Dukh instituta," TsGIAL, fond 733, opis' 88, ed. khr. 28, pp. 1–2 (March 23, 1848); and "Pis'ma Uvarova" (September 12, 1848), fond 733, opis' 34, ed. khr. 3, pp. 1–5. Egorov, "Universitety," p. 257; Rozhdestvenskii, *Obzor*, pp. 260–61; Shevyrev, *Istoriia*, pp. 509–10; Uva-

rov, *Otchet za 1848*, pp. 136–40; "Pis'mo Uvarova k popechiteliu Moskovskago okruga" (February 26, 1849), GIM, fond 404; M. P. Pogodin, "Prebyvanie Ministra narodnago prosveshcheniia v Moskve," *Moskvitianin* 10 (1848): 1–10.

29. Nikitenko, *Diary* (entries of December 1–December 20, 1848), pp. 117–20.

30. Barsukov, *Pogodin*, X, p. 124; "Pis'ma I. I. Davydova k M. P. Pogodinu" (March 20, 1849), ROBIL, fond 231, ed. 5; Maksimov, *Sovremennik*, p. 240; Nifontov, *1848*, p. 200; Semevskii, "Materialy," p. 226; Davydov, "O naznachenii russkikh universitetov i uchastii ikh v obshchestvennom obrazovanii," *Sovremennik* 14, No. 3 (March 1849): 37–46.

31. Uvarov's compilations for the Third Section are located in TsGIAL, fond 733, opis' 90, ed. khr. 129, pp. 2–10 (January 21, 1849); Nikitenko, *Diary* (entry of April 4, 1849), p. 124; "Pis'mo Uvarova" (March 18, 1849), GIM, fond 404, ed. 15.

32. "Pis'mo Uvarova" (April 22, 1849), ROBIL, fond 1179, no. 13; Nifontov, *1848*, pp. 119–200; Rozhdestvenskii, *Obzor*, p. 262; "Tsenzura" 7 (1903): 148–53.

33. On the Petrashevtsy, consult V. I. Semevskii, *M. V. Butashevich-Petrashevskii i petrashevtsy* (Moscow, 1922); S. N. Valk, ed., *Delo petrashevtsev*, I–III (Moscow, 1937–1951); N. V. Riasanovsky, "Fourierism in Russia: An Estimate of the Petrashevtsy," *American Slavic and East European Review* 12, No. 3 (October 1953): 289–302; Frank, *Dostoevsky*, pp. 239–57; Lincoln, *Nicholas I*, pp. 303–11.

34. "O priniatii studentov universiteta kazennoe soderzhanie so vtorogo kursa ili goda ucheniia," TsGIAL, fond 733, opis' 90, ed. khr. 116, pp. 4–9; "Ob ogranichenii chisla studentov v universitetakh 300-mi," TsGIAL, fond 733, opis' 88, no. 35, pp. 1–2 (May 6 and May 19, 1849); "O sokrashenii chisla studentov do 300," TsGIAL, fond 733, opis' 34, ed. khr., pp. 1–35 (January 26–August 1, 1849); "Ob umenshenii chisla studentov v universitetakh do 300 chelovek v kazhdom," TsGIAL, fond 733, opis' 90, ed. khr. 127, pp. 1–35 (April 30–September 25, 1849); SPMNP, II, 2: 1066 (April 30, 1849); 1008–70 (May 11, 1849); 1101–2 (August 1, 1849); and 1104 (September 25, 1849); Nifontov, *1848*, pp. 201–2; Rozhdestvenskii, *Obzor*, p. 226.

35. "Pis'mo k neustanovlennomy litsu (kuzenu)" (July 26, 1849), PD, fond 3, opis' 1, no. 2048; and "Pis'mo Uvarova" (July 26, 1849), GIM, fond 590; Barsukov, *Pogodin*, X, p. 543; "Pis'ma Davydova k Pogodinu" (September 16 and October 2, 1849), ROBIL, fond 231, no. 9. His resignation is located in TsGIAL, fond 735, opis' 1, no. 479, p. 432; the royal family's reaction is found in "Grudeva," p. 434.

36. Allister, "Reform," pp. 258–59; Wortman, *Russian Legal Consciousness*, pp. 164, 183; Rozhdestvenskii, "Posledniaia stranitsa iz istorii politiki narodnago prosveshcheniia Imperatora Nikolaia I-ogo (Komitet grafa Bludova, 1849–1856)," *Russkii istoricheskii zhurnal* 3–4 (1917): 37–59; S. R., "Protoierei N. F. Raevskii," *RS* 126 (June 1906): 575; Nikitenko, *Diary* (entry of June 2, 1853), p. 136.

37. The record of the new minister's immediate actions are located in TsGIAL, fond 733, opis' 90, ed. 126 (October 8–November 2, 1849); Shirinskii-Shikhmatov, *Otchet za 1849*, p. 46 (presented to the tsar on January 26, 1850). The tsar is quoted in A. Kornilov, *Nineteenth-Century Russia* (New York, 1966): 202–3; the new minister is quoted in Riasanovsky, *History*, p. 365.

38. Nikitenko, *Diary* (entry of March 16, 1850), p. 124. Buturlin's requests for lithographed copies of lectures (dating from June 9, 1849, through August 5, 1849) are found in TsGIAL, fond 735, opis' 10, no. 228, pp. 2–36. On the

Falloux Law, consult F. Ponteil, *Histoire de l'Enseignement en France, 1789–1964* (Paris, 1966).

39. "Prekrashchenie na vremia prepodavaniia gosudarstvennago prava Evropeiskikh derzhav," TsGIAL, fond 733, opis' 25, ed. 81 (July 6–August 18, 1849); *SPMNP*, II, 2: 1104–5 (October 1, 1849); 1116–18 (November 7, 1849); 1131–32 (January 12, 1850); 1133–34 (January 26, 1850); 1135–38 (January 26, 1850); 1158–61 (March 12, 1850); 1166–81 (April 12, 1850); 1182–85 (April 12, 1850); Rozhdestvenskii, *Obzor*, pp. 262–64; Egorov, "Politika," pp. 71–75; Shmid, *Istoriia*, p. 386.

40. Riasanovsky, *History*, p. 365; Berlin, "1848," p. 13; Nikitenko, *Diary* (entry of March 18, 1850), p. 125. Kavelin is quoted in W. B. Lincoln, *Nikolai Miliutin: An Enlightened Russian Bureaucrat* (Newtonville, Mass., 1977), p. 35.

41. "Avtograf Uvarova" (c. 1850), GIM, fond 445, ed. 230.

42. Vetrinskii, *T. N. Granovskii*, pp. 122–23, 302; Chizhevskii, *Gegel'*, pp. 150–51; Netting, "Liberalism," p. 217.

43. Uvarov, "Os'moe ianvaria 1851 goda," *Sovremennik* 26, No. 3 (March 1851): 1–6; "Literaturnye vospominaniia," *Sovremennik* 6 (June 1851): 37–42; "Vospominanie ob akademike Fr. Grefe," *Uchenye zapiski Akademii nauk po I i III otd.* 1 (1853): 1–13 (first read at an Academy meeting on February 6, 1852).

44. "Podvigaetsia li vpered istoricheskaia dostovernost'?" *Sovremennik* 1 (January 1850): 121–28 (also published as separate brochures in French: *La Certitude historique est-elle en progrès?* [St. Petersburg, 1850, and Dorpat, 1852]); "Pis'ma k M. P. Pogodinu" (March 2, 1851), ROBIL, fond 231, ed. 36.

45. *De Bulgariorum utrarumque origine et sedibus antiquissimus* (Dorpat, 1853), 89 pp.; *Propilei: Sbornik statei po klassicheskoi drevnosti*, I–III (Moscow, 1850–1853); *De provinciarum imperii orientalis administrandarum forma mutata inde a Constantino Magno, usque ad Justinianum* (Dorpat, 1858); "Marlo, odin iz predshestvennikov Shekspera. Ocherk iz istorii angliiskoi dramy," *Russkoe slovo* 2 (1859): 5–53; "Marlo" continues in *Russkoe slovo* 3 (1859): 221–84.

46. "Polozhenie o nagradakh grafa Uvarova (November 7, 1858)," *Sbornik postanovlenii i rasporiazhenii, otnosiashchikhsia do Imp. Akademii nauk* (St. Petersburg, 1869), pp. 50–53.

47. Apparently, the Soviet government is restoring Porech'e and making it a national museum. An archival worker gave me this information, later denied by officials; the area around Mozhaisk is closed to foreigners because of its military importance.

48. Davydov, "Selo Porech'e," *Moskvitianin*, 5, No. 9 (1841): 156–90; Pogodin, "Dlia biografii grafa S. S. Uvarova," *RS* 9, No. 12 (1871): 2079; Pogodin, "Shkol'nye vospominaniia, 1814–1820," *Vestnik Evropy* 8 (1868): 618–19; Barsukov, *Pogodin*, VI, p. 147; "Grudeva," p. 433; "Arkhiv Briullovykh," *RS* 10 (1900): 177–95; *Ukazatel' Poretskago muzeuma dlia posetitelei* (Moscow, 1853); M. F. Shcherbin, "Grafu S. S. Uvarovu, pri otkrytii pamiatnika Zhukovskomu v sele Porech'e," *RA* 2 (1906): 127–28; P. M. Leont'ev, "Bakhicheskii pamiatnik grafa S. S. Uvarova," *Propilei* 1 (1851): 135–43; S. S. Uvarov, "O drevneklassicheskom pamiatnike, perevezennom iz Rima v Porech'e," *Uchenye zapiski Imp. akademii nauk po I i III otdeleniiam* 1 (1852): 51–57 (first read at an Academy meeting on October 10, 1851); in 1854, the last article was printed as a pamphlet.

The guest lists are located in GIM, fond 17, no. 29; "Porech'e," ROBIL, ed. 18, no. 3, pp. 122–23; "Pis'ma P. A. Pletneva" (August 24, 1848), PD, fond 234, opis' 3, no. 671; "Pis'mo Uvarova k A. P. Briullovu" (December 23, 1852), PD, fond 265, opis' 2, no. 313; "Pis'ma A. I. Lebedeva k M. P. Pogodinu" (April 15, 1853), ROBIL, fond 231, no. 18.

49. The prescriptions are located in GIM, fond 17, no. 29, pp. 26–27; "Pis'ma Davydova k Pogodinu" (March 3–December 4, 1851, and October 7, 1852), ROBIL, fond 231, ed. 10; "Piatidesiatiletnyi iubilei grafa S. S. Uvarova," *Moskovskiia vedomosti* (April 9, 1853), p. 43; "Po otnosheniiu . . . prosheniia grafa Uvarova ob uvol'nenii ego ot dolzhnosti prezidenta Akademii nauk" (August 3–September 4, 1854), TsGIAL, fond 735, opis' 10, ed. khr. 271; K. N. Lebedev, "Iz zapisok senatora K. N. Lebedeva," *RA* 1 (1893): 289; Barsukov, *Pogodin*, XII, p. 435.

50. Along with his serfs, Uvarov left his son his estate, his library, and his works of art; his house serfs were to be freed, with a monetary award to be ascertained by his son. Uvarov's daughter received his house in St. Petersburg and 12,000 rubles ("Zaveshchanie" [October 30, 1849], GIM, fond 17, no. 9).

51. The eulogies and description of Uvarov's death are located in GIM, fond 17, no. 9, 29, pp. 4–5; "Pis'ma Lacosta k M. P. Pogodinu" (September 3, 1855), ROBIL, fond 231, no. 40, ed. 60, p. 5; "Panikhida v Imp. universiteta sv. Vladimira za upokoi dushi grafa S. S. Uvarova," *ZMNP* 8, No. 10 (1855): 19; "Otpevanie telegrafa S. S. Uvarova i panikhida o upokoenii dushi ego," *ZMNP* 9 (1855): 86–88; Menshchikov, "Elegeia," *ZMNP* 1 (February 1856): 25–28 (written in Greek); *Moskovskiia vedomosti* 107 (September 6, 1855); *Moskovskiia vedomosti* 109 (September 10, 1855); M. Longinov, "Vospominanie o grafe S. S. Uvarove," *Sovremennik* 10 (1855): 119–24; the last quotation is in N. Barsukov, *Zhizn' i trudy P. M. Stroeva* (St. Petersburg, 1878), p. 520. On the grand duchess as a rare "liberal" in the family, see W. Bruce Lincoln, "The Circle of the Grand Duchess Yelena Pavlovna, 1847–1861," *Slavonic and East European Review* 47, No. 112 (July 1970): 373–87.

SELECTED BIBLIOGRAPHY

Archival material cited throughout this work will not be included in the bibliography since these sources are unavailable to the general reader. For those scholars with access to Soviet archives, the notes make clear the location of the documents used in preparing this monograph.

UVAROV'S PUBLISHED WORKS

À la mémoire de l'Empereur Alexandre. St. Petersburg, 1826.
À la mémoire de l'Imperatrice Elisabeth. St. Petersburg, 1827.
À la mémoire de l'Imperatrice Marie. St. Petersburg, 1829.
À la mémoire de la Princesse Lieven. St. Petersburg, 1828.
Appel à l'Europe. St. Petersburg, 1815.
"Coup d'oeil sur l'état de la littérature russe." *Le Conservateur impartial,* 77 (September 25, 1817).
"De l'administration de la plupart des gouvernements de la Russie centrale." *Materialy sobrannye dlia vysochaishei uchrezhdennoi komissii o preobrazovanii gubernskikh i uezdnykh uchrezhdenii,* I. St. Petersburg, 1870, pp. 68–72.
De Bulgariorum utrarumque origine et sedibus antiquissimus. Dorpat, 1853.
De provinciarum imperii orientalis administrandarum forma mutata inde a Constantine Magno usque ad Justinianum. Dorpat, 1858.
"Deistviia pravitel'stva: Obozrenie istekshago piatiletiia." *ZMNP* 21, No. 4 (1839): 1–36.
Desiatiletie Ministerstva narodnago prosveshcheniia, 1833–1843. St. Petersburg, 1864.
Discours du Président de l'Académie imperiale des Sciences prononcé dans la séance solennelle du 29 decembre 1826, à l'occasion de la fête séculaire de l'Académie. St. Petersburg, 1827.
"Doklad grafa Uvarova Imp. Mikol I-mu" (1847). *Nashe minule* 2 (1918): 171–77.
"Dva pis'ma Ministra prosveshcheniia grafa S. S. Uvarova k shefu zhandarmov grafu A. K. Benkendorf" (1832–1833). *RA* 23, No. 1 (1885): 366–70.
Éloge funèbre de Moreau. St. Petersburg, 1813. Translations include *Freir Rede auf Moreau.* Riga, 1814; *Funeral Oration Pronounced in Honor of Moreau.* New York and Boston, 1814; "Istoricheskiia izvestie o Moro." *Vestnik Evropy* 78 (January–February 1814): 148–56, 224–31.

L'Empereur Alexandre et Buonaparte. St. Petersburg, 1814.

Esquisses politiques et littéraires. Paris, 1848. Includes "Des Vues de Napoléon sur l'Italie," "Stein et Pozzo di Borgo," "Le Prince de Ligne," "Examen critique de la fable d'Hercule, commentée par Dupuis," "Mémoire sur les tragiques grecs," "Notice sur Goethe," "Vues générales sur la philosophie de la littérature," "Venise," and "Rome."

Essai sur les Mystères d'Éleusis. St. Petersburg, 1812, 1815, and 1816. Translations include *Essay on the Mysteries of Éleusis.* London, 1817; "Issledovanie ob elevsinskikh tainstvakh." Translated by I. I. Vvedenskii. *Sovremennik* 2 (February 1846): 77–108.

Études de philologie et de critique. St. Petersburg, 1843, and Paris, 1845. Includes "Projet d'une académie asiatique," "Éssai sur les Mystères d'Éleusis," "Nonnos von Panopolis, der Dichter," "Über das Vorhomerische Zeitalter," "Examen critique de la fable d'Hercule, commentée par Dupuis," "Mémoire sur les tragiques grecs," "Vues générales sur la philosophie de la littérature," "Notice sur Goethe," and "Le Prince de Ligne."

Examen critique de la fable d'Hercule. St. Petersburg, 1817.

"K istorii klassitsizma v Rossii: Mnenie S. S. Uvarova (1826)." *RA* 37, No. 12 (1899): 465–68.

Lettre à M. le Sécretaire perpetuel de l'Académie imperiale des Sciences. Lué à l'Académie le 6/18 février 1852. St. Petersburg, 1852.

"Literaturnye vospominaniia." *Sovremennik* 27, No. 6 (1851): 37–42. Signed pseudonymously, A. B.

"Littérature russe: Essai en vers et en prose par M. de Batushchoff." *Le Conservateur impartial* 83 (October 16, 1817).

"Marlo, odin iz predshestvennikov Shekspera. Ocherk iz istorii angliiskoi dramy." *Russkoe slovo* 2 (1859: 5–53. Concludes in *Russkoe slovo* 3 (1859): 221–84.

Mémoires sur les tragiques grecs. St. Petersburg, 1824. (Paper read to the Academy of Sciences on November 24, 1820.) Translated as "O trekh grecheskikh tragikakh." Translated by F. Somov. *Syn otechestva* (May 1825): 134–37. The Somov translation concludes in *Syn otechestva* 11 (June 1825): 282–93.

Nonnos von Panopolis, der Dichter. St. Petersburg, 1818.

"O drevne-klassicheskom pamiatnike, perevezennom iz Rima v Porech'e." In *Uchenyia zapiski Imp. Akademii nauk po I i III otdeleniiam.* St. Petersburg, 1852. (Paper read on October 10, 1851; seventeen pamphlets also printed.)

"O narodonaselenii v Rossii." *Chteniia Imp. Akademii nauk* 1 (1831): 114–28 (paper read on December 29, 1830).

O prepodavanii istorii otnositel'no k narodnomu vospitaniiu. St. Petersburg, 1813.

"O skotovodstve voobshche i o sostoianii onago v Porech'e, podmoskovorom imenii G. pochetnago chlena S. S. Uvarova." *Zemledel'cheskii zhurnal* 23 (1828): 198–227.

"Obshchii vzgliad na filosofiiu slovesnosti." *Severnoe obozrenie* 1 (1848): 1–10. Translation into Russian of "Vues générales sur la philosophie de la littérature." Also published separately in St. Petersburg, 1848.

"Os'moe ianvaria 1851 goda." *Sovremennik* 26, No. 3 (1851): 1–6.

"Otchety." *ZMNP.* Uvarov's annual summary of his ministry's activity appeared in the April (No. 4) issue of the *Zhurnal* from 1834 to 1849 and was often published separately.

"Otvet V. V. Kapnistu na pis'mo ego ob eksametre." *Chteniia v Besede liubitelei russkago slova* 17 (1815): 47–67.

"Pis'mo grafu A. K. Razumovskomu: Pervonachal'naia pros'ba Pezaroviusa o razreshenii emu izdavat' ezhenedel'nyi zhurnal, 'Obshchenarodnykh rossiiskikh izvestii'" (1812). *RS* 33, No. 1 (1902): 175–76.

"Pis'mo k baronu Shteinu" (1813). *RA* 9, No. 2 (1871): 129–34.

"Pis'mo k Nikolaiu Ivanovichu Gnedichu o Grecheskom ekzametre." *Chteniia v Besede liubitelei russkago slova* 13 (1813): 56–68.

"Pis'mo k Speranskomu" (1819). *RS* 27, No. 10 (1896): 158–84.

"Pis'mo k Speranskomu" (1819). *V Pamiat' grafa M. M. Speranskago* 1771–1872. St. Petersburg, 1872, pp. 233–34.

"Pis'ma k V. A. Zhukovskomu" (1811–1845). *RA* 9, No. 2 (1871): 157–70.

"Podvigaetsia li vpered istoricheskaia dostovernost'?" *Sovremennik* 26, No. 1 (1851): 121–28. Translated as *La Certitude historique est-elle en progrès?* St. Petersburg, 1850, and Dorpat, 1852.

"Poslednyie minuty zhizhni generala-ot-kavalerii F. P. Uvarova, uchastnika otechestvennoi voiny 1812 g." *RS* 44, No. 8 (August 1913): 353–54.

"Predislovie." *ZMNP* 1, No. 1 (1834): iii–vii.

Le Prince de Ligne. St. Petersburg, 1815.

Proekt tsenzurnago ustava vnesennyi v gosudarstvennyi sovet grafom Uvarovym, v 1849 gody, i neodobrennyi sovetom. St. Petersburg, 1864.

Projet d'une académie asiatique. St. Petersburg, 1810. Translations include *Ideen zu einer asiatischen Akademie.* Translated by A. von Hauenschild. Berlin, 1811; "Mysli o zavedenii v Rossii akademii aziatskoi." Translated by V. Zhukovskii. *Vestnik Evropy* 1 (1811): 27–52. The Zhukovskii translation concludes in *Vestnik Evropy* 2 (1811): 96–120.

"Puteshestviia: Otryvok iz zapisok 1805 goda." *Syn otechestva* 8, No. 47 (1829), 109–16. Signed pseudonymously, A. B.

Rech' prezidenta Im. A. N. popechitelia Peterburgskago uchebnago okruga v torzhestvennom sobrannii Glavnago pedagogicheskago instituta 22 marta 1818. St. Petersburg, 1818. Translation as *Tale af Kuratoren for den Peterborgske Underwisings Anfang S. S. Ouwaroff, holden i det Pedagogiske Central-Institut a 22 marts* 1818. Copenhagen, 1820.

"Rech' S. S. Uvarova, proiznesennaia v chrezvychainom sobranii konferentsii Glavnago pedagogicheskago instituta 14 fevralia 1819 g." *Severnaia pochta* 16 (February 22, 1819). Concludes in *Severnaia pochta* 17 (February 26, 1819).

"S predstavleniem otcheta Tainago sovetnika Uvarova po obozreniiu Imp. Moskovskago universiteta i gimnazii." *SPMNP*, II, 1: 502–32 (December 4, 1832).

"Slovo o Goethe." *Uchenyia zapiski Imperatorskago Moskovskago universiteta* 1 (1833): 74–94 (paper read on March 22, 1833). Also published as *Notice sur Goethe.* St. Petersburg, 1842.

"Smes': O stikhotvorenii Gete." *Syn otechestva* 4, No. 9 (February 27, 1813): 134–36.

Stein et Pozzo di Borgo (St. Petersburg, 1846, and Paris, 1847). Translations include *Shtein i Potstso-di-Borgo.* Translated by M. Rozberg. Dorpat, 1847; and *Stein and Pozzo di Borgo.* Translated by D. F. Campbell. London, 1847.

"Stikhi." *Severnyi vestnik* 8 (November 1805): 188–92.

"Sur l'avantage de mourir jeune." In *Almanach des muses* (1813).

"Tri bumagi S. S. Uvarova" (1847). *RA* 4 (1866): 1066–69.

"Tsirkuliarnoe predlozhenie g. upravliaiushchego Ministerstvom narodnago prosveshcheniia nachalstvam uchebnykh okrugov, 'O vstuplenii v upravlenie Ministerstvom.'" *ZMNP* 1, No. 1 (1834): xlix–xlx.

Über das Vorhomerische Zeitalter. St. Petersburg, 1819.

"Vospominanie ob akademike Fr. Grefe." *Uchenye zapiski Akademii nauk po I i III otd.* St. Petersburg, 1853 (paper read at meeting of the Academy on February 6, 1852).

"Vsepoddaneishaia dokladnaia zapiska o stat'e 'Filosoficheskiia pis'ma' v Zhurnale 'Teleskop' ot 20 Okt. 1836 g." *RA* 22, No. 3 (1884): 459–61.

PUBLISHED PRIMARY SOURCES

Afanas'ev, A. N. "Moskovskii universitet, 1843–1849 gg." *RS* 17, No. 8 (1886): 357–94.

Akademiia nauk. *Katalog izdanii Imp. Akademii nauk.* St. Petersburg, 1912. "Polozhenie o nagradakh grafa Uvarova (November 7, 1858)." *Sbornik postanovlenii i rasporiazhenii, otnosiashchikhsia do Imp. Akademii nauk.* St. Petersburg, 1869.

———. "Séance solennelle de l'Académie tenue en l'honneur de son président M. S. d'Ouvaroff le 12 janvier 1843." *Recueil des actes des séances publiques de l'Académie imperiale des Sciences.* St. Petersburg, 1843.

Aksakov, K. S. *Vospominaniia studentstva.* St. Petersburg, 1911.

Aksakov, S. T. *Sobranie sochinenii.* 6 vols. St. Petersburg, 1909.

Androssov, V. "O predelakh, v koikh dolzhny byt izuchaemy i prepodavaemy prava politicheskoe i narodnoe." *ZMNP* 4, No. 12 (1834): 367–85.

Annenkov, P. V. "Dve zimy v provintsii i derevne. S ianvaria 1849 do avgust 1851 goda." *Byloe* 18 (1922): 4–18.

———. *The Extraordinary Decade: Literary Memoirs.* Translated by I. R. Titunik and edited by A. P. Mendel. Ann Arbor, 1968.

———. *Literaturnye vospominaniia.* Moscow, 1960.

———. *Materialy dlia biografii A. S. Pushkina.* St. Petersburg, 1855.

Arkheograficheskaia ekspeditsiia Akademii nauk, 1828–1834: Sbornik materialov. Leningrad, 1930.

Arndt, E. M. *Meine Wanderungen und Wandelungen mit dem Reichsfreiherrn H. R. F. von Stein.* Berlin, 1858.

Ashevskii, S. "Iz istorii Moskovskago universiteta." *Mir Bozhii* 14, No. 3 (1905): 109–16.

Baader, Franz von. *Lettres inédites de Franz von Baader.* Edited by E. Susini. 3 vols. Paris, 1942.

Batiushkov, K. N. *Sochineniia.* St. Petersburg, 1885–1887.

Belinskii, V. *Pol'noe sobranie sochinenii.* Moscow, 1955.

Bludova, A. D. "Vospominaniia grafini A. D. Bludovoi." *RA* 27, No. 1 (1889): 39–112.

Bogoliubov, V. F. "Pis'ma V. F. Bogoliubova k kniaziu Aleksandru Borisovichu Kurakinu." *RA* 31, No. 10 (1893): 233–46. Concludes in *RA* 11 (1893): 257–315.

Boguslavskii, P. G. "Istoricheskie razskazy i anekdoty." *RS* 11, No. 1 (1880): 173–84.

Bolkhovitinova, E. "Pis'ma mitropolita Evgeniia Bolkhovitinova k V. G. Anastasevichu, 1820." *RA* 27, No. 2 (1889): 321–88.

Borgo, P. *Iz besedy Potstso di Borgo s baronom Meiendorfom v Vene v 1832 godu.* St. Petersburg, 1910.

———. "Zametka gr. Potstso di Borgo o nem samom." *Sbornik Imperatorskago russkago istoricheskago obshchestva* 2 (1868): 158–63.

Bradke, E. F. von. "Avtobiograficheskiia zapiski." *RA* 13, No. 3 (1875): 257–94.

Bre, O. de. "Vospominaniia: Imperator Nikolai i ego spodvizhniki." *RS* 33, No. 1 (1902): 115–39.

Briullov, K. P. "Arkhiv Briullovykh." *RS* 31, No. 10 (1900): 177–95.

Bulgakov, A. Ia. "Iz pis'em A. Ia. Bulgakova k bratu." *RA* 39, No. 1 (1901): 46–94. This item concludes in several issues of *RA*, as listed here. *RA* 39, No. 2 (1901): 260–315. *RA* 39, No. 3 (1901): 398–469. *RA* 39, No. 6 (1901): 161–238. *RA* 39, No. 7 (1901): 339–437. *RA* 39, No. 9 (1901): 1–43. *RA* 40, No. 1 (1902): 42–157.

Bulgarin, F. *Rossiia v istoricheskom, staticheskom, geograficheskom i literaturnom otnosheniiakh.* 6 vols. St. Petersburg, 1837.

Burke, E. *Reflections on the Revolution in France.* New York, 1955.

Buslaev, F. "Vospominaniia." *Vestnik Evropy* 6, No. 11 (1891): 1–56, 513–48.

Buturlin, M. D. "Zapiski grafa M. D. Buturlina." *RA* 39, No. 11 (1901): 384–421.

Chaadaev, P. Ia. *Sochineniia i pis'ma P. Ia. Chaadaeva.* Edited by M. O. Gershenzon. Moscow, 1914.

Chateaubriand. *Memoirs.* Translated by R. Balick. New York, 1961.

———.*Oeuvres complètes.* 7 vols. Paris, 1828.

Celebrated Speeches of Chatham, Burke and Erskine. Philadelphia, 1835.

Cherevin, P. D. "O prepodavanii istorii detiam." *Vestnik Evropy* 1 (January–February 1825): 117–29.

Chistiakov, M. "Chateaubriand." *ZMNP* 41 (February 1849): 1–52.

Condorcet, M. *Esquisse d'un tableau historique des progrès de l'esprit humain.* Paris, 1966.

Custine, A. de. *Journey for Our Time.* Edited and translated by P. P. Kohler. Chicago, 1951.

———. *La Russie en* 1839. 4 vols. Brussels, 1843.

Davydov, I. I. "O naznachenii russkikh universitetov i uchastii ikh v obshchestvennom obrazovanii." *Sovremennik* 14, No. 3 (1849): 37–46. Written under Uvarov's direction.

———. "Pis'ma I. I. Davydova k A. A. Prokopovichu-Antonskomu." *RA* 27, No. 3 (1889): 542–65.

———. "Selo Porech'e." *Moskvitianin* 5, No. 9 (1841): 156–90.

———. "Vozmozhna li u nas germanskaia filosofiia?" *Moskvitianin* 2, No. 3 (1842): 385–401.

———. "Vzgliad na zhizn' Uvarova, kak muzha gosudarstvennago, kak pisatelia i kak cheloveka." *Izvestiia Imperatorskii Akademii nauk* 5 (1856): 14–22.

Delariu, F. M. "D. M. Delariu i A. S. Pushkin." *RS* 11, No. 9 (1880): 217–19.

Dmitriev, I. I. "Pis'ma 1806–1823 godov I. I. Dmitrieva k A. I. Turgeneva." *RA* 5 (1867): 1072–1138.

Dolgorukov, N. V. "Iz zapisok kniazia N. V. Dolgorukova." *RA* 30, No. 11 (1892): 261–90.

Dondukov-Korsakov, A. M. *Moi vospominaniia.* St. Petersburg, 1902–1903.

Dorn, B. *Das Asiatische Museum der kaiserlichen Akademie der Wissenschaften zu St. Petersburg.* St. Petersburg, 1846.

Dvadtsatipiatiletie Evropy v tsarstvovanie Aleksandra I. 2 vols. St. Petersburg, 1831.

Elagina, E. I. "Iz vospominanii E. I. Elaginoi." *RA* 40, No. 3 (1902): 476–80.

Elizaveta Alekseevna. "Pis'mo imperatritsy Elizavety Alekseevny k S. S. Uvarovu." *RS* 15, No. 11 (1884): 389.

Fisher, A. "O khode obrazovaniia v Rossii i ob uchastii kakoe dolzhna prinimat' v nem filosofiia." *ZMNP* 5, No. 1 (1835): 28–68.

———. "O noveishem estestvennom prave." *ZMNP* 9, No. 1 (1836): 1–19.

Fisher, K. I. "Zapiski senatora K. I. Fishera." *Istoricheskii vestnik* 3, No. 1 (1908): 439–60.

Fletcher, G. *Of the Russe Commonwealth, 1591.* Introduction by R. Pipes. Cambridge, Mass., 1966.

Freiherr vom Stein. Edited by M. L. E. Lehmann. 6 vols. Leipzig, 1905.

F. U. "Graf S. S. Uvarov." *Biblioteka dlia chteniia* 136, No. 3 (1856): 66–79.

Fuss, M. P. "Coup d'oeil historique sur le dernier quart-de-siècle de l'existence de l'Académie imperiale des Sciences de Saint-Pétersbourg." In *Recueil des actes des séances publiques de l'Académie imperiale des Sciences.* St. Petersburg, 1843.

Gavriila, A. *Istoriia russkoi filosofii*. Kazan, 1940.
Gay, P., ed. *The Enlightenment: A Comprehensive Anthology*. New York, 1973.
Glinka, F. "Podrobnyi otchet drugu o priiatnom vechere v obshchestve pros-veshchennykh liudei." *Syn otechestva* 45, No. 19 (1818): 22–36.
Gnedich, N. I. "Razsuzhdenie o prichinakh, zamedliaiushchikh uspekhi nashei slovesnosti." In *Opisanie torzhestvennago otkrytiia Imp. publichnoi biblioteki, byvshago ianvaria 2 dnia 1814 goda*. St. Petersburg, 1814.
————. "Pis'mo k S. S. Uvarovu." *Chteniia v Besede liubitelei russkago slova* 13 (1813): 67–72.
Gogol', N. V. "Plan prepodavaniia vseobshchei istorii." *ZMNP* 1, No. 2 (1834).
————. *Pol'noe sobranie sochinenii*. Moscow, 1940.
Golokhvastov, D. P. "K istorii Moskovskago universiteta." *RA* 25, No. 2 (1887): 245–51.
————. "Ob ukraino-slavianskom obshchestve: Iz bumag D. P. Golokhvastova." *RA* 30, No. 7 (1892): 334–59.
Golovine, I. *Russia under the Autocrat, Nicholas I*. New York, 1970.
Golubinskii, F. A. *Biograficheskie ocherki*. Moscow, 1855.
Grech, N. I. "F. V. Bulgarin, 1789–1859." *RS* 2, No. 11 (1871): 483–523.
————. *Zapiski o moei zhizni*. St. Petersburg, 1886.
Griboedov, A. S. *Sobranie sochinenii*. Edited by I. A. Shliankin. St. Petersburg, 1889.
Grudev, G. V. "Iz razskazov G. V. Grudeva." *RA* 36, No. 11 (1898): 426–39.
Guizot, F. *Historical Essays and Lectures*. Chicago, 1972.
————. "Isotoriia prosveshcheniia i grazhdanskago obrazovaniia." *ZMNP* 1, No. 3 (1834): 428–452.
————. *Memoirs to Illustrate the History of My Time*. Translated by J. W. Cole. 3 vols. London, 1860.
Gumbol'dt, A. *Perepiska Aleksandra Gumbol'dta s uchenymi i gosudarstvennymi deia-teliami Rossii*. Moscow, 1962.
Hegel, G. W. F. *The Philosophy of History*. New York, 1956
Herder, J. G. *Auch eine Philosophie der Geschichte zur Bildung der Menscheit*. N.p., 1774.
————. *Reflections on the Philosophy of the History of Mankind*. Chicago, 1968.
Hertzen, A. I. *My Past and Thoughts*. 2 vols. Translated by C. Garnett. New York, 1968.
I. Kh. "Za Pushkina." *RA* 26, No. 2 (1888): 500–501.
I. S. "Kriticheskoe obozrenie kantovoi religii v predelakh odnogo razuma." *ZMNP* 17, No. 1 (1838): 44–99.
"Iubilei prezidenta AN, S. S. Uvarova." *Moskvitianin* 2, No. 3 (1843): 265–86.
Ivanitskii, N. I. "Iz avtobiografii N. I. Ivanitskago." *RA* 47, No. 10 (1909): 126–80.
Ivanovskii, A. "O nachalakh postepennago usovershenstvovaniia nashego go-sudarstva." *ZMNP* 13, No. 1 (1837): 1–15.
"Iz istorii 'Obshchestva sv. Kirilla i Mefodiia' (1847): Ustav i pravila, prokla-matsii." *Byloe*, February 1906, pp. 66–68.
"Iz zapisok damy." *RA* 20, No. 1 (1882): 206–19.
Kapnist, V. V. *Sochineniia Kapnista*. Edited by A. Smirdin. St. Petersburg, 1849.
Karamzin, N. M. *Izbrannye sochineniia*. 2 vols. Moscow, 1964.
————. *Karamzin's Memoir on Ancient and Modern Russia*. Edited by and intro-duced by R. Pipes. Cambridge, Mass., 1959.
————. *Neizdannye sochineniia i perepiska*. St. Petersburg, 1862.
————. "Pis'ma N. M. Karamzina k A. I. Turgenevu." *RS* 30, No. 2 (1899): 463–80.

_____. "Pis'ma N. M. Karamzina k S. S. Uvarovu." *Syn otechestva* 44, No. 8 (1818): 79–80.

Kireevskii, I. V. "Pis'ma I. V. Kireevskago k A. S. Khomiakovu." *RA* 47, No. 5 (1909): 109–14.

Klaproth, J. *Archiv für Asiatische Literatur, Geschichte und Sprachkunde.* St. Petersburg, 1810.

Kliuchevskii, V. O., et al. *Vospominaniia o studencheskoi zhizni.* Moscow, 1889.

Kolmakov, N. M. "Ocherki i vospominaniia N. M. Kolmakova." *RS* 22, No. 5 (1891): 449–69.

Korf, M. A. "Iz zapisok barona M. A. Korfa." *RS* 31, No. 2 (1900): 545–88.

Kostomarov, N. I. *Avtobiografiia.* Edited by V. Kotel'nikov. Moscow, 1922.

Kristina. "Perepiska Kristina s kniazhnoi Turkestanovoi, 1813–1815." *RA* 20, No. 2 (1882): 1–236.

Kroneberg, I. "O izuchenii slovesnosti." *ZMNP* 8 (November 1835): 255–89.

Krusenstern, A. de. *Précis du système, des progrès et de l'état de l'instruction publique en Russie.* Warsaw, 1845.

Kunitsyn, A. P. "O konstitutsii." *Syn otechestva* 45 (1818): 202–11.

_____. "Rassmotrenie rechi." *Syn otechestva* 46 (1819): 136–46, 174–91.

Kutorga, S. "Vzgliad na izuchenii estestvennoi istorii." *ZMNP* 25, No. 11 (1835): 290–300

Kutuzov, N. "O prichinakh blagodenstviia i velichiia narodov." *Syn otechestva* 49, No. 1 (1820): 3–20.

Lebedev; K. N. "Iz zapisok senatora K. N. Lebedeva. 1855." This item concludes in succeeding issues of *RA*, as listed here. *RA* 26, No. 1 (1888): 481–88, 617–28; *RA* 26, No. 2 (1888): 133–44, 232–43, 345–66; *RA* 26, No. 3 (1888): 249–70, 455–67.

Leduc, L. "Essai biographique et critique." *Esquisses politiques et littéraires.* Paris, 1848.

Leont'ev, P. M. "Bakkhicheskii pamiatnik grafa S. S. Uvarova." *Propilei: Sbornik statei po klassicheskoi drevnosti* 1 (1851): 135–43.

Ligne, Charles-Joseph, Prince de. *Mélanges militaires, littéraires, sentimentaires.* 37 vols. in 12. Paris, 1827.

Lilienthal, M. *My Travels in Russia.* New York, 1937.

Longinov, M. N. "Vospominanie o grafe S. S. Uvarove." *Sovremennik* 53, No. 10 (1885): 119–24.

Loransi, P. S. "O dukhe ucheniia." *ZMNP* 11 (August 1836): 586–601.

Lozinskii, S. G. *Opisanie del vyshego arkhiva Ministerstva narodnago prosveshcheniia: Kazennye evreiskie uchilishcha.* Petrograd, 1920.

Magnitskii, M. L. "Dva mneniia." *RA* 2, No. 3 (1874): 321–27.

_____. "Instruktsiia k D. M. Makseevu." *RA* 5 (1867): 1643–47.

_____. "Rech' k Imperatorskomu Kazanskomu universitetu 15 sentiabria 1825 goda." *Chteniia v Imperatorskom Obshchestve istorii i drevnostei rossiiskikh pri moskovskom universitete* 4 (1861): 160–61.

Maistre, J. de. *Considérations sur la France.* Paris, 1936.

_____. *Lettres et opuscules inédites.* 2 vols. Paris, 1851.

_____. *On God and Society.* Chicago, 1959.

_____. *Quatre chapitres inédites sur la Russie.* Paris, 1859.

_____. *Soirées de Saint-Pétersbourg.* Utrecht, 1821.

_____. *The Works of Joseph de Maistre.* Edited by Jack Lively. New York, 1965.

Maksimov, S. V. "Literaturnaia ekspeditsia." *RS* 11, No. 2 (1890): 17–50.

Maksimovich, M. "O znachenii i proizkhozhdenie slova." *ZMNP* 5, No. 1 (1835): 14–27.

————. "Ob uchastii i znachenii Kieva v obshchei zhizni Rossii." *ZMNP* 16 (October 1837): 1–29.

Mallet du Pan, M. "Considerations on the Nature of the French Revolution." In *Political Tracts*. Vol. V. London, 1793.

Martynov, N. S. "Iz bumag N. S. Martynova." *RA* 31, No. 8 (1893): 585–606.

Ministerstvo narodnago prosveshcheniia. *Sbornik postanovlenii po Ministerstvu narodnago prosveshcheniia*. 15 vols. St. Petersburg, 1875–1902. I: 1802–1815 (St. Petersburg, 1864); II: 1825–55 (St. Petersburg, 1876).

————. *Staticheskie materialy dlia opredeleniia obshchestvennago polozheniia lishch', poluvshikh obrazovanie v Imperatorskom universiteta s 1802–1852 goda*. St. Petersburg, 1862.

"Mnenie o uchrezhdenii universiteta v Sankt-Peterburge (grafa Severina Pototskago)." *Chteniia v Imp. Obshchestve istorii i drevnostei Rossiiskikh pri Moskovskom universitete* 4 (December 1860): 308–13.

Montesquieu, C. *The Spirit of the Laws*. New York, 1949.

Moscow University. *Biblioteka*. Moscow, 1845.

————. *Biograficheskii slovar' Moskovskago universiteta*. 2 vols. in 1. Moscow, 1855.

Mukhanov, N. A. "Iz dnevnika N. A. Mukhanova." *RA* 35, No. 4 (1897): 653–57.

Mukhanov, V. A. "Iz drevnikh zapisok V. A. Mukhanova." *RA* 35, No. 1 (1897): 45–109.

————. "Iz novonaidennykh zapisnykh knizhek V. A. Mukhanova." *RA* 38, No. 2 (1900): 316.

Murav'ev-Apostol, I. M. "Pis'ma iz Moskvy v Nizhnii Novgorod." *Syn otechestva* 8, Nos. 35 and 36 (1813): 89–97 and 129–39, respectively. Concludes in *Syn otechestva* 9, Nos. 44 and 45 (1813): 211–34 and 259–70, respectively; *Syn otechestva* 10, No. 49 (1813): 137–55; *Syn otechestva* 11, Nos. 3 and 4 (1814): 97–109 and 62–73, respectively; and *Syn otechestva* 12, No. 7 (1814): 19–30.

Nadezhdin, N. I. "Ob istoricheskikh trudakh v Rossii." *Biblioteka dlia chteniia* 20 (1837): 93–136.

Nevolin, K. "O soedinenii teorii s praktikoiu v izuchenii zakonov i v deloproizvodstve." *ZMNP* 8 (December 1835): 443–75.

Nikiforov, D. *Vospominaniia iz vremen imperatora Nikolaia I*. Moscow, 1903.

Nikitenko, A. V. *The Diary of a Russian Censor*. Edited and translated by H. S. Jacobson. Amherst, Mass., 1975.

————. *Dnevnik*. 3 vols. Leningrad, 1955.

Nikolai Pavlovich. "Iz pisem Nikolaia Pavlovicha k kniaziu I. F. Paskevichu." *RA* 48, No. 3 (1910): 321–56.

"Notice of: 'Essai sur les Mystères d'Éleusis.' 2nd ed. St. Petersburg, 1815." *Classical Journal* 13, No. 26 (1816): 399–406; 27 (1816), 165–71; 28 (1817): 117–23.

Novitskii, O. "Ob uprekakh, delaemykh filosofii v teoreticheskom i prakticheskom otnoshenii, ikh sil' i vazhnosti." *ZMNP* 17 (February 1838): 229–329.

"O litsakh, komandirovannykh Ministerstvom narodnago prosveshcheniia za granitsu dlia prigotovleniia k zvaniiu professorov i prepodavatelei s 1808 po 1860 god." *ZMNP* 121 (January 1864): 335–54.

"O metode Belia i Lankastera." *Syn otechestva* 96, No. 21 (1817): 26–35.

"O periodicheskikh izdaniiakh vo Frantsi." *ZMNP* 1, No. 1 (1834): 118–22.

Obolenskii, M. A. "Pis'ma kniazia M. A. Obolenskago k V. A. Polenovu (1839–1851)." *RA* 20, No. 1 (1882): 249–96.

"Obozrenie khoda i uspekhov prepodavaniia aziatskikh iazykov pri Kazanskom universiteta." *ZMNP* 39, No. 1 (1843): 49–78.

"Obshchestvo literaturov v Nizhnem Novgorode v 1812 godu." *Severnaia pchela* 72 (March 30, 1845): 285–86.

Ochkin, A. "O sostoianii narodnago prosveshcheniia v Prussii." *ZMNP* 1, No. 1 (1834): 61–80.

Odoevskii, V. F. *Izbrannye pedagogicheskie sochineniia.* Moscow, 1955.

———. *Russian Nights.* Translated by O. Koshansky-Olienikov and R. Matlaw. New York, 1965.

Olenin, A. N. *O knemakakh u drevnykh grekov, ili ponozhkakh: Pis'mo A. N. Olenina k S. S. Uvarovu (May 25, 1815).* St. Petersburg, 1872.

Ooma, F. A. "Vospominaniia." *RA* 44, No. 6 (1896): 217–72.

Ostaf'evskii arkhiv kniazei Viazemskikh. Edited by S. D. Sheremetev and V. I. Saitov. 8 vols. St. Petersburg, 1899–1913.

"Otryvok iz zapisok starago diplomata, 1855." *Bibliograficheskie zapiski* 1, No. 10 (1858): 291–308. Concludes in *Bibliograficheskie zapiski* 1, No. 11 (1858): 323–31.

Ozhe-de-Rankur, N. "V dvukh universitetakh." *RS* 27, No. 6 (1896): 571–82.

Panaev, I. I. *Literaturnye vospominaniia.* Moscow, 1950.

Pirogov, N. I. *Izbrannye pedagogicheskie sochineniia.* Moscow, 1952.

Pletnev, P. A. "O narodnosti v literature." *ZMNP* 1, No. 1 (1834): 1–30.

———. "Pamiati grafa S. S. Uvarova, prezidenta Imperatorskoi Akademii nauk." *Uchenye zapiski.* Vol. I (1856), pp. liii–cxxv.

———. *Sochineniia i perepiska.* Edited by Ia. K. Grot. 3 vols. St. Petersburg, 1896.

Pnin, I. I. *Sochineniia.* Moscow, 1934.

Pogodin, M. P. "Dlia biografii graf S. S. Uvarova." *RA* 9, No. 12 (1871): 2078–2107.

———. *God v chuzhikh kraiakh.* Moscow, 1844.

———. *Istoriko-politicheskie pis'ma i zapiski vpodalzhenii voiny, 1853–1856.* Moscow, 1874.

———. "O vseobshchei istorii." *ZMNP* 1, No. 1 (1834): 31–44.

———. "Obuchenie drevnim iazykam v Rossii." *RA* 40, No. 1 (1902): 163–88.

———. "Petr Velikii." *Moskvitianin* 1, No. 1 (1841): 3–29.

———. "Pis'ma M. P. Pogodina k S. P. Shevyrevu." *RA* 20, No. 3 (1882): 67–126.

———. *Pis'ma i stati M. Pogodina o politike Rossii v otnoshenii slavianskikh narodov i zapadnoi Evropy.* Paris, 1861.

———. "Prebyvanie Ministra narodnago prosveshcheniia v Moskve." *Moskvitianin* 8, No. 10 (1848): 1–10.

———. "Shkolnyia vospominaniia, 1814–1820." *Vestnik Evropy* 4, No. 8 (1868): 605–30.

Polevoi, K. A. *Zapiski.* St. Petersburg, 1888.

Polevoi, N. A. "Novaia Svetlana." *RA* 23, No. 1 (1885): 649–59.

Polevye. "Iz pis'em brat'ev Polevykh k V. K. Karlgofu." *RA* 50, No. 3 (1912): 419–25.

Politsyn, N. A. "Manifesty, napisannye Shishkovym v otechestvennuiu voinu, i patrioticheskoe ikh znachenie." *RS* 43, No. 6 (1912):477–91.

Polnoe sobranie zakonov Rossiiskoi imperii, 1649–1916. 240 vols. St. Petersburg, 1830–1916.

"Pravoslavie—istochnik spaseniia otechestva." *ZMNP* 61 (January 1849): 1–30.

"Proekt ustava obshchestva uchrezhdeniia uchilishch po metode vzaimnago obucheniia Belia i Lankastera (1818)." *RS* 1 180–82.

Pushkin, A. S. *Dnevnik Pushkina, 1833–1835.* Edited by B. L. Modzalevskii. Moscow, 1923.

———. *Epigrammy*. Moscow, 1979.

———. *The Letters of Alexander Pushkin*. Translated by J. Thomas Shaw. 3 vols. Bloomington, Ind., 1963.

———. *Polnoe sobranie sochinenii*. vols. Moscow, 1936.

———. *Pushkin bez tsenzury*. London, 1972.

———. "Pushkin o Batiushkove." *RA* 32, No. 1 (1894): 528–55.

Pushkin, V.L. *Sochineniia*. Edited by V. I. Saitov. St. Petersburg, 1893.

Raeff, M., ed. *The Decembrist Movement*. ENglewood Cliffs, N.J., 1966.

———. *Plans for Political Reform in Imperial Russia*, 1730–1905. Englewood Cliffs, N.J., 1966.

———. *Russian Intellectual History: An Anthology*. New York, 1966.

Robert, C., "Les deux panslavismes." *Revue des deux mondes* 16 (October 1946): 452–83.

Robertson, W. *The Progress of Society in Europe*. Edited by Felix Gilbert. Chicago, 1972.

Rozberg, M. "Glavnyia svoistva grecheskoi i rimskoi slovesnosti." *ZMNP* 3 (July 1834): 1–26.

———. "Ob istoricheskkom znachenii Rossii." *ZMNP* 17 (January 1938): 1–16.

Saint-Pierre, Charles, Abbé de. *Abrège du projet de paix*. Paris, 1729.

Sazonov, N.I. "Pis'ma N. I. Sazonova k Gertsenu." *Literaturnoe nasledstvo* 42 (1955): 522–45.

Schlegel, F. *The Aesthetic and Miscellaneous Works of Friedrich von Schlegel*. Translated by E. J. Millington. London, 1881.

———. *Briefe von und an Friedrich und Dorothea Schlegel*. Edited by J. Körner. Berlin, 1926.

———. *A Course of Lectures of Modern History*. Translated by L. Purcell and R. Whitelock. London, 1886.

———. *The Philosophy of History*. Translated by J. B. Robertson. London, 1852.

Semevmskii, V. I. "Materialy po istorii tsenzury v Rossii." *Gotos minuvshego* 3 (March 1913): 218–228.

Shcherbatov, Prince M. M. *On the Corruption of Morals in Russia*. Edited by A. Lentin. Cambridge, Eng., 1969.

Shcherbin, N. F. "Grafu S. S. Uvarovu, pri otkrytii pamiatnika Zhukovskomu v sele Porech'e." *RA* 44, No. 2 (1906): 127–28.

Shchkin, P. I., ed. *Bumagi, otnosiahchiiasia do Otechestvennoi voiny 1812 goda*. 10 vols. Moscow, 1908.

Shelgunov, N. V. *Vospominaniia*. Moscow, 1923.

Shevyrev, S. P., *Istoriia Imperatorskago Moskovskago universiteta*, 1755–1855. Moscow, 1855.

———. "O tseli v vospitanii." *ZMNP* 73 (March 1852): 134–51.

———. "Ob otnoshenii semeinago vospitaniia k gosudarstvennomu." *ZMNP* 35 (July 1842): 1–52. Concluded in *AMNP* 35 (August 1842): 63–111.

———. "Vstuplenie v pedagogiiu." *ZMNP* 73 (January 1852): 9–42.

———. "Vzgliad russkago na sovremennoe obrazovnie Evropy." *Moskvitianin* 1, No. 1 (1841): 219–96.

Shil'der, N. K. "Dva donosa v 1831 godu: Vsepoddanneishiia pis'ma M. Magnitskago imperatoru Nikolaiu ob illuminatakh." *RS* 30, No. 3 (11899 60731

Shishkov, A. S. *Zapiski, mneniia i perepiska*. Edited by N. Kisilev and I. Samarin. Berlin, 1870.

Smirnov, A. O. "A. S. Pushkin po zapiskam A. O. Smirnovoi." *RA* 37, No. 6 (1899): 310–99.

Sobolevskii, S. A. "Vyderzhki iz zagranichnykh pis'em S.A. Sobolevskago k S. P. Shevyrevu." *RA* 47, No. 2 (1909): 475–511.

Solov'ev, I. M., ed. *Russkie universitety v ikh ustavkh i vospominaniiakh sovremennikov.* St. Petersburg, n.d.

Speranskii, M. M. *Plan' gosudarstvennago preobrazovaniia.* Moscow, 1905.

_____. "Pis'ma Speranskago k A. A. Stolypinu." *RA* 7 (1869): 1681–1709. Concludes in *RA* 8 (1870): 1125–55.

_____. "Pis'mo M. M. Speranskago—S. S. Uvarovu po povodu izbraniia ego pochetnym chlenom Akademii nauk." *RS* 34, No. 3 (1903): 444.

Sreznevskii, N. I. "Evropeiskie sistemy prosveshcheniia v ikh sovremennom sostoianii." *ZMNP* 20 (November 1838): 251–64.

Staël, G. de. *De l'Allemagne.* Paris, 1835.

_____. *Ten Years of Exile.* Translated by D. Beik. New York, 1972.

Starchevskii, A. "Vospominaniia starago literatora." *Istoricheskii vestnik* 6, No. 10 (September 1886): 46–84.

Sturdza, A. S. "Vospominaniia o N. M. Karamzine." *Moskvitianin* 6, Nos. 9–10 (1846): 145–54.

Tiutchev, F. I. "Na I. I. D." *RA* 22, No. 1 (1884): 243.

_____. "Pis'ma." *Literaturnoe nasledstvo* 19–20 (1935): 582–83.

Tolstoi, D. N. "Pis'ma grafa D. N. Tolstago k grafu M. D. Buturlinu." *RA* 50, No. 3 (1912): 352–68.

Turgenev, A. I. "Aleksandr I. Turgenev v ego pis'makh, 1827–1845." *RS* 12, No. 6 (1881): 187–206. Concludes in *RS* 13, No. 5 (1882): 443–62.

Turgenev, N. I. *Dekabrist N. I. Turgenev: Pis'ma k bratu S. I. Turgenevu.* Moscow, 1936.

_____. *La Russie et les Russes.* 3 vols. Paris, 1847.

_____. *O nravstvennom otnoshenii Rossii k Evrope.* Leipzig, 1869.

Ustrialov, N. G. *Istoricheskoe obozrenie tsarstvovaniia gosudaria imperatora Nikolaia I.* St. Petersburg, 1847.

_____. *O sisteme pragmaticheskoi russkoi istorii.* St. Petersburg, 1836.

_____. *Russkaia istoriia.* St. Petersburg, 1839.

_____. "Vospominaniia o moei zhizni." *Drevniaia i novaia Rossiia,* January 1877, pp. 26–42 and August 1880, pp. 603–86.

Viazemskii, P. A. "Iz pis'em Viazemskago k Zhukovskomu." *RA* 38, No. 3 (1900): 355–90.

_____. "Pis'ma kniazia P. A. Viazemskago iz Peterburga v chuzhie kraia k A. O. Smirnovoi," *RA* 26, No. 2 (1888): 292–304.

_____. *Polnoe sobranie sochinenii,* 10 vols. St. Petersburg, 1886.

Vigel', F. F. *Zapiski.* 5 vols. Moscow, 1892.

Vologzhanin. "Pamiatnye zametki Vologzhanina." *RA* 5 (1867): 1646–1707.

"Vospominaniia pervago kamer-pazha." *RS* 6, No. 4 (1875): 769–96.

"Vyderzhki iz staroi zapisnoi knizhki, nachatoi v 1813 godu." *RA* 14, No. 1 (1876): 60–70. Concludes in *RA* 14, No. 10 (1876): 155–61.

"Vzgliad na soderzhanie Zhurnala Ministerstva narodnago prosveshcheniia za minuvshee piatiletie." *ZMNP* 21 (January 1839): 1–23.

Welcker, K. T. *Die Letzten Grunde von Recht, Staat, und Strafe.* Giessen, 1813.

Wolf, F. A. *Erziehung, Schule, Universität.* Leipzig, 1835.

Zakrevskii, A. A. "Pis'mo grafa A. A. Zakrevskago k popechiteliu Moskovskago universiteta D. P. Golokhvastovu." *RA* 25, No. 2 (1887): 522–23.

"Zamechaniia frantsuzskikh gazet' kasatel'no rasporiazheniia russkago pravitel'stva o chastnykh pansionakh." *ZMNP* 2 (April 1834): 138–45.

Zavadovskii, V. P. "Imperator Nikolai Pavlovich v ego rechi k deputatam S.-Peterburgskago dvorianstva." *RS* 14 (1883): 593–96.

Zhukovskii, V. A. "Pis'ma." *RA* 38, No. 9 (1900): 5–54.

_____. "Pis'ma Zhukovskago k Pushkinu." *RA* 47, No. 2 (1909): 152–57.

————. "Pis'ma Zhukovskago k Turgenevu." *RA* 38, Nos. 1–12 (1895). Special supplement, pp. 1–310.

————. "Razskaz V. A. Zhukovskago o pervom ego predstavlenii imperatritse Marii Feodorovni." *RA* 3 (1865): 803–6.

————. *Sobranie sochinenii.* 4 vols. Moscow, 1960.

SECONDARY SOURCES

A. Ia. "Kollegiia inostrannykh del'." *Entsiklopedicheskii slovar'*, XXX (1895), p. 696.

Aizenshtok, I. "Frantsuzskie pisateli v otsenkakh tsarskoi tsenzury." *Literaturnoe nasledstvo* 33–34 (1939): 769–858.

Akademiia nauk. *Aziatskoi muzei rossiiskoi akademii nauk, 1818–1918.* Petrograd, 1920.

————. *Katalog izdanii Imp. Akademii nauk: Periodicheskiia izdaniia, sborniki, otchety i serii s 1726 goda po 1912 goda.* St. Petersburg, 1912.

————. *Ocherk istorii muzeev Imperatorskoi Akademii nauk.* St. Petersburg, 1865.

————. *Sobranie aktov torzhestvennago zasedaniia Imp. Spb. AN byvshago po sluchaiu prazdnovaniia stoletniago eia sushchestvovaniia 19 dekabria 1826 goda.* St. Petersburg, 1827.

Alekseev, M. P., ed. *Ot klassitsizma k romantizmu.* Leningrad, 1970.

————. *Rannie romanticheskie veianiia: Iz istorii mezhdunarodnykh sviazei russkoi literatury.* Leningrad, 1972.

Aleshintsev, I. *Istoriia gimnazicheskago obrazovaniia v Rossii.* St. Petersburg, 1912.

————. *Soslovnyi vopros i politika v istorii nashikh gimnazii.* St. Petersburg, 1908.

Allister, S. H. "The Reform of Higher Education in Russia during the reign of Nicholas I, 1825–1855." Ph.D. diss., Princeton University, 1974.

Alston, P. L. *Education and the State in Tsarist Russia.* Stanford, Calif., 1969.

Anderson, B. A., and A. J. Coale. *Human Fertility in Russia since the Nineteenth Century.* Princeton, N.J., 1979.

Anderson, R. "Secondary Education in Mid-Nineteenth Century France." *Past and Present* 53 (November 1971): 121–46.

Andress, J. M. *Johann Gottfried Herder as an Educator.* New York, 1916.

Anichkov, E. V. "Ocherk Pushkinskago perioda." In *Istoriia Rossii v XIX veke.* Vol. II. St. Petersburg, 1910.

Annenkov, P. V. *A. S. Pushkin v Aleksandrovskuiu epokhu.* St. Petersburg, 1874.

Aris, R. *History of Political Thought in Germany from 1789 to 1815.* London, 1936.

Aristov, V. V. "Dissertatsii kirillo-mefodievtsa I. A. Posiady." *Opisanie rukopisei nauchnoi biblioteki im. N. I. Lobachevskogo* 11 (1962): 21–39.

Armstrong, J. A. *The European Administrative Elite.* Princeton, N.J., 1973.

Arnould, L. *La Providence et le bonheur d'après Bossuet et Joseph de Maistre.* Paris, 1917.

Aronson, M. and S. Reiser. *Literaturnye kruzhki i salony.* Leningrad, 1929.

Arsenev, K. "Zapiski Guizot." *Russkii vestnik* 29 (October 1860): 479–537.

Artz, F. B. *The Development of Technical Education in France, 1500–1850.* Cambridge, Mass., 1966.

Avineri, S. *Hegel's Theory of the Modern State.* Cambridge, Eng., 1972.

Baehr, S. L. "From History to National Myth: *Translatio imperii* in Eighteenth-Century Russia." *Russian Review* 27, No. 1 (January 1978): 1–14.

Bagalei, D. I. *Kratkii ocherk istorii Khar'kovskago universiteta za pervye sto let ego sushchestvovaniia.* Khar'kov, 1906.

————. *Opyt' istorii Khar'kovskago universiteta.* 2 vols. Khar'kov, 1894.

Baker, K. M. *Condorcet: From Natural Philosophy to Social Mathematics.* Chicago, 1975.

Bakounine, T. *Le Répertoire biographique des Francs-maçons russes.* Brussels, 1940.

Balmuth, D. *Censorship in Russia, 1865–1905.* Washington, D.C., 1979.

———. "The Origins of the Tsarist Epoch of Censorship Terror." *American Slavic and East European Review* 19 (December 1960): 497–520.

Bamford, T. W. "Public Schools and Social Class, 1801–1850." *British Journal of Sociology* 12 (1961): 224–35.

Barnard, H., ed. *German Educational Reformers.* Hartford, Conn., 1878.

Baron, S. W. *The Russian Jew under Tsars and Soviets.* New York, 1964.

Barsukov, N. "S. S. Uvarov i admiral Shishkov." *RA* 20, No. 6 (1882): 226–28.

———. "Zametka ob A. S. Khomiakove." *RA* 23, No. 3 (1885): 158–60.

———. *Zhizn' i trudy M. P. Pogodina.* 22 vols. St. Petersburg, 1888–1910.

———. *Zhizn' i trudy P. M. Stroeva.* St. Petersburg, 1878.

Bartenev, P. I. *Deviatnadtsatyi vek. Istoricheskii sbornik.* Moscow, 1872.

Bartol'd, V. *Istoriia izucheniia vostoka v Evrope i Rossii.* Leningrad, 1925.

Barzun, J. *Darwin, Marx, Wagner: Critique of a Heritage.* New York, 1958.

Bauer, J. *Lives of the Brothers Humboldt.* Translated by H. Klencke. New York, 1853.

Baumer, F. A. *Modern European Thought: Continuity and Change in Ideas, 1600–1950.* New York, 1977.

Baziiants, A. P. *Lazarevskii institut vostochnykh iazykov.* Moscow, 1959.

Beauvois, D. *Lumières et société en Europe de l'est: L'Université de Vilna et les écoles polonaises de l'empire russe, 1803–1832.* 2 vols. Paris, 1977.

Becker, C. *The Heavenly City of the Eighteenth-Century Philosophers.* New Haven, Conn., 1961.

Beletskii, A. V. "Vopros ob obrazovanie russkikh evreev v tsarstvovanie imperatora Nikolaia I-go." Published in *Russkaia shkola,* 1893, in the following issues: 1 (January): 12–28; 2 (February): 9–20; 3 (March): 10–31; 4 (April): 13–33; 5 (May): 13–29; 7 (July): 12–27; and 11 (November): 10–28.

Belokurov, S. A. *'Delo Fletchera,' 1848–1864 gg.* Moscow, 1910.

Berlin, I. *The Hedgehog and the Fox: An Essay on Tolstoy's View of History.* New York, 1970.

———. *Russian Thinkers.* Edited by H. Hardy and A. Kelly. New York, 1978.

Besançon, A. *Éducation et société en Russie dans le second tiers du XIXᵉ siècle.* Paris, 1974.

Binswanger, P. *Wilhelm von Humboldt.* Leipzig, 1937.

Birn, R. *Crisis, Absolutism, Revolution: Europe, 1648–1789/91.* Hillsdale, Minn., 1977.

Black, C. *The Dynamics of Modernization: A Study in Comparative History.* New York, 1966.

Black, C., et al. *The Modernization of Japan and Russia: A Comparative Study.* New York, 1975.

Black, J. L. *Citizens for the Fatherland: Education, Educators and Pedagogical Ideals in Eighteenth-Century Russia.* Boulder, Colo., 1979.

———. *Nicholas Karamzin and Russian Society in the Nineteenth Century: A Study in Russian Political and Historical Thought.* Toronto, 1975.

Blackwell, W. L. *The Beginnnings of Russian Industrialization, 1800–1860.* Princeton, N.J., 1968.

Blagoi, D. *Istoriia russkoi literatury XVIII veka.* Moscow, 1951.

———. "Sotsial'no-politicheskoe litso Arzamasa." *Arzamas i arzamasskie protokoly.* Leningrad, 1933.

————. *Tvorcheskii put' Pushkina (1813–1826).* Moscow, 1950.

Bled, V. du. *Le Prince de Ligne et ses contemporains.* Paris, 1890.

Bloch, J. G. *Finansy Rossii XIX stoletia: Istoriia-Statistika.* 4 vols. St. Petersburg, 1882.

Bobrov, E. *Literatura i prosveshchenie v Rossii XIX v.* 3 vols. in 1. St. Petersburg, 1901.

Bograd, V. E. *Zhurnal 'Sovremennik' 1847–1866.* Moscow, 1959.

Borovkova-Maikova, M. S., ed. *Arzamas i arzamasskie protokoly.* Leningrad, 1933.

Borozdin, A. "Shishkov." *Entsiklopedicheskii slovar',* LXXVIII (1903), pp. 611–15.

Borozdin, I. N. "Universitety v Rossii v pervoi polovine XIX veke. "In *Istoriia Rossii v XIX veke.* Vol. II. St. Petersburg, 1910.

Bortnikov, A. I. "Kirillo-mefodievskoe obshchestvo: Glavnye idei i tseli." *Trudy istoricheskogo fakul'teta Kievskogo universiteta* 1 (1940): 221–71.

Bourquin, M. *Histoire de Sainte Alliance.* Geneva, 1954.

Braudel, F. *La Méditerranée et le monde méditerranéen à l'epoque de Philippe II.* Paris, 1949.

Brodskii, N. L. *Literaturnye salony i kruzhki.* Moscow, 1930.

Brower, D. *Training the Nihilists: Education and Radicalism in Tsarist Russia.* Ithaca, 1975.

Brown, E. J. *Stankevich and His Moscow Circle, 1830–1840.* Stanford, Calif., 1961.

Brush, E. P. *Guizot in the Early Years of the Orleanist Monarchy.* Springfield, Ill., 1929.

Bulich, N. N. *Ocherki po istorii russkoi literatury i prosveshcheniia s nachala XIX veka.* St. Petersburg, 1902.

Bullen, R. *Palmerston, Guizot and the Collapse of the Entente Cordiale.* London, 1974.

Bury, J. B. *The Idea of Progress: An Inquiry into Its Origin and Growth.* New York, 1932.

Byrnes, R. F. "Russian Conservative Thought before the Revolution." In *Russia under the Last Tsar.* Edited by T. G. Stavrou. Minneapolis, 1969.

Carèrre d'Encausse, Hélène. *Decline of an Empire: The Soviet Socialist Republics in Revolt.* New York, 1979.

Charnoluskii, V. I. "Narodnoe obrazovanie v pervoi polovine XIX veke." In *Istoriia Rossii v XIX veke.* Vol. IV. St. Petersburg, 1910.

Chizhevskii, D. I. "Baader i Rossiia." *Novyi Zhurnal* 35 (1953): 301–10.

————. *Gegel v Rossii.* Paris, 1939.

————. *History of Nineteenth-Century Russian Literature.* Nashville, 1974.

————. *Outline of Comparative Slavic Literatures.* Vol. I of *Survey of Slavic Civilization.* Boston, 1952.

————. *Russian Intellectual History.* Translated by J. C. Osborne. Ann Arbor, 1978.

Christian, D. "The Political Ideals of Michael Speransky." *Slavonic and East European Review* 44, No. 2 (April 1976): 192–213.

Christoff, P. *The Third Heart: Some Intellectual-Ideological Currents and Cross-Currents in Russia, 1800–1830.* The Hague, 1970.

Chubashev, I. V. *Ocherki po istorii doshkol'nogo vospitaniia v Rossii.* Moscow, 1955.

Chumikov, A. "General-gubernatorstvo kniazia A. A. Suvorova v pribaltiiskom krae." *RA* 27, No. 3 (1890): 58–88.

————. "Letopis' zabav i shalostei derptskikh studentov." *RS* 21, No. 2 (1890): 341–70.

————. "Peterburgskii universitet polveka nazad." *RA* 26, No. 3 (1888): 120–50.

_____. "Studencheskiia korporatsii v Peterburgskom universitete v 1830–1840 gg." *RS* 12, No. 2 (1881): 367–80.

Clarke, M. L. *Classical Education in Britain, 1500–1900.* Cambridge, Eng., 1959.

Cobban, A. *Edmund Burke and the Revolt against the Eighteenth Century.* New York, 1960.

Coker, F. W. *Organismic Theories of the State: Nineteenth-Century Interpretations of the State as an Organism or as Person.* Vol. XXXVIII of *Studies in History, Economics and Public Law.* New York, 1910.

Collart, P. *Nonnos de Panopolis.* Paris, 1931.

Crankshaw, E. *The Shadow of the Winter Palace: The Drift to Revolution, 1825–1917.* New York, 1976.

Dantsig, B. M. "Iz istorii izucheniia blizhnego vostoka v Rossii (vtoraia polovina XVIII v.)." *Ocherki po istorii russkago vostokovedeniia* 6 (1963): 134–86.

Darlington, T. *Education in Russia.* Vol. XXIII of Special Reports on Educational Subjects. London, 1909.

Decaunes, L. *Réformes et projets de réforme de l'enseignement français de la révolution à nos jours.* Paris, 1962.

Dementev, A. *Ocherki po istorii russkoi zhurnalistiki, 1840–1850gg.* Moscow, 1951.

Dikii, A. *Evrei v Rossii i v SSSR.* New York, 1967.

D'Ippolito, G. *Studi Nonniani: L'Epillio nelle Dionisiache.* Palermo, 1964.

Dmitrev, S. S. "Le Voyage agronomique du professeur Iu. A. Linovskii en France en 1842–1844." *La Russie et l'Europe: XVIᵉ–XXᵉ siècle.* Paris, 1970.

Dolgorukov, P. V. *Rossiiskaia rodoslovnaia kniga.* 4 vols. St. Petersburg, 1854–1857.

"Dragoman: posviashchaetsia pamiati grafa S. S. Uvarova." *RA* 34, No. 10 (1886): 203–20.

Drizen, N. V. *Dramaticheskaia tsenzura dvukh epokh, 1825–1881.* St. Petersburg, 1917.

Droz, J. *L'Allemagne et la révolution française.* Paris, 1949.

_____. *Europe between Revolutions, 1815–1848.* New York, 1967.

Druzhinin, N. M. "Prosveshchennyi absoliutizm v Rossii." In *Absoliutizm v Rossii (XVII–XVIII vv.).* Edited by N. M. Druzhinin. Moscow, 1964.

Dubnow, S. M. *History of the Jews in Russia and Poland.* 2 vols. Philadelphia, 1918.

Dudley, C. S. *An Analysis of the System of the Bible Society throughout Its Different Parts.* London, 1821.

Durkheim, É. *Education and Sociology.* Translated by S. D. Fox. Glencoe, Ill., 1956.

Durylin, S. N. "Drug Gete." *Literaturnoe nasledstvo* 4–6 (1932): 186–217.

_____. "G-zha de Stal' i ee russkie otnosheniia." *Literaturnoe nasledstvo* 33–34 (1939): 215–330.

Dzhivelegov, A. K., ed. *Oteshchestvennaia voina i russkoe obshchestvo, 1812–1912.* 10 vols. Moscow, 1912.

Edwards, D. W. "Count Joseph Marie de Maistre and Russian Educational Policy, 1803–1826." *Slavic Review* 36, No. 1 (March 1977): 54–75.

Egorov, Iu. N. "Reaktsionnaia politika tsarizma v voprosakh universitetskogo obrazovaniia v 30–50kh gg. XIX v." *Istoricheskie nauki* 3 (1960): 60–75.

_____. "Russkie universitety i studencheskoe dvizhenie vo vtoroi polovine 1830 do 1850 gg. XIX veka." Unpublished candidate's diss., Leningrad State University, 1958.

Egunov, A. N. *Gomer v russkikh perevodakh XVIII–XIX vekov.* Moscow, 1964.

Ehrhard, M. *V. A. Joukovskii et le préromantisme russe.* Paris, 1938.

El'iashevich, V. B., et al. *Moskovskii universitet, 1755–1930.* Paris, 1930.

Emmons, T. *The Russian Landed Gentry and the Peasant Emancipation of* 1861. Cambridge, Mass., 1968.

Engel'gardt, N. A. *Ocherk istorii russkoi tsenzury v sviazi s razvitiem pechati (1703–1903).* St. Petersburg, 1904.

————. "Ocherki nikolaevskoi tsenzury." *Istoricheskii vestnik* 85 (September 1901): 850–73. Concludes in *Istoricheskii vestnik* 86 (October 1901): 156–79.

————. "Samoderzhavie i biurokratiia v tsarstvovanii imperatora Nikolaia I." *Russkii vestnik* 182, Nos. 11–12 (1902): 465–75.

Enikolonov, I. K. *A. S. Griboedov v Gruzii i Persii.* Tiflis, U.S.S.R., 1929.

Epstein, K. *The Genesis of German Conservatism.* Princeton, N.J., 1966.

Ergang, R. R. *Herder and the Foundations of German Nationalism.* New York, 1931.

Falbork, G. A., and V. Charnoluskii. *Narodnoe obrazovanie v Rossii.* St. Petersburg, 1900.

Fanger, D. *The Creation of Nikolai Gogol.* Cambridge, Mass., 1979.

Fedosov, I. A. "Prosveshchennyi absoliutizm v Rossii." *Vosprosy istorii* 9 (1970): 34–55.

Feinberg, I. L. *Nezavershennye raboty Pushkina.* Moscow, 1958.

Feoktistov, E. *Materialy dlia istoriia prosveshcheniia v Rossii.* Vol. I of *Magnitskii.* St. Petersburg, 1865.

Flint, R. *Historical Philosophy in France.* New York, 1894.

Florinsky, M. T. *Russia: A History and an Interpretation.* 2 vols. New York, 1947.

Florovskii, G. V. *Puti russkago bogosloviia.* Paris, 1937.

Flynn, J. T. "The Affair of Kostomarov's Dissertation: A Case Study of Official Nationalism in Practice." *Slavonic and East European Review* 52, No. 127 (April 1974): 188–96.

————. "Magnitskii's Purge of Kazan University: A Case Study in the Uses of Reaction in Nineteenth-Century Russia." *Journal of Modern History* 43, No. 4 (1971): 598–614.

————. "The Role of the Jesuits in the Politics of Russian Education, 1801–1820." *Catholic Historical Review* 41, No. 2 (July 1970): 249–65.

————. "Tuition and Social Class in the Russian Universities: S. S. Uvarov and 'Reaction' in the Russia of Nicholas I." *Slavic Review* 35, No. 2 (June 1976): 232–48.

————. "The Universities in the Russia of Alexander I: Patterns of Reform and Reaction." Ph.D. diss., Clark University, 1964.

————. "The Universities, The Gentry and the Russian Imperial Services, 1815–1825." *Canadian Slavic Studies* 2, No. 4 (Winter 1968): 486–503.

————. "S. S. Uvarov's 'Liberal' Years." *Jahrbücher für Geschichte Osteuropas* 20, No. 4 (1972): 481–91.

————. "V. N. Karazin, The Gentry, and Kharkov University." *Slavic Review* 28, No. 2 (1969): 209–20.

Frank, J. L. *Dostoevsky: The Seeds of Revolt, 1821–1849.* Princeton, N.J., 1976.

Frank, S.L. *Etiudy o Pushkine.* Munich, 1957.

————. *Pushkin kak politicheskii myslitel'.* Belgrade, 1937.

Frantsev, V. I. *I. Sreznevskii i slavianstvo.* Petrograd, 1914.

Frieden, N. M. *Russian Physicians in an Era of Reform, 1856–1905.* Princeton, N.J., 1981.

Friedenthal, R. *Goethe: His Life and Times.* London, 1963.

Frommett, B. *Ocherki po istorii studentchestva v Rossii.* St. Petersburg, 1912.

Gabov, G. *Obshchestvenno-politicheskie i filosofskie vzgliady dekabristov.* Moscow, 1953.

Gagliardo, J. G. *Enlightened Despotism.* New York, 1967.

Galskoy, C. "The Ministry of Education under Nicholas I, 1826–1836." Ph.D. diss., Stanford University, 1977.

Garratt, G. T., ed. *The Legacy of India*. Oxford, 1937.

Gay, P. *Voltaire's Politics: The Poet as Realist*. New York, 1965.

Georgievskii, A. I. *Predpolozhennaia reforma nashei srednei shkoly*. St. Petersburg, 1901.

Gerbod, P. *La Condition universitaire en France au XIXe siècle*. Paris, 1965.

Gershenzon, M. O., ed. *Epokha Nikolaia I*. Moscow, 1911.

Gillel'son, M. I. *Derzhavin i Karamzin v literaturnom dvizhenii XVIII–nachala XIX veka*. Leningrad, 1969.

———. *Molodoi Pushkin i arzamasskoe bratstvo*. Leningrad, 1974.

———. *P. A. Viazemskii: Zhizn' i tvorchestvo*. Moscow, 1969.

Ginsburg, S. M. "Max Lilienthal's Activities in Russia: New Documents." *Publications of the American Jewish Historical Society* 35 (1939): 39–51.

———. "Russkoe pravitel'stvo i vopros ob obrazovanii evreev v pervoi polovine XIX veke." In *Kazennye evreishie uchilishcha*. Edited by S. G. Lozinskii. Petrograd, 1920.

Glasenapp, H. "Indien in der Dichtung und Forschung des Deutschen Ostens." *Schriften der Königlichen deutschen gesellschaft zu Königsburg Presse* 5 (1930): 5–47.

Glatigny, M. *Histoire de l'enseignement en France*. Paris, 1949.

Gnuchev, V. F. *Materialy dlia istorii ekspeditsii Akademii nauk v XVIII i XIX vekakh*. Moscow, 1940.

Goetze, P. von. *Fürst Alexander Nikolajewitsch Galitzin und seine Zeit*. Leipzig, 1882.

———. "Iz zapisok P. O. Fon-Getse: Kniaz A. N. Golitsyn i ego vremia." *RA* 40, No. 9 (1902): 66–107. Concludes in *RA* 11 (1902): 321–29.

Golovin, V. F. *Russkii roman i russkoe obshchestvo*. St. Petersburg, 1897.

Goncharuk, P. *Istoricheskie vzgliady Kirillo-Mefodievtsev, 1846–1847*. Kiev, 1970.

Gontard, M. *L'Enseignement primaire en France de la révolution à la loi Guizot (1789–1833)*. Paris, n.d.

Gooch, G. P. *Germany and the French Revolution*. New York, 1920.

———. *History and Historians in the Nineteenth Century*. Boston, 1959.

Gorchakov, A. M. "Litseiskie lektsii: Entsiklopediia prav." *Krasnyi arkhiv* 1, No. 80 (1937): 90–129.

Gorodetskii, V. P., ed. *Istoriia russkoi kritiki*. 2 vols. Moscow, 1958.

Görres, J. *Mythengeschichte der Asiatischen Welt*. Heidelberg, 1810.

"Graf S. S. Uvarov." *Vsemirnaia illustratsiia* 59 (1870): 123.

Greenburg, L. *The Jews in Russia*. 2 vols. New Haven, 1951.

Grigor'ev, V. V. *Imperatorskii S. Peterburgskii universitet*. St. Petersburg, 1870.

———. *Istoricheskii ocherk russkoi shkoly*. Moscow, 1900.

Grigor'ian, K. N., ed. *Russkii romantizm*. Moscow, 1978.

Grimsted, P. K. *The Foreign Ministers of Alexander I*. Berkeley, Calif., 1969.

Grossman, L. "Bal'zak v Rossii." *Literaturnoe nasledstvo* 31–32 (1937): 150–373.

Grot, Ia. K. "K istorii slavianskago samosoznaniia i slavianskikh sochuvstvii v russkom obshchestve (Iz 40kh godov XIX stoletiia)." *Pravitel'stvennyi vestnik*. Nos. 195–98.

———. *Piatidesiatiletie otdeleniia russkago iazyka i slovesnosti Imp. Akademii nauk, 1841–1891*. St. Petersburg, 1892.

Guerrier, W. *Leibnitz in seinen Beziehungen zu Russland und Peter dem Grossen*. St. Petersburg, 1873.

Gus, M. S. *Gogol' i nikolaevskaia Rossiia*. Moscow, 1957.

Halevy, A. *Jewish Schools under Czarism and Communism: A Struggle for Cultural Identity*. New York, 1976.

Hans, N. *History of Russian Educational Policy, 1701–1917.* London, 1931.
———. *The Russian Tradition in Education.* London, 1963.
Hare, R. *Pioneers of Russian Social Thought.* New York, 1964.
Harnack, O. "Goethes Beziehungen zu russischen Schriftstellern." *Zeitschrift für Vergleichende literatur-geschichte und Renaissance-Literatur* 5 (1890): 269–70.
Hessen, J. "Die russische Regierung und die westerropaischen Juden." *Monatsschrift für Geschichte und Wissenschaft des Judentums* 42 (1913): 256–71, 482–500.
Highet, G. *The Classical Tradition: Greek and Roman Influences on Western Literature.* Oxford, 1949.
Hingley, R. *Russian Writers and Society, 1825–1904.* New York, 1967.
Hoch, S., and W. Augustine. "The Tax Censuses and the Decline of the Serf Population in Imperial Russia, 1833–1858." *Slavic Review* 73, No. 3 (September 1979): 403–25.
Hofmann, M. L. *Pouchkine.* Paris, 1931.
Hollingsworth, B. "A. P. Kunitsyn and the Social Movement in Russia under Alexander I." *Slavonic and East European Review* 43, No. 100 (1964): 115–29.
———. "Arzamas: Portrait of a Literary Society." *Slavonic and East European Review* 44, No. 103 (1966): 306–26.
———. "Lancastrian Schools in Russia." *Durham Research Review* 5 (1966): 59–74.
Iagich, I. V. *Istoriia slavianskoi filologii.* St. Petersburg, 1910.
Iatsimirskii, A. I. "N. M. Karamzin." In *Istoriia russkoi literatury.* Edited by D. N. Ovsianiko-Kulikovskii. Moscow, 1910.
Ikonnikov, V. "Russkie universitety v sviazi s khodom obshchestvennago obrazovaniia." *Vestnik Evropy* 5, No. 9 (1876): 161–206. Concludes in *Vestnik Evropy* 5, No. 10 (1876): 492–550; and *Vestnik Evropy* 5, No. 11 (1876): 73–132.
Istoricheskiia svedeniia o tsenzure v Rossii. St. Petersburg, 1862.
"Istoriia 'Teleskopa.' " *RA* 22, No. 2 (1884): 453–461.
Istrin, V. "Druzheskoe literaturnoe obshchestvo 1801 g." *ZMNP* 8 (1910): 271–307.
———. "Russkie studenty v Gettingene v 1802–1804 gg (Po materialam arkhiva brat'ev Turgenevykh)." *ZMNP* 7 (1910): 80–144.
"Iu. N. Bartenev." *RA* 35, No. 12 (1897): 614–60.
Iusupov, P. F. *Russkii romantizm nachala XIX veka i natsional'nye kultury.* Moscow, 1970.
Iuzefovich, M. "Neskol'ko slov ob imperatore Nikolae." *RA* 8 (1870): 999–1008.
"I. V. Kireevskii." *RA* 32, No. 2 (1894): 326–48.
Ivanov, V. F. *Ot Petra Pervago do nashikh dnei: Russkaia intelligentsia i masonstvo.* Khargin, 1934.
Ivanov-Razumnik, V. *Istoriia russkoi obshchestvennoi mysli.* St. Petersburg, 1914.
Ivanovskii, A. *Biograficheskii ocherk I. M. Snegireva.* St. Petersburg, 1871.
Jagoditsch, R. "Goethe und seine russischen Zeitgenossen." *Germanoslavica* 1 (1931–1932): 347–81.
Jenkyns, R. *The Victorians and Ancient Greece.* Cambridge, Mass., 1980.
Johnson, D. *Guizot: Aspects of French History, 1787–1874.* Toronto, 1963.
Johnson, W. H. E. *Russia's Educational Heritage.* Pittsburgh, 1950.
K 125 letiiu Kazanskago universiteta. Kazan, 1930.
Kabuzan, V. M. *Narodonaselenie Rossii v XVIII–pervoi polovine XIX v.* Moscow, 1963.
Kabuzan, V. M., and S. M. Troitskii. "Izmeneniia v chislennosti, udel'nom vese i razmeshchenii dvorianstva v Rossii v 1782–1858 gg." *Istoriia SSSR* 4 (July–August 1971): 153–69.

Kalugin, N. N. "Studenty Moskovskago universiteta v byloe vremia." *RA* 45, No. 11 (1907): 423-29.

Kamenskii, Z. A. *Filosofskie idei russkogo prosveshcheniia.* Moscow, 1971.

———. *Russkaia filosofiia nachala XIX veka: Shelling.* Moscow, 1980.

Kapterev, P. F. *Istoriia russkoi pedagogii.* St. Petersburg, 1897.

Karatygin, P. "Severnaia pchela, 1825 1859 *RA* 20, No. 2 (1882): 241-303.

Karlinsky, S. *The Sexual Labyrinth of Nikolai Gogol.* Cambridge, Mass., 1976.

Katkov, M. N., ed. *Nasha uchebnaia reforma.* Moscow, 1890.

Kennan, G. F. *The Marquis de Custine and His Russia in 1839.* Princeton, N.J., 1971.

Khalanskii, M. "K istorii vozniknoveniia Arzamasa." *Mirnyi trud* 1, No. 1 (1902): 57-60.

Khar'kov University. *Khar'kovskii gosudarstvennyi universitet im. A. M. Gor'kogo za 150 let.* Khar'kov, 1955.

Kirpichnikov, A. "K biografii A. S. Pushkina." *RS* 30, No. 5 (1899): 263-66.

———. "Lessing." *Ensiklopedicheskii slovar',* XXXIV (1896), pp. 595-98.

———. "Novye materialy dlia istorii 'Arzamasa' (po dokumentam Porechenskago arkhiva)." *RS* 30, No. 5 (1899): 337-51.

Kisliagina, L. G. *Formirovanie obshchestvenno-politcheskikh vzgliadov N. M. Karamzina, 1785-1803 gg.* Moscow, 1976.

"K istorii russkoi literatury: Popytki brat'ev A. A. i M. A. Bestuzhevykh izdavat' zhurnal." *RS* 31, No. 9 (1900): 391-94.

"K istorii tsarstvovaniia imperatora Nikolaia I." *RS* 27, No. 6 (1896): 553-70.

Kizevetter, A. A. *Istoricheskie ocherki.* Moscow, 1912.

———. "Vnutrennaia politika v tsarstvovanie Nikolaia Pavlovicha." *Istoriia Rossii v XIX veke.* Vol. I. St. Petersburg, 1910.

Kizevetter, A. A., V. B. El'iashevich, and M. M. Novikov, eds. *Moskovskii universitet, 1755-1930.* Paris, 1930.

Kniazev, G. A., and A. V. Kol'tsov. *Kratkii ocherk istorii Akademii nauk SSSR.* Moscow, 1964.

"Kniaz G. Shcherbatov o grafe Uvarove." *Sovremennaia letopis'.* Nos. 5, 6, and 7 (February 1, 8, and 15, 1870).

Kniazkov, S. A., and N. I. Serbov. *Ocherk istorii narodnago obrazovannia v Rossii do epokhi reform Aleksandra II.* Moscow, 1911.

"Knizhnye redkosti." *RA* 30, No. 2 (1892): 233-58.

Kobeko, D. F. *Imperatorskii Tsarskosel'skii litsei.* St. Petersburg, 1911.

Kochubinskii, A. A. "Graf S. G. Stroganov: Iz istorii nashikh universitetov 30kh godov." *Vestnik Evropy* 4, No. 7 (1896): 165-96. Concludes in *Vestnik Evropy* 8 (1896): 471-90.

———. *Nachal'nye gody russkago slavianovedeniia.* Odessa, 1888.

Kolbasin, E. "I. I. Martynov—perevodchik grecheskikh klassikov." *Sovremennik* 56, No. 3 (1856): 1-46. Concludes in *Sovremennik* 56, No. 4 (1856): 75-126.

Kononov, A. N. *Istoriia izucheniia tiurkskikh iazykov v Rossii dooktiabrskii period.* Leningrad, 1972.

Korbut, M. K. *Kazanskii gosudarstvennyi universitet im. V. I. Ul'ianova-Lenina za 125 let, 1804/05-1929/30.* 2 vols. Kazan, 1930.

Korf, M. A. *Zhizn' grafa Speranskago.* 2 vols. St. Petersburg, 1861.

Korf, S. A. *Dvorianstvo i ego soslovnoe upravlenie za stoletie 1762-1855 godov.* St. Petersburg, 1906.

Kornilov, A. *Nineteenth-Century Russia.* New York, 1966.

Kosachevskaia, E. M. *M. A. Balug'ianskii i Peterburgskii universitet pervoi chetverti XIX veka.* Leningrad, 1971.

Kovalevskii, E. *Graf Bludov i ego vremia.* St. Petersburg, 1866.

———. *L'Instruction publique en Russie.* St. Petersburg, 1905.

Kovalevskii, M. N. "Sredniaia shkola." In *Istoriia Rossii v XIX veke.* Vol. IV. St. Petersburg, 1910.

Koyré, A. *La Philosophie et le problème national en Russie au début du XIXe siècle.* Paris, 1929.

Kozmin, N. K. "N. I. Nadezhdin, professor Moskovskago universiteta." *ZMNP* 361, No. 9 (1905): 1–41. Concludes in *ZMNP* 366, No. 5 (1907), 124–37.

―――. "Nikolai Polevoi i ego otnosheniia k tsenzure." *RS* 31, No. 2 (1900): 415–32.

―――. *Ocherki iz istorii russkago romantizma.* St. Petersburg, 1903.

Krachkovskii, I. Iu. *Ocherki po istorii russkoi arabistiki.* Moscow, 1950.

Krasnobaev, B. I. *Ocherki istorii russkoi kul'tury XVIII veka.* Moscow, 1972.

Krieger, L. *An Essay on the Theory of Enlightened Despotism.* Chicago, 1975.

―――. *The German Idea of Freedom.* Chicago, 1975.

Kuhn, H. *Das Wartburgfest.* Weimar, 1913.

Kuleshov, V. I. *Literaturnye sviazi Rossii i zapadnoi Evropy v XIX veke (pervaia polovina).* Moscow, 1965.

―――. *'Otechestvennye zapiski' i literatura 40kh godov XIX veka.* Moscow, 1958.

Kulikov, S. N. "Bal'zak: neopublikovannye pis'ma." *Zven'ia* 3–4 (1934): 289–98.

Kulikova, A. M. "Proekty vostokovednogo obrazovaniia v Rossii (XVIII–1-ia pol. XIX v.)." *Narody Azii i Afriki* 4 (1970): 133–139.

"Kurakiny." *Entsiklopedicheskii slovar',* XXXI (1895), p. 61.

Kushelev, N. "Unichtozhenie masonskikh lozh v Rossii." *RS* 8, No. 4 (1877): 642–65.

Kuznetsov, B. G. *Lomonosov, Lobachevskii, Mendeleev: Ocherki zhizni i mirovozreniia.* Moscow, 1945.

Lach, D. F. *Asia in the Making of Europe.* 2 vols. Chicago, 1970.

―――. *Contributions of China to German Civilization, 1648–1740.* Chicago, 1944.

Lalaev, M. S. *Imperator Nikolai I, zizhditel' russkoi shkoly.* St. Petersburg, 1896.

Landa, S. S. *Dukh revoliutsionnykh preobrazovanii . . . Iz istorii formirovaniia ideologii i politicheskoi organizatsii dekabristov 1816–1825.* Moscow, 1975.

Langer, W. L. *Political and Social Upheaval, 1832–1852.* New York, 1969.

Leary, D. B. *Education and Autocracy in Russia: From the Origins to the Bolsheviki.* University of Buffalo Studies, vol. I. Buffalo, 1919.

Lebedev, N. A. *Istoricheskii vzgliad na uchrezhdenie uchilishch, shkol, uchebnykh zavedenii i uchenykh obshchest . . . c 1025 po 1855 god.* St. Petersburg, 1875.

Leighton, L. G. *Russian Romanticism: Two Essays.* The Hague, 1975.

Lemke, M. *Nikolaevskie zhandarmy i literatura, 1826–1855 gg.* St. Petersburg, 1907.

Leningrad University. *Leningradskii universitet, 1819–1944.* Moscow, 1945.

―――. *Leningradskii universitet v vospominaniiakh sovremennikov.* Vol. I of *Petersburgskii universitet, 1819–1895.* Leningrad, 1963.

―――. *Ocherki po istorii Leningradskogo universiteta.* 2 vols. Leningrad, 1962.

Levitats, I. *The Jewish Community in Russia, 1772–1884.* New York, 1943.

Liashchenko, P. I. *Istoriia narodnago khoziaistva SSSR.* 2 vols. Leningrad, 1952.

Lincoln, W. B. "The Circle of the Grand Duchess Yelena Pavlovna, 1847–1861." *Slavonic and East European Review* 48, No. 112 (July 1970): 373–87.

―――. "The Genesis of an 'Enlightened' Bureaucracy in Russia, 1826–1856." *Jahrbücher für Geschichte Osteuropas* 20, No. 3 (September 1972): 321–30.

―――. "The Ministers of Nicholas I: A Brief Inquiry into Their Backgrounds and Service Career." *Russian Review* 24, No. 3 (July 1975): 308–23.

―――. *Nikolai Miliutin: An Enlightened Russian Bureaucrat.* Newtonville, Mass., 1977.

―――. *Nicholas I.* Bloomington, Ind., 1978.

———. *In the Vanguard of Reform: Russia's Enlightened Bureaucrats, 1825–1861*. DeKalb, Ill., 1982.

Linkov, Ia. I. *Ocherki istorii krest'ianskogo dvizheniia v Rossii v 1825–1861 gg*. Moscow, 1952.

Literaturnye vzgliady i tvorchestvo slavianofilov (1830–1850 gody). Moscow, 1978.

Lozinskii, S. G. *Opisanie del'byvshego arkhiva Ministerstva narodnago prosveshcheniia: Kazennye evreiskie uchilishcha*. Petrograd, 1920.

Lubac, H. de. *La Rencontre du Bouddhisme et de l'occident*. Paris, 1952.

Luciani, G. *Le Livre de la genèse du peuple ukrainien*. Paris, 1956.

Lunin, B. V. *Sredniaia Aziia v dorevoliutsionnom i sovetskom vostokovedenii*. Tashkent, 1965.

Luppov, S. V., ed. *Istoriia biblioteki Akademii nauk SSSR*. Moscow, 1964.

McClelland, J. C. *Autocrats and Academics: Education, Culture, and Society in Tsarist Russia*. Chicago, 1979.

McConnell, A. *Tsar Alexander I*. New York, 1970.

McGrew, R. E. *Russia and the Cholera, 1823–1832*. Madison, Wis., 1965.

McPherson, R. G. *Theory of Higher Education in Nineteenth-Century England*. Athens, Ga., 1959.

Maikov, L. *Batiushkov, ego zhizn' i sochineniia*. St. Petersburg, 1896.

Maikov, P. "Vvedenie russkago iazyka v Ostzeiskikh guberniiakh." *RS* 38, No. 4 (1907): 60.

Maksimov, V. E. *'Sovremennik' v 40–50 gg*. Leningrad, 1934.

Malia, Martin. *Alexander Herzen and the Birth of Russian Socialism*. New York, 1961.

Malinovskii, V. P. "Ocherki po istorii nachal'noi shkoly." *Russkaia shkola* 9 (September 1912): 84–112.

Malnick, B. "A. A. Shakhovskoi." *Slavonic and East European Review* 32, No. 78 (December 1953): 29–51.

"M. A. Maksimovich." *RA* 12, No. 12 (1874): 1056–87.

Mannheim, K. *Essays in Sociology and Social Psychology*. Edited by Paul Kecskemeti. New York, 1953.

Marker, G. J. "Publishing and the Formation of a Reading Public in Eighteenth-Century Russia." Ph.D. diss., University of California, 1977.

Masaryk, T. G. *The Spirit of Russia*. Translated by Robert Bass. 3 vols. London, 1967.

Medynskii, E. N. *Istoriia russkoi pedagogiki*. Moscow, 1936.

Mel'gunov, S. P. *Dela i liudi aleksandrovskago vremeni*. Berlin, 1923.

———. "Epokha 'ofitsial'noi narodnosti' i krepostnoe pravo." In *Velikaia reforma: Russkoe obshchestvo i krestianskii vopros v proshlom i nastoiashchem*. Vol. III. Edited by A. K. Dzhivelegov. Moscow, 1911.

———. *Iz istorii studencheskikh obshchestv v russkikh universitetakh*. Moscow, 1904.

Mesniakov, A. S., ed. *Kontekst-1972*. Moscow, 1973.

Meyer, K. "Die Entstehung der 'Universitätsfrage' in Russland. Zum Verhältnis von Universität, Staat und Gesellschaft zu Beginn des neunzehnten Jahrhunderts." *Forschüngen für Osteuropaischen Geschichte* 25 (1978): 229–38.

Michel, H. *L'Idée de l'état*. Paris, 1896.

Mikhailov, A. A. "Revoliutsiia 1848 goda i slavianofil'stvo." *Uchenye zapiski Leningradskogo gosudarstvennogo universiteta* 73 (1940): 48–74.

Mikhailovich, I. *Snegirev: Biograficheskii ocherk*. St. Petersburg, 1871.

Miliband, S. D., ed. *Biobibliograficheskii slovar' sovetskikh vostokovedov*. Moscow, 1975.

Miliukov, P. *Ocherki po istorii russkoi kul'tury*. 3 vols. in 4. Paris, 1930–1937.

———. "Universitety v Rossii." *Entsiklopedicheskii slovar'* 68 (1902): 788–800.

Miliukov, R., and A. Kirpichnikov. "Karamzin kak istorik i literator." *Entsiklopedicheskii slovar'*, XXVII (1895): 442–47.

Ministerstvo narodnago prosveshcheniia. *Sravnitel'naia tablitsa ustavov universitetov 1884, 1863, 1835 i 1804 gg.* St. Petersburg, 1901.

Mirsky, D. S. *A History of Russian Literature: From Its Beginnings to 1900.* New York, 1958.

Mitropol'skii, I. A. "G. V. Grudev." *RA* 34, No. 1 (1896): 638–40.

Mogilianskii, A. P. "A. S. Pushkin i V. F. Odoevskii kak sozdateli." *Izvestiia AN SSSR* 6, No. 3 (1949): 209–26.

Monas, S. "Bureaucracy in Russia under Nicholas I." In *Russia: Essays in History and Literature.* Edited by L. Legters. Leiden, 1972.

————. "Shishkov, Bulgarin and the Russian Censorship." *Harvard Slavic Studies* 4 (1957): 127–47.

————. *The Third Section: Police and Society in Russia under Nicholas I.* Cambridge, Mass., 1961.

Moody, J. N. *French Education since Napoleon.* Syracuse, N.Y., 1978.

Morakhovets, E. A., ed. *Krest'ianskoe dvizhenie, 1827–1869.* Moscow, 1931.

Mordovchenko, N. I. *Russkaia kritika pervoi chetvert XIX veka.* Moscow, 1959.

Morgulis, M. G. "K istorii obrazovaniia russkikh evreev." *Evreiskaia biblioteka* 1 (1871): 135–89.

Mulhern, J. *A History of Education: A Social Interpretation.* New York, 1959.

Muret, Charlotte T. *French Royalist Doctrines since the Revolution.* New York, 1933.

Musgrave, P. W. *Society and Education in England since 1800.* London, 1968.

Myers, P. V. *The Modernization of Education in Nineteenth Century Europe.* St. Louis, 1977.

Mylonas, G. E. *Eleusis and the Eleusinian Mysteries.* Princeton, N.J., 1961.

Nazarevskii, I. T. "Istoricheskii ocherk zakonodatel'stva po nachal'nomu obrazovaniiu v Rossii." *ZMNP* 357 (February 1905): 149–86. Concludes in *ZMNP* 358 (March 1905): 1–37.

Nazarevskii, V. V. *Tsarstvovanie imperatora Nikolaia I, 1825–1855.* Moscow, 1910.

N. D. "K istorii russkoi tsenzury (1814–1820/gg.)." *RS* 31, No. 12 (1900): 643–64.

Nechaevskii, V., and S. Durylin. "P. A. Viazemskii i Frantsiia." *Literaturnoe nasledstvo* 21–22 (1937): 77–148.

Nesmes-Desmarets, R. de. *Les Doctrines politiques de Royer-Collard.* Paris, 1908.

Netting, A. G. "Russian Liberalism: The Years of Promise, 1842–1855." Ph.D. diss., Columbia University, 1967.

Nikitenko, A. *Aleksandr I. Galich, byvshii professor S.-Peterburgskago universiteta.* St. Petersburg, 1869.

"N. M. Karamzin." *RA* 49, No. 8 (1911): 553–93.

Nolde, B. E. *Iurii Samarin i ego vremia.* Paris, 1926.

O'Boyle, L. "The Problem of an Excess of Educated Men in Western Europe, 1800–1850." *Journal of Modern History* 42 (1970): 471–95.

Okol'skii, A. *Ob otnoshenii gosudarstva k narodnomu obrazovaniiu.* St. Petersburg, 1872.

Oncken, W. *Wartburg.* Berlin, 1907.

Orlik, O. V. *Peredovaia Rossiia i revoliutsionnaia Frantsiia.* Moscow, 1973.

————. *Rossiia i frantsuzskaia revoliutsiia 1830 goda.* Moscow, 1968.

Orlov, O. V., and V. I. Fedorov. *Russkaia literatura XVIII veka.* Moscow, 1973.

Orlov, V. N. *Nikolai Polevoi: Materialy po istorii russkoi literatury i zhurnalistiki tridtsatykh godov.* Leningrad, 1934.

Orlovsky, D. T. *The Limits of Reform: The Ministry of Internal Affairs in Imperial Russia, 1802–1881.* Cambridge, Mass., 1981.

Ostroglazov, V. "Kholera v Moskve v 1830 godu." *RA* 9 (1893): 93–106.

Ostrovitianov, K. V., ed. *Istoriia Akademii nauk SSSR.* 3 vols. Moscow, 1964.

Panachin, F. G. *Pedagogicheskoe obrazovanie v Rossii. Istoriko-pedagogicheskie ocherki.* Moscow, 1979.

Parker, H. T. *The Cult of Antiquity and the French Revolutionaries*. New York, 1965.
Paulsen, F. *German Education Past and Present*. London, 1908.
Pekarskii, P. *Istoriia AN v Peterburge*. St. Petersburg, 1870.
Pelech, O. "Toward a Historical Sociology of the Ukrainian Ideologues in the Russian Empire of the 1830's and 1840's." Ph.D. diss., Princeton University, 1976.
Pertz, G. H. *Das Leben des Ministers Freiherr vom Stein*. 6 vols. Berlin, 1851.
Petukhov, E. V. *Imperatorskii Iur'evskii, byvshii Derptskii, universitet za sto let ego sushchestvovaniia (1802–1902)*. 2 vols. Iur'ev, 1902.
Pfeiffer, R. *History of Classical Scholarship from the Beginnings to the End of the Hellenistic Age*. Oxford, 1968.
Philippson, D. *Max Lilienthal: American Rabbi, Life and Writings*. New York, 1915.
———. "Max Lilienthal in Russia." *Hebrew Union College Annual, XII–XIII* (1937–1938), pp. 825–39.
Piatkovskii, A. P. *Iz istorii nashego literaturnago i obshchestvennago razvitiia*. St. Petersburg, 1889.
Piksanov, N. K. *A. S. Griboedov*. St. Petersburg, 1911.
———. "Publitsistika Aleksandrovskoi epokhi." In *Istoriia russkoi literatury XIX v.* Edited by D. N. Ovsianiko-Kulikovskii. Moscow, 1910.
Pintner, W. M. "The Russian Civil Service on the Eve of the Great Reforms." *Social History*, Spring 1975, pp. 55–68.
———. *Russian Economic Policy under Nicholas I*. Ithaca, N.Y., 1967.
———. "The Social Characteristics of the Early Nineteenth-Century Bureaucracy." *Slavic Review* 29 (September 1970): 429–43.
Pipes, R. "Karamzin's Conception of the Monarchy." *Harvard Slavic Studies* 4 (1957): 35–58.
———. *Russian Conservatism in the Second Half of the Nineteenth Century*. Moscow, 1970. Paper delivered to 13th International Congress of Historical Sciences, Moscow, August 16–23, 1970.
———, ed. *The Russian Intelligentsia*. New York, 1961.
Plakans, A. "Peasants, Intellectuals, and Nationalism in the Russian Baltic Provinces." *Journal of Modern History* 46, No. 3 (1974): 445–75.
Pogodin, A. "Goethe in Russland." *Germanoslavica* 1 (1931–1932): 333–47.
Pogozhev, A. "Votchinnye fabriki i ikh fabrichnye." *Vestnik Evropy* 4 (July 1889): 5–43.
Polievktov, M. A. *Nikolai I: Biografiia i obzor tsarstvovaniia*. Moscow, 1918.
Ponomarev, S. I. "M. A. Maksimovich." *ZMNP* 158 (October 1871): 175–249.
Ponteil, F. *Histoire de l'enseignement en France, 1789–1964*. Paris, 1966.
Popov, A. N. "Graf Mestr i iezuity v Rossii." *RA* 30, No. 6 (1892): 159–96.
———. *Snosheniie Rossii s Rimom c 1845 po 1850 god*. St. Petersburg, 1871.
Popov, N. "Obshchestvo liubilelei otechestvennoi slovesnosti i periodicheskaia literatura v Kazani, s 1805 po 1834 god." *Russkii vestnik* 23, No. 9 (1859): 52–98.
Posner, S. *Evrei v obshchei shkole*. St. Petersburg, 1914.
Potiquet, A. *L'Institut national de France: Ses diverses organizations*. Paris, 1871.
Pouthas, C. *Guizot pendant la restauration*. Paris, 1923.
Poznanskii, V. V. *Ocherk formirovaniia russkoi natsional'noi kul'tury: Pervaia polovina XIX veka*. Moscow, 1975.
———. *Ocherki istorii russkoi kul'tury pervoi poloviny XIX veka*. Moscow, 1970.
Presniakov, A. E. *Emperor Nicholas I of Russia: The Apogee of Autocracy, 1825–1855*. Edited and translated by J. C. Zacek. Gulf Breeze, Fla., 1974.
———. "Samoderzhavie Nikolaia I." *Russkoe proshloe* 2 (1923): 3–21.
"Prikliucheniia Lifliandtsa v Peterburge." *RA* 16, No. 3 (1878): 436–68.
Prost, A. *Histoire de l'enseignement en France, 1800–1967*. Paris, 1968.

Pugachev, V. V. *Evoliutsiia obshchestvenno-politicheskikh vzgliadov Pushkina.* Gorky, 1967.

——. "Predistoriia soiuza Blagodenstviia i pushkinskaia oda 'Volnost'." In *Issledovaniia i materialy.* Vol. IV. Moscow, 1962.

——. "K voprosu o politicheskie vzgliadakh S. S. Uvarova v 1810-e gody." *Uchenye zapiski seriia istoriko-filologicheskaia Gor'kovskii g. universitet, im. N. I. Lobachevskogo* 72 (1964): 125–32.

Pypin, A. N. *Belinskii, ego zhizn' i perepiska.* 2 vols. in 1. St. Petersburg, 1876.

——. *Istoriia russkoi etnografii.* 4 vols. St. Petersburg, 1890–1892.

——. *Kharakteristiki literaturnykh mnenii: 1820–1850.* St. Petersburg, 1906.

——. *Obshchestvennoe dvizhenie v Rossii pri Aleksandr I.* St. Petersburg, 1900.

——. *Religioznyia dvizheniia pri Aleksandr I.* Petrograd, 1916.

——. *Russkoe masonstvo.* Petrograd, 1916.

Radharkrishnan, S. *Eastern Religions and Western Thought.* Oxford, 1939.

Raeff, M. *Michael Speransky: Statesman of Imperial Russia.* The Hague, 1957.

——. *Origins of the Russian Intelligentsia: The Eighteenth-Century Nobility.* New York, 1966.

——. "Russian Youth on the Eve of Romanticism: Andrei I. Turgenev and His Circle." *Revolution and Politics in Russia: Essays in Memory of B. I. Nicholaevsky.* Edited by A. and J. Rabinowitch. Bloomington, Ind., 1972.

——. "The Well-Ordered Police State and the Development of Modernity in Seventeenth- and Eighteenth-Century Europe: An Attempt at a Comparative Approach." *American Historical Review* 80, No. 5 (December 1975): 1221–43.

Raikov, B. E. "Evoliutsionnaia ideia v trudakh russkikh akademikov XVIII i pervoi poloviny XIX veka." *Vestnik Akademii nauk SSSR* 3 (1946): 37–46.

——. *Karl Ber, ego zhizn' i trudy.* Moscow, 1961.

——. *Russkie biologi-evoliutsionisty do Darvina.* Moscow, 1951.

Ramer, S. C. "The Traditional and the Modern in the Writings of Ivan Pnin." *Slavic Review* 34, No. 3 (September 1975): 539–59.

Rath, R. "Training for Citizenship in the Austrian Elementary Schools during the Reign of Francis I." *Journal of Central European Affairs* 4, No. 2 (1944): 147–64.

Ratynskii, N. A. "Dvor i pravitel'stvo sto let nazad." *RA* 24, No. 2 (1886):149–76.

Raumer, K. von. *Contributions to the History and Improvement of the German Universities.* New York, 1859.

Reisner, E. H. *Nationalism and Education since 1789: A Social and Political History of Modern Education.* New York, 1923.

Remy, A. F. J. *The Influence of India and Persia on the Poetry of Germany.* New York, 1966.

Riasanovsky, N. V. "Fourierism in Russia: An Estimate of the Petraševcy." *American Slavic and East European Review* 12, No. 3 (October 1953):289–302.

——. *A History of Russia.* New York, 1969.

——. "On Lammenais, Chaadaev, and the Romantic Revolt in France and Russia." *American Historical Review* 82, No. 5 (December 1977): 1165–86.

——. *Nicholas I and Official Nationality in Russia, 1825–1855.* Berkeley, Calif., 1967.

——. *A Parting of Ways: Government and the Educated Public in Russia, 1801–1855.* Oxford, 1976.

——. "Pogodin and Shevyrev in Russian Intellectual History." *Harvard Slavic Studies* 4 (1957): 149–67.

——. "Russia and Asia: Two Nineteenth-Century Russian Views." *California Slavic Studies* 1 (1960): 170–82.

——. *Russia and the West in the Teaching of the Slavophiles: A Study of Romantic Ideology.* Cambridge, Mass., 1952.

Ringer, F. K. *Education and Society in Modern Europe*. Bloomington, Ind., 1979.

Rober, A. N. "Organizatsiia uchebnoi chasti v gimnaziiakh." *Russkii vestnik* 27, No. 9 (1860): 53–73, 242–78.

Rogger, H., and E. Weber. *The European Right: A Historical Profile*. Berkeley, Calif., 1966.

Romanovich-Slavatinskii, A. V. *Dvorianstvo v Rossii ot nachala XVIII veka do otmeny krepostnago prava*. St. Petersburg, 1870.

"Rossiiskoe bibleiskoe obshchestvo, 1812–1826 gg." *Vestnik Evropy* 4, No. 8 (1868): 639–712. Concludes in *Vestnik Evropy* 5, No. 9 (1868):231–37; *Vestnik Evropy* 5, No. 11 (1868): 222–85; and *Vestnik Evropy* 5, No. 12 (1868): 708–68.

Rouët de Journel, M. J. *Un Collège de Jésuites à Saint-Pétersbourg, 1800–1816*. Paris, 1822.

Rozenburg, V., and V. Iakushkina. *Russkaia pechat' i tsenzura v proshlom i nastoiashchem*. Moscow, 1905.

Rozhdestvenskii, S. V. *Istoricheskii obzor deiatel'nosti Ministerstva narodnago prosveshcheniia, 1802–1902*. St. Petersburg, 1902.

_____. "Posledniaia stranitsa iz istorii politiki narodnago prosveshcheniia Imperatora Nikolaia I-ogo (Komitet grafa Bludova, 1849–1856)." *Russkii istoricheskii zhurnal* 3–4 (1917): 37–59.

_____. "Soslovnyi vopros v russkikh universitetakh v pervoi chetverti XIX v." *ZMNP* 9, No. 5 (1907): 83–107.

_____. "Vopros o narodnom obrazovanii i sotsial'naia problema v epokhu Aleksandra I." *Russkoe proshloe* 5 (1923): 35–49.

Rudakov, V. "Gimnaziia." *Entsiklopedicheskii slovar'*, XVI (1893), pp. 694–707.

Rusk, R. R. *Doctrines of the Great Educators*. London, 1918.

Russkaia literatura i folklor: Pervaia polovina XIX veka. Leningrad, 1976.

Ruud, C. A. *Fighting Words: Imperial Censorship and the Russian Press, 1804–1906*. Toronto, 1982.

Ryndziunskii, P. G. *Gorodskoe grazhdanstvo doreformennoi Rossii*. Moscow, 1958.

Ryskin, E. I. *Zhurnal A. S. Pushkina 'Sovremennik' 1836–1837*. Moscow, 1967.

Rzhevskii, V. "Ob otnoshenii gimnazii k universitety." *Russkii vestnik* 27, No. 6 (1860): 514–60.

Said, E. *Orientalism*. New York, 1979.

St. Petersburg University. *Materialy dlia istorii fakul'teta vostochnykh iazykov*. 2 vols. St. Petersburg, 1905–1906.

Sakulin, P. N. *Iz Istorii russkago idealizma: Kniaz V. F. Odoevskii*. Moscow, 1913.

_____. "Literaturnye techeniia v Aleksandrovskuiu epokhu." In *Istoriia russkoi literatury XIX v.* Edited by D. N. Ovsianiko-Kulikovskii. Moscow, 1910.

_____. "Russkaia literatura vo vtoroi chetverti veka." In *Istoriia Rossii v XIX veke*. Vol. II. St. Petersburg, 1910.

Sandys, J. E. *A History of Classical Scholarship*. 3 vols. 1908–1921. Reprint. New York, 1964.

Sauzin, L. *Adam Müller: Sa vie et son oeuvre*. Paris, 1937.

Savant, J. *Alexandre de Rennenkampf et ses amis*. Paris, 1846.

_____. "Predpolozheniia ob uchrezhdenii vostochnoi akademii v S. Peterburge, 1733 i 1810." *ZMNP* 2 (February 1856): 27–36.

Savel'ev, P. S.. *O zhizni i trudakh de Sasi*. St. Petersburg, 1839.

_____. *O zhizni i uchenykh trudakh Frena*. St. Petersburg, 1855.

Sawatsky, W. W. "Prince Alexander N. Golitsyn (1773–1844): Tsarist Minister of Piety." Ph.D. diss., University of Minnesota, 1976.

Schaffstein, F. *Wilhelm von Humboldt, ein Lebensbild*. Frankfurt, 1952.

Schapiro, J. S. *Condorcet and the Rise of Liberalism*. New York, 1934.

Schapiro, L. *Rationalism and Nationalism in Russian Nineteenth-Century Political Thought*. London, 1967.

Schiemann, T. *Geschichte Russlands unter Kaiser Nikolaus I.* 4 vols. Berlin, 1919.
————. "Imperator Nikolai Pavlovich." *RA* 40, No. 3 (1902): 459–75.
Schmid, G. "Goethe and Uwarow und ihr Briefwechsel." *Russische Revue* 28, No. 17 (1888): 131–82.
————. "Zur Russischen Gelehrtengeschichte: S. S. Uwarow und Chr. Fr. Gräfe." *Russische Revue* 26 (1886): 77–109.
Schnabel, F. *Deutsche Geschichte im neunzehnten Jahrhundert.* 4 vols. Berlin, 1929–1937.
Schwab, R. *La Renaissance orientale.* Paris, 1950.
Sechkarev, V. *Schellings Einfluss in der russischen Literatur der 20er und 30er Jahre des XIX Jahrhunderts.* Berlin, 1939.
Seeley, Sir J.-R. *Life and Times of Stein.* 2 vols. Boston, 1879.
Selle, G. von. *Die Georg-August Universität zu Göttingen, 1737–1937.* Göttingen, 1937.
Semenov, L. S. *Rossiia i Angliia: Ekonomicheskie otnosheniia v seredine XIX veka.* Leningrad, 1975.
Semevskii, V. I. "Kirillo-Mefodievskoe obshchestvo, 1846–1847." *Golos minuvshago* 10–12 (October–December 1918): 101–58.
————. *M. V. Butashevich-Petrashevskii i petrashevtsy.* Moscow, 1922.
————. *Krest'ianskii vopros v tsarstvovanie Imperatora Nikolaia.* St. Petersburg, 1888.
Seton-Watson, H. *The Russian Empire, 1801–1917.* Oxford, 1967.
Shavaev, M. F., ed. *Ocherki istorii shkoly i pedagogicheskoi mysli narodov SSSR: XVIII v.–pervaia polovina XIX v.* Moscow, 1973.
Shchapov, A. P. "Sotsialno-pedagogicheskaia istoriia umstvennago razvitiia russkago naroda." *Sochineniia A. P. Shchapova.* Vol. III. St. Petersburg, 1908.
Shchebal'skii, P. "A. S. Shiskov, ego soiuzniki i protivniki." *Russkii vestnik* 90 (November 1870): 192–254.
Shchegolev, P. E. *Iz zhizni i tvorchestva Pushkina.* Moscow, 1931.
Shchegolev, P. I. "Imperator Nikolai I, 1826–1831." *Istoricheskii vestnik* 95 (January 1904): 138–66.
Shcherbatov, G. "Kharakter i znachenie grafa S. S. Uvarova." *S.-Peterburgskiia vedomosti.* Nos. 334 and 335 (December 4, 1869, and December 5, 1869).
Shebunin, A. N. "Brat'ia Turgenevy i dvorianskoe obshchestvo aleksandrovskoi epokhi." *Dekabrist N. I. Turgenev.* Moscow, 1936.
Shepelev, L. E. *Otmenennye istoriei chiny, zvaniia i tituly v rossiiskoi imperii.* Leningrad, 1977.
Shestakov, P. D. "Graf D. A. Tolstoi." *RS* 22, No. 2 (1891): 387–405.
Shil'der, N. K. *Imperator Aleksandr pervyi: Ego zhizn' i tsarstvovanie.* St. Petersburg, 1898.
————. *Imperator Nikolai Pervyi: Ego zhizn' i tsarstvovanie.* 2 vols. St. Petersburg, 1903.
Shmid, E. K. *Istoriia srednikh uchebnykh zavedenii v Rossii.* St. Petersburg, 1877–1878.
Shpet, G. *Ocherk razvitiia russkoi filosofii.* Petrograd, 1922.
Shugurov, M. "Cherty russkoi politiki v 1819 godu." *RA* 5 (1867): 262–78.
Shul'gin, V. Ia. "Istoricheskoe obozrenie uchebnykh zavedenii v iugozapadnoi Rossii s kontsa XVIII veka do otkrytiia universiteta v Kieve: Istoriia universiteta sv. Vladimira." *Russkoe slovo* 10 (October 1859): 1–62.
————. *Istoriia Universiteta sv. Vladimira.* St. Petersburg, 1860.
Sidorov, E. "Literaturnoe obshchestvo 'Arzamas.'" *ZMNP 325*, No. 6 (1901): 357–91. Concludes in *ZMNP* 336, No. 7 (1901): 47–92.
Silber, K. *Pestalozzi: The Man and His Work.* New York, 1960.
Simkhovitch, V. G. "The History of the School in Russia." *Educational Review* 3 (May 1907): 486–522.

Simmons, E. J., ed. *Continuity and Change in Russian and Soviet Thought*. Cambridge, Mass., 1955.

Sinel, A. *The Classroom and the Chancellery: State Educational Reform in Russia under Count Dmitry Tolstoi*. Cambridge, Mass., 1973.

_____. "Problems in the Periodization of Russian Education: A Tentative Solution." *Slavic and European Education Review* 2 (1977): 54–61.

_____. "The Socialization of the Russian Bureaucratic Elite: Life at the Tsarskoe Selo Lyceum and the School of Jurisprudence." *Russian History* 3 (1976): 1–31.

Skabichevskii, A. M. *Ocherki istorii russkoi tsenzury, 1700–1863*. St. Petersburg, 1892.

_____. "Ocherki umstvennago razvitiia nashego obshchestva, 1825–1860." *Otechestvennye zapiski* 192, No. 10 (1870): 255–321. Concludes in succeeding issues as listed here: *Otechestvennye zapiski* 193, No. 11 (1870): 1–62; *Otechestvennye zapiski* 194, Nos. 2 and 6 (1871): 361–64 and 85–123, respectively; *Otechestvennye zapiski* 195, No. 3 (1871): 73–110; *Otechestvennye zapiski* 198, No. 10 (1871): 442–84; *Otechestvennye zapiski* 199, No. 11 (1871): 207–42; *Otechestvennye zapiski* 201, No. 4 (1872): 373–410; *Otechestvennye zapiski* 202, Nos. 5 and 6 (1872): 55–88 and 395–430, respectively.

Skachkov, P. E. *Ocherki istorii russkago kitaevedeniia*. Moscow, 1977.

_____. *Russko-kitaiskie otnosheniia 1689–1916: Ofitsial'nye dokumenty*. Moscow, 1958.

_____, ed. *Kitaiskaia khudozhestvennaia literatura: Bibliografiia russkikh perevodov i kriticheskoi literatury na russkom iazyke*. Moscow, 1957.

Smirnov, N. A. *Ocherki istorii izucheniia Islama v SSSR*. Moscow, 1954.

Soboleva, E. V. *Borba za reorganizatsiiu peterburgskoi Akademii nauk v seredine XIX veka*. Leningrad, 1971.

Solov'ev, E. *Ocherki iz istorii russkoi literatury XIX veka*. St. Petersburg, 1907.

Soltau, R. H. *French Political Thought in the Nineteenth Century*. New York, 1959.

Sommerfeld, S. *Indienschau und Indiendeutung romantischer Philosophen*. Zurich, 1943.

Spasovich, V. D. "Piatidesiatiletie S.-Peterburgskago universiteta." In *Sobranie sochinenii*. Vol. IV. St. Petersburg, 1889–1902.

Spring, H. P. *Chateaubriand at the Crossways*. New York, 1924.

Squire, P. S. *The Third Department: The Establishment and Practices of Political Police in the Russia of Nicholas I*. New York, 1968.

Stanislawski, M. *Tsar Nicholas I and the Jews: The Transformation of Jewish Society in Russia, 1825–1855*. Philadelphia, 1983.

Staniukovich, T. V. *Kunstkamera Peterburgskoi Akademii nauk*. Leningrad, 1953.

Stankevich, A. *Granovskii: Biograficheskii ocherk*. Moscow, 1914.

Starr, S. F. *Decentralization and Self-Government in Russia, 1830–1870*. Princeton, N.J., 1972.

Stasov, V. "Tsenzura v tsarstvovanie imperatora Nikolaia I." *RS* 34, No. 2 (1903): 305–28. Concludes in *RS* 34, Nos. 3 (1903): 571–91; 4 (1903): 163–84; 5 (1903): 379–96; 6 (1903): 643–71; 7 (1903): 137–57; 8 (1903): 405–37.

Stasiulevich, M. "O 'Zapiske' i 'Programma uchebnika vseobshchei istorii,' sostavlennykh v 1850 g. T. N. Granovskim." *Vestnik Evropy* 3 (September 1866):1–12.

Steinger, C. S. "Condorcet's Report on Public Education." *The Social Studies*, January 1970, pp. 20–25.

_____. "Government Policy and the University of St. Petersburg, 1819–1849." Ph.D. diss., The Ohio State University, 1971.

Stepanov, M., and F. Vermale. "Zhosef de Mestr v Rossii." *Literaturnoe nasledstvo* 29–30 (1937): 577–726.

Stilman, L. "Freedom and Repression in Prerevolutionary Russian Literature." In *Continuity and Change in Russian and Soviet Thought*. Edited by E. J. Simmons. Cambridge, Mass., 1955.

Stoiunin, V. Ia. "Konservatory sorokovykh godov." *Istoricheskii vestnik* 7 (1882): 1–28.

Stone, L., ed. *The University in Society*. Vol. I. Princeton, N.J., 1974.

Sturdza, A. S. "Beseda liubitelei russkago slova i Arzamas." *Moskvitianin* 6, No. 21 (1851): 3–22.

Sturt, M. *The Education of the People*. London, 1967.

Styker, L. P. *For the Defense: Thomas Erskine, the Most Enlightened Liberal of His Times, 1750–1823*. New York, 1947.

Sukhomlinov, M. I. *Istoriia Rossiiskoi akademii*. 8 vols. St. Petersburg, 1874–1888.

———. *Izsledovaniia i stati po russkoi literature i prosveshcheniiu*. 2 vols. St. Petersburg, 1889.

———. *Materialy dlia istorii obrazovaniia v Rossii v tsarstvovanie imp. Aleksandra*. Vol. I. St. Petersburg, 1866.

———. "Osobennosti poeticheskago tvorchestva A. N. Maikova." *RS* 30, No. 3 (1899): 481–98.

———. "Unichtozhenie dissertatsii N. I. Kostomarova." *Sbornik statei iz 'Drevnei i novoi Rossii'* 3, No. 9 (1875): 42–55.

Sweet, P. R. *Wilhelm von Humboldt: A Biography. 1808–1835*. Vol. II. Columbus, O., 1979.

Tairova, P. V. "Proekt I. O. Pototskogo otnositel'no sozdaniia Aziatskoi akademii v Rossii." *Narody Azii i Afriki* 2 (1973): 202–7.

Tarle, E. V. "Samoderzhavie Nikolaia I i frantsuzskoe obshchestvennoe mnenie." *Byloe* 1, No. 9 (1906): 12–42. Concludes in *Byloe* 1, No. 10 (1906): 138–59.

———. *Zapad i Rossiia*. Petrograd, 1918.

Thaden, E. "The Beginnings of Romantic Nationalism in Russia." *American Slavic and East European Review* 3, No. 4 (1954): 500–21.

———. *Conservative Nationalism in Nineteenth-Century Russia*. Seattle, Wash., 1964.

Tikhomirov, N. M., ed. *Istoriia Moskovskogo universiteta*. 2 vols. Moscow, 1955.

Timoshchuk, V. V. "Imperatritsa Elizaveta Alekseevna, supruga Imperatora Aleksandra I." *RS* 41, No. 4 (1910): 159–76.

Tomashevskii, B. *Pushkin: Kniga pervaia (1813–1824)*. Moscow, 1956.

Tompkins, S. R. "The Russian Bible Society: A Case of Religious Xenophobia." *American Slavic and East European Review* 7 (October 1948): 251–68.

Torke, H. J. "Continuity and Change in the Relations between Bureaucracy and Society in Russia, 1613–1861." *Canadian Slavic Studies* 5, No. 4 (Winter 1971): 457–76.

———. *Das russische Beamtentum in der ersten Hälfe des 19 Jahrhunderts*. Berlin, 1967.

Trevor-Roper, H. "The Historical Philosophy of the Enlightenment." In *Studies on Voltaire and the Eighteenth Century*. Vol. XXVII. Edited by T. Besterman. Geneva, 1963.

Trotskii, I. *Trete otdelenie pri Nikolae I*. Moscow, 1930.

Tseitlin, A. "Zapiska Pushkina o narodnom vospitanii." *Literaturnyi sovremennik* 1 (January 1937): 266–91.

Tucker, R. C. *The Marxian Revolutionary Idea*. New York, 1969.

Tugan-Baranovskii, M. *Russkaia fabrika v proshlom i nastoiashchem*. St. Petersburg, 1898.

Tymms, R. *German Romantic Literature, 1795–1830*. London, 1954.

Tynianov, Iu. N. *Arkhaisty i novatory* (Leningrad, 1929).

Universitet i politika. St. Petersburg, 1906.

University of Berlin. *Wilhelm von Humboldt, 1767–1967*. Halle, 1967.

Ushakova, L. A. *T. N. Granovskii i ego rol' v ideinoi bor'be Rossii 30kh–40kh godov XIX veka*. Tomsk, 1956.

Valk, S. N., ed. *Delo petrashevtsev*. 3 vols. Moscow, 1937–1951.

Vasilchikov, A. A. *Semeistvo Razumovskikh.* 5 vols. St. Petersburg, 1890–1894.

Vaughan, M., and M. Archer. *Social Conflict and Educational Change in England and France, 1789–1848.* Cambridge, Eng., 1971.

Vernadskii, V. I. "Pamiati akademika K. M. fon Bera." *Trudy Komissii po istorii znanii.* Leningrad, 1927.

Vernadsky, G. *La Charte constitutionelle de l'empire russe de l'an 1820.* Translated by S. Oldenbourg. Paris, 1933.

―――. "Reforms under Czar Alexander I: French and American Influences." *Review of Politics* 9, No. 1 (January 1947): 47–64.

Veselovskii, Iu. "Sentimentalizm v zapadno-evropeiskoi i russkoi literature." *Entsiklopedicheskii slovar'*, LVIII (1900), pp. 536–39.

Veselovskii, N. I. "Svedeniia ob ofitsial'nom prepodavanii vostochnykh iazykov v Rossii." *Trudy tret'iago mezhdunarodnogo s'ezda orientalistov v S.-Peterburge, 1876.* Edited by V. V. Grigor'ev. St. Petersburg, 1879–1880.

Veselovskii, S. B., ed. *Smutnoe vremia: Arzamasskie pomestnye akty (1578–1618 gg.).* Moscow, 1915.

Vessel', N. Kh. "Nachal'noe obrazovanie i narodnyia uchilishcha v zapadnoi Evrope i Rossii." *Russkaia shkola* 2, No. 5 (1891): 36–55. Concludes in *Russkaia shkola* 2, No. 6 (1891): 12–44.

Vetrinskii, Ch. *T. N. Granovskii i ego vremia: Istoricheskii ocherk.* St. Petersburg, 1905.

Viazemskii, P. P. "A. S. Pushkin (1816–1837)." *RA* 22, No. 2 (1884): 375–440.

Vinogradov, P. G. "Granovskii." *Russkaia mysl'* 4, No. 4 (1893): 44–66.

Vintergal'ter, E. I. *Sto let Pulkovskoi observatorii.* Moscow, 1945.

Vipper, R. "Gosudarstvennyia idei Shteina." *Russkaia mysl'* 8, No. 2 (1891):1–18.

Vladimirskii-Budanov, M. F. *Istoriia Imperatorskago Universiteta sv. Vladimira.* Kiev, 1884.

Volk, S. S. *Istoricheskie vzgliady Dekabristov.* Moscow, 1958.

Vorob'ev-Desiatovskii, V. S. "Russkii indianist G. S. Lebedev (1749–1817)." *Ocherki po istorii russkago vostokovedeniia* 2 (1956): 57–62.

Voronov, A. S. *Istorichesko-statisticheskoe obozrenie uchebnykh zavedenii Spb. okruga.* 2 vols. St. Petersburg, 1849–1855.

V. P. "Uvarovy." *Entsiklopedicheskii slovar'*, LXVII (1902), p. 420.

V. R. "N. N. Novosiltsev." *Entsiklopedicheskii slovar'*, XLI (1897), p. 295.

Vucinich, A. *Science in Russian Culture: A History to 1860.* Stanford, Calif., 1963.

Vucinich, W., ed. *Russia and Asia: Essays on the Influence of Russia on Asian Peoples.* Stanford, Calif., 1972.

Vyverberg, H. *Historical Pessimism in the French Enlightenment.* Cambridge, Mass., 1958.

Walicki, A. *A History of Russian Thought from the Enlightenment to Marxism.* Stanford, Calif., 1979.

―――. *The Slavophile Controversy: History of a Conservative Utopia in Nineteenth-Century Russian Thought.* Translated by H. Andrews-Rusiecka. Oxford, 1975.

Walker, M., ed. *Metternich's Europe.* New York, 1968.

Weston, J. C. "Edmund Burke's View of History." *Review of Politics* 33, No. 2 (April 1961): 203–29.

White, H. *Metahistory: The Historical Imagination in Nineteenth-Century Europe.* Baltimore, 1975.

Whittaker, C. H. "Count S. S. Uvarov: Conservatism and National Enlightenment in Pre-Reform Russia." Ph.D. diss., Indiana University, 1971.

―――. "The Ideology of Sergei Uvarov: An Interpretive Essay." *Russian Review* 37, No. 2 (April 1978): 158–76.

―――. "The Impact of the Oriental Renaissance in Russia: The Case of Sergeij Uvarov." *Jahrbücher für Geschichte Osteuropas* 26, No. 4 (1978): 503–24.

————. "One Use of History in Education: A Lesson in Patience." *Slavic and European Education Review* 2, No. 2 (1978): 29–38.

————. "The Women's Movement during the Reign of Alexander II." *Journal of Modern History* 48, No. 2 (June 1976): 35–69.

Willson, A. L. *A Mythical Image: The Ideal of India in German Romanticism.* Durham, N.C., 1964.

Wischnitzer, M. "Goettingenskie gody N. I. Turgeneva." *Minuvshie gody* 1, No. 4 (1908): 184–218. Concludes in *Minuvshie gody* 1, Nos. 5–6 (1908): 216–41.

————. *Die Universität Göttingen und die Entwicklung der liberalen Ideen in Russland im ersten Viertel des 19 Jahrhunderts.* Berlin, 1907.

Woltner, M. *Das wolgadeutsche Bildungswesen und die russische Schulpolitik.* Leipzig, 1937.

Woodward, E. L. *Three Studies in European Conservatism: Metternick, Guizot, The Catholic Church in the Nineteenth Century.* Hamden, Conn., 1963.

Wortman, R. S. *The Development of a Russian Legal Consciousness.* Chicago, 1976.

Yaney, G. L. *The Systematization of Russian Government: Social Evolution in the Domestic Administration of Imperial Russia, 1711–1905.* Chicago, 1973.

Zabel, E. "Goethe und Russland." *Jahrbuch der Goethe-Gesellschaft.* Weimar, 1921.

Zablotskii-Desiatovskii, A. P. *Graf P. D. Kiselev i ego vremia.* St. Petersburg, 1882.

Zaborov, P. R. "Vol'ter v Rossii kontsa XVIII–nachala XIX veka." *Ot klassitsizma k romantizmu.* Edited by M. P. Alekseev. Leningrad, 1970.

————. "Zhermena de Stal'i russkaia literatura pervoi treti XIX veka." *Rannie romanticheskie veianiia.* Edited by M. P. Alekseev. Leningrad, 1972.

Zacek, J. C. "The Lancastrian School Movement in Russia." *Slavonic and East European Review* 45, No. 105 (July 1967): 343–67.

————. "The Russian Bible Society, 1812–1926." Ph. D. diss., Columbia University, 1964.

————. "The Russian Bible Society and the Catholic Church." *Canadian Slavic Studies* 5, No. 1 (1971): 35–50.

————. "The Russian Bible Society and the Russian Orthodox Church." *Church History* 35 (December 1966): 411–37.

Zagoskin, N. P. *Istoriia Imp. Kazanskogo universiteta za pervyia sto let ego sushchestvovaniia (1804–1904).* 4 vols. Kazan, 1902–1906.

Zaionchkovskii, P. A. *Kirillo-Mefodievskoe obshchestvo.* Moscow, 1959.

————. *Pravitel'stvennyi apparat samoderzhavnoi Rossii v XIX v.* Moscow, 1978.

————. "Vysshaia biurokratiia nakanune Krymskoi voiny." *Istoriia SSSR* 4 (July–August, 1974): 154–64.

Zavitnevich, V. "Znachenie pervykh slavianofilov v dele uiasneniia idea narodnosti i sambytnosti." *Trudy Kievskoi dukh. Akademii za 1891.* Kiev, 1891.

Zdobnov, N. V. *Istoriia russkoi bibliografii ot drevnago perioda do nachala XX veka.* 2 vols. Moscow, 1944–1948.

Zotov, P. *Tridtsatiletie Evropy v tsarstvovanie imperatora Nikolai I.* 2 vols. St. Petersburg, 1857.

Zotov, V. R. "Peterburg v 40kh godakh." *Istoricheskii vestnik* 39 (1890):29–53, 324–43, 553–72. Concludes in *Istoricheskii vestnik* 40 (1890): 93–115, 290–319, 535–59.

INDEX

A